AUTOMOTIVE ENGINES AND ENGINE PERFORMANCE

James D. Halderman

Edited by Jeffrey Rehkopf

Taken from

Automotive Engines, Seventh Edition

By James D. Halderman

Automotive Engine Performance, Fourth Edition

By James D. Halderman

PEARSON

Boston   Columbus   Indianapolis   New York   San Francisco   Upper Saddle River
Amsterdam   Cape Town   Dubai   London   Madrid   Milan   Munich   Paris   Montréal
Toronto   Delhi   Mexico City   São Paulo   Sydney   Hong Kong   Seoul   Singapore   Taipei   Toky

Editorial Director: Vernon Anthony
Senior Acquisitions Editor: Lindsey
   Prudhomme Gill
Editorial Assistant: Nancy Kesterson
Director of Marketing: David Gesell
Senior Marketing Coordinator: Alicia
   Wozniak
Program Manager: Maren Beckman
Project Manager: Holly Shufeldt

Senior Art Director: Jayne Conte
Cover Designer: Karen Noferi
Media Project Manager: April Cleland
**Full-Service Project Management and
   Composition:** Integra Software
   Services, Ltd.
Printer/Binder: Courier Digital Solutions
Cover Printer: Courier Digital Solutions

Taken from:
Automotive Engines, Seventh Edition
By James D. Halderman
Copyright © 2011 by Pearson Education

Automotive Engine Performance, Fourth Edition
By James D. Halderman
Copyright © 2014 by Pearson Education

Portions of material contained herein have been reprinted with permission of General Motors LLC, License Agreement # 1310944. GM ASEP is a trademark of General Motors LLC, used with permission. While portions of this work contains copyrighted works of General Motors, used with permission, General Motors does not assume any responsibility for this work or the factual accuracy of its contents.

Credits and acknowledgments borrowed from other sources and reproduced, with permission, in this textbook appear on the appropriate page within the text.

Many of the designations by manufacturers and sellers to distinguish their products are claimed as trademarks. Where those designations appear in this book, and the publisher was aware of a trademark claim, the designations have been printed in initial caps or all caps.

10 9 8 7 6 5 4 3

ISBN 10:   0-13-352598-8
ISBN 13: 978-0-13-352598-4

BRIEF CONTENTS

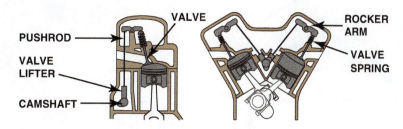

OVERHEAD VALVE (OHV) - CAMSHAFT IN CYLINDER BLOCK

PUSHROD

VALVE

VALVE LIFTER

CAMSHAFT

ROCKER ARM

VALVE SPRING

OVERHEAD CAM (OHC) - CAMSHAFT IN CYLINDER HEAD

SOHC

DOHC

FIGURE 1–14 There are a variety of valve train designs. (*Courtesy of General Motors*)

? FREQUENTLY ASKED QUESTION

What Is a Rotary Engine?

A successful alternative engine design is the **rotary engine**, also called the **Wankel engine** after its inventor, Felix Heinrich Wankel (1902–1988), a German inventor. The Mazda RX-7 and RX-8 represent the only long-term use of the rotary engine. The rotating combustion chamber engine runs very smoothly, and it produces high power for its size and weight.

The basic rotating combustion chamber engine has a triangle-shaped rotor turning in a housing. The housing is in the shape of a geometric figure called a two-lobed epitrochoid. A seal on each corner, or apex, of the rotor is in constant contact with the housing, so the rotor must turn with an eccentric motion. This means that the center of the rotor moves around the center of the engine. The eccentric motion can be seen in ● **FIGURE 1–16.**

FIGURE 1–15 A DOHC engine uses a camshaft for the intake valves and a separate camshaft for the exhaust valves in each cylinder head.

same standard for direction of rotation. A few transverse engines, and some marine applications, may differ from this standard.

ENGINE MEASUREMENT

BORE The diameter of a cylinder is called the **bore**. The larger the bore, the greater the area on which the gases have to work. Pressure is measured in units, such as pounds per square inch (PSI). The greater the area (in square inches), the higher the force exerted by the pistons to rotate the crankshaft. ● **SEE FIGURE 1–18.**

to which the power is applied to drive the vehicle. This is called the **principal end** of the engine. The **nonprincipal end** of the engine is opposite the principal end and is generally referred to as the *front* of the engine, where the accessory belts are used. ● **SEE FIGURE 1–17.**

Therefore, in most rear-wheel-drive vehicles, the engine is mounted longitudinally with the principal end at the rear of the engine. Most transversely mounted engines also adhere to the

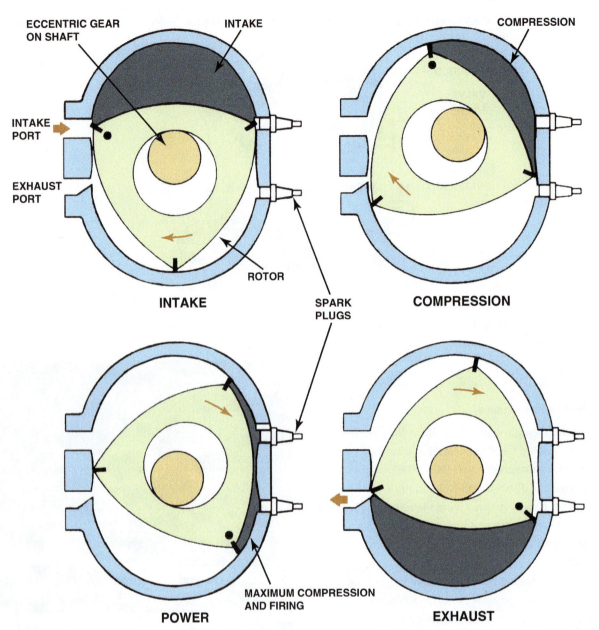

FIGURE 1–16 A rotary engine operates on the four-stroke cycle but uses a rotor instead of a piston and crankshaft to achieve intake, compression, power, and exhaust stroke.

STROKE The **stroke** of an engine is the distance the piston travels from top dead center (TDC) to bottom dead center (BDC). This distance is determined by the throw of the crankshaft. The throw is the distance from the centerline of the crankshaft to the centerline of the crankshaft rod journal. The throw is one-half of the stroke. ● **SEE FIGURE 1–19.**

The longer this distance is, the greater the amount of air-fuel mixture that can be drawn into the cylinder. The more air-fuel mixture inside the cylinder, the more force will result when the mixture is ignited.

NOTE: Changing the connecting rod length does *not* change the stroke of an engine. Changing the connecting rod only changes the position of the piston in the cylinder. Only the crankshaft determines the stroke of an engine.

DISPLACEMENT Engine size is described as displacement. **Displacement** is the cubic inch (cu. in.) or cubic centimeter (cc) volume displaced or how much air is moved by all of the pistons. A liter (L) is equal to 1,000 cubic centimeters; therefore, most engines today are identified by their displacement in liters.

1 Liter = 1,000 cubic centimeters

1 Liter = 61 cubic inch

1 cu. in. = 16.4 cubic centimeters

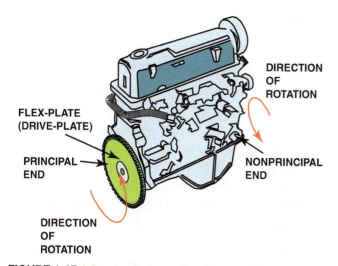

FIGURE 1-17 Inline 4-cylinder engine showing principal and nonprincipal ends. Normal direction of rotation is clockwise (CW) as viewed from the front or accessory belt (nonprincipal) end.

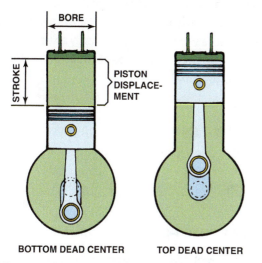

BOTTOM DEAD CENTER   TOP DEAD CENTER

FIGURE 1-18 The bore and stroke of pistons are used to calculate an engine's displacement.

CONVERSION

- To convert cubic inches to liters, divide cubic inches by 61.02.

$$\text{Liters} = \frac{\text{Cubic inches}}{61.02}$$

- To convert liters into cubic inches, multiply by 61.02.

$$\text{Cubic inches} = \text{Liters} \times 61.02$$

CALCULATING CUBIC INCH DISPLACEMENT
The formula to calculate the displacement of an engine is basically

FIGURE 1-19 The distance between the centerline of the main bearing journal and the centerline of the connecting rod journal determines the stroke of the engine. This photo shows a V-6 with a splayed crankshaft used to even out the power strokes on a 90-degree, V-6 engine design.

? FREQUENTLY ASKED QUESTION

What is the Atkinson Cycle?

In 1882, James Atkinson, a British engineer, invented an engine that achieved a higher efficiency than the Otto cycle but produced lower power at low engine speeds. The Atkinson cycle engine was produced in limited numbers until 1890, when sales dropped, and the company that manufactured the engines finally went out of business in 1893.

However, the one key feature of the Atkinson cycle that remains in use today is that the intake valve is held open longer than normal to allow a reverse flow into the intake manifold. This reduces the effective compression ratio and engine displacement and allows the expansion to exceed the compression ratio while retaining a normal compression pressure. This is desirable for good fuel economy because the compression ratio in a spark ignition engine is limited by the octane rating of the fuel used, while a high expansion delivers a longer power stroke and reduces the heat wasted in the exhaust. This increases the efficiency of the engine because more work is being achieved. The Atkinson cycle engine design is commonly used in hybrid electric vehicles.

the formula for determining the volume of a cylinder multiplied by the number of cylinders.

The formula is:

Cubic inches displacement = π (pi) $\times$ R^2 $\times$ Stroke $\times$ Number of cylinder

R = Radius of the cylinder or one-half of the bore.

The πR^2 part is the formula for the area of a circle.

Applying the formula to a 6-cylinder engine:

- Bore = 4.000 inch
- Stroke = 3.000 inch
- π = 3.14
- R = 2 inches
- R^2 = 4 (2^2 or 2 $\times$ 2)

  Cubic inches = 3.14 $\times$ 4 (R^2) $\times$ 3 (stroke) $\times$ 6 (number of cylinders).

  Cubic inches = 226 cubic inches

Because 1 cubic inch equals 16.4 cubic centimeters, this engine displacement equals 3,706 cubic centimeters or, rounded to 3,700 cubic centimeters, 3.7 liters. ● **SEE CHART 1–1** for an example of engine sizes for a variety of bore and stroke measurements.

ENGINE SIZE CONVERSION Many vehicle manufacturers will round the displacement so the calculated cubic inch displacement may not agree with the published displacement value. ● **SEE CHART 1–2.**

COMPRESSION RATIO

DEFINITION **Compression ratio (CR)** is the ratio of the difference in the cylinder volume when the piston is at the bottom of the stroke to the volume in the cylinder above the piston when the piston is at the top of the stroke. The compression ratio of an engine is an important consideration when rebuilding or repairing an engine. ● **SEE FIGURE 1–20.**

If Compression Is Lower	If Compression Is Higher
Lower power	Higher power possible
Poorer fuel economy	Better fuel economy possible
Easier engine cranking	Harder to crank engine, especially when hot
More advanced ignition timing possible without spark knock (detonation)	Less ignition timing required to prevent spark knock (detonation)

TECH TIP

How Fast Can an Engine Rotate?

Most passenger vehicle engines are designed to rotate at low speed for the following reasons.

- Maximum efficiency is achieved at low engine speed. A diesel engine used in a large ship, for example, will rotate at about 50 RPM for maximum efficiency.
- Piston ring friction is the highest point of friction in the engine. The slower the engine speed, the less loss to friction from the piston rings.

However, horsepower is what is needed to get a vehicle down the road quickly. Horsepower is torque times engine speed divided by 5,252. Therefore, a high engine speed usually indicates a high horsepower. For example, a Formula 1 race car is limited to 2.4 liter V-8 but uses a 1.6 in. (40 mm) stroke. This extremely short stroke means that the engine can easily achieve the upper limit allowed by the rules of 18 000 RPM while producing over 700 horsepower.

CALCULATING COMPRESSION RATIO The compression ratio (CR) calculation uses the formula:

$$CR = \frac{\text{Volume in cylinder with piston at bottom of cylinder}}{\text{Volume in cylinder with piston at top center}}$$

● **SEE FIGURE 1–21.**

For example: What is the compression ratio of an engine with 50.3 cu. inches displacement in one cylinder and a combustion chamber volume of 6.7 cu. inches?

$$CR = \frac{50.3 + 6.7 \text{ cu. inches}}{6.7 \text{ cu. inches}} = \frac{57.0}{6.7} = 8.5$$

CHANGING COMPRESSION RATIO Any time an engine is modified, the compression ratio should be checked to make sure it is either the same as it was originally or has been changed to match the desired compression ratio. Factors that can affect compression ratio include:

- **Head gasket thickness.** A thicker than stock gasket will decrease the compression ratio and a thinner than stock gasket will increase the compression ratio.
- **Increasing the cylinder size.** If the bore or stroke is increased, a greater amount of air will be compressed into the combustion chamber, which will increase the compression ratio.

V-8 ENGINE

Stroke	3.50	3.75	3.875	4.00	4.125
Bore	Cubic Inches	Cubic Inches	Cubic Inches	Cubic Inches	Cubic Inches
3.00	199	212	219	226	233
3.125	214	229	237	244	252
3.250	232	249	257	265	274
3.375	251	269	277	286	295
3.500	269	288	298	308	317
3.625	288	309	319	330	339
3.750	309	332	343	354	365
3.875	331	354	366	378	390
4.00	352	377	389	402	414
4.125	373	399	413	426	439

6-CYLINDER ENGINE

Stroke	3.50	3.75	3.875	4.00	4.125
Bore	Cubic Inches	Cubic Inches	Cubic Inches	Cubic Inches	Cubic Inches
3.00	148	159	164	169	175
3.125	161	172	178	184	190
3.250	174	186	193	199	205
3.375	188	201	208	215	222
3.500	202	216	223	228	238
3.625	216	232	239	247	255
3.750	232	249	257	265	273
3.875	248	266	275	283	292
4.00	264	283	292	301	311
4.125	280	299	309	319	329

4-CYLINDER ENGINE

Stroke	3.50	3.75	3.875	4.00	4.125
Bore	Cubic Inches	Cubic Inches	Cubic Inches	Cubic Inches	Cubic Inches
3.00	99	106	110	113	117
3.125	107	115	119	123	126
3.250	116	124	129	133	137
3.375	125	134	139	143	148
3.500	135	144	149	152	159
3.625	144	158	160	165	170
3.750	155	166	171	177	182
3.875	165	177	183	189	195
4.00	176	188	195	201	207
4.125	186	200	206	213	220

CHART 1–1

To find the cubic inch displacement, find the bore that is closest to the actual value, then go across to the closest stroke value.

		Liters to Cubic Inches			
Liters	Cubic Inches	Liters	Cubic Inches	Liters	Cubic Inches
1.0	61	3.2	196	5.4	330
1.3	79	3.3	200 / 201	5.7	350
1.4	85	3.4	204	5.8	351
1.5	91	3.5	215	6.0	366 / 368
1.6	97 / 98	3.7	225	6.1	370
1.7	105	3.8	229 / 231 / 232	6.2	381
1.8	107 / 110 / 112	3.9	239 / 240	6.4	389 / 390 / 391
1.9	116	4.0	241 / 244	6.5	396
2.0	121 / 122	4.1	250 / 252	6.6	400
2.1	128	4.2	255 / 258	6.9	420
2.2	132 / 133 / 134 / 135	4.3	260 / 262 / 265	7.0	425 / 427 / 428 / 429
2.3	138 / 140	4.4	267	7.2	440
2.4	149	4.5	273	7.3	445
2.5	150 / 153	4.6	280 / 281	7.4	454
2.6	156 / 159	4.8	292	7.5	460
2.8	171 / 173	4.9	300 / 301	7.8	475 / 477
2.9	177	5.0	302 / 304 / 305 / 307	8.0	488
3.0	181 / 182 / 183	5.2	318	8.8	534
3.1	191	5.3	327		

CHART 1–2

Liters to cubic inches is often not exact and can result in representing several different engine sizes based on their advertised size in liters.

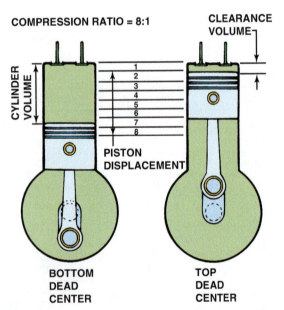

FIGURE 1–20 Compression ratio is the ratio of the total cylinder volume (when the piston is at the bottom of its stroke) to the clearance volume (when the piston is at the top of its stroke).

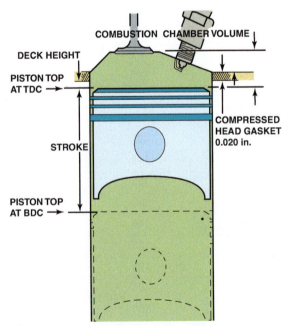

FIGURE 1–21 Combustion chamber volume is the volume above the piston with the piston is at top dead center.

TORQUE AND HORSEPOWER

DEFINITION OF TORQUE Torque is the term used to describe a rotating force that may or may not result in motion. Torque is measured as the amount of force multiplied by the length of the lever through which it acts. If you use a 1 ft long wrench to apply 10 pounds (lb) of force to the end of the wrench to turn a bolt, then you are exerting 10 pound-feet (lb-ft) of torque. ● **SEE FIGURE 1–22.**

Torque is the twisting force measured at the end of the crankshaft and measured on a dynamometer. Engine torque is always expressed at a specific engine speed (RPM) or range of engine speeds where the torque is at the maximum. For example, an engine may be listed as producing 275 pound-feet @ 2400 RPM.

The metric unit for torque is newton-meters, because the newton is the metric unit for force and the distance is expressed in meters.

1 pound-foot = 1.3558 newton-meters

1 newton-meter = 0.7376 pound-foot

WORK **Work** is defined as an actually accomplishing movement when torque is applied to an object. A service technician can apply torque to a bolt in an attempt to loosen it, yet no work is done until the bolt actually moves. Work is calculated by multiplying the applied force (in pounds) by the distance the object moves (in feet). If you applied 100 pounds of force to move an object 10 feet, then you accomplished 1000 foot-pounds of work (100 pounds × 10 feet = 1000 foot pounds). ● **SEE FIGURE 1–23.**

NOTE: The designations for torque and work are often confusing. Torque is expressed in pound-feet because it represents a force exerted a certain distance from the object and acts as a lever. Work, however, is expressed in foot-pounds because work is the movement over a certain distance (feet) multiplied by the force applied (pounds). Engines produce torque and service technicians exert torque represented by the unit pound-feet.

DEFINITION OF POWER The term *power* means the rate of doing work. Power equals work divided by time. Work is achieved when a certain amount of mass (weight) is moved a certain distance by a force. Whether the object is moved in 10 seconds or 10 minutes does not make a difference in the amount of work accomplished, but it does affect the amount of

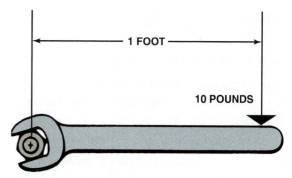

FIGURE 1–22 Torque is a twisting force equal to the distance from the pivot point times the force applied expressed in units called pound-feet (lb-ft) or newton-meters (N-m).

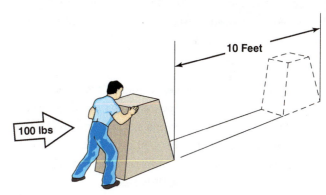

FIGURE 1–23 Work is calculated by multiplying force times distance. If you exert 100 pounds of force for 10 feet, you have done 1000 foot-pounds of work.

? **FREQUENTLY ASKED QUESTION**

Is Torque ft-lb or lb-ft?

The definition of torque is a force (lb) applied to an object times the distance from that object (ft). Therefore, based on the definition of the term, torque should be:

lb-ft (a force times a distance)

Newton-meter (N-m) (a force times a distance)

However, torque is commonly labeled, even on some torque wrenches as ft-lb.

---

power needed. Power is expressed in units of foot-pounds per minute and power also includes the engine speed (RPM) where the maximum power is achieved. For example, an engine may be listed as producing 280 hp @ 4400 RPM.

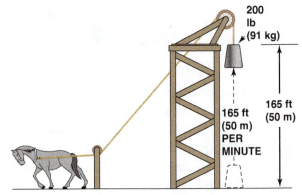

FIGURE 1–24 One horsepower is equal to 33,000 foot-pounds (200 lbs. × 165 ft) of work per minute.

HORSEPOWER

The power an engine produces is called horsepower (hp). One **horsepower** is the power required to move 550 pounds one foot in one second, or 33,000 pounds one foot in one minute (550 lb × 60 sec = 33,000 lb). This is expressed as 500 foot-pounds (ft-lb) per second or 33,000 foot-pounds per minute. ● **SEE FIGURE 1–24.**

The actual horsepower produced by an engine is measured with a **dynamometer.** A dynamometer (often abbreviated as **dyno** or **dyn**) places a load on the engine and measures the amount of twisting force the engine crankshaft places against the load. The load holds the engine speed, so it is called a **brake.** The horsepower derived from a dynamometer is called **brake horsepower (bhp).** The dynamometer actually measures the torque output of the engine. Torque is a rotating force that may or may not cause movement. The horsepower is calculated from the torque readings at various engine speeds (in revolutions per minute or RPM).

Horsepower is torque times RPM divided by 5252.

$$\text{Horsepower} = \frac{\text{Torque} \times \text{RPM}}{5252}$$

Torque is what the driver "feels" as the vehicle is being accelerated. A small engine operating at a high RPM may have the same horsepower as a large engine operating at a low RPM.

SAE standards for measuring horsepower include gross and net horsepower ratings. **SAE gross horsepower** is the maximum power an engine develops without some accessories in operation. **SAE net horsepower** is the power an

engine develops as installed in the vehicle. A summary of the differences is given in the following table.

SAE Gross Horsepower	SAE Net Horsepower
No air cleaner or filter	Stock air cleaner or filter
No cooling fan	Stock cooling fan
No alternator	Stock alternator
No mufflers	Stock exhaust system
No emission controls	Full emission and noise control

Ratings are about 20% lower for the net rating method. Before 1971, most manufacturers used gross horsepower rating (the higher method) for advertising purposes. After 1971, the manufacturers started advertising only SAE net-rated horsepower.

HORSEPOWER AND ALTITUDE

Because the density of the air is lower at high altitude, the power that a normal engine can develop is greatly reduced at high altitude.

According to SAE conversion factors, a nonsupercharged or nonturbocharged engine loses about 3% of its power for every 1,000 feet (300 m) of altitude.

Therefore, an engine that develops 200 brake horsepower at sea level will only produce about 116 brake horsepower at the top of Pike's Peak in Colorado at 14,110 feet (4,300 m) (3% × 14 − 42%). Supercharged and turbocharged engines are not as greatly affected by altitude as normally aspirated engines, (engines that intake air at normal atmospheric pressure).

SUMMARY

1. The four strokes of the four-stroke cycle are intake, compression, power, and exhaust.

2. Engines are classified by number and arrangement of cylinders and by number and location of valves and camshafts, as well as by type of mounting, fuel used, cooling method, and type of air induction.

3. Most engines rotate clockwise as viewed from the front (accessory) end of the engine. The SAE standard is counterclockwise as viewed from the principal (flywheel) end of the engine.

4. Engine size is called displacement and represents the volume displaced by all of the pistons.

REVIEW QUESTIONS

1. What are the strokes of a four stroke cycle?

2. If an engine at sea level produces 100 hp, how many horsepower would it develop at 6,000 ft of altitude?

CHAPTER QUIZ

1. All overhead valve engines _____.
   a. Use an overhead camshaft
   b. Have the valves located in the cylinder head
   c. Operate by the two-stroke cycle
   d. Use the camshaft to close the valves

2. An SOHC V-8 engine has how many camshafts?
   a. One   c. Three
   b. Two   d. Four

3. The coolant flow through the radiator is controlled by the _____.
   a. Size of the passages in the block
   b. Thermostat
   c. Cooling fan(s)
   d. Water pump

4. Torque is expressed in units of _____.
   a. Pound-feet
   b. Foot-pounds
   c. Foot-pounds per minute
   d. Pound-feet per second

5. Horsepower is expressed in units of _____.
   a. Pound-feet
   b. Foot-pounds
   c. Foot-pounds per minute
   d. Pound-feet per second

6. A normally aspirated automobile engine loses about _____ power per 1,000 ft of altitude.
   a. 1%   c. 5%
   b. 3%   d. 6%

7. One cylinder of an automotive four-stroke cycle engine completes a cycle every _____.
   a. 90 degrees
   b. 180 degrees
   c. 360 degrees
   d. 720 degrees

8. How many rotations of the crankshaft are required to complete each stroke of a four-stroke cycle engine?
   a. One-fourth
   b. One-half
   c. One
   d. Two

9. A rotating force is called _____.
   a. Horsepower
   b. Torque
   c. Combustion pressure
   d. Eccentric movement

10. Technician A says that a crankshaft determines the stroke of an engine. Technician B says that the length of the connecting rod determines the stroke of an engine. Which technician is correct?
   a. Technician A only
   b. Technician B only
   c. Both Technicians A and B
   d. Neither Technician A nor B

chapter 2

DIESEL ENGINE OPERATION

FIGURE 2–1 Diesel engines are becoming more common in both trucks and passenger cars. (*Ecotec 2.0L CDTI, Courtesy of General Motors*)

DIESEL ENGINES

FUNDAMENTALS In 1892, a German engineer named Rudolf Diesel perfected the compression ignition engine that bears his name. The diesel engine uses heat created by compression to ignite the fuel, so it requires no spark ignition system. ● **SEE FIGURE 2–1.**

The diesel engine requires compression ratios of 16:1 and higher. Incoming air is compressed until its temperature reaches about 1,000°F (540°C). This is called **heat of compression.** As the piston reaches the top of its compression stroke, fuel is injected into the cylinder, where it is ignited by the hot air. ● **SEE FIGURE 2–2.**

As the fuel burns, it expands and produces power. Because of the very high compression and torque output of a diesel engine, it is made heavier and stronger than the same size gasoline-powered engine.

A diesel engine uses a fuel system with a precision **injection pump** and individual fuel injectors. The pump delivers fuel to the injectors at a high pressure and at timed intervals. Each injector

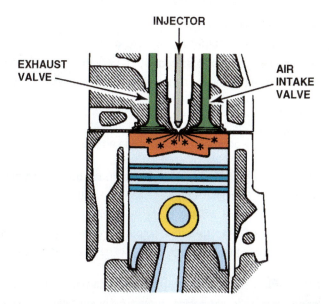

FIGURE 2–2 Diesel combustion occurs when fuel is injected into the hot, highly compressed air in the cylinder.

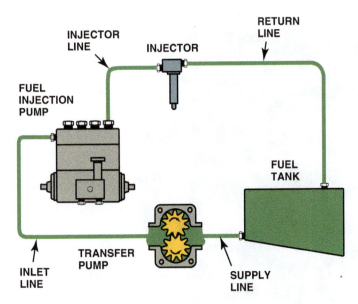

FIGURE 2–3 A basic injector pump type of automotive diesel fuel–injection system.

FIGURE 2–4 This engine cutaway shows the construction of a diesel engine. Note the thick cylinder walls and heavyduty construction. (*Courtesy of General Motors*)

sprays fuel into the combustion chamber at the precise moment required for efficient combustion. ● **SEE FIGURE 2–3.**

ADVANTAGES AND DISADVANTAGES
A diesel engine has several advantages compared to a similar size gasoline-powered engine, including:

1. More torque output
2. Greater fuel economy
3. Long service life

A diesel engine has several disadvantages compared to a similar size gasoline-powered engine, including:

1. Engine noise, especially when cold and/or at idle speed
2. Exhaust smell
3. Cold weather startability
4. Vacuum pump that is needed to supply the vacuum needs of the heat, ventilation, and air-conditioning system
5. Heavier than a gasoline engine
6. Fuel availability
7. Extra cost compared to a gasoline engine

CONSTRUCTION
Diesel engines must be constructed heavier than gasoline engines because of the tremendous pressures that are created in the cylinders during operation. ● **SEE CHART 2–1.** The torque output of a diesel engine is often double or more than the same size gasoline-powered engines.

AIR-FUEL RATIOS
In a diesel engine, air is not controlled by a throttle as in a gasoline engine. Instead, the amount of fuel injected is varied to control power and speed. The air-fuel mixture in a diesel engine can vary from as lean as 85:1 at idle to as rich as 20:1

System or Component	Diesel Engine	Gasoline Engine
Block	Cast iron and heavy (● SEE FIGURE 2–4)	Cast iron or aluminum and as light as possible
Cylinder head	Cast iron or aluminum	Cast iron or aluminum
Compression ratio	17:1 to 25:1	8:1 to 12:1
Peak engine speed	2000 to 2500 RPM	5000 to 8000 RPM
Pistons	Aluminum with combustion pockets and heavy-duty connecting rods	Aluminum, usually flat top or with valve relief but no combustion pockets

CHART 2–1

Comparison between a typical gasoline and a diesel engine.

at full load. This higher air-fuel ratio and the increased compression pressures make the diesel engine more fuel efficient than a gasoline engine, in part because diesel engines do not suffer from throttling losses. Throttling losses involve the power needed in a gasoline engine to draw air past a closed or partially closed throttle.

In a gasoline engine, the speed and power are controlled by the throttle valve, which controls the amount of air entering the engine. Adding more fuel to the cylinders of a gasoline engine without adding more air (oxygen) will not increase the speed or power of the engine. In a diesel engine, speed and power are not controlled by the amount of air entering the cylinders because the engine air intake is always wide open. Therefore, the engine always has enough oxygen to burn the fuel in the cylinder and will increase speed (and power) when additional fuel is supplied.

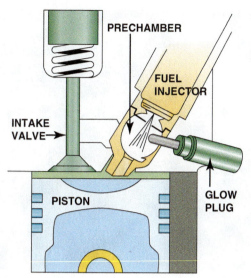

FIGURE 2–5 An indirect injection diesel engine uses a prechamber and a glow plug.

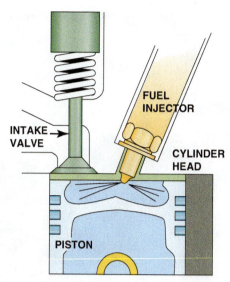

FIGURE 2–6 A direct injection diesel engine injects the fuel directly into the combustion chamber. Many designs do not use a glow plug.

NOTE: Most newer diesel engines are equipped with a throttle valve. This valve is used by the emission control system and is not designed to control the speed of the engine.

INDIRECT AND DIRECT INJECTION

In an **indirect injection** (abbreviated **IDI**) diesel engine, fuel is injected into a small prechamber, which is connected to the cylinder by a narrow opening. The initial combustion takes place in this prechamber. This has the effect of slowing the rate of combustion, which tends to reduce noise. ● **SEE FIGURE 2–5.**

All indirect diesel injection engines require the use of a glow plug which is an electrical heater that helps start the combustion process.

In a **direct injection** (abbreviated **DI**) diesel engine, fuel is injected directly into the cylinder. The piston incorporates a depression where initial combustion takes place. Direct injection diesel engines are generally more efficient than indirect injection engines, but have a tendency to produce greater amounts of noise. ● **SEE FIGURE 2–6.**

While some direct injection diesel engines use glow plugs to help cold starting and to reduce emissions, many direct injection diesel engines do not use glow plugs.

DIESEL FUEL IGNITION

Ignition occurs in a diesel engine by injecting fuel into the air charge, which has been heated by compression to a temperature greater than the ignition point of the fuel or about 1,000°F (538°C). The chemical reaction of burning the fuel creates heat, which causes the gases to expand, forcing the piston to rotate the crankshaft. A four-stroke diesel engine requires two rotations of the crankshaft to complete one cycle.

- On the intake stroke, the piston passes TDC, the intake valve(s) opens, and filtered air enters the cylinder, while the exhaust valve(s) remains open for a few degrees

to allow all of the exhaust gases to escape from the previous combustion event.

- On the compression stroke, after the piston passes BDC, the intake valve(s) closes and the piston travels up to TDC (completion of the first crankshaft rotation).

- On the power stroke, the piston nears TDC on the compression stroke and diesel fuel is injected into the cylinder by the injectors. The ignition of the fuel does not start immediately but the heat of compression starts the combustion phases in the cylinder. During this power stroke, the piston passes TDC and the expanding gases force the piston down, rotating the crankshaft.

- On the exhaust stroke, as the piston passes BDC, the exhaust valve(s) opens and the exhaust gases start to flow out of the cylinder. This continues as the piston travels up to TDC, pumping the spent gases out of the cylinder. At TDC, the second crankshaft rotation is complete.

THREE PHASES OF COMBUSTION

There are three distinct phases or parts to the combustion in a diesel engine.

1. **Ignition delay.** Near the end of the compression stroke, fuel injection begins, but ignition does not begin immediately. This period is called *ignition delay*.

2. **Rapid combustion.** This phase of combustion occurs when the fuel first starts to burn, creating a sudden rise in cylinder pressure. It is this sudden and rapid

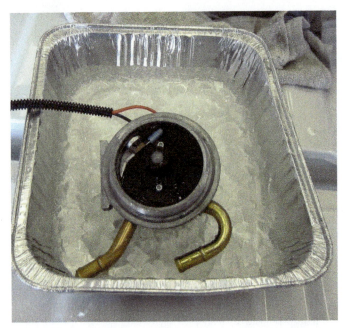

FIGURE 2–7 A fuel temperature sensor is being tested using an ice bath.

FIGURE 2–8 A typical distributor-type diesel injection pump showing the pump, lines, and fuel filter.

rise in combustion chamber pressure that causes the characteristic diesel engine knock.

3. **Controlled combustion.** After the rapid combustion occurs, the rest of the fuel in the combustion chamber begins to burn and injection continues. This process occurs in an area near the injector that contains fuel surrounded by air. This fuel burns as it mixes with the air.

FUEL TANK AND LIFT PUMP

PARTS INVOLVED A fuel tank used on a vehicle equipped with a diesel engine differs from the one used with a gasoline engine in the following ways.

- The filler neck is larger for diesel fuel. The nozzle size is 15/16 inch (24 mm) instead of 13/16 inch (21 mm) for gasoline filler necks. Truck stop diesel nozzles for large over-the-road truck are usually larger, 1.25 inch or 1.5 inch (32 mm or 38 mm) to allow for faster fueling of large-capacity fuel tanks.

- There are no evaporative emission control devices or a charcoal (carbon) canister. Diesel fuel is not as volatile as gasoline and, therefore, diesel vehicles do not have evaporative emission control devices.

The diesel fuel is usually drawn from the fuel tank by a separate pump, called a **lift pump** and delivers the fuel to the injection pump. Between the fuel tank and the lift pump is a **water-fuel separator.** Water is heavier than diesel and sinks to the bottom

of the separator. Part of normal routine maintenance on a vehicle equipped with a diesel engine is to drain the water from the water-fuel separator. A float is often used inside the separator, which is connected to a warning light on the dash that lights if the water reaches a level where it needs to be drained. The water separator is often part of the fuel filter assembly. Both the fuel filter and the water separator are common maintenance items.

NOTE: Water can cause corrosive damage and wear to diesel engine parts because it is not a good lubricant. Water cannot be atomized by a diesel fuel injector nozzle and will often "blow out" the nozzle tip.

Many diesel engines also use a *fuel temperature sensor*. The computer uses this information to adjust fuel delivery based on the density of the fuel. ● SEE FIGURE 2–7.

INJECTION PUMP

NEED FOR HIGH-PRESSURE FUEL PUMP On older diesel engines an injection pump is used to increase the pressure of the diesel fuel from the very low values of the lift pump to the extremely high pressures needed for injection.

- The lift pump is a *low-pressure, high-volume pump.*

- The high-pressure injection pump is a *high-pressure, low-volume pump.*

Injection pumps are usually driven by a gear off the camshaft at the front of the engine. As the injection pump shaft rotates, the diesel fuel is fed from a fill port to a high-pressure chamber. If a distributor-type injection pump is used, the fuel is forced out of the injection port to the correct injector nozzle through the high-pressure line. ● SEE FIGURE 2–8.

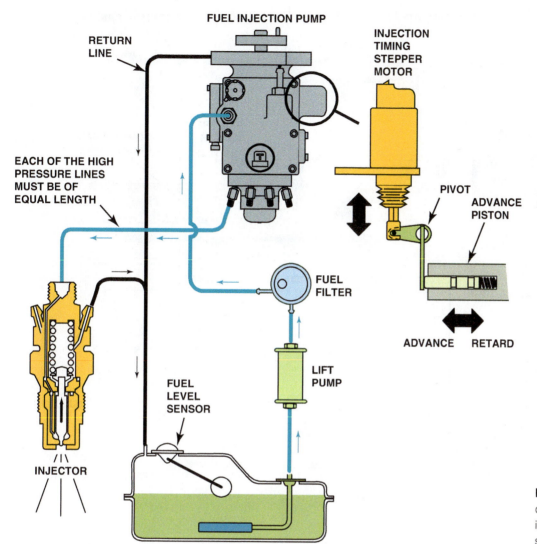

FUEL INJECTION PUMP

RETURN LINE

EACH OF THE HIGH PRESSURE LINES MUST BE OF EQUAL LENGTH

INJECTION TIMING STEPPER MOTOR

PIVOT

ADVANCE PISTON

FUEL FILTER

ADVANCE   RETARD

LIFT PUMP

FUEL LEVEL SENSOR

INJECTOR

FUEL TANK

FIGURE 2–9 A schematic of Standadyne diesel fuel–injection pump assembly showing all of the related components.

NOTE: Because of the very tight tolerances in a diesel engine, the smallest amount of dirt can cause excessive damage to the engine and to the fuel-injection system.

DISTRIBUTOR INJECTION PUMP   A distributor diesel injection pump is a high-pressure pump assembly with lines leading to each individual injector. The high-pressure lines between the distributor and the injectors must be the exact same length to ensure proper injection timing. The high-pressure fuel causes the injectors to open. Due to the internal friction of the lines, there is a slight delay before fuel pressure opens the injector nozzle. The injection pump itself creates the injection advance needed for engine speeds above idle often by using a stepper motor attached to the advance piston, and the fuel is then discharged into the lines. ● **SEE FIGURE 2–9.**

NOTE: The lines expand to some extent during an injection event. This is how timing checks are performed. The pulsing of the injector line is picked up by a probe used to detect the injection event similar to a timing light used to detect a spark on a gasoline engine.

HIGH-PRESSURE COMMON RAIL   Newer diesel engines use a fuel delivery system referred to as a **high-pressure common rail (HPCR)** design. Diesel fuel under high pressure, over 20 000 PSI (138,000 kPa), is applied to the injectors, which are opened by a solenoid controlled by the computer. Because the injectors are computer controlled, the combustion process can be precisely controlled to provide maximum engine efficiency with the lowest possible noise and exhaust emissions. ● **SEE FIGURE 2–10.**

HEUI SYSTEM

PRINCIPLES OF OPERATION   Some non-GM diesel engines use a system called **hydraulic electronic unit injection** system, or **HEUI** system. The components used include:

- High-pressure engine oil pump and reservoir
- Pressure regulator for the engine oil
- Passages in the cylinder head for flow of fuel to the injectors

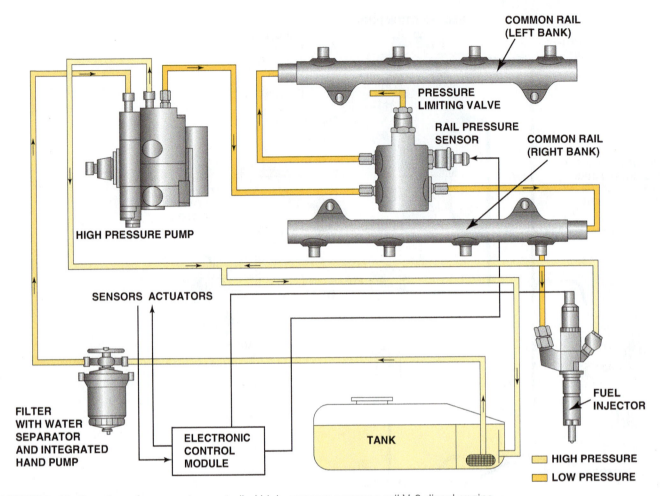

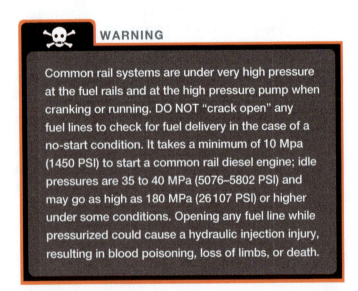

FIGURE 2–10 Overview of a computer-controlled high-pressure common rail V-8 diesel engine.

NOTE: Loosening or removing any of the high-pressure pipes may require that the pipe be replaced with a new one. No amount of tightening will keep it from leaking.

OPERATION The engine oil is pressurized to provide an opening pressure strong enough to overcome the fuel pressure when the solenoid is commanded to open by the PCM. The system functions as follows:

- Fuel is drawn from the tank by the tandem fuel pump, which circulates fuel at low pressure through the fuel filter/water separator/fuel heater bowl and then fuel is directed back to the fuel pump where fuel is pumped at high pressure into the cylinder head fuel galleries.

- The injectors, which are hydraulically actuated by engine oil pressure from the high-pressure oil pump, are then fired by the powertrain control module (PCM). The control system for the fuel injectors is the PCM, and the injectors are fired based on sensor inputs received by the PCM. ● **SEE FIGURE 2–11.**

HEUI injectors rely on O-rings to keep fuel and oil from mixing or escaping, causing performance problems or engine damage. HEUI injectors use five O-rings. The three external O-rings should be replaced with updated O-rings if they fail.

FIGURE 2–11 A HEUI injector. The O-ring grooves indicate the location of the O-rings that seal the fuel section of the injector from coolant and from the engine oil.

The two internal O-rings are not replaceable and if these fail, the injector(s) must be replaced. The most common symptoms of injector O-ring trouble include:

- Oil getting in the fuel
- The fuel filter element turning black
- Long cranking times before starting
- Sluggish performance
- Reduction in power
- Increased oil consumption (This often accompanies O-ring problems or any fault that lets fuel in the oil.)

DIESEL INJECTOR NOZZLES

PARTS INVOLVED Diesel injector nozzles are spring-loaded closed valves that spray fuel directly into the combustion chamber or precombustion chamber when the injector is opened. Injector nozzles are threaded or clamped into the cylinder head, one for each cylinder, and are replaceable as an assembly.

The tip of the injector nozzle has many holes to deliver an atomized spray of diesel fuel into the cylinder. Parts of a diesel injector nozzle include:

- **Heat shield.** This is the outer shell of the injector nozzle and may have external threads where it seals in the cylinder head.
- **Injector body.** This is the inner part of the nozzle and contains the injector needle valve and spring, and threads into the outer heat shield.

 **TECH TIP**

Never Allow a Diesel Engine to Run Out of Fuel

If a gasoline-powered vehicle runs out of gasoline, it is an inconvenience and a possible additional expense to get some gasoline. However, if a vehicle equipped with a diesel engine runs out of fuel, it can be a major concern.

Besides adding diesel fuel to the tank, the other problem is getting all of the air out of the pump, lines, and injectors so the engine will operate correctly.

The procedure usually involves cranking the engine long enough to get liquid diesel fuel back into the system, but at the same time keeping cranking time short enough to avoid overheating the starter. Consult service information for the exact service procedure if the diesel engine runs out of fuel.

NOTE: Some diesel engines, such as the General Motors Duramax V-8, are equipped with a priming pump located under the hood on top of the fuel filter. Pushing down and releasing the priming pump with a vent valve open will purge any trapped air from the system. Always follow the vehicle manufacturer's instructions.

- **Diesel injector needle valve.** This precision-machined valve and the tip of the needle seal against the injector body when it is closed. When the valve is open, diesel fuel is sprayed into the combustion chamber. This passage is controlled by a computer-controlled solenoid on diesel engines equipped with computer-controlled injection.
- **Injector pressure chamber.** The pressure chamber is a machined cavity in the injector body around the tip of the injector needle. Injection pump pressure forces fuel into this chamber, forcing the needle valve open.

DIESEL INJECTOR NOZZLE OPERATION The electric solenoid attached to the injector nozzle is computer controlled and opens to allow fuel to flow into the injector pressure chamber. ● **SEE FIGURE 2–12.**

The fuel flows down through a fuel passage in the injector body and into the pressure chamber. The high fuel pressure in the pressure chamber forces the needle valve upward, compressing the needle valve return spring and forcing the needle valve open.

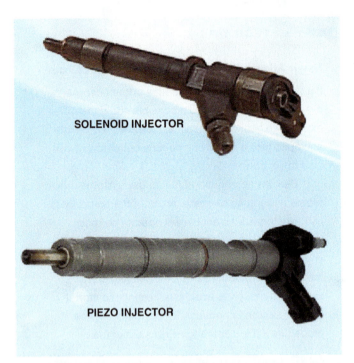

FIGURE 2–12 Typical computer-controlled diesel engine fuel injectors. (*Courtesy of General Motors*)

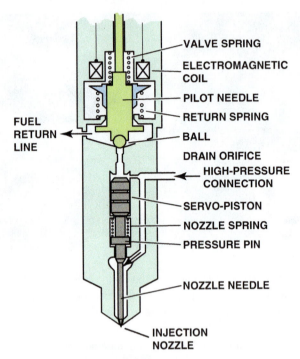

VALVE SPRING
ELECTROMAGNETIC COIL
PILOT NEEDLE
RETURN SPRING
FUEL RETURN LINE
BALL
DRAIN ORIFICE
HIGH-PRESSURE CONNECTION
SERVO-PISTON
NOZZLE SPRING
PRESSURE PIN
NOZZLE NEEDLE
INJECTION NOZZLE

FIGURE 2–13 A solenoid-type Duramax injector, showing all the internal parts. The operating voltage is about 48 volts.

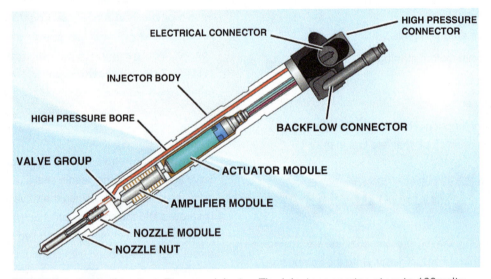

HIGH PRESSURE CONNECTOR
ELECTRICAL CONNECTOR
INJECTOR BODY
HIGH PRESSURE BORE
VALVE GROUP
BACKFLOW CONNECTOR
ACTUATOR MODULE
AMPLIFIER MODULE
NOZZLE MODULE
NOZZLE NUT

FIGURE 2–14 A piezo-type Duramax injector. The injector operates at up to 160 volts. (*Courtesy of General Motors*)

When the needle valve opens, diesel fuel is discharged into the combustion chamber in a hollow cone spray pattern.

Any fuel that leaks past the needle valve returns to the fuel tank through a return passage and line. ● SEE FIGURES 2–13 AND 2–14.

CAUTION: Before working on any high-voltage fuel injection system, be aware of the following procedures: Do NOT make contact with the fuel injection harness, Engine Control Module (ECM), or fuel injectors while the ignition is ON or in RUN position.

Wait 5 minutes after key OFF before you attempt to disconnect or test engine control components. This allows the ECM to discharge the high voltage.

Do NOT use the ECM case as a ground while jump-starting. Failure to follow procedures exactly as written may result in serious injury or death. Refer to Service Information for proper safety procedures before servicing high voltage systems or their components.

GLOW PLUGS

PURPOSE AND FUNCTION
Glow plugs are always used in diesel engines equipped with a precombustion chamber and may be used in direct injection diesel engines to aid starting. A **glow plug** is a heating element that uses up to 12 volts from the battery and aids in the starting of a cold engine by providing heat to help the fuel to ignite. ● **SEE FIGURE 2–15.**

As the temperature of the glow plug increases, the resistance of the heating element inside increases, thereby reducing the current in amperes needed by the glow plugs.

OPERATION
Most glow plugs used in newer vehicles are controlled by the powertrain control module (PCM) which monitors coolant temperature and intake air temperature. The glow plugs are turned on or pulsed on or off depending on the temperature of the engine. The PCM will also keep the glow plug turned on after the engine starts, to reduce white exhaust smoke (unburned fuel) and to improve idle quality after starting. ● **SEE FIGURE 2–16.**

The "wait to start" lamp (if equipped) will light when the engine and the outside temperatures are low to allow time for the glow plugs to get hot.

HEATED INLET AIR
Some diesel engines may use an electrical heater to warm the intake air to help in cold weather starting and running. ● **SEE FIGURE 2–17.**

ENGINE-DRIVEN VACUUM PUMP

Because a diesel engine is unthrottled, it creates very little vacuum in the intake manifold. Several engine and vehicle components operate using vacuum, such as the exhaust gas recirculation (EGR) valve and the heating and ventilation blend and air doors. Most diesels used in cars and light trucks are equipped with an engine-driven vacuum pump to supply the vacuum for these components.

DIESEL FUEL HEATERS

Diesel fuel heaters help prevent power loss and stalling in cold weather. The heater is placed in the fuel line between the tank and the primary filter. Some coolant heaters are thermostatically controlled, which allows fuel to bypass the heater once it has reached operating temperature.

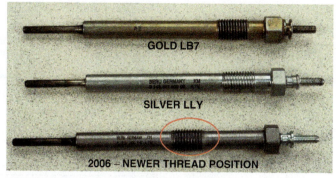

FIGURE 2–15 Duramax diesel glow plugs are different, depending on the year of manufacture of the engine. The gold colored plug operates at 12–14 volts and is not interchangeable with the silver plugs that operate at 4.7 volts. Note also the thread location. (*Courtesy of General Motors*)

? FREQUENTLY ASKED QUESTION

How Can You Tell If Gasoline Has Been Added to the Diesel Fuel by Mistake?

If gasoline has been accidentally added to diesel fuel and is burned in a diesel engine, the result can be very damaging to the engine. The gasoline can ignite faster than diesel fuel, which would tend to increase the temperature of combustion. This high temperature can harm injectors and glow plugs, as well as pistons, head gaskets, and other major diesel engine components. If contaminated fuel is suspected, first smell the fuel at the filler neck. If the fuel smells like gasoline, then the tank should be drained and refilled with diesel fuel. If the smell test does not indicate a gasoline or any rancid smell, then test a sample for proper specific gravity.

NOTE: Diesel fuel designed for on-road use should be green. Red diesel fuel (high sulfur) should only be found in off-road or farm equipment.

ACCELERATOR PEDAL POSITION SENSOR

Some light-truck diesel engines are equipped with an electronic throttle to control the amount of fuel injected into the engine. Although a diesel engine does not normally use a throttle in the air intake, these engines may also have a

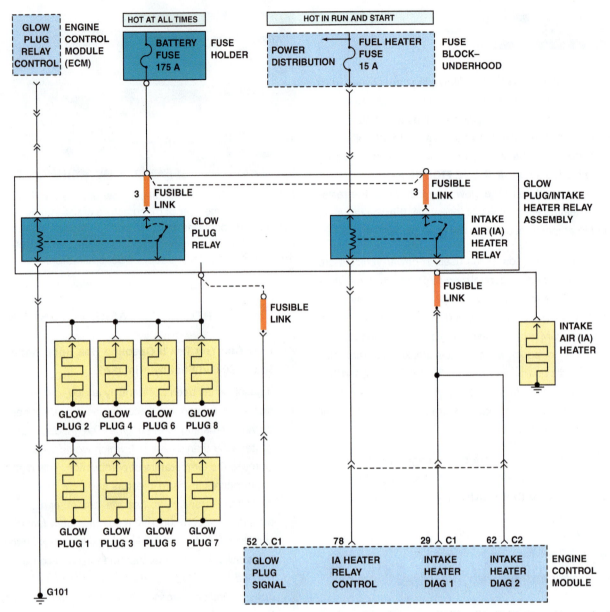

FIGURE 2–16 A schematic of a typical glow plug circuit. Notice that the glow plug relay and intake air heater relay are both computer controlled.

throttle housing and plate as part of the emission control system. Instead of a mechanical link from the accelerator pedal to the diesel injection pump, a throttle-by-wire system uses an accelerator pedal position (APP) sensor. To ensure safety, it consists of three separate sensors that change in voltage as the accelerator pedal is depressed.
● **SEE FIGURE 2–18.**

The computer checks for errors by comparing the voltage output of each of the three sensors inside the APP and compares them to what they should be if there are no faults. If an error is detected, the engine and vehicle speed are often reduced.

DIESEL ENGINE TURBOCHARGERS

TURBOCHARGED DIESELS A turbocharger greatly increases engine power by pumping additional compressed air into the combustion chambers. This allows a greater quantity of fuel to be burned in the cylinders resulting in greater power output. In a turbocharger, the turbine wheel spins as exhaust gas flows out of the engine and drives the turbine blades. The turbine spins the compressor wheel at the opposite end of

FIGURE 2–17 This heater is used to warm the intake air during cold weather operation. (*Courtesy of General Motors*)

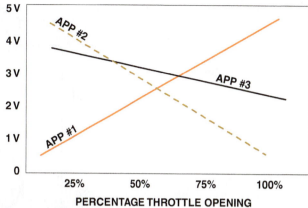

FIGURE 2–18 A typical accelerator pedal position (APP) sensor uses two or three different sensors in one package with each creating a different voltage as the accelerator is moved.

the turbine shaft, pumping air into the intake system. ● **SEE FIGURE 2–19.**

AIR CHARGE COOLER

The first component in a typical turbocharger system is an air filter through which ambient air passes before entering the compressor. The air is compressed, which raises its density (mass/unit volume). All currently produced light-duty diesels use an **air charge cooler** whose purpose is to cool the compressed air to further raise the air density. Cooler air entering the engine means more power can be produced by the engine. ● **SEE FIGURE 2–20.**

VARIABLE TURBOCHARGER

A variable turbocharger is used on many diesel engines for boost control. Boost pressure is controlled independent of engine speed and a wastegate is not needed. The adjustable vanes mount to a unison ring that allows the vanes to move. As the position of the unison ring rotates, the vanes change angle. The vanes are opened to minimize flow at the turbine and exhaust back pressure at low engine speeds. To increase turbine speed, the vanes are closed. The velocity of the exhaust gases increases, as does the speed of the turbine. The unison ring is connected to a cam that is positioned by a rack-and-pinion gear. The turbocharger's vane position actuator solenoid connects to a hydraulic piston, which moves the rack to rotate the pinion gear and cam. ● **SEE FIGURE 2–21.**

FIGURE 2–19 A turbocharger is used to increase the power and torque of the engine. (*Courtesy of General Motors*)

The turbocharger vane position control solenoid valve is used to advance the unison ring's relationship to the turbine and thereby articulate the vanes. This solenoid actuates a spool valve that applies oil pressure to either side of a piston. Oil flow has three modes: apply, hold, and release.

- *Apply* moves the vanes toward a closed position.
- *Hold* maintains the vanes in a fixed position.
- *Release* moves the vanes toward the open position.

The turbocharger vane position actuation is controlled by the ECM, which can change turbine boost efficiency independent of engine speed. The ECM provides a control signal to the valve solenoid along with a low-side reference. A pulse-width-modulated signal from the ECM moves the valve to the desired position.

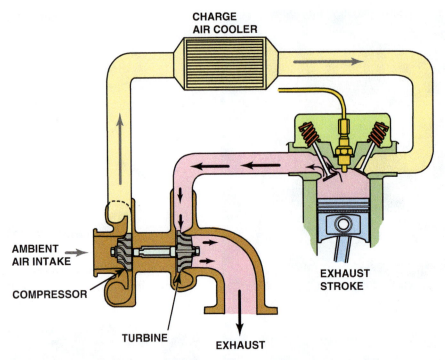

FIGURE 2–20 An air charge cooler is used to cool the compressed air.

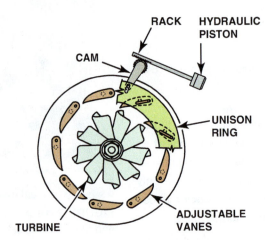

FIGURE 2–21 A variable vane turbocharger allows the boost to be controlled without the need of a wastegate.

SUMMARY

1. A diesel engine uses heat of compression to ignite the diesel fuel when it is injected into the compressed air in the combustion chamber.

2. There are two basic designs of combustion chambers used in diesel engines. Indirect injection (IDI) uses a pre-combustion chamber, whereas direct injection (DI) occurs directly into the combustion chamber.

3. The three phases of diesel combustion include:
   a. Ignition delay
   b. Rapid combustion
   c. Controlled combustion

4. The typical diesel engine fuel system consists of the fuel tank, lift pump, water-fuel separator, and fuel filter.

5. The engine-driven injection pump supplies high-pressure diesel fuel to the injectors.

6. The two most common types of fuel injection used in diesel engines are:
   a. Distributor-type injection pump
   b. Common rail design where all of the injectors are fed from the same fuel supply from a rail under high pressure.

7. Injector nozzles are either opened by the high-pressure pulse from the distributor pump or electrically by the computer on a common rail design.

8. Glow plugs are used to help start a cold diesel engine and help prevent excessive white smoke during warm-up.

1. What is the difference between direct injection and indirect injection?

2. What are the three phases of diesel ignition?

3. What are the two most commonly used types of diesel injection systems?

4. Why are glow plugs kept working after the engine starts?

CHAPTER QUIZ

1. How is diesel fuel ignited in a warm diesel engine?
   a. Glow plugs
   b. Heat of compression
   c. Spark plugs
   d. Distributorless ignition system

2. Which type of diesel injection produces less noise?
   a. Indirect injection (IDI)
   b. Common rail
   c. Direct injection
   d. Distributor injection

3. Which diesel injection system requires the use of a glow plug?
   a. Indirect injection (IDI)
   b. High-pressure common rail
   c. Direct injection
   d. Distributor injection

4. The three phases of diesel ignition include _____.
   a. Glow plug ignition, fast burn, slow burn
   b. Slow burn, fast burn, slow burn
   c. Ignition delay, rapid combustion, controlled combustion
   d. Glow plug ignition, ignition delay, controlled combustion

5. What fuel system component is used in a vehicle equipped with a diesel engine that is seldom used on the same vehicle when it is equipped with a gasoline engine?
   a. Fuel filter
   b. Fuel supply line
   c. Fuel return line
   d. Water-fuel separator

6. The diesel injection pump is usually driven by a _____.
   a. Gear off the camshaft
   b. Belt off the crankshaft
   c. Shaft drive off the crankshaft
   d. Chain drive off the camshaft

7. Which diesel system supplies high-pressure diesel fuel to all of the injectors all of the time?
   a. Distributor
   b. Inline
   c. High-pressure common rail
   d. Rotary

8. Glow plugs should have high resistance when _____ and lower resistance when _____.
   a. Cold/warm
   b. Warm/cold
   c. Wet/dry
   d. Dry/wet

9. Technician A says that glow plugs are used to help start a diesel engine and are shut off as soon as the engine starts. Technician B says that the glow plugs are turned off as soon as a flame is detected in the combustion chamber. Which technician is correct?
   a. Technician A only
   b. Technician B only
   c. Both Technicians A and B
   d. Neither Technician A nor B

10. The injectors on a common rail diesel engine are opened by _____.
    a. Vibration
    b. Voltage from the ECM
    c. A vacuum pulse
    d. High voltage resistors

chapter 3
COOLANT

LEARNING OBJECTIVES

After studying this chapter, the reader should be able to:

1. Describe the various types of antifreeze coolants.
2. Discuss recycling coolant.
3. Discuss how to test coolant.

This chapter will help you prepare for ASE certification test A1 Engine Repair, content area "D" (Lubrication and Cooling Systems Diagnosis and Repair).

KEY TERMS

DEX-COOL® 34
Electrolysis 38
Embittered coolant 35
Ethylene glycol based coolant 33
Galvanic activity 38
Hybrid organic acid technology (HOAT) 34
Inorganic acid technology (IAT) 34
Organic acid technology (OAT) 34
Passivation 39
Phosphate hybrid organic acid technology (PHOAT) 34
Refractometer 37

GM STC OBJECTIVES

GM Service Technical College topics covered in this chapter are:

1. The purpose and composition of engine coolant. (00510.01W-R2)
2. The components of the engine cooling system.
3. Normal and abnormal engine coolant.

COOLANT FUNDAMENTALS

PURPOSE OF COOLANT   Coolant is used in the cooling system because it:

1. Transfers heat from the engine to the radiator

2. Protects the engine and the cooling system from rust and corrosion

3. Prevents freezing in cold climates

Coolant is a mixture of antifreeze and water. Water is able to absorb more heat per gallon than any other liquid coolant. Under standard conditions, the following occurs.

- Water boils at 212°F (100°C) at sea level.

- Water freezes at 32°F (0°C).

- When water freezes, it increases in volume by about 9%. The expansion of the freezing water can easily crack engine blocks, cylinder heads, and radiators.

A curve depicting freezing point as compared with the percentage of antifreeze mixture is shown in ● **FIGURE 3–1**.

FREEZING/BOILING TEMPERATURES   It should be noted that the freezing point increases as the antifreeze concentration is increased above 60%. The normal mixture is 50% antifreeze and 50% water. Ethylene glycol antifreeze contains:

- Anticorrosion additives

- Rust inhibitors

- Water pump lubricants

At the maximum level of protection, an ethylene glycol concentration of 60% will absorb about 85% as much heat as will water. Ethylene glycol based antifreeze also has a higher boiling point than water. A curve depicting freezing point as compared with the percentage of antifreeze mixture is shown in ● **FIGURE 3–2**.

If the coolant boils, it vaporizes and does not act as a cooling agent because it is not in liquid form or in contact with the cooling surfaces.

All coolants have rust and corrosion inhibitors to help protect the metals in the engine and cooling systems.

COOLANT COMPOSITION   All manufacturers recommend the use of **ethylene glycol based coolant**, which contains:

- Ethylene glycol (EG): 47%

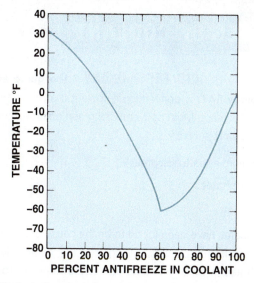

FIGURE 3–1 Graph showing the relationship of the freezing point of the coolant to the percentage of antifreeze used in the coolant.

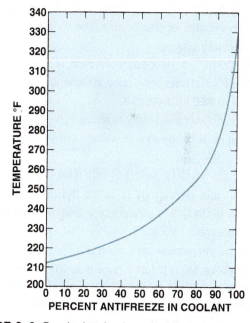

FIGURE 3–2 Graph showing how the boiling point of the coolant increases as the percentage of antifreeze in the coolant increases.

- Water: 50%

- Additives: 3%

Regardless of the type of coolant and its color, the only difference among all original equipment coolants is in the additives. This means that about 97% of all coolants are the same. The only difference is in the additive package and color used to help identify the coolant.

TYPES OF COOLANT

INORGANIC ACID TECHNOLOGY
Inorganic additive technology (IAT) is conventional coolant that has been used for over 50 years. Most conventional green antifreeze contains inorganic salts such as:

- Sodium silicate (silicates)
- Phosphates
- Borates

Silicates have been found to be the cause of erosive wear to water pump impellers. The color of IAT coolant is green. Phosphates in these coolants can cause deposits to form if used with water that is hard (contains minerals). IAT coolants used in new vehicles were phased out in the mid-1990s.

ORGANIC ACID TECHNOLOGY
Organic acid technology (OAT) coolant contains ethylene glycol, but does not contain silicates or phosphates. The color of this type of coolant is usually orange.

DEX-COOL®, developed by Havoline, is just one brand of OAT coolant, which has been used in General Motors vehicles since 1996. ● **SEE FIGURE 3–3.**

These coolants are usually available in premix or as a pure coolant that must be mixed with water.

HYBRID ORGANIC ACID TECHNOLOGY
A newer variation of this technology is called **hybrid organic acid technology (HOAT).** It is similar to the OAT-type antifreeze as it uses organic acid salts (carboxylates) that are not abrasive to water pumps, yet provide the correct pH. The pH of the coolant is usually above 11. A pH of 7 is neutral, with lower numbers indicating an acidic solution and higher numbers indicating an alkaline solution. If the pH is too high, the coolant can cause scaling and reduce the heat transferability of the coolant. If the pH is too low, the resulting acidic solution could cause corrosion of the engine components exposed to the coolant.

HOAT coolants can be green, orange, yellow, gold, pink, red, or blue.

PHOSPHATE HYBRID ORGANIC ACID TECHNOLOGY
Phosphate hybrid organic acid technology (PHOAT) is used in some imported and import-based domestic vehicles, and is ethylene glycol based. This coolant is available in a 55% coolant/45% water premix.

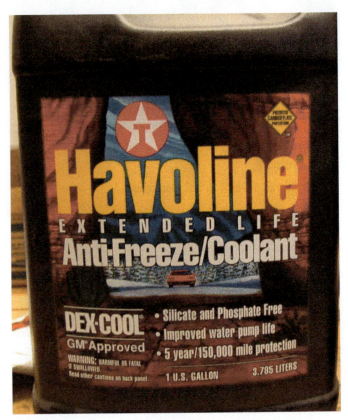

FIGURE 3–3 Havoline was the first company to make and market OAT coolant. General Motors uses the term DEX-COOL®.

- Concentration: 55%
- Boiling point (with 15 PSI pressure cap): 270°F (132°C)
- Freezing point: −47°F (−44°C)
- Color: Dark green
- Embittered (made to taste bitter so animals will not drink it)

The use of PHOAT coolant in these engines is required to be assured of proper protection of the material used in the engine. It is also only available in premix containers to ensure that the water used meets specifications.

WATER

INTRODUCTION
Water is half of the coolant and can have an effect on the corrosion protection of coolant due to variations in its quality, which is often unknown. As a result, many vehicle manufacturers are specifying the use of premix

FIGURE 3–4 Embittered coolants may or may not be labeled as such, depending on the manufacturer.

What Is "Pet Friendly" Antifreeze?

Conventional ethylene glycol antifreeze used by all vehicle manufacturers is attractive to pets and animals because it has a sweet taste. Ethylene glycol is fatal to any animal if swallowed, so any spill should be cleaned up quickly. There are two types of coolant that are safer for use around pets than the conventional type.

- **Propylene glycol (PG).** This type of antifreeze is less attractive to pets and animals because it is not as sweet, but it is still harmful if swallowed. This type of coolant, including the Sierra brand, should not be mixed with any other ethylene glycol based coolant.

  CAUTION: Some vehicle manufacturers do not recommend the use of propylene glycol coolant. Check the recommendation in the owner manual or service information before using it in a vehicle.

- **Embittered coolant.** This coolant has a small amount of a substance that makes it taste bitter and therefore not appealing to animals. The embittering agent used in ethylene glycol (EG) antifreeze is usually denatonium benzoate, added at the rate of 30 ppm. Oregon and California require all coolant sold in these states since 2004 to be embittered. ● **SEE FIGURE 3–4.**

If 50% Is Good, 100% Must Be Better

A vehicle owner said that the cooling system of his vehicle would never freeze or rust. He said that he used 100% antifreeze (ethylene glycol) instead of a 50/50 mixture with water.

However, after the temperature dropped to –20°F (–29°C), the radiator froze and cracked. (Pure antifreeze freezes at about 0°F [–18°C].) After thawing, the radiator had to be repaired. The owner was lucky that the engine block did not also crack.

For best freeze protection with good heat transfer, use a 50/50 mixture of antifreeze and water. A 50/50 mixture of antifreeze and water is the best compromise between temperature protection and the heat transfer that is necessary for cooling system operation. Do not exceed 70% antifreeze (30% water). As the percentage of antifreeze increases, the boiling temperature increases, and freezing protection increases (up to 70% antifreeze), but the heat transfer performance of the mixture decreases.

What Makes Some Water Bad for Coolant?

City water is treated with chlorine, which, if the levels are high enough, can cause corrosion problems when used with coolants. Well water may contain iron or other minerals that can affect the coolant and may increase the corrosion or cause electrolysis. Due to the fact that the water quality is often unknown and could affect the engine, many vehicle manufacturers are specifying the use of pre-mixed coolant. In pre-mix coolant, the water is usually de-ionized and meets the standards for use in coolant.

coolants only. The main reason is that not only can the water/coolant ratio be maintained, but also the quality of the water can be controlled.

PROPERTIES Water is about half of the coolant and is used because of the following qualities.

1. It is inexpensive.

2. It is an efficient heat exchange fluid because of its excellent thermal conductivity (the ability of a material to conduct heat).

3. It has good specific heat capacity, meaning it takes more heat energy to increase the temperature, versus one with low specific heat capacity.

4. The boiling point is 212°F (100°C) (at sea level).

5. The freezing point is 32°F (0°C).

HYBRID/ELECTRIC VEHICLE PRECAUTIONS When servicing any of the cooling systems on GM hybrid/electric vehicles, which includes the pumps, reservoirs, hoses, air separators, radiators, Power Inverter Module (PIM), high-voltage battery assembly, engine or heater system, it is important to use the proper coolant and water mixture.

The Power Electronics/Charging and Battery Cooling systems require a 50/50 mix of DEX-COOL® and de-ionized water. This mixture is available in a pre-mix with bitterant. The pre-mixed coolant is no longer available without the bitterant chemical. Bitterant is a chemical that is added to products to make them smell or taste extremely bitter and is required in some states.[1]

COOLANT FREEZING/ BOILING TEMPERATURES

FREEZING POINT An antifreeze and water mixture is an example wherein the freezing point differs from the freezing point of either pure antifreeze or pure water.

	Freezing Point
Pure water	32°F (0°C)
Pure antifreeze*	0°F (−18°C)
50/50 mixture	−34°F (−37°C)
70% antifreeze/30% water	−84°F (−64°C)

*Pure antifreeze is usually 95% ethylene glycol, 2% to 3% water, and 2% to 3% additives.

Depending on the exact percentage of water used, antifreeze (not premixed), as sold in containers, freezes at about 0°F (−18°C). Premixed coolant will freeze at about −34°F (−37°C).

[1]GM Techlink, April 2012.

Why Are Most Coolants 50/50 Mixed with Water?

According to the freezing point, it appears that the lowest freezing point of coolant is achieved when 70% antifreeze is used with 30% water. While the freezing temperature is lower, the high concentrate of antifreeze reduces the heat transferability of the coolant. Therefore, most vehicle manufacturers specify a 50/50 mixture of antifreeze and water to achieve the best balance between freeze protection and heat conductivity.

BOILING POINT The boiling point of antifreeze and water is also a factor of mixture concentrations.

	Boiling Point at Sea Level	Boiling Point with 15 PSI Pressure Cap
Pure water	212°F (100°C)	257°F (125°C)
50/50 mixture	218°F (103°C)	265°F (130°C)
70/30 mixture	225°F (107°C)	276°F (136°C)

COOLANT TESTING

Normal coolant tests include:

- **Visual inspection.** Coolant should be clean and bright.

- **Freeze/boiling point.** A high freezing point or low boiling point indicates dilution (too much water).

- **pH.** The wrong pH indicates buffer loss, which is used to help maintain the pH level.

- **Coolant voltage.** A high voltage indicates the wrong pH or a stray current flow.

Various methods are used to test coolant.

HYDROMETER TESTING Coolant can be checked using a coolant hydrometer. The hydrometer measures the density of the coolant. The higher the density, more the concentration of antifreeze in the water. Most coolant hydrometers read the freezing and boiling points of the coolant. ● **SEE FIGURE 3–5.**

If the engine is overheating and the hydrometer reading is near −50°F (−60°C), suspect that pure 100% antifreeze is present. For best results, the coolant should have a freezing point lower than −20°F (−29°C) and a boiling point above 234°F (112°).

FIGURE 3–5 Checking the freezing temperature of the coolant using a hydrometer.

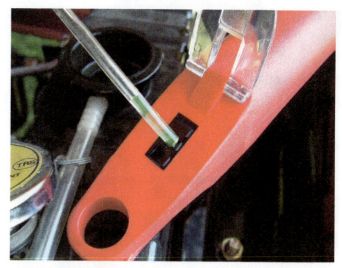

FIGURE 3–7 Cover the lens with the coolant sample and then close the lens cover.

FIGURE 3–6 A refractometer can be used to check the specific gravity of coolant and diesel exhaust fluid.

🔧 **TECH TIP**

Ignore the Wind Chill Factor

The wind chill factor is a temperature that combines the actual temperature and the wind speed to determine the overall heat loss effect on open skin. Because it is the heat loss factor for open skin, the wind chill temperature is *not* to be considered when determining antifreeze protection levels.

Although moving air makes it feel colder, the actual temperature is not changed by the wind, and the engine coolant will not be affected by the wind chill. If you are not convinced, try placing a thermometer in a room and wait until a stable reading is obtained. Now turn on a fan and have the air blow across the thermometer. The temperature will not change.

REFRACTOMETER

A **refractometer** is a tester used to test the freezing point of coolant by placing a few drops of coolant on the prism surface. The technician then holds the unit up to light and looks through the eyepiece for the location of the shadow on the display. **SEE FIGURES 3–6 AND 3–7.**

A refractometer measures the extent to which light is bent (refracted) to determine the index of refraction of a liquid sample.

The refractive index is commonly used for the following:

- To determine the purity of a coolant by comparing its refractive index to the value for the pure substance
- To determine the concentration of a solute in a solution by comparing the solution's refractive index to a standard curve
- **SEE FIGURE 3–8.**

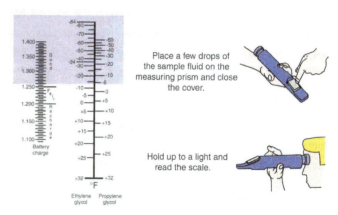

Place a few drops of the sample fluid on the measuring prism and close the cover.

Hold up to a light and read the scale.

FIGURE 3–8 Using a refractometer is an accurate method to check the freezing point of coolant.

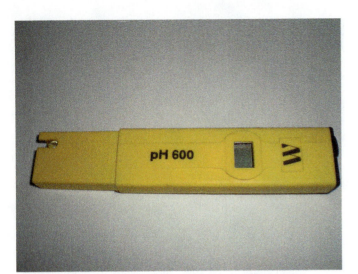

FIGURE 3–9 A meter that measures the actual pH of the coolant can be used for all coolants, unlike many test strips that cannot be used to test the pH of red or orange coolants.

PH The term *pH* comes from a French word, meaning "power of hydrogen," and is a measure of acidity or alkalinity of a solution.

- Less than 7 pH is considered acidic.
- Greater than 7 pH is considered alkaline.

The pH of new coolant varies according to the type of coolant used. Typical pH values for new coolant include:

IAT: 9 to 10.5 new

OAT: 7.5 to 8.5 new (G30 and G34 designations)

HOAT: 7.5 to 8.5 new (G05, G48, G11, or G12 designation)

PHOAT: 7.5 to 8.5 new

When testing for pH, use either a test strip or a pH meter. If using a test strip be sure that it is calibrated to test the type of coolant being used in the vehicle.

Used coolant pH readings are usually lower than when the coolant is new and range from between 7.5 and 10 for IAT and lower for used OAT, HOAT, and PHOAT coolants. For best results use a pH tester that measures the actual pH of the coolant. ● **SEE FIGURE 3–9.**

GALVANIC ACTIVITY **Galvanic activity** is the flow of an electrical current as a result of two different metals in a liquid, which acts like a battery. Galvanic activity does *not* require an outside source of voltage. The two different metals, usually iron and aluminum, become the plates of the battery and the coolant is the electrolyte. The higher the electrical conductivity of the coolant, the greater is the amount of corrosion. ● **SEE FIGURE 3–10.**

BI-METAL CORROSION

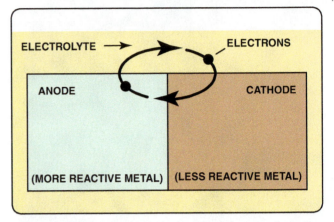

FIGURE 3–10 Galvanic activity is created by two dissimilar metals in contact with a liquid, in this case coolant.

ELECTROLYSIS **Electrolysis** requires the use of an outside voltage source. The source is usually due to a poor electrical ground connection.

- Electrical flow through the cooling system may cause metal to dissolve into the coolant.
- This metal transfer can eat holes in a heater core or radiator.
- Electrolysis holes will usually start from the inside and have a dark coloration.

TESTING FOR GALVANIC ACTIVITY AND ELECTROLYSIS A voltmeter set to read DC volts is used to test for galvanic activity and electrolysis. To check for excessive voltage caused by galvanic activity or electrolysis, perform the following steps.

STEP 1 Allow the engine to cool and then carefully remove the pressure cap from the radiator.

STEP 2 Set the voltmeter to DC volts and connect the black meter lead to a good engine ground.

STEP 3 Place the red meter lead into the coolant.

STEP 4 Read the meter. If the voltage is above 0.5 V, this indicates excessive galvanic activity. Normal readings should be less than 0.2 V (200 mV). Flush and refill the cooling system.

STEP 5 To test for excessive electrolysis, start the engine and turn on all electrical accessories, including the headlights on high beam.

STEP 6 Read the voltmeter. If the reading is higher than 0.5 V, check for improper body ground wires or connections. Normal readings should be less than 0.3 V (300 mV).

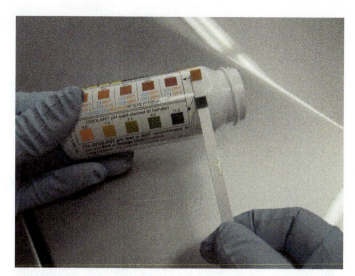

FIGURE 3–11 A test strip can be used to determine the pH and percentage of glycol of the coolant. The percentage of glycol determines the freezing and boiling temperatures, as shown on the bottle that contains the test strips.

TEST STRIP TESTING Test strips can be used to check one or more of the following:

- Freeze point
- Boiling point
- Level of pH

Test strips will change color when they are dipped into the coolant, and the color change is compared to the container. Test strips are fairly accurate, easy to use, and inexpensive.

For best results, use test strips that are new and have been stored in a sealed bottle. Using older test strips may affect the accuracy. ● **SEE FIGURE 3–11.**

COOLANT REPLACEMENT ISSUES

INTERVALS Coolant should be replaced according to the vehicle manufacturer's recommended interval.

- For most new vehicles using OAT (DEX-COOL®) or HOAT type coolant, this interval may be every five years or 150,000 miles (241,000 km), whichever occurs first.

- If the coolant is changed from a long life to a conventional IAT coolant, the replacement interval needs to be changed to every two years or 24,000 miles (39,000 km), whichever occurs first.

PASSIVATION **Passivation** is a chemical reaction that takes place between coolant additives and the metal that it protects. This means that a chemical barrier is created between the coolant and the metals of the engine. When changing coolants, passivation can take from a few days to a few weeks.

- Each chemical package does its own passivation.
- If you change chemical packages, passivation has to start over.

Therefore, because of passivation concerns, most experts agree that for best results do not change types of coolants. Always use what the vehicle manufacturer recommends. Always check service information for the exact recommended replacement interval for the vehicle being serviced.

RECYCLING COOLANT Coolant (antifreeze and water) should be recycled. Used coolant may contain heavy metals, such as lead, aluminum, and iron, which are absorbed by the coolant during its use in the engine.

Recycle machines filter out these metals and dirt and reinstall the depleted acids. The recycled coolant, restored to be like new, can be reinstalled into the vehicle.

General Motors supports the use of recycled engine coolant for warranty repairs/service, provided a GM-approved engine coolant recycling system is used.

Only current licensed and approved providers of DEX-COOL® should be used in GM vehicles. Products that are advertised as "COMPATIBLE" or "RECOMMENDED" for use with DEX-COOL® have not been tested or approved by General Motors. Non-approved coolants may degrade the coolant system integrity and will no longer be considered a 5 yr/150,000 mile (240,000 km) coolant.[2]

---

[2]GM TSB 00-06-02-006D

1. All coolants are ethylene glycol-based. Some aftermarket coolants use propylene glycol.
2. Used coolant should be recycled whenever possible.
3. The freezing temperature of the coolant can be tested using a hydrometer or refractometer.
4. Proper cooling system maintenance usually calls for replacing the coolant every two years or every 24,000 miles (36,000 km) for IAT coolant. For most new vehicles using OAT (DEX-COOL®) or HOAT type coolant, this interval may be every five years or 150,000 miles (241,000 km), whichever occurs first.

REVIEW QUESTIONS

1. What types of coolant are used in vehicles?
2. Why is a 50/50 mixture of antifreeze and water commonly used as a coolant?
3. What are the differences among IAT, OAT, HOAT, and PHOAT coolants?
4. What are some of the heavy metals that can be present in used coolant?
5. What is the difference between galvanic activity and electrolysis?

CHAPTER QUIZ

1. Coolant is water and _____.
   a. Methanol
   b. Glycerin
   c. Kerosene
   d. Ethylene glycol

2. As the percentage of antifreeze in the coolant increases, _____.
   a. The freeze point decreases (up to a point)
   b. The boiling point decreases
   c. The heat transfer increases
   d. All of the above

3. Adding a chemical to make ethylene glycol coolant bitter to the taste is called _____.
   a. Passivation
   b. Refractometer
   c. Embittered
   d. Electrolysis

4. A refractometer is used to measure coolant _____.
   a. Freezing point
   b. Temperature
   c. Color
   d. Viscosity

5. DEX-COOL is what type of coolant?
   a. IAT
   b. OAT
   c. HOAT
   d. PHOAT

6. PHOAT coolant is what color?
   a. Dark green
   b. Red
   c. Orange
   d. Blue

7. DEX-COOL® is _____.
   a. Propylene glycol
   b. Ethylene glycol
   c. Is silicate and phosphate free
   d. Both b and c

8. Two technicians are discussing testing coolant for proper pH. Technician A says that coolant has a pH above 7 when new and becomes lower with use in an engine. Technician B says that OAT and HOAT coolants have a lower pH when new compared to the old green IAT coolant. Which technician is correct?
   a. Technician A only
   b. Technician B only
   c. Both Technicians A and B
   d. Neither Technician A nor B

9. What type of water is recommended for use when mixing with coolant?
   a. Ironized water
   b. De-ionized water
   c. Mineral water
   d. Ice water

10. A voltmeter was used to check the coolant and a reading of 0.2 volt with the engine off was measured. A reading of 0.8 volt was measured with the engine running and all electrical accessories turned on. Technician A says that the coolant should be flushed to solve the galvanic activity. Technician B says that the ground wires and connections should be inspected and repaired to solve the electrolysis problem. Which technician is correct?
   a. Technician A only
   b. Technician B only
   c. Both Technicians A and B
   d. Neither Technician A nor B

chapter 4

COOLING SYSTEM OPERATION AND DIAGNOSIS

LEARNING OBJECTIVES

After studying this chapter, the reader should be able to:

1. Describe how coolant flows through an engine.
2. Discuss the operation of the thermostat.
3. Explain the purpose and function of the radiator pressure cap.
4. Describe the operation and service of water pumps.
5. Discuss how to diagnose cooling system problems.

This chapter will help you prepare for ASE certification test A1 Engine Repair, content area "D" (Lubrication and Cooling Systems Diagnosis and Repair).

KEY TERMS

Bar 49
Bleed holes 53
Bypass 44
Centrifugal pump 50
Coolant recovery system 49
Cooling fins 47
Core tubes 47
Impeller 51
Parallel flow system 52
Reverse cooling 50
Scroll 51
Series flow system 53
Series-parallel flow system 53
Silicone coupling 54
Steam slits 53
Surge tank 49
Thermostatic spring 54

GM STC OBJECTIVES

GM Service Technical College topics covered in this chapter are:

1. The components of the engine cooling system. (00510.01W-R2)
2. Normal and abnormal engine coolant.
3. Engine coolant system service inspection procedures.
4. Perform cooling system tests (pressure, combustion leakage, and temperature); determine needed repairs.
5. Test and replace thermostat.

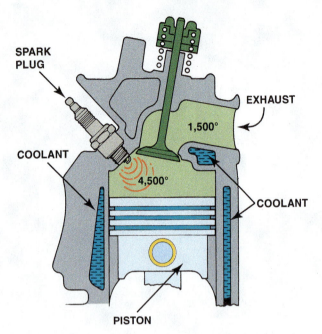

FIGURE 4–1 Typical combustion and exhaust temperatures.

Labels in figure: SPARK PLUG, EXHAUST, 1,500°, COOLANT, 4,500°, COOLANT, PISTON

COOLING SYSTEM

PURPOSE AND FUNCTION   Satisfactory cooling system operation depends on the design and operating conditions of the system. The design is based on heat output of the engine, radiator size, type of coolant, size of water pump (coolant pump), type of fan, thermostat, and system pressure. The cooling system must allow the engine to warm up to the required operating temperature as rapidly as possible and then maintain that temperature.

Peak combustion temperatures in the engine run from 4,000°F to 6,000°F (2,200°C to 3,300°C). The combustion temperatures will *average* between 1,200°F and 1,700°F (650°C and 925°C). Continued temperatures as high as this would weaken engine parts, so heat must be removed from the engine. The cooling system keeps the head and cylinder walls at a temperature that is within the range for maximum efficiency. The cooling system removes about one-third of the heat created in the engine. Another third escapes to the exhaust system. ● **SEE FIGURE 4–1.**

LOW-TEMPERATURE ENGINE PROBLEMS   Engine operating temperatures must be above a minimum temperature for proper engine operation. If the coolant temperature does not reach the specified temperature as determined by the thermostat, then the following engine-related faults can occur.

- A P0128 diagnostic trouble code (DTC) can be set. This code indicates "coolant temperature below thermostat regulating temperature," which is usually caused by a defective thermostat staying open or partially open.

- Moisture created during the combustion process can condense and flow into the oil. *For each gallon of fuel used, moisture equal to a gallon of water is produced.* The condensed moisture combines with unburned hydrocarbons and additives to form carbonic acid, sulfuric acid, nitric acid, hydrobromic acid, and hydrochloric acid.

To reduce cold engine problems and to help start engines in cold climates, most manufacturers offer block heaters as an option. These block heaters are plugged into household current (110 volts AC) and the heating element warms the coolant.

HIGH-TEMPERATURE ENGINE PROBLEMS   Maximum temperature limits are required to protect the engine. Higher than normal temperatures can cause the following engine-related issues.

- High temperatures will oxidize the engine oil producing hard carbon and varnish. The varnish will cause the hydraulic valve lifter plungers to stick. Higher than normal temperatures will also cause the oil to become thinner (lower viscosity than normal). Thinned oil will also get into the combustion chamber by going past the piston rings and through valve guides to cause excessive oil consumption.

- The combustion process is very sensitive to temperature. High coolant temperatures raise the combustion temperatures to a point that may cause detonation (also called spark knock or ping) to occur.

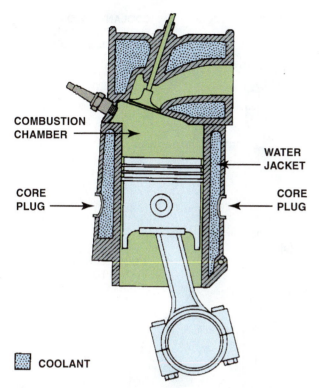

FIGURE 4–2 Coolant circulates through the water jackets in the engine block and cylinder head.

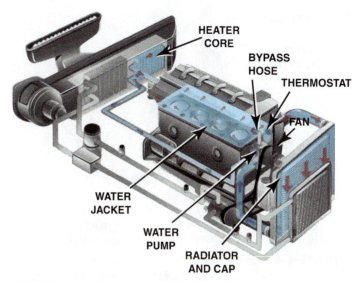

FIGURE 4–3 Coolant flow through a typical engine cooling system. (*Courtesy of General Motors*)

COOLING SYSTEM OPERATION

PURPOSE AND FUNCTION Coolant flows through the engine, where it picks up heat. It then flows to the radiator, where the heat is given up to the outside air. The coolant continually recirculates through the cooling system, as illustrated in ● **FIGURES 4–2 AND 4–3.**

COOLING SYSTEM OPERATION The temperature of the coolant rises as much as 15°F (8°C) as it goes through the engine and cools as it goes through the radiator. *The coolant flow rate may be as high as 1 gallon (4 liters) per minute for each horsepower the engine produces.*

Hot coolant comes out of the thermostat housing on the top of the engine on most engines. The engine coolant outlet is connected to the radiator by the upper radiator hose and clamps. The coolant in the radiator is cooled by air flowing through the radiator. As the coolant moves through the radiator, it cools. The cooler coolant leaves the radiator through an outlet and the lower radiator hose, and then flows to the inlet side of the water pump, where it is recirculated through the engine.

NOTE: Some engine designs such as General Motor's 4.8, 5.3, 5.7, and 6.0 liter V-8s place the thermostat on the inlet side of the water pump. As the cooled coolant hits the thermostat, the thermostat closes until the coolant temperature again causes it to open. Placing the thermostat in the inlet side of the water pump therefore reduces the rapid temperature changes that could cause stress in the engine, especially if aluminum heads are used with a cast iron block.

Radiators are designed for the maximum rate of heat transfer using minimum space. Cooling airflow through the radiator is aided by a belt- or electric motor–driven cooling fan.

THERMOSTATS

PURPOSE AND FUNCTION There is a normal operating temperature range between low-temperature and high-temperature extremes. The thermostat controls the minimum normal temperature. The thermostat is a temperature-controlled valve placed at the engine coolant outlet on most engines.

THERMOSTAT OPERATION An encapsulated wax-based plastic pellet heat sensor is located on the engine side of the thermostatic valve. As the engine warms, heat swells the heat sensor. ● **SEE FIGURE 4–4.**

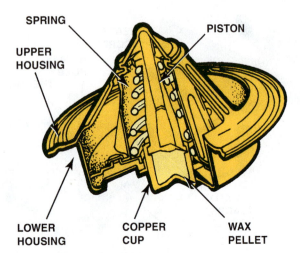

FIGURE 4–4 A cross section of a typical wax-actuated thermostat showing the position of the wax pellet and spring.

A mechanical link, connected to the heat sensor, opens the thermostat valve. As the thermostat begins to open, it allows some coolant to flow to the radiator, where it is cooled. The remaining part of the coolant continues to flow through the bypass, thereby bypassing the thermostat and flowing back through the engine. ● **SEE FIGURE 4–5.**

The rated temperature of the thermostat indicates the temperature at which the thermostat starts to open. The thermostat is fully open at about 20°F higher than its opening temperature. ● **SEE CHART 4–1.**

If the radiator, water pump, and coolant passages are functioning correctly, the engine should always be operating within the opening and fully open temperature range of the thermostat. ● **SEE FIGURE 4–6.**

NOTE: A bypass around the closed thermostat allows a small part of the coolant to circulate within the engine during warm-up. It is a small passage that leads from the engine side of the thermostat to the inlet side of the water pump. It allows some coolant to bypass the thermostat even when the thermostat is open. The bypass may be cast or drilled into the engine and pump parts. ● SEE FIGURES 4–7 AND 4–8.

The bypass aids in uniform engine warm-up. Its operation eliminates hot spots and prevents the building of excessive coolant pressure in the engine when the thermostat is closed.

ELECTRIC THERMOSTAT
On some engines the thermostat has an electric heating grid that is controlled by the engine control module (ECM). Both the coolant and the heater grid, depending on the load conditions of the engine, can heat the wax pellet. The heater grid is pulse-width modulated (PWM) to ground by the ECM; this results in more efficient fuel

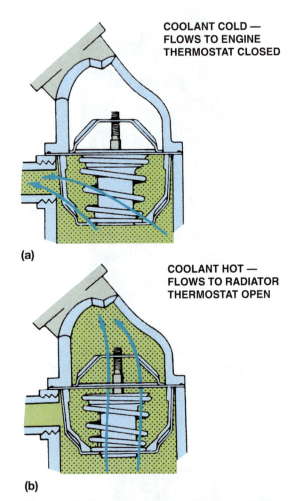

FIGURE 4–5 (a) When the engine is cold, the coolant flows through the bypass. (b) When the thermostat opens, the coolant can flow to the radiator.

THERMOSTAT TEMPERATURE RATING	STARTS TO OPEN	FULLY OPEN
180°F	180°F	200°F
195°F	195°F	215°F

CHART 4–1

The temperature of the coolant depends on the rating of the thermostat.

consumption and reduced emissions in city driving and low-speed cruising. ● **SEE FIGURE 4–9.**

THERMOSTAT TESTING There are three basic methods used to check the operation of the thermostat.

1. **Hot water method.** If the thermostat is removed from the vehicle and is closed, insert a 0.015 inch (0.4 mm) feeler gauge in the opening so that the thermostat will hang on the feeler gauge. The thermostat should then be suspended by the feeler gauge in a container of water or

FIGURE 4–6 A thermostat stuck in the open position caused the engine to operate too cold. If a thermostat is stuck closed, this can cause the engine to overheat.

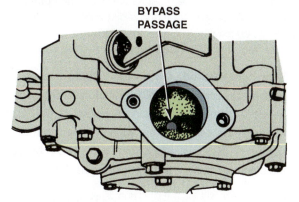

BYPASS PASSAGE

FIGURE 4–7 This internal bypass passage in the thermostat housing directs cold coolant to the water pump.

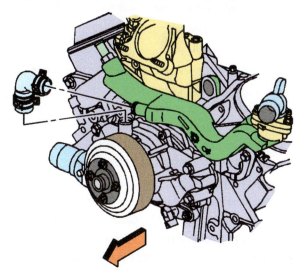

FIGURE 4–8 The water pump may have an external bypass tube and hose. (*Courtesy of General Motors*)

coolant along with a thermometer. The container should be heated until the thermostat opens enough to release and fall from the feeler gauge. The temperature at which the thermostat falls is the opening temperature of the thermostat. If it is within 5°F (4°C) of the temperature stamped

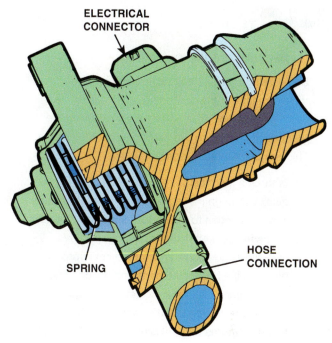

ELECTRICAL CONNECTOR

SPRING

HOSE CONNECTION

FIGURE 4–9 The electric thermostat is warmed by the coolant or an electric heater. (*Courtesy of General Motors*)

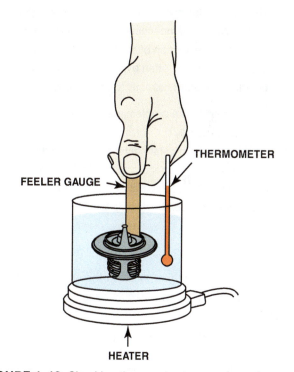

THERMOMETER

FEELER GAUGE

HEATER

FIGURE 4–10 Checking the opening temperature of a thermostat.

on the thermostat, the thermostat is satisfactory for use. If the temperature difference is greater, the thermostat should be replaced. ● **SEE FIGURE 4–10.**

2. **Infrared thermometer method.** An infrared thermometer (also called a pyrometer) can be used to measure the temperature of the coolant near the thermostat. The area on the engine side of the thermostat should be at the

Do Not Take Out the Thermostat!

Some vehicle owners and technicians remove the thermostat in the cooling system to "cure" an overheating problem. In some cases, removing the thermostat can *cause* overheating rather than stop it. This is true for three reasons.

1. Without a thermostat the coolant can flow more quickly through the radiator. The thermostat adds some restriction to the coolant flow, and therefore keeps the coolant in the radiator longer. This also allows additional time for the heat transfer between the hot engine parts and the coolant. The presence of the thermostat thus ensures a greater reduction in the coolant temperature before it returns to the engine.

2. Heat transfer is greater with a greater difference between the coolant temperature and air temperature. Therefore, when coolant flow rate is increased (no thermostat), the temperature difference is reduced.

3. Without the restriction of the thermostat, much of the coolant flow often bypasses the radiator entirely and returns directly to the engine.

   If overheating is a problem, removing the thermostat will usually not solve the problem. Remember, the thermostat controls the temperature of the engine coolant by opening at a certain temperature and closing when the temperature falls below the minimum rated temperature of the thermostat.

highest temperature that exists in the engine. A properly operating cooling system should cause the pyrometer to read as follows:

- As the engine warms, the temperature reaches near thermostat opening temperature.
- As the thermostat opens, the temperature drops just as the thermostat opens, sending coolant to the radiator.
- As the thermostat cycles, the temperature should range between the opening temperature of the thermostat and 20°F (11°C) above the opening temperature.

NOTE: If the temperature rises higher than 20°F (11°C) above the opening temperature of the thermostat, inspect the cooling system for a restriction or low coolant flow. A clogged radiator could also cause the excessive temperature rise.

FIGURE 4–11 Some thermostats are an integral part of the housing. This thermostat and radiator hose housing is serviced as an assembly. Some thermostats snap into the engine radiator fill tube underneath the pressure cap.

3. **Scan tool method.** A scan tool can be used on many vehicles to read the actual temperature of the coolant as detected by the engine coolant temperature (ECT) sensor. Although the sensor or the wiring to and from the sensor may be defective, at least the scan tool can indicate what the computer "thinks" is the engine coolant temperature.

THERMOSTAT REPLACEMENT Two important things about a thermostat include:

1. An overheating engine *may* result from a faulty thermostat.

2. An engine that does not get warm enough *always* indicates a faulty thermostat.

To replace the thermostat, coolant will have to be drained from the radiator drain petcock to lower the coolant level below the thermostat. It is not necessary to completely drain the system. The hose should be removed from the thermostat housing neck and then the housing removed to expose the thermostat. ● **SEE FIGURES 4–11 AND 4–12.**

The gasket flanges of the engine and thermostat housing should be cleaned, and the gasket surface of the housing must be flat. The thermostat should be placed in the engine with the sensing pellet *toward* the engine. Make sure that the thermostat position is correct, and install the thermostat housing with a new gasket or O-ring.

CAUTION: Failure to set the thermostat into the recessed groove will cause the housing to become tilted when tightened. If this happens and the housing bolts are tightened, the housing will usually crack, creating a leak.

The upper hose should then be installed and the system refilled. Install the correct size of radiator hose clamp. ● **SEE FIGURES 4-13 AND 4-14.**

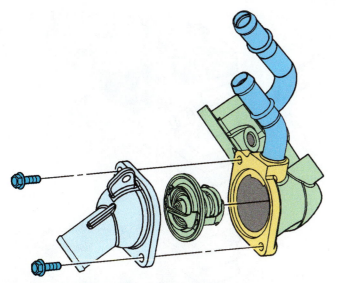

FIGURE 4–12 The thermostat can be removed after removing the bolts and cover. (*Courtesy of General Motors*)

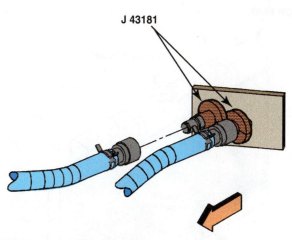

FIGURE 4–14 Some coolant hoses may have a quick-connect fitting that requires a special tool to disconnect. (*Courtesy of General Motors*)

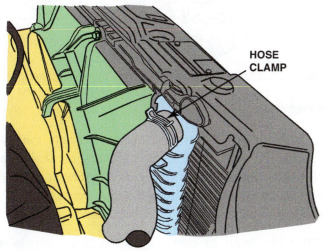

FIGURE 4–13 A spring-type hose clamp, as used on many General Motors vehicles. (*Courtesy of General Motors*)

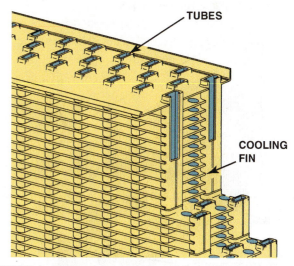

FIGURE 4–15 The tubes and fins of the radiator core.

RADIATORS

TYPES The two types of radiator cores in common use in most vehicles are:

- Serpentine fin core
- Plate fin core

In each of these types, the coolant flows through oval-shaped **core tubes**. Heat is transferred through the tube wall and soldered joint to **cooling fins**. The fins are exposed to the air that flows through the radiator, which removes heat from the radiator and carries it away. ● **SEE FIGURES 4–15 AND 4–16.**

Older automobile radiators were made from yellow brass. Since the 1980s, most radiators have been made from aluminum with nylon-reinforced plastic side tanks. These materials are corrosion resistant, have good heat transferability, and are easily formed.

Core tubes are made from 0.0045 to 0.012 inch (0.1 to 0.3 mm) thicksheet of brass or aluminum, using the thinnest possible materials for each application. The metal is rolled into round tubes and the joints are sealed with a locking seam.

The two basic designs of radiators include:

1. **Down-flow radiators.** This design was used mostly in older vehicles, where the coolant entered the radiator at the top and flowed downward, exiting the radiator at the bottom.

2. **Cross-flow radiators.** Most radiators use a cross-flow design, where the coolant flows from one side of the radiator to the opposite side.

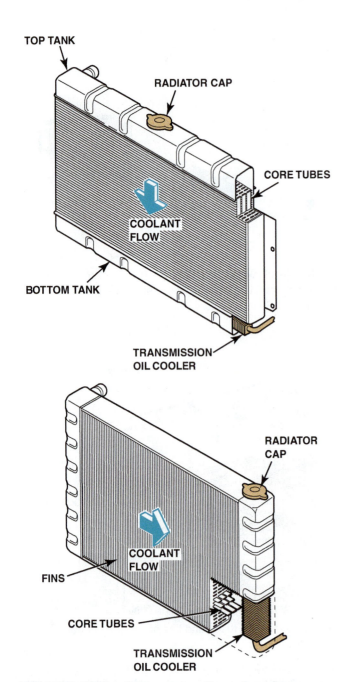

FIGURE 4–16 A radiator may be either a down-flow or a cross-flow type.

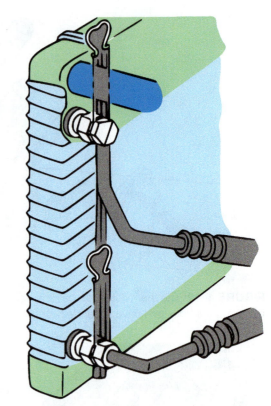

FIGURE 4–17 Many vehicles equipped with an automatic transmission use a transmission fluid cooler installed in one of the radiator tanks.

HOW RADIATORS WORK

The main limitation of heat transfer in a cooling system is in the transfer from the radiator to the air. Heat transfers from the water to the fins as much as seven times faster than heat transfers from the fins to the air, assuming equal surface exposure. The radiator must be capable of removing an amount of heat energy approximately equal to the heat energy of the power produced by the engine. *Each horsepower is equivalent to 42 BTUs (10,800 calories) per minute.* As the engine power is increased, the heat-removing requirement of the cooling system is also increased.

With a given frontal area, radiator capacity may be increased by increasing the core thickness, packing more material into the same volume, or both. The radiator capacity may also be increased by placing a shroud around the fan so that more air will be pulled through the radiator.

NOTE: The lower air dam in the front of the vehicle is used to help direct the air through the radiator. If this air dam is broken or missing, the engine may overheat, especially during highway driving due to the reduced airflow through the radiator.

When a transmission oil cooler is used in the radiator, it is placed in the outlet tank, where the coolant has the lowest temperature. ● **SEE FIGURE 4–17.**

PRESSURE CAPS

OPERATION

On many radiators the filler neck is fitted with a pressure cap. ● **SEE FIGURE 4–18.** The cap has a spring-loaded valve that closes the cooling system vent. This causes cooling pressure to build up to the pressure setting of the cap. At this point, the valve will release the excess

FIGURE 4–18 Many radiator caps are mounted on the radiator.

TECH TIP

Working Better Under Pressure

A problem that sometimes occurs with a high-pressure cooling system involves the water pump. For the pump to function, the inlet side of the pump must have a lower pressure than its outlet side. If inlet pressure is lowered too much, the coolant at the pump inlet can boil, producing vapor. The pump will then spin the coolant vapors and not pump coolant. This condition is called *pump cavitation*. Therefore, a radiator cap could be the cause of an overheating problem. A pump will not pump enough coolant if not kept under the proper pressure for preventing vaporization of the coolant.

pressure to prevent system damage. Engine cooling systems are pressurized to raise the boiling temperature of the coolant.

- *The boiling temperature will increase by approximately 3°F (1.6°C) for each pound of increase in pressure.*
- At sea level, water will boil at 212°F (100°C). With a 15 PSI (100 kPa) pressure cap, water will boil at 257°F (125°C), which is a maximum operating temperature for an engine.

FUNCTIONS The specified coolant system temperature serves two functions.

1. It allows the engine to run at an efficient temperature, close to 200°F (93°C), with no danger of boiling the coolant.
2. The higher the coolant temperature, the more heat the cooling system can transfer. The heat transferred by the cooling system is proportional to the temperature difference between the coolant and the outside air. This characteristic has led to the design of small, high-pressure radiators that are capable of handling large quantities of heat. For proper cooling, the system must have the right pressure cap correctly installed.

A vacuum valve is part of the pressure cap and is used to allow coolant to flow back into the radiator when the coolant cools down and contracts. ● **SEE FIGURE 4–19.**

NOTE: The proper operation of the pressure cap is especially important at high altitudes. The boiling point of water is lowered by about 1°F for every 550 ft increase in altitude. Therefore, in Denver, Colorado (altitude 5,280 ft), the boiling point of water is about 202°F, and at the top of Pike's Peak in Colorado (14,110 ft) water boils at 186°F.

METRIC RADIATOR CAPS According to the *SAE Handbook,* all radiator caps must indicate their nominal (normal) pressure rating. Most original equipment radiator caps are rated at about 14 to 16 PSI (97 to 110 kPa).

However, some vehicles use radiator pressure indicated in a unit called a **bar.** One bar is the pressure of the atmosphere at sea level, or about 14.7 PSI. The conversions in ● **CHART 4–2** can be used when replacing a radiator cap, to make certain it matches the pressure rating of the original.

COOLANT RECOVERY SYSTEMS

PURPOSE AND FUNCTION Excess pressure usually forces some coolant from the system through an overflow. Most cooling systems connect the overflow to a plastic reservoir to hold excess coolant while the system is hot. ● **SEE FIGURE 4–20.**

When the system cools, the pressure in the cooling system is reduced and a partial vacuum forms. This vacuum pulls the coolant from the plastic container back into the cooling system, keeping the system full. Because of this action, the system is called a **coolant recovery system.** A vacuum valve allows coolant to reenter the system as the system cools so that the radiator parts will not collapse under the partial vacuum.

SURGE TANK Some vehicles use a **surge tank,** which is located at the highest level of the cooling system and holds about 1 quart (1 liter) of coolant. A hose attaches to the bottom

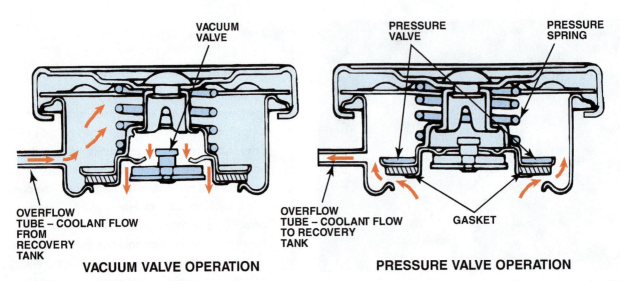

VACUUM VALVE OPERATION

PRESSURE VALVE OPERATION

FIGURE 4–19 The pressure valve maintains the system pressure and allows excess pressure to vent. The vacuum valve allows coolant to return to the system from the recovery tank.

BAR OR ATMOSPHERES	POUNDS PER SQUARE INCH (PSI)
1.1	16
1.0	15
0.9	13
0.8	12
0.7	10
0.6	9
0.5	7

CHART 4–2

Comparison showing the metric pressure as shown on the top of the cap to pounds per square inch (PSI).

of the surge tank to the inlet side of the water pump. A smaller bleed hose attaches to the side of the surge tank to the highest point of the radiator. The bleed line allows some coolant circulation through the surge tank, and air in the system will rise below the radiator cap and be forced from the system if the pressure in the system exceeds the rating of the radiator cap. ● **SEE FIGURE 4–21.**

WATER PUMPS

OPERATION The water pump (also called a coolant pump) is driven by one of two methods.

- Crankshaft belt
- Camshaft

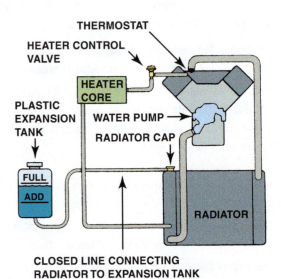

CLOSED LINE CONNECTING
RADIATOR TO EXPANSION TANK

FIGURE 4–20 The level in the coolant recovery system raises and lowers with engine temperature.

Coolant recirculates from the radiator to the engine and back to the radiator. Low-temperature coolant leaves the radiator by the bottom outlet. It is pumped into the warm engine block, where it picks up some heat. From the block, the warm coolant flows to the hot cylinder head, where it picks up more heat.

NOTE: Some engines use reverse cooling. This means that the coolant flows from the radiator to the cylinder head(s) before flowing to the engine block.

Water pumps are not positive displacement pumps. The water pump is a **centrifugal pump** that can move a

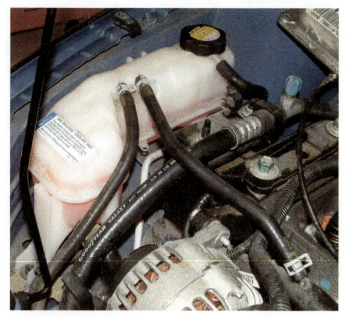

FIGURE 4–21 Some vehicles use a surge tank, which is located at the highest level of the cooling system, with a radiator cap.

FIGURE 4–23 A demonstration engine running on a stand, showing the amount of coolant flow that actually occurs through the cooling system.

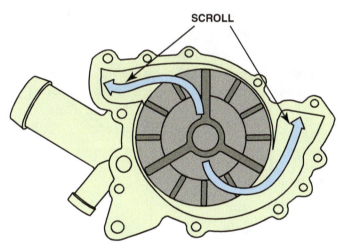

SCROLL

FIGURE 4–22 Coolant flow through the impeller and scroll of a coolant pump for a V-type engine.

? **FREQUENTLY ASKED QUESTION**

How Much Coolant Can a Water Pump Move?

A typical water pump can move a maximum of about 7,500 gallons (28,000 liters) of coolant per hour, or recirculate the coolant in the engine over 20 times per minute. This means that a water pump could be used to empty a typical private swimming pool in an hour! The slower the engine speed, the less power is consumed by the water pump. However, even at 35 mph (56 km/h), the typical water pump still moves about 2,000 gallons (7,500 liters) per hour or 0.5 gallon (2 liters) per second! ● **SEE FIGURE 4–23.**

large volume of coolant without increasing the pressure of the coolant. The pump pulls coolant in at the center of the **impeller**. Centrifugal force throws the coolant outward so that it is discharged at the impeller tips. ● **SEE FIGURE 4–22.**

As engine speeds increase, more heat is produced by the engine and more cooling capacity is required. The pump impeller speed increases as the engine speed increases to provide extra coolant flow at the very time it is needed.

The coolant leaving the pump impeller is fed through a **scroll**. The scroll is a smoothly curved passage that changes the fluid flow direction with minimum loss in velocity. The scroll is connected to the front of the engine so as to direct the coolant into the engine block. On V-type engines, two outlets are often used, one for each cylinder bank. Occasionally, diverters are necessary in the water pump scroll to equalize coolant flow between the cylinder banks of a V-type engine in order to equalize the cooling.

FIGURE 4–24 This severely corroded water pump could not circulate enough coolant to keep the engine cool. As a result, the engine overheated and blew a head gasket.

WEEP HOLE

FIGURE 4–25 The bleed weep hole in the water pump allows coolant to leak out of the pump and not be forced into the bearing. If the bearing failed, more serious damage could result.

WATER PUMP SERVICE
A worn impeller on a water pump can reduce the amount of coolant flow through the engine. ● SEE FIGURE 4–24.

If the seal of the water pump fails, coolant will leak out of the weep hole. The hole allows coolant to escape without getting trapped and forced into the water pump bearing assembly. ● SEE FIGURE 4–25.

The hole allows coolant to escape without getting trapped and forced into the water pump bearing assembly.

If the bearing is defective, the pump will usually be noisy and will have to be replaced. Before replacing a water pump that has failed because of a loose or noisy bearing, check all of the following:

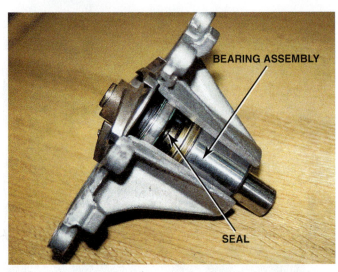

BEARING ASSEMBLY

SEAL

FIGURE 4–26 A cutaway of a typical water pump showing the long bearing assembly and the seal. The weep hole is located between the seal and the bearing. If the seal fails, then coolant flows out of the weep hole to prevent the coolant from damaging the bearing.

🔧 **TECH TIP**

Release the Belt Tension Before Checking a Water Pump

The technician should release water pump belt tension before checking for water pump bearing looseness. To test a water pump bearing, it is normal to check the fan for movement; however, if the drive belt is tight, any looseness in the bearing will not be felt.

---

1. Drive belt tension
2. Bent fan
3. Fan for balance

If the water pump drive belt is too tight, excessive force may be exerted against the pump bearing. If the cooling fan is bent or out of balance, the resulting vibration can damage the water pump bearing. ● SEE FIGURE 4–26.

COOLANT FLOW IN THE ENGINE

TYPES OF SYSTEMS
Coolant flows through the engine in one of the following ways.

- **Parallel flow system.** In the **parallel flow system,** coolant flows into the block under pressure and then crosses the head gasket to the head through main coolant passages beside *each* cylinder.

- **Series flow system.** In the **series flow system**, the coolant flows around all the cylinders on each bank. All the coolant flows to the *rear* of the block, where large main coolant passages allow the coolant to flow across the head gasket. The coolant then enters the rear of the heads. In the heads, the coolant flows forward to a crossover passage on the intake manifold outlet at the *highest point* in the engine cooling passage. This is usually located at the front of the engine. The outlet is either on the heads or in the intake manifold.

- **Series-parallel flow system.** Some engines use a combination of these two coolant flow systems and call it a **series-parallel flow system**. Any steam that develops will go directly to the top of the radiator. In series flow systems, **bleed holes** or **steam slits** in the gasket, block, and head perform the function of letting out the steam.

COOLANT FLOW AND HEAD GASKET DESIGN Most V-type engines use cylinder heads that are interchangeable side to side, but not all engines. Therefore, based on the design of the cooling system and flow through the engine, it is very important to double check that the cylinder head is matched to the block and that the head gasket is installed correctly (end for end) so that all of the cooling passages are open to allow the proper flow of coolant through the system. ● **SEE FIGURE 4–27.**

ENGINE OIL COOLER The coolant can also be directed through an oil cooler to cool the oil during high-temperature conditions. The oil cooler also helps to warm the engine oil when the engine is first started in cold weather. Because the coolant usually reaches operating temperature before the oil, the cooler can also heat the cold engine oil so it reaches normal operating temperature more quickly, thereby helping to reduce engine wear. ● **SEE FIGURE 4–28.**

COOLING FANS

ELECTRONICALLY CONTROLLED COOLING FAN

Two types of electric cooling fans used on many engines include:

- One two-speed cooling fan
- Two cooling fans (one for normal cooling and one for high heat conditions)

FIGURE 4–27 A Chevrolet V-8 block that shows the large coolant holes and the smaller gas vent or bleed holes that must match the head gasket when the engine is assembled.

COOLANT PASSAGE

GAS VENT

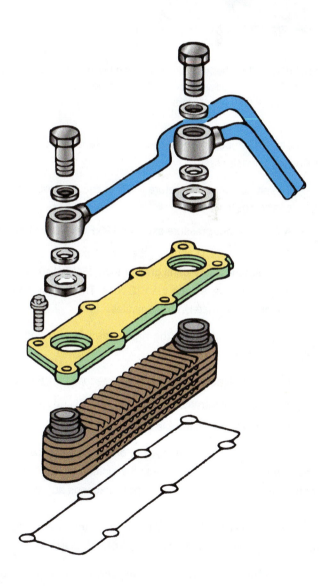

FIGURE 4–28 This engine oil cooler mounts in the water jacket of the engine block. (*Courtesy of General Motors*)

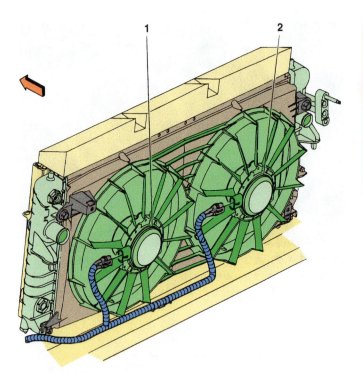

FIGURE 4–29 These cooling fans can be individually controlled by the powertrain control module (PCM). (*Courtesy of General Motors*)

The PCM commands low-speed fans on under the following conditions.

- Engine coolant temperature (ECT) exceeds approximately 223°F (106°C).
- A/C refrigerant pressure exceeds 190 PSI (1,310 kPa).
- After the vehicle is shut off, the engine coolant temperature at key-off is greater than 284°F (140°C) and system voltage is more than 12 volts. The fan(s) will stay on for approximately three minutes.

The PCM commands the high-speed fan on under the following conditions:

- Engine coolant temperature (ECT) reaches 230°F (110°C).
- A/C refrigerant pressure exceeds 240 PSI (1,655 kPa).
- Certain diagnostic trouble codes (DTCs) set.

To prevent a fan from cycling on and off excessively at idle, the fan may not turn off until the ignition switch is moved to the off position or the vehicle speed exceeds approximately 10 mph (16 km/h).

Many rear-wheel-drive vehicles and all transverse engines drive the fan with an electric motor. ● **SEE FIGURE 4–29.**

NOTE: Most electric cooling fans are computer controlled. To save energy, the cooling fans are turned off whenever the vehicle is traveling faster than 35 mph

WARNING

Some electric cooling fans can come on after the engine is off without warning. Always keep hands and fingers away from the cooling fan blades unless the electrical connector has been disconnected to prevent the fan from coming on. Always follow all warnings and cautions.

(55 km/h). The ram air caused by the vehicle speed is enough to keep the radiator cool. Of course, if the computer senses that the temperature is still too high, the computer will turn on the cooling fan, to "high," if possible, in an attempt to cool the engine to avoid severe engine damage.

THERMOSTATIC FANS On some rear-wheel-drive vehicles, a thermostatic cooling fan is driven by a belt from the crankshaft. It turns faster as the engine turns faster. Generally, the engine is required to produce more power at higher speeds. Therefore, the cooling system will also transfer more heat. Increased fan speed aids in the required cooling. Engine heat also becomes critical at low engine speeds in traffic where the vehicle moves slowly. The thermostatic fan is designed so that it uses little power at high engine speeds and minimizes noise. Three types of thermostatic fans include:

1. **Silicone coupling.** The **silicone coupling** fan drive is mounted between the drive pulley and the fan.

   NOTE: When diagnosing an overheating problem, look carefully at the cooling fan. If silicone is leaking, then the fan may not be able to function correctly and should be replaced.

2. **Thermostatic spring.** A second type of thermal fan has a **thermostatic spring** added to the silicone coupling fan drive. The thermostatic spring operates a valve that allows the fan to freewheel when the radiator is cold. As the radiator warms to about 150°F (65°C), the air hitting the thermostatic spring will cause the spring to change its shape. The new shape of the spring opens a valve that allows the drive to operate like the silicone coupling drive. When the engine is very cold, the fan may operate at high speeds for a short time until the drive fluid warms slightly. The silicone fluid will then flow into a reservoir to let the fan speed drop to idle. ● **SEE FIGURE 4–30.**

FIGURE 4–30 A typical engine-driven thermostatic spring cooling fan.

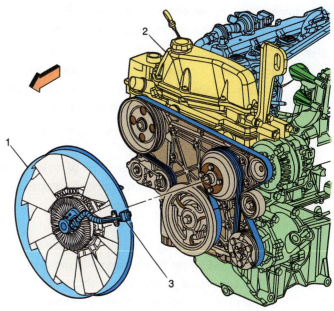

FIGURE 4–31 An electronically controlled fan hub showing the fan (1), the engine (2), and the electrical connector (3). (*Courtesy of General Motors*)

TECH TIP

Be Sure to Always Use a Fan Shroud

A fan shroud forces the fan to draw air through the radiator. If a fan shroud is not used, then air is drawn from around the fan and will reduce the airflow through the radiator. Many overheating problems are a result of not replacing the factory shroud after engine work or body repair work to the front of the vehicle.

3. Another version of the silicone fan coupling uses an internal solenoid to control the flow of the viscous fluid within the fan hub. The solenoid is controlled by a relay, which in turn is controlled by the vehicle's powertrain control module (PCM). ● **SEE FIGURE 4–31.**

The fan is designed to move enough air at the lowest fan speed to cool the engine when it is at its highest coolant temperature. The fan shroud is used to increase the cooling system efficiency. The fan or fan clutch may be bolted or threaded onto the water pump fan hub. ● **SEE FIGURE 4–31.**

HEATER CORES

PURPOSE AND FUNCTION Most of the heat absorbed from the engine by the cooling system is wasted. Some of this heat, however, is recovered by the vehicle heater. Heated coolant is passed through tubes in the small core of the heater.

FIGURE 4–32 A typical heater core installed in a heating, ventilation, and air-conditioning (HVAC) housing assembly.

Air is passed across the heater fins and is then sent to the passenger compartment. In some vehicles, the heater and air conditioning work in series to maintain vehicle compartment temperature. ● **SEE FIGURE 4–32.**

HEATER PROBLEM DIAGNOSIS When the heater does not produce the desired amount of heat, many owners and technicians replace the thermostat before doing any other troubleshooting. It is true that a defective thermostat is the reason for the *engine* not to reach normal operating temperature, but there are many other causes besides a defective thermostat that can result in lack of heat from the heater. To determine the exact cause, follow this procedure.

STEP 1 After the engine has been operated, feel the upper radiator hose. If the engine is up to proper operating temperature, the upper radiator hose should be too hot to hold. The hose should also be pressurized.

  a. If the hose is not hot enough, replace the thermostat.

  b. If the hose is not pressurized, test or replace the radiator pressure cap if it will not hold the specified pressure.

  c. If okay, see step 2.

STEP 2 With the engine running, feel both heater hoses. (The heater should be set to the maximum heat position.) Both hoses should be too hot to hold. If both hoses are warm (not hot) or cool, check the heater control valve for proper operation (if equipped). If one hose is hot and the other (return) is just warm or cool, remove both hoses from the heater core or engine and flush the heater core with water from a garden hose.

STEP 3 If both heater hoses are hot and there is still a lack of heating concern, then the fault is most likely due to an airflow blend door malfunction. Check service information for the exact procedure to follow.

NOTE: Heat from the heater that "comes and goes" is most likely the result of low coolant level. Usually with the engine at idle, there is enough coolant flow through the heater. At higher engine speeds, however, the lack of coolant through the heads and block prevents sufficient flow through the heater.

COOLING SYSTEM TESTING

VISUAL INSPECTION Many cooling system faults can be found by performing a thorough visual inspection. Items that can be inspected visually include:

- Water pump drive belt for tension or faults
- Cooling fan for faults
- Heater and radiator hoses for condition and leaks
- Coolant overflow or surge tank coolant level
- Evidence of coolant loss
- Radiator condition ● **SEE FIGURE 4–33.**

FIGURE 4–33 A heavily corroded radiator from a vehicle that was overheating. A visual inspection discovered that the corrosion had eaten away many of the cooling fins, yet did not leak. This radiator was replaced and it solved the overheating problem.

FIGURE 4–34 Pressure testing the cooling system. A typical hand-operated pressure tester applies pressure equal to the radiator cap pressure. The pressure should hold; if it drops, this indicates a leak somewhere in the cooling system. An adapter is needed for vehicles that use a threaded pressure cap.

PRESSURE TESTING Pressure testing using a hand-operated pressure tester is a quick and easy cooling system test. The radiator cap is removed (engine cold!) and the tester is attached in the place of the radiator cap. By operating the plunger on the pump, the entire cooling system is pressurized. ● **SEE FIGURE 4–34.**

CAUTION: Do not pump up the pressure beyond that specified by the vehicle manufacturer. Most systems should not be pressurized beyond 14 PSI (100 kPa).

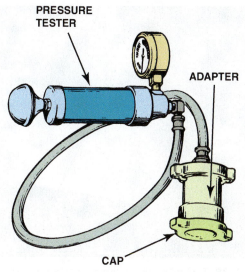

FIGURE 4–35 The pressure cap should be checked for proper operation using a pressure tester as part of the cooling system diagnosis.

FIGURE 4–36 Use dye specifically made for coolant when checking for leaks using a black light.

FIGURE 4–37 When an engine overheats, often the coolant overflow container boils.

If a greater pressure is used, it may cause the water pump, radiator, heater core, or hoses to fail.

If the cooling system is free from leaks, the pressure should stay and not drop. If the pressure drops, look for evidence of leaks anywhere in the cooling system, including:

1. Heater hoses
2. Radiator hoses
3. Radiator
4. Heater core
5. Cylinder head
6. Core plugs in the side of the block or cylinder head

Pressure testing should be performed whenever there is a leak or suspected leak. The pressure tester can also be used to test the radiator cap. An adapter is used to connect the pressure tester to the radiator cap. Replace any cap that will not hold pressure. ● **SEE FIGURE 4–35.**

COOLANT DYE LEAK TESTING One of the best methods to check for a coolant leak is to use a fluorescent dye in the coolant, one that is specifically designed for coolant. Operate the vehicle with the dye in the coolant until the engine reaches normal operating temperature. Use a black light to inspect all areas of the cooling system. When there is a leak, it will be easy to spot because the dye in the coolant will be seen as bright green. ● **SEE FIGURE 4–36.**

COOLANT TEMPERATURE WARNING LIGHT

PURPOSE AND FUNCTION Most vehicles are equipped with a heat sensor for the engine operating temperature indicator light. If the warning light comes on during driving (or the temperature gauge goes into the red danger zone), then the coolant temperature is about 250°F to 258°F (120°C to 126°C), which is still *below* the boiling point of the coolant (assuming a properly operating pressure cap and system). ● **SEE FIGURE 4–37.**

PRECAUTIONS If the coolant temperature warning light comes on, follow these steps.

STEP 1 Shut off the air conditioning and turn on the heater. The heater will help rid the engine of extra heat. Set the blower speed to high.

STEP 2 If possible, shut the engine off and let it cool. (This may take over an hour.)

STEP 3 Never remove the radiator cap when the engine is hot.

STEP 4 Do *not* continue to drive with the hot light on, or serious damage to your engine could result.

STEP 5 If the engine does not feel or smell hot, it is possible that the problem is a faulty hot light sensor or gauge. Continue to drive, but to be safe, stop occasionally and check for any evidence of overheating or coolant loss.

COMMON CAUSES OF OVERHEATING
Overheating can be caused by defects in the cooling system, such as the following:

1. Low coolant level
2. Plugged, dirty, or blocked radiator
3. Defective fan clutch or electric fan
4. Incorrect ignition timing (if adjustable)
5. Low engine oil level
6. Broken fan drive belt
7. Defective radiator cap
8. Dragging brakes
9. Frozen coolant (in freezing weather)
10. Defective thermostat
11. Defective water pump (the impeller slipping on the shaft internally)
12. Blocked cooling passages in the block or cylinder head(s)

COOLING SYSTEM INSPECTION

COOLANT LEVEL
The cooling system is one of the most maintenance-free systems in the engine. Normal maintenance involves an occasional check on the coolant level. It should also include a visual inspection for signs of coolant system leaks and for the condition of the coolant hoses and fan drive belts.

CAUTION: The coolant level should only be checked when the engine is cool. Removing the pressure cap

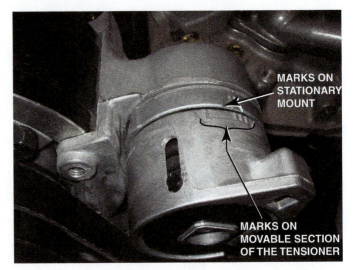

MARKS ON STATIONARY MOUNT

MARKS ON MOVABLE SECTION OF THE TENSIONER

FIGURE 4–38 Typical marks on an accessory drive belt tensioner.

from a hot engine will release the cooling system pressure while the coolant temperature is above its atmospheric boiling temperature. When the cap is removed, the pressure will instantly drop to atmospheric pressure level, causing the coolant to boil immediately. Vapors from the boiling liquid will blow coolant from the system. Coolant will be lost, and someone may be injured or burned by the high-temperature coolant that is blown out of the filler opening.

ACCESSORY DRIVE BELT TENSION
Drive belt condition and proper installation are important for the proper operation of the cooling system.

There are a number of ways vehicle manufacturers specify that the belt tension is within factory specifications.

1. **Belt tension gauge.** A belt tension gauge is needed to achieve the specified belt tension. Install the belt and operate the engine with all of the accessories turned on, to run in the belt for at least five minutes. Adjust the tension of the accessory drive belt to factory specifications or use ● **CHART 4–3** for an example of the proper tension based on the size of the belt. Replace any serpentine belt that has more than three cracks in any one rib that appears in a 3 inch span.

2. **Marks on the tensioner.** Many tensioners have marks that indicate the normal operating tension range for the accessory drive belt. Check service information for the location of the tensioner mark. ● **SEE FIGURE 4–38.**

3. **Torque wrench reading.** Some vehicle manufacturers specify that a beam-type torque wrench be used to determine the torque needed to rotate the tensioner. If the

NUMBER OF RIBS USED	TENSION RANGE (LB.)
3	45 to 60
4	60 to 80
5	75 to 100
6	90 to 125
7	105 to 145

CHART 4–3

The number of ribs determines the tension range of the belt.

 **TECH TIP**

The Water Spray Trick

Lower-than-normal alternator output could be the result of a loose or slipping drive belt. All belts (V and serpentine multigroove) use an interference angle between the angle of the Vs of the belt and the angle of the Vs on the pulley. A belt wears this interference angle off the edges of the V of the belt. As a result, the belt may start to slip and make a squealing sound even if tensioned properly.

A common trick to determine if the noise is from the belt is to spray water from a squirt bottle at the belt with the engine running. If the noise stops, the belt is the cause of the noise. The water quickly evaporates and therefore, water just finds the problem—it does not provide a short-term fix.

torque reading is below specifications, the tensioner must be replaced.

4. **Deflection.** Depress the belt between the two pulleys that are the farthest apart and the flex or deflection should be about 1/2 inch.

COOLING SYSTEM SERVICE

FLUSHING COOLANT Flushing the cooling system includes the following steps.

STEP 1 Drain the system (dispose of the old coolant correctly).

STEP 2 Fill the system with clean water and flushing/cleaning chemical.

STEP 3 Start the engine until it reaches operating temperature with the heater on.

STEP 4 Drain the system and fill with clean water.

FIGURE 4–39 Many vehicle manufacturers recommend that the bleeder valve be opened whenever refilling the cooling system.

STEP 5 Repeat until drain water runs clear (any remaining flush agent will upset pH).

STEP 6 Fill the system with 50/50 antifreeze/water mix or pre-mixed coolant.

STEP 7 Start the engine until it reaches operating temperature with the heater on.

STEP 8 Adjust coolant level as needed.

Bleeding the air out of the cooling system is important because air can prevent proper operation of the heater and can cause the engine to overheat. ●**SEE FIGURE 4–39.**

In most systems, small air pockets can occur. The engine must be thoroughly warmed to open the thermostat. This allows full coolant flow to remove the air pockets. The heater must also be turned to full heat. On some vehicles a special tool can be used to remove all of the air from the system. Always refer to service information for the proper procedure. ●**SEE FIGURE 4–40.**

NOTE: The Vac-n-Fill system is a required tool when servicing the Chevrolet Volt and some other GM vehicles. The Volt high voltage battery cooling system MUST be filled using the Vac-n-Fill equipment.

COOLANT EXCHANGE MACHINE Many coolant exchange machines are able to perform one or more of the following operations.

- Exchange old coolant with new coolant
- Flush the cooling system
- Pressure or vacuum check the cooling system for leaks

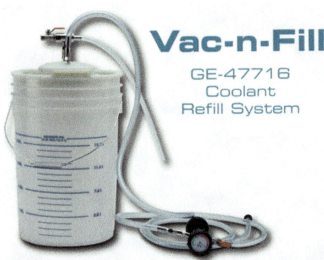

Vac-n-Fill

GE-47716
Coolant
Refill System

FIGURE 4–40 The Vac-n-Fill is recommended on most vehicles. It is a required tool when servicing the Chevy Volt. (*Courtesy of General Motors*)

FIGURE 4–41 Using a coolant exchange machine helps eliminate the problem of air getting into the system which can cause overheating or lack of heat due to air pockets getting trapped in the system.

TECH TIP

Always Replace the Pressure Cap

Replace the old radiator cap with a new cap with the same pressure rating. The cap can be located on the following:

1. Radiator
2. Coolant recovery reservoir
3. Upper radiator hose

☠ WARNING

Never remove a pressure cap from a hot engine. When the pressure is removed from the system, the coolant will immediately boil and will expand upward, throwing scalding coolant in all directions. Hot coolant can cause serious burns.

The use of a coolant exchange machine pulls a vacuum on the cooling system which helps illuminate air pockets from forming during coolant replacement. If an air pocket were to occur, the following symptoms may occur.

1. **Lack of heat from the heater.** Air rises and can form in the heater core, which will prevent coolant from flowing.

2. **Overheating.** The engine can overheat due to the lack of proper coolant flow through the system.

Always follow the operating instructions for the coolant exchange machine being used. ● **SEE FIGURE 4–41.**

HOSE INSPECTION Coolant system hoses are critical to engine cooling. As the hoses get old, they become either soft or brittle and sometimes swell in diameter. Their condition depends on their material and on the engine service conditions. If a hose breaks while the engine is running, all coolant will be lost. A hose should be replaced any time it appears to be abnormal. ● **SEE FIGURE 4–42.**

NOTE: To make hose removal easier and to avoid possible damage to the radiator, use a utility knife and slit the hose lengthwise. Then simply peel the hose off.

The hose and hose clamp should be positioned so that the clamp is close to the bead on the neck. This is especially important on aluminum hose necks to avoid corrosion. When the hoses are in place and the drain petcock is closed, the cooling system can be refilled with the correct coolant mixture.

DISPOSING OF USED COOLANT Used coolant drained from vehicles should be disposed of according to state or local laws. Some communities permit draining into the sewer. Ethylene glycol will easily biodegrade. There could be problems with groundwater contamination, however, if coolant is spilled on open ground. Check with recycling companies authorized by local or state governments for the exact method recommended for disposal in your area.

CLEANING THE RADIATOR EXTERIOR Overheating can result from exterior and interior radiator plugging. External plugging is caused by dirt and insects. This type of plugging can be seen if you look straight through the radiator while a light is held behind it. It is most likely to occur on off-road vehicles. The plugged exterior of the radiator core can usually be cleaned with water pressure from a hose. The water is aimed at the *engine side* of the radiator. The water should flow freely through the core at all locations. If this does not clean the core, the radiator should be removed for cleaning at a radiator shop.

TECH TIP

Always Use Heater Hoses Designed for Coolant

Many heater hoses are sizes that can also be used for other purposes such as oil lines. Always check and use hose that states it is designed for heater or cooling system use. ● **SEE FIGURE 4–43.**

TECH TIP

Quick and Easy Cooling System Problem Diagnosis

1. If overheating occurs in slow stop-and-go traffic, the usual cause is low airflow through the radiator. Check for airflow blockages or cooling fan malfunction.
2. If overheating occurs at highway speeds, the cause is usually a radiator or coolant circulation problem. Check for a restricted or clogged radiator.

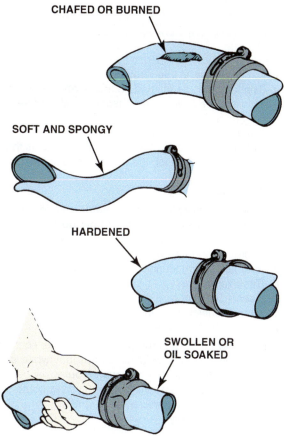

FIGURE 4–42 All cooling system hoses should be checked for wear or damage.

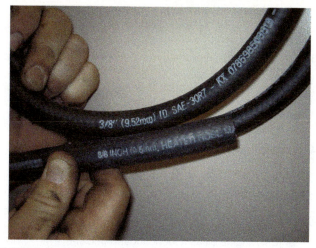

FIGURE 4–43 The top 3/8 inch hose is designed for oil and similar liquids, whereas the 3/8 inch hose below is labeled "heater hose" and is designed for coolant.

SUMMARY

1. The purpose and function of the cooling system is to maintain proper engine operating temperature.

2. The thermostat controls engine coolant temperature by opening at its rated opening temperature to allow coolant to flow through the radiator.

3. Coolant fans are designed to draw air through the radiator to aid in the heat transfer process, drawing the heat from the coolant and transferring it to the outside air through the radiator.

4. The cooling system should be tested for leaks using a hand-operated pressure pump.

5. Water pumps are usually engine driven and circulate coolant through the engine and the radiator when the thermostat opens.

6. Coolant flows through the radiator hoses to and from the engine and through heater hoses to send heated coolant to the heater core in the passenger compartment.

REVIEW QUESTIONS

1. What is normal operating coolant temperature?
2. Explain the flow of coolant through the engine and radiator.
3. Why is a cooling system pressurized?
4. What is the purpose of the coolant system bypass?
5. Describe how to perform a drain, flush, and refill procedure on a cooling system.
6. Explain the operation of a thermostatic cooling fan.
7. Describe how to diagnose a heater problem.
8. What are 10 common causes of overheating?

CHAPTER QUIZ

1. The upper radiator collapses when the engine cools. What is the most likely cause?
   a. Defective upper radiator hose
   b. Missing spring from the upper radiator hose, which is used to keep it from collapsing
   c. Defective thermostat
   d. Defective pressure cap

2. What can be done to prevent air from getting trapped in the cooling system when the coolant is replaced?
   a. Pour the coolant into the radiator slowly.
   b. Use a coolant exchange machine that draws a vacuum on the system.
   c. Open the air bleeder valves while adding coolant.
   d. Either b or c

3. Heat transfer is improved from the coolant to the air when the _____.
   a. Temperature difference is great
   b. Temperature difference is small
   c. Coolant is 95% antifreeze
   d. Both a and c

4. A water pump is a positive displacement type of pump.
   a. True
   b. False

5. Water pumps _____.
   a. Work only at idle and low speeds and are disengaged at higher speeds
   b. Use engine oil as a lubricant and coolant
   c. Are driven by the engine crankshaft or camshaft
   d. Disengage during freezing weather to prevent radiator failure

6. What diagnostic trouble code (DTC) could be set if the thermostat is defective?
   a. P0300
   b. P0171
   c. P0440
   d. P0128

7. Which statement is *true* about thermostats?
   a. The temperature marked on the thermostat is the temperature at which the thermostat should be fully open.
   b. Thermostats often cause overheating.
   c. The temperature marked on the thermostat is the temperature at which the thermostat should start to open.
   d. Both a and b

8. Technician A says that the radiator should always be inspected for leaks and proper flow before installing a rebuilt engine. Technician B says that overheating during slow city driving can only be due to a defective electric cooling fan. Which technician is correct?
   a. Technician A only
   b. Technician B only
   c. Both Technicians A and B
   d. Neither Technician A nor B

9. A customer complains that the heater works sometimes, but sometimes only cold air comes out while driving. Technician A says that the water pump is defective. Technician B says that the cooling system could be low on coolant. Which technician is correct?
   a. Technician A only
   b. Technician B only
   c. Both Technicians A and B
   d. Neither Technician A nor B

10. The normal operating temperature (coolant temperature) of an engine equipped with a 195°F thermostat is _____.
    a. 175°F to 195°F
    b. 185°F to 205°F
    c. 195°F to 215°F
    d. 175°F to 215°F

LEARNING OBJECTIVES

After studying this chapter, the reader should be able to:

1. Describe the importance and the role of engine oil.
2. Describe the various oil specifications.
3. Discuss the importance of the vehicle manufacturer's requirements.
4. Discuss how to change oil.

This chapter will help you prepare for ASE certification test A1 Engine Repair, content area "D" (Lubrication and Cooling Systems Diagnosis and Repair).

KEY TERMS

Additive package 67
American Petroleum Institute (API) 65
Antidrainback valve 72
Association des Constructeurs Européens d'Automobiles (ACEA) 66
Bypass valve 73
HTHS 67
International Lubricant Standardization and

Approval Committee (ILSAC) 66
Japanese Automobile Standards Organization (JASO) 67
Miscible 64
Oil Life System (OLS) 74
Pour point 64
SAPS 67
Society of Automotive Engineers (SAE) 64
Viscosity index (VI) 64

 ## STC OBJECTIVES

GM Service Technical College topics covered in this chapter are:

1. The purpose and composition of engine oil. (00510.01W-R2)
2. Normal and abnormal engine oil.
3. General Motors specified engine oils.

INTRODUCTION

Engine oil has a major effect on the proper operation and life of any engine. Engine oil provides the following functions in every engine.

- Lubricates moving parts
- Helps cool engine parts
- Helps seal piston rings
- Helps to neutralize acids created by the by-products of combustion
- Reduces friction in the engine
- Helps to prevent rust and corrosion

As a result of these many factors, the specified engine oil must be used and replaced at the specified mileage or time intervals.

PROPERTIES OF ENGINE OIL

The most important property of engine oil is its thickness or viscosity.

- As oil is cooled, it gets thicker.
- As oil is heated, it gets thinner.

Therefore, its viscosity changes with temperature. The oil must not be too thick at low temperatures to allow the engine to start. The lowest temperature at which oil will pour is called its **pour point.** An index of the change in viscosity between the cold and hot extremes is called the **viscosity index (VI).** All oils with a high viscosity index thin less with heat than do oils with a low viscosity index. Oils must also be **miscible,** meaning they are capable of mixing with other oils (brands and viscosities, for example) without causing any problems such as sludge.

SAE RATING

TERMINOLOGY   Engine oils are sold with a **Society of Automotive Engineers (SAE)** grade number, which indicates the viscosity range into which the oil fits. Oils tested at 212°F (100°C) have a number with no letter following. For example,

FIGURE 5–1 The SAE viscosity rating required is often printed on the engine oil filler cap.

SAE 30 indicates that the oil has only been checked at 212°F (100°C). This oil's viscosity falls within the SAE 30 grade number range when the oil is hot. Oils tested at 0°F (−18°C) are rated with a number and the letter *W*, which means *winter* and indicates that the viscosity was tested at 0°F, such as SAE 20W.

MULTIGRADE ENGINE OIL   An SAE 5W-30 multigrade oil meets the SAE 5W viscosity specification when cooled to 0°F (−18°C), and meets the SAE 30 viscosity specification when tested at 212°F (100°C).

Most vehicle manufacturers recommend the following multiviscosity engine oils.

- SAE 5W-30
- SAE 10W-30
- ● **SEE FIGURE 5–1.**

Oil with a high viscosity has a higher resistance to flow and is thicker than lower viscosity oil. Thick oil is not necessarily good oil and thin oil is not necessarily bad oil. Generally, the following items can be considered in the selection of engine oil within the recommended viscosity range.

- Thinner oil
  1. Improved cold engine starting
  2. Improved fuel economy
- Thicker oil
  1. Improved protection at higher temperatures
  2. Reduced fuel economy

NOTE: Always use the specified viscosity engine oil.

FIGURE 5–2 API doughnut for a SAE 5W-30, SM engine oil. When compared to a reference oil, the "energy conserving" designation indicates a 1.1% better fuel economy for SAE 10W-30 oils and 0.5% better fuel economy for SAE 5W-30 oils.

 **TECH TIP**

Three Oil Change Facts

Three facts that are important to know when changing oil are:

1. *Recommended SAE viscosity* (thickness) for the temperature range that is anticipated before the next oil change (such as SAE 5W-30)
2. *Quality rating* as recommended by the engine or vehicle manufacturer such as API SM and other specified rating such as the ILSAC and vehicle manufacturer's specifications
3. *Recommended oil change interval* (time or mileage) (usually every 5,000 miles or every six months)

API RATING

DEFINITION The **American Petroleum Institute (API),** working with the engine manufacturers and oil companies, has established an engine oil performance classification. Oils are tested and rated in production automotive engines. The oil container is printed with the API classification of the oil. The API performance or service classification and the SAE grade marking are the only information available to help determine which oil is satisfactory for use in an engine. ● **SEE FIGURE 5–2** for a typical API oil container "doughnut."

GASOLINE ENGINE RATINGS In gasoline engine ratings, the letter *S* means *service,* but can also indicate spark ignition engines. The rating system is open ended so that newer, improved ratings can be readily added as necessary (the letter *I* is skipped to avoid confusion with the number one).

SA Straight mineral oil (no additives), not suitable for use in any engine

SB Nondetergent oil with additives to control wear and oil oxidation

SC Obsolete (1964)

SD Obsolete (1968)

SE Obsolete (1972)

SF Obsolete (1980)

SG Obsolete (1988)

SH Obsolete (1993–1997)

SJ Obsolete (1997–2001)

SL 2001–2003

SM 2004–2010

SN 2011+

NOTE: Vehicles built since about 1996 that use roller valve lifers can use the newer, higher rated engine oil classifications where older, now obsolete ratings were specified. Newly overhauled antique cars or engines also can use the newer, improved oils, as the appropriate SAE viscosity grade is used for the anticipated temperature range.

DIESEL ENGINE RATINGS Diesel classifications begin with the letter *C,* which stands for *commercial,* but can also indicate compression ignition or diesel engines.

CA Obsolete

CB Obsolete

CC Obsolete

CD Minimum rating for use in a diesel engine service

CE Designed for certain turbocharged or super-charged heavy-duty diesel engine service

CF For off-road indirect injected diesel engine service

CF-2 Two-stroke diesel engine service

CF-4 High-speed four-stroke cycle diesel engine service

FIGURE 5–3 The International Lubricant Standardization and Approval Committee (ILSAC) starburst symbol. If this symbol is on the front of the container of oil, then it is acceptable for use in almost any gasoline engine.

CG-4   Severe-duty high-speed four-stroke diesel engine service

CI-4   Severe-duty high-speed four-stroke diesel engine service

CJ-4   Required for use in all 2007 and newer diesels using ultra-low-sulfur diesel (ULSD) fuel

ILSAC OIL RATING

DEFINITION   The **International Lubricant Standardization and Approval Committee (ILSAC)** developed an oil rating that consolidates the SAE viscosity rating and the API quality rating. If an engine oil meets the standards, a "starburst" symbol is displayed on the *front* of the oil container. If the starburst is present, the vehicle owner and technician know that the oil is suitable for use in almost any gasoline engine. ● **SEE FIGURE 5–3.**

ILSAC RATINGS

- The original GF-1 (gasoline fueled) rating in 1993
- Updated to GF-2 in 1997
- Updated to GF-3 in 2000
- Updated to GF-4 in 2004
- Updated to GF-5 in 2010

For more information, visit www.gf-5.com.

EUROPEAN OIL RATING SYSTEM

DEFINITION   The **Association des Constructeurs Européens d'Automobiles (ACEA)** rates the oil according to the following:

- Gasoline engine oils

  ACEA A1   Low-friction low-viscosity oil (not suitable for some engines)

  ACEA A2   General-purpose oil intended for normal oil change intervals; not suitable for some engines or extended oil drain intervals in any engine

  ACEA A3   Designed for high-performance engines and/or extended oil drain intervals and under all temperature ranges

  ACEA A4   Designed to meet the requirements for gasoline direct injection (GDI) engines

  ACEA A5   Low-viscosity low-friction oil not suitable for some engines

- Diesel engine oils

  ACEA B1   Low-viscosity oil designed for use in a passenger vehicle diesel engine that is equipped with an indirect injection system; not suitable for some diesel engines

  ACEA B2   Designed for use in passenger vehicle diesel engines using indirect injection and using normal oil drain intervals

  ACEA B3   Intended for use in a high-performance indirect injected passenger vehicle diesel engine and under extended oil drain interval conditions

  ACEA B4   Intended for year-round use in direct injected passenger vehicle diesel engines; can be used in an indirect injected diesel engine

  ACEA B5   Designed for extended oil drain intervals; not suitable for some engines

  ACEA C1, C2, C3   Specifications for catalyst compatible oils, which have limits on the amount of sulfur, zinc, and other additives that could harm the catalytic converter

Starting in 2004, the ACEA began using combined ratings such as A1/B1, A3/B3, A3/B4, and A5/B5.

- ACEA oil also requires low levels of sulfated ash, phosphorous, and sulfur, abbreviated **SAPS,** and has a high temperature/high shear rate viscosity, abbreviated **HTHS.**

- C ratings are catalytic converter compatible oils and include:

C1: basically A5/B5 oil with low SAPS, low HTHS
C2: A5/B5 with low HTHS and mid-level SAPS
C3: A5/B5 with high HTHS and mid-level SAPS
C4: low SAPS; high HTHS ● **SEE FIGURE 5–4.**

JAPANESE OIL RATINGS

The **Japanese Automobile Standards Organization (JASO)** also publishes oil standards. The JASO tests use small Japanese engines, and their ratings require more stringent valve train wear standards than oil ratings in other countries. However, most Japanese brand vehicles specify SAE, API, and ILSAC rating standards for use in the engine.

ENGINE OIL ADDITIVES

Oil producers are careful to check the compatibility of the oil additives they use. A number of chemicals that will help each other can be used for each of the additive requirements. The balanced additives are called an **additive package.**

ADDITIVES TO IMPROVE THE BASE OIL

- **Viscosity index (VI) improver.** Modifies the viscosity of the base fluid so that it changes less as the temperature rises; allows the lubricant to operate over a wider temperature range (● **SEE FIGURE 5–5.**)

- **Pour point depressant.** Keeps the lubricant flowing at low temperatures

- **Antifoam agents.** Foam reduces the effectiveness of a lubricant. The antifoam agents reduce/stop foaming when the oil is agitated or aerated.

ADDITIVES TO PROTECT THE BASE OIL

- **Antioxidants.** Slow the breakdown of the base fluid caused by oxygen (air) and heat (Oxidation is the main cause of lubricant degradation in service.)

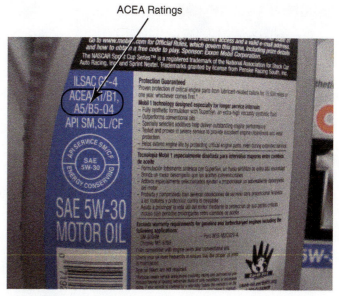

ACEA Ratings

FIGURE 5–4 ACEA ratings are included on the back of the oil container if it meets any of the standards. ACEA ratings apply to European vehicles only.

FIGURE 5–5 Viscosity index (VI) improver is a polymer and feels like finely ground foam rubber. When dissolved in the oil, it expands when hot to keep the oil from thinning.

- **Oxidants.** Prevent acid formation (corrosion) in the form of sludges, varnishes

- **Total base number (TBN).** The reserve alkalinity used to neutralize the acids created during the combustion process (Typical TBN levels are between 60 and 100, which is dependent on the fuel sulfur level. The higher the sulfur percentage in the fuel, the higher the TBN required. The higher the total base number of oil, the longer it can be used in an engine. Long-life oils usually have higher total base numbers than other oils.)

ADDITIVES TO PROTECT THE ENGINE

- **Rust inhibitor.** Inhibits the action of water on ferrous metal such as steel
- **Corrosion inhibitor.** Protects nonferrous metals such as copper
- **Antiwear additive.** Forms a protective layer on metal surfaces to reduce friction and prevent wear when no lubricant film is present
- **Extreme pressure additive.** Functions only when heavy loads and temperatures are occurring

OIL BRAND COMPATIBILITY

Many technicians and vehicle owners have their favorite brand of engine oil. The choice is often made as a result of marketing and advertising, as well as comments from friends, relatives, and technicians. If your brand of engine oil is not performing up to your expectations, then you may wish to change brands. For example, some owners experience lower oil pressure with a certain brand than they do with other brands with the same SAE viscosity rating.

- Most experts agree that oil change is the most important regularly scheduled maintenance for an engine.
- It is also wise to check the oil level regularly and add oil when needed.
- According to SAE standard J-357, all engine oils must be miscible (compatible) with all other brands of engine oil.
- Therefore, any brand of engine oil can be used as long as it meets the viscosity and API standards recommended by the vehicle manufacturer. Even though many people prefer a particular brand, be assured that, according to API and SAE, any major brand name engine oil can be used.

SYNTHETIC OIL

DEFINITION Synthetic engine oils have been available for years for military, commercial, and general public use. The term *synthetic* means that it is a manufactured product and not refined from a naturally occurring substance, as engine oil (petroleum base) is refined from crude oil. Synthetic oil is processed from several different base stocks using several different methods.

TECH TIP

Dirty Engine Oil Can Cause Oil Burning

Service technicians have known for a long time that some of their customers never change the engine oil. Often these customers believe that because their engine uses oil and they add a new quart every week, they are doing the same thing as changing the oil. But dirty, oxidized engine oil could cause piston rings to stick and not seal the cylinder. Therefore, when the oil and filter are changed, the clean oil may free the piston rings, especially if the vehicle is driven on a long trip during which the oil is allowed to reach the normal operating temperature.

FIGURE 5–6 Mobil 1 synthetic engine oil is used by several vehicle manufacturers in new engines.

API GROUPS According to the American Petroleum Institute, engine oil is classified into the following groups.

- **Group I.** Mineral, nonsynthetic base oil with few if any additives; suitable for light lubricating needs and rust protection, not for use in an engine
- **Group II.** Mineral oil with quality additive packages; includes most conventional engine oils
- **Group III.** Hydrogenated (hydroisomerized) synthetic compounds commonly referred to as hydrowaxes or hydrocracked oil; the lowest costing synthetic engine oil; includes Castrol Syntec
- **Group IV.** Synthetic oils made from mineral oil and monomolecular oil called polyalpholefin (POA); includes Mobil 1 (● **SEE FIGURE 5–6.**)
- **Group V.** Nonmineral sources such as alcohol from corn called diesters or polyolesters; includes Red Line synthetic oil

Groups III, IV, and V are considered to be synthetic because the molecular structure of the finished product does not occur naturally, but is man-made through chemical processes. All synthetic engine oils perform better than group II (mineral) oils, especially when tested according to the Noack Volatility Test ASTM D-5800. This test procedure measures the ability of an oil to stay in grade after it has been heated to 300°F (150°C) for one hour. The oil is then measured for percentage of weight loss. As the lighter components boil off, the oil's viscosity will increase.

ADVANTAGE OF SYNTHETIC OIL. The major advantage of using synthetic engine oil is its ability to remain fluid at very low temperatures. ● **SEE FIGURE 5–7.**

This characteristic of synthetic oil makes it popular in colder climates where cold-engine cranking is important.

DISADVANTAGE OF SYNTHETIC OIL. The major disadvantage is cost. The cost of synthetic engine oils can be four to five times the cost of petroleum-based engine oils.

SYNTHETIC BLENDS A synthetic blend indicates that some synthetic oil is mixed with petroleum base engine oil; however, the percentage of synthetic used in the blend is unknown.

VEHICLE-SPECIFIC SPECIFICATIONS

BACKGROUND Some oils can meet industry specifications, such as SAE, API, and/or ILSAC ratings, but not pass the tests specified by the vehicle manufacturer.

VEHICLE MANUFACTURER–SPECIFIC OIL SPECIFICATIONS The oil used should meet the specifications of the vehicle manufacturer, which include the following:

- **BMW**

  Longlife-98 and longlife-01 (abbreviated LL-01), LL-04

- **General Motors**

  GM 6094M

  GM 4718M (synthetic oil specification)

  Dexos 1 (all GM gasoline engines, 2011+)

  Dexos 2 (all GM diesel engines, 2011+)

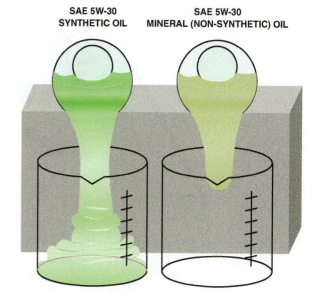

FIGURE 5–7 Both oils have been cooled to –20°F (–29°C). Notice that the synthetic oil on the left flows more freely than the mineral oil on the right even though both are SAE 5W-30.

- **Ford**

  WSS-M2C153-H

  WSS-M2C929-A (low viscosity rating, SAE 5W-20)

  WSS-M2C930-A

  WSS-M2C931-A

  WSS-M2C934-A

- **Chrysler**

  MS-6395 (2005+ vehicles)

  MS-10725 (2004 and older)

- **Honda/Acura**

  HTO-06 (turbocharged engine only)

- **Mercedes**

  229.3, 229.5, 229.1, 229.3, 229.31, 229.5, and 229.51

- **Volkswagen (VW and Audi)**

  502.00, 505.00, 505.01, 503, 503.01, 505, 506 diesel, 506.1 diesel, and 507 diesel

Be sure to use the oil that meets all of the specifications, especially during the warranty period.

NOTE: Most Asian brand vehicle manufactures do not specify any specifications other than SAE, API, and ILSAC. These vehicles include:

- **Acura/Honda**
- **Toyota/Lexus/Scion**
- **Kia**
- **Hyundai**
- **Nissan/Infinity**
- **Mitsubishi**
- **Mazda**
- **Suzuki**

FIGURE 5–8 The first commercially successful oil well was drilled in Titusville, Pennsylvania. (*Courtesy of General Motors*)

HIGH MILEAGE OILS

DEFINITION   A "high mileage oil" is sold for use in vehicles that have over 75,000 miles and are, therefore, nearing the eight-year, 80,000-mile catalytic converter warranty period.

Usually higher viscosity and lack of friction-reducing additives mean that most high mileage oils cannot meet ILSAC GF-4 rating and are, therefore, not recommended for use in most engines.

DIFFERENCES

- Esters are added to swell oil seals (main and valve-stem seals).
- The oil is used only in engines with higher than 75,000 miles.
- The oil usually does not have the energy rating of conventional oils (i.e., will not meet the specifications for use according to the owner manual in most cases).

ENGINE OIL MYTHS[1]

Over the years a number of engine oil myths have persisted. Here are some facts to pass along to customers that will help debunk the fiction behind these myths.

THE PENNSYLVANIA CRUDE MYTH   This myth is based on a misapplication of truth. In 1859, the first commercially

---
[1]General Motors TechLink December 2007, revised 2013

successful oil well was drilled in Titusville, Pennsylvania. ●**SEE FIGURE 5–8**.

This myth started before World War II, claiming that the only good oils were those made from pure Pennsylvania crude oil. At the time, only minimal refining was done to make engine oil from crude oil. Under these refining conditions, Pennsylvania crude oil made better engine oil than Texas crude or California crude. Today, with modern refining methods, almost any crude can be made into good engine oil.

THE DETERGENT OIL MYTH   The next myth was that modern detergent engine oils are bad for older engines. This myth started after World War II, when the government no longer needed all of the available detergent oil for the war effort, and detergent oil hit the market as "heavy-duty" oil.

Many prewar cars had been driven way past their normal life, their engines were full of sludge and deposits, and the piston rings were completely worn out. Massive piston deposits were the only thing standing between merely high oil consumption and horrendous oil consumption. After a thorough purge by the new detergent oil, increased oil consumption was a possible consequence.

If detergent oils had been available to the public during the war, preventing the massive deposit buildup from occurring in the first place, this myth never would have started. Amazingly, there are still a few people today, 60 years later, who believe that they need to use nondetergent oil in their older cars.

THE SYNTHETIC OIL MYTH   This myth says that new engine break-in will not occur with synthetic oils. This one was apparently started by an aircraft engine manufacturer who put out a bulletin that said so. The fact is that Mobil 1 synthetic oil has been the factory-fill for many millions of engines. Clearly, they have broken in quite well, and that should put this one to rest.

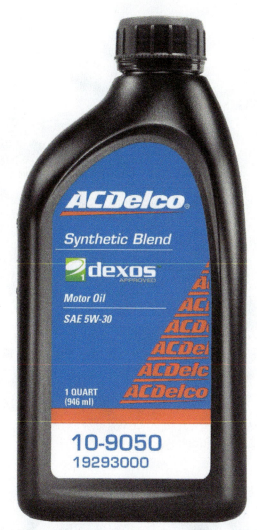

FIGURE 5–9 Beginning with model year 2011, General Motors specifies dexos1™ oil for gasoline engines and dexos2™ for diesel engines. Visit www.gmdexos.com for more information. (*Courtesy of General Motors*)

SYNTHETIC OILS ARE BETTER THAN CONVENTIONAL MINERAL OILS MYTH

When Mobil 1 was introduced in 1973, the term "synthetic" meant the oil was synthesized from a petrochemical by combining two or more molecules into a short chain-length polymer to make polyalpha olefin (PAO). PAO oil was made at a chemical plant, unlike conventional mineral oil, which was produced from petroleum at a refinery.

PAO oils were very pure and, thus, more expensive than conventional mineral oils. However, over time, refining technology has improved to the point where conventional mineral oils have become so highly refined through molecular transformation and rearrangement processes that these oils also have come to be called "synthetic" by some oil marketers. The result is that today the term "synthetic" means whatever the marketer wants it to mean, and this opinion has been upheld in court. Whether bottles of dexos™ oils are labeled Synthetic or Synthetic Blend is not important. What is important is that the bottle of oil that has the dexos™ symbol has passed all the testing requirements of the dexos™ specification for use in General Motors engines. ● **SEE FIGURE 5–9**.

THE STARBURST OIL MYTH

The latest myth promoted by the antique and collector car press says that Starburst/API SN engine oils (called Starburst for the shape of the symbol on the container) are bad for older engines because the amount of antiwear additive in them has been reduced. The antiwear additive being discussed is zinc dithiophosphate (ZDP).

Before debunking this myth, we need to look at the history of ZDP usage. For over 60 years, ZDP has been used as an additive in engine oils to provide wear protection and oxidation stability. ZDP was first added to engine oil to control copper/lead bearing corrosion. Oils with a phosphorus level in the 0.03% range passed a corrosion test that was introduced in 1942.

In the mid-1950s, when the use of high-lift camshafts increased the potential for scuffing and wear, the phosphorus level contributed by ZDP was increased to the 0.08% range. In addition, the industry developed a battery of oil tests (called sequences), two of which were valve train scuffing and wear tests.

These tests showed that a higher level of ZDP was good for flat-tappet valve train scuffing and wear, but it turned out that more was not better. While break-in scuffing was reduced by using more phosphorus, longer-term wear increased when phosphorus rose above 0.14%. At about 0.20% phosphorus, the ZDP started attacking the grain boundaries in the iron, resulting in camshaft spalling.

By the 1970s, increased antioxidancy was needed to protect the oil in high-load engines, which otherwise could thicken to a point where the engine could no longer pump it. Because ZDP was an inexpensive and effective antioxidant, it was used to place the phosphorus level in the 0.10% range.

However, since phosphorus is a poison for exhaust catalysts, ZDP levels have been reduced over the last 10 to 15 years. It's now down to a maximum of 0.08% for Starburst oils. This was supported by the introduction of modern ashless antioxidants that contain no phosphorus.

Enough history. Let's get back to the myth that Starburst oils are no good for older engines. The argument put forth is that while these oils work perfectly well in modern, gasoline engines equipped with roller camshafts, they will cause catastrophic wear in older engines equipped with flat-tappet camshafts. The facts say otherwise.

Backward compatibility was of great importance when the Starburst oil standards were developed by a group of experts from the manufacturers, oil companies, and oil additive companies. In addition, multiple oil and additive companies ran no-harm tests on older engines with the new oils; and no problems were uncovered.

The Starburst specification contains two valve train wear tests that all Starburst oil formulations must pass:

- Sequence IVA tests for camshaft scuffing and wear using a single overhead camshaft engine with slider finger (not roller) followers.
- Sequence IIIG evaluates cam and lifter wear using a V-6 engine with a flat-tappet system, similar to those used in the 1980s.

Those who hold onto the myth are ignoring the fact that the Starburst oils contain about the same percentage of ZDP as the oils that solved the *camshaft scuffing* and wear issues back in the 1950s. (True, they do contain less ZDP than the oils that solved the oil thickening issues in the 1960s, but that's because they now contain high levels of ashless antioxidants that were not commercially available in the 1960s.)

Despite the pains taken in developing special flat-tappet camshaft wear tests that Starburst oils must pass and the fact that the ZDP level of these oils is comparable to the level found necessary to protect flat-tappet camshafts in the past, there will still be those who will want to believe the myth that new oils will wear out older engines. Like other myths before it, history teaches us that it will probably take 60 or 70 years for this one also to die.[1]

OIL FILTERS

CONSTRUCTION The oil within the engine is pumped from the oil pan through the filter before it goes into the engine lubricating system passages. The filter is made from either closely packed cloth fibers or a porous paper. Large particles are trapped by the filter. Microscopic particles will flow through the filter pores. These particles are so small that they can flow through the bearing oil film and not touch the surfaces, so they do no damage. ● **SEE FIGURE 5–10.**

[1]General Motors TechLink December 2007, revised 2013

FIGURE 5–10 A cartridge-type oil filter as used on many newer engines. (*Courtesy of General Motors*)

OIL DRAIN-BACK VALVE

FIGURE 5–11 A rubber diaphragm acts as an antidrainback valve to keep the oil in the filter when the engine is stopped and the oil pressure drops to zero.

OIL FILTER VALVES Many oil filters are equipped with an **antidrainback valve** that prevents oil from draining out of the filter when the engine is shut off. ● **SEE FIGURE 5–11.**

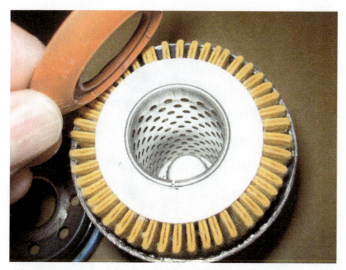

FIGURE 5–12 A cutaway of a typical spin-on oil filter. Engine oil enters the filter through the small holes around the center of the filter and flows through the pleated paper filtering media and out the large hole in the center of the filter. The center metal cylinder with holes is designed to keep the paper filter from collapsing under the pressure. The bypass valve can be built into the center on the oil filter or is part of the oil filter housing and located in the engine.

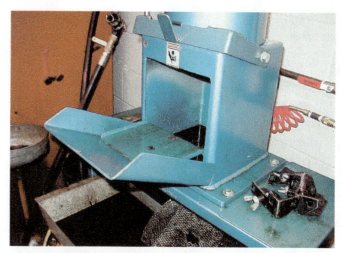

FIGURE 5–13 A typical filter crusher. The hydraulic ram forces out most of the oil from the filter. The oil is trapped underneath the crusher and is recycled.

This valve keeps oil in the filter and allows the engine to receive immediate lubrication as soon as the engine starts.

Either the engine or the filter is provided with a **bypass valve** that will allow the oil to go around the filter element. ● **SEE FIGURE 5–12.**

The bypass allows the engine to be lubricated with dirty oil, rather than having no lubrication, if the filter becomes plugged. The oil also goes through the bypass when the oil is cold and thick.

OIL FILTER DISPOSAL Oil filters should be crushed and/or drained of oil before discarding. After the oil has been drained, the filter can usually be disposed of as regular metal scrap. Always check and follow local, state, or regional oil filter disposal rules, regulations, and procedures. ● **SEE FIGURE 5–13.**

OIL CHANGE

INTERVALS All vehicle and engine manufacturers recommend a maximum oil change interval. The recommended intervals are usually expressed in terms of mileage or elapsed time, whichever milestone is reached first.

For vehicles not equipped with an oil life monitoring system, an oil change interval of 7,500 to 12,000 miles

(12,000 to 19,000 km) or every six months is recommended. The important thing to remember is that these are recommended *maximum* intervals and they should be shortened substantially if the vehicle is operated under other than normal, ideal conditions.

SEVERE SERVICE If any one of the conditions in the following list exists, it is considered severe service. The oil change interval recommendation usually drops to 3,000 miles (5,000 km) or every three months.

1. Operating in dusty areas
2. Towing a trailer
3. Short-trip driving, especially during cold weather (The definition of a short trip varies among manufacturers, but it is usually defined as 4 to 15 miles (6 to 24 km) each time the engine is started.)
4. Operating in temperatures below freezing point (32°F, 0°C)
5. Operating at idle speed for extended periods of time (such as normally occurs in police or taxi service)

Because most vehicles driven during cold weather are driven on short trips, technicians and automotive experts recommend changing the oil every 2,000 to 3,000 miles or every two to three months, whichever occurs first.

OIL LIFE MONITORS Most vehicles built since the mid-1990s are equipped with a warning system that lets the driver know when the engine oil should be changed. The two basic types of oil change monitoring systems include:

■ **Mileage only.** The service light will come on based on mileage only and may include a service "A" or "B" based

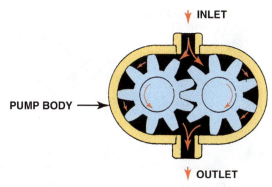

FIGURE 6–6 In an external gear-type oil pump, the oil flows through the pump around the outside of each gear. This is an example of a positive displacement pump, wherein everything entering the pump must leave the pump.

The oil pump is driven from the end of the distributor shaft, often with a hexagon-shaped shaft. Some engines have a short shaft with a gear that meshes with the cam gear to drive both the distributor and oil pump. With a distributor-driven oil pump, the pump turns at one-half the engine speed. On crankshaft-driven oil pump systems, the oil pump assembly is often made as part of the engine's front cover so that it turns at the same speed as the crankshaft.

TYPES OF OIL PUMPS

All oil pumps are called **positive displacement pumps**, and each rotation of the pump delivers the same volume of oil; therefore, everything that enters must exit. Also a positive displacement pump will deliver more oil and higher pressure as the speed of the pump increases. Most automotive engines use one of two types of oil pumps, either gear or rotor.

- **External gear type.** A gear-type oil pump is usually driven by a shaft from the distributor, which is driven by the camshaft. As a result, this type of pump rotates at half the engine (crankshaft) speed. The gear-type oil pump consists of two spur gears in a close-fit housing—one gear is driven while the other idles. As the gear teeth come out of mesh, they tend to leave a space, which is filled by oil drawn through the pump inlet. When the pump is pumping, oil is carried around the *outside* of each gear in the space between the gear teeth and the housing. As the teeth mesh in the center, oil is forced from the teeth into an oil passage, thus producing oil pressure. ●**SEE FIGURE 6–6.**

- **Internal/external gear type.** This type of oil pump is driven by the crankshaft and operates at engine speed. In this style of oil pump, two gears and a crescent stationary element are used. ●**SEE FIGURE 6–7.**

- **Rotor type.** The rotor-type oil pump is driven by a shaft from the distributor and uses a special lobe-shape gear

FIGURE 6–7 A typical internal/external oil pump mounted in the front cover of the engine that is driven by the crankshaft.

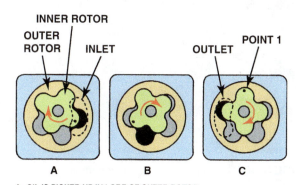

A. OIL IS PICKED UP IN LOBE OF OUTER ROTOR.
B. OIL IS MOVED IN LOBE OF OUTER ROTOR TO OUTLET.
C. OIL IS FORCED OUT OF OUTLET BECAUSE THE INNER AND OUTER ROTORS MESH TOO TIGHTLY AT POINT 1 AND THE OIL CANNOT PASS THROUGH.

FIGURE 6–8 The operation of a rotor-type oil pump.

meshing with the inside of a lobed rotor. The center lobed section is driven and the outer section idles. As the lobes separate, oil is drawn in just as it is drawn into gear-type pumps. As the pump rotates, it carries oil around and between the lobes. As the lobes mesh, they force the oil out from between them under pressure in the same manner as the gear-type pump. The pump is sized so that it will maintain a pressure of at least 10 PSI (70 kPa) in the oil gallery when the engine is hot and idling. Pressure will increase because the engine-driven pump also rotates faster. ●**SEE FIGURE 6–8.**

- **Gerotor type.** This type of positive displacement oil pump uses an inner and an outer rotor. The term is derived from two words: "*generated rotor,*" or **gerotor**. The inner rotor has one fewer teeth than the outer rotor and both rotate. ●**SEE FIGURE 6–9.**

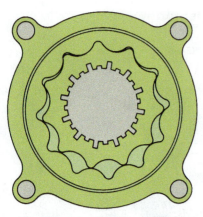

FIGURE 6–9 Gerotor-type oil pump is driven by the crankshaft.

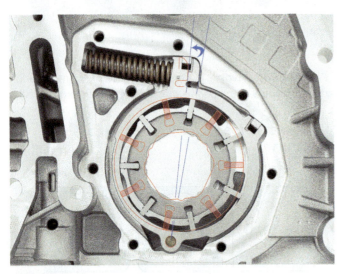

FIGURE 6–10 The oil pump rotor housing moves (blue arrow) to change the size of the pumping chamber (red outlines). *(Courtesy of General Motors)*

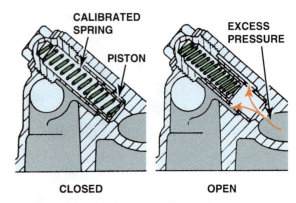

FIGURE 6–11 Oil pressure relief valves are spring loaded. The stronger the spring tension, the higher the oil pressure.

VARIABLE DISPLACEMENT OIL PUMP

Some General Motors engines use variable displacement oil pumps. The pump rotor assembly uses a hub and sliding vanes that spin inside a rotor housing. The housing is hinged so that it can be moved by spring or actuator oil pressure, thus changing the volume of oil displaced by the pump. ● **SEE FIGURE 6–10.**

The Engine Control Module (ECM), determines flow requirements based on engine loads. The ECM electrically commands an oil control valve (OCV) assembly to accordingly increase or decrease oil volume and pressure.

During cold starts or high engine-load conditions, the OCV is in the OFF position, and the internal pressure chamber lever within the oil pump is offset, creating high oil pressure and volume. During low load conditions, the OCV is commanded ON by the ECM, sending oil pressure into the high pressure chambers. This shifts the internal pressure chamber lever, causing a low volume and low pressure state. This state

results in improved engine efficiency and fuel mileage. When the OCV valve is turned off, spring pressure returns the internal pressure chamber lever to the high pressure position, and oil is exhausted out of the pump, through the OCV valve and back to the oil pan.

OIL PRESSURE REGULATION

In engines with a full-pressure lubricating system, maximum pressure is limited with a pressure *relief valve.* The relief valve (sometimes called the **pressure regulating valve**) is located at the outlet of the pump. The relief valve controls maximum pressure by bleeding off oil to the inlet side of the pump. ● **SEE FIGURE 6–11.**

The relief valve spring tension determines the maximum oil pressure. If a pressure relief valve is not used, the engine oil pressure will continue to increase as the engine speed increases. Maximum pressure is usually limited to the lowest pressure that will deliver enough lubricating oil to all engine parts that need to be lubricated.

The oil pump is made so that it is large enough to provide pressure at low engine speeds and small enough that it will not **cavitate** at high speed. Cavitation occurs when the pump tries to pull oil faster than it can flow from the pan to the pickup. When it cannot get enough oil, it will pull air. This puts air pockets or cavities in the oil stream. A pump is cavitating when it is pulling air or vapors.

NOTE: The reason for sheet metal covers over the pickup screen is to prevent cavitation. Oil is trapped under the cover, which helps prevent the oil pump from drawing in air, especially during sudden stops or during rapid acceleration.

After the oil leaves the pump, it first flows through the oil filter and then is delivered to the moving parts through drilled oil passages. ● **SEE FIGURE 6–12.**

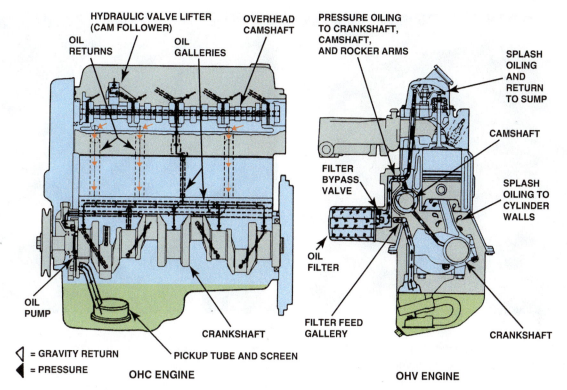

FIGURE 6–12 A typical engine design that uses both pressure and splash lubrication. Oil travels under pressure through the galleries (passages) to reach the top of the engine. Other parts are lubricated as the oil flows back down into the oil pan or is splashed onto parts.

FACTORS AFFECTING OIL PRESSURE

Oil pressure can only be produced when the oil pump has a capacity larger than all the "leaks" in the engine.

- **Leaks.** The leaks are the clearances at end points of the lubrication system. The end points are at the edges of bearings, the rocker arms, the connecting rod spit holes, and so on. These clearances are designed into the engine and are necessary for its proper operation. As the engine parts wear and clearance becomes greater, more oil will leak out. In other words, warn main or rod bearings are often the cause of lower than normal oil pressure.

- **Oil pump capacity.** The oil pump must supply extra oil for any leaks. The capacity of the oil pump results from its size, rotating speed, and physical condition. When the pump is rotating slowly as the engine idles, oil pump capacity is low. *If the leaks are greater than the pump capacity, engine oil pressure is low.* As the engine speed increases, the pump capacity increases and the pump tries to force more oil out of the leaks. This causes the pressure to rise until it reaches the regulated maximum pressure.

NOTE: A clogged oil pump pickup screen can cause lower than normal oil pressure because the amount of oil delivered by the pump is reduced by the clogged screen.

- **Viscosity of the engine oil.** The viscosity of the oil affects both the pump capacity and the oil leakage. Thin oil or oil of very low viscosity slips past the edges of the pump and flows freely from the leaks. Hot oil has a low viscosity, and therefore, a hot engine often has low oil pressure. Cold oil is more viscous (thicker) than hot oil. This results

(a)

(b)

FIGURE 6–13 (a) A visual inspection indicated that this pump cover was worn. (b) An embedded particle of something was found on one of the gears, making this pump worthless except for scrap metal.

in higher pressures, even with the cold engine idling. High oil pressure occurs with a cold engine, because the oil relief valve must open farther to release excess oil than is necessary with a hot engine. This larger opening increases the spring compression force, which in turn increases the oil pressure. Putting higher viscosity oil in an engine will raise the engine oil pressure to the regulated setting of the relief valve at a lower engine speed.

OIL PUMP CHECKS The cover is removed to check the condition of the oil pump.

- **Visual inspection.** The gears and housing are examined for scoring. If the gears and housing are heavily scored, the entire pump should be replaced. ● **SEE FIGURE 6–13.**

- **Measurements.** If they are lightly scored, the clearances in the pump should be measured. These clearances include the space between the gears and housing, the space between the teeth of the two gears, and the space between the side of the gear and the pump cover. A feeler gauge is often used to make these measurements. Gauging plastic can be used to measure the space between the side of the gears and the cover. The oil pump should be replaced when excessive clearance or scoring is found.

On most engines, the oil pump should be replaced as part of any engine work, especially if the cause for the repair is lack of lubrication.

NOTE: The oil pump is the "garbage pit" of the entire engine. Any and all debris is often forced through the gears and housing of an oil pump. ● SEE FIGURE 6–14.

Always refer to the manufacturer's specifications when checking the oil pump for wear. Typical oil pump clearances include the following:

1. End plate clearance: 0.0015 inch (0.04 mm)
2. Side (rotor) clearance: 0.012 inch (0.30 mm)
3. Rotor tip clearance: 0.010 inch (0.25 mm)
4. Gear end play clearance: 0.004 inch (0.10 mm)

All parts should also be inspected closely for wear. Check the relief valve for scoring and check the condition of the spring. When installing the oil pump, coat the sealing surfaces with engine assembly lubricant. This lubricant helps draw oil from the oil pan on initial start-up.

OIL PASSAGES

PURPOSE AND FUNCTION Oil from the oil pump first flows through the oil filter, and then goes through a drilled hole that intersects with a drilled main oil **gallery**, or longitudinal header. This is a long hole drilled from the front of the block to the back.

- Inline engines use one oil gallery.
- V-type engines may use two or three galleries.

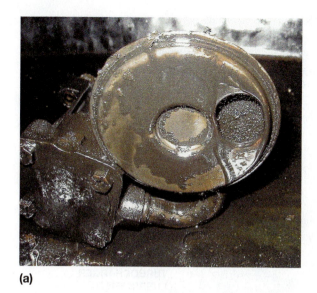

(a)

(b)

FIGURE 6–14 (a) The oil pump is the only part in an engine that gets unfiltered engine oil. The oil is drawn up from the bottom of the oil pan and is pressurized before flowing to the oil filter. (b) If debris gets into an oil pump, the drive or distributor shaft can twist and/or break. When this occurs, the engine will lose all oil pressure.

Passages drilled through the block bulkheads allow the oil to go from the main oil gallery to the main and cam bearings. ● SEE FIGURE 6–15.

In some engines, oil goes to the cam bearings first, and then to the main bearings. It is important that the oil holes in the bearings match with the drilled passages in the bearing saddles so that the bearing can be properly lubricated. Over a long period of use, bearings will wear. This wear causes excess clearance. The excess clearance will allow too much oil to leak from the side of the bearing. When this happens, there will be little or no oil left for bearings located farther downstream in the lubricating system. This is a major cause of bearing failure. To aid in bearing failure diagnosis, on most engines, the last rod bearing to receive oil pressure is typically the bearing farthest from the oil pump. If this bearing fails, then suspect low oil pressure as the probable cause.

VALVE TRAIN LUBRICATION The oil gallery may intersect or have drilled passages to the valve lifter bores to lubricate the lifters. When hydraulic lifters are used, the oil pressure in the gallery keeps refilling them. On some engines, oil from the lifters goes up the center of a hollow pushrod to lubricate the pushrod ends, the rocker arm pivot, and the valve stem tip. In other engines, an oil passage is drilled from either the gallery or a cam bearing to the block deck, where it matches with a head gasket hole and a hole drilled in the head to carry the oil to a rocker arm shaft. Some engines use an enlarged bolt hole to carry lubrication oil around the rocker shaft cap screw to the rocker arm shaft.

Holes in the bottom of the rocker arm shaft allow lubrication of the rocker arm pivot. Rocker arm assemblies need only a surface coating of oil, so the oil flow to the rocker assembly is minimized using restrictions or metered openings. The restriction or metering disk is in the lifter when the rocker assembly is lubricated through the pushrod. Oil that seeps from the rocker assemblies is returned to the oil pan through drain holes. These oil drain holes are often placed so that the oil drains on the camshaft or cam drive gears to lubricate them. Oil drain holes can be either machined or cast into the cylinder heads and block. ● SEE FIGURE 6–16.

Some engines have means of directing a positive oil flow to the cam drive gears or chain. This may include either of the following:

- Nozzle
- Chamfer on a bearing parting surface, which allows oil to spray on the loaded portion of the cam drive mechanism

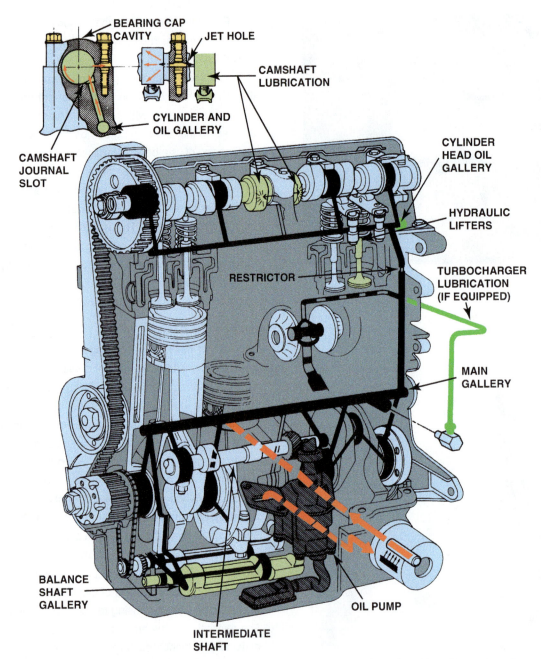

FIGURE 6–15 An intermediate shaft drives the oil pump on this overhead camshaft engine. Note the main gallery and other drilled passages in the block and cylinder head.

OIL PANS

PURPOSE AND FUNCTION The oil pan is where engine oil is used for lubricating the engine. Another name for the oil pan is a **sump**. As the vehicle accelerates, brakes, or turns rapidly, the oil tends to move around in the pan. Pan baffles and oil pan shapes are often used to keep the oil inlet under the oil at all times. As the crankshaft rotates, it acts like a fan and causes air within the crankcase to rotate with it. This can cause a strong draft on the oil, churning it so that air bubbles enter the oil, which then causes oil foaming. Oil with air will not lubricate like liquid oil, so oil foaming can cause bearings to fail. A baffle or **windage tray** is sometimes installed in engines to eliminate the oil churning problem. This may be an added part, as shown in ● **SEE FIGURE 6–17,** or it may be a part of the oil pan.

Windage trays have the good side effect of reducing the amount of air disturbed by the crankshaft, so that less power is drained from the engine at high crankshaft speeds.

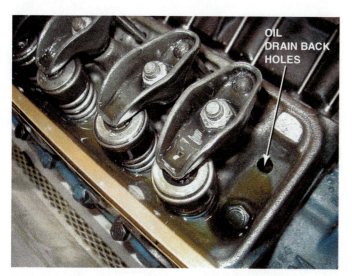

FIGURE 6–16 Oil is sent to the rocker arms on this Chevrolet V-8 engine through the hollow pushrods. The oil returns to the oil pan through the oil drainback holes in the cylinder head.

OIL DRAIN BACK HOLES

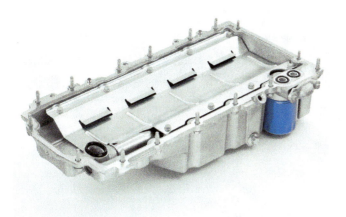

FIGURE 6–17 An oil pan with a windage tray used to keep oil from being churned up by the rotating crankshaft. (*Courtesy of General Motors*)

DRY SUMP SYSTEM

CONSTRUCTION AND OPERATION The term *sump* is used to describe a location where oil is stored or held. In most engines, oil is held in the oil pan and the oil pump draws the oil from the bottom. This type of system is called a **wet sump** oil system. In a **dry sump** system, the oil pan is shallow and the oil is pumped into a remote reservoir. In this reservoir, the oil is cooled and any trapped air is allowed to escape before being pumped back to the engine. A dry sump system uses an externally mounted oil reservoir. ● **SEE FIGURE 6–18.**

?   FREQUENTLY ASKED QUESTION

Why Is It Called a Windage Tray?

A windage tray is a plate or baffle installed under the crankshaft and is used to help prevent aeration of the oil. Where does the wind come from? Pistons push air down into the crankcase as they move from top dead center to bottom dead center. The pistons also draw air and oil upward when moving from bottom dead center to top dead center. At high engine speeds, this causes a great deal of airflow, which can easily aerate the oil. Therefore, a windage tray is used to help prevent this movement of air (wind) from affecting the oil in the pan. Try the following:

- Take an oil pan and add a few quarts (liters) of oil.
- Then take an electric hair dryer and use it to blow air into the oil pan.

Oil will be thrown everywhere, which helps illustrate why windage trays are used in all newer engines.

ADVANTAGES   The advantages of a dry sump system are as follows:

1. A shallow oil pan allows the engine to be mounted lower in the vehicle to improve cornering.

2. The oil capacity can be greatly expanded because the size of the reservoir is not limited. A larger quantity of oil means that the oil temperature can be controlled.

3. A dry sump system allows the vehicle to corner and brake for long periods, which is not able to be done with a wet sump system due to the oil being thrown to one side and away from the oil pickup.

4. A dry sump system also allows the engine to develop more power as the oil is kept away from the moving crankshaft.

DISADVANTAGES   A dry sump system has the following disadvantages.

1. The system is expensive as it requires components and plumbing not needed in a wet sump system.

2. The system is complex because the plumbing and connections, plus the extra components, result in more places where oil leaks can occur and change the way

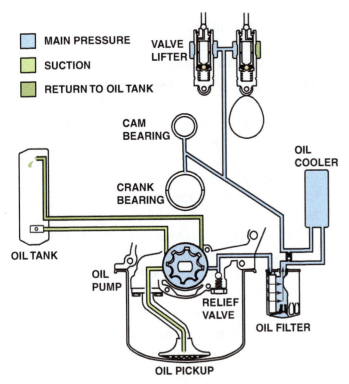

- MAIN PRESSURE
- SUCTION
- RETURN TO OIL TANK

VALVE LIFTER

CAM BEARING

CRANK BEARING

OIL TANK

OIL PUMP

RELIEF VALVE

OIL PICKUP

OIL COOLER

OIL FILTER

FIGURE 6–18 A dry sump system as used in a Chevrolet Corvette.

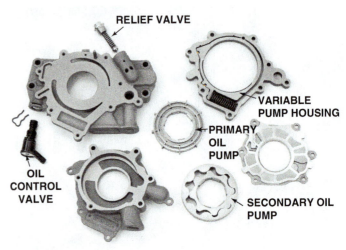

RELIEF VALVE

VARIABLE PUMP HOUSING

PRIMARY OIL PUMP

OIL CONTROL VALVE

SECONDARY OIL PUMP

FIGURE 6–19 The components of a Corvette dry sump oil pump assembly. (*Courtesy of General Motors*)

routine maintenance is handled. A dry sump oil system is used in most motor sport vehicles and is standard on certain high-performance production vehicles, such as some models of the Chevrolet Corvette, Porsche, and BMW. ● SEE FIGURE 6–19.

OIL COOLERS

Oil temperature must be controlled on many high-performance or turbocharged engines. A larger capacity oil pan helps to control oil temperature. Some engines use remote mounted oil coolers. Coolant flows through the oil cooler to help warm the oil when the engine is cold and cool the oil when the engine is hot. Oil temperature should be:

- Above 212°F (100°C) to boil off any accumulated moisture
- Below 280°F to 300°F (138°C to 148°C)
  ● SEE FIGURE 6–20.

In addition to the engine oil cooler, many diesel and high-performance version engines use the engine oil to cool the

OIL COOLER

OIL FILTER

FIGURE 6–20 Oil is cooled by the flow of coolant through the oil filter adaptor.

pistons. An oil jet is directed through a nozzle to the back of the piston head where heat is absorbed into the oil and carried away when the oil returns to the oil pan. The oil jet nozzle is bolted onto the engine block and sprays upward onto the back of the piston head. ● SEE FIGURE 6–21.

FIGURE 6–21 The piston oil cooler jet sprays oil onto the back of the piston head. (*Courtesy of General Motors*)

? FREQUENTLY ASKED QUESTION

What Is Acceptable Oil Consumption?

There are a number of opinions regarding what is acceptable oil consumption. Most vehicle owners do not want their engine to use any oil between oil changes even if they do not change it more often than every 7,500 miles (12,000 km). Engineers have improved machining operations and piston ring designs to help eliminate oil consumption.

Many stationary or industrial engines are not driven on the road, so they do not accumulate miles but still may consume excessive oil.

A general rule for "acceptable" oil consumption is that it should be about 0.002 to 0.004 pound per horsepower per hour. To figure, use the following:

$$\frac{1.82 \times \textbf{Quarts used}}{\textbf{Operating hp} \times \textbf{Total hours}} = \textbf{Pound/hp/hr}$$

Therefore, oil consumption is based on the amount of work an engine performs. Although the formula may not be viable for vehicle engines used for daily transportation, it may be for the marine or industrial engine builder. Generally, oil consumption that is greater than 1 quart for every 600 miles (1 liter per 1,000 km) is considered to be excessive with a motor vehicle.

SUMMARY

1. Viscosity is the oil's thickness or resistance to flow.
2. Normal engine oil pump pressure ranges from 10 to 60 PSI (200 to 400 kPa) or 10 PSI for every 1000 engine RPM.
3. Hydrodynamic oil pressure around engine bearings is usually over 1,000 PSI (6,900 kPa).
4. The oil pump is driven directly by the crankshaft or by a gear or shaft from the camshaft.

REVIEW QUESTIONS

1. What causes a wedge-shaped film to form in the oil?
2. What is hydrodynamic lubrication?
3. Explain why internal engine leakage affects oil pressure.
4. Describe how the oil flows from the oil pump, through the filter and main engine bearings, to the valve train.
5. What is the purpose of a windage tray?

1. Normal oil pump pressure in an engine is _____ PSI.
   a. 3 to 7
   c. 100 to 150
   b. 10 to 60
   d. 180 to 210

2. Two technicians are discussing oil pumps. Technician A says that many oil pumps are driven directly off the front of the crankshaft. Technician B says that some are driven from the distributor if the engine uses a distributor-type ignition system. Which technician is correct?
   a. Technician A only
   b. Technician B only
   c. Both Technicians A and B
   d. Neither Technician A nor B

3. A typical oil pump can pump how many gallons per minute?
   a. 3 to 6 gallons
   c. 10 to 60 gallons
   b. 6 to 10 gallons
   d. 50 to 100 gallons

4. In typical engine lubrication systems, what components are the last to receive oil and the first to suffer from a lack of oil or oil pressure?
   a. Main bearings
   c. Valve train components
   b. Rod bearings
   d. Oil filters

5. Hydrodynamic lubrication, created by the wedging action of oil between the crankshaft journal and the bearing, can be as high as _____ PSI.
   a. 60
   c. 500
   b. 120
   d. 1,000

6. What type of oil pump is driven by the crankshaft?
   a. Gerotor
   b. External gear
   c. Internal/external gear
   d. Both a and c

7. Lower than specified oil pressure is measured on a high mileage engine. Technician A says that worn main or rod bearings could be the cause. Technician B says that a clogged oil pump pickup screen could be the cause. Which technician is correct?
   a. Technician A only
   b. Technician B only
   c. Both Technicians A and B
   d. Neither Technician A nor B

8. Oil passages in an engine block are usually called _____.
   a. Galleries
   c. Runners
   b. Holes
   d. Pathways

9. Why is a dry sump system used in some high-performance vehicles?
   a. It allows the vehicle to corner or brake for long periods
   b. It allows the engine to develop more power
   c. It allows for a greater oil capacity so that oil temperatures can be controlled
   d. All of the above

10. An engine oil cooler uses _____ to cool the oil.
    a. Coolant
    b. Turbo flow
    c. Air-conditioning evaporator output
    d. Automatic transmission fluid after it flows through the radiator

chapter 7
INTAKE AND EXHAUST SYSTEMS

LEARNING OBJECTIVES

After studying this chapter, the reader should be able to:

1. Discuss the purpose and function of intake air (induction) system components.
2. Explain the differences between throttle-body fuel-injection manifolds and port fuel-injection manifolds.
3. List the materials used in exhaust manifolds and exhaust systems.
4. Describe the purpose and function of the exhaust system components.

This chapter will help you prepare for ASE Engine Performance (A8) certification test content area "C" (Air Induction and Exhaust Systems Diagnosis and Repair).

KEY TERMS

EGR 99
Hangers 102
Helmholtz resonator 96
Micron 94
Plenum 98

GM STC OBJECTIVES

GM Service Technical College topics covered in this chapter are:

1. The purpose of induction systems. (06510.05W)
2. The purpose, location, and types of air induction system components.
3. The operation of air induction systems.
4. The purpose of exhaust systems.
5. Common exhaust system designs.
6. Exhaust system components.

INTAKE AIR FILTRATION

NEED FOR AIR FILTERING Gasoline must be mixed with air to form a combustible mixture. Air movement into an engine occurs due to low pressure (vacuum) being created in the engine. ● **SEE FIGURE 7–1.**

Air contains dirt and other materials that cannot be allowed to reach the engine. Just as fuel filters are used to clean impurities from gasoline, an air cleaner and filter are used to remove contaminants from the air. The three main jobs of the air cleaner and filter include:

1. Clean the air before it is mixed with fuel
2. Silence intake noise
3. Act as a flame arrester in case of a backfire

The automotive engine uses about 9,000 gallons (34,000 liters) of air for every gallon of gasoline burned at an air-fuel ratio of 14.7:1 by weight. Without proper filtering of the air before it enters the engine, dust and dirt in the air can seriously damage engine parts and shorten engine life.

Abrasive particles can cause wear any place inside the engine where two surfaces move against each other, such as piston rings against the cylinder wall. The dirt particles then pass by the piston rings and into the crankcase. From the crankcase, the particles circulate throughout the engine in the oil. Large amounts of abrasive particles in the oil can damage other moving engine parts.

The filter that cleans the intake air is in a two-piece air cleaner housing made either of:

- Stamped steel or
- Composite (usually nylon reinforced plastic) materials.

AIR FILTER ELEMENTS The paper air filter element is the most common type of filter. It is made of a chemically treated paper stock that contains tiny passages in the fibers. These passages form an indirect path for the airflow to follow. The airflow passes through several fiber surfaces, each of which traps microscopic particles of dust, dirt, and carbon. Most air filters are capable of trapping dirt and other particles larger than 10 to 25 microns in size. One **micron** is equal to 0.000039 inch.

NOTE: Only objects that are about 40 microns or larger in size are visible to the human eye. A human hair is about 50 microns in diameter.

● **SEE FIGURE 7–2.**

FILTER REPLACEMENT Manufacturers recommend cleaning or replacing the air filter element at periodic intervals,

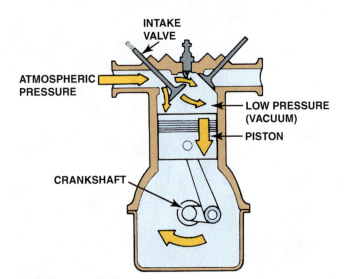

FIGURE 7–1 Downward movement of the piston lowers the air pressure inside the combustion chamber. The pressure differential between the atmosphere and the inside of the engine forces air into the engine.

FIGURE 7–2 Dust and dirt in the air are trapped in the air filter so they do not enter the engine.

usually listed in terms of distance driven or months of service. The distance and time intervals are based on so-called normal driving. More frequent air filter replacement is necessary when the vehicle is driven under dusty, dirty, or other severe conditions.

It is best to replace a filter element before it becomes too dirty to be effective. A dirty air filter that passes contaminants can cause engine wear.

REMOTELY MOUNTED AIR FILTERS AND DUCTS Air cleaner and duct design depend on a number of factors such as the size, shape, and location of other engine compartment components, as well as the vehicle body structure.

FIGURE 7–3 Most air filter housings are located on the side of the engine compartment and use flexible rubber hose to direct the airflow into the throttle body of the engine.

The throttle body may be mounted vertically, horizontally, or at an angle, depending on the vehicle.

Some systems also have a mass airflow (MAF) sensor between the throttle body and the air cleaner. Because placing the air cleaner housing next to the throttle body would cause engine and vehicle design problems, it is more efficient to use this remote air cleaner placement. ● **SEE FIGURE 7–3.**

Turbocharged engines present a similar problem. The air cleaner connects to the air inlet elbow at the turbocharger. However, the tremendous heat generated by the turbocharger makes it impractical to place the air cleaner housing too close to the turbocharger. Remote air cleaners are connected to the turbocharger air inlet elbow or fuel-injection throttle body by composite ducting that is usually retained by clamps. The ducting used may be rigid or flexible, but all connections must be airtight.

HYDROCARBON (HC) ABSORBER Some vehicles may have a pad- or paper-like component glued to the inner surface of the air cleaner cover or intake air duct. This is a hydrocarbon (HC) absorber that is used to collect the small amounts of HC vapor that may be present inside the duct system when the engine is turned off. When the engine is started the vapors are drawn into the engine and burned. ● **SEE FIGURE 7–4.**

NOTE: The absorber should not be removed or washed in any way. If found to be saturated or loose, the duct or air cleaner cover should be replaced.

AIR FILTER RESTRICTION INDICATOR Some vehicles, especially pickup trucks that are often driven in dusty conditions, are equipped with an air filter restriction indicator.

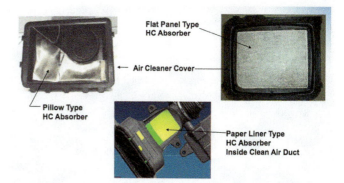

FIGURE 7–4 The HC absorber may be one of three types and is part of the duct or cover. (*Courtesy of General Motors*)

FIGURE 7–5 A typical air filter restriction indicator used on a General Motors truck engine. The indicator turns red when it detects enough restriction to require a filter replacement.

The purpose of this device is to give a visual warning when the air filter is restricted and needs to be replaced. The device operates by detecting the slight drop in pressure that occurs when an air filter is restricted. The calibration before the red warning bar or "replace air filter" message appears varies, but is usually:

- 15 to 20 inch of water (inch H_2O) for gasoline engines
- 20 to 30 inch of water (inch H_2O) for diesel engines

The unit of inches of water is used to measure the difference in air pressure before and after the air filter. The unit is very small, because 28 inch of water is equal to a pound per square inch (PSI).

Some air filter restriction indicators, especially on diesel engines, include an electrical switch used to light a dash-mounted warning lamp when the air filter needs to be replaced. ● **SEE FIGURE 7–5.**

(a)

(b)

FIGURE 7–6 (a) Note the discovery as the air filter housing was opened during service on this vehicle. The nuts were obviously deposited by squirrels (or some other animal). (b) Not only was the housing filled with nuts, but also this air filter was extremely dirty, indicating that this vehicle had not been serviced for a long time.

 TECH TIP

Always Check the Air Filter

Always inspect the air filter and the air intake system carefully during routine service. Debris or objects deposited by animals can cause a restriction to the airflow and can reduce engine performance.
● **SEE FIGURE 7–6.**

 FREQUENTLY ASKED QUESTION

What Does This Tube Do?

What is the purpose of the odd-shaped tube attached to the inlet duct between the air filter and the throttle body, as seen in ● **FIGURE 7–7?**

The tube shape is designed to dampen out certain resonant frequencies that can occur at specific engine speeds. The length and shape of this tube are designed to absorb shock waves that are created in the air intake system and to provide a reservoir for the air that will then be released into the airstream during cycles of lower pressure. This resonance tube is often called a **Helmholtz resonator**, named for the discoverer of the relationship between shape and value of frequency, Herman L. F. von Helmholtz (1821 to 1894) of the University of Hönizsberg in East Prussia. The overall effect of these resonance tubes is to reduce the noise of the air entering the engine.

RESONANCE TUBE

FIGURE 7–7 A resonance tube, called a Helmholtz resonator, is used on the intake duct between the air filter and the throttle body to reduce air intake noise during engine acceleration.

THROTTLE-BODY INJECTION INTAKE MANIFOLDS

TERMINOLOGY The *intake manifold* is also called an *inlet manifold*. Smooth engine operation can only occur when each combustion chamber produces the same pressure as every other chamber in the engine. For this to be achieved, each cylinder must receive an intake charge exactly like the charge going into the other cylinders in quality and quantity. The charges must have the same physical properties and the same air-fuel mixture.

A throttle-body fuel injector forces finely divided droplets of liquid fuel into the incoming air to form a combustible air-fuel mixture. ● **SEE FIGURE 7–8** for an example of a typical throttle-body injection (TBI) unit.

FIGURE 7–8 A throttle-body injection (TBI) unit used on a GM V-6 engine.

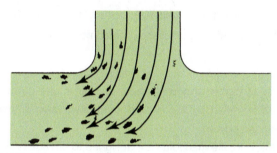

FIGURE 7–9 Heavy fuel droplets separate as they flow around an abrupt bend in an intake manifold.

INTAKE AIR SPEEDS These droplets start to evaporate as soon as they leave the throttle-body injector nozzles. *The droplets stay in the charge as long as the charge flows at high velocities.* At maximum engine speed, these velocities may reach 300 ft per second. Separation of the droplets from the charge as it passes through the manifold occurs when the velocity drops below 50 ft per second. Intake charge velocities at idle speeds are often below this value. When separation occurs—at low engine speeds—extra fuel must be supplied to the charge in order to have a combustible mixture reach the combustion chamber.

Manifold sizes and shapes represent a compromise.

- They must have a cross section large enough to allow charge flow for maximum power.

- The cross section must be small enough that the flow velocities of the charge will be high enough to keep the fuel droplets in suspension. This is required so that equal mixtures reach each cylinder. Manifold cross–sectional size is one reason why engines designed especially for racing will not run at low engine speeds.

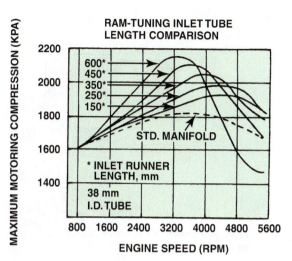

FIGURE 7–10 The graph shows the effect of sonic tuning of the intake manifold runners. The longer runners increase the torque peak and move it to a lower RPM. The 600 mm intake runner is about 24 inch long.

- Racing manifolds must be large enough to reach maximum horsepower. This size, however, allows the charge to move slowly, and the fuel will separate from the charge at low engine speeds. Fuel separation leads to poor accelerator response. ● **SEE FIGURE 7–9.**

Standard passenger vehicle engines are primarily designed for economy during light-load, partial-throttle operation. Their manifolds, therefore, have a much smaller cross-sectional area than do those of racing engines. This small size will help keep flow velocities of the charge high throughout the normal operating speed range of the engine.

PORT FUEL-INJECTION INTAKE MANIFOLDS

TERMINOLOGY The size and shape of port fuel-injected engine intake manifolds can be optimized because the only thing in the manifold is air. The fuel injector is located in the intake manifold about 3 to 4 inch (70 to 100 mm) from the intake valve. Therefore, the runner length and shape are designed for tuning only. There is no need to keep an air-fuel mixture thoroughly mixed (homogenized) throughout its trip from the TBI unit to the intake valve. Intake manifold runners are tuned to improve engine performance.

- Long runners build low-RPM torque.

- Shorter runners provide maximum high-RPM power.

● **SEE FIGURES 7–10 AND 7–11.**

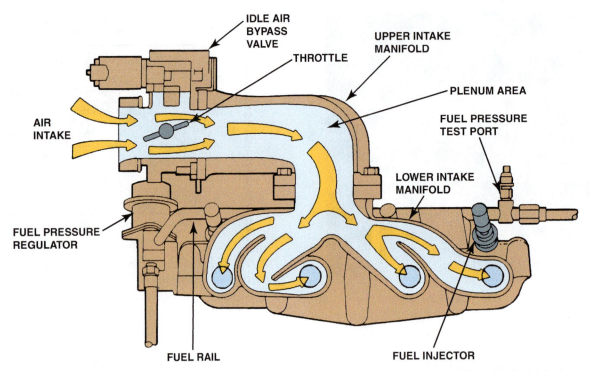

FIGURE 7-11 Airflow through the large diameter upper intake manifold is distributed to smaller diameter individual runners in the lower manifold in this two-piece manifold design.

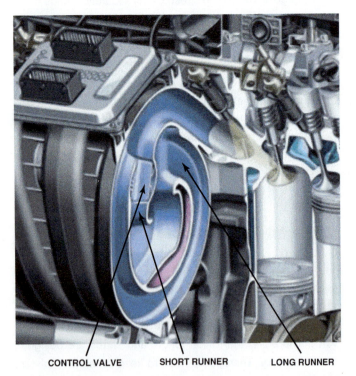

FIGURE 7-12 The air flowing into the engine can be directed through long or short runners for best performance and fuel economy. (*Courtesy of General Motors*)

VARIABLE INTAKE MANIFOLDS Some engines with four valve heads utilize a dual or variable intake runner design. At lower engine speeds, long intake runners provide low-speed torque. At higher engine speeds, shorter intake runners are opened by means of a computer-controlled valve to increase high-speed power.

Many intake manifolds are designed to provide both short runners best for higher engine speed power and longer runners best for lower engine speed torque. The valve(s) that control the flow of air through the passages of the intake manifold are computer controlled. ● **SEE FIGURE 7-12.**

PLASTIC INTAKE MANIFOLDS Most intake manifolds are made from thermoplastic molded from fiberglass-reinforced nylon by either casting or by injection molding. Some manifolds are molded in two parts and bonded together. Plastic intake manifolds are lighter than aluminum manifolds and can better insulate engine heat from the fuel injectors.

Plastic intake manifolds have smoother interior surfaces than do other types of manifolds, resulting in greater airflow. ● **SEE FIGURE 7-13.**

UPPER AND LOWER INTAKE MANIFOLDS Many intake manifolds are constructed in two parts.

- A lower section attaches to the cylinder heads and includes passages from the intake ports.
- An upper manifold, usually called the **plenum**, connects to the lower unit and includes the long passages needed to help provide the ram effect that helps the

FIGURE 7–13 This molded (plastic) intake manifold is designed for a V-8 engine. Also shown is the acoustic shield that helps reduce engine noise. (*Corvette; Courtesy of General Motors*)

engine deliver maximum torque at low engine speeds. The throttle body attaches to the upper intake.

The use of a two-part intake manifold allows for easier manufacturing as well as assembly, but can create additional locations for leaks.

If the lower intake manifold gasket leaks, not only could a vacuum leak occur affecting the operation of the engine, but a coolant leak or an oil leak can also occur if the manifold has coolant flowing through it. A leak at the gasket(s) of the upper intake manifold usually results in a vacuum (air) leak only.

EXHAUST GAS RECIRCULATION PASSAGES

PURPOSE AND FUNCTION To reduce the emission of oxides of nitrogen (NOx), engines have been equipped with **exhaust gas recirculation (EGR)** valves. From 1973 until recently, they were used on almost all vehicles. Most EGR valves are mounted on the intake manifold. Because of the efficiency of computer-controlled fuel injection, some newer engines do not require an EGR system to meet emission standards. These engines' variable valve timing to close the exhaust valve sooner than normal, trapping some exhaust in the cylinder, is an alternative to using an EGR valve.

On engines with EGR systems, the EGR valve opens at speeds above idle on a warm engine. When open, the valve allows a small portion of the exhaust gas (5% to 10%) to enter the intake manifold.

The EGR system has some means of interconnecting the exhaust and intake manifolds. The EGR valve controls the gas flow through the passages.

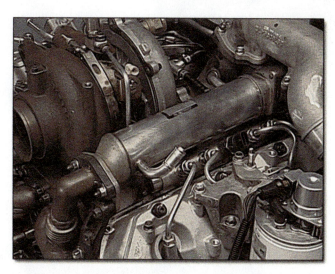

FIGURE 7–14 The EGR cooler may be a long EGR tube or a water cooled EGR cooler (shown). (*Courtesy of General Motors*)

- On V-type engines, the intake manifold crossover is used as a source of exhaust gas for the EGR system. A cast passage connects the exhaust crossover to the EGR valve.
- On inline-type engines, an external tube is generally used to carry exhaust gas to the EGR valve.

EXHAUST GAS COOLERS The exhaust gases are more effective in reducing oxides of nitrogen (NOx) emissions if gases are cooled before being drawn into the cylinders. This can be accomplished by extending the length of the EGR tubes or with the use of an EGR cooler that uses the engine coolant to cool the gases. ● SEE FIGURE 7–14.

EXHAUST MANIFOLDS

PURPOSE AND FUNCTION The exhaust manifold is designed to collect high-temperature spent gases from the individual head exhaust ports and direct them into a single outlet connected to the exhaust system. ● SEE FIGURE 7–15.

The exhaust gases are routed through exhaust pipes, then to the catalytic converter, to the muffler, to the resonator (if used) and on to the tailpipe, where they are vented to the atmosphere. The exhaust system is designed to meet the following needs.

- Provide the least possible amount of restriction or backpressure
- Keep the exhaust noise at a minimum

Exhaust gas temperature will vary according to the power produced by the engine. The manifold must be designed to operate at both engine idle and continuous full power. Under

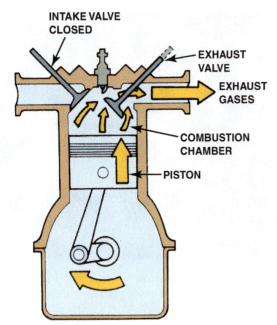

FIGURE 7–15 The exhaust gases are pushed out of the cylinder by the piston on the exhaust stroke.

FIGURE 7–16 This exhaust manifold is cast from stainless steel alloy. (*Ecotec 2.0L I-4 VVT DI Turbo; Courtesy of General Motors*)

full-power conditions, the exhaust manifold can become red-hot, causing a great deal of expansion.

The temperature of an exhaust manifold can exceed 1,500°F (815°C).

CONSTRUCTION   Most exhaust manifolds are made from the following:

- Cast iron or stainless steel alloy ● **SEE FIGURE 7-16.**
- Steel tubing

During vehicle operation, manifold temperatures usually reach the high-temperature extremes. The manifold is bolted to the head in a way that will allow expansion and contraction.

Many exhaust manifolds have heat shields to help keep exhaust heat off the spark plug wires and to help keep the heat from escaping to improve exhaust emissions.

FIGURE 7–17 This engine uses a tuned exhaust manifold; note the shielding around the spark plug boots. (*6.2L LT1; Courtesy of General Motors*)

Exhaust systems are especially designed for the engine-chassis combination. The exhaust system length, pipe size, and silencer are designed, where possible, to make use of the tuning effect within the exhaust system. Tuning occurs when the exhaust pulses from the cylinders are emptied into the manifold between the pulses of other cylinders. ● **SEE FIGURE 7–17.**

? FREQUENTLY ASKED QUESTION

How Can a Cracked Exhaust Manifold Affect Engine Performance?

Cracks in an exhaust manifold will not only allow exhaust gases to escape and cause noise, but will also allow air to enter the exhaust manifold. ● **SEE FIGURE 7–18.**

Exhaust flows from the cylinders as individual puffs or pressure pulses. Behind each of these pressure pulses, a low pressure (below atmospheric pressure) is created. Outside air at atmospheric pressure is then drawn into the exhaust manifold through the crack. This outside air contains 21% oxygen and is measured by the oxygen sensor (O2S). The air passing the O2S signals the engine computer that the engine is operating too lean (excess oxygen) and the computer, not knowing that the lean indicator is false, adds additional fuel to the engine. The result is that the engine will be operating richer (more fuel than normal) and spark plugs could become fouled by fuel, causing poor engine operation.

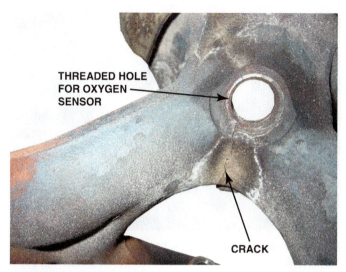

FIGURE 7–18 A crack in an exhaust manifold is often not visible because a heat shield usually covers the area. A crack in the exhaust manifold upstream of the oxygen sensor can fool the sensor and affect engine operation.

EXHAUST MANIFOLD GASKETS

Exhaust heat will expand the manifold more than it will expand the head. The heat causes the exhaust manifold to slide on the sealing surface of the head. The heat also causes thermal stress. When the manifold is removed from the engine for service, the stress is relieved, which may cause the manifold to warp slightly. Exhaust manifold gaskets are included in gasket sets to seal slightly warped exhaust manifolds. These gaskets *should* be used, even if the engine did not originally use exhaust manifold gaskets. When an exhaust manifold gasket has facing on one side only, put the facing side against the head and put the manifold against the perforated metal core. The manifold can slide on the metal of the gasket just as it slid on the sealing surface of the head.

Gaskets are used on new engines with tubing- or header-type exhaust manifolds. They may have several layers of steel for high-temperature sealing. The layers are spot welded together. Some are embossed where special sealing is needed. ● SEE FIGURE 7–19.

Many new engines do not use gaskets with cast exhaust manifolds. The flat surface of the new cast-iron exhaust manifold fits tightly against the flat surface of the new head.

INTEGRATED EXHAUST MANIFOLD

Some new GM engines achieve more power, better fuel economy, and fewer emissions by combining the exhaust manifold and the cylinder head into a single aluminum casting. Each integrated exhaust manifold cylinder head replaces a cast iron exhaust manifold, six bolts, a gasket, a heat shield, and three bolts. By eliminating this joint, the potential for a gasket failure is eliminated. And the change reduces engine weight by 13 lbs. or 6 kg per engine.

FIGURE 7–19 Typical exhaust manifold gaskets. Note how they are laminated to allow the exhaust manifold to expand and contract due to heating and cooling.

FIGURE 7–20 The new design integrated exhaust manifold cylinder head (R) is compared to the older style cylinder head (L). (*Courtesy of General Motors*)

Extensive simulation and bench testing was performed to perfect cylinder-head airflow. Exhaust flow is 10 percent better than the previous V-6 engine. With the catalytic converter closer to the engine exhaust point, the emissions reduction process begins sooner, resulting in lower emissions. The new cylinder heads decrease the overall width of the engine by 4.6 inches (117 mm) for significantly more packaging space in the engine bay making underhood work easier.[1] ● SEE FIGURE 7–20.

MUFFLERS

PURPOSE AND FUNCTION

When the exhaust valve opens, it rapidly releases high-pressure gas. This sends a strong air pressure wave through the atmosphere inside the exhaust system, which produces a sound we call "explosion". It is the same sound produced when the high-pressure gases from burned gunpowder are released from a gun. In an engine, the pulses are released one after another. The explosions come so fast that they blend together in a steady roar.

[1] media.gm.com, "Head Games: 2012 Chevy Camaro Adds Power, Saves Fuel," May 16, 2011.

FIGURE 7–21 Exhaust gases expand and cool as they travel through passages in the muffler.

FIGURE 7–22 A hole in the muffler allows condensed water to escape.

? **FREQUENTLY ASKED QUESTION**

Why Is There a Hole in My Muffler?

Many mufflers are equipped with a small hole in the lower rear part to drain accumulated water. About 1 gallon of water is produced in the form of steam for each gallon of gasoline burned. The water is formed when gasoline is burned in the cylinder. Water consists of two molecules of hydrogen and one molecule of oxygen (H_2O). The hydrogen (H) comes from the fuel and the oxygen (O) comes from the air. During combustion, the hydrogen from the fuel combines with some of the oxygen in the air to form water vapor. The water vapor condenses on the cooler surfaces of the exhaust system, especially in the muffler, until the vehicle has been driven long enough to fully warm the exhaust above the boiling point of water (212°F [100°C]). ● **SEE FIGURE 7–22.**

Sound is air vibration. When the vibrations are large, the sound is loud. The muffler catches the large bursts of high-pressure exhaust gas from the cylinder, smoothing out the pressure pulses and allowing them to be released at an even and constant rate. It does this through the use of perforated tubes within the muffler chamber. The smooth-flowing gases are released to the tailpipe. In this way, the muffler silences engine exhaust noise. ● **SEE FIGURE 7–21.**

CONSTRUCTION Most mufflers have a larger inlet diameter than outlet diameter. As the exhaust enters the muffler, it expands and cools. The cooler exhaust is denser and occupies less volume. The diameter of the outlet of the muffler and the diameter of the tailpipe can be reduced with no decrease in efficiency.

Sometimes resonators are used in the exhaust system and the catalytic converter also acts as a muffler. They provide additional expansion space at critical points in the exhaust system to smooth out the exhaust gas flow.

The tailpipe carries the exhaust gases from the muffler to the air, away from the vehicle. In most cases, the tailpipe exit is at the rear of the vehicle, below the rear bumper. In some cases, the exhaust is released at the side of the vehicle, just ahead of or just behind the rear wheel.

The muffler and tailpipe are supported with brackets, called **hangers**, which help to isolate the exhaust noise from the rest of the vehicle. The types of exhaust system hangers include:

- Rubberized fabric with metal ends that hold the muffler and tailpipe in position so that they do not touch any metal part, to isolate the exhaust noise from the rest of the vehicle

- Rubber material that looks like large rubber bands, which slip over the hooks on the exhaust system and the hooks attached to the body of the vehicle

SUMMARY

1. All air entering an engine must be filtered.

2. Engines that use throttle-body injection units are equipped with intake manifolds that keep the airflow speed through the manifold at 50 to 300 ft per second.

3. Most intake manifolds have an EGR valve that regulates the amount of recirculated exhaust that enters the engine to reduce NOx emissions.

4. Exhaust manifolds can be made from cast iron or steel tubing.

5. The exhaust system also contains a catalytic converter, exhaust pipes, and muffler. The entire exhaust system is supported by rubber hangers that isolate the noise and vibration of the exhaust from the rest of the vehicle.

1. Why is it necessary to have intake charge velocities of about 50 ft per second?

2. Why can port fuel-injected engines use larger (and longer) intake manifolds and still operate at low engine speed?

3. What is a tuned runner in an intake manifold?

4. How does a muffler quiet exhaust noise?

CHAPTER QUIZ

1. Intake charge velocity has to be _____ to prevent fuel droplet separation.
   a. 25 ft per second
   b. 50 ft per second
   c. 100 ft per second
   d. 300 ft per second

2. The air filter restriction indicator uses what to detect when it signals to replace the filter?
   a. Number of hours of engine operation
   b. Number of miles or vehicle travel
   c. The amount of light that can pasts through the filter
   d. The amount of restriction measured in inches of water

3. Why are the EGR gases cooled before entering the engine on some engines?
   a. Cool exhaust gas is more effective at controlling NOx emissions
   b. To help prevent the exhaust from slowing down
   c. To prevent damage to the intake valve
   d. To prevent heating the air-fuel mixture in the cylinder

4. The air-fuel mixture flows through the intake manifold on what type of system?
   a. Port fuel-injection systems
   b. Throttle-body fuel-injection systems
   c. Both a port-injected and throttle-body injected engine
   d. Any fuel-injected engine

5. Air filters can remove particles and dirt as small as _____.
   a. 5 to 10 microns
   b. 10 to 25 microns
   c. 30 to 40 microns
   d. 40 to 50 microns

6. Why do many port fuel-injected engines use long intake manifold runners?
   a. To reduce exhaust emissions
   b. To heat the incoming air
   c. To increase high-RPM power
   d. To increase low-RPM torque

7. Exhaust passages are included in some intake manifolds. Technician A says that the exhaust passages are used for exhaust gas recirculation (EGR) systems. Technician B says that the upper intake is often called the plenum. Which technician is correct?
   a. Technician A only
   b. Technician B only
   c. Both Technicians A and B
   d. Neither Technician A nor B

8. The upper portion of a two-part intake manifold is often called the _____.
   a. Housing
   b. Lower part
   c. Plenum
   d. Vacuum chamber

9. Technician A says that a cracked exhaust manifold can affect engine operation. Technician B says that a leaking lower intake manifold gasket could cause a vacuum leak. Which technician is correct?
   a. Technician A only
   b. Technician B only
   c. Both Technicians A and B
   d. Neither Technician A nor B

10. Technician A says that some intake manifolds are plastic. Technician B says that some intake manifolds are constructed in two parts or sections: upper and lower. Which technician is correct?
   a. Technician A only
   b. Technician B only
   c. Both Technicians A and B
   d. Neither Technician A nor B

chapter 8
TURBOCHARGING AND SUPERCHARGING

LEARNING OBJECTIVES

After studying this chapter, the reader should be able to:

1. Explain the difference between a turbocharger and a supercharger.
2. Describe how the boost levels are controlled.
3. Discuss maintenance procedures for turbochargers and superchargers.

This chapter will help you prepare for ASE Engine Performance (A8) certification test content area "C" (Air Induction and Exhaust Systems Diagnosis and Repair).

KEY TERMS

Boost 106
BOV 112
Bypass valve 108
CBV 112
Charge air cooler (CAC) 112
Dump valve 112
Forced induction systems 106
Intercooler 112
Naturally (normally) aspirated 106

Positive displacement 108
Roots supercharger 108
Supercharger 107
Turbocharger 109
Turbo lag 111
Vent valve 112
Volumetric efficiency 105
Wastegate 112

GM STC OBJECTIVES

GM Service Technical College topics covered in this chapter are:

1. The purpose of induction systems. (06510.05W)
2. The purpose of forced induction systems.
3. How to recognize various forced induction systems.
4. Types of forced induction systems and their operation.

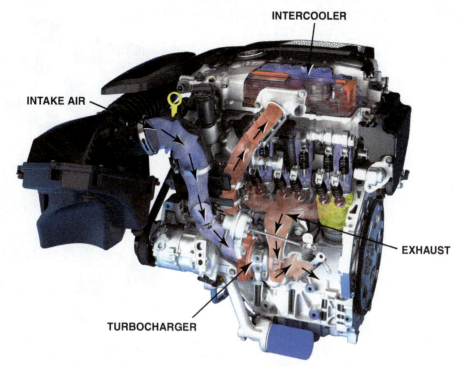

INTERCOOLER

INTAKE AIR

EXHAUST

TURBOCHARGER

FIGURE 8–1 A turbocharger uses energy from the exhaust to drive a compressor wheel that compresses the intake air. The heat from the compressed intake air is passed through a cooler and then forced into the engine cylinders. (*Courtesy of General Motors*)

AIRFLOW REQUIREMENTS

Naturally aspirated engines with throttle plates use atmospheric pressure to push an air-fuel mixture into the combustion chamber vacuum created by the down stroke of a piston. The mixture is then compressed before ignition to increase the force of the burning, expanding gases. The greater the compression of the air-fuel mixture, the higher the engine power output resulting from combustion.

A four-stroke engine can take in only a definite amount of air, and how much fuel it needs for proper combustion depends on how much air it takes in. Engineers calculate engine airflow requirements using three factors.

1. Engine displacement
2. Engine revolutions per minute (RPM)
3. Volumetric efficiency

VOLUMETRIC EFFICIENCY **Volumetric efficiency** is a measure of how well an engine breathes. It is a comparison of the actual volume of air-fuel mixture drawn into an engine to the theoretical maximum volume that could be drawn in. Volumetric efficiency is expressed as a percentage. If the engine takes

in the airflow volume slowly, a cylinder might fill to capacity. It takes a definite amount of time for the airflow to pass through all the curves of the intake manifold and valve port. Therefore, volumetric efficiency decreases as engine speed increases due to the shorter amount of time for the cylinders to be filled with air during the intake stroke. At high speed, it may drop to as low as 50%.

The average stock gasoline engine never reaches 100% volumetric efficiency. A new engine is about 85% efficient. A race engine usually has 95% or better volumetric efficiency. These figures apply only to naturally aspirated engines. However, with either turbochargers or superchargers, engines can easily achieve more than 100% volumetric efficiency. Many vehicles are equipped with a supercharger or a turbocharger to increase power. ● SEE FIGURE 8–1.

FORCED INDUCTION PRINCIPLES

PURPOSE AND FUNCTION The amount of force an air-fuel charge produces when it is ignited is largely a function of the charge density. Charge density is a term used to define

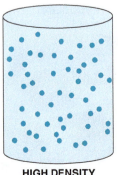

LOW DENSITY **HIGH DENSITY**

FIGURE 8–2 The more air and fuel that can be packed in a cylinder, the greater the density of the air-fuel charge.

FIGURE 8–3 This is a supercharger with an air-to-coolant charge air cooler. It is belt driven; the coolant pipes are just above the drive pulley. (*Corvette 6.2L V-8 SC; Courtesy of General Motors*)

the amount of the air-fuel charge introduced into the cylinders. Density is the mass of a substance in a given amount of space. ● **SEE FIGURE 8–2.**

The greater the density of an air-fuel charge forced into a cylinder, the greater the force it produces when ignited, and the greater the engine power.

An engine that uses atmospheric pressure for its intake charge is called a **naturally (normally) aspirated** engine. A better way to increase air density is to use some type of air pump such as a turbocharger or supercharger ● **SEE FIGURE 8–3 AND FIGURE 8–4.**

When air is pumped into the cylinder, the combustion chamber receives an increase of air pressure known as **boost,** and can be measured in:

- Pounds per square inch (PSI)
- Atmospheres (ATM) (1 atmosphere is 14.7 PSI)
- Bars (1 bar is 14.7 PSI)

FIGURE 8–4 A four cylinder engine showing the turbocharger mounted on the side. (*Ecotec 2.0L I-4 VVT DI Turbo; Courtesy of General Motors*)

While boost pressure increases air density, friction heats air in motion and causes an increase in temperature. This increase in temperature works in the opposite direction, decreasing air density. Because of these and other variables, an increase in pressure does not always result in greater air density.

FORCED INDUCTION **Forced induction systems** use an air pump to pack a denser air-fuel charge into the cylinders. Because the density of the air-fuel charge is greater, the following occurs.

- The weight of the air-fuel charge is higher.
- Power is increased because it is directly related to the weight of an air-fuel charge consumed within a given time period.

Pumping air into the intake system under pressure forces it through the bends and restrictions of the air intake system at a greater speed than it would travel under normal atmospheric pressure. This added pressure allows more air to enter the intake port before the intake valve closes. By increasing the airflow into the intake, more fuel can be mixed with the air while still maintaining the same air-fuel ratio. The denser the air-fuel charge entering the engine during its intake stroke, the greater the potential energy released during combustion. In addition to the increased power resulting from combustion, there are several other advantages of supercharging an engine, including:

- It increases the air-fuel charge density to provide high-compression pressure when power is required,

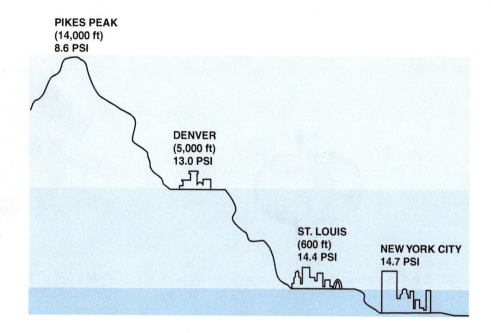

FIGURE 8–5 Atmospheric pressure decreases with increases in altitude.

PIKES PEAK
(14,000 ft)
8.6 PSI

DENVER
(5,000 ft)
13.0 PSI

ST. LOUIS
(600 ft)
14.4 PSI

NEW YORK CITY
14.7 PSI

but allows the engine to run on lower pressures when additional power is not required.

- The pumped air pushes the remaining exhaust from the combustion chamber during intake and exhaust valve overlap. (Overlap is when both the intake and exhaust valves are partially open when the piston is near the top—at the end of the exhaust stroke and the beginning of the intake stroke.)
- The forced airflow and removal of hot exhaust gases lowers the temperature of the cylinder head, pistons, and valves, and helps extend the life of the engine.

A supercharger or turbocharger pressurizes air to greater than atmospheric pressure. The pressurization above atmospheric pressure, or boost, can be measured in the same way as atmospheric pressure. Atmospheric pressure drops as altitude increases, but boost pressure remains the same. If a supercharger develops 12 PSI (83 kPa) boost at sea level, it will develop the same amount at a 5,000 ft altitude because boost pressure is measured inside the intake manifold. ● **SEE FIGURE 8–5.**

BOOST AND COMPRESSION RATIOS Boost increases the amount of air drawn into the cylinder during the intake stroke. This extra air causes the effective compression ratio to be greater than the mechanical compression ratio designed into the engine. The higher the boost pressure, the greater the compression ratio. This means that any engine that uses a supercharger or turbocharger must use all of the following engine components.

- Forged pistons, to withstand the increased combustion pressures
- Stronger than normal connecting rods
- Piston oil squirters that direct a stream of oil to the underneath part of the piston, to keep piston temperatures under control
- Lower compression ratio compared to a naturally aspirated engine
  ● **SEE CHART 8–1.**

SUPERCHARGERS

A **supercharger** is an engine-driven air pump that supplies more than the normal amount of air into the intake manifold and boosts engine torque and power. A supercharger provides an instantaneous increase in power without any delay. However, a supercharger, because it is driven by the engine, requires horsepower to operate and is not as efficient as a turbocharger.

A supercharger is an air pump mechanically driven by the engine itself. Gears, shafts, chains, or belts from the crankshaft can all be used to turn the pump. This means that the air pump or supercharger pumps air in direct relation to engine speed.

TYPES OF SUPERCHARGERS There are two general types of superchargers.

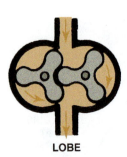

LOBE

FIGURE 8–6 A roots-type supercharger uses two lobes to force the air around the outside of the housing and into the intake manifold.

FIGURE 8–7 The supercharger vanes are fitted closely together but do not actually touch. (*Corvette ZR1; Courtesy of General Motors*)

Final Compression Ratio Chart at Various Boost Levels										
	Blower Boost (PSI)									
Comp Ratio	2	4	6	8	10	12	14	16	18	20
6.5	7.4	8.3	9.2	10	10.9	11.8	12.7	13.6	14.5	15.3
7	8	8.9	9.9	10.8	11.8	12.7	13.6	14.5	15.3	16.2
7.5	8.5	9.5	10.6	11.6	12.6	13.6	14.6	15.7	16.7	17.8
8	9.1	10.2	11.3	12.4	13.4	14.5	15.6	16.7	17.8	18.9
8.5	9.7	10.8	12	13.1	14.3	15.4	16.6	17.8	18.9	19.8
9	10.2	11.4	12.7	13.9	15.1	16.3	17.6	18.8	20	21.2
9.5	10.8	12.1	13.4	14.7	16	17.3	18.5	19.8	21.1	22.4
10	11.4	12.7	14.1	15.4	16.8	18.2	19.5	20.9	22.2	23.6

CHART 8–1

The effective compression ratio compared to the boost pressure.

- **Roots type.** Named for Philander and Francis Roots, two brothers from Connersville, Indiana, the **roots supercharger** was patented in 1860 as a type of water pump to be used in mines. Later, it was used to move air and is used today on two-stroke-cycle Detroit diesel engines and other supercharged engines. The roots-type supercharger is called a **positive displacement** design, because all of the air that enters is forced through the unit. Early applications included the GMC 6-71 (used originally on GMC diesel engines that had 6 cylinders each with 71 cu. inches) and some later 3800 V-6 GM engines. The roots-type supercharger is used today on some Chevrolet and Cadillac high performance models. ●**SEE FIGURES 8–6 AND 8–7.**

- **Centrifugal supercharger.** A centrifugal supercharger is similar to a turbocharger, but is mechanically driven by the engine instead of being powered by the hot exhaust gases. A centrifugal supercharger is not a positive displacement pump and all of the air that enters is not forced through the unit. Air enters a centrifugal supercharger housing in the center and exits at the outer edges of the compressor wheels at a much higher speed due to centrifugal force. The speed of the blades has to be higher than engine speed so a smaller pulley is used on the supercharger and the crankshaft overdrives the impeller through an internal gear box achieving about seven times the speed of the engine. Examples of centrifugal superchargers include Vortech and Paxton.

SUPERCHARGER BOOST CONTROL Many factory installed superchargers are equipped with a **bypass valve** that allows intake air to flow directly into the intake manifold, bypassing the supercharger. The computer controls the bypass valve actuator. ●**SEE FIGURE 8–8.**

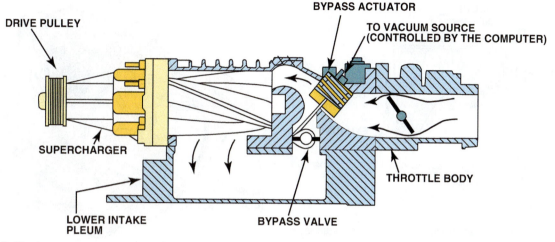

FIGURE 8–8 The bypass actuator opens the bypass valve to control boost pressure.

 TECH TIP

Faster Moves More Air

One of the high-performance measures that can be used to increase horsepower on a supercharged engine is to install a smaller diameter pulley. The smaller the pulley diameter, the faster the supercharger will rotate and the higher the potential boost pressure will be. The change will require a shorter belt, and the extra boost could cause serious engine damage.

The airflow is directed around the supercharger whenever any of the following conditions occur.

- The boost pressure, as measured by the MAP sensor, indicates that the intake manifold pressure is reaching the predetermined boost level.
- During deceleration, to prevent excessive pressure buildup in the intake.
- Reverse gear is selected.

SUPERCHARGER SERVICE
Superchargers are usually lubricated with synthetic engine oil inside the unit. This oil level should be checked and replaced as specified by the vehicle or supercharger manufacturer. The drive belt should also be inspected and replaced as necessary. The air filter should be replaced regularly, and always use the filter specified for a supercharged engine. Many factory supercharger systems use a separate cooling system for the charge air cooler located under the supercharger. Check service information for the exact service procedures to follow. ● SEE FIGURE 8–9.

FIGURE 8–9 A supercharger cutaway display showing the roots-type blower and charge air cooler (intercooler). The air charge cooler is used to reduce the temperature of the compressed air before it enters the engine to increase the air charge density.

TURBOCHARGERS

PURPOSE AND FUNCTION
The major disadvantage of a supercharger is that takes some of the engine power to drive the unit. In some installations, as much as 20% of the engine power is used by a mechanical supercharger. A **turbocharger** uses the heat of the exhaust to power a turbine wheel and therefore does not directly reduce engine power. In a naturally

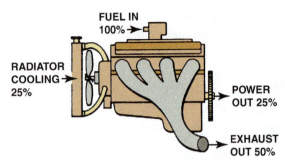

FIGURE 8–10 A turbocharger uses some of the heat energy that would normally be wasted.

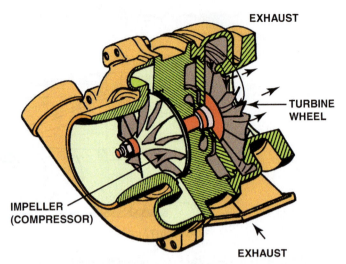

FIGURE 8–11 A turbine wheel is turned by the expanding exhaust gases.

aspirated engine, about half of the heat energy contained in the fuel goes out the exhaust system. However, some engine power is lost due to the exhaust restriction. This loss in power is regained, though, to perform other work and the combustion heat energy lost in the engine exhaust (as much as 40% to 50%) can be harnessed to do useful work. Another 25% is lost through radiator cooling. Only about 25% is actually converted to mechanical power. A mechanically driven pump uses some of this mechanical output, but a turbocharger gets its energy from the exhaust gases, converting more of the fuel's heat energy into useful mechanical energy. ● SEE FIGURE 8–10.

TURBOCHARGER DESIGN A turbocharger turbine looks much like a typical centrifugal pump used for supercharging.

Hot exhaust gases flow from the combustion chamber to the *turbine wheel*. The gases are heated and expanded as they leave the engine. It is not the speed of force of the exhaust gases that forces the turbine wheel to turn, as is commonly thought, but the expansion of hot gases against the turbine wheel's blades.

A turbocharger consists of two chambers connected with a center housing. The two chambers contain a turbine wheel and an *impeller* (compressor) *wheel* connected by a shaft which passes through the center housing. ● SEE FIGURE 8–11.

To take full advantage of the exhaust heat which provides the rotating force, a turbocharger must be positioned as close as possible to the exhaust manifold. This allows the hot exhaust to pass directly into the unit with minimal heat loss. As exhaust gas enters the turbocharger, it rotates the turbine blades. The turbine wheel and compressor wheel are on the same shaft so that they turn at the same speed. Rotation of the compressor wheel draws air in through a central inlet and centrifugal force pumps it through an outlet at the edge of the housing. A pair of bearings in the center housing supports the turbine and compressor wheel shaft, and is lubricated by engine oil. ● SEE FIGURE 8–12.

Both the turbine and compressor wheels must operate with extremely close clearances to minimize possible leakage

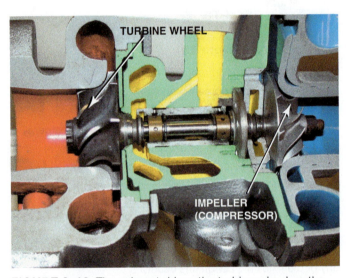

FIGURE 8–12 The exhaust drives the turbine wheel on the left which is connected to the impeller wheel on the right through a shaft. The bushings that support the shaft are lubricated with engine oil under pressure.

around their blades. Any leakage around the turbine blades causes a dissipation of the heat energy required for compressor rotation. Leakage around the compressor blades prevents the turbocharger from developing its full boost pressure.

TURBOCHARGER OPERATION When the engine is started and runs at low speed, both exhaust heat and pressure are low and the turbine runs at a low speed (approximately 1000 RPM). Because the compressor does not turn fast enough to develop boost pressure, air simply passes through it and the engine works like any naturally aspirated engine. As the engine runs faster or load increases, both exhaust heat and flow increase, causing the turbine and compressor wheels to rotate faster. Since there is very little rotating resistance on

FIGURE 8–13 Engine oil is fed to the center of the turbocharger (marked in red) to lubricate the bushings and returns to the oil pan through a return line. The coolant pipe is also shown (marked in green). (*Ecotec 1.6L SIDI Turbo; Courtesy of General Motors*)

the turbocharger shaft, the turbine and compressor wheels accelerate as the exhaust heat energy increases. When an engine is running at full power, the typical turbocharger rotates at speeds between 100000 and 150000 RPM.

LUBRICATION AND COOLING The turbocharger is lubricated by engine oil through an oil line to the center bearing assembly. Lubricating oil also helps to cool the bearings. The high rotating speeds and extremely close clearances of the turbine and compressor wheels in their housings require equally critical bearing clearances. The bearings must keep radial clearances of 0.003 to 0.006 inches (0.08 to 0.15 mm). Axial clearance (endplay) must be maintained at 0.001 to 0.003 inches (0.025 to 0.08 mm). ● **SEE FIGURE 8–13.**

All late-model turbochargers have liquid-cooled center bearings to prevent heat damage. In a liquid-cooled turbocharger, engine coolant is circulated through passages cast in the center housing to draw off the excess heat. This allows the bearings to run cooler and minimize the probability of oil coking when the engine is shut down.

BEARING "COKING" If the engine is decelerated to idle and then shut off immediately, engine lubricant stops flowing to the center housing bearings while the turbocharger is still spinning at thousands of RPM. The oil in the center housing is then subjected to extreme heat and can gradually "coke" or oxidize. The coked oil can clog passages and will reduce the

life of the turbocharger. Engine deceleration from full power to idle requires only a second or two because of its internal friction, pumping resistance, and drivetrain load. The turbocharger, however, has no such load on its shaft, and is already turning many times faster than the engine at top speed. As a result, it can take as much as a minute or more after the engine has returned to idle speed before the turbocharger also has returned to idle.

TURBOCHARGER SIZE AND RESPONSE TIME A time lag occurs between an increase in engine speed and the increase in the speed of the turbocharger. This delay between acceleration and turbo boost is called **turbo lag.** Like any material, moving exhaust gas has inertia. Inertia also is present in the turbine and compressor wheels, as well as the intake airflow. Unlike a supercharger, the turbocharger cannot supply an adequate amount of boost at low speed.

Turbocharger response time is directly related to the size of the turbine and compressor wheels. Small wheels accelerate rapidly; large wheels accelerate slowly. While small wheels would seem to have an advantage over larger ones, they may not have enough airflow capacity for an engine. To minimize turbo lag, the intake and exhaust breathing capacities of an engine must be matched to the exhaust and intake airflow capabilities of the turbocharger.

BOOST CONTROL

PURPOSE AND FUNCTION Both supercharged and turbocharged systems are designed to provide a pressure greater than atmospheric pressure in the intake manifold. This increased pressure forces additional amounts of air into the combustion chamber over what would normally be forced in by atmospheric pressure. This increased charge increases engine power. The amount of "boost" (or pressure in the intake manifold) is measured in pounds per square inch (PSI), in inches of mercury (in. Hg), in bars, or in atmospheres. The following values will vary due to altitude and weather conditions (barometric pressure).

    1 atmosphere = 14.7 PSI

    1 atmosphere = 29.50 inch Hg

    1 atmosphere = 1 bar

    1 bar = 14.7 PSI

BOOST CONTROL FACTORS The higher the level of boost (pressure), the greater the horsepower output potential. However, other factors must be considered when increasing boost pressure.

FIGURE 8–14 The unit in front of this engine that looks like a radiator is the charge air cooler (intercooler), which cools the air after it has been compressed by the turbocharger. (*Courtesy of General Motors*)

1. As boost pressure increases, the temperature of the air also increases.

2. As the temperature of the air increases, combustion temperatures also increase, as well as the possibility of detonation.

3. Power can be increased by cooling the compressed air after it leaves the turbocharger. *The power can be increased about 1% per 10°F by which the air is cooled.* This device is called a **charge air cooler (CAC) or intercooler**. It is similar to a radiator, wherein outside air can pass through, cooling the pressurized heated air. The CAC is located between the turbocharger and the intake manifold. ● **SEE FIGURE 8–14.** Some CACs use engine coolant to cool the hot compressed air that flows from the turbocharger to the intake.

4. As boost pressure increases, combustion temperature and pressures increase, which, if not limited, can do severe engine damage. The maximum exhaust gas temperature must be 1,550°F (840°C). Higher temperatures decrease the durability of the turbocharger *and* the engine.

WASTEGATE Turbochargers use exhaust gases to increase boost, which causes the engine to make more exhaust gases, which in turn increases the boost from the turbocharger. To prevent overboost and severe engine damage, most turbocharger systems use a wastegate. A **wastegate** is a valve similar to a door that can open and close. It is a bypass valve at the exhaust inlet to the turbine, which allows all of the exhaust into the turbine, or it can route part of the exhaust past the turbine to the exhaust system. If the valve is closed, all of the exhaust travels to the turbocharger. When a predetermined amount of boost pressure develops in the intake manifold, the wastegate

Boost Is the Result of Restriction

The boost pressure of a turbocharger (or supercharger) is commonly measured in pounds per square inch. If a cylinder head is restricted because of small valves and ports, the turbocharger will quickly provide boost. Boost results when the air being forced into the cylinder heads cannot flow into the cylinders fast enough and "piles up" in the intake manifold, increasing boost pressure. If an engine had large valves and ports, the turbocharger could provide a much greater *amount* of air into the engine at the same boost pressure as an identical engine with smaller valves and ports. Therefore, by increasing the size of the valves, a turbocharged or supercharged engine will be capable of producing much greater power.

valve is opened. As the valve opens, most of the exhaust flows directly out the exhaust system, bypassing the turbocharger. With less exhaust flowing across the vanes of the turbocharger, the turbocharger decreases in speed, and boost pressure is reduced. When the boost pressure drops, the wastegate valve closes to direct the exhaust over the turbocharger vanes to again allow the boost pressure to rise. Wastegate operation is a continuous process to control boost pressure.

The wastegate is the pressure control valve of a turbocharger system. It is usually controlled by the engine control computer through a boost control solenoid, also called a wastegate control valve. ● **SEE FIGURE 8–15.**

RELIEF VALVES A wastegate controls the exhaust side of the turbocharger. A relief valve controls the intake side. A relief valve vents pressurized air from the connecting pipe between the outlet of the turbocharger and the throttle whenever the throttle is closed during boost, such as during shifts. If the pressure is not released, the turbocharger turbine wheel will slow down, creating a lag when the throttle is opened again after a shift has been completed. There are two basic types of relief valves.

1. **Compressor bypass valve (CBV).** This type of relief valve routes the pressurized air to the inlet side of the turbocharger for reuse and is quiet during operation.

2. **Blow-off valve (BOV).** Also called a **dump valve** or **vent valve,** the BOV features an adjustable spring design that keeps the valve closed until a sudden release of the throttle.

FIGURE 8–15 A wastegate is used on many turbocharged engines to control maximum boost pressure. The wastegate is controlled by a computer-controlled valve.

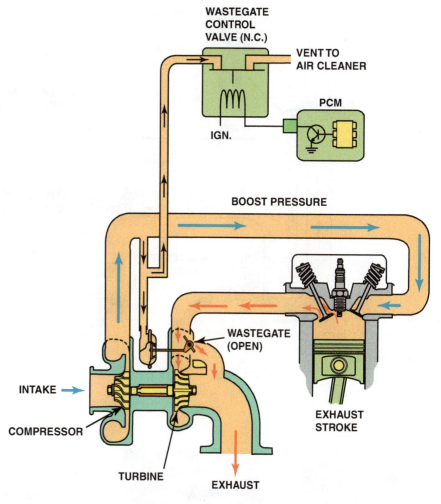

The resulting pressure increase opens the valve and vents the pressurized air directly into the atmosphere. This type of relief valve is noisy in operation and creates a whooshing sound when the valve opens. ● **SEE FIGURE 8–16.**

TURBOCHARGER FAILURES

If properly maintained, the turbocharger is a trouble-free device. However, to prevent problems, the following must be met.

- The turbocharger bearings must be constantly lubricated with clean engine oil. Turbocharged engines usually have specified oil changes at more frequent intervals than non-turbocharged engines. Always use the specified engine oil, which is likely to be vehicle specific and synthetic.

- Dirt particles and other contamination must be kept out of the intake and exhaust housings.

- Whenever a basic engine bearing (crankshaft or camshaft) has been damaged, the turbocharger must be flushed with clean engine oil after the bearing has been replaced.

TECH TIP

If One Is Good, Two Are Better

A turbocharger uses the exhaust from the engine to spin a turbine, which is connected to an impeller inside a turbocharger. This impeller then forces air into the engine under pressure, higher than is normally achieved without a turbocharger. The more air that can be forced into an engine, the greater the power potential. A V-type engine has two exhaust manifolds and so two small turbochargers can be used to help force greater quantities of air into an engine, as shown in ● **FIGURE 8–17.**

- If the turbocharger is damaged, the engine oil must be drained and flushed and the oil filter replaced as part of the repair procedure.

SYMPTOMS OF FAILURE When turbochargers fail to function correctly, a noticeable drop in power occurs. To restore proper operation, the turbocharger must be rebuilt,

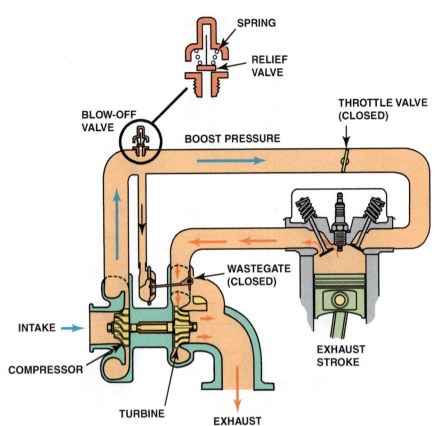

SPRING

RELIEF VALVE

BLOW-OFF VALVE

BOOST PRESSURE

THROTTLE VALVE (CLOSED)

WASTEGATE (CLOSED)

INTAKE

COMPRESSOR

EXHAUST STROKE

TURBINE

EXHAUST

FIGURE 8–16 A blow-off valve is used in some turbocharged systems to relieve boost pressure during deceleration.

FIGURE 8–17 A dual turbocharger system installed on a small block Chevrolet V-8 engine.

repaired, or replaced. It is not possible to simply remove the turbocharger, seal any openings, and maintain decent driveability. Bearing failure is a common cause of turbocharger failure, and replacement bearings are usually only available to rebuilders. Another common turbocharger problem is excessive and continuous oil consumption resulting in blue exhaust smoke. Turbochargers use small rings similar to piston rings on the shaft to prevent exhaust (combustion gases) from entering

the central bearing. Because there are no seals to keep oil in, excessive oil consumption is usually caused by the following:

1. Plugged positive crankcase ventilation (PCV) system, resulting in excessive crankcase pressures forcing oil into the air inlet (This failure is not related to the turbocharger, but the turbocharger is often blamed.)

2. Clogged air filter, which causes a low-pressure area in the inlet, drawing oil past the turbo shaft rings and into the intake manifold.

3. Clogged oil return (drain) line from the turbocharger to the oil pan (sump), which can cause the engine oil pressure to force oil past the turbocharger's shaft rings and into the intake *and* exhaust manifolds (Obviously, oil being forced into both the intake and exhaust would create lots of smoke.)

PREVENTING TURBOCHARGER FAILURES To help prevent turbocharger failures, the wise vehicle owner should follow the vehicle manufacturer's recommended routine service procedures. The most critical of these services include:

- Regular oil changes (synthetic oil would be best)
- Regular air filter replacement intervals
- Performing any other inspections and services recommended such as cleaning the intercooler.

SUMMARY

1. Volumetric efficiency is a comparison of the actual volume of air-fuel mixture drawn into the engine to the theoretical maximum volume that can be drawn into the cylinder.

2. A supercharger operates from the engine by a drive belt and, although it consumes some engine power, it forces a greater amount of air into the cylinders for even more power.

3. There are two types of superchargers: roots-type and centrifugal.

4. A turbocharger uses the normally wasted heat energy of the exhaust to turn an impeller at high speed. The impeller is linked to a turbine wheel on the same shaft and is used to force air into the engine.

5. A bypass valve is used to control the boost pressure on most factory installed superchargers.

6. A charge air cooler (CAC) is used on many turbocharged and some supercharged engines to reduce the temperature of air entering the engine for increased power.

7. A wastegate is used on most turbocharger systems to limit and control boost pressures, as well as a relief valve, to keep the speed of the turbine wheel from slowing down during engine deceleration.

REVIEW QUESTIONS

1. What are the reasons why supercharging increases engine power?

2. How does the bypass valve work on a supercharged engine?

3. What are the advantages and disadvantages of supercharging?

4. What are the advantages and disadvantages of turbocharging?

5. What turbocharger control valves are needed for proper engine operation?

CHAPTER QUIZ

1. Boost pressure is generally measured in _____.
   a. inch Hg
   b. inch H_2O
   c. PSI
   d. inch lb

2. Two types of superchargers include _____.
   a. Rotary and reciprocating
   b. Roots-type and centrifugal
   c. Double and single acting
   d. Turbine and piston

3. Which valve is used on a factory supercharger to limit boost?
   a. Bypass valve
   b. Blow-off valve
   c. Wastegate
   d. Air valve

4. How are most superchargers lubricated?
   a. By engine oil under pressure through lines from the engine
   b. By an internal oil reservoir
   c. By greased bearings
   d. No lubrication is needed because the incoming air cools the supercharger

5. How are most turbochargers lubricated?
   a. By engine oil under pressure through lines from the engine
   b. By an internal oil reservoir
   c. By greased bearings
   d. No lubrication is needed because the incoming air cools the supercharger

6. Two technicians are discussing the term *turbo lag*. Technician A says that it refers to the delay between when the exhaust leaves the cylinder and when it contacts the turbine blades of the turbocharger. Technician B says that it refers to the delay in boost pressure that occurs when the throttle is first opened. Which technician is correct?
   a. Technician A only
   b. Technician B only
   c. Both Technicians A and B
   d. Neither Technician A nor B

7. What is the purpose of charge air cooler (intercooler)?
   a. To reduce the temperature of the air entering the engine
   b. To cool the turbocharger
   c. To cool the engine oil on a turbocharged engine
   d. To cool the exhaust before it enters the turbocharger

8. Which type of relief valve used on a turbocharged engine is noisy?
   a. Bypass valve
   b. BOV
   c. Dump valve
   d. Both b and c

9. Technician A says that a stuck open wastegate can cause the engine to burn oil. Technician B says that a clogged PCV system can cause the engine to burn oil. Which technician is correct?
   a. Technician A only
   b. Technician B only
   c. Both Technicians A and B
   d. Neither Technician A nor B

10. What service operation is *most* important on engines equipped with a turbocharger?
   a. Replacing the air filter regularly
   b. Replacing the fuel filter regularly
   c. Regular oil changes
   d. Regular exhaust system maintenance

chapter 9
ENGINE CONDITION DIAGNOSIS

If there is an engine operation problem, then the cause could be any one of many components, including the engine itself. The condition of the engine should be tested anytime the operation of the engine is not satisfactory.

TYPICAL ENGINE-RELATED COMPLAINTS

Many driveability problems are *not* caused by engine mechanical problems. A thorough inspection and testing of the ignition and fuel systems should be performed before testing for mechanical engine problems.

Typical engine mechanical-related complaints include the following:

- Excessive oil consumption
- Engine misfiring
- Loss of power
- Smoke from the engine or exhaust
- Engine noise

OIL CONSUMPTION

All engines require oil to lubricate and protect the load bearing and internal moving parts from wear including cylinder walls, pistons, and piston rings. When a piston moves down its cylinder, a thin film of oil is left on the cylinder wall. During the power stroke, part of this oil layer is consumed in the combustion process. As a result, varying rates of oil consumption are accepted as normal in all engines.[1]

In the past, engine oil consumption was always higher for a brand new engine during break-in, settled down to a long period of low consumption during the normal service life, and then began to increase as the engine finally wore out. Modern engines, with closer piston ring clearances, higher quality ring material, and carefully prepared cylinder bores, require almost no break-in procedures at all. Refer to the vehicle owner's manual for any special break-in requirements.

In older vehicles, using 1 quart or less every 600 miles is considered to be normal; but when more than that, the engine needs attention. At that level, the oil being burned in the combustion chamber will form significant deposits on the intake valve, piston crown, cylinder head, and spark plug.

TECH TIP

A check of the spark plugs may indicate whether the oil is coming past the valves or the rings. An engine pulling oil past the valve guides may have deposits built up on one side of the plug electrodes on the side nearest the intake valve. Oil passing the rings will more likely cause deposits all over the end of the plug.

Today's engines use much less oil. For example, General Motors' Service Information explains that normal oil consumption is 1 quart every 2,000 miles, rather than every 600 miles—quite an improvement. Oil can enter the combustion chamber either past the piston rings or past the valve guides.

Oil passing the piston rings can be due to:

- Piston and cylinder bore wear or cylinder scoring
- Stuck worn, or broken rings
- Rings installed incorrectly
- Using oil with too low viscosity or diluted with fuel
- Excessive crankcase pressure
- Excessive oil thrown onto the cylinder walls

Oil passing the valve guides can be due to:

- Worn valve guides and/or valve stems
- Worn or damaged valve stem seals
- Valve stem seals "hardened" by heat and age
- Clogged oil drain-back holes in the head

OTHER FACTORS AFFECTING OIL CONSUMPTION[1]

Many factors can affect a customer's concern with oil consumption. Driving habits and vehicle maintenance vary from owner to owner. Thoroughly evaluate each case before deciding whether the vehicle in question has abnormal engine oil consumption.

- **Gasket and External Leaks.** Inspect the oil pan and engine covers for leakage due to over-tightened, damaged, or out of place gaskets. Inspect oil lines and fittings for signs of leakage.

- **Improper Reading of the Oil Level Indicator (Dipstick).** Verify that the dipstick tube is fully seated in the block. When checking the oil level, make sure the dipstick is wiped clean before taking an oil level reading and fully depress the dipstick until the shoulder bottoms out on the dipstick tube.

- **Not Waiting Long Enough After Running Engine to Check Oil Level.** Some engines require more time than others for the oil to drain back into the crankcase. To assure a sufficient amount of oil has drained back to the crankcase, and an accurate reading can be obtained, the vehicle should be allowed to sit for at least 15 minutes, after the engine has been shut off, before taking an oil level reading.

- **Improper Oil Fill After an Oil Change.** Following an oil change, verify that the proper amount and type of oil was put in the engine and that the oil level on the dipstick is not above the full mark or below the add marks.

- **Aggressive Driving, High Speed, or High RPM Driving.** Aggressive driving and/or continuous driving at high speeds/high RPMs will increase oil consumption. Because this may not always be an everyday occurrence, it is hard to determine exactly how much the oil economy will be affected. A higher rate of oil consumption is normal for vehicles equipped with manual transmissions that are driven aggressively.

- **Towing or Heavy Usage.** Towing a trailer will increase oil consumption; large frontal area trailers will further increase the work required from the engine, especially at highway speeds, and thus increase the rate of oil consumption.

- **Crankcase Ventilation System.** Verify that the positive crankcase ventilation (PCV) system is operating properly. Blockages, restrictions, or damage to the PCV system can result in increased oil use.

- **Oil Dilution (Fuel and Water).** On vehicles that are usually driven short distances, less than 8 km (5 mi), especially in colder weather, unburned fuel and condensation generated from cold engine operation may not get hot enough to evaporate out of the oil. When this occurs, the dipstick may indicate that the oil level is over-full. Subsequent driving on a trip of sufficient distance to enable normal engine operating temperature for 30 minutes or more, in order to vaporize excess moisture and fuel, may give the customer the impression of excessive oil consumption.

- **Engine Temperature.** If an engine is run at overheated temperatures (see Owner's Manual or Service Manual) for more than brief periods, oil will oxidize at a faster than normal rate. In addition, gaskets may distort, piston rings may stick, and excessive wear may result. Verify that all cooling system components are in proper working order.

FREQUENTLY ASKED QUESTION

What Is "Aggressive" Driving?

Aggressive driving means driving at a high RPM (3000 RPM to redline), with frequent braking (slowing down the vehicle). Vehicles that are driven aggressively may consume engine oil at a rate of up to 0.946 L (1 quart) every 805 km (500 mi). This is normal for a vehicle that is driven aggressively. No repair is necessary. This characteristic, however, does require the owner to check the engine oil level at sufficiently frequent intervals, to assure the oil level remains within the recommended operating range. As the Owner's Manual recommends, the oil level should be checked every time the vehicle is refueled.[*]

- **Engine Wear.** Piston scuffing, excessive piston-to-wall clearance, tapered or out of round cylinders, worn, damaged or improperly installed valve guides, seals, and piston rings will all cause an increase in oil consumption.

ENGINE SMOKE DIAGNOSIS

The color of engine exhaust smoke can indicate what engine problem might exist. ● **SEE CHART 9–1.**

THE DRIVER IS YOUR BEST RESOURCE

The driver of the vehicle knows a lot about the vehicle and how it is driven. *Before* diagnosis is started, always ask the following questions:

- When did the problem first occur?
- Under what conditions does it occur?

1. Cold or hot?
2. Acceleration, cruise, or deceleration?
3. How far was it driven?
4. What recent repairs have been performed?

After the nature and scope of the problem are determined, the complaint should be verified before further diagnostic tests are performed.

---

[1] Information from General Motors TSB 01-06-01-011G, September 28, 2011.

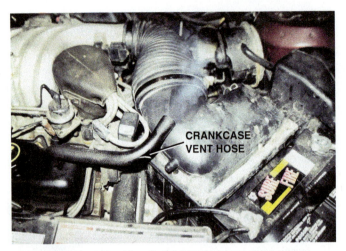

FIGURE 9–1 Blowby gases coming out of the crankcase vent hose. Excessive amounts of combustion gases flow past the piston rings and into the crankcase.

FIGURE 9–2 White steam is usually an indication of a blown (defective) cylinder head gasket that allows engine coolant to flow into the combustion chamber where it is turned to steam.

TYPICAL EXHAUST SMOKE COLOR	POSSIBLE CAUSES
Blue	Blue exhaust indicates that the engine is burning oil. Oil is getting into the combustion chamber either past the piston rings or past the valve stem seals. Blue smoke only after start-up is usually due to defective valve stem seals. ● **SEE FIGURE 9–1.**
Black	Black exhaust smoke is due to excessive fuel being burned in the combustion chamber. Typical causes include a defective or misadjusted throttle body, leaking fuel injector, or excessive fuel-pump pressure.
White (steam)	White smoke or steam from the exhaust is normal during cold weather and represents condensed steam. Every engine creates about 1 gallon of water for each gallon of gasoline burned. If the steam from the exhaust is excessive, then water (coolant) is getting into the combustion chamber. Typical causes include a defective cylinder head gasket, a cracked cylinder head, or in severe cases a cracked block. ● **SEE FIGURE 9–2.**

Note: White smoke can also be created when automatic transmission fluid (ATF) is burned. A common source of ATF getting into the engine is through a defective vacuum modulator valve used on older automatic transmissions.

CHART 9-1

Exhaust smoke colors and possible causes.

VISUAL CHECKS

The first and most important "test" that can be performed is a careful visual inspection.

OIL LEVEL AND CONDITION   The first area for visual inspection is oil level and condition.

1. Oil level–oil should be to the proper level
2. Oil condition
   a. Using a match or lighter, try to light the oil on the dipstick; if the oil flames up, gasoline is present in the engine oil.
   b. Drip some of the engine oil from the dipstick onto the hot exhaust manifold. If the oil bubbles or boils, there is coolant (water) in the oil.
   c. Check for grittiness by rubbing the oil between your fingers.

COOLANT LEVEL AND CONDITION   Most mechanical engine problems are caused by overheating. The proper operation of the cooling system is critical to the life of any engine.

NOTE: Check the coolant level in the radiator only if the radiator is cool. If the radiator is hot and the radiator cap is removed, the drop in pressure above the coolant

Your Nose Knows

Whenever diagnosing any vehicle try to use all senses including the smell. Some smells and their cause include:

- **Gasoline:** Gasoline smell: If there is a smell of gas when opening the hood, something is leaking. If the exhaust smells like gasoline or unburned fuel, then a fault with the ignition system is a likely cause. Unburned fuel due to lean air-fuel mixture causing a lean misfire is also possible.
- **Sweet smell:** A coolant leak often gives off a sweet smell especially if the leaking coolant flows onto the hot exhaust.
- **Exhaust smell:** Check for an exhaust leak including a possible cracked exhaust manifold, which can be difficult to find because it often does not make noise.

will cause the coolant to boil immediately and can cause severe burns when the coolant explosively expands upward and outward from the radiator opening.

The cooling system should be inspected for the following conditions:

1. The coolant level in the coolant recovery container should be within the limits indicated on the overflow bottle. If this level is too low or the coolant recovery container is empty, then check the level of coolant in the radiator (only when cool) and also check the operation of the pressure cap.

2. The coolant should be checked with a hydrometer for boiling and freezing temperature. This test indicates if the concentration of the antifreeze is sufficient for proper protection.

3. Pressure-test the cooling system and look for leakage. Coolant leakage can often be seen around hoses or cooling system components because it will often cause:
   a. A grayish white stain
   b. A rusty color stain
   c. Dye stains from antifreeze (greenish or yellowish depending on the type of coolant)

4. Check for cool areas of the radiator indicating clogged sections.

5. Check operation and condition of the fan clutch, fan, and coolant pump drive belt.

What's Leaking?

The color of the leaks observed under a vehicle can help the technician determine and correct the cause. Some leaks, such as condensate (water) from the air-conditioning system, are normal, whereas a brake fluid leak is very dangerous. The following are colors of common leaks:

Sooty Black	Engine Oil
Yellow, green, blue, or orange	Antifreeze (coolant)
Red	Automatic transmission fluid
Murky brown	Brake or power steering fluid or very neglected antifreeze (coolant)
Clear	Air-conditioning condensate (water) (normal)

6. Check for damaged or missing air-flow deflectors or air dams. If missing, the engine may run hot at highway speeds.

7. Some vehicles are equipped with electrically controlled shutters in the lower grill; refer to service information (SI) for the procedure to verify proper operation.

OIL LEAKS Oil leaks can lead to severe engine damage if the resulting low oil level is not corrected. Besides causing an oily mess where the vehicle is parked, the oil leak can cause blue smoke to occur under the hood as leaking oil drips on the exhaust system. *Finding* the location of the oil leak can often be difficult. ● **SEE FIGURES 9–3 AND 9–4.** To help find the source of oil leaks follow these steps:

STEP 1 Clean the engine or area around the suspected oil leak. Use a high-powered hot-water spray to wash the engine. While the engine is running, spray the entire engine and the engine compartment. Avoid letting the water come into direct contact with the air inlet and ignition distributor or ignition coil(s).

NOTE: If the engine starts to run rough or stalls when the engine gets wet, then the secondary ignition wires (spark plug wires) or distributor cap may be defective or have weak insulation. Be certain to wipe all wires and the distributor cap dry with a soft, dry cloth if the engine stalls.

An alternative method is to spray a degreaser on the engine, then start and run the engine until warm. Engine heat helps the degreaser penetrate the grease and dirt. Use a water hose to rinse off the engine and engine compartment.

FIGURE 9–3 What looks like an oil pan gasket leak can be a rocker cover gasket leak. Always look up and look for the highest place you see oil leaking; that should be repaired first.

FIGURE 9–5 Using a black light to spot leaks after adding dye to the oil.

FIGURE 9–4 The transmission and flexplate (flywheel) were removed to check the exact location of this oil leak. The rear main seal and/or the oil pan gasket could be the cause of this leak.

STEP 2 If the oil leak is not visible or oil seems to be coming from "everywhere," use a white talcum powder. The leaking oil will show as a dark area on the white powder. See the Tech Tip, "The Foot Powder Spray Trick."

STEP 3 Fluorescent dye can be added to the engine oil. Add about 1/2 oz (15 cc) of dye per 5 quarts of engine oil. Start the engine and allow it to run about 10 minutes to thoroughly mix the dye throughout the engine. A black light can then be shown around every suspected oil leak location. The black light will easily show all oil leak locations because the dye will show as a bright yellow/green area. ● **SEE FIGURE 9–5**.

NOTE: Fluorescent dye works best with clean oil.

FIGURE 9–6 An accessory belt tensioner. Most tensioners have a mark that indicates normal operating location. If the belt has stretched, this indicator mark will be outside of the normal range. Anything wrong with the belt or tensioner can cause noise.

ENGINE NOISE DIAGNOSIS

An engine knocking noise is often difficult to diagnose. ● **SEE CHART 9–2.** Several items that can cause a deep engine knock include:

- **Valves clicking.** This can happen because of lack of oil to the lifters. This noise is most noticeable at idle when the oil pressure is the lowest.

- **Torque converter.** The attaching bolts or nuts may be loose on the flex plate. This noise is most noticeable at idle or when there is no load on the engine.

- **Cracked flex plate.** The noise of a cracked flex plate is often mistaken for a rod- or main-bearing noise.

- **Loose or defective drive belts or tensioners.** If an accessory drive belt is loose or defective, the flopping noise often sounds similar to a bearing knock. ● **SEE FIGURE 9–6.**

- **Piston pin knock.** This knocking noise is usually not affected by load on the cylinder. If the clearance is too great, a double knock noise is heard when the engine idles. If all cylinders are grounded out one at a time and the noise does not change, a defective piston pin could be the cause.

- **Piston slap.** A piston slap is usually caused by an undersized or improperly shaped piston or oversized cylinder bore. A piston slap is most noticeable when the

TYPICAL NOISES	POSSIBLE CAUSES
Clicking noise– like the clicking of a ballpoint pen	1. Loose spark plug 2. Loose accessory mount (for air-conditioning compressor, alternator, power steering pump, etc.) 3. Loose rocker arm 4. Worn rocker arm pedestal 5. Fuel pump (broken mechanical fuel pump return spring) 6. Worn camshaft 7. Exhaust leak. ● SEE FIGURE 9–7.
Clacking noise- like tapping on metal	1. Worn piston pin 2. Broken piston 3. Excessive valve clearance 4. Timing chain hitting cover
Knock-like knocking on a door	1. Rod bearing(s) 2. Main bearing(s) 3. Thrust bearing(s) 4. Loose torque converter 5. Cracked flex plate (drive plate)
Rattle-like a baby rattle	1. Manifold heat control valve 2. Broken harmonic balancer 3. Loose accessory mounts 4. Loose accessory drive belt or tensioner
Clatter-like rolling marbles	1. Rod bearings 2. Piston pin 3. Loose timing chain
Whine-like an electric motor running	1. Alternator bearing 2. Drive belt 3. Power steering 4. Belt noise (accessory or timing)
Clunk-like a door closing	1. Engine mount 2. Drive axle shaft U-joint or constant velocity (CV) joint

CHART 9–2

Engine-related noises and possible causes.

engine is cold and tends to decrease or stop making noise as the piston expands during engine operation.

- **Timing chain noise.** An excessively loose timing chain can cause a severe knocking noise when the chain hits the timing chain cover. This noise can often sound like a rod-bearing knock.

- **Rod-bearing noise.** The noise from a defective rod bearing is usually load sensitive and changes in intensity as the load on the engine increases and decreases. A rod-bearing failure can often be detected by grounding out the spark plugs one cylinder at a time. If the knocking

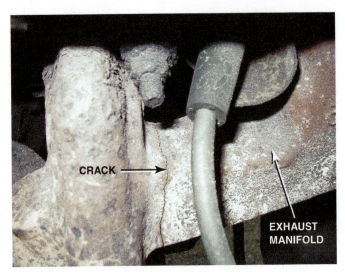

FIGURE 9–7 A cracked exhaust manifold.

Engine Noise and Cost

A light ticking noise often heard at one-half engine speed and associated with valve train noise is a less serious problem than many deep-sounding knocking noises. Generally, the deeper the sound of the engine noise, the more the owner will have to pay for repairs. A light "tick tick tick," though often not cheap, is usually far less expensive than a deep "knock knock knock" from the engine.

noise decreases or is eliminated when a particular cylinder is grounded (disabled), then the grounded cylinder is the one from which the noise is originating.

- **Main-bearing knock.** A main-bearing knock often cannot be isolated to a particular cylinder. The sound can vary in intensity and may disappear at times depending on engine load.

Regardless of the type of loud knocking noise, after the external causes of the knocking noise have been eliminated, the engine should be disassembled and carefully inspected to determine the exact cause.

OIL PRESSURE TESTING

Proper oil pressure is very important for the operation of any engine. *Low oil pressure can cause engine wear, and engine wear can cause low oil pressure.*

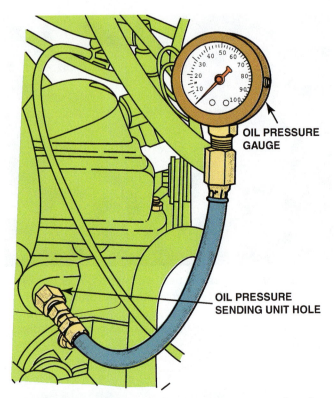

FIGURE 9–8 To measure engine oil pressure, remove the oil pressure sending (sender) unit usually located near the oil filter. Screw the pressure gauge into the oil pressure sending unit hole.

If main thrust or rod bearings are worn, oil pressure is reduced because of leakage of the oil around the bearings. Oil pressure testing is usually performed with the following steps:

STEP 1 Operate the engine until normal operating temperature is achieved.

STEP 2 With the engine off, remove the oil pressure sending unit or sender, usually located near the oil filter. Thread an oil pressure gauge into the threaded hole. Most of the time an adapter is needed in order to attach the oil pressure gauge; refer to service information for the proper tools. ● **SEE FIGURES 9–8 AND 9–9.**

STEP 3 Start the engine and observe the gauge. Record the oil pressure at idle and at 2500 RPM. Most vehicle manufacturers recommend a minimum oil pressure of 10 PSI per 1000 RPM. Therefore, at 2500 RPM, the oil pressure should be at least 25 PSI. Always compare your test results with the manufacturer's recommended oil pressure.

Besides engine bearing wear, other possible causes for low oil pressure include:

- Low oil level
- Diluted oil
- Stuck oil pressure relief valve

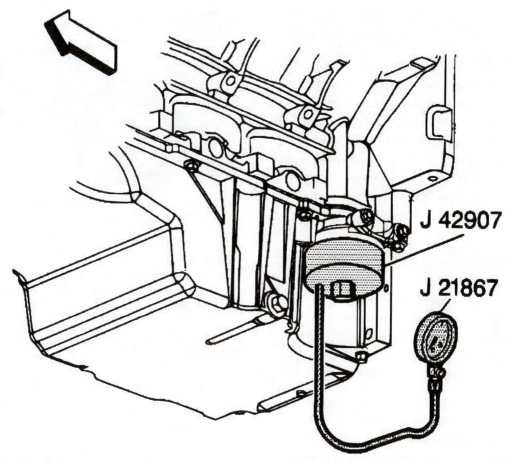

FIGURE 9–9 Some engines can use an adapter at the oil filter mount for checking oil pressure. (*Courtesy of General Motors*)

NOTE: Oil pressure specifications for GM engines at idle range from 10 to 35 PSI, depending on the engine. Always refer to service information (SI) when diagnosing an engine.

OIL PRESSURE WARNING LAMP

The red oil pressure warning lamp in the dash usually lights when the oil pressure is less than 4 to 7 PSI, depending on vehicle and engine. The oil light should not be on during driving. If the oil warning lamp is on, stop the engine immediately. Always confirm oil pressure with a reliable mechanical gauge before performing engine repairs. The sending unit or circuit may be defective.

COMPRESSION TEST

CRANKING COMPRESSION TEST An engine **compression test** is one of the fundamental engine diagnostic tests that can be performed. For smooth engine operation, all cylinders must have equal compression. An engine can lose compression by leakage of air through one or more of only three routes:

- Intake or exhaust valve
- Piston rings (or piston, if there is a hole)
- Cylinder head gasket

If any of the preceding indicators of head gasket failure occur, remove the cylinder head(s) and check all of the following:

1. Head gasket
2. Sealing surfaces—for warpage
3. Castings—for cracks

DASH WARNING LIGHTS

Most vehicles are equipped with several dash warning lights often called "telltale" or "idiot" lights. These lights are often the only warning a driver receives that there may be engine problems. A summary of typical dash warning lights and their meanings follows.

OIL (ENGINE) LIGHT   The red oil light indicates that the engine oil pressure is too low (usually lights when oil pressure is 4 to 7 PSI [20 to 50 kPa]). Normal oil pressure should be 10 to 60 PSI (70 to 400 kPa) or 10 PSI per 1000 engine RPM.

When this light comes on, the driver should shut off the engine immediately and check the oil level and condition for possible dilution with gasoline caused by a fuel system fault. If the oil level is okay, then there is a possible serious engine problem or a possible defective oil pressure sending (sender) unit. The automotive technician should always check the oil pressure using a reliable mechanical oil pressure gauge if low oil pressure is suspected.

COOLANT TEMPERATURE LIGHT   Most vehicles are equipped with a coolant temperature gauge or dash warning light. The warning light may be labeled "coolant," "hot," or "temperature." If the coolant temperature warning light comes on during driving, this usually indicates that the coolant temperature is above a safe level, or above about 250°F (120°C). Normal coolant temperature should be about 200°F to 220°F (90°C to 105°C).

If the coolant temperature light comes on during driving, the following steps should be followed to prevent possible engine damage:

1. Turn off the air conditioning and turn on the heater. The heater will help get rid of some of the heat in the cooling system.
2. Raise the engine speed in neutral or park to increase the circulation of coolant through the radiator.
3. If possible, turn the engine off and allow it to cool (this may take over an hour).
4. Do not continue driving with the coolant temperature light on (or the gauge reading in the red warning section or above 260°F) or serious engine damage may result.

NOTE: If the engine does not feel or smell hot, it is possible that the problem is a faulty coolant temperature sensor or gauge.

COMPRESSION TEST

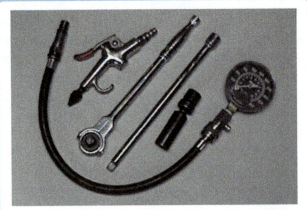

1 The tools and equipment needed to perform a compression test include a compression gauge, an air nozzle, and the socket ratchets and extensions that may be necessary to remove the spark plugs from the engine.

2 To prevent ignition and fuel-injection operation while the engine is being cranked, remove both the fuel-injection fuse and the ignition fuse. If the fuses cannot be removed, disconnect the wiring connectors for the injectors and the ignition system.

3 Before removing the spark plugs, use an air nozzle to blow away any dirt that may be around the spark plug. This step helps prevent debris from getting into the engine when the spark plugs are removed.

4 Remove all of the spark plugs. Be sure to mark the spark plug wires so that they can be reinstalled onto the correct spark plugs after the compression test has been performed.

5 Select the proper adapter for the compression gauge. The threads on the adapter should match those on the spark plug.

6 If necessary, connect a battery charger to the battery before starting the compression test. It is important that consistent cranking speed be available for each cylinder being tested.

7 Press the accelerator pedal to the floor and crank the engine. Make a note of the reading on the gauge after the first "puff," which indicates the first compression stroke that occurred on that cylinder as the engine was being rotated. If the first puff reading is low and the reading gradually increases with each puff, weak or worn piston rings may be indicated.

8 After the engine has been cranked for four "puffs," stop cranking the engine and observe the compression gauge.

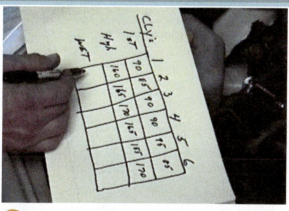

9 Record the first puff and this final reading for each cylinder. The final readings should all be within 70% of each other.

10 If a cylinder(s) is lower than most of the others, use an oil can and use two squirts of engine oil into the cylinder and repeat the compression test. This is called performing a wet compression test.

11 If the gauge reading is now much higher than the first test results, then the cause of the low compression is due to worn or defective piston rings. The oil in the cylinder temporarily seals the rings, which causes the higher reading.

SUMMARY

1. The first step in diagnosing engine condition is to perform a thorough visual inspection, including a check of oil and coolant levels and condition.

2. Oil leaks can be found by using a white powder or a fluorescent dye and a black light.

3. Many engine-related problems make a characteristic noise.

4. A compression test can be used to test the condition of valves and piston rings.

5. A cylinder leakage test fills the cylinder with compressed air, and the gauge indicates the percentage of leakage.

6. A cylinder balance test indicates whether all cylinders are working okay.

7. Testing engine vacuum is another procedure that can help the service technician determine engine condition.

REVIEW QUESTIONS

1. Describe the visual checks that should be performed on an engine if a mechanical malfunction is suspected.

2. List three items that could cause excessive oil consumption.

3. List three items that could cause engine noises.

4. Describe how to perform a compression test and how to determine what is wrong with an engine based on a compression test result.

5. Describe the cylinder leakage test.

6. Describe how a vacuum gauge would indicate if the valves were sticking in their guides.

7. Describe the test procedure for determining if the exhaust system is restricted (clogged) using a vacuum gauge.

CHAPTER QUIZ

1. Technician A says that the paper test could detect a burned valve. Technician B says that a grayish white stain on the engine could be a coolant leak. Which technician is correct?
   a. Technician A only
   b. Technician B only
   c. Both Technicians A and B
   d. Neither Technician A nor B

2. Two technicians are discussing oil leaks. Technician A says that an oil leak can be found using a fluorescent dye in the oil with a black light to check for leaks. Technician B says that a white spray powder can be used to locate oil leaks. Which technician is correct?
   a. Technician A only
   b. Technician B only
   c. Both Technicians A and B
   d. Neither Technician A nor B

3. Which of the following is the *least likely* to cause an engine noise?
   a. Carbon on the pistons
   b. Cracked exhaust manifold
   c. Loose accessory drive belt
   d. Vacuum leak

4. A good gasoline engine should produce how much compression during a running (dynamic) compression test at idle?
   a. 150 to 200 PSI
   b. 100 to 150 PSI
   c. 60 to 90 PSI
   d. 30 to 60 PSI

5. A smoothly operating engine depends on _____.
   a. High compression on most cylinders
   b. Equal compression between cylinders
   c. Cylinder compression levels above 100 PSI (700 kPa) and within 70 PSI (500 kPa) of each other
   d. Compression levels below 100 PSI (700 kPa) on most cylinders

6. A good reading for a cylinder leakage test would be _____.
   a. Within 20% between cylinders
   b. All cylinders below 20% leakage
   c. All cylinders above 20% leakage
   d. All cylinders above 70% leakage and within 7% of each other

7. Technician A says that during a power balance test, the cylinder that causes the biggest RPM drop is the weak cylinder. Technician B says that if one spark plug wire is grounded out and the engine speed does not drop, a weak or dead cylinder is indicated. Which technician is correct?
   a. Technician A only
   b. Technician B only
   c. Both Technicians A and B
   d. Neither Technician A nor B

8. *Cranking* vacuum should be _____.
   a. 2.5 inches Hg or higher
   b. Over 25 inches Hg
   c. 17 to 21 inches Hg
   d. 6 to 16 inches Hg

9. Technician A says that a leaking head gasket can be tested for using a chemical tester. Technician B says that leaking head gasket can be found using an exhaust gas analyzer.
   a. Technician A only
   b. Technician B only
   c. Both Technicians A and B
   d. Neither Technician A nor B

10. The low oil pressure warning light usually comes on _____.
   a. Whenever an oil change is required
   b. Whenever oil pressure drops dangerously low (4 to 7 PSI)
   c. Whenever the oil filter bypass valve opens
   d. Whenever the oil filter antidrainback valve opens

chapter 10
IN-VEHICLE ENGINE SERVICE

LEARNING OBJECTIVES

After studying this chapter, the reader should be able to:

1. Diagnose and replace the thermostat.
2. Diagnose and replace the water pump.
3. Diagnose and replace an intake manifold gasket.
4. Determine and verify correct cam timing.
5. Replace a timing a belt.
6. Describe how to adjust valves.
7. Explain hybrid engine precautions.

This chapter will help you prepare for Engine Repair (A1) ASE certification test content area "A" (General Engine Diagnosis).

KEY TERMS

EREV 144

Fretting 142

HEV 144

Idle stop 144

Skewed 141

GM STC OBJECTIVES

GM Service Technical College topics covered in this chapter are:

1. Perform on-vehicle engine repairs using General Motors service information and procedures.
2. Test and replace thermostat.
3. Inspect, remove, and replace water pump.
4. Remove a cylinder head.
5. Remove and install the engine valve timing components.

THERMOSTAT REPLACEMENT

FAILURE PATTERNS   All thermostat valves move during operation to maintain the desired coolant temperature. Thermostats can fail in the following ways.

- **Stuck open.** If a thermostat fails open or partially open, the operating temperature of the engine will be less than normal. ● SEE FIGURE 10–1.

- **Stuck closed.** If the thermostat fails closed or almost closed, the engine will likely overheat.

- **Stuck partially open.** This will cause the engine to warm up slowly if at all. This condition can cause the powertrain control module (PCM) to set a P0128 diagnostic trouble code (DTC) which means that the engine coolant temperature does not reach the specified temperature.

- **Skewed.** A **skewed** thermostat works, but not within the correct temperature range. Therefore, the engine could overheat or operate cooler than normal or even do both.

REPLACEMENT PROCEDURE   Before replacing the thermostat, double-check that the cooling system problem is not due to another fault, such as being low on coolant or an inoperative cooling fan. Check service information for the specified procedure to follow to replace the thermostat. Most recommended procedures include the following steps.

STEP 1   Allow the engine to cool for several hours so the engine and the coolant should be at room temperature.

STEP 2   Drain the coolant into a suitable container. Most vehicle manufacturers recommend that new coolant be used and the old coolant disposed of properly or recycled.

STEP 3   Remove any necessary components to get access to the thermostat.

STEP 4   Remove the thermostat housing and thermostat.

STEP 5   Replace the thermostat housing gasket and thermostat. Torque all fasteners to specifications.

STEP 6   Refill the cooling system with the specified coolant and bleed any trapped air from the system.

STEP 7   Pressurize the cooling system to verify that there are no leaks around the thermostat housing.

STEP 8   Run the engine until it reaches normal operating temperature and check for leaks.

STEP 9   Verify that the engine is reaching correct operating temperature.

FIGURE 10–1 If the thermostat has a jiggle valve, it should be placed toward the top to allow air to escape. If a thermostat were to become stuck open or open too soon, this can set a diagnostic trouble code P0128 (coolant temperature below thermostat regulating temperature).

WATER PUMP REPLACEMENT

NEED FOR REPLACEMENT   A water pump will require replacement if any of the following conditions are present.

- Leaking coolant from the weep hole
- Bearing noisy or loose
- Lack of proper coolant flow caused by worn or slipping impeller blades

REPLACEMENT GUIDELINES   After diagnosis has been confirmed that the water pump requires replacement, check service information for the exact procedure to follow. The steps usually include the following:

STEP 1   Allow the engine to cool to room temperature.

STEP 2   Drain the coolant and dispose of properly or recycle.

STEP 3   Remove engine components to gain access to the water pump as specified in service information.

STEP 4   Remove the water pump assembly.

STEP 5   Clean the gasket surfaces and install the new water pump using a new gasket or seal as needed. ● SEE FIGURE 10–2. Torque all fasteners to factory specifications.

FIGURE 10–2 Use caution if using a steel scraper to remove a gasket from aluminum parts. It is best to use a wood or plastic scraper.

STEP 6   Install removed engine components.

STEP 7   Fill the cooling system with the specified coolant.

STEP 8   Run the engine, check for leaks, and verify proper operation.

INTAKE MANIFOLD GASKET INSPECTION

CAUSES OF FAILURE   Many V-type engines leak oil, coolant, or experience an air (vacuum) leak caused by a leaking intake manifold gasket. This failure can be contributed to one or more of the following:

1. Expansion/contraction rate difference between the cast-iron head and the aluminum intake manifold can cause the intake manifold gasket to be damaged by the relative motion of the head and intake manifold. This type of failure is called **fretting**.

2. Plastic (Nylon 6.6) gasket deterioration caused by the coolant. ● **SEE FIGURE 10–3.**

DIAGNOSIS OF LEAKING INTAKE MANIFOLD GASKET   Because intake manifold gaskets are used to seal oil, air, and coolant in most cases, determining that the intake manifold gasket is the root cause can be a challenge. To diagnose a possible leaking intake manifold gasket, perform the following tests.

FIGURE 10–3 An intake manifold gasket that failed and allowed coolant to be drawn into the cylinder(s).

Visual inspection. Check for evidence of oil or coolant between the intake manifold and the cylinder heads.

Coolant level. Check the coolant level and determine if the level has been dropping. A leaking intake manifold gasket can cause coolant to leak and then evaporate, leaving no evidence of the leak.

Air (vacuum) leak. If there is a stored DTC for a lean exhaust (P0171, P0172, or P0174), a leaking intake manifold gasket could be the cause. Use propane to check if the engine changes in speed or sound when dispensed around the intake manifold gasket. If the engine changes in speed or sound, then this test verifies that an air leak is present.

INTAKE MANIFOLD GASKET REPLACEMENT

When replacing the intake manifold gasket, always check service information for the exact procedure to follow. The steps usually include the following:

STEP 1   Be sure the engine has been off for about an hour and then drain the coolant into a suitable container.

STEP 2   Remove covers and other specified parts needed to get access to the retaining bolts.

STEP 3   To help ensure that the manifold does not warp when removed, loosen all fasteners in the reverse order of the tightening sequence. This means that the bolts should be loosened starting at the ends and working toward the center.

STEP 4   Remove the upper intake manifold (plenum), if equipped, and inspect for faults. ● **SEE FIGURE 10–4.**

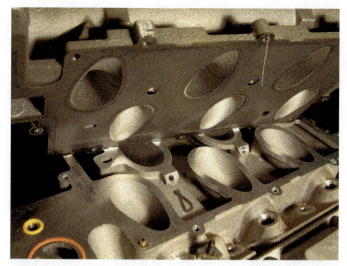

FIGURE 10–4 Remove the upper intake manifold.

FIGURE 10–5 This manifold has two bolts that are not visible with the upper manifold in place.

STEP 5 Remove the lower intake manifold, using the same bolt removal procedure of starting at the ends and working toward the center. Some engines may have bolts hidden under the upper manifold. ● **SEE FIGURES 10–5 AND 10–6.**

STEP 6 Thoroughly clean the area and replace the intake manifold if needed. Check that the correct replacement manifold is being used, and even the current part could look different from the original.

STEP 7 Install the intake manifold using new gaskets as specified. Some designs use gaskets that are reusable. Replace as needed.

STEP 8 Torque all fasteners to factory specifications and in the proper sequences. The tightening sequences usually start at the center and work outward to the ends.

CAUTION: Double-check the torque specifications and be sure to use the correct values. Many intake manifolds use fasteners that are torqued to values expressed in pound-inches and not pound-feet.

STEP 9 Reinstall all parts needed to allow the engine to start and run, including refilling the coolant if needed.

STEP 10 Start the engine and check for leaks and proper engine operation.

STEP 11 Reset the idle if specified, using a scan tool.

STEP 12 Install all of the remaining parts and perform a test drive to verify proper operation and no leaks.

STEP 13 Check and replace the air filter if needed.

STEP 14 Change the engine oil if the intake manifold leak could have caused coolant to leak into the engine, which would contaminate the oil.

FIGURE 10–6 Carefully remove the lower manifold. Don't drop any parts into the engine.

TIMING BELT REPLACEMENT

NEED FOR REPLACEMENT Timing belts have a limited service and a specified replacement interval ranging from 60,000 miles (97,000 km) to about 100,000 miles (161,000 km). Timing belts are required to be replaced if any of the following conditions occur.

- Meets or exceeds the vehicle manufacturer's recommended timing belt replacement interval.
- The timing belt has been contaminated with coolant or engine oil.
- The timing belt has failed (missing belt teeth or broken).

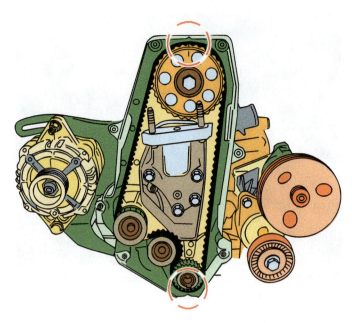

FIGURE 10-7 Make sure that the timing marks are lined up before removing the old belt. (*Courtesy of General Motors*)

TIMING BELT REPLACEMENT GUIDELINES Before replacing the timing belt, check service information for the recommended procedure to follow. Most timing belt replacement procedures include the following steps.

STEP 1 Allow the engine to cool before starting to remove components to help eliminate the possibility of personal injury or warpage of the parts.

STEP 2 Remove all necessary components to gain access to the timing belt and timing marks.

STEP 3 If the timing belt is not broken, rotate the engine until the camshaft and crankshaft timing marks are aligned according to the specified marks. ● **SEE FIGURE 10–7.**

STEP 4 Loosen or remove the tensioner as needed to remove the timing belt.

STEP 5 Replace the timing belt and any other recommended items. Components that some vehicle manufacturers recommend replacing in addition to the timing belt include:

- Tensioner assembly and idler pulley, if equipped
- Water pump
- Camshaft oil seal(s)
- Front crankshaft seal

STEP 6 Check (verify) that the camshaft timing is correct by rotating the engine several revolutions, then recheck the timing marks.

STEP 7 Install enough components to allow the engine to start to verify proper operation. Check for any leaks, especially if seals have been replaced.

STEP 8 Complete the reassembly of the engine and perform a test drive before returning the vehicle to the customer.

HYBRID ENGINE PRECAUTIONS

HYBRID VEHICLE ENGINE OPERATION Gasoline engines used in **hybrid electric vehicles (HEVs)** and in **extended range electric vehicles (EREVs)** can be a hazard to be around under some conditions. These vehicles are designed to stop the gasoline engines unless needed. This feature is called **idle stop**. This means that the engine is not running, but could start at any time if the computer detects the need to charge the hybrid batteries or any other issue that requires the gasoline engine to start and run.

PRECAUTIONS Always check service information for the exact procedures to follow when working around or under the hood of a hybrid electric vehicle. These precautions could include:

- Before working under the hood or around the engine, be sure that the ignition is off and the key is out of the ignition.
- Check that the "Ready" light is off. ● **SEE FIGURE 10–8.**
- Do not touch any circuits that have orange electrical wires or conduit. The orange color indicates dangerous high-voltage wires, which could cause serious injury or death if touched.
- Always use high-voltage linesman's gloves whenever depowering the high-voltage system.

HYBRID ENGINE SERVICE The gasoline engine in most hybrid electric vehicles specifies low viscosity engine oil as a way to achieve maximum fuel economy. ● **SEE FIGURE 10–9.** The viscosity required is often:

- SAE 0W-20
- SAE 5W-20

Many shops do not keep this viscosity in stock so preparations need to be made to get and use the specified engine oil.

In addition to engine oil, some hybrid electric vehicles require special spark plugs. Check service information for the specified service procedures and parts needed if a hybrid electric vehicle is being serviced.

FIGURE 10–8 Some hybrid electric vehicles have a ready light. If the ready light is on, the engine can start at anytime without warning.

FIGURE 10–9 Always use the viscosity of oil as specified on the oil fill cap.

GASOLINE DIRECT INJECTION SERVICE

NOISE ISSUES Gasoline direct-injection systems operate at high pressure and the injectors can often be heard with the engine running and the hood open. This noise can be a customer concern because the clicking sound is similar to noisy valves. If a noise issue is the customer concern, check the following:

- Check a similar vehicle to determine if the sound is louder or more noticeable than normal.

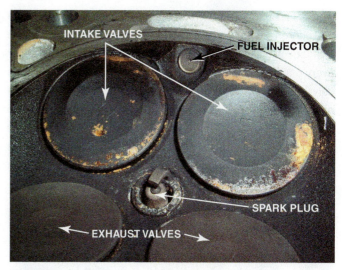

FIGURE 10–10 The gasoline direct-injection fuel injector is exposed to combustion carbon and fuel residue.

- Check that nothing under the hood is touching the fuel rail. If another line or hose is in contact with the fuel rail, the sound of the injectors clicking can be transmitted throughout the engine, making the sound more noticeable.
- Check service information (SI) for any technical service bulletins (TSBs) that may include new clips or sound insulators to help reduce the noise.

CARBON ISSUES Carbon deposits can be an issue in engines equipped with gasoline direct-injection systems. Carbon can affect engine operation by accumulating in two places:

- On the injector itself. Because the injector tip is in the combustion chamber, fuel residue can accumulate on the injector, reducing its ability to provide the proper spray pattern and amount of fuel. Some injector designs are more likely to be affected by carbon than others. For example, an injector that uses small holes may tend to become clogged more easily than an injector using a single slit opening, where the fuel being sprayed out tends to blast away any carbon. ● **SEE FIGURE 10–10.**
- The backside of the intake valve. This is a common place for fuel residue and carbon to accumulate on engines equipped with gasoline direct injection. The accumulation of carbon on the intake valve can become so severe that the engine will start and idle, but lack power to accelerate the vehicle. The carbon deposits restrict the airflow into the cylinder enough to decrease engine power.

NOTE: Using the manufacturer specified engine oil and changing it at the proper intervals will help to minimize or eliminate this problem.

CARBON CLEANING.   Most experts recommend the use of Techron®, a fuel system dispersant, to help keep carbon from accumulating. The use of a dispersant every six months or every 6,000 miles has proven to help prevent injector and intake valve deposits. If the lack of power is discovered and there are no stored diagnostic trouble codes, a conventional carbon cleaning procedure will likely restore power if the intake valves are coated. In severe cases, a special carbon removal process will be needed to clean the backside of the valves. Check service information for the specified procedures to follow.

REMOVING AND REPLACING THE CYLINDER HEAD AND GASKET

When the diagnosis indicates cylinder head leakage, keep in mind that head gasket failure is generally the result of another problem. Overheating is usually its cause, and the source of this problem has to be located and repaired in order to do the job properly. There may be additional damage that is not clearly visible, even with the head off. The cylinder head, block, and cylinder bores should be carefully checked for warpage, cracking, or scoring.

NOTE: If torque-to-yield bolts are used for the head or manifold, they should be replaced. Refer to service information (SI) for the proper procedures.

1 After removing the intake manifold and any accessories out of the way, remove the exhaust manifolds.

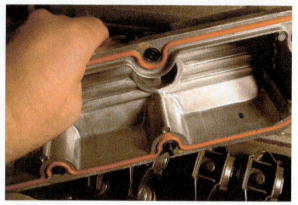

2 Unbolt and remove the valve covers.

3 Remove the rocker arm assemblies. Be careful to keep them in order.

4 Remove all of the push rods. This is a simple way to keep everything in order.

5 Break loose all of the head bolts in the reverse order of the specified tightening sequence. Once all the bolts are loose, remove them.

6 Carefully remove the cylinder head from the engine.

CONTINUED ▶

HEAD GASKET REPLACEMENT (CONTINUED)

7 Protect the cylinders with clean rags. Scrape off the old gasket material and inspect the surface.

8 The new head gasket usually will have markings that show how the gasket is to be installed. This arrow marking should point toward the front of the engine.

9 Follow service information for the proper torque procedure. This engine torques to 37 lb/ft and then another 120 degrees.

10 Install the pushrods and rocker arms, then torque to specification.

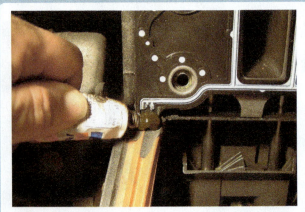

11 Install the new intake manifold gaskets and seals. Use sealing compound at each of the four corners as shown.

12 After placing the intake manifold in position, start all the bolts by hand before tightening them to specification. Finish the job by re-installing the exhaust manifolds and accessories previously removed.

1. Thermostats can fail in
   - Stuck open
   - Stuck closed
   - Stuck partially open
   - Skewed

2. A water pump should
   conditions are present.
   - Leaking from the wee
   - Noisy bearing
   - Loose bearing
   - Lack of normal circul

3. A leaking intake manifo
   into the oil or oil into th
   such as a poor running

a timing belt is replaced, most vehicle manufacturers
commend that the following items be replaced and
sembly, if equipped.
oner assembly
r pump
haft seal(s)
crankshaft seal

orking on hybrid electric vehicles (HEVs), be sure
key is off and out of the ignition and the READY
ff.

REVIEW QUES

1. How can a thermostat fa
2. How can a water pump f
3. What will happen to the
   ket fails?

t timing belts be replaced?

important that the READY light be out on the
re working under the hood of a hybrid electric

CHAPTER QUIZ

1. A thermostat can fail in w
   a. Stuck open
   b. Stuck closed

2. A skewed thermostat mea
   a. Working, but not at the
   b. Not working
   c. Missing the thermo wa
   d. Contaminated with coo

3. Coolant drained from the c
   thermostat or water pump
   a. Reused
   b. Disposed of properly or
   c. Filtered and reinstalled
   d. Poured down a toilet

4. A water pump can fail to
   flow of coolant through th
   happened?
   a. The coolant is leaking fr
   b. The bearing is noisy.
   c. The impeller blades are
   d. A bearing failure has cau

5. Intake manifold gaskets on a V-type engine can fail due to
   what factor?
   a. Fretting
   b. Coolant damage
   c. Relative movement between the intake manifold and
      the cylinder head
   d. All of the above

e thermostat can cause the powertrain control
set what diagnostic trouble code (DTC)?
   c. P0128
   d. P0300

oving an intake manifold, the bolts are easy to
nove.
   b. False

specifications for many intake manifolds are in

   nches   c. Ft-lb per minute
   eet   d. Lb-ft per second

acing a timing belt, many experts and vehi-
cturers recommend what other part(s) to be

   r assembly   c. Camshaft oil seal(s)
   mp   d. All of the above

ric vehicles usually require special engine oil
osity?
   30   c. SAE 0W-20
   -30   d. SAE 5W-40

chapter 11
ENGINE REMOVAL AND DISASSEMBLY

LEARNING OBJECTIVES

After studying this chapter, the reader should be able to:

1. Explain the differences between a long-block assembly and a short-block assembly.
2. Describe how to remove an engine from a vehicle.
3. Explain how to remove engine accessory components, such as the covers and valve train components.
4. Discuss how to remove cylinder heads without causing warpage.
5. List the steps necessary to remove a piston from a cylinder.
6. Explain how to remove a valve from a cylinder head.

This chapter will help you prepare for ASE Engine Repair (A1) certification test content areas "B" (Cylinder Head and Valve Train Diagnosis and Repair) and "C" (Engine Block Diagnosis and Repair).

GM STC OBJECTIVES

GM Service Technical College topics covered in this chapter are:

1. Perform engine removal following General Motors service information and procedures.
2. Remove cylinder wall ridges.

KEY TERMS

Freshening 151
Long block 151
Rebuilding 151
Short block 151
Vibration damper 157

ENGINE REPAIR OPTIONS

TECHNICIAN AND OWNER DECISION The decision to repair an engine should be based on all the information about the engine that is available to the service technician and the vehicle owner.

- In some cases, the engine might not be worth repairing. It is the responsibility of the technician to discuss the advantages and disadvantages of the different repair options with the customer.

- The customer, who is paying for the repair, must make the final decision on the reconditioning procedure to be followed. The repair might involve replacing a worn component instead of reconditioning. The decision will be based on the recommendation of the service technician.

REPAIR OPTIONS Most customers want to spend the least amount of money possible, so they have only the faulty component repaired. This is the correct procedure in many cases. Examples of component repairs include:

- **Component replacement.** Timing chain replacement is an example of a component repair due to wear that can cause a loss of engine performance. If testing indicates that the timing chain has excessive slack, the front of the engine can be disassembled and the actual slack measured. Usually a slack of 0.5 inch (13 mm) or more indicates that the timing chain and gears need to be replaced. ● SEE FIGURE 11–1.

- **Valve job.** Valve leakage is corrected by doing a valve job. This does not necessarily correct the customer's concerns, however. Stopping valve leakage improves manifold vacuum. After completing a valve job, the greater manifold vacuum may draw the oil past worn piston rings and into the combustion chamber during the intake stroke, causing oil consumption to increase.

- **Minor overhaul.** A minor overhaul can usually be done without removing the engine from the chassis. It requires removal of both the head and the oil pan. The overhaul is usually done when the engine lacks power, has poor fuel economy, uses an excessive amount of oil, produces visible tailpipe emissions, runs rough, or is hard to start. It is still only a repair procedure. Parts normally replaced include the piston rings, rod bearings, gaskets, and valves. Other engine problems may be noticed after the oil pan is removed and the piston and rod assemblies are taken out. The customer should be informed about any

FIGURE 11–1 A worn timing sprocket that resulted in a retarded valve timing and reduced engine performance.

other engine problem, in order to authorize the service that the engine requires. In the high-performance industry, this procedure is called **freshening** the engine.

- **Major overhaul.** A complete engine reconditioning job is called **rebuilding.** Sometimes, this type of reconditioning is called a major overhaul. To rebuild the engine, the engine must be removed from the chassis and be completely disassembled. All serviceable parts are reconditioned to either new or service standards. All bearings, gaskets, and seals are replaced. When the reconditioning is done properly, a rebuilt engine should operate like a new engine.

- **Short block.** The quickest way to get a vehicle back in service is to exchange the faulty engine for a different one. In an older vehicle, the engine may be replaced with a used engine from a salvage yard. In some cases, only a reconditioned block, including the crankshaft, rods, and pistons, is used. This replacement assembly is called a **short block.** The original heads, valve train, oil pump, and all external components are reconditioned and used on the short block.

- **Long block.** The replacement assembly is called a **long block** when the reconditioned assembly includes the heads and valve train. Many automotive machine shops maintain a stock of short and long blocks of popular engines. Usually, the original engine parts, called the core, are exchanged for the reconditioned assembly. The core parts are reconditioned by the automotive machine shop and put back in stock for the next customer.

- **Crate engines.** Crate engines are new engines built by the engine manufacturer and sold through vehicle dealers. ● SEE FIGURE 11–2.

FIGURE 11–2 A crate engine from General Motors to be used in a restored muscle car. Using a complete new engine costs more than rebuilding an existing engine, but it has a warranty and uses all new parts. (*Courtesy of General Motors*)

- **Remanufactured engines.** Some engines are remanufactured and can be replaced in a day or two, greatly reducing the amount of time the customer is without a vehicle. The engine cores are completely disassembled, and each serviceable part is reconditioned with specialized machinery. Engines are then assembled on an engine assembly line similar to the original manufacturer's assembly line. The parts that are assembled together as an engine have not come out of the same engine. The remanufactured engine usually has new pistons, valves, and lifters, together with other parts that are normally replaced in a rebuilt engine. All clearances and fits in the remanufactured engine are the same as in a new engine. A remanufactured engine should give service as good as that of a new engine, and it will cost about half as much. Remanufactured engines usually carry a warranty. This means that they will be replaced if they fail during the period of the warranty. They may even cost less than a rebuilt engine, because much of the reconditioning is done by specialized machines rather than by expensive skilled labor.

ENGINE REMOVAL

CHECK SERVICE INFORMATION Whenever any engine-related work is being performed, always print out the specified procedure as published in service information to avoid doing any harm to the vehicle or the engine.

USUAL ENGINE REMOVAL PROCEDURES The procedures that are usually specified include:

- **Remove the hood.** Removing the hood allows easier access to all of the components around the engine. Store the hood in a place where it will not be damaged. Some technicians place a fender cover on the roof of the vehicle and then place the hood upside down on top of the fender cover.

- **Clean the engine area.** The engine exterior and the engine compartment should be cleaned before work is begun. Using a power washer is the most commonly used way to clean the engine compartment area. A clean engine is easier to work on, and the cleaning not only helps to keep dirt out of the engine, but also minimizes accidental damage from slipping tools.

- **Disconnect the battery negative (–) cable.** Disconnect the positive cable and then remove the battery from the vehicle if it could interfere with the removal of the engine.

- **Remove the air cleaner assembly.** Remove the hoses and other components of the air intake system. Mark or bag and tag all fasteners.

- **Remove all accessories.** Those that usually need to be removed include the alternator, engine driven fan, and AIR pump, if equipped.

- **Drain the coolant.** Draining coolant from the radiator and the engine block help reduce the chance of coolant getting into the cylinders when the cylinder head is removed. Dispose of the used coolant properly.

- **Remove the radiator.** Disconnect the transmission oil cooler lines and radiator hoses from the radiator. Removing the radiator helps provide room for moving the engine during removal and helps prevent the possibility of damage.

- **Disconnect the exhaust system.** On some engines, it may be easier to remove the exhaust manifold(s) from the cylinder head(s), whereas on others, it may be easier to disconnect the exhaust pipe from the manifold(s).

- **Recover the air-conditioning refrigerant.** Set the air-conditioning compressor aside and do not open the system unless absolutely necessary. If the air-conditioning system has to be opened to remove components, then the refrigerant must be recovered. Tape or cover all open refrigerant fittings and hoses to prevent contaminates from entering the A/C system. Check service information for the exact procedures to follow.

A Picture Is Worth a Thousand Words

Take pictures with a cell phone camera, digital camera, or a video camcorder of the engine being removed. These pictures will be worth their weight in gold when it comes time to reassemble or reinstall the engine. It is very difficult for anyone to remember the *exact* location of every bracket, wire, and hose. Referring back to the photos of the engine before work was started will help you restore the vehicle to like-new condition.

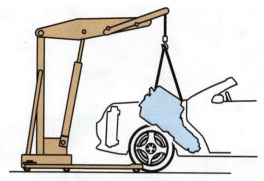

FIGURE 11–3 An engine must be tipped as it is pulled from the chassis.

Tag and Bag

All components and fasteners should be marked for future reference. Large components should be marked or a tag installed that identifies the part. Smaller parts and fasteners should be placed in plastic bags and labeled as to what they are used for, such as the water pump bolts.

- **Remove the power steering pump.** Remove the fasteners to the power steering pump and set aside the pump and hoses.

- **Drain the engine oil.** Draining the engine oil and removing the oil filter also helps prevent fluid loss during the removal process.

- **Disconnect fuel lines.** Disconnect and plug all fuel supply and return lines.

- **Disconnect wiring and vacuum hoses.** Mark and remove all vacuum hoses and electrical wiring attached to the engine.

PROCEDURE FOR ENGINE REMOVAL   There are two ways to remove the engine.

1. The engine can be lifted out of the chassis with the transmission/transaxle attached.

2. The transmission/transaxle can be separated from the engine and left in the chassis.

The method to be used must be determined before the engine is removed from the vehicle.

- **Rear-wheel-drive vehicle.** The removal procedure for most rear-wheel-drive vehicles includes the following steps.

  STEP 1   Under the vehicle, remove the driveshaft (propeller shaft) and disconnect the exhaust pipes. Also remove the engine (motor) mounts. In some installations, it may be necessary to loosen the steering linkage idler arm to give clearance. The transmission controls and wiring need to be disconnected at the connectors, and clutch linkages disconnected and labeled.

  STEP 2   Attach a sling, either a chain or lift cable, to one of the following:

- Factory-installed lifting hooks
- Intake manifold
- Cylinder head bolts, on top of the engine

An engine lift hoist chain or cable is attached and snugged to take most of the weight. This leaves the engine resting on the mounts.

NOTE: For the best results, use the factory-installed lifting hooks that are attached to the engine. These hooks are used in the assembly plant to install the engine and are usually in the best location to remove the engine.

STEP 3   Remove the rear cross-member, and lower the transmission. Cover the extension housing with a plug or a plastic bag to help prevent the automatic transmission fluid from leaking during the removal process. If the engine alone is being removed, the transmission retaining bolts and torque converter fasteners will need to be removed. Check service information for exact procedures to follow when removing an automatic transmission.

STEP 4   The front of the engine must come almost straight up as the transmission slides from under the floor pan. The engine and transmission are hoisted free of the automobile, swung clear, and lowered on an open floor area. ● **SEE FIGURE 11–3.**

FIGURE 11–4 When removing just the engine from a front-wheel-drive vehicle, the transaxle must be supported. Shown here is a typical fixture that can be used to hold the engine if the transaxle is removed or to hold the transaxle if the engine is removed.

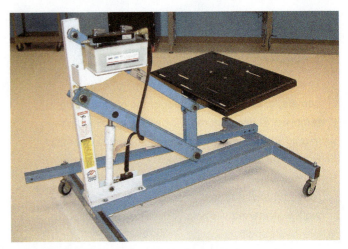

FIGURE 11–5 An engine lift platform can be used when removing or installing the complete engine and cradle assembly from the bottom of the vehicle.

- **Front-wheel-drive vehicle.** Check service information for the exact procedure to follow to remove the engine from a front-wheel-drive vehicle. Depending on the vehicle, the engine could be removed from the top or lowered and removed from underneath on many front-wheel-drive vehicles. Typical steps include:

STEP 1 Disconnect units that might interfere with engine removal, including the steering unit, engine electrical harness, and radiator.

STEP 2 Disconnect the torque converter and bell housing bolts and clutch linkage if required.

STEP 3 Often special holding fixtures are required to help hold the transaxle in place while removing the engine. ● SEE FIGURE 11–4.

STEP 4 If removing the engine and transmission assembly from underneath, the upper strut and lower engine cradle fasteners will have to be removed. Use an engine lift table or rack to support the complete assembly as it is removed from the vehicle. **SEE FIGURES 11–5 AND 11–6.**

CAUTION: When removing the complete engine/ transmission/cradle assembly make sure that the vehicle is properly positioned on the hoist. When the weight of the drivetrain is removed from the vehicle it becomes very light in the front and could become unbalanced and fall at the rear.

RACK AND PINION STEERING GEAR

CRADLE

FIGURE 11–6 The entire cradle, which included the engine, transaxle, and steering gear, was removed and placed onto a stand. The rear cylinder head has been removed to check for the root cause of a coolant leak.

ENGINE DISASSEMBLY

MOUNTING THE ENGINE ON A STAND Engines should be installed to a sturdy engine stand. For safety, always check the following:

- Always use at least four grade 8 bolts when mounting an engine to an engine stand. Using low-quality nongraded bolts or fewer than four bolts can cause the engine to fall. Also check to ensure that the proper threads of bolts

FIGURE 11–7 Always use graded bolts—either grade 5 or 8 bolts—whenever mounting an engine to a stand.

FIGURE 11–8 Keeping the pushrods and the lifters sorted by cylinder, including the spark plugs, is a wise way to proceed when disassembling the cylinder heads.

are being used. Some engines use fractional threads, whereas others use metric threads.

- Install the bolts so that at least 1/2 inch (13 mm) of thread is engaged in the back of the engine to ensure that the fasteners are securely attached to the engine block.

- Check that the engine is properly balanced on the engine stand before work is started on the engine. ● **SEE FIGURE 11–7**.

DISASSEMBLING A CAM-IN-BLOCK (OHV) ENGINE

Check service information for the specified engine disassembly procedure. Read, understand, and follow all safety instructions. Following are the usual steps involved.

STEP 1 Engines should be cold before disassembly to minimize the chance of warpage of the components that are being removed.

STEP 2 Removal of the rocker arm covers gives the first opportunity to see inside a part of the engine. Examine the rocker arms, valve springs, and valve tips for obvious defects. Remove the rocker arms and pushrods and, if they are to be reused, place them in a location so that the rockers and the pushrods can be installed back to their original location. ● **SEE FIGURE 11–8**.

STEP 3 Remove the intake manifold bolts and lift off the manifold. Use care to avoid damaging the parting surface as the gasket is loosened. When the intake manifold and lifter valley cover (if equipped) are off of

V-type engines, the technician has another opportunity to examine the interior of the engine. On some V-type engines, it is possible to see the condition of the cam at the bottom of the lifter valley.

STEP 4 The lifters can be removed at this time if they are causing the problem or if the engine valve train is to be serviced.

STEP 5 Remove the cylinder head bolts (also called cap screws) following the reverse of the installation procedure. Loosening the fasteners at the ends of the cylinder head first, then working toward the center, helps reduce the chance of warpage to the cylinder head. Be sure to notice and mark the head bolt locations as they are often different lengths depending on their location in the head. Carefully lift the head from the block deck. If the head gasket is stuck, carefully pry the head to loosen the gasket. Use care not to scratch the block or head machined surfaces. The combustion chamber in the head and the top of the piston should be given a thorough visual examination. ● **SEE FIGURE 11–9**.

- Check the cylinder head and head gasket for signs of leakage.

- A normal combustion chamber is coated with a layer of hard, light-colored deposits.

- If the combustion chamber has been running too hot, the deposits will be very thin and white.

FIGURE 11–9 Sometimes after the cylinder head has been removed, the engine condition is discovered to be so major that the entire engine may need to be replaced rather than overhauled.

NUMBERS STAMPED ON CONNECTING ROD AND ROD CAP

FIGURE 11–10 These connecting rods were numbered from the factory. If they are not, then they should be marked.

OVERHEAD CAMSHAFT (OHC) ENGINE DISASSEMBLY

Disassembling an overhead camshaft engine differs from a cam-in-block (OHV) engine. Check service information for the specified disassembly procedure for the engine being serviced. Read, understand, and follow all safety notices and warnings included in the instructions to help avoid causing damage to parts or components during the disassembly process. The usual steps include:

STEP 1 Remove the intake and exhaust manifolds if they have not already been removed and bag and tag all fasteners.

STEP 2 Remove the crankshaft harmonic balancer pulley that will allow access to the timing chain or belt cover.

STEP 3 Remove the timing belt/chain cover(s) and then the timing belt(s) or chain(s).

STEP 4 With most overhead camshaft engines, the camshaft(s) must be removed before removing the cylinder head due to location of the head bolts.

STEP 5 Remove the cylinder head by removing the cylinder head bolts in the opposite order of assembly. This means to loosen the outermost fasteners first, then work toward the center of the cylinder head.

STEP 6 Carefully lift the cylinder head from the block.

DISASSEMBLY OF THE SHORT BLOCK

REMOVING THE OIL PAN Most engine builders prefer to remove the oil pan before turning the engine upside down so the that the technician can inspect for any oil pan deposits first. Deposits are a good indication of the condition and care taken of the engine.

Heavy sludge indicates infrequent oil changes; hard carbon indicates overheating. The oil pump pickup screen should be checked to see how much plugging exists. After removing the oil pan, turn the engine upside down.

MARKING CONNECTING RODS AND CAPS The connecting rod caps should be marked (numbered) so that they can be reassembled in exactly the same position. If the connecting rods are not marked from the factory, then they should be marked using a number stamp, electric pencil, or permanent marker. ● **SEE FIGURE 11–10.**

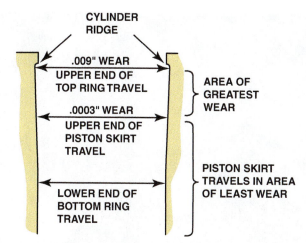

FIGURE 11–11 Most of the cylinder wear is on the top inch just below the cylinder ridge. This wear is due to the heat and combustion pressures that occur when the piston is near the top of the cylinder.

FIGURE 11–12 This ridge is being removed with one type of ridge reamer before the piston assemblies are removed from the engine.

CAUTION: Some vehicle manufacturers warn *not* to use a punch or an electric pencil on powdered metal connecting rods. Use only a permanent marker to label powdered metal rods. If in doubt as to the type of rod that is in the engine, use a marker to be safe.

REMOVING THE CYLINDER RIDGE Before the pistons can be removed from the block, the ridge must be removed. Piston wear against the cylinder wall leaves an upper ridge, because the top ring does not travel all the way to the top of the cylinder. Ridge removal is necessary to avoid catching a ring on the ridge and breaking the piston. ● **SEE FIGURE 11–11.**

The ridge is removed with a cutting tool that has a guide to help prevent accidental cutting below the ridge. ● **SEE FIGURE 11–12.**

PISTON REMOVAL Removing the piston and rod assembly includes the following steps.

STEP 1 Rotate the engine until the piston that is to be removed is at bottom dead center (BDC).

STEP 2 Remove connecting rod nuts from the rod so that the rod cap with its bearing half can be removed.

STEP 3 Fit the rod bolts with protectors to keep the bolt threads from damaging the crankshaft journals, and then carefully remove the piston and rod assemblies.

STEP 4 After removal of each piston, replace the rod cap and nuts to avoid losing or mismatching them.

 **TECH TIP**

Measure the Cylinder Bore Before Further Disassembly

As soon as the cylinder head has been removed from the engine, take a measurement of the cylinder bore. This is done for the following reasons.

- To verify that the engine size is the same as specified by the vehicle identification number (VIN)
- To measure the bore and compare it to factory specifications, to help the technician determine if the cylinder(s) are too worn to use or cannot be restored

ENGINE ROTATING ASSEMBLIES REMOVAL

HARMONIC BALANCER REMOVAL The next step after the water pump has been removed is to remove the crankshaft **vibration damper** (also called a *harmonic balancer*). The bolt and washer that hold the damper are removed. The damper should be removed only with the correct type puller. ● **SEE FIGURE 11–13.**

If a hook-type puller is used around the edge of the damper, it may pull the damper ring from the hub. If this happens, the damper assembly will have to be replaced with

FIGURE 11–13 Puller being used to pull the vibration damper from the crankshaft.

FIGURE 11–14 When the timing chain cover was removed, the broken timing gear explained why this GM 4.3 liter V-6 engine stopped running.

a new assembly. With the damper assembly off, the timing cover can be removed, exposing the timing gear or timing chain. Examine these parts for excessive wear and looseness. ● **SEE FIGURE 11–14.**

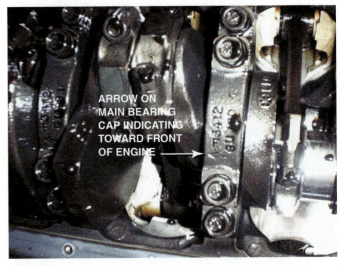

FIGURE 11–15 Most engines such as this Chevrolet V-8 with four-bolt main bearing caps have arrows marked on the bearing caps which should point to the front of the engine.

Bolted cam sprockets can be removed to free the timing chain. On some engines this will require removal of the crankshaft gear at the same time. Pressed-on gears and sprockets are removed from the shaft *only* if they are faulty. They are removed after the camshaft is removed from the block. It is necessary to remove the camshaft thrust plate retaining screws when they are used.

CAMSHAFT REMOVAL   The camshaft and balance shafts, if equipped, can be removed at this time, or they can be removed after the crankshaft is out. For best results, insert long bolts into the camshaft threaded holes to serve as handles for removing (or installing) a camshaft. It must be carefully eased from the engine to avoid damaging the cam bearings or cam lobes. This is done most easily with the front of the engine pointing up. Bearing surfaces are soft and scratch easily, and the cam lobes are hard and can chip easily.

CRANKSHAFT AND MAIN BEARING REMOVAL   The main bearing caps should be checked for position markings before they are removed. If they are not marked, use steel number stamps to mark them and also be sure to indicate which side of each main cap faces to the front of the engine. ● **SEE FIGURE 11–15.**

They have been machined in place and will not fit perfectly in any other location. After marking, they can be removed to free the crankshaft. When the crankshaft is removed, the main bearing caps and bearings are reinstalled on the block to reduce the chance of damage to the caps.

BLOCK INSPECTION   After the pistons and crankshaft have been removed, remove all cups and plugs and carefully inspect the block for faults that could affect whether the engine can be rebuilt. ● **SEE FIGURE 11–16.**

FIGURE 11–16 This small block Chevrolet V-8 had water standing in the cylinders, causing a lot of rust, which was discovered as soon as the head was removed.

Further detailed inspection should be completed after the components have been cleaned.

CYLINDER HEAD DISASSEMBLY

OHV ENGINE CYLINDER HEADS After the heads are removed and placed on the bench, the valves can be removed.

CAUTION: Always wear safety glasses when working on a cylinder head. Valve springs can release quickly, causing valve parts to fly.

To disassemble a cylinder head, perform the following steps.

STEP 1 Tap the valve spring retainer with a brass hammer, hitting the retainer on an angle to "break the taper" of the valve keepers (locks).

STEP 2 Using a valve spring compressor, compress the valve spring far enough to expose the keepers. ● **SEE FIGURE 11–18**.

STEP 3 Remove the two keepers using a magnet.

STEP 4 After the valve keepers have been removed, slowly release the compressor to remove and to free the valve retainer and spring.

STEP 5 The valve tip edge and keeper (lock) area should be lightly filed or stoned to remove any burrs *before* sliding the valve from the head. Burrs will scratch the valve guide.

STEP 6 Remove all valve stem seals and the metal spring seats that are used on aluminum heads.

STEP 7 When all valves are removed following the same procedure, carefully inspect the valve springs, retainers, keepers (locks), guides, and seats.

PARAFFIN WAX

FIGURE 11–17 A torch is used to heat gallery plugs. Paraffin wax is then applied and allowed to flow around the threads. This procedure results in easier removal of the plugs and other threaded fasteners that cannot otherwise be loosened.

 **TECH TIP**

The Wax Trick

Before the engine block can be thoroughly cleaned, all oil gallery plugs must be removed. A popular trick of the trade for plug removal involves heating the plug (not the surrounding metal) with an oxyacetylene torch. The heat tends to expand the plug and make it tighter in the block. Do not overheat.

As the plug is cooling, touch the plug with paraffin wax (beeswax or candle wax may be used). ● **SEE FIGURE 11–17**.

The wax will be drawn down around the threads of the plug by capillary action as the plug cools and contracts. After being allowed to cool, the plug is easily removed.

OHC ENGINE CYLINDER HEADS After the heads are removed and placed on the bench, the valves can be removed after the camshaft is removed. Often a special valve spring compressor is required to reach the valve retainers. Always read, understand, and follow all vehicle manufacturer's instructions. Refer to Chapter 13 for more information on cylinder head disassembly.

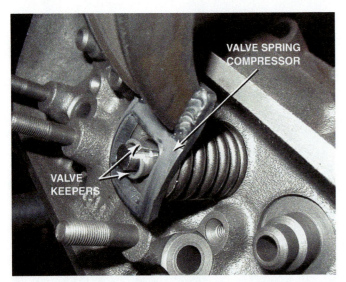

FIGURE 11–18 A valve spring compressor is used to compress the valve spring before removing the keepers (locks).

TECH TIP

Mark It to Be Safe

Whenever you disassemble anything, it is always wise to mark the location of parts, bolts, hoses, and other items that could be incorrectly assembled. Remember, the first part removed will be the last part that is assembled. If you think you will remember where everything goes—forget it! It just does not happen in the real world.

One popular trick is to use correction fluid to mark the location of parts before they are removed. Most of these products are alcohol or water based, dry quickly, and usually contain a brush in the cap for easy use.

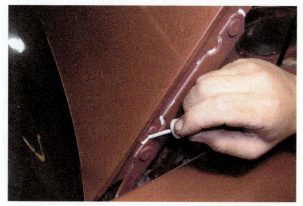

1 Before beginning work on removing the engine, mark and remove the hood and place it in a safe location.

2 Disconnect the negative battery cable and cover it with tape to prevent accidental re-connection.

3 Drain the coolant and dispose of properly.

4 Disconnect all cooling system and heater hoses and remove the radiator.

5 Remove the accessory drive belt(s) and set the alternator, power steering pump, and air-conditioning compressor aside.

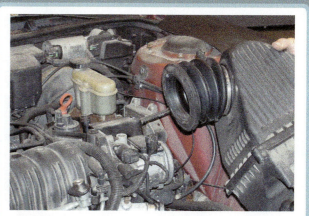

6 Remove the air intake system including the air filter housing as needed.

CONTINUED ▶

7 Remove the electrical connector from all sensors and label.

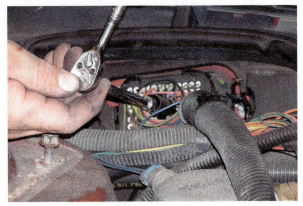

8 Disconnect the engine wiring harness connector at the bulkhead.

9 Safely hoist the vehicle and disconnect the exhaust system from the exhaust manifolds.

10 Mark and then remove the fasteners connecting the flex plate to the torque converter.

11 Lower the vehicle and remove the engine mount bolts and transaxle bell housing fasteners.

12 Secure the lifting chain to the engine hooks and carefully remove the engine from the vehicle.

(a)

(b)

(c)

(d)

FIGURE 12–13 (a) Before welding, the crack is ground out using a carbide grinder. (b) Here the technician is practicing using the special cast-iron welding torch before welding the cracked cylinder head. (c) This is the finished welded crack before final machining. (d) Note the finished cylinder head after the crack has been repaired using welding.

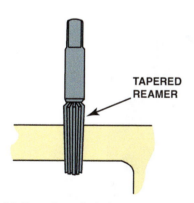

TAPERED REAMER

FIGURE 12–14 Reaming a hole for a tapered plug.

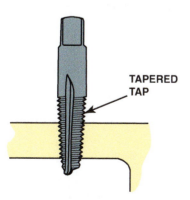

TAPERED TAP

FIGURE 12–15 Tapping a tapered hole for a plug.

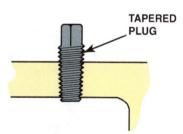

TAPERED PLUG

FIGURE 12–16 Screwing a tapered plug in the hole.

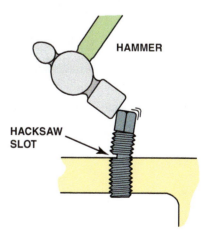

HAMMER

HACKSAW SLOT

FIGURE 12–17 Cutting the plug with a hacksaw.

the full depth or thickness of the cast metal. After the first plug is installed on each end, a new hole is drilled with the tap drill so that it cuts into the edge of the first plug. This new hole is reamed and tapped, and a plug is inserted as before. The plug should fit about one-fourth of the way into the first plug to lock it into place ● **SEE FIGURE 12–18.**

Interlocking plugs are placed along the entire crack, alternating slightly from side to side. The exposed ends of the plugs are peened over with a hammer to help secure them in place. The surface of the plugs is then ground or filed down nearly to the gasket surface. In the combustion chamber and at the ports, the plugs are ground down to the original surface using a hand grinder. The gasket surface of the head must be resurfaced after the crack has been repaired. ● **SEE FIGURE 12–19** for an example of a cylinder head repair using plugs.

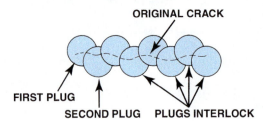

FIGURE 12–18 Interlocking plugs.

(a)

(b)

(c)

FIGURE 12–19 (a) A hole is drilled and tapped for the plugs. (b) The plugs are installed. (c) After final machining, the cylinder head can be returned to useful service.

SUMMARY

1. Mechanical cleaning with scrapers is used to remove deposits.

2. Abrasive pads, wire, and abrasive rubber finger wheels should never be used to clean aluminum parts.

3. Most chemical cleaners are strong soaps called caustic materials.

4. Always use aluminum-safe chemicals when cleaning aluminum parts or components.

5. Thermal cleaning is done in a pyrolytic oven in temperatures as high as 800°F (425°C) to turn grease and dirt into harmless ash deposits.

6. Blasters use metal shot or glass beads to clean parts. All of the metal shot or glass beads must be thoroughly cleaned from the part so as not to cause engine problems.

7. All parts should be checked for cracks using magnetic, dye-penetrant, fluorescent-penetrant, or pressure testing methods.

8. Cracks can be repaired by welding or by plugging.

REVIEW QUESTIONS

1. Describe five methods that could be used to clean engines or engine parts.

2. Explain magnetic crack inspection, dye-penetrant testing, and fluorescent-penetrant testing methods and where each can be used.

3. How can engine block and cylinder heads be repaired if cracked?

CHAPTER QUIZ

1. GM recommends that gasket surfaces be cleaned with _____.
   a. A grinding disc
   b. Plastic razor blades
   c. A finger grinder
   d. A soft buffing tool

2. What actually does the cleaning when using steam?
   a. Heat from the steam
   b. Pressure behind the steam
   c. Abrasives used
   d. Both a and b

3. Aqueous-based cleaning means _____.
   a. Water based
   b. Abrasive based
   c. Strong chemical based
   d. All of the above

4. A pyrolytic oven is used to clean parts; however, caution should be used to limit the temperature, to prevent damaging engine parts. What are the maximum recommended temperatures?
   a. 300°F (150°C) for all engine parts
   b. 600°F (315°C) for aluminum parts
   c. 800°F (425°C) for cast iron
   d. Both b and c

5. Which media is best to use for cleaning parts as it does not need to be thoroughly cleaned after using?
   a. Baking soda
   b. Stainless steel shot
   c. Glass beads
   d. Aluminum shot

6. Cleaning chemicals are usually either a caustic material or an acid material. Which of the following statements is true?
   a. Both caustics and acids have a pH of 7 if rated according to distilled water.
   b. An acid is lower than 7 and a caustic is higher than 7 on the pH scale.
   c. An acid is higher than 7 and a caustic is lower than 7 on the pH scale.
   d. Pure water is a 1 and a strong acid is a 14 on the pH scale.

7. Many cleaning methods involve chemicals that are hazardous to use. The least hazardous method is generally considered to be the _____.
   a. Pyrolytic oven
   b. Hot vapor tank
   c. Hot soak tank
   d. Cold soak tank

8. Magnetic crack inspection_____.
   a. Uses a red dye to detect cracks in aluminum
   b. Uses a black light to detect cracks in iron parts
   c. Uses a fine iron powder to detect cracks in iron parts
   d. Uses a magnet to remove cracks from iron parts

9. Technician A says that engine parts should be cleaned before a thorough test can be done to detect cracks. Technician B says that pressure testing can be used to find cracks in blocks or cylinder heads. Which technician is correct?
   a. Technician A only
   b. Technician B only
   c. Both Technicians A and B
   d. Neither Technician A nor B

10. Plugging can be used to repair cracks _____.
   a. In cast-iron cylinder heads
   b. In aluminum cylinder heads
   c. In both cast-iron and aluminum cylinder heads
   d. Only in cast-iron blocks

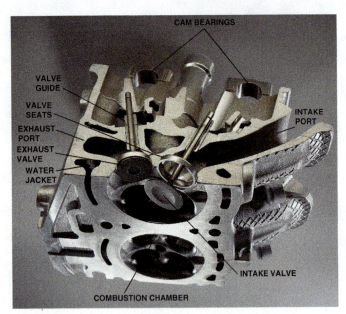

FIGURE 13–1 The seats and guides for the valves are in the cylinder head as well as the camshaft and the entire valve train if it is an overhead camshaft design. (*Courtesy of General Motors*)

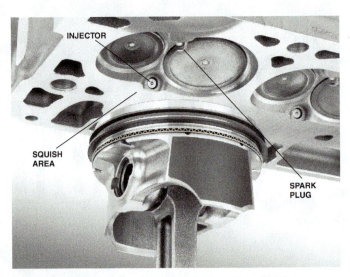

FIGURE 13–2 A wedge-shaped combustion chamber, showing the squish area where the air-fuel mixture is squeezed, causing turbulence that pushes the mixture toward the spark plug. This cylinder head features direct fuel injection into the combustion chamber. (*Courtesy of General Motors*)

INTRODUCTION

The repair and reconditioning of cylinder heads represents the most frequent engine repair operation of any engine component. The highest temperatures and pressures in the entire engine are located in the combustion chamber of the cylinder head. Its valves must open and close thousands of times when the engine is operated.

CYLINDER HEADS

CONSTRUCTION Cylinder heads support the valves and valve train, and contain passages for the flow of intake, exhaust gases, coolant, and sometimes engine oil. In an overhead camshaft design engine, the cylinder head also supports all of the valve train components including the camshaft, rocker arms, or followers, as well as the intake and exhaust valves and valve guides. ● SEE FIGURE 13–1.

DESIGN FEATURES Most cylinder head designs incorporate the following design factors to achieve fast burning of the air-fuel mixture and to reduce exhaust emissions.

- **Squish area.** This is an area of the combustion chamber where the piston nearly contacts the cylinder head. When the piston is moving upward toward the cylinder head, the air-fuel mixture is rapidly pushed out of the squish area, causing turbulence. Turbulence helps mix the air and fuel, thereby ensuring a more uniform and complete combustion. ● SEE FIGURE 13–2.

- **Quench area.** The squish area can also be the quench area where the air-fuel mixture is cooled by the cylinder head. The quench area is the flat area of the combustion chamber that is above the flat area of the piston. As the piston moves upward on the compression stroke, the air-fuel mixture is forced from this area as the piston gets near the top. The quench area operates at lower temperatures than the rest of the combustion chamber and can cause the gasoline vapors to condense on these cooler surfaces, thereby helping to reduce detonation caused by the autoignition of the end gases in the combustion chamber.

- **Spark plug placement.** The best spark plug placement is at the center of the combustion chamber. ● SEE FIGURE 13–3.

  The closer to the center, the shorter the flames travel to all edges of the combustion chamber, which also reduces abnormal combustion (ping or spark knock). While it is best to have the spark plug in the center, some combustion chamber designs do not allow this, due to valve size, combustion chamber design, and valve placement. Some engines use two spark plugs per cylinder to achieve rapid combustion needed to meet exhaust emissions standards.

FIGURE 13–3 Locating the spark plug in the center of the combustion chamber reduces the distance the flame front must travel. (*Courtesy of General Motors*)

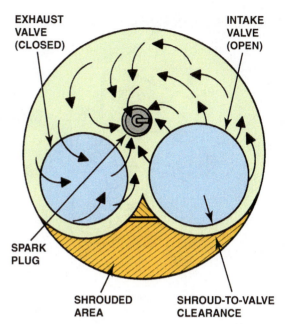

EXHAUST VALVE (CLOSED)

INTAKE VALVE (OPEN)

SPARK PLUG

SHROUDED AREA

SHROUD-TO-VALVE CLEARANCE

FIGURE 13–4 The shrouded area around the intake valve causes the intake mixture to swirl as it enters the combustion chamber.

- **Surface-to-volume ratio.** This ratio is an important design consideration for combustion chambers. A typical surface-to-volume ratio is 7.5:1, which means the surface area of the combustion chamber divided by the volume is 7.5. If the ratio is too high, there is a lot of surface area where fuel can adhere, causing an increase in unburned hydrocarbon (HC) emissions. The cool cylinder head causes some of the air-fuel mixture to condense, resulting in a layer of liquid fuel on the surfaces of the combustion chamber. This layer of condensed fuel will not burn because it is not surrounded by oxygen needed for combustion. As a result, this unburned fuel is pushed out of the cylinder by the piston on the exhaust stroke.

- **Valve shrouding.** Shrouding means that the valve is kept close to the walls of the combustion chamber to help increase mixture turbulence. Although shrouding the intake valve can help swirl and increase turbulence, it also reduces the flow into the engine at higher engine speeds thus reducing efficiency. ● **SEE FIGURE 13–4.**

- **Crossflow valve placement.** Valve placement in the cylinder head is an important factor in breathing efficiency. By placing the intake and the exhaust valves on the opposite sides of the combustion chamber, an easy path from the intake port through the combustion chamber to the exhaust port is provided. This is called a **crossflow head** design. ● **SEE FIGURE 13–5.**

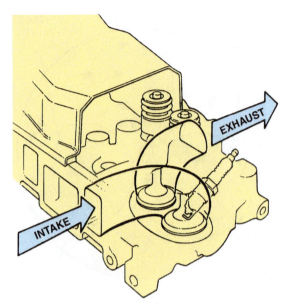

FIGURE 13–5 An older cross flow cylinder head design, where the flow into and out of the combustion chamber is from opposite sides of the cylinder head.

COMBUSTION CHAMBER DESIGNS Combustion chamber shape has an effect on engine power and efficiency. The combustion chamber is created as two parts.

- The upper part consists of the cylinder head and cylinder walls.
- The lower part is the top of the piston.

The most commonly used combustion chamber shapes include:

- **Wedge.** Commonly found on many two-valve pushrod engines (cam-in-block) designs
- **Pentroof.** Commonly found on many four-valve overhead camshaft design engines
- **Hemispherical.** Found on both cam-in-block and overhead camshaft design engines

FOUR-VALVE CYLINDER HEADS Adding more than two valves per cylinder permits more flow into and out of the engine with greater velocity without excessive valve duration. **Valve duration** is the number of degrees by which the crankshaft rotates when the valve is off the valve seat. Increased valve duration increases valve overlap. The valve overlap occurs when both valves are open at the same time at the end of the exhaust stroke and at the beginning of the intake stroke. At lower engine speeds, the gases can move back and forth between the open valves. Therefore, the greater valve duration hurts low engine speed performance and driveability, but it allows for more air-fuel mixture to enter the engine for better high-speed power.

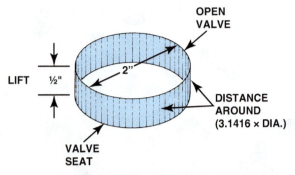

OPENING AREA = DISTANCE × LIFT

FIGURE 13–6 Method for measuring the valve opening space.

The maximum amount of flow through the opening area of a valve depends on the distance around the valve and the degree to which it lifts open. ● **SEE FIGURE 13–6.**

Using normal opening lift of about 25% of the valve head diameter as an example, if the intake valve is 2 inch diameter, the normal amount of lift off the seat (not cam lobe height) is 25% of 2 inch, or 1/2 (0.5) inch. However, the amount of air-fuel mixture that can enter a cylinder depends on the total area around the valve, not just the amount of lift. The distance around a valve is calculated by the equation:

pi $\times$ D or

3.1416 $\times$ Valve diameter

● **SEE FIGURE 13–7.**

More total area under the valve is possible when two smaller valves are used rather than one larger valve at the same valve lift. The smaller valves allow smooth low-speed operation (because of increased velocity of the mixture as it enters the cylinder as a result of smaller intake ports). Good high-speed performance is also possible because of the increased valve area and lighter weight valves. ● **SEE FIGURE 13–8.**

When four valves are used, either the combustion chamber has a pentroof design, with each pair of valves in line, or it is hemispherical, with each valve on its own axis. ● **SEE FIGURE 13–9.**

Four valves on the pentroof design will be operated with dual overhead camshafts or with single overhead camshafts and rocker arms. When four valves are used, it is possible to place the spark plug at the center of the combustion chamber.

INTAKE AND EXHAUST PORTS

PURPOSE AND FUNCTION The part of the intake or exhaust system passage that is cast in the cylinder head is called a **port.** Ports lead from the manifolds to the valves. The

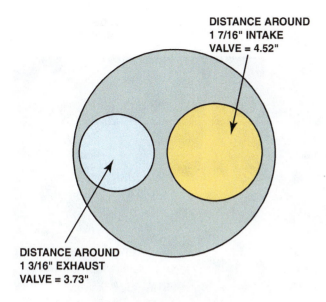

DISTANCE AROUND
1 7/16" INTAKE
VALVE = 4.52"

DISTANCE AROUND
1 3/16" EXHAUST
VALVE = 3.73"

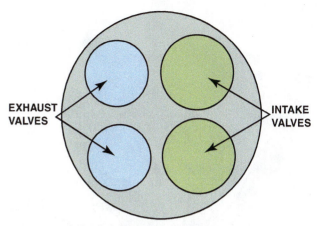

EXHAUST
VALVES

INTAKE
VALVES

FIGURE 13–8 Typical four-valve head. The total area of opening of two small intake valves and two smaller exhaust valves is greater than the area of a two-valve head using much larger valves. The smaller valves also permit the use of smaller intake runners for better low-speed engine response.

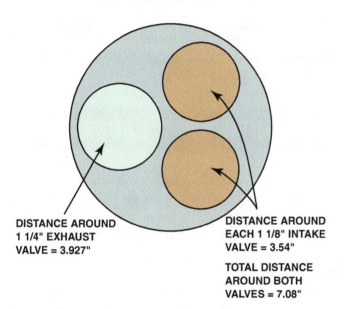

DISTANCE AROUND
1 1/4" EXHAUST
VALVE = 3.927"

DISTANCE AROUND
EACH 1 1/8" INTAKE
VALVE = 3.54"

TOTAL DISTANCE
AROUND BOTH
VALVES = 7.08"

FIGURE 13–7 Comparing the valve opening areas between a two- and three-valve combustion chamber when the valves are open.

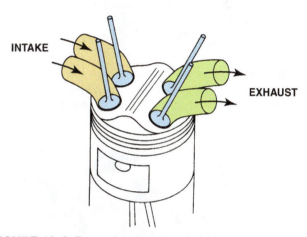

INTAKE

EXHAUST

FIGURE 13–9 Four valves in a pentroof combustion chamber.

most desirable port shape is not always possible because of space requirements in the head. Space is required for the head bolt bosses, valve guides, cooling passages, and pushrod openings. Inline engines may have both intake and exhaust ports located on the same side of the engine. On some older engines two cylinders share the same port because of the restricted space available. Shared ports are called **Siamese ports.**

Larger ports and better breathing are possible in engines that have the intake port on one side of the head and the exhaust port on the opposite side. Sometimes a restricting hump within a port may actually increase the airflow capacity of the port.

It does this by redirecting the flow to an area of the port that is large enough to handle the flow. Modifications in the field, such as **porting** or **relieving,** would result in restricting the flow of such a carefully designed port.

INTAKE PORTS The intake port in a cylinder head designed for use with a carburetor or throttle-body-type fuel injection is relatively long, whereas the exhaust port is short. On engines designed for use with port fuel injection, the cylinder head ports are designed to help promote swirl in the combustion chamber, as shown in ● **FIGURE 13–10.**

The intake ports on four-valve cylinder heads are often oval shaped to help improve airflow to the individual intake valves. On a direct-injected cylinder head the ports are matched to the intake manifold, with the injectors spraying fuel directly into the combustion chamber. ● **SEE FIGURE 13–11**

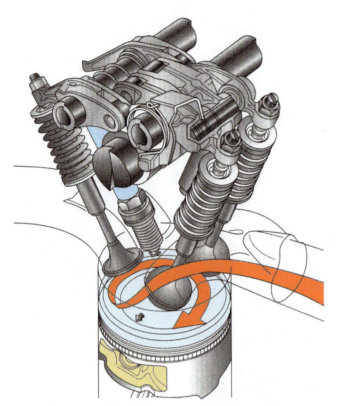

FIGURE 13–10 The intake manifold design and combustion chamber design both work together to cause the air-fuel mixture to swirl as it enters the combustion chamber.

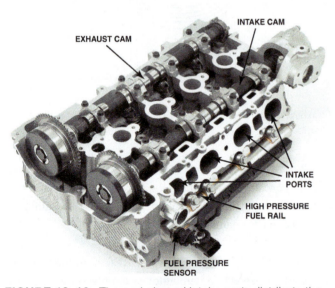

FIGURE 13–12 The oval-shaped intake ports distribute the intake air to each of the two intake valves more efficiently. (*Direct-injection cylinder head; Courtesy of General Motors*)

EXHAUST PORTS

EXHAUST PORTS Like the intake ports, exhaust ports are designed to allow the free flow of exhaust gases from the engine. The length of the exhaust ports is shorter than the intake ports to help reduce the amount of heat transferred to the coolant. ● **SEE FIGURE 13–12.**

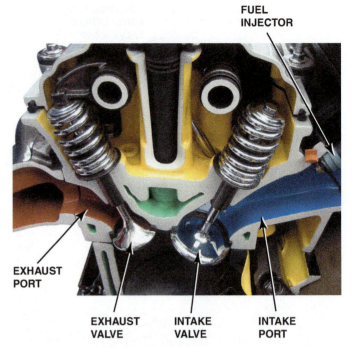

FIGURE 13–11 A port-injected engine showing the straight free-flowing intake and exhaust ports.

CYLINDER HEAD PASSAGES

COOLANT FLOW PASSAGES The engine is designed so that coolant will flow from the coolest portion of the engine to the warmest portion. The water pump takes the coolant from the radiator. The coolant is circulated through the block, where it is directed all around the cylinders. The coolant then flows upward through the gasket to the cooling passages cast into the cylinder head. The heated coolant is collected at a common point and returned to the radiator to be cooled and recycled.

NOTE: Reversed-flow cooling systems, used on some General Motors V-8 engines, send the coolant from the radiator to the cylinder heads first. This results in a cooler cylinder head and allows for more spark advance without engine-damaging detonation.

Typical coolant passages in a head are shown in ● **FIGURE 13–13.**

HEAD GASKET HOLES There are relatively large holes in the gasket surface of the head leading to the head cooling passages. The openings between the head and the block are usually too large for the correct coolant flow. When the openings are too large, the head gasket performs an important coolant flow function. Special-size and smaller holes are made in the gasket.

FIGURE 13–13 A cutaway head showing the coolant passages in green.

FIGURE 13–14 Coolant flows through the cylinder head, and the passages are sealed by the head gasket. Notice that this gasket had been leaking coolant into the cylinder (see circle).

These holes correct the coolant flow rate at each opening. Therefore, it is important that the head gasket be installed correctly for proper engine cooling. ● **SEE FIGURE 13–14.**

LUBRICATING OIL PASSAGES

Lubricating oil is delivered to the overhead valve mechanism, either through the valve pushrods or through drilled passages in the head and block casting. There are special openings in the head gasket to allow the oil to pass between the block and head without leaking. After the oil passes through the valve mechanisms, it returns to the oil pan through oil drainback holes. Some engines have drilled oil return holes, but most engines have large cast holes that allow the oil to return freely to the engine oil pan. The cast holes are large and do not easily become plugged.

NOTE: Many aluminum cylinder heads have smaller-than-normal drainback holes. If an engine has excessive oil consumption, check the drain holes before removing the engine.

FIGURE 13–15 Camshafts are commonly held in place using bearing caps bolted to the cylinder head. (*Courtesy of General Motors*)

CYLINDER HEAD SERVICING

CYLINDER HEAD SERVICING SEQUENCE Although not all cylinder heads require all service operations, cylinder heads should be reconditioned using the following sequence.

1. Disassemble and thoroughly clean the heads.
2. Check for cracks and repair as necessary.
3. Check the surface that contacts the engine block and machine, if necessary. (See discussion later in the chapter.)
4. Check valve guides and replace or service, as necessary. (See discussion later in the chapter.)
5. Grind valves and reinstall them in the cylinder head with new valve stem seals. (See Chapter 14.)

DISASSEMBLING OVERHEAD CAMSHAFT HEAD

The overhead camshaft will have either one-piece bearings in a solid bearing support or split bearings and a bearing cap. When one-piece bearings are used, the valve springs will have to be compressed with a fixture or the finger follower will have to be removed before the camshaft can be pulled out endwise. When bearing caps are used, they should be loosened alternately so that bending loads are not placed on either the cam or bearing caps. ● **SEE FIGURES 13–15 AND 13–16.**

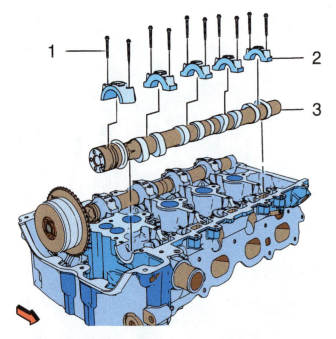

FIGURE 13–16 Loosen the bearing cap bolts (1) one turn at a time until all spring tension is released from the cam (3), then remove the caps (2). (*Courtesy of General Motors*)

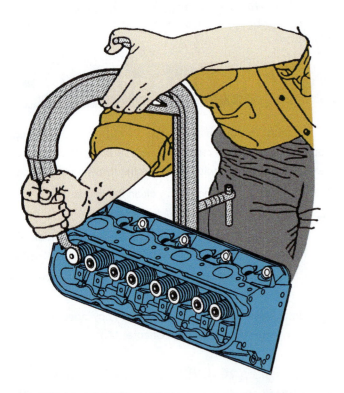

FIGURE 13–17 A valve spring compressor is used to remove the valve keepers. (*Courtesy of General Motors*)

VALVE TRAIN DISASSEMBLY Disassemble the cylinder head as discussed in Chapter 11. All valve train components that are to be reused must be kept together. As wear occurs, parts are worn together. ● **SEE FIGURES 13–17 AND 13–18.**

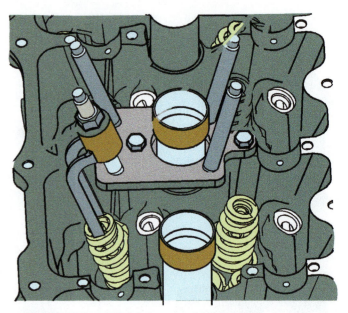

FIGURE 13–18 A special tool may be required when disassembling overhead cam or multivalve cylinder heads. (*Courtesy of General Motors*)

FIGURE 13–19 Pushrods can be kept labeled if stuck through a cardboard box. Individual parts become worn together. Using cardboard is a crude but effective material to keep all valve train parts together and labeled exactly as they came from the engine.

- Be sure to keep the top part of the pushrod at the top.
- Keep the rocker arms with the same pushrods as they wear together. ● **SEE FIGURE 13–19.**
- Intake and exhaust valve springs can be different and must be kept with the correct valve.

CYLINDER HEAD INSPECTION The surface must be thoroughly cleaned and inspected as follows:

STEP 1 After removing the old gasket material, use a file and draw it across the surface of the head to remove any small burrs.

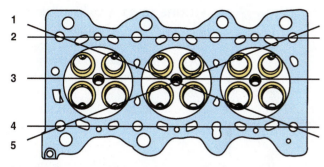

FIGURE 13–20 Cylinder heads should be checked in five planes for warpage, distortion, bend, and twist.

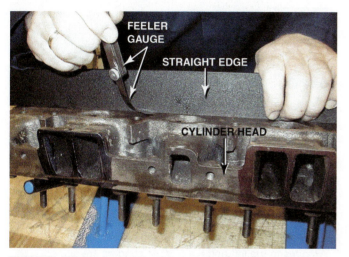

FIGURE 13–21 A precision ground straightedge and a feeler gauge are used to check the cylinder head for flatness.

STEP 2 The head should be checked with a straightedge in five planes. Checking the cylinder head gasket surface in five planes checks the head for **warpage, distortion, bend,** and **twist.** ● SEE FIGURE 13–20.

These defects are determined by trying to slide a 0.004 inch (0.1 mm) feeler gauge under a precision straightedge held against the head surface. The clearance between the cylinder head and the straightedge should not vary by over 0.002 inch (0.05 mm) in any 6 inch (15 cm) length, or by more than 0.004 inch overall. Always check the manufacturer's recommended specifications. ● SEE FIGURE 13–21.

NOTE:

1. **The cylinder head surface that mates with the top deck of the block is often called the fire deck.**

2. **Always check the cylinder head thickness and specifications to be sure that material can be safely removed from the surface. Some manufacturers do not recommend *any* machining, but rather require cylinder head replacement if cylinder head surface flatness is not within specifications.**

FIGURE 13–22 A cast-iron cylinder head being resurfaced using a surface grinder.

CYLINDER HEAD RESURFACING

REFINISHING METHODS Two common resurfacing methods are:

- Milling or broaching
- Grinding

A **milling** type of resurfacer uses metal-cutting tool bits fastened in a disc. This type is also called a *broach*. The disc is the rotating workhead of the mill.

The **surface grinder** type uses a large-diameter abrasive wheel. Both types of resurfacing can be done with table-type and with precision-type surfacers. With a table-type surfacer, the head or block is passed over the cutting head that extends slightly above a worktable. The abrasive wheel is dressed before grinding begins. The wheel head is adjusted to just touch the surface. At this point, the feed is calibrated to zero. This is necessary so that the operator knows exactly the size of the cut being made. Light cuts are taken. The abrasive wheel cuts are limited to 0.005 inch (0.015 mm). ● SEE FIGURE 13–22.

The abrasive wheel surface should be wire brushed after each five passes, and the wheel should be redressed after grinding each 0.1 inch (2.5 mm). The mill-type cutting wheel can remove up to 0.03 inch (0.075 mm) on each pass. A special mill-cutting tool or a dull grinding wheel is used when aluminum heads are being resurfaced.

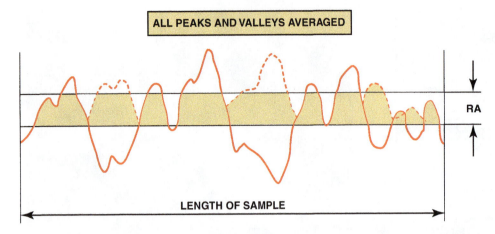

ALL PEAKS AND VALLEYS AVERAGED

RA

LENGTH OF SAMPLE

FIGURE 13–23 A graph showing a typical rough surface as would be viewed through a magnifying glass. RA is an abbreviation indicating the average height of all peaks and valleys.

NOTE: Resurfacing the cylinder head changes the compression ratio of the engine by about 1/10 point per 0.01 inch of removed material. For example, the compression ratio would be increased from 9.0:1 to 9.2:1 if 0.02 inch were removed from a typical cylinder head.

SURFACE FINISH The surface finish of a reconditioned part is as important as the size of the part. Surface finish is measured in units called microinches (abbreviated "μ in."). The symbol in front of the inch abbreviation is the Greek letter *mu.* One microinch equals 0.000001 inch, or 0.025 micrometer (μ m). The finish classification in microinches gives the distance between the highest peak and the deepest valley. The usual method of expressing surface finish is by the **arithmetic average roughness height (RA),** that is, the average of the distances of all peaks and valleys from the mean (average) line. Surface finish is measured using a machine with a diamond stylus. ● **SEE FIGURE 13–23.**

Another classification of surface finish, which is becoming obsolete, is called the **root-mean-square (RMS).** The RMS is a slightly higher number and can be obtained by multiplying RA × 1.11.

Typical surface finish roughness recommendations for cast-iron and aluminum cylinder heads and blocks include the following:

Cast Iron

Maximum: 110 RA (125 RMS) (Rough surfaces can limit gasket movement and conformity.)

Minimum: 30 RA (33 RMS) (Smoother surfaces increase the tendency of the gasket to flow and *reduce* gasket sealing ability.)

Recommended range: 60 to 100 RA (65 to 110 RMS)

TECH TIP

The Potato Chip Problem

Most cylinder heads are warped or twisted in the shape of a typical potato chip (high at the ends and dipped in the center). After a cylinder head is ground, the surface *should* be perfectly flat. A common problem involves grinding the cylinder head in both directions while it is being held on the table that moves to the left and right. Most grinders are angled by about 4 degrees. The lower part of the stone should be the cutting edge. If grinding occurs along the angled part of the stone, then too much heat is generated. This heat warps the head (or block) upward in the middle. The stone then removes this material, and the end result is a slight (about 0.0015 inch) depression in the center of the finished surface. To help prevent this from happening, always feed the grinder in the forward direction only (especially during removal of the last 0.003 inch of material).

Aluminum

Maximum: 60 RA (65 RMS)

Minimum: 30 RA (33 RMS)

Recommended range: 50 to 60 RA (55 to 65 RMS)

The rougher the surface is, the higher the microinch finish measurement will be. Typical preferred microinch finish standards for other engine components include the following:

Crank and rod journal:	10 to 14 RA (12 to 15 RMS)
Honed cylinder:	18 to 32 RA (20 to 35 RMS)
Connecting rod big end:	45 to 72 RA (50 to 80 RMS)

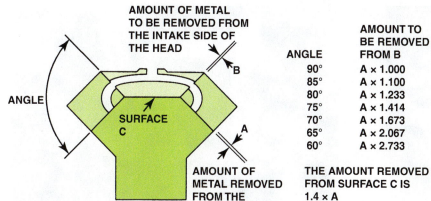

AMOUNT OF METAL TO BE REMOVED FROM THE INTAKE SIDE OF THE HEAD

ANGLE

SURFACE C

B

A

AMOUNT OF METAL REMOVED FROM THE RESURFACED HEAD

ANGLE	AMOUNT TO BE REMOVED FROM B
90°	A × 1.000
85°	A × 1.100
80°	A × 1.233
75°	A × 1.414
70°	A × 1.673
65°	A × 2.067
60°	A × 2.733

THE AMOUNT REMOVED FROM SURFACE C IS 1.4 × A

FIGURE 13–24 The material that must be removed for a good manifold fit.

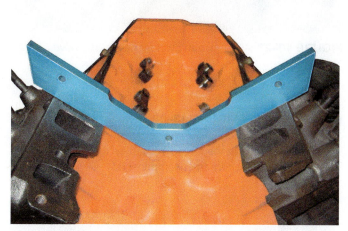

FIGURE 13–25 Using an intake manifold template to check for the proper angles after the cylinder heads have been machined.

INTAKE MANIFOLD ALIGNMENT

PURPOSE The intake manifold of a V-type engine may no longer fit correctly after the gasket surfaces of the heads are ground. The ports and the assembly bolt holes may no longer match. The intake manifold surface must be resurfaced to remove enough metal to rematch the ports and bolt holes. The amount of metal that must be removed depends on the angle between the head gasket surface and the intake manifold gasket surface. ● SEE FIGURE 13–24.

PROCEDURE Automotive machine shops that perform head resurfacing have tables that specify the exact amount of metal to be removed. It is usually necessary to also remove some metal from both the front and the back gasket surfaces of closed-type intake manifolds used on V-type engines. This is necessary to provide a good gasket seal that will prevent oil leakage from the lifter valley. ● SEE FIGURE 13–25.

CAUTION: Do not remove any more material than is necessary to restore a flat cylinder head-to-block surface. Some manufacturers limit *total* material that can be removed from the block deck and cylinder head to 0.008 inch (0.2 mm). Removal of material from the cylinder head of an overhead camshaft engine shortens the distance between the camshaft and the crankshaft. This causes the valve timing to be *retarded*

VALVE GUIDES

TYPES The valve guide supports the valve stem so that the valve face will remain perfectly centered, or **concentric,** with the valve seat. The valve guide is generally integral with the head casting in cast-iron heads for better heat transfer and for lower manufacturing costs. ● SEE FIGURE 13–26.

Removable or pressed-in **valve guides** and **valve seat inserts** are always used in aluminum heads. ● SEE FIGURE 13–27.

No matter how good the valves or seats are, they cannot operate properly if the valve guide is not accurate. In use, the valve opening mechanism pushes the valve tip sideways. This is the major cause of valve stem and guide wear. The movement of the valve causes both the top and bottom ends of the guide to wear until the guide has bell-mouth shapes at both ends. ● SEE FIGURE 13–28.

VALVE STEM-TO-GUIDE CLEARANCE Engine manufacturers usually recommend the following valve stem-to-guide clearances.

- Intake valve: 0.001 to 0.003 inch (0.025 to 0.076 mm)
- Exhaust valve: 0.002 to 0.004 inch (0.05 to 0.1 mm)

Be sure to check the exact specifications for the engine being serviced. The exhaust valve clearance is greater than the

FIGURE 13–26 An integral valve guide is simply a guide that has been drilled into the cast-iron cylinder head.

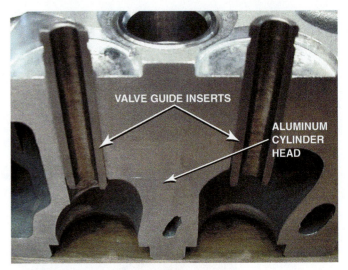

FIGURE 13–27 All aluminum cylinder heads use valve guide inserts.

FIGURE 13–28 Valve guides often wear to a bell-mouth shape to both ends due to the forces exerted on the valve by the valve train components.

intake valve clearance because the exhaust valve runs hotter and therefore expands more than the intake valve.

Excessive valve stem-to-guide clearance can cause excessive oil consumption. The intake valve guide is exposed to manifold vacuum that can draw oil from the top of the cylinder head down into the combustion chamber. In this situation, valves can also run hotter than usual because much of the heat in the valve is transferred to the cylinder head through the valve guide.

HINT: A human hair is about 0.002 inch (0.05 mm) in diameter. Therefore, the typical clearance between a valve stem and the valve guide is only the thickness of a human hair.

MEASURING VALVE GUIDES Valves should be measured for stem wear before valve guides are measured. The valve guide is measured in the middle with a small-hole gauge. The gauge size is checked with a micrometer. The guide is then checked at each end.

The expanded part of the ball should be placed crosswise to the engine where the greatest amount of valve guide wear exists. The dimension of the valve stem diameter is subtracted from the dimension of the valve guide diameter. If the clearance exceeds the specified clearance, then the valve guide will have to be reconditioned. ● **SEE FIGURES 13–29 AND 13–30.**

Valve stem-to-guide clearance can also be checked using a dial indicator (gauge) to measure the amount of movement of the valve when lifted off the valve seat. ● **SEE FIGURE 13–31.**

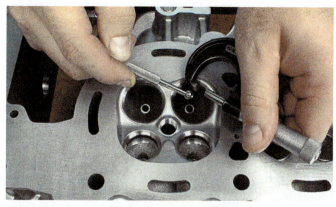

FIGURE 13–29 A small-hole gauge and a micrometer are being used to measure the valve guide. The guide should be measured in three places: at the top, middle, and bottom.

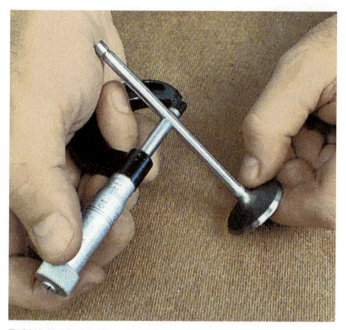

FIGURE 13–30 The diameter of the valve stem is being measured using a micrometer. The difference between the inside diameter of the valve guide and the diameter of the valve stem is the valve guide-to-stem clearance.

OVERSIZE STEM VALVES

Some domestic vehicle manufacturers that have integral valve guides in their engines recommend reaming worn valve guides and installing new valves with **oversize (OS) stems.** When a valve guide is worn, the valve stem is also likely to be worn. In this case, new valves are required. If new valves are used, they can just as well have oversize stems as standard stems. Typically, available sizes include 0.003, 0.005, 0.015, and 0.03 inch OS. The valve guide is reamed or honed to the correct size to fit the oversize stem of the new valve.

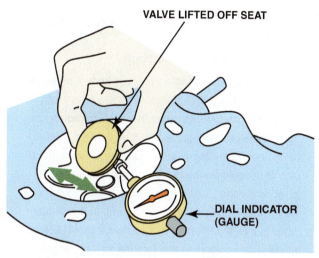

VALVE LIFTED OFF SEAT

DIAL INDICATOR (GAUGE)

FIGURE 13–31 Measuring valve guide-to-stem clearance with a dial indicator while rocking the stem in the direction of normal thrust. The reading on the dial indicator should be compared to specifications because it does not give the guide-to-stem clearance directly. The valve is usually held open to its maximum operating lift.

🔧 **TECH TIP**

Tight Is Not Always Right

Many engine manufacturers specify a valve stem-to-guide clearance of 0.001 to 0.003 inch (0.025 to 0.076 mm). However, some vehicles, especially those equipped with aluminum cylinder heads, may specify a much greater clearance. For example, the General Motors LS1 5.7L V-8 allows up to 0.004 inch (0.105 mm) clearance. This amount of clearance feels loose to those technicians accustomed to normal valve stem clearance specifications. Although this large amount of clearance may seem excessive, remember that the valve stem increases in diameter as the engine warms up. Therefore, the *operating* clearance is smaller than the clearance measured at room temperature. Always double-check factory specifications before replacing a valve guide for excessive wear.

The resulting clearance of the valve stem in the guide is the same as the original clearance. The oil clearance and the heat transfer properties of the original valve and guide are not changed when new valves with oversize stems are installed.

NOTE: Many remanufacturers of cylinder heads use oversize valve stems to simplify production.

What Is Valve Guide Knurling?

In an old and now outdated process known as **valve guide knurling,** a tool is rotated as it is driven into the guide. The tool *displaces* the metal to reduce the hole diameter of the guide. Knurling is ideally suited to engines with integral valve guides (guides that are part of the cylinder head and are nonremovable). It is recommended that knurling not be used to correct wear exceeding 0.006 inch (0.15 mm). In the displacing process, the knurling tool pushes a small tapered wheel or dull threading tool into the wall of the guide hole. This makes a groove in the wall of the guide, similar to a threading operation without removing any metal.

The metal piles up along the edge of the groove just as dirt would pile up along the edge of a tire track as the tire rolled through soft dirt. (The dirt would be displaced from under the wheel to form a small ridge alongside the tire track.) ● **SEE FIGURE 13–32.**

The knurling tool is driven by an electric drill and an attached speed reducer that slows the rotating speed of the knurling tool. The reamers that accompany the knurling set will ream just enough to provide the correct valve stem clearance for commercial reconditioning standards. The valve guides are honed to size in the precision shop when precise fits are desired. Clearances of knurled valve guides are usually one-half of the new valve guide clearances. Such small clearance can be used because knurling leaves so many small oil rings down the length of the guide for lubrication.

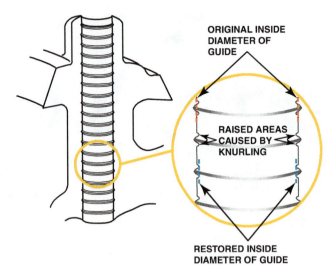

FIGURE 13–32 Sectional view of a knurled valve guide.

Right Side Up

When replacing valve guides, it is important that the recommended procedures be followed. Most manufacturers specify that replaceable guides be driven from the combustion chamber side toward the rocker arm side. For example, big block Chevrolet V-8 heads (396, 402, 427, and 454 cu.[3]) have a 0.004 inch (0.05 mm) taper (small end toward the combustion chamber).

Other manufacturers, however, may recommend driving the old guide from the rocker arm side to prevent any carbon buildup on the guide from damaging the guide bore. Always check the manufacturer's recommended procedures before attempting to replace a valve guide.

After the valve guide height is measured, the worn guide is pressed from the head with a proper fitting *driver.* ● **SEE FIGURE 13–33.**

The driver has a stem to fit the guide opening and a shoulder that pushes on the end of the guide. If the guide has a flange, care should be taken to ensure that the guide is pushed out from the correct end, usually from the port side and toward the rocker arm side. The new guide is pressed into the guide bore using the same driver. Make sure that the guide is pressed to the correct depth. After the guides are replaced, they are reamed or honed to the proper inside diameter.

Replacement valve guides can also be installed to repair worn integral guides. Both **cast-iron** and **bronze guides** are available.

VALVE GUIDE REPLACEMENT

PURPOSE When an engine is designed with replaceable valve guides, their replacement is always recommended when the valve assembly is being reconditioned. The original valve guide height should be measured before the guide is removed so that the new guide can be properly positioned.

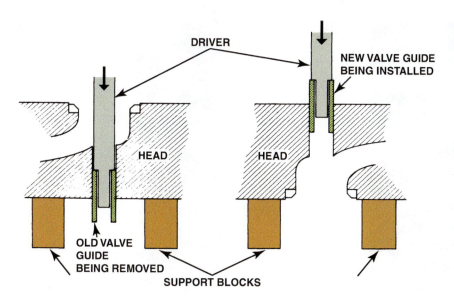

DRIVER

NEW VALVE GUIDE
BEING INSTALLED

HEAD

HEAD

OLD VALVE
GUIDE
BEING REMOVED

SUPPORT BLOCKS

FIGURE 13–33 Valve guide replacement procedure.

VALVE GUIDE SIZES
Three common valve guide sizes are as follows:

- 5/16 or 0.313 inch
- 11/32 or 0.343 inch
- 3/8 or 0.375 inch

VALVE GUIDE INSERTS
When the integral valve guide is badly worn, it can be reconditioned using an insert. This repair method is usually preferred in heavy-duty and high-speed engines. Two types of guide inserts are commonly used for guide repair.

- **Thin-walled bronze alloy sleeve bushing**
- **Spiral bronze alloy bushing**

The thin-walled bronze sleeve bushings are also called **bronze guide liners.** The valve guide rebuilding kit used to install each of these bushings includes all of the reamers, installing sleeves, broaches, burnishing tools, and cutoff tools that are needed to install and properly size the bushings.

The valve guide must be bored to a large enough size to accept the thin-walled insert sleeve. The boring tool is held in alignment by a rugged fixture. One type is shown in ● **FIGURE 13–34.**

Depending on the make of the equipment, the boring fixture is aligned with the valve guide hole, the valve seat, or the head gasket surface. First, the boring fixture is properly aligned. The guide is then bored, making a hole somewhat smaller than the insert sleeve that will be used. The bored hole is reamed to make a precise smooth hole that is still slightly smaller than the insert sleeve. The insert sleeve is installed with a press fit that holds it in the guide. The press fit also helps to maintain normal

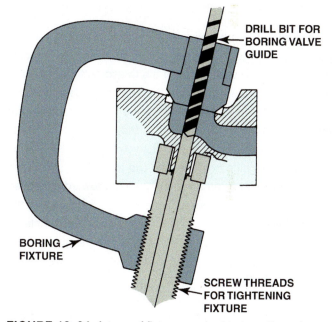

DRILL BIT FOR
BORING VALVE
GUIDE

BORING
FIXTURE

SCREW THREADS
FOR TIGHTENING
FIXTURE

FIGURE 13–34 A type of fixture required to bore the valve guide to accept a thin-walled insert sleeve.

heat transfer from the valve to the head. The thin-walled insert sleeve is held in an installing sleeve. A driver is used to press the insert from the installing sleeve into the guide. A broach is then pressed through the insert sleeve to firmly seat it in the guide. The broach is designed to put a knurl in the guide to aid in lubrication. The insert sleeve is then trimmed to the valve guide length. Finally, the insert sleeve is reamed or honed to provide the required valve stem clearance. A very close clearance of 0.0005 inch (one-half of one-thousandth of an inch) (0.013 mm) is often used with the bronze thin-walled insert sleeve. ● **SEE FIGURE 13–35.**

FIGURE 13–35 Trimming the top of the thin-walled insert.

FIGURE 13–36 Installed spiral bronze insert bushing.

SPIRAL BRONZE INSERT BUSHINGS The spiral bronze alloy insert bushing is screwed into a thread that is put in the valve guide. The tap used to cut threads in the valve guide has a long pilot ahead of the thread-cutting portion of the tap. This aids in restoring the original guide alignment. The long pilot is placed in the guide from the valve seat end. A power driver is attached to the end of the pilot that extends from the spring end of the valve guide. The threads are cut in the guide from the seat end toward the spring end as the power driver turns the tap, pulling it toward the driver. The tap is stopped before it comes out of the guide, and the power driver is removed. The thread is carefully completed by hand to avoid breaking either the end of the guide or the tap. An installed spiral bronze insert bushing can be seen in
● **FIGURE 13–36.**

The spiral bronze bushing is tightened on an inserting tool. This holds it securely in the wound-up position so that it can be screwed into the spring end of the guide. It is screwed in until the bottom of the bushing is flush with the seat end of the

guide. The holding tool is removed, and the bushing material is trimmed to one coil *above* the spring end of the guide. The end of the bushing is temporarily secured with a plastic serrated bushing retainer and a worm gear clamp. This holds the bushing in place as a broach is driven through the bushing to firmly seat it in the threads. The bushing is reamed or honed to size before the temporary bushing retainer is removed. The final step is to trim the end of the bushing with a special cutoff tool that is included in the bushing installation tool set. This type of spiral bronze bushing can be removed by using a pick to free the end of the bushing. It can then be stripped out and a new bushing inserted in the original threads in the guide hole. New threads do not have to be put in the guide. The spiral bushing design has natural spiral grooves to hold oil for lubrication. The valve stem clearances are the same as those used for knurling and for the thin-walled insert (about one-half of the standard recommended clearance).

SUMMARY

1. The most commonly used combustion chamber types include hemispherical, wedge, and pentroof.

2. Coolant and lubricating openings and passages are located throughout most cylinder heads.

3. Cylinder head resurfacing machines include grinders and milling machines.

4. Valve guides should be checked for wear using a ball gauge or a dial indicator. Typical valve stem-to-guide clearance is 0.001 to 0.003 inch for intake valves and 0.002 to 0.004 inch for exhaust valves.

5. Valve guide repair options include use of oversize stem valves, replacement valve guides, valve guide inserts, and knurling of the original valve guide.

1. What is meant by the term *crossflow head*?
2. What is a Siamese port?
3. What is the recommended cylinder head reconditioning sequence?
4. What are the advantages of using four valves per cylinder?

CHAPTER QUIZ

1. Cylinder heads with four valves flow more air than those with two valves because they _____.
   a. Have a greater open area
   b. Use a higher lift camshaft
   c. Increase the velocity of the air
   d. Both a and c

2. Technician A says that a two-valve cylinder head can be used with gasoline direct injection. Technician B says that gasoline direct injection can be used on a four-valve cylinder head. Which technician is correct?
   a. Technician A only
   b. Technician B only
   c. Both Technicians A and B
   d. Neither Technician A nor B

3. Technician A says that a four-valve engine uses three intake valves and one exhaust valve. Technician B says that it uses three exhaust valves and one intake valve. Which technician is correct?
   a. Technician A only
   b. Technician B only
   c. Both Technicians A and B
   d. Neither Technician A nor B

4. The gasket surface of a cylinder head, as measured with a precision straightedge, should have a maximum variation of _____.
   a. 0.002 inch in any 6 inch length, or 0.004 inch overall
   b. 0.001 inch in any 6 inch length, or 0.004 inch overall
   c. 0.020 inch in any 10 inch length, or 0.02 inch overall
   d. 0.004 inch in any 10 inch length, or 0.008 inch overall

5. How are the valve guides formed in an aluminum cylinder head?
   a. They are drilled and honed into the aluminum
   b. Pressed-in inserts are used
   c. The head is drilled and then knurled
   d. Formed-in-place bronze tubes

6. Some vehicle manufacturers recommend repairing integral guides with _____.
   a. OS stem valves
   b. Knurling
   c. Replacement valve guides
   d. Valve guide inserts

7. Typical valve stem-to-guide clearance is _____.
   a. 0.03 to 0.045 inch (0.8 to 1 mm)
   b. 0.015 to 0.02 inch (0.4 to 0.5 mm)
   c. 0.005 to 0.01 inch (0.13 to 0.25 mm)
   d. 0.001 to 0.004 inch (0.03 to 0.05 mm)

8. What other engine component may have to be machined if the cylinder heads are machined on a V-type engine?
   a. Exhaust manifold
   b. Intake manifold
   c. Block deck
   d. Distributor mount (if the vehicle is so equipped)

9. Which type of valve guide is most used in a cast-iron head?
   a. Integral
   b. Bronze
   c. Powdered metal (PM)
   d. Thin-walled sleeve type

10. Which statement is true about surface finish?
    a. Cast-iron surfaces should be smoother than aluminum surfaces.
    b. The rougher the surface, the higher the microinch finish measurement.
    c. The smoother the surface, the higher the microinch finish measurement.
    d. A cylinder head should be much smoother than a crankshaft journal.

chapter 14

VALVE AND SEAT SERVICE

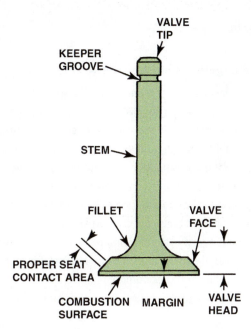

FIGURE 14–1 Identification of the parts of a valve.

INTAKE AND EXHAUST VALVES

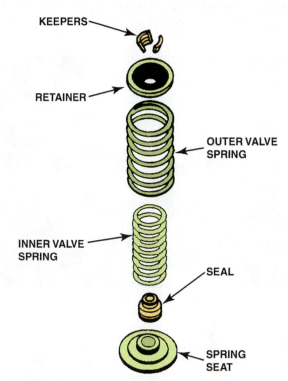

FIGURE 14–2 Typical valve spring and related components. Dual valve springs are used to reduce valve train vibrations and a spring seat is used to protect aluminum heads.

TERMINOLOGY Automotive engine valves are of a **poppet valve** design. The term *poppet* refers to the shape of the valve and their operation in automotive engines. The valve is opened by means of a valve train that is operated by a cam. The cam is timed to the piston position and crankshaft cycle. The valve is closed by one or more springs.

A typical valve is shown in ● **FIGURE 14–1.**

Intake valves control the inlet of cool, low-pressure induction charges. Exhaust valves handle hot, high-pressure exhaust gases. This means that exhaust valves are exposed to more severe operating conditions. They are, therefore, made from much higher quality materials than the intake valves, which makes them more expensive.

The valve is held in place and is positioned in the head by the **valve guide.** The portion of the valve that seals against the **valve seat** in the cylinder head is called the **valve face.** The face and seat will have an angle of either 30 or 45 degrees, which are the nominal angles; actual service angles may vary. Most engines use a nominal 45-degree valve and seat angle.

PARTS INVOLVED

- A **valve spring** holds the valve against the seat.
- The valve *keepers* (also called **locks**) secure the spring **retainer** to the stem of the valve.

For valve removal, it is necessary to compress the spring and remove the valve keepers. Then the spring, valve seals,

and valve can be removed from the head. Typical valve spring and related components are shown in ● **FIGURE 14–2.**

VALVE SIZE RELATIONSHIPS

Extensive testing has shown that a normal relationship exists between the different dimensions of valves.

- **Intake valves.** Engines with cylinder bores that measure from 3 to 8 inch (80 to 200 mm) will have intake valve head diameters that measure approximately 45% of the bore size. The intake valve must be larger than the exhaust valve to handle the same mass of gas. The larger intake valve controls low-velocity, low-density gases. The distance the valve opens is close to 25% of the valve head diameter.

- **Exhaust valves.** The exhaust valve head diameter is approximately 38% of the cylinder bore size. Exhaust valve heads are, therefore, approximately 85% of the size of intake valve heads. The exhaust valve, however, controls high-velocity, high-pressure, denser gases. These gases can be handled by a smaller valve.● **SEE FIGURE 14–3.**

VALVE MATERIALS

- **Alloy steel.** Alloys used in exhaust valve materials are largely of chromium for oxidation resistance, with small amounts of nickel, manganese, and nitrogen added. Heat-treating is used whenever it is necessary to produce special valve properties.

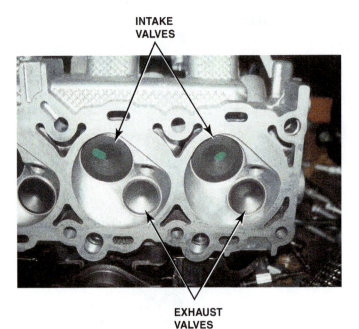

INTAKE
VALVES

EXHAUST
VALVES

FIGURE 14–3 The intake valve is larger than the exhaust valve because the intake charge is being drawn into the combustion chamber at a low speed due to differences in pressure between atmospheric pressure and the pressure (vacuum) inside the cylinder. The exhaust is actually pushed out by the piston and, therefore, the size of the valve does not need to be as large, leaving more room in the cylinder head for the larger intake valve.

- **Stellite®.** An alloy of nickel, chromium, and tungsten, **Stellite®** is nonmagnetic. Some valves use this product only on the tip of the valve to help reduce wear in places where the rocker arm contacts the valve stem on engines that do not use a roller rocker arm. Stellite® is also used on some valve faces.

  NOTE: If the valve tip is made from Stellite® do NOT grind the tip when reconditioning the valve.

- **Inconal®.** A type of alloy containing nickel, chrome, and iron and is used mostly in racing engines.

- **Titanium.** About half the weight of conventional valves, titanium allows lower tension on valve springs resulting in higher RPM engine operation. The valve stems are often moly coated to help prevent sticking in the valve guide.

  NOTE: Titanium valves should not be ground or machined in any way. They should be replaced if damaged or worn.

- **Stainless steel.** Used in many heavy-duty applications, stainless steel often uses chrome-plated valve stems and Stellite tips to improve long-term durability.

TECH TIP

Hot Engine + Cold Weather = Trouble

Serious valve damage can occur if cold air reaches hot exhaust valves soon after the engine is turned off. An engine equipped with exhaust headers and/or straight-through mufflers can allow cold air a direct path to the hot exhaust valve. The exhaust valve can warp and/or crack as a result of rapid cooling. This can easily occur during cold windy weather when the wind can blow cold outside air directly up the exhaust system. Using reverse-flow mufflers with tailpipes and a catalytic converter reduces the possibilities of this occurring.

- **Aluminized.** The valve is aluminized where corrosion may be a problem. Aluminized valve facing reduces valve recession when unleaded gasoline is used. Aluminum oxide forms to separate the valve steel from the cast-iron seat to keep the face metal from sticking.

TWO-MATERIAL VALVES   Some exhaust valves are manufactured from two different materials when a one-piece design cannot meet the desired hardness and corrosion resistance specifications. The joint cannot be seen after valves have been used. The valve heads are made from special alloys that can operate at high temperatures, have physical strength, resist lead oxide corrosion, and have indentation resistance. These heads are welded to stems that have good wear resistance properties. These types of valves are usually welded together using a process called **inertia friction welding.** Inertia friction welding is performed by spinning one end and then forcing the two pieces together until the materials reach their melting temperature. Then the parts are held together until they fuse, resulting in a uniform weld between two different materials. ● **FIGURE 14–4** shows an inertia welded valve before final machining.

SODIUM-FILLED VALVES   Some heavy-duty applications use hollow stem exhaust valves that are partially filled with metallic sodium. The sodium in the valve becomes a liquid at operating temperatures. As it splashes back and forth in the valve stem, the sodium transfers heat from the valve head to the valve stem. The heat goes through the valve guide into the coolant. In general, a one-piece valve design using properly selected materials will provide satisfactory service for automotive engines. ● **SEE FIGURE 14–5.**

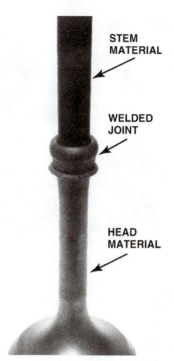

FIGURE 14–4 Inertia welded valve stem and head before machining.

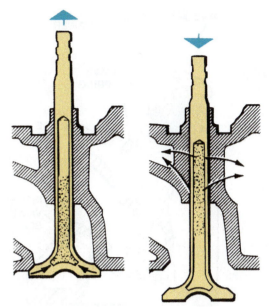

FIGURE 14–5 A sodium-filled valve uses a hollow stem, which is partially filled with metallic sodium (a liquid when hot) to conduct heat away from the head of the valve.

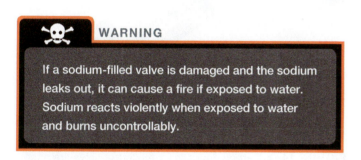

WARNING

If a sodium-filled valve is damaged and the sodium leaks out, it can cause a fire if exposed to water. Sodium reacts violently when exposed to water and burns uncontrollably.

VALVE SEATS

INTEGRAL SEATS The valve face closes against a valve seat to seal the combustion chamber. The seat is generally formed as part of the cast-iron head of automotive engines, called an **integral seat.** ● **SEE FIGURE 14–6.**

The seats are usually induction hardened so that unleaded gasoline can be used. This minimizes valve recession as the engine operates. Valve recession is the wearing away of the seat, so that the valve sits further into the head.

INSERT SEATS An **insert seat** fits into a machined recess in the steel or aluminum cylinder head. Insert seats are used in *all* aluminum head engines and in applications for which corrosion and wear resistance are critical. Aluminum heads also include insert valve guides.

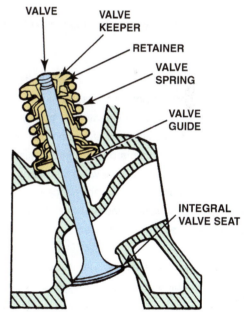

FIGURE 14–6 Integral valve seats are machined directly into the cast-iron cylinder head and are induction hardened to prevent wear.

The exhaust valve seat runs as much as 180°F (100°C) *cooler* in aluminum heads than in cast-iron heads, because aluminum conducts heat faster than cast iron. Insert seats are also used to recondition integral valve seats that have been badly damaged. ● **SEE FIGURE 14–7.**

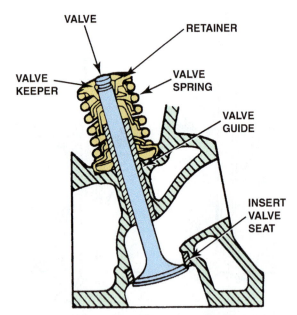

FIGURE 14–7 Insert valve seats are a separate part that is interference fitted to a counterbore in the cylinder head.

FIGURE 14–8 Typical intake valve seat wear.

VALVE FAULT DIAGNOSIS

Careful inspection of the cylinder head and valves can often reveal the root cause of failure.

POOR VALVE SEATING Poor seating results from too small a valve lash, hard carbon deposits, valve stem deposits, excessive valve stem-to-guide clearances, or out-of-square valve guide and seat. A valve seat recession can result from improper valve lash adjustments on solid lifter engines. It can also result from misadjustments on a valve train using hydraulic lifters. The valve clearance will also be reduced as a result of valve head cupping or valve face and seat wear. ● **FIGURE 14–8** shows typical intake valve and seat wear.

CARBON DEPOSITS If there is a large clearance between the valve stem and guide or faulty valve stem seals, too much oil will go down the stem. This will increase deposits, as shown on the intake valve in ● **FIGURE 14–9.**

In addition, a large valve guide clearance will allow the valve to cock or lean sideways, especially with the effect of the rocker arm action. Continued cocking keeps the valve from seating properly and causes it to leak, burning the valve face. ● **SEE FIGURE 14–10.**

Sometimes, the cylinder head will warp slightly as the head is tightened to the block deck during assembly. In other cases, heating and cooling will cause warpage. When head warpage causes valve guide and seat misalignment, the valve cannot seat properly and it will leak, burning the valve face.

FIGURE 14–9 Carbon deposits on the intake valve are often caused by oil getting past the valve stems or fuel deposits.

EXCESSIVE TEMPERATURES High valve temperatures occur when the valve does not seat properly. Root causes include the following:

1. Cooling system passages in the head may be partially blocked by faulty casting or by deposits built up from the coolant. A corroded head gasket will change the coolant flow. This can cause overheating when the coolant is allowed to flow to the wrong places.

2. Extremely high temperatures are also produced by preignition and by detonation. These conditions are the result of abnormal combustion. Both of these produce a very rapid increase in temperature that can cause uneven heating. The rapid increase in temperature will give a **thermal shock** to the valve. (A thermal shock is a sudden change in temperature.) The shock will often cause radial cracks in the valve. The cracks will allow the combustion gases to escape and gutter the valve face. ● **SEE FIGURE 14–11.**

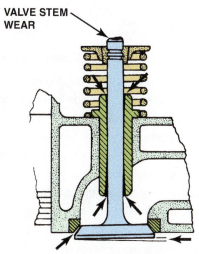

FIGURE 14–10 Excessive wear of the valve stem or guide can cause the valve to seat in a cocked position.

FIGURE 14–11 Valve face guttering caused by thermal shock.

VALVE SEAT EROSION Valve seats can wear especially in those engines that were designed for use with leaded gasoline (prior to 1975). Without lead, the valve movement against the seat tears away tiny iron oxide particles during engine operation. The valve movement causes these particles of iron oxide to act like valve grinding compound, cutting into the valve seat surface. As the valve seat is eroded, the valve recedes further into the cylinder head. When the valve seat erodes, the valve lash decreases. This can lead to valve burning because the valve may not close all the way.

HIGH-VELOCITY SEATING High-velocity seating is indicated by excessive valve face wear, valve seat recession, and impact failure. It can be caused by excessive lash in

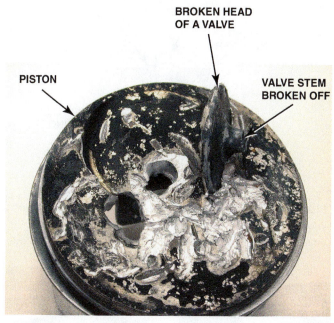

FIGURE 14–12 This valve broke off at the stem causing severe engine damage.

mechanical lifters and by collapsed hydraulic lifters. Lash allows the valve to hit the seat without the effects of the cam ramp to ease the valve onto its seat. Excessive lash may also be caused by wear of parts, such as the cam, lifter base, pushrod ends, rocker arm pivot, and valve tip. Weak or broken valve springs allow the valves to float away from the cam lobes so that the valves are uncontrolled as they hit the seat.

Impact breakage may occur under the valve head or at the valve keeper grooves. The break lines radiate from the starting point. Impact breakage may also cause the valve head to fall into the combustion chamber. In most cases, it will ruin the piston before the engine can be stopped. This situation causes catastrophic engine damage and is described in the field by several terms, including:

- Sucking a valve
- Dropping a valve
- Swallowing a valve ● **SEE FIGURE 14–12.**

VALVE SPRINGS

PURPOSE AND FUNCTION A valve spring holds the valve against the seat when the valve is not being opened. One end of the valve spring is seated against the head. The other end of the spring is attached under compression to the valve stem through a valve spring retainer and a valve spring keeper (lock). ● **SEE FIGURE 14–13.**

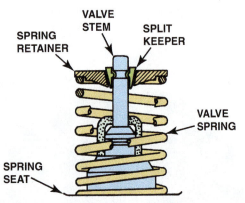

FIGURE 14–13 A retainer and two split keepers hold the spring in place on the valve. A steel spring seat is used on aluminum heads. Otherwise, the spring seat is a machined area in the head.

FIGURE 14–14 Valve spring types (*left to right*): coil spring with equally spaced coils; spring with damper inside spring coil; variable rate spring with a damper; taper wound (beehive) coil spring.

SPRING MATERIALS AND DESIGN

Valves usually have a single inexpensive valve spring. The springs are generally made of chromium vanadium alloy steel. When one spring cannot control the valve, another spring or damper is added. Some valve springs use a flat coiled damper inside the spring. The damper helps to reduce valve seat wear. This eliminates spring surge and adds some valve spring tension. The normal valve spring winds up as it is compressed. This causes a small but important turning motion as the valve closes on the seat. The turning motion helps to keep the wear even around the valve face. ● SEE FIGURE 14–14.

Multiple valve springs are used where large camshaft lobe lifts are required and a single spring does not have enough strength to control the valve.

- If dual coil springs are wrapped in same direction, they are used for extra tension.

- If the inner spring or flat damper is wrapped in the opposite direction, it is used as a damper to control spring oscillations. This is done to control valve spring surge and to prevent excessive valve rotation. These are sometimes called *surge dampers*.

Valve spring surge is the tendency of a valve spring to vibrate.

Valve Seat Recession and Engine Performance

If unleaded fuel is used in an engine without hardened valve seats, valve seat recession is likely to occur over time. Without removing the cylinder heads, how can a technician identify valve seat recession?

As the valve seat wears up into the cylinder head, the valve itself also is located further up in the head. As this wear occurs, the valve clearance (lash) *decreases*. If hydraulic lifters are used on the engine, this wear will go undetected until the reduction in valve clearance finally removes all clearance (bottoms out) in the lifter. When this occurs, the valve does not seat fully, and compression, power, and fuel economy are drastically reduced. With the valve not closing completely, the valve cannot release its heat and will burn or begin to melt. If the valve burns, the engine will miss and not idle smoothly.

If solid lifters are used on the engine, the decrease in valve clearance will first show up as a rough idle only when the engine is hot. As the valve seat recedes farther into the head, low power, rough idle, poor performance, and lower fuel economy will be noticed sooner than if the engine were equipped with hydraulic lifters.

To summarize, refer to the following symptoms as valve seat recession occurs.

1. Valve lash (clearance) decreases (valves are *not* noisy).
2. The engine idles roughly when hot as a result of reduced valve clearance.
3. Missing occurs, and the engine exhibits low power and poor fuel economy, along with a rough idle, as the valve seat recedes farther into the head.
4. As valves burn, the engine continues to run poorly; the symptoms include difficulty in starting (hot and cold engine), backfiring, and low engine power.

NOTE: If valve lash is adjustable, valve burning can be prevented by adjusting the valve lash regularly. Remember, as the seat recedes, the valve itself recedes, which decreases the valve clearance. Many technicians do not think of adjusting valves unless they are noisy. If, during the valve adjustment procedure, a *decrease* in valve lash is noticed, then valve seat recession could be occurring.

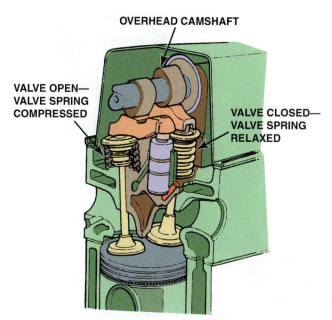

FIGURE 14–15 Valve springs maintain tension in the valve train when the valve is open to prevent valve float, but must not exert so much tension that the cam lobes and lifters begin to wear.

 FREQUENTLY ASKED QUESTION

What Is Valve Float?

Valve float occurs when the valve continues to stay open after the camshaft lobe has moved from under the lifter. This happens when the inertia of the valve train overcomes the valve spring tension at high engine speeds. ● **SEE FIGURE 14–15.**

VARIABLE RATE SPRINGS

Variable rate springs, also called *progressive rate* or *variable pitch springs,* have uneven spacing between the coils. Where nonprogressive rate (linear) valve springs provide the same rate through all heights, a variable rate valve spring has a different spring rate depending on how much it is compressed. One advantage of using a variable rate spring is that it provides a low seat pressure and still provides the rate needed for high lift camshaft designs. This type of spring is used to help control valve surge.

VALVE SPRING INSPECTION

Valve springs close the valves after they have been opened by the cam. They must close squarely to form a tight seal and to prevent valve stem and guide wear. It is necessary, therefore, that the springs be square and have the proper amount of closing force. The valve springs are checked for squareness by rotating them on a flat

FIGURE 14–16 All valve springs should be checked for squareness by using a square on a flat surface and rotating the spring while checking. The spring should be replaced if more than 1/16 inch (1.6 mm) is measured between the top of the spring and the square.

surface with a square held against the side. They should be within 1/16 (1.6 mm) of being square. Out-of-square springs will have to be replaced. ● **SEE FIGURE 14–16.**

Only the springs that are square should be checked to determine their compressed force. The surge damper is often specified to be *removed* from the valve spring when the spring force is being checked. Check service information for the exact procedure to follow for the engine being checked. A valve spring scale is used to measure the valve spring force at a specific height measurement. ● **SEE FIGURE 14–17.**

Another type uses a torque wrench on a lever system to measure the valve spring force. Valve springs are checked for the following:

1. Free height (or length) without being compressed, should be within 1/16 (0.06) inch of specifications.

2. Pressure with valve closed and height as per specifications

3. Pressure with valve open and height as per specifications

Most specifications allow for variations of plus or minus 10% from the published figures.

VALVE KEEPERS AND ROTATORS

VALVE KEEPERS

Valve keepers (locks) are used on the end of the valve stem to retain the spring. The inside surfaces of the keeper use a variety of grooves or beads. The design depends on the holding requirements. The outside of the keeper fits into a cone-shaped seat in the center of the valve spring retainer. ● **SEE FIGURE 14–18.**

FIGURE 14–17 One popular type of valve spring tester used to measure the compressed force of valve springs. Specifications usually include (1) free height (height without being compressed), (2) pressure at installed height with the valve closed, and (3) pressure with the valve open to the height specified.

VALVE ROTATORS

Some valve spring retainers have built-in devices called valve rotators. They cause the valve to rotate in a controlled manner as it is opened. The purposes and functions of valve rotators include the following:

- Help prevent carbon buildup from forming by providing a "wiping" action of the valve face
- Reduce hot spots on the valves by constantly turning them
- Help to even out the wear on the valve face and seat
- Improve valve guide lubrication
- The two types of valve rotators are free and positive.
- **Free rotators** simply take the pressure off the valve to allow engine vibration to rotate the valve. ● SEE FIGURE 14–19.
- **Positive rotators** use the opening of the valve to force the valve to rotate. One type of positive rotator uses small steel balls and slight ramps. Each ball moves down its ramp to turn the rotator sections as the valve opens. A second type uses a coil spring. The spring lies down as the valve opens. This action turns the rotator body in

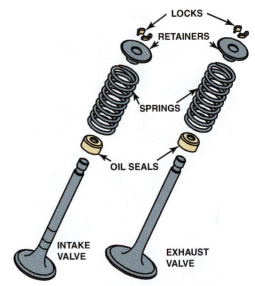

FIGURE 14–18 Valve keepers (also called locks) are tapered so they wedge into a tapered hole in the retainer.

FIGURE 14–19 Notice that there is no gap between the two keepers (ends butted together). As a result, the valve is free to rotate because the retainer applies a force, holding the keepers in place but not tight against the stem of the valve. Most engines, however, do not use free rotators and, therefore, have a gap between the keepers.

relation to the collar. Valve rotators are only used when it is desirable to increase the valve service life, because rotors cost more than plain retainers. ● SEE FIGURE 14–20.

VALVE RECONDITIONING PROCEDURE

After proper cleaning, inspection, and measurement procedures have been completed, valve reconditioning, usually called a "valve job," can be performed using the following sequence.

BALL-TYPE

SPRING-TYPE

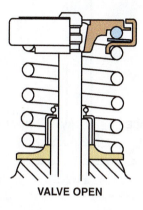
VALVE OPEN

BALL-TYPE

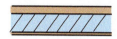
SPRING-TYPE

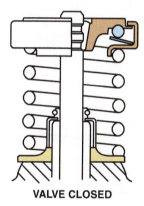
VALVE CLOSED

FIGURE 14–20 Type of valve rotator operation. Ball-type operation is on the left and spring-type operation is on the right.

STEP 1 The valve stem is lightly ground and chamfered. This step helps to ensure that the valve will rest in the collet (holder of the valve stem during valve grinding) of the valve grinder correctly. This process is often called **truing** the valve tip.

STEP 2 The face of the valve is ground to the proper angle using a valve grinder.

STEP 3 The valve seat is ground in the head. (The seat must be matched to the valve that will be used in that position.)

STEP 4 Valve spring installed height and valve stem height are checked and corrected as necessary.

STEP 5 After a thorough cleaning, the cylinder head should be assembled with new valve stem seals installed.

VALVE FACE GRINDING

PURPOSE AND FUNCTION   Each valve grinder operates somewhat differently. The operation manual that comes with the grinder should be followed for lubrication, adjustment, and specific operating procedures. The general procedures given in the following paragraphs apply to all valve resurfacer equipment. Set the grinder head at the **valve face angle** as specified by the vehicle manufacturer.

CAUTION: Safety glasses should *always* be worn for valve and seat reconditioning work. During grinding operations, fine hot chips fly from the grinding stones.

NOTE: Some valve grinders use the end of the valve to center the valve while grinding. If the tip of the valve is not square with the stem, the face of the valve may be ground improperly.

The valve stem is clamped in the work head as close to the fillet under the valve head as possible to prevent vibrations. The work head motor is turned on to rotate the valve. The wheel head motor is turned on to rotate the grinding wheel. The coolant flow is adjusted to flush the material away, but not so much that it splashes.

For best results perform the following:

- The rotating grinding wheel is fed slowly to the rotating valve face.

- Light grinding is done as the valve is moved back and forth across the grinding wheel face.

- Do not feed the valve into the grinding stone more than 0.001 to 0.002 inch at one time.

- The valve is never moved off the edge of the grinding wheel. It is ground only enough to clean the face.
  ● **SEE FIGURE 14–21.**

MARGIN   The margin is the distance between the head of the valve and the seat of the value. This distance should be 0.03 inch (0.8 mm). Some vehicle manufacturers specify a minimum margin of less than 0.03 inch for some engines, especially for intake valves. Always check service information for the exact specifications for the engine being serviced.
● **SEE FIGURE 14–22.**

NOTE: To help visualize a 0.03 inch margin, note that this dimension is equal to about 1/32 inch or the thickness of a U.S. dime.

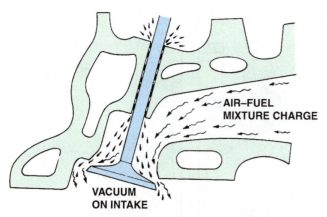

FIGURE 14–40 Engine vacuum can draw oil past the valve guides and into the combustion chamber. The use of valve stem seals limits the amount of oil that is drawn into the engine. If the seals or guides are defective, excessive blue (oil) smoke is most often observed during engine start-up.

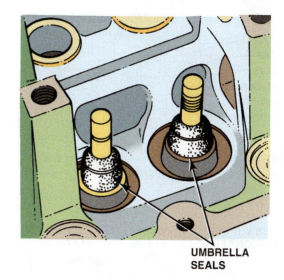

UMBRELLA SEALS

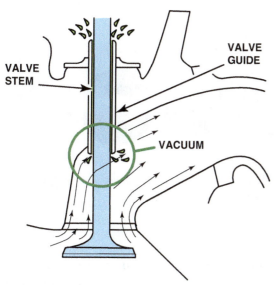

FIGURE 14–41 Engine oil can also be drawn past the exhaust valve guide because of a small vacuum created by the flow of exhaust gases. Any oil drawn past the guide would simply be forced out through the exhaust system and not enter the engine. Some engine manufacturers do not use valve stem seals on the exhaust valves.

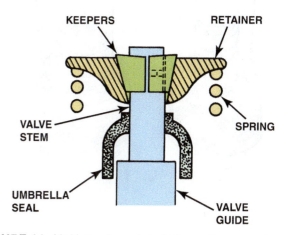

FIGURE 14–42 Umbrella seals install over the valve stems and cover the guide.

VALVE STEM SEALS

PURPOSE AND FUNCTION
Leakage past the valve guides is a major oil consumption problem in any overhead valve or overhead cam engine. A high vacuum exists in the intake port, as shown in ● FIGURE 14–40.

Most engine manufacturers use valve stem seals on the exhaust valve, because a weak vacuum in the exhaust port area can draw oil into the exhaust stream, as illustrated in ● FIGURE 14–41.

Valve stem seals are used on overhead valve engines to control the amount of oil used to lubricate the valve stem as it moves in the guide. The stem and guide will scuff if they do not have enough oil. Too much oil will cause excessive oil consumption and will cause heavy carbon deposits to build up on the spark plug nose and on the valves.

TYPES OF VALVE STEM SEALS
The types of valve stem seals include the following:

- The *umbrella valve stem seal* holds tightly on the valve stem and moves up and down with the valve. Any oil that spills off the rocker arms is deflected out over the valve guide, much as water is deflected over an umbrella. As a result, umbrella valve stem seals are often called *deflector valve stem seals*. ● SEE FIGURE 14–42.

- The *O-ring valve stem seal* used on Chevrolet engines keeps oil from leaking between the valve stem and valve

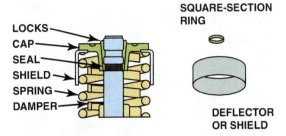

FIGURE 14–43 A small square cut O-ring is installed under the retainer in a groove in the valve under the groove(s) used for the keepers (locks).

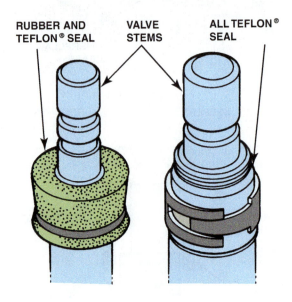

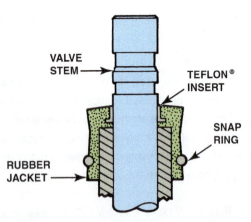

FIGURE 14–44 Positive valve stem seals are the most effective type because they remain stationary on the valve guide and wipe the oil from the stem as the valve moves up and down.

spring retainer. The oil is deflected over the retainer and shield. The assembly controls oil like an umbrella-type oil seal. Both types of valve stem seals allow only the correct amount of oil to reach the valve guide to lubricate the valve stem. The rest of the oil flows back to the oil pan. ● **SEE FIGURE 14–43.**

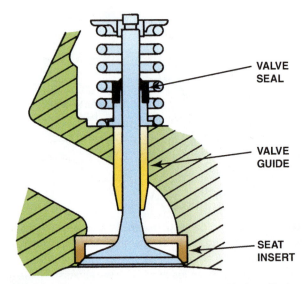

FIGURE 14–45 The positive valve stem seal is installed on the valve guide.

FIGURE 14–46 An assortment of shapes, colors, and materials of positive valve stem seals.

■ *Positive valve stem seals* hold tightly around the valve guide, and the valve stem moves through the seal. The Teflon® wiping ring wipes the excess oil from the valve stem. ● **SEE FIGURES 14–44 and 14–45.**

VALVE SEAL MATERIALS
Valve stem seals are made from many different types of materials. They may be made from nylon or teflon, but most valve stem seals are made from synthetic rubber. Three types of synthetic rubbers are in common use.

■ Nitrile (Nitril)
■ Polyacrylate
■ Viton

Nitrile is the oldest valve stem seal material. It has a low cost and a low useful temperature. Engine temperatures have increased with increased emission controls and improved

Purchase Engine Parts from a Known Manufacturer

It is interesting to note that an automotive service technician cannot tell the difference between these synthetic rubber valve stem seals if they have come out of the same mold for the same engine. Often suppliers that package gasket sets for sale at a low price will include low-temperature nitrile, even when the engine needs higher-temperature polyacrylate. The best chances of getting the correct valve stem seal material for an engine is to purchase gaskets and seals packaged by a major brand gasket company.

Check Before Bolting It On

Using new assembled cylinder heads, whether aluminum or cast iron, is a popular engine buildup option. However, experience has shown that metal shavings and casting sand are often found inside the passages.

Before bolting on these "ready to install" heads, disassemble them and clean all passages. Often machine shavings are found under the valves. If this debris were to get into the engine, the results would be extreme wear or damage to the pistons, rings, block, and bearings. This cleaning may take several hours, but how much is your engine worth?

efficiencies, which made it necessary to use premium polyacrylate, even with its higher cost. In many cases, it is being retrofit to the older engines because it will last much longer than nitrile. Diesel engines and engines used for racing, heavy trucks, and trailer towing, along with turbocharging, operate at still higher temperatures. These engines may require expensive Viton valve stem seals that operate at higher temperatures. ● **SEE FIGURE 14–46.**

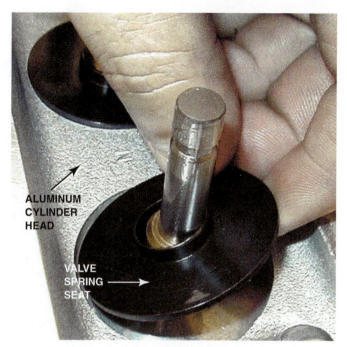

FIGURE 14–47 A metal valve spring seat must be used between the valve spring and the aluminum cylinder head. Some aluminum cylinder heads use a combination valve spring seat and valve stem seal.

INSTALLING THE VALVES

PROCEDURE Assembling a cylinder head includes the following steps.

STEP 1 Clean the reconditioned cylinder head thoroughly with soap and water to wash away any remaining grit and metal shavings from the valve grinding operation.

STEP 2 Valves are assembled in the head, one at a time. The valve guide and stem are given a liberal coating of engine oil, and the valve is installed in its guide.

STEP 3 Umbrella or positive valve stem seals are installed. Push umbrella seals down until they touch the valve guide. Use a plastic sleeve over the tip of the valve when installing positive seals to prevent damage to the seal lip. Make sure that the positive seal is fully seated on the valve guide and that it is square.

STEP 4 Install the valve spring seat if assembling an aluminum head. Hold the valve against the valve seat as the valve spring, valve seal, and retainer are placed over the valve stem. One end of the valve spring compressor pushes on the retainer to compress the spring. ● **SEE FIGURES 14–47 AND 14–48.**

STEP 5 The O-ring type of valve stem seal, if used, is installed in the lower groove. The valve keepers are installed while the valve spring is compressed. Using grease helps to keep them attached to the valve stem as the valve spring compressor is released.

STEP 6 Release the valve spring compressor slowly and carefully while making sure that the valve keepers seat properly between the valve stem grooves and the retainer.

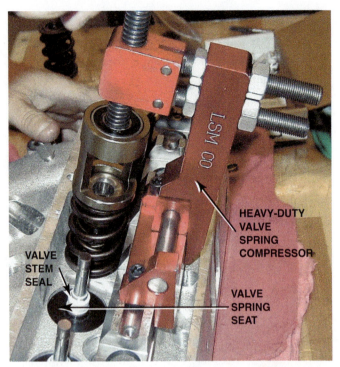

FIGURE 14-48 Assembling a race engine using a heavy-duty valve spring compressor.

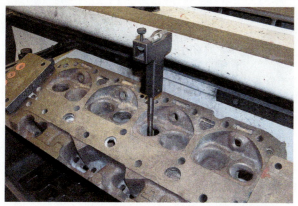

1 After the valve guide has been replaced or checked for being within specification, insert a pilot into the valve guide.

2 Level the bubble on the pilot by moving the cylinder head, which is clamped to a seat/guide machine.

3 Select the proper seat insert for the application. Consult guide manufacturer's literature for recommendations.

4 Select the correct cutter and check that the cutting bits are sharp.

5 Carefully measure the exact outside diameter (O.D.) of the valve seat.

6 Adjust the diameter of the cutter bit to achieve the specified interference fit for the valve seat.

CONTINUED ▶

7 Install the pilot into the valve guide to support the seat cutter.

8 Install the seat cutter onto the pilot.

9 Adjust the depth of cut, using the new valve seat to set it to the same depth as the thickness of the seat.

10 With the cylinder head still firmly attached to the seat and guide machine, start the cutter motor and cut the head until it reaches the stop.

11 The finish cut valve seat pocket. Be sure to use a vacuum to remove all of the metal shavings from the cutting operation.

12 Place the chilled valve seat over the pilot being sure that the chamfer is facing toward the head as shown. (Gloves should be worn.)

13 Install the correct size driver onto the valve seat.

14 Using the air hammer or press, press the valve seat into the valve pocket.

15 A new valve seat is now ready to be machined or cut.

SUMMARY

1. The exhaust valve is about 85% of the size of the intake valve.

2. Valve springs should be tested for squareness and proper spring force.

3. Two designs of valve rotators are "free" and "positive."

4. Valve grinding should start with truing the valve tip; then the face should be refinished. A pilot is placed into the valve guide to position the stone or cutter correctly for resurfacing the valve seat.

5. The installed height should be checked and corrected with valve spring inserts, if needed.

6. Valve stem height should be checked and the top of the valve ground, if necessary.

7. After a thorough cleaning, the cylinder head should be assembled using new valve stem seals.

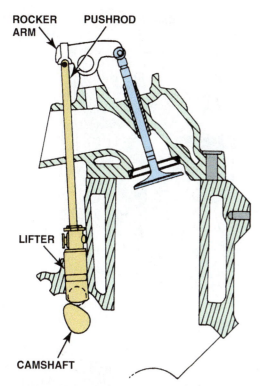

FIGURE 15–27 Overhead valve engines are also known as pushrod engines because of the long pushrod that extends from the lifter to the rocker arm.

FIGURE 15–28 When the timing chain broke, the valves stopped moving up and down but the pistons kept moving and hit the valves causing the pushrods to bend.

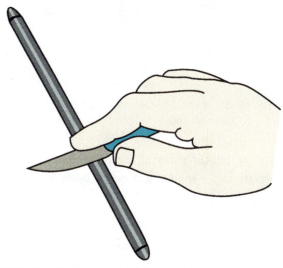

FIGURE 15–29 Hardened pushrods should be used in any engine that uses pushrod guides (plates). To determine if the pushrod is hardened, simply try to scratch the side of the pushrod with a pocketknife.

 TECH TIP

Hollow Pushrod Dirt

Many engine rebuilders and remanufacturers do not reuse old hollow pushrods. Dirt, carbon, and other debris are difficult to thoroughly clean from inside a hollow pushrod. When an engine is run with used pushrods, the trapped particles can be dislodged and ruin new bearings and other new engine parts. Therefore, for best results, consider purchasing new hollow pushrods instead of trying to clean and reuse the originals.

TECH TIP

The Scratch Test

All pushrods used with guide plates *must* be hardened on the sides and on the tips. To easily determine if a pushrod is hardened, simply use a sharp pocketknife to scrape the wall of the pushrod. A heat-treated pushrod will not scratch. ● **SEE FIGURE 15–29.**

PUSHRODS

PURPOSE AND FUNCTION   Pushrods transfer the lifting motion of the valve train from the cam lobe and lifters to the rocker arms. ● **SEE FIGURE 15–27.**

TYPES OF PUSHRODS   Pushrods are designed to be as light as possible and still maintain their strength. They may be either solid or hollow. If they are to be used as passages for oil to lubricate rocker arms, they *must* be hollow. Pushrods use a convex ball on the lower end that seats in the lifter. The rocker arm end is also a convex ball, unless there is an adjustment screw in the pushrod end of the rocker arm. In this case, the rocker arm end of the pushrod has a concave socket. It mates with the convex ball on the adjustment screw in the rocker arm.

All pushrods should be rolled on a flat surface to check for straightness. ● **SEE FIGURE 15–28.**

The tolerance in the valve train allows for some machining of engine parts without the need to change pushrod length.

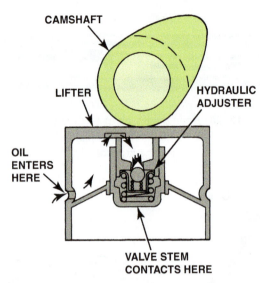

FIGURE 15–30 Hydraulic lifters may be built into bucket-type lifters on some overhead camshaft engines.

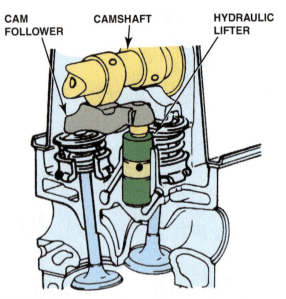

FIGURE 15–31 The use of cam followers allows the use of hydraulic lifters with an overhead camshaft design.

However, if one or more of the following changes have been made to an engine, a different pushrod length may be necessary.

- Block deck height machined
- Cylinder head deck height machined
- Camshaft base circle size reduced
- Valve length increased
- Lifter design changed

OVERHEAD CAMSHAFT VALVE TRAINS

Overhead camshaft engines use several different types of valve opening designs.

1. One type opens the valves directly with a **bucket.** ● **SEE FIGURE 15–30.**

2. The second type uses a **cam follower,** also called a **finger follower,** that provides an opening ratio similar to that of a rocker arm. Finger followers open the valves by approximately 1 1/2 times the cam lift. The pivot point of the finger follower may have a mechanical adjustment or it may have an automatic hydraulic adjustment. ● **SEE FIGURE 15–31.**

3. A third type moves the rocker arm directly through a hydraulic lifter.

4. In the fourth design, some newer engines have the hydraulic adjustment in the rocker arm and are commonly called **hydraulic lash adjusters (HLA).** ● **SEE FIGURE 15–32.**

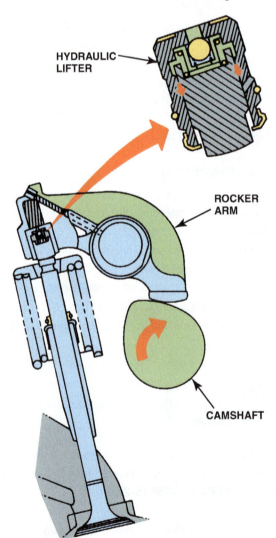

FIGURE 15–32 Hydraulic lash adjusters (HLA) are built into the rocker arm on some OHC engines. Sometimes hydraulic lash adjusters may not bleed down properly if the wrong viscosity (SAE rating) oil is used.

CAMSHAFT SPECIFICATIONS

DURATION Camshaft duration is the number of degrees of *crankshaft* (not camshaft) rotation for which a valve is lifted off the seat.

The specification for duration can be expressed by several different methods, which must be considered when comparing one cam with another. The three most commonly used methods include:

1. **Duration of valve opening at zero lash (clearance).** If a hydraulic lifter is used, the lash is zero. If a solid lifter is used, this method of expression refers to the duration of the opening of the valve after the specified clearance (lash) between the rocker arm and the valve stem tip has been closed.

2. **Duration at 0.05 inch lifter (tappet) lift.** Because this specification method eliminates all valve lash clearances and compensates for lifter (tappet) styles, it is the preferred method to use when comparing one camshaft with another. Another method used to specify duration of some factory camshafts is to specify crankshaft duration at 0.01 inch lifter lift. The important point to remember is that the technician must be sure to use equivalent specification methods when comparing or selecting camshafts.

   NOTE: Fractions of a degree are commonly expressed in units called minutes ('). Sixty (60) minutes equal one degree (1°). For example, 45' = 3/4 degree, 30' = 1/2 degree, and 15' = 1/4 degree.

3. **SAE camshaft specifications.** SAE's recommended practice is to measure all valve events at 0.006 inch (0.15 mm) valve lift. This method differs from the usual method used by vehicle or camshaft manufacturers. Whenever comparing valve timing events, be certain that the exact same methods are used on all camshafts being compared.

VALVE OVERLAP Another camshaft specification is the number of degrees of overlap. **Valve (camshaft) overlap** is the number of degrees of crankshaft rotation during which both intake and exhaust valves are open. In other words, overlap occurs at the beginning of the intake stroke and at the end of the exhaust stoke. All camshafts provide for some overlap to improve engine performance and efficiency, especially at higher engine speeds.

- A lower amount of overlap results in smoother idle and low-engine speed operation, but it also means that a lower amount of power is available at higher engine speeds.

- A greater valve overlap causes rougher engine idle, with decreased power at low speeds, but it also means that high-speed power is improved.

Example 1: A camshaft with 50 degrees (or less) of overlap may be used in an engine in which low-speed torque and smooth idle qualities are desired. Engines used with overdrive automatic transmissions benefit from the low-speed torque and fuel economy benefits of a small-overlap cam.

Example 2: A camshaft with 100 degrees of overlap is more suitable for use with a manual transmission, with which high-RPM power is desired. An engine equipped with a camshaft with over 100 degrees of overlap tends to idle roughly and exhibit poorer low-engine speed response and lowered fuel economy. ● SEE FIGURE 15–33.

CALCULATING VALVE OVERLAP An engine features a camshaft where the intake valve starts to open at 19 degrees before top dead center (BTDC) and the exhaust valve is open until 22 degrees after top dead center (ATDC).

To determine overlap, total the number of degrees for which the intake valve is open BTDC (19 degrees) and the number of degrees for which the exhaust valve is open ATDC (22 degrees) are added:

$$\text{Valve overlap} = 19 + 22 = 41 \text{ degrees}$$

LOBE CENTERS Another camshaft specification that creates some confusion is the angle of the centerlines of the intake and exhaust lobes. This separation between the centerlines of the intake and exhaust lobes is called:

- **Lobe center**
- **Lobe separation**
- **Lobe displacement angle (LDA)**
- **Lobe spread**

The lob center's measurement is measured in degrees. ● SEE FIGURE 15–34.

Two camshafts with identical lift and duration can vary greatly in operation because of variation in the angle between the lobe centerlines.

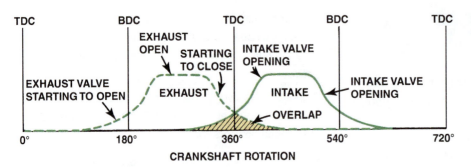

FIGURE 15–33 Graphic representation of a typical camshaft showing the relationship between the intake and exhaust valves. The shaded area represents the overlap period of 100 degrees.

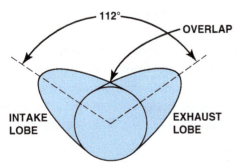

FIGURE 15–34 As the lobe center angle decreases, the overlap increases, with no other changes in the lobe profile lift and duration.

1. The smaller the angle between the lobe centerlines, the greater the amount of overlap. For example, 108 degrees is a narrower lobe center angle.

2. The larger the angle between the lobe centerlines, the less the amount of overlap. For example, 114 degrees is a wider lobe center angle.

NOTE: Some engines that are equipped with dual overhead camshafts and four valves per cylinder use a different camshaft profile for each of the intake and exhaust valves. For example, one intake valve for each cylinder could have a cam profile designed for maximum low-speed torque. The other intake valve for each cylinder could be designed for higher engine speed power. This results in an engine that is able to produce a high torque over a broad engine speed range.

To find the degree of separation between intake and exhaust lobes of a cam, use the following formula:

$$\frac{(\text{Intake duration} + \text{Exhaust duration})}{4} - \frac{\text{Overlap}}{2}$$
$$= \text{Number of degrees of separation}$$

● **SEE FIGURE 15–35.**

The lobe separation angle can be determined by transferring the intake and exhaust duration and overlap into the formula, as follows:

Intake duration = 15 degrees + 180 degrees + 59 degrees = 254 degrees

Exhaust duration = 59 degrees + 180 degrees + 15 degrees = 254 degrees

Overlap = 15 degrees + 15 degrees = 30 degrees

The lobe separation angle can be calculated by taking the center of the intake lobe use: Intake valve duration plus exhaust valve duration divided by 4 minus the overlap divided by 2.

$$\frac{(254 + 254)}{4} - \frac{30}{2} = \frac{508}{4} - \frac{30}{2}$$
$$= 127 - 15 = 112 \text{ degrees (lobe separation angle)}$$

● **SEE CHART 15–1** for what effect a change in lobe separation angle (LSA) has on engine operation.

CAM TIMING SPECIFICATIONS Cam timing specifications are stated in terms of the angle of the crankshaft in relation to top dead center (TDC) or bottom dead center (BDC) when the valves open and close.

■ **Intake valve.** The intake valves should open slightly before the piston reaches TDC and starts down on the intake stroke. This ensures that the valve is fully open when the piston travels downward on the intake stroke. The flow through a partially open valve (especially a valve ground at 45 degrees instead of 30 degrees) is greatly reduced as compared with that when the valve is in its fully open position. The intake valve closes after the piston reaches BDC because the air-fuel mixture has inertia, or the tendency of matter to remain in motion. Even after the piston stops traveling downward on the intake stroke and starts upward on the compression stroke, the inertia of the air-fuel mixture can still be used to

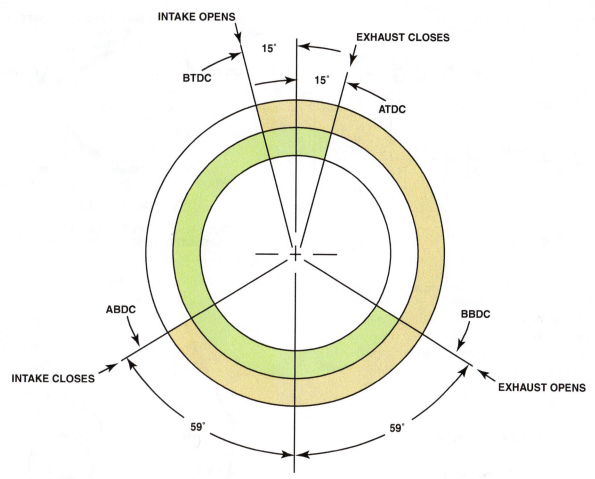

FIGURE 15–35 Typical cam timing diagram.

LOBE SEPARATION ANGLE (LSA)	NARROWER	WIDER
Valve overlap	Greater	Less
Intake valve opening	Sooner	Later
Intake valve closing	Sooner	Later
Exhaust valve opening	Later	Sooner
Exhaust valve closing	Later	Sooner
Idle quality	Worst	Better

CHART 15–1

Changing the lobe separation angle has major effect on engine operation.

draw in additional charge. Typical intake valve specifications are to open at 19 degrees before top dead center (BTDC) and close at 46 degrees after bottom dead center (ABDC).

- **Exhaust valve.** The exhaust valve opens while the piston is traveling down on the power stroke, before the piston starts up on the exhaust stroke. Opening the exhaust

valve before the piston starts up on the exhaust stroke ensures that the combustion pressure is released and the exhaust valve is mostly open when the piston starts up. The exhaust valve does not close until after the piston has traveled past TDC and is starting down on the intake stroke. Because of inertia of the exhaust, some of the burned gases continue to flow out the exhaust valve after the piston is past TDC. This can leave a partial vacuum in the combustion chamber to start pulling in the fresh charge. This partial vacuum is called **scavenging** and helps bring in a fresh air-fuel charge into the cylinders. Typical exhaust valve specifications are to open at 49 degrees before bottom dead center (BBDC) and close at 22 degrees after top dead center (ATDC).

CAM TIMING CHART During the four strokes of a four-stroke cycle gasoline engine, the crankshaft revolves 720 degrees (it makes two complete revolutions [2 × 360 = 720 degrees]). Camshaft specifications are given in crankshaft degrees. In the example in ● **FIGURE 15–36,** the intake valve

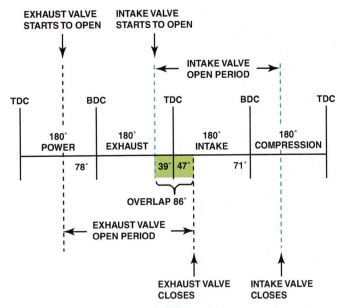

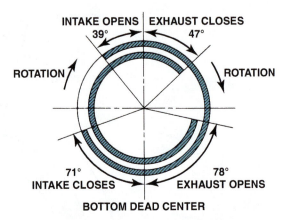

THIS VALVE TIMING DIAGRAM SHOWS TWO
REVOLUTIONS (720°) OF THE CRANKSHAFT

FIGURE 15–37 Typical camshaft valve timing diagram with the same specifications as those shown in Figure 15–36.

FIGURE 15–36 Typical high-performance camshaft specifications on a straight-line graph. Intake valve duration = 39 + 180 + 71 = 290 degrees. Exhaust valve duration = 7 + 180 + 47 = 234 degrees. Because intake and exhaust valve specifications are different, the camshaft grind is called asymmetrical.

starts to open at 39 degrees BTDC, remains open through the entire 180 degrees of the intake stroke, and does not close until 71 degrees ATDC.

Therefore, the duration of the intake valve is 39 degrees + 180 degrees + 71 degrees, or 290 degrees.

The exhaust valve of the example camshaft opens at 78 degrees BBDC and closes at 47 degrees ATDC. When the exhaust valve specifications are added to the intake valve specifications in the diagram, the overlap period is easily observed. The overlap in the example is 39 degrees + 47 degrees, or 86 degrees. The duration of the exhaust valve opening is 78 degrees + 180 degrees + 47 degrees, or 305 degrees. Because the specifications of this camshaft indicate close to and over 300 degrees of duration, this camshaft should only be used where power is more important than fuel economy.

The usual method of drawing a camshaft timing diagram is in a circle illustrating two revolutions (720 degrees) of the crankshaft. ● **SEE FIGURE 15–37** for an example of a typical camshaft timing diagram for a camshaft with the same specifications as the one illustrated in Figure 15–36.

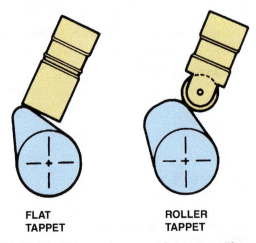

FIGURE 15–38 Older engines used flat-bottom lifters, whereas all engines since the 1990s use roller lifters.

valve train. Older-style lifters have a relatively flat surface that slides on the cam.

Most lifters, however, are designed with a roller to follow the cam contour. Roller lifters are used primarily in production engines to reduce valve train friction (by up to 8%). This friction reduction can increase fuel economy and help to offset the greater manufacturing cost. ● **SEE FIGURE 15–38.**

All roller lifters must use a retainer or a guide plate to prevent lifter rotation. The retainer ensures that the roller is kept in line with the cam. ● **SEE FIGURE 15–39.**

VALVE LASH Valve train clearance is also called **valve lash,** which is needed to help compensate for thermal expansion and wear. Valve train clearance must not be excessive, or it will cause noise or result in premature failure. Two methods are commonly used to make the necessary valve clearance adjustments.

LIFTERS OR TAPPETS

PURPOSE AND FUNCTION Valve lifters or tappets follow the contour or shape of the camshaft lobe. This arrangement changes the rotary cam motion to a reciprocating motion in the

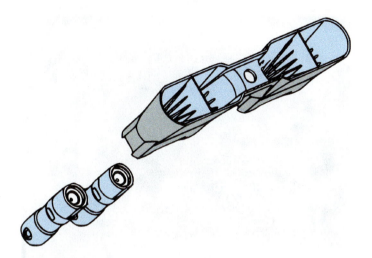

FIGURE 15–39 The lifter retainer keeps the roller lifters from rotating. (*Courtesy of General Motors*)

- One involves a **solid valve lifter,** which can be adjusted mechanically at the rocker arm or by changing shims on certain overhead camshaft engines.

- The other involves a lifter with an automatic hydraulic adjustment built into the lifter body, called a **hydraulic valve lifter.**

SOLID LIFTERS

Overhead valve engines with mechanical lifters have an adjustment screw at the pushrod end of the rocker arm or an adjustment nut at the ball pivot. Adjustable pushrods are available for specific applications.

Valve trains using solid lifters must run with some clearance to ensure positive valve closure, regardless of the engine temperature. This clearance is matched by a gradual rise in the cam contour, called a **ramp.** (Hydraulic lifter camshafts do not have this ramp.) The ramp will take up the clearance before the valve begins to open. The camshaft lobe also has a closing ramp to ensure quiet operation.

A lifter is solid in the sense that it transfers motion directly from the cam to the pushrod or valve. Its physical construction is that of a lightweight cylinder, either hollow or with a small-diameter center section and full-diameter ends. In some types that transfer oil through the pushrod, the external appearance is the same as for hydraulic lifters. ● **SEE FIGURE 15–40.**

HYDRAULIC LIFTERS

A hydraulic lifter consists primarily of a hollow cylinder body enclosing a closely fit hollow plunger, a check valve, and a pushrod cup. Lifters that feed oil up through the pushrod have a metering disc or restrictor valve located under the pushrod cup. Engine oil under pressure is fed through an engine passage to the exterior lifter body. An undercut portion allows the oil under pressure to surround

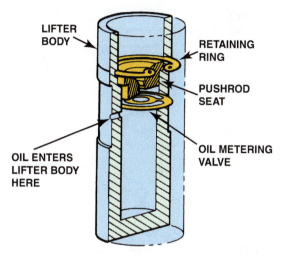

FIGURE 15–40 A cutaway of a flat-bottom solid lifter. Because this type of lifter contains a retaining ring and oil holes, it is sometimes confused with a hydraulic lifter that also contains additional parts. The holes in this lifter are designed to supply oil to the rocker arms through a hollow pushrod.

the lifter body. Oil under pressure goes through holes in the undercut section into the center of the plunger. From there, it goes down through the check valve to a clearance space between the bottom of the plunger and the interior bottom of the lifter body. It fills this space with oil at engine pressure. Slight leakage allowance is designed into the lifter so that the air can bleed out and the lifter can leak down if it should become overfilled.

The pushrod fits into a cup in the top, open end of the lifter plunger. Holes in the pushrod cup, pushrod end, and hollow pushrod allow oil to transfer from the lifter piston center, past a metering disc or restrictor valve, and up through the pushrod to the rocker arm. Oil leaving the rocker arm lubricates the rocker arm assembly.

As the cam starts to push the lifter against the valve train, the oil below the lifter plunger is squeezed and tries to return to the lifter plunger center. A lifter check valve, either ball or disc type, traps the oil below the lifter plunger. This hydraulically locks the operating length of the lifter. The hydraulic lifter then opens the engine valve as would a solid lifter. When the lifter returns to the base circle of the cam, engine oil pressure again works to replace any oil that may have leaked out of the lifter. ● **SEE FIGURE 15–41.**

The job of the hydraulic lifter is to take up all clearance in the valve train. Occasionally, engines are run at excessive speeds. This tends to throw the valve open, causing **valve float.** During valve float, clearance exists in the valve train. The hydraulic lifter will take up this clearance as it is designed to do. When this occurs, it will keep the valve from closing on the seat, a process called **pump-up.** Pump-up will not occur when the engine is operated in the speed range for which it is designed.

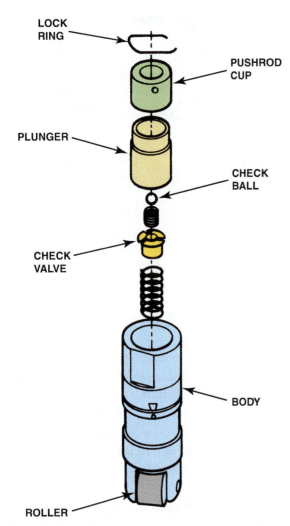

LOCK RING

PUSHROD CUP

PLUNGER

CHECK BALL

CHECK VALVE

BODY

ROLLER

FIGURE 15–41 An exploded view of a hydraulic roller lifter.

PUSHROD PUNCHED THROUGH ROCKER ARM

FIGURE 15–42 The cause of a misfire diagnostic trouble code was discovered to be a pushrod that had worn through the rocker arm on a General Motors 3.1 liter V-6 engine.

an engine equipped with flat-bottom lifters should be operated at a fast idle of about 2500 RPM during the first 10 minutes of engine operation. The high idle speed helps ensure that there is enough splash oil to properly lubricate and break in a new camshaft and lifters.

VALVE TRAIN LUBRICATION

The lifters in an overhead valve (OHV) engine are lubricated through oil passages drilled through the block. The engine oil then flows through the lifter, and up through the hollow pushrod where the oil flows to lubricate and cool the rocker arm, valve, and valve spring.

CAMSHAFT LUBRICATION The bearing surfaces of the camshaft are lubricated by oil under pressure from the engine oil pump. The camshaft lobes in overhead valve (OHV) engines are lubricated by splash oil thrown up by the movement of the crankshaft counterweights and connecting rods. At low engine speed there is less splash lubrication than occurs at higher engine speeds. This is the major reason why

VALVE TRAIN PROBLEM DIAGNOSIS

SYMPTOMS A camshaft with a partially worn lobe is often difficult to diagnose. Sometimes a valve "tick, tick, tick" noise is heard if the cam lobe is worn. The ticking noise can be intermittent, which makes it harder to determine the cause. If the engine has an overhead camshaft (OHC), it is usually relatively easy to remove the cam cover and make a visual inspection of all cam lobes and the rest of the valve train. In an overhead valve (OHV) engine, the camshaft is in the block, where easy visual inspection is not possible. However, it always pays to perform a visual inspection. ● **SEE FIGURE 15–42.**

VALVE NOISE DIAGNOSIS Valve lifters are often noisy, especially at engine start-up. When the engine is off, some valves are open. The valve spring pressure forces the inner plunger to leak down (oil is forced out of the lifter). Therefore, many vehicle manufacturers consider valve ticking at one-half engine speed after start-up to be normal, especially if the

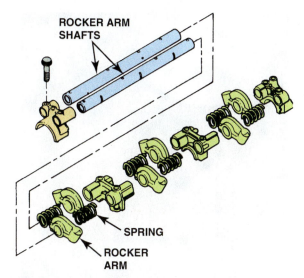

ROCKER ARM SHAFTS

SPRING

ROCKER ARM

FIGURE 15–43 Shaft-mounted rocker arms are held in position by an assortment of springs, spacers, and washers, which should be removed so that the entire shaft can be inspected for wear.

engine is quiet after 10 to 30 seconds. Be sure that the engine is equipped with the correct oil filter, and that the filter has an internal check valve. If in doubt, use an original equipment oil filter. If all of the valves are noisy, check the oil level. If low, the oil may have been **aerated** (air mixed with the oil), which would prevent proper operation of the hydraulic lifter. Aeration can be caused by:

- Low oil pressure, which can also cause all valves to be noisy

- Too high oil level, which can also cause noisy valve lifters (The crankshaft counterweights create foam as they rotate through the oil. This foam can travel through the oiling systems to the lifters. The foam in the lifters prevents normal operation and allows the valves to make noise.)

If the valves are abnormally noisy, remove the valve cover and use a stethoscope to listen or apply pressure to the rocker arms to determine which valves or valve train parts may be causing the noise. Check for all of the following items.

- Valve lash too loose

- Worn camshaft lobe

- Dirty, stuck, or worn lifters

- Worn rocker arm (if the vehicle is so equipped)

 **TECH TIP**

The Rotating Pushrod Test

To quickly and easily test whether the camshaft is okay, observe if the pushrods are rotating when the engine is running. This test will work on any overhead valve pushrod engine that uses flat-bottom lifters. Due to the slight angle on the cam lobe and lifter offset, the lifter (and pushrod) should rotate whenever the engine is running. To check, simply remove the rocker arm cover and observe the pushrods when the engine is running. If one or more pushrods are *not* rotating, this camshaft and/or the lifter for that particular valve is worn and needs to be replaced.

REAL WORLD FIX

The Noisy Camshaft

The owner of an overhead cam 4-cylinder engine complained of a noisy engine. After taking the vehicle to several technicians and getting high estimates to replace the camshaft and followers, the owner tried to find a less expensive solution. Finally, another technician replaced the serpentine drive belt on the front of the engine and "cured" the "camshaft" noise for a fraction of the previous estimates.

Remember, accessory drive belts can often make noises similar to valve or bad bearing types of noises. Many engines have been disassembled and/or overhauled because of a noise that was later determined to be from one of the following:

- Loose or defective accessory drive belt(s)
- Loose torque converter-to-flex plate (drive plate) bolts (nuts)
- Defective mechanical fuel pump (if equipped)

- Worn rocker arm shaft (**SEE FIGURE 15–43.**)

- Worn or bent pushrods (if the vehicle is so equipped)

- Broken or weak valve springs

- Sticking or warped valves

Any of the above can cause the engine to idle roughly, misfire, or even backfire during acceleration.

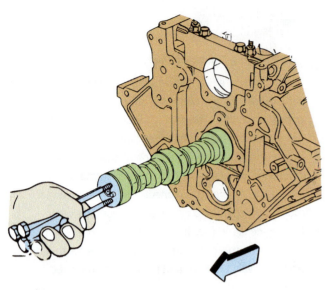

FIGURE 15–44 Long bolts threaded into the camshaft make removal easier. (*Courtesy of General Motors*)

CAMSHAFT REMOVAL

If the engine is of an overhead valve (OHV) design, the camshaft is usually located in the block above the crankshaft. The timing chain and gears (if the vehicle is so equipped) should be removed after the timing chain (gear) cover is removed. Loosen the rocker arms (or rocker arm shaft) and remove the pushrods. Then remove the valve lifters before removing the camshaft from the block. **SEE FIGURE 15–44.**

NOTE: Be sure to keep the pushrods and rocker arms together if they are to be reused.

MEASURING CAMSHAFTS

TOTAL INDICATOR RUNOUT All camshafts should be checked for straightness by placing them on V-blocks and measuring the cam bearings for runout by using a dial

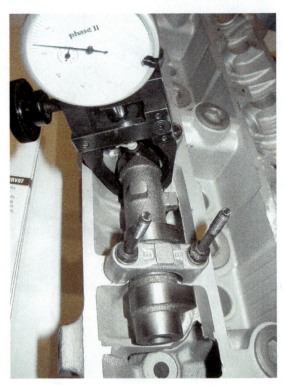

FIGURE 15–45 A dial indicator being used to measure cam lobe height.

indicator. The maximum **total indicator runout (TIR)** (also called total indicated runout) should be less than 0.002 inch (0.05 mm).

CAM LOBE HEIGHT Sometimes the camshaft lobe height needs to be measured to verify the exact camshaft that is installed in the engine. This can be done by attaching a dial indicator and then slowly rotating the engine while observing the indicator and comparing the measurement to factory specifications. ● **SEE FIGURE 15–45.**

SUMMARY

1. The camshaft rotates at one-half the crankshaft speed.
2. The pushrods will keep rotating while the engine is running if the camshaft and lifters are okay.
3. When the camshaft is placed in the engine block above the crankshaft, it is a cam-in-block design, also called an overhead valve engine.
4. An overhead cam design places the camshaft in the cylinder head, above or near the valves. There may be one

camshaft (single overhead cam) or two cams; one for the intake valves and one for the exhaust valves (double overhead cam).

5. Camshafts are driven by timing chains, timing belts, or timing gears.
6. In many engines, camshaft lobe lift is transferred to the tip of the valve stem to open the valve by the use of a rocker arm, bucket, or follower.

7. Valve lifters may be solid, which require adjustment, or hydraulically self-adjusting.

8. On a cam-in-block engine pushrods transfer camshaft lobe movement upward from the camshaft to the rocker arm.

9. Camshaft duration is the number of degrees of crankshaft rotation for which the valve is lifted off the seat.

10. Valve lift is usually expressed in decimal inches and represents the distance that the valve is lifted off the valve seat.

11. Valve overlap is the number of crankshaft degrees for which both intake and exhaust valves are open at the same time.

REVIEW QUESTIONS

1. Explain why the lift and duration and lobe displacement angle (LDA) dimension of the camshaft determine the power characteristics of the engine.

2. List the terms that mean the same as lobe displacement angle (LDA).

3. Describe the operation of a hydraulic lifter.

CHAPTER QUIZ

1. The camshaft makes _____ for every revolution of the crankshaft.
   a. One-quarter revolution
   b. One-half revolution
   c. One revolution
   d. Two revolutions

2. Flat-bottom valve lifters rotate during operation because of the _____ of the camshaft.
   a. Taper of the lobe
   b. Thrust plate
   c. Chain tensioner
   d. Bearings

3. If lift and duration remain constant and the lobe center angle decreases, then _____.
   a. The valve overlap decreases
   b. The effective lift increases
   c. The effective duration increases
   d. The valve overlap increases

4. Which timing chain type is also called a "silent chain"?
   a. Roller
   b. Morse
   c. Flat link
   d. Both b and c

5. The camshaft may operate all of these EXCEPT _____.
   a. Water pump
   b. High pressure fuel pump
   c. Oil pump
   d. Valves

6. Many technicians always use new pushrods because _____.
   a. They are less expensive to buy than clean
   b. All of the dirt cannot be cleaned out from the hollow center
   c. They wear at both ends
   d. They shrink in length if removed from an engine

7. A DOHC V-6 has how many camshafts?
   a. 4
   b. 3
   c. 2
   d. 1

8. The intake valve opens at 39 degrees BTDC and closes at 71 degrees ABDC. The exhaust valve opens at 78 degrees BBDC and closes at 47 degrees ATDC. Which answer is correct?
   a. Intake valve duration is 110 degrees.
   b. Exhaust valve duration is 125 degrees.
   c. Overlap is 86 degrees.
   d. Both a and b

9. Hydraulic valve lifters can make a ticking noise when the engine is running if _____.
   a. The valve lash is too close
   b. The valve lash is too loose
   c. The lobe centerline is over 110 degrees
   d. Both a and c

10. Hydraulic lifters or hydraulic lash adjusters (HLA) may not bleed down properly and cause an engine miss if _____.
    a. The engine oil is 1 quart low
    b. The wrong API-rated engine oil is used
    c. The wrong SAE-rated engine oil is used
    d. Both a and b

chapter 16

VARIABLE VALVE TIMING SYSTEMS

LEARNING OBJECTIVES

After studying this chapter, the reader should be able to:

1. List the reasons for variable valve timing.
2. Discuss the various types of variable valve timing.
3. Explain how to diagnose variable valve timing faults.

This chapter will help you prepare for Engine Repair (A8) ASE certification test content area "A" (General Engine Diagnosis).

KEY TERMS

Active fuel management (AFM) 250
Cylinder cutoff system 250
Displacement on demand (DOD) 250
EVCP 245
Oil control valve (OCV) 243
PWM 246
Spline phaser 244
Vane phaser 244
Variable displacement system 250
VTEC 249
VVT 244

GM STC OBJECTIVES

GM Service Technical College topics covered in this chapter are:

1. Perform camshaft position actuator service and diagnosis.
2. Perform on-vehicle testing for an AFM concern.
3. Perform variable valve-timing diagnosis using on-vehicle testing.

CAMSHAFT POSITION CHART

DRIVING CONDITION	CHANGE IN CAMSHAFT POSITION	OBJECTIVE	RESULT
Idle	No change	Minimize valve overlap	Stabilize idle speed
Light engine load	Retard valve timing	Decrease valve overlap	Stable engine output
Medium engine load	Advance valve timing	Increase valve overlap	Better fuel economy with lower emissions
Low to medium RPM with heavy load	Advance valve timing	Advance intake valve closing	Improve low to midrange torque
High RPM with heavy load	Retard valve timing	Retard intake valve closing	Improve engine output

CHART 16–1

An overview of how variable valve timing is able to improve engine performance and reduce exhaust emissions.

PRINCIPLES OF VARIABLE VALVE TIMING

PURPOSE OF VARIABLE VALVE TIMING

Conventional camshafts are permanently synchronized to the crankshaft so that they operate the valves at a specific point in each combustion cycle. In an engine, the intake valve opens slightly before the piston reaches the top of the cylinder and closes about 60 degrees after the piston reaches the bottom of the stroke on every cycle, regardless of the engine speed or load.

Variable-cam timing allows the valves to be operated at different points in the combustion cycle, to improve performance.

There are three basic types of variable valve timing used on vehicles:

1. Exhaust camshaft variable action only on overhead camshaft engines, such as the inline 4.2-liter engine used in some General Motors vehicles.

2. Intake and exhaust camshaft variable action on both camshafts used in many General Motors engines.

3. Overhead valve, cam-in-block engines use variable valve timing by changing the relationship of the camshaft to the crankshaft. ● SEE CHART 16–1.

Variable camshaft timing is used on many engines including General Motors four, five, six, and 8 cylinder engines.

On a system that controls the intake camshaft only, the camshaft timing is advanced at low engine speed, closing the intake valves earlier to improve low RPM torque. At high engine speeds, the camshaft is retarded by using engine oil pressure against a helical gear to rotate the camshaft. When the camshaft is retarded, the intake valve closing is delayed, improving cylinder filling at higher engine speeds.

Variable cam timing can be used to control exhaust cam timing only. Engines that use this system, such as the 4.2 liter GM inline six-cylinder engines, can eliminate the exhaust gas recirculation (EGR) valve because the computer can close the exhaust valve sooner than normal, trapping some exhaust gases in the combustion chamber and therefore eliminating the need for an EGR valve. Some engines use variable camshaft timing on both intake and exhaust cylinder cams.

PARTS AND OPERATION

The camshaft position actuator **oil control valve (OCV)** directs oil from the oil feed in the head to the appropriate camshaft position actuator oil passages. There is one OCV for each camshaft position actuator. The OCV is sealed and mounted to the front cover. The ported end of the OCV is inserted into the cylinder head with a sliding fit. A filter screen protects each OCV oil port from any contamination in the oil supply.

The camshaft position actuator is mounted at the front end of the camshaft and the timing notch in the nose of the camshaft aligns with the dowel pin in the camshaft position actuator to ensure proper cam timing and camshaft position actuator oil hole alignment. ● SEE FIGURE 16–1.

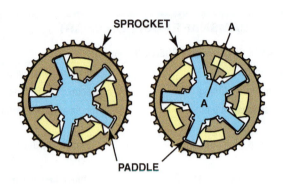

FIGURE 16-1 Camshaft rotation during advance and retard.

SPROCKET

A

PADDLE

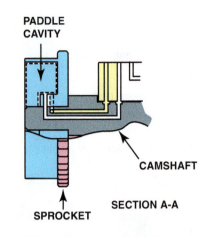

PADDLE CAVITY

CAMSHAFT

SPROCKET

SECTION A-A

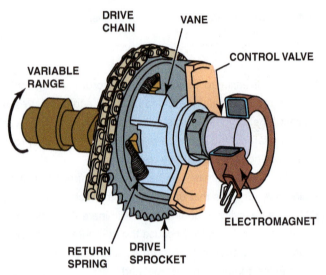

DRIVE CHAIN

VANE

CONTROL VALVE

VARIABLE RANGE

ELECTROMAGNET

RETURN SPRING

DRIVE SPROCKET

FIGURE 16-2 The camshaft is rotated in relation to the camshaft by the PCM to provide changes in valve timing.

INTAKE AND EXHAUST CAMSHAFT PHASING CHART

CAMSHAFT PHASING CHANGED	IMPROVES
Exhaust cam phasing	Reduces NO_X exhaust emissions
Exhaust cam phasing	Increases fuel economy (reduced pumping losses)
Intake cam phasing	Increases low-speed torque
Intake cam phasing	Increases high-speed power

CHART 16-2

By varying the intake camshaft timing, engine performance is improved. By varying the exhaust camshaft timing, the exhaust emissions and fuel consumption are reduced.

OPERATION AND COMPONENTS The GM 3900 V-6 engine is an example of an overhead valve (OHV) cam-in-block engine that uses variable valve timing (VVT) and active fuel management (displacement on demand—DOD).

The variable valve timing system uses electronically controlled, hydraulic gear–driven cam phaser that can alter the relationship of the camshaft from 15 degrees retard to 25 degrees advance (40 degrees overall) relative to the crankshaft. By using **variable valve timing (VVT)**, engineers were able to eliminate the EGR valve and still be able to meet the standards for oxides of nitrogen (NO_X). The VVT also works in conjunction with an active manifold that gives the engine a broader torque curve.

A valve in the intake manifold creates a longer path for intake air at low speeds, improving combustion efficiency and torque output. At higher speed the valve opens creating a shorter air path for maximum power production. ● **SEE FIGURE 16-2.**

Varying the exhaust and/or the intake camshaft position allows for reduced exhaust emissions and improved performance. ● **SEE CHART 16-2.**

By varying the exhaust cam phasing, vehicle manufacturers are able to meet newer NO_X reduction standards and eliminate the exhaust gas recirculation (EGR) valve. By using exhaust cam phasing, the PCM can close the exhaust valves sooner than usual, thereby trapping some exhaust gases in the combustion chamber. General Motors uses one or two actuators that allow the camshaft piston to change by up to 50 degrees in relation to the crankshaft position.

There are two types of cam phasing devices used on General Motors engines:

- **Spline phaser**—used on overhead camshaft (OHC) engines

- **Vane phaser**—used on overhead camshaft (OHC) and overhead valve (OHV) cam-in-block engines

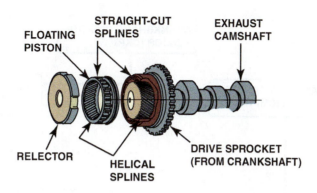

FLOATING PISTON

STRAIGHT-CUT SPLINES

EXHAUST CAMSHAFT

RELECTOR

HELICAL SPLINES

DRIVE SPROCKET (FROM CRANKSHAFT)

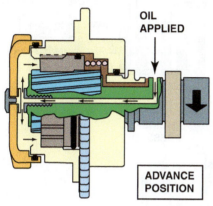

OIL APPLIED

ADVANCE POSITION

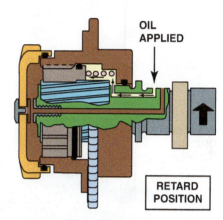

OIL APPLIED

RETARD POSITION

FIGURE 16–3 Spline cam phaser assembly.

SPLINE PHASER SYSTEM

The spline phaser system is also called the **exhaust valve cam phaser (EVCP)** and consists of the following components:

- Engine control module (ECM)
- Four-way pulse-width-modulated (PWM) control valve
- Cam phaser assembly
- Camshaft position (CMP) sensor
- **SEE FIGURE 16–3**.

SPLINE PHASER SYSTEM OPERATION

On the 4200 inline six-cylinder engine used in the Chevrolet Trailblazer, the pulse-width-modulated (PWM) control valve is located on the front passenger side of the cylinder head. Oil pressure is regulated by the control valve and then directed to the ports in the cylinder head leading to the camshaft and cam phaser position. The cam phaser is located on the exhaust cams and is part of the exhaust cam sprocket. When the ECM commands an increase in oil pressure, the piston is moved inside the cam phaser and rides along the helical splines, which compresses the coil spring. This movement causes the cam phaser gear and the camshaft to move in an opposite direction, thereby retarding the cam timing. ● **SEE FIGURE 16–4**.

TECH TIP

Check the Screen on the Control Valve If There Are Problems

If a NO$_x$ emission failure at a state inspection occurs or a diagnostic trouble code (DTC) is set related to the cam timing, remove the control valve and check for a clogged oil screen. A lack of regular oil changes can cause the screen to become clogged, thereby preventing proper operation. A rough idle is a common complaint because the spring may not be able to return the camshaft to the idle position after a long highway trip. ● **SEE FIGURE 16–5**.

VANE PHASER SYSTEM ON AN OVERHEAD CAMSHAFT ENGINE

The vane phaser system used on overhead camshaft (OHC) engines uses a camshaft piston (CMP) sensor on each camshaft. Each camshaft has its own actuator and its own oil control valve (OCV). Instead of using a piston along a helical spline, the vane phaser uses a rotor with four vanes, which is connected to the end of the camshaft.

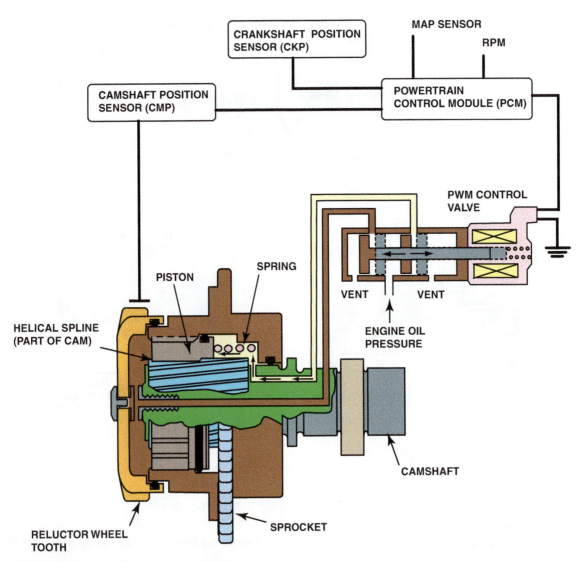

FIGURE 16–4 A spline phaser.

FIGURE 16–5 The screen(s) protects the solenoid valve from dirt and debris that can cause the valve to stick. This fault can set a P0017 diagnostic trouble code (crankshaft position–camshaft position correlation error).

The rotor is located inside the stator, which is bolted to the cam sprocket. The stator and rotor are not connected. Oil pressure is controlled on both sides of the vanes of the rotor, which creates a hydraulic link between the two parts. The oil control valve varies the balance of pressure on either side of the vanes and thereby controls the position of the camshaft. A return spring is used under the reluctor of the phaser to help return it to the home or zero degrees position. ● **SEE FIGURE 16–6.**

MAGNETICALLY CONTROLLED VANE PHASER A magnetically controlled vane phaser is controlled by the ECM by using a 12 volt **pulse-width-modulated (PWM)** signal to an electromagnet, which operates the oil control valve (OCV). A magnetically controlled vane phaser is used on many General Motors engines that use overhead camshafts on both the intake and exhaust. The OCV directs pressurized engine oil

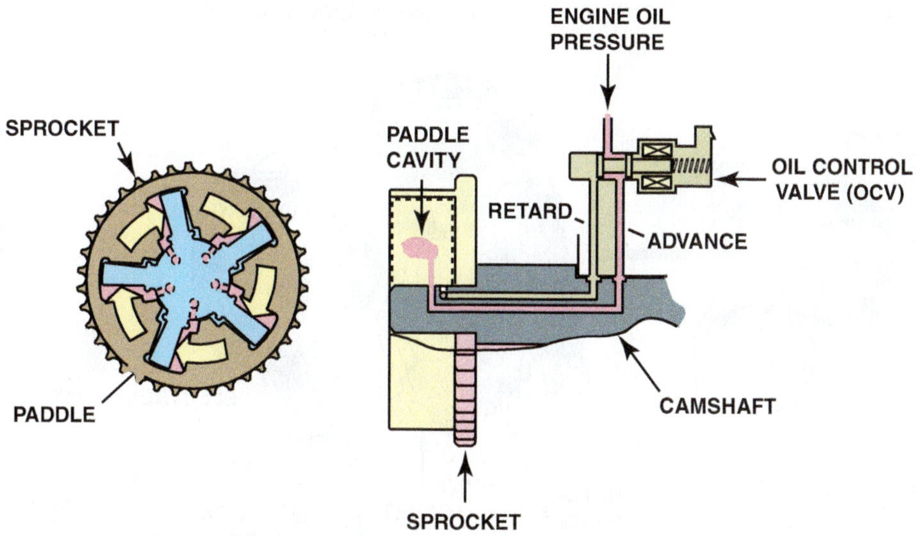

FIGURE 16–6 A vane phaser is used to move the camshaft using changes of oil pressure from the oil control valve.

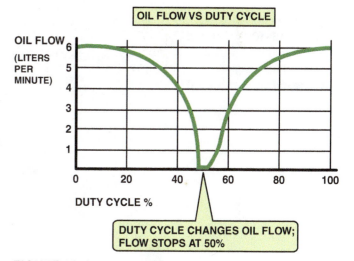

FIGURE 16–7 A magnetically controlled vane phaser. (*Courtesy of General Motors*)

FIGURE 16–8 When the PCM commands 50% duty cycle, the oil flow through the phaser drops to zero.

to either advance or retard chambers of the camshaft actuator to change the camshaft position in relation to the crankshaft position. ● **FIGURES 16–7, 16–8, AND 16–9.**

The following occurs when the pulse width is changed:

- **0% pulse width—** The oil is directed to the advance chamber of the exhaust camshaft actuator and the retard chamber of the intake camshaft activator.

- **50% pulse width—** The PCM is holding the cam in the calculated position based on engine RPM and load. At 50% pulse width, the oil flow through the phaser drops to zero.

- **100% pulse width—** The oil is directed to the retard chamber of the exhaust camshaft actuator and the advance chamber of the intake camshaft actuator.

The cam phasing is continuously variable with a range from 40 degrees for the intake camshaft and 50 degrees for the exhaust camshaft. The PCM uses the following sensors to determine the best position of the camshaft for maximum power and lowest possible exhaust emissions:

- Engine speed (RPM)
- MAP sensor
- Crankshaft position (CKP) sensor
- Camshaft position (CMP) sensor
- Barometric pressure (BARO) sensor

CAM-IN-BLOCK ENGINE CAM PHASER Overhead valve engines that use a cam-in-block design use a magnetically controlled cam phaser to vary the camshaft in relation to the crankshaft. This type of phaser is not capable of changing the duration of valve opening or valve lift.

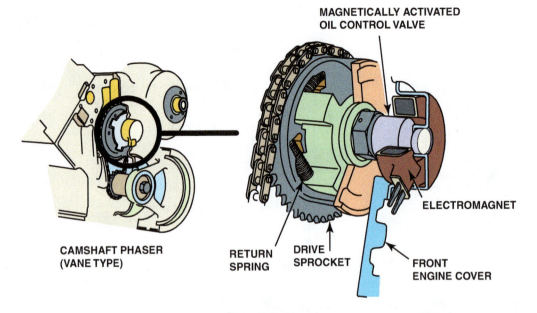

FIGURE 16–9 The cam phaser is located at the front of the camshaft.

MAGNETICALLY ACTIVATED OIL CONTROL VALVE

ELECTROMAGNET

CAMSHAFT PHASER (VANE TYPE)

RETURN SPRING

DRIVE SPROCKET

FRONT ENGINE COVER

FIGURE 16–10 A camshaft position actuator used in a cam-in-block engine. (*Courtesy of General Motors*)

? **FREQUENTLY ASKED QUESTION**

What Happens When the Engine Stops?

When the engine stops, the oil pressure drops to zero and a spring-loaded locking pin is used to keep the camshaft locked to prevent noise at engine start. When the engine starts, oil pressure releases the locking pin.

Inside the camshaft actuator is a rotor with vanes that are attached to the camshaft. Oil pressure is supplied to the vanes, which causes the camshaft to rotate in relation to the crankshaft. The camshaft actuator solenoid valve directs the flow of oil to either the advance or retard side vanes of the actuator.
● **SEE FIGURE 16–10**.

The ECM sends a pulse-width-modulated (PWM) signal to the camshaft actuator magnet. The movement of the pintle is used to direct oil flow to the actuator. The higher the duty cycle is, the greater the movement in the valve position and change in camshaft timing.

DIAGNOSIS OF VARIABLE VALVE TIMING SYSTEMS

The diagnostic procedure as specified by most vehicle manufacturers usually includes the following steps:

STEP 1 Verify the customer concern. This will usually be a check engine light (malfunction indicator light or MIL), as the engine performance effects would be minor under most operating conditions.

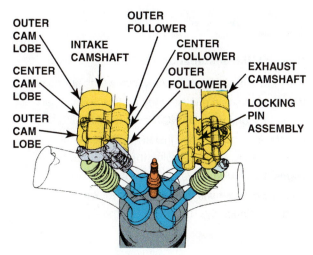

FIGURE 16–11 Engine oil pressure is used to switch cam lobes on a VTEC system.

Intake Valve Lift Control
Delivering optimum airflow on demand to maximize fuel economy

FIGURE 16–12 The lift control system uses two different cam profiles. (*Impala RPO LKW; Courtesy of General Motors*)

STEP 2 Check for stored diagnostic trouble codes (DTCs). Typical variable valve timing–related DTCs include:

P0011—Intake cam position is over advanced bank 1

P0021—Intake cam position is over advanced bank 2

P0012—Intake cam position is over retarded bank 1

P0022—Intake cam position is over retarded bank 2

STEP 3 Use a scan tool and check for duty cycle on the cam phaser solenoid while operating the vehicle at a steady road speed. The commanded pulse width should be 50%. If the pulse width is not 50%, then the PCM is trying to move the phaser to its commanded position and the phaser has not reacted properly. A PWM signal of higher or lower than 50% usually indicates a stuck phaser assembly.

STEP 4 Check the solenoid for proper resistance. If a scan tool with bidirectional control is available, connect an ammeter and measure the current as the solenoid is being commanded on by the scan tool.

STEP 5 Check for proper engine oil pressure. Low oil pressure or restricted flow to the cam phaser can be the cause of many diagnostic trouble codes.

STEP 6 Determine the root cause of the problem and clear all DTCs.

STEP 7 Road-test the vehicle to verify the fault has been corrected.

VARIABLE VALVE LIFT AND DURATION SYSTEMS

VARIABLE VALVE LIFT SYSTEMS

Variable camshafts include the system used by some Saturn models called Variable Valve Timing and Lift Electronic Control or **VTEC**. This system uses two different camshafts for low and high RPM. When the engine is operating at idle and speeds below about 4000 RPM, the valves are opened by camshafts that are optimized by maximum torque and fuel economy. When engine speed reaches a predetermined speed, depending on the exact make and model, the computer turns on a solenoid, which opens a spool valve. When the spool valve opens, engine oil pressure pushes against pins that lock the three intake rocker arms together. With the rocker arms lashed, the valves must follow the profile of the high RPM cam lobe in the center. This process of switching from the low-speed camshaft profile to the high-speed profile takes about 100 milliseconds (0.1 sec). ● **SEE FIGURE 16–11**.

The latest design for variable lift and duration is called intake valve lift control. The rocker arm is able to switch between low- and high-lift cam profiles, actuated by an oil control valve through a dual-feed hydraulic lash adjuster. ● **SEE FIGURE 16–12**.

In low-lift mode, the engine pumps only the air it needs to meet driver demands. As needed, the high-lift mode provides the full output capability of the engine.[1] ● **SEE FIGURE 16–13**.

---

[1]General Motors TechLink © April 2013

Low-Lift Profile = Airflow is controlled to deliver just what is needed for normal driving

LOW LIFT(4.0 mm)

Intake Valve Lift Control
Delivering optimum airflow on demand to maximize fuel economy

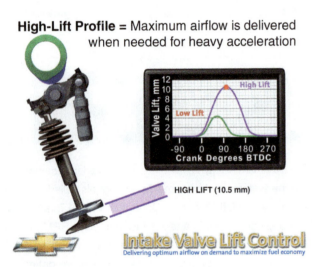

High-Lift Profile = Maximum airflow is delivered when needed for heavy acceleration

HIGH LIFT (10.5 mm)

Intake Valve Lift Control
Delivering optimum airflow on demand to maximize fuel economy

FIGURE 16–13 The system changes between low- and high-lift modes as needed. (*Courtesy of General Motors*)

VARIABLE DISPLACEMENT SYSTEMS

PURPOSE AND FUNCTION   Some engines are designed to be operated on four of eight or three of six cylinders during low-load conditions to improve fuel economy. The powertrain computer monitors engine speed, coolant temperature, throttle position, and load. It also determines when to deactivate cylinders.

Systems that can deactivate cylinders are called:

- Cylinder cutoff system
- Variable displacement system
- Displacement on Demand (DOD) (now called **Active Fuel Management**)

PARTS AND OPERATION   The key to this process is the use of two-stage hydraulic valve lifters. In normal operation, the inner and outer lifter sleeves are held together by a pin and operate as an assembly. When the computer determines that the cylinder can be deactivated, oil pressure is delivered to a passage, which depresses the pin and allows the outer portion of the lifter to follow the contour of the cam while the inner portion remains stationary, keeping the valve closed. The electronic operation is achieved through the use of lifter oil manifold containing solenoids to control the oil flow, which is used to activate or deactivate the cylinders. ● **SEE FIGURES 16–14 AND 16–15.**

AFM DETAILS[2]   On V-8 engines with the Active Fuel Management (AFM) system, the Engine Control Module (ECM) will typically deactivate cylinders 1 and 7 on the left bank, and cylinders 4 and 6 on the right bank, switching to V-4 mode. During this time, the ECM energizes solenoids on the valve lifter oil manifold (VLOM) assembly, which is bolted to the top of the engine block. The VLOM assembly has four electronically operated, normally closed solenoids.

When energized, the solenoids direct pressurized oil to the intake and exhaust lifters. This pressurized oil deactivates both the intake and exhaust lifters for AFM cylinders 1, 7, 4, and 6. When driving conditions require V-8 mode, the solenoids are de-energized, reactivating the lifters.

There are two types of lifters, AFM and non-AFM. AFM lifters are similar to what are used in non-AFM engines. The lifter guide is notched so that it will only fit one way into the engine block. ● **SEE FIGURE 16–16.**

The ECM is responsible for all engine control functions, therefore the ECM controls the AFM system as well. The ECM

[2]General Motors course #16050.12D2 Participant Guide © 2013

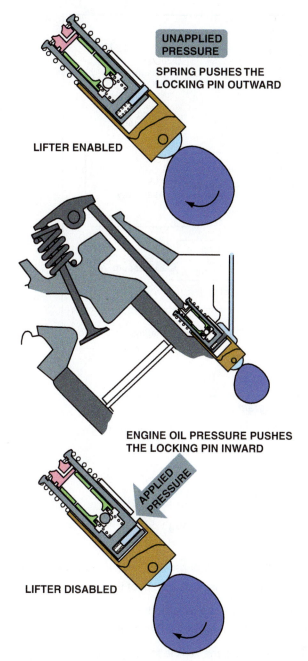

UNAPPLIED PRESSURE

SPRING PUSHES THE LOCKING PIN OUTWARD

LIFTER ENABLED

ENGINE OIL PRESSURE PUSHES THE LOCKING PIN INWARD

APPLIED PRESSURE

LIFTER DISABLED

FIGURE 16–14 Oil pressure applied to the locking pin causes the inside of the lifter to freely move inside the outer shell of the lifter, thereby keeping the valve closed.

is equipped with a low-side driver for each VLOM solenoid.
● **SEE FIGURE 16–17**.

All enable criteria must happen for AFM to operate. Refer to service information for the complete list of enable criteria. Typically these include:

- The transmission must be in third or forth gear.

- Oil pressure should be between 172 and 517 kPa (25–75 PSI).

- Engine speed should be between 900 and 3000 RPM.

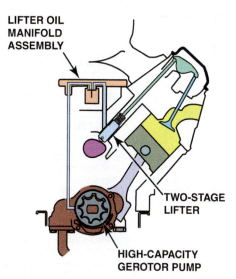

LIFTER OIL MANIFOLD ASSEMBLY

TWO-STAGE LIFTER

HIGH-CAPACITY GEROTOR PUMP

FIGURE 16–15 Active fuel management includes many different components and changes to the oiling system, which makes routine oil changes even more important on engines equipped with this system.

FIGURE 16–16 The AFM lifter is on the left and the non-AFM lifter is on the right. Note the notch in the lifter guide. (*Courtesy of General Motors*)

- Engine oil temperature should be between 20°C and 150°C (68°F–302°F).

- System voltage should be between 11 and 18 volts.

During AFM operation, the fuel injectors are shut off, but the spark plugs will continue to spark. The ECM will interrupt continuous AFM operation after 10 minutes and then return to AFM operation within one minute, if enable criteria are still met. This happens so that the system can maintain heat in the cylinder. It also prevents fouling of the spark plugs.

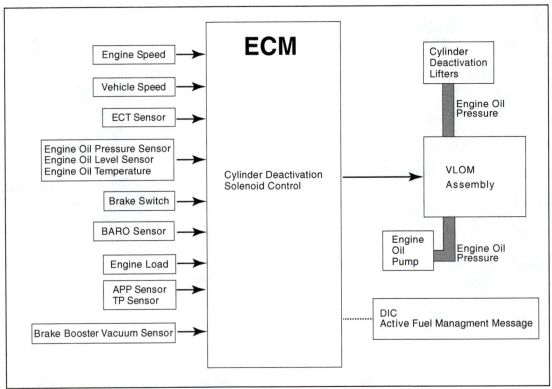

AFM System – ECM Inputs diagram

FIGURE 16–17 The ECM uses these inputs when controlling the active fuel management solenoids. (*Courtesy of General Motors*)

Transitions into and out of AFM are seamless and can only be observed using the scan tool. Some vehicles display a message on the Driver Information Center (DIC). Refer to service information for the specific vehicle application.[3] ● **SEE FIGURE 16–18**.

ACTIVE FUEL MANAGMENT SYSTEM DIAGNOSIS

The diagnosis of the variable displacement system usually starts as a result of a check engine light (malfunction indicator lamp or MIL). The diagnostic procedure specified by the vehicle manufacturer usually includes the following steps:

STEP 1 Verify the customer concern. With a cylinder deactivation system, the customer concern could be lower than expected fuel economy.

STEP 2 Check for any stored diagnostic trouble codes. A fault code set for an emission-related fault could cause the PCM to disable cylinder deactivation.

STEP 3 Perform a thorough visual inspection, including checking the oil level and condition.

STEP 4 Check scan tool data for related parameters to see if any of the sensors are out of the normal range.

STEP 5 Determine the root cause and perform the repair as specified in service information (SI).

STEP 6 Test-drive the vehicle to verify proper operation.

Always refer to DTCs when diagnosing AFM systems. If a fault occurs within a particular solenoid control circuit, a DTC will set for that cylinder. Refer to service information for a complete list of DTCs for the AFM system. The scan tool allows viewing of cylinder deactivation data while the AFM system is operating. The data include:

- Engine Mode (V-4 or V-8)
- Solenoid Status (ON or OFF)
- Circuit Status (COMPLETE or INCOMPLETE)

The scan tool can also be used to manually switch the engine operating mode and any AFM cylinder can be individually deactivated for testing. ● **SEE FIGURE 16–19**.

[3]General Motors course #16050.12D2 Participant Guide © 2013

FIGURE 16–18 The driver information display on a Chevrolet Impala with a 5.3 liter V-8 equipped with active fuel management. The transition between four-cylinder mode and eight-cylinder mode is so smooth that most drivers are not aware that the switch is occurring.

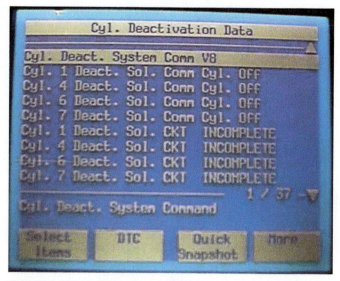

FIGURE 16–19 The scan tool allows you to view the status of each solenoid. (*Courtesy of General Motors*)

AFM COMPRESSION TEST GM service information has a number of diagnostic tests concerning the AFM system, including oil pressure tests and resistance tests. One test that verifies the operation of the AFM system is the AFM compression test.

If the resistance checks and oil pressure test are within specifications, perform the AFM compression test. This test is a functional test of the VLOM and valve lifters. The procedure tests the ability of the system to go in and out of AFM operation when commanded by the scan tool. The pressure values on the compression gauge are not critical; it is more important to observe the ON/OFF switching action of the solenoids and valve lifters.

Before beginning the compression test, make sure the engine oil level is correct.

- Disable the ignition and fuel injection systems for the cylinder to be tested.
- Install the compression gauge, and start the engine.
- Using the scan tool, command the solenoid ON.
- Release the pressure on the compression gauge, and note the gauge reading. The reading should be less than 172 kPa (25 PSI).
- Using the scan tool, de-energize the solenoid or activate the cylinder.
- The compression gauge reading should quickly increase to approximately 345 kPa (50 PSI) or higher.[4]

---

[4] General Motors course #16050.12D2 Participant Guide © 2013.

SUMMARY

1. Variable valve timing is used to improve engine performance and reduce exhaust emissions.

2. Intake cam phasing is used to improve low-speed torque and high-speed power.

3. Exhaust cam phasing is used to reduce exhaust emissions and increase fuel economy by reducing pumping losses.

4. Variable valve timing or overhead valve, cam-in-block engines are used to reduce NO_X emissions.

5. Variable valve timing faults are often the result of extended oil change intervals, which can clog the screen on the cam phaser. As a result of the clogged screen, oil cannot

flow to and adjust the valve timing, thereby setting valve timing-related DTCs.

6. Oil flow to the phasers is controlled by the powertrain control module (PCM). If a 50% duty cycle is shown on a scan tool, this means that the phaser has reached the commanded position.

7. If the duty cycle is other than 50% while operating the vehicle under steady conditions, this means that there is a fault in the system because the cam phaser is not able to reach the commanded position.

8. Variable valve timing and lift electronic control (VTEC) is used on some General Motors vehicles to improve performance.

9. Common variable valve timing diagnostic trouble codes include P0011, P0021, P0012, and P0022.

10. Cylinder deactivation systems improve fuel economy by disabling half of the cylinders during certain driving conditions, such as steady speed cruising.

REVIEW QUESTIONS

1. What is the advantage of varying the intake camshaft timing?

2. What is the advantage of varying the exhaust camshaft timing?

3. Why must the engine oil be changed regularly on an engine equipped with variable valve timing?

4. What sensors does the PCM monitor to determine the best camshaft timing?

5. What diagnostic trouble codes are associated with the variable valve timing (VVT) system?

6. Explain the operation of the General Motors AFM system.

CHAPTER QUIZ

1. Variable valve timing can be found on which type of engines?
   a. Cam-in-block
   b. SOHC
   c. DOHC
   d. All of the above

2. To reduce oxides of nitrogen (NO_X) exhaust emissions, which camshaft is varied?
   a. Exhaust camshaft only
   b. Intake camshaft only
   c. Both the intake and exhaust camshaft
   d. The exhaust camshaft is advanced and the intake camshaft is advanced.

3. To increase engine performance, which camshaft is varied?
   a. Exhaust camshaft only
   b. Intake camshaft only
   c. Both the intake and exhaust camshaft
   d. The exhaust camshaft is advanced and the intake camshaft is advanced.

4. What is the commanded pulse width of the camshaft phaser that results in no oil flow to the phaser?
   a. 0%
   b. 25%
   c. 50%
   d. 100%

5. What sensors are used by the PCM to determine the best position of the camshafts for maximum power and lowest possible exhaust emissions?
   a. Engine speed (RPM)
   b. Crankshaft position (CKP) sensor
   c. Camshaft position (CMP) sensor
   d. All of the above

6. How is the camshaft actuator controlled?
   a. On only when conditions are right
   b. Pulse-width-modulated (PWM) signal
   c. Spring-loaded to the correct position based on engine speed
   d. Vacuum-controlled valve

7. If the engine oil is not changed regularly, what is the most likely fault that can occur to an engine equipped with variable valve timing (VVT)?
   a. Low oil pressure DTC
   b. A no-start condition because the camshaft cannot rotate
   c. The filter screens on the actuator control valve become clogged
   d. Any of the above

8. How quickly can the rocker arms be switched from the low-speed camshaft profile to the high-speed camshaft profile on a vehicle equipped with a VTEC system?
   a. 50 milliseconds
   b. 100 milliseconds
   c. 250 milliseconds
   d. 500 milliseconds

9. Which DTC may be set if there is a problem with the bank 1 intake cam position?
   a. P0300
   b. P0420
   c. P0011 or P0012
   d. P0021 or P0022

10. When the AFM solenoids are turned on, the _____ are inactivated, causing the intake and exhaust valves to not open.
   a. Valve springs
   b. Lifters
   c. Push rods
   d. Cam phasers

PISTONS

PURPOSE AND FUNCTION All engine power is developed by burning fuel mixed with air in the combustion chamber. Heat from the combustion causes the burned gas to increase in pressure. The force of this pressure is converted into useful work through the piston, connecting rod, and crankshaft. Therefore, the piston serves three purposes.

1. **Transfers force.** The piston transfers the force of combustion to the crankshaft through the connecting rod.

2. **Seals the combustion chamber.** The piston and piston rings seal the compressed air during the compression stroke and the combustion gases on the power stroke.

3. **Conducts heat.** The piston transfers heat from the combustion chamber to the cylinder walls through the piston rings and to the engine oil through the piston.

PARTS INVOLVED The **piston** forms a movable bottom to the combustion chamber. ● **SEE FIGURE 17–1.**

The piston is attached to the connecting rod with a **piston pin,** also called a **wrist pin.** The piston pin is allowed to have a rocking movement because of a swivel joint at the piston end of the connecting rod. The crankshaft changes the up-and-down (reciprocating) motion of the pistons into rotary motion. The connecting rod is connected to a part of the crankshaft called a **crank throw, crankpin,** or **connecting rod bearing journal.**

Piston rings seal the small space between the piston and cylinder wall, keeping the pressure above the piston. When the pressure builds up in the combustion chamber, it pushes on the piston. The piston, in turn, pushes on the piston pin and upper end of the connecting rod. The lower end of the connecting rod pushes on the crank throw. This provides the force to turn the crankshaft. As the crankshaft turns, it develops inertia. *Inertia is the force that causes the crankshaft to continue rotating.* This action will bring the piston back to its original position, where it will be ready for the next power stroke. While the engine is running, the combustion cycle keeps repeating as the piston reciprocates (moves up and down) and the crankshaft rotates.

PISTON OPERATION When the engine is running, the piston starts at the top of the cylinder. As it moves downward, it accelerates until it reaches a maximum velocity slightly before it is halfway down. The piston comes to a stop at the bottom of the cylinder at 180 degrees of crankshaft rotation. During the next 180 degrees of crankshaft rotation, the piston moves upward. It accelerates to reach a maximum velocity slightly above the halfway point and then comes to a stop at the top of

FIGURE 17–1 The piston seals the bottom of the combustion chamber and is attached to a connecting rod.

the stroke. Thus, the piston starts, accelerates, and stops twice in each crankshaft revolution.

NOTE: A typical piston in an engine operating at 4000 RPM accelerates from 0 to 60 mph (97 km/h) in about 0.004 second (4 ms) as it travels about halfway down the cylinder.

This reciprocating action of the piston produces large *inertia forces.* Inertia is the force that causes a part that is at rest to stay at rest or a part that is in motion to stay in motion. The lighter the piston, the lesser the inertia force developed. Less the inertia will allow higher engine operating speeds. For this reason, pistons are made to be as light as possible while still having the strength that is needed.

The piston operates with its top or head exposed to the hot combustion gases, whereas the skirt contacts the relatively cool cylinder wall. This results in a temperature difference of about 275°F (147°C) between the top and bottom of the piston.

PISTON CONSTRUCTION

PISTON RING GROOVES Piston ring **grooves** are located between the piston head and skirt. The width of the grooves, the width of the **lands** between the ring grooves, and the number of rings are major factors in determining minimum

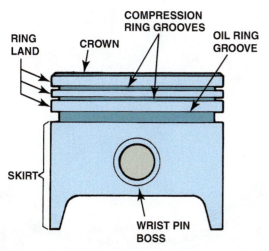

FIGURE 17–2 All pistons share the same parts in common.

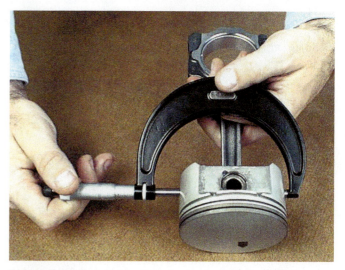

FIGURE 17–3 A piston diameter is measured across the thrust surfaces.

FIGURE 17–4 A cast piston showing the sprues which were used to fill the mold with molten aluminum alloy.

TECH TIP

Piston Weight Is Important!

All pistons in an engine should weigh the same to help ensure a balanced engine. Piston weight becomes a factor when changing pistons. Most aluminum pistons range in weight from 10 to 30 ounces (280 to 850 grams) (1 oz = 28.35 g). *A typical paper clip weighs 1 g.* If the cylinder has been bored, larger replacement pistons are obviously required. If the replacement pistons weigh more, this puts additional inertia loads on the rod bearings. Therefore, to help prevent rod bearing failure on an overhauled engine, the replacement pistons should not weigh more than the original pistons.

CAUTION: Some less expensive replacement cast pistons or high-performance forged pistons are much heavier than the stock pistons, even in the stock bore size. This means that the crankshaft may need heavy metal added to the counterweights of the crankshaft for the engine to be balanced.

For the same reason, if one piston is being replaced, all pistons should be replaced or at least checked and corrected to ensure the same weight.

piston height. The outside diameter of the lands is about 0.02 to 0.04 inch (0.5 to 1 mm) smaller than the **skirt** diameter.
● SEE FIGURE 17–2.
 ● SEE FIGURE 17–3 for an example of how to measure the diameter of a piston.

CAST PISTONS
Cast aluminum pistons usually are made using *gravity die casting*. In this process, molten aluminum alloy and about 10% silicon are poured into a mold. The silicon is used to increase the strength and help control the expansion of the piston when it gets hot. Other metals used in the aluminum alloy include copper, nickel, manganese, and magnesium.
● SEE FIGURE 17–4.

HYPEREUTECTIC PISTONS
A standard cast aluminum piston contains about 9% to 12% silicon and is called a *eutectic* piston. To add strength, the silicon content is increased to about 16%, and the resulting piston is called a **hypereutectic** piston. Other advantages of a hypereutectic piston are its 25% weight reduction and lower expansion rate. The disadvantage of hypereutectic pistons is their higher cost, because they are more difficult to cast and machine.

Hypereutectic pistons are commonly used in the aftermarket and as original equipment in many turbocharged and supercharged engines.

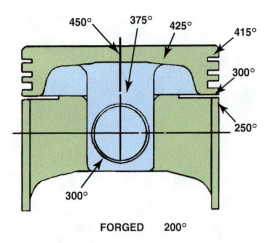

FORGED 200°

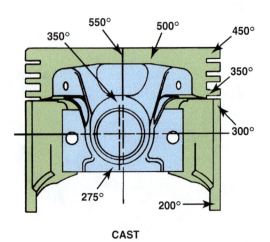

CAST

FIGURE 17–5 The top of the piston temperature can be 100°F (38°C) lower on a forged piston compared to a cast piston.

FIGURE 17–6 Valve reliefs are used to provide valve clearance. (*Courtesy of General Motors*)

NOTE: Some engines do not use valve reliefs because this requires that the thickness of the top of the piston be increased to provide the necessary strength. The thicker the top of the piston, the lower down from the top the top piston ring sits. To reduce unburned hydrocarbon (HC) exhaust emissions, engineers attempt to place the top piston ring as close to the top of the piston as possible to prevent the unburned fuel from being trapped (and not burned) between the top of the piston and the top of the top piston ring.

Recesses machined or cast into the tops of the pistons for valve clearance are commonly called:

- Eyebrows
- Valve reliefs
- Valve pockets

The depth of the eyebrows has a major effect on the compression ratio and is necessary to provide clearance for the valves if the timing belt or chain of an overhead camshaft engine should break. Without the eyebrows, the pistons could hit the valves near TDC if the valves are not operating (closing) because of nonrotation of the camshaft. If an engine is designed not to have the pistons hitting the valves, in cases the timing belt or chain breaks, the engine is called **freewheeling.** ● **SEE FIGURE 17–6.**

FORGED PISTONS High-performance engines need pistons with added strength. Forged pistons have a dense grain structure and are very strong. Forged pistons are often used in turbocharged or supercharged engines. Because forged pistons are less porous than cast pistons, they conduct heat more quickly. Forged pistons generally run about 20% cooler than cast pistons. ● **SEE FIGURE 17–5.**

PISTON HEAD DESIGNS Because the piston head forms a portion of the combustion chamber, its shape is vital to the combustion process. Many newer engines have *flat-top* pistons. Some of these flat-top pistons come so close to the cylinder head that *recesses* are cut in the piston top for valve clearance. Pistons used in high-powered engines may have raised domes or *pop-ups* on the piston heads. These are used to increase the compression ratio. Pistons used in other engines may be provided with a depression or a *dish*. The varying depths of the dish provide different compression ratios required by different engine models.

GASOLINE DIRECT-INJECTION DESIGNS Engines using spark-ignited direct injection (SIDI) have the fuel injected directly into the combustion chamber. The piston head is

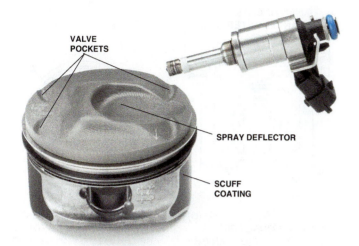

FIGURE 17–7 The piston head is shaped to direct the injection spray upward toward the spark plug. (*Courtesy of General Motors*)

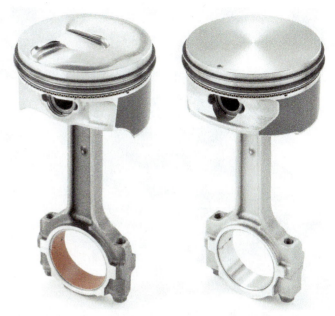

FIGURE 17–8 A comparison of a direct-injected piston (left) and a port-injected piston (right) from two different model years of the same engine. (*Courtesy of General Motors*)

shaped so that the injected fuel is directed and concentrated around the spark plug tip, making it easier to ignite the air-fuel mixture. ● SEE FIGURES 17–7 AND 17–8.

SLIPPER SKIRT PISTONS
A **slipper skirt** design piston is shorter on the two sides that are not thrust surfaces. Advantages of using a slipper skirt design include:

- Lighter weight
- Allows for a shorter overall engine height, because the crankshaft counterweights can be closer to the piston when they are at the bottom of the stroke

Most engines today use a slipper skirt piston design.

CAM GROUND PISTONS
Aluminum pistons expand when they get hot. A method of expansion control was devised using a **cam ground** piston skirt. With this design, the piston thrust surfaces closely fit the cylinder, and the piston pin boss diameter is fitted loosely. As the cam ground piston is heated, it expands along the piston pin so that it becomes nearly round at its normal operating temperatures. A cam ground piston skirt is illustrated in ● FIGURE 17–9.

PISTON FINISH
The finish on piston skirts varies with the manufacturer, but all are designed to help reduce scuffing. Scuffing is a condition where the metal of the piston actually contacts the cylinder wall. When the piston stops at the top of the cylinder, welds or transfer of metal from one part to the other can take place. Scuffing can be reduced by coating the piston skirts with tin 0.0005 inch (0.0125 mm) thick or a moly graphite coating. ● SEE FIGURE 17–10.

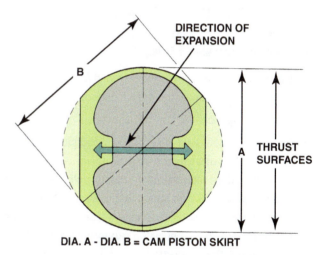

FIGURE 17–9 Piston cam shape. The largest diameter is across the thrust surfaces and perpendicular to the piston pin (labeled A).

PISTON HEAD SIZE
The top or head of the piston is smaller in diameter than the rest of the piston. The top of the piston is exposed to the most heat and therefore tends to expand more than the rest of the piston. ● SEE FIGURE 17–11.

Most pistons have horizontal separation slots that act as **heat dams.** These slots reduce heat transfer from the hot piston head to the lower skirt. This, in turn, keeps the skirt temperature lower to reduce skirt expansion. Because the slot is placed in the oil ring groove, it can be used for oil drainback and expansion control.

FIGURE 17–10 A moly graphite coating on this piston from a General Motors 3800 V-6 engine helps to prevent piston scuffing.

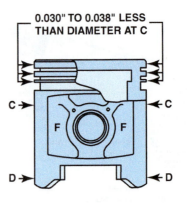

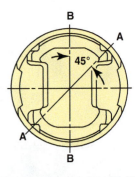

0.030" TO 0.038" LESS THAN DIAMETER AT C

45°

DIAMETERS AT (C) AND (D) CAN BE EQUAL OR DIAMETER AT (D) CAN BE 0.0015" GREATER THAN (C).

THE ELLIPTICAL SHAPE OF THE PISTON SKIRT SHOULD BE 0.010" TO 0.012" LESS AT DIAMETER (A) THAN ACROSS THE THRUST FACES AT DIAMETER (B). MEASUREMENT IS MADE 1/8" BELOW LOWER RING GROOVE.

FIGURE 17–11 The head of the piston is smaller in diameter than the skirt of the piston to allow it to expand when the engine is running.

PISTON STRUT INSERTS
A major development in expansion control occurred when the piston aluminum was cast around two stiff steel **struts.**

- The struts add strength to the piston in the piston pin area where additional strength is needed.
- The struts help control thermal expansion.
- Pistons with steel strut inserts allow good piston-to-cylinder wall clearance at normal temperatures. At the same time, they allow the cold operating clearance to be as small as 0.0005 inch (one-half thousandth of an inch) (0.0127 mm). This small clearance will prevent cold piston slap and noise. A typical piston expansion control strut is visible in ● **FIGURE 17–12.**

STEEL STRUT

FIGURE 17–12 Steel struts cast inside the piston help control expansion and add strength to the piston pin area.

PISTON PINS

TERMINOLOGY
Piston pins are used to attach the piston to the connecting rod. Piston pins are also known as *wrist pins* or *gudgeon pins*, a British term. The piston pin transfers the force produced by combustion chamber pressures and piston inertia to the connecting rod. The piston pin is made from high-quality steel in the shape of a tube to make it both strong and light. Sometimes, the interior hole of the piston pin is tapered, so it is large at the ends and small in the middle of the pin. This gives the pin strength that is proportional to the location of the load placed on it. A double-taper hole such as this is more expensive to manufacture, so it is used only where its weight advantage merits the extra cost. ● **SEE FIGURE 17–13.**

PISTON PIN OFFSET
Some piston pin holes are not centered in the piston. They are located toward the **major thrust surface,** approximately 0.062 inch (1.57 mm) from the piston centerline, as shown in ● **FIGURE 17–14.**

Pin offset is designed to reduce piston slap and the noise that can result as the large end of the connecting rod crosses over top dead center.

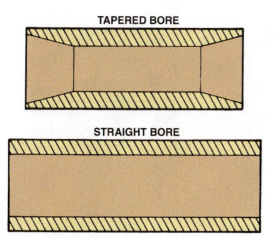

FIGURE 17–13 Most piston pins are hollow to reduce weight and have a straight bore. Some pins have a tapered bore to reinforce the pin.

- **Minor thrust.** The minor thrust side of the piston head has a greater area than the major side. This is caused by the pin offset. As the piston moves up in the cylinder on the compression stroke, it rides against the minor thrust surface. When compression pressure becomes high enough, the greater head area on the minor side causes the piston to cock slightly in the cylinder. This keeps the *top* of the minor thrust surface on the cylinder. It forces the *bottom* of the major thrust surface to contact the cylinder wall. As the piston approaches top center, both thrust surfaces are in contact with the cylinder wall.

- **Major thrust.** When the crankshaft crosses over top center, the force on the connecting rod moves the entire piston toward the major thrust surface. The lower portion of the major thrust surface has already been in contact with the cylinder wall. The rest of the piston skirt slips into full contact just after the crossover point, thereby controlling piston slap. This action is illustrated in ● **FIGURE 17–15.**

Off-setting the piston toward the minor thrust surface would provide a better mechanical advantage. It also would cause less piston-to-cylinder friction, and increase piston noise. For these reasons, the offset is often placed toward the minor thrust surface in racing engines. Noise and durability are not as important in racing engines as maximum performance.

NOTE: Not all piston pins are offset. In fact, many engines operate without the offset to help reduce friction and improve power and fuel economy.

PISTON PIN FIT
The finish and size of piston pins are closely controlled. Piston pins have a smooth, mirrorlike finish. Their size is held to tens of thousandths of an inch so that exact fits can be maintained. If the piston pin is loose in the piston or

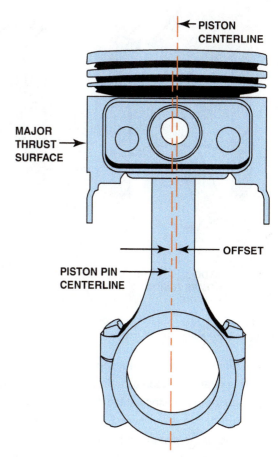

FIGURE 17–14 Piston pin offset toward the major thrust surface.

 FREQUENTLY ASKED QUESTION

Which Side Is the Major Thrust Side?

The thrust side is the side the rod points to when the piston is on the power stroke. Any V-block engine (V-6 or V-8) that rotates clockwise is viewed from the front of the engine. The left bank piston thrust side faces the inside (center) of the engine. The right bank piston thrust side faces the outside of the block. This rule, called the *left-hand rule,* states the following:

- Stand at the rear of the engine and point toward the front of the engine.
- Raise your thumb straight up, indicating the top of the engine.
- Point your other fingers toward the right. This represents the major thrust side of the piston.

Always assemble the connecting rods onto the rods so that the notch or "F" on the piston is pointing toward the front of the engine and the oil squirt hole on the connecting rod is pointing toward the major thrust side with your left hand.

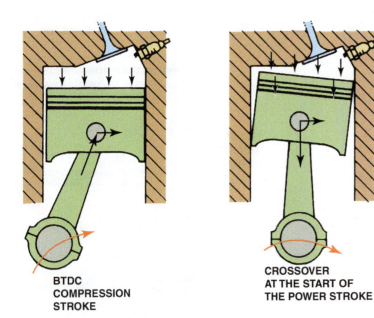

BTDC
COMPRESSION
STROKE

CROSSOVER
AT THE START OF
THE POWER STROKE

ATDC
POWER STROKE

FIGURE 17–15 Engine rotation and rod angle during the power stroke cause the piston to press harder against one side of the cylinder, called the major thrust surface.

in the connecting rod, it will make a sound while the engine is running. This is often described as a **double knock.** The noise is created when the piston stops at top dead center and occurs again as it starts to move downward, creating a doubleknock or rattling sound. If the piston pin is too tight in the piston, it will restrict piston expansion along the pin diameter and lead to piston scuffing. Normal piston pin clearances range from 0.0005 to 0.0007 inch (0.0126 to 0.018 mm).

PISTON PIN RETAINING METHODS

FULL FLOATING   **Full-floating** piston pins are free to "float" in the connecting rod and the piston. Often, a bronze bushing is installed in the small end of the connecting rod to support the piston pin. Full-floating pins require a retaining device to keep the piston pin from moving endwise and scrape against the cylinder wall. Most full-floating piston pins use some type of **lock ring** to retain the piston pin. There are two common types of lock rings.

- One is an internal snap ring that fits into a groove in the piston pin bore. These internal snap rings or "circle clips" are commonly called "circlips."

- The other is a "spiral lock" ring, which is a wound flat ring with two or three layers made from hardened steel. The spiral lock is inserted into a groove cut into the piston pin bore by starting with the bottom layer and twisting the spiral ring into place until all layers are in the groove.

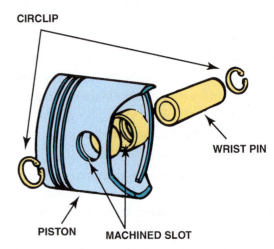

CIRCLIP

WRIST PIN

PISTON   MACHINED SLOT

FIGURE 17–16 Circlips hold full-floating piston pins in place.

Full-floating piston pins are most often used in high-performance modified engines and in diesel engines. ● **SEE FIGURE 17–16.**

Some engines use aluminum or plastic plugs in both ends of the piston pin. These plugs touch the cylinder wall without scoring, to hold the piston pin centered in the piston.

INTERFERENCE FIT   Another method of retaining the piston pin in the connecting rod is to make the connecting rod hole slightly smaller than the piston pin. The pin is installed by heating the rod to expand the hole or by pressing the pin into the rod. This retaining method will securely hold the pin. ● **SEE FIGURE 17–17.**

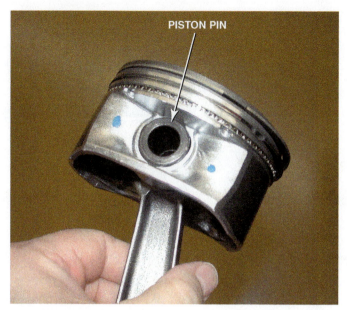

FIGURE 17–17 A typical interference fit piston pin.

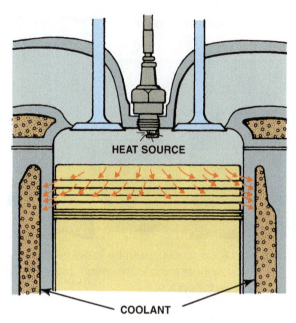

FIGURE 17–18 The rings conduct heat from the piston to the cylinder wall.

 REAL WORLD FIX

Big Problem, No Noise

Sometimes the piston pin can "walk" off the center of the piston and score the cylinder wall. This scoring is often not noticed because this type of wear does not create noise. Because the piston pin is below the piston rings, little combustion pressure is lost past the rings until the groove worn by the piston pin has worn the piston rings.

Troubleshooting the exact cause of the increased oil consumption is difficult because the damage done to the oil control rings by the groove usually affects only one cylinder.

Often, compression tests indicate good compression because of the cylinder seals, especially at the top. More than one technician has been surprised to see the cylinder gouged by a piston pin when the cylinder head has been removed for service. In such a case, the cost of the engine repair immediately increases far beyond that of normal cylinder head service.

This press or shrink fit is called an **interference fit.** Care must be taken to have the correct hole sizes, and the pin must be centered in the connecting rod. Because the interference fit method is the least expensive to use, it is found in the majority of engines.

PISTON RINGS

PURPOSE AND FUNCTION Piston rings serve several major functions in engines.

- They form a sliding combustion chamber seal that prevents the high-pressure combustion gases from leaking past the piston.
- They keep engine oil from getting into the combustion chamber.
- The rings transfer some of the piston heat to the cylinder wall, where it is removed from the engine through the cooling system. ● **SEE FIGURE 17–18.**

CLASSIFICATIONS Piston rings are classified into two types.

1. Two **compression rings,** located toward the top of the piston
2. One **oil control ring,** located below the compression rings

COMPRESSION RINGS A compression ring is designed to form a seal between the moving piston and the cylinder wall. This is necessary to get maximum power from the combustion pressure. At the same time, the compression ring must keep

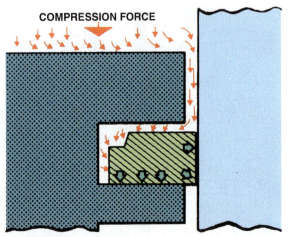

FIGURE 17-19 Combustion chamber pressure forces the ring against the cylinder wall and the bottom of the ring groove to effectively seal the cylinder.

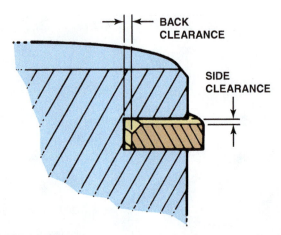

FIGURE 17-20 The side and back clearances must be correct for the compression rings to seal properly.

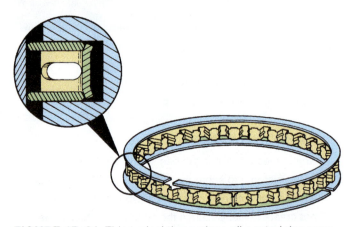

FIGURE 17-21 This typical three-piece oil control ring uses a hump-type stainless steel spacer-expander. The expander separates the two steel rails and presses them against the cylinder wall.

friction at a minimum. This is made possible by providing only enough static or built-in mechanical tension to hold the ring in contact with the cylinder wall during the intake stroke. Combustion chamber pressure during the compression, power, and exhaust strokes is applied to the top and back of the ring. This pressure will add extra force on the ring that is required to seal the combustion chamber during these strokes. ● **FIGURE 17-19** illustrates how the combustion chamber pressure adds force to the ring.

The space in the ring groove above the ring is called the **side clearance** and the space behind the ring is called the **back clearance.** ● **SEE FIGURE 17-20.**

OIL CONTROL RINGS   The scraping action of the oil control ring allows oil to return through the expander and openings in the piston.

Steel spring expanders were placed in the ring groove behind the ring to improve static radial tension. They forced the ring to conform to the cylinder wall. Many expander designs are used. On the three-piece ring, a spacer expander lies between the top and bottom rails. The spacer expander keeps the rails separated and pushes them out against the cylinder wall. ● **SEE FIGURE 17-21.**

RING GAP   The piston **ring gap** will allow some leakage past the top compression ring. This leakage is useful in providing pressure on the second ring to develop a dynamic sealing force. The amount of piston ring gap is critical.

- **Too much gap.** A ring gap that is too great will allow excessive **blowby.** Blowby is the leakage of combustion gases past the rings. Blowby will blow oil from the cylinder wall. This oil loss is followed by piston ring scuffing.

- **Too little gap.** A ring gap that is too little will allow the piston ring ends to touch together when the engine is hot. Ring end touching increases the mechanical force against the cylinder wall, causing excessive wear and possible engine failure.

A butt-type piston ring gap is the most common type used in automotive engines. Some low-speed industrial engines and some diesel engines use a more expensive tapered or seal-cut ring gap. These gaps are necessary to reduce losses of the high-pressure combustion gases. At low speeds, the gases have more time to leak through the gap. Typical ring gaps are illustrated in ● **FIGURE 17-22.**

PISTON RING SHAPES   As engine speeds have increased, inertia forces on the piston rings have also increased. As a result, engine manufacturers have found it desirable to reduce inertia forces on the rings by reducing their weight. This has

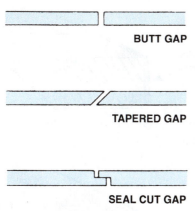

FIGURE 17–22 Typical piston ring gaps.

BUTT GAP

TAPERED GAP

SEAL CUT GAP

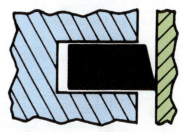

TAPER FACE

FIGURE 17–23 The taper face ring provides oil control by scraping the cylinder wall. This style of ring must be installed right side up or the ring will not seal and oil will be drawn into the combustion chamber.

been done by reducing the thickness of the piston ring from 1/4 inch. (6 mm) to as little as 1/16 inch. (1.6 mm). There are several types of piston rings.

- **Taper face ring** will contact the cylinder wall at the lower edge of the piston ring. ● **SEE FIGURE 17–23.**

  When either a chamfer or counterbore relief is made on the *upper inside* corner of the piston ring, the ring cross section is unbalanced, causing the ring to twist in the groove in a positive direction.

- **Positive twist ring** will give the same wall contact as the taper face ring. It will also provide a line contact seal on the bottom side of the groove. Sometimes, twist and a taper face are used on the same compression ring.

  Some second rings are notched on the *outer lower* corner. This, too, provides a positive ring twist. The sharp, lower outer corner becomes a scraper that helps in oil control, but this type of ring has less compression control than the preceding types.

- **Reverse twist ring** is produced by chamfering the ring's *lower inner* corner. This seals the lower outer section of the ring and piston ring groove, thus improving oil control. Reverse twist rings require a greater taper face or barrel face to maintain the desired ring face-to-cylinder wall contact. ● **SEE FIGURE 17–24.**

  Another style of positive twist ring has a counterbore at the lower outside edge. ● **SEE FIGURE 17–25.**

- **Scraper ring** does a good job of oil control and is usually recommended for use at the second compression ring.

- **Barrel face ring** can replace the outer ring taper on some rings. The barrel is 0.0003 inch per 0.1 inch (0.0076 mm

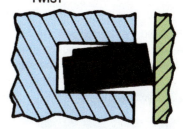

POSITIVE TORSIONAL TWIST

REVERSE TORSIONAL TWIST

FIGURE 17–24 Torsional twist rings provide better compression sealing and oil control than regular taper rings.

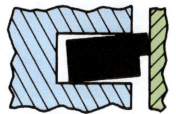

SCRAPER FACE

FIGURE 17–25 Scraper-type rings provide improved oil control.

per 0.254 mm) of piston ring width. Barrel faces are found on rectangular rings and on torsionally twisted rings. ● **SEE FIGURE 17–26.**

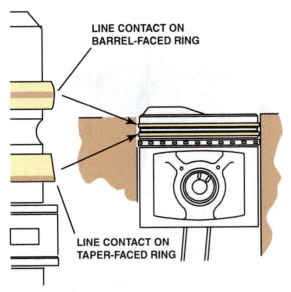

FIGURE 17–26 The upper barrel face ring has a line showing contact with the cylinder wall. The second taper face ring shows contact along the lower edge of the ring.

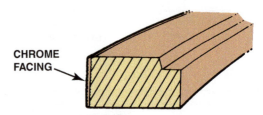

FIGURE 17–27 The chrome facing on this compression ring is about 0.004 inch (0.10 mm) thick.

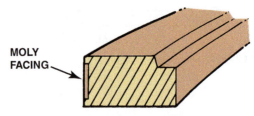

FIGURE 17–28 The moly facing on this compression ring is about 0.005 inch (0.13 mm) thick.

PISTON RING CONSTRUCTION

PISTON RING MATERIALS   The first piston rings were made with a simple rectangular cross section, modified with tapers, chamfers, counterbores, slots, rails, and expanders. Piston ring materials can include:

- Plain cast iron
- Pearlitic cast iron
- Nodular cast iron
- Steel
- **Ductile iron** (This is also used as a piston ring material in some automotive engines, which is very flexible and can be twisted without breaking.)

CHROMIUM PISTON RINGS   A chromium facing on cast iron rings greatly increases piston ring life, especially where abrasive materials are present in the air. During manufacture, the chromium-plated ring is slightly chamfered at the outer corners. About 0.004 inch (0.01 mm) of chrome is then plated on the ring face. Chromium-faced rings are then prelapped or honed before they are packaged and shipped to the customer. The finished chromium facing is shown in a sectional view in ● **FIGURE 17–27.**

MOLYBDENUM PISTON RINGS   Early in the 1960s, molybdenum piston ring faces were introduced. These rings proved to have good service life, especially under scuffing

conditions. The plasma method is a spray method used to deposit molybdenum on cast iron to produce a long-wearing and low-friction piston ring. The plasma method involves an electric arc plasma (ionized gas) that generates an extremely high temperature to melt the molybdenum and spray-deposit a molten powder of it onto a piston ring. Therefore, plasma rings are molybdenum (moly) rings that have the moly coating applied by the plasma method. Most molybdenum face piston rings have a groove that is 0.004 to 0.008 inch (0.1 to 0.2 mm) deep cut into the ring face. This groove is filled with molybdenum, using a metallic (or plasma) spray method, so that there is a cast-iron edge above and below the molybdenum. This edge may be chamfered in some applications. A sectional view of a molybdenum face ring is shown in ● **FIGURE 17–28.**

Molybdenum face piston rings will survive under high-temperature and scuffing conditions better than chromium face rings. Under abrasive wear conditions, chromium face rings will have a better service life. There is little measurable difference between these two facing materials with respect to blowby, oil control, break-in, and horsepower. Piston rings with either of these two types of facings are far better than plain cast-iron rings with phosphorus coatings. A molybdenum face ring, when used, will be found in the top groove, and a plain cast-iron or chromium face ring will be found in the second groove.

MOLY-CHROME-CARBIDE RINGS   Rings with moly-chrome-carbide coating are also used in some original equipment (OE) and replacement applications. The coating has properties that include the hardness of the chrome and carbide combined with the heat resistance of molybdenum.

CERAMIC-COATED RINGS The ceramic-coated ring surface is created by applying a ceramic coating to the ring using a process called *physical vapor deposition (PVD)*. Ceramic-coated rings are also being used where additional heat resistance is needed, such as in some heavy-duty, turbocharged, or supercharged engines. For example, the General Motors Duramax 6.6 liter diesel engine uses ceramic-coated rings.

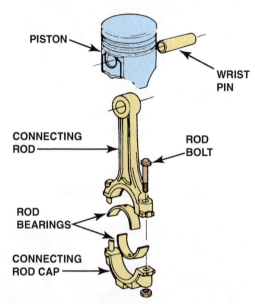

FIGURE 17–29 The connecting rod is the most highly stressed part of any engine because combustion pressure tries to compress it and piston inertia tries to pull it apart.

CONNECTING RODS

PURPOSE AND FUNCTION The connecting rod transfers the force and reciprocating motion of the piston to the crankshaft. The small end of the connecting rod reciprocates with the piston. The large end rotates with the crankpin. ● **SEE FIGURE 17–29.**

These dynamic motions make it desirable to keep the connecting rod as light as possible while still having a rigid beam section. ● **SEE FIGURE 17–30.**

Connecting rods are manufactured by casting, forging, and powdered (sintered) metal processes.

CONNECTING ROD DESIGN The big end of the connecting rod must be a perfect circle. Once a rod and cap are initially machined, they must remain a "matched set," due to the precise

FIGURE 17–30 The I-beam shape (top rod) is the most common, but the H-beam shape is common in high-performance and racing engine applications.

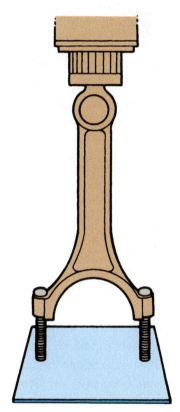

FIGURE 17–31 Rod bolts are quickly removed using a press.

machining required to obtain a perfect circle. Therefore, the rod caps must not be interchanged. Assembly bolt holes are closely reamed in both the cap and connecting rod to ensure alignment. The connecting rod bolts have *piloting surfaces* that closely fit these reamed holes. The fitting of the connecting rod bolts is so tight that a press must be used to remove the bolts when they are to be replaced, as shown in ● **FIGURE 17–31.**

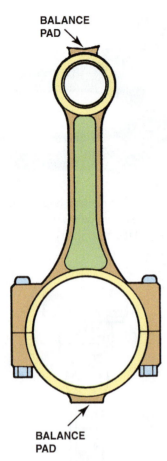

BALANCE
PAD

BALANCE
PAD

FIGURE 17–32 Some rods have balancing pads on each end of the connecting rod.

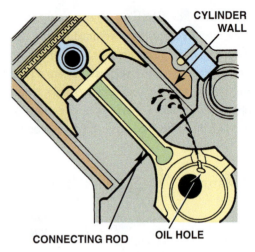

CYLINDER
WALL

CONNECTING ROD   OIL HOLE

FIGURE 17–33 Some connecting rods have spit holes to help lubricate the cylinder wall or piston pin.

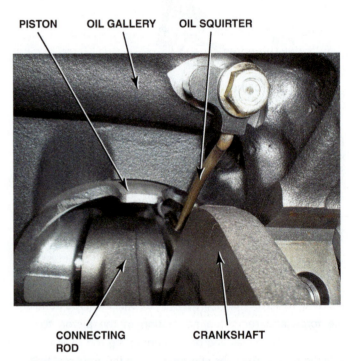

PISTON   OIL GALLERY   OIL SQUIRTER

CONNECTING
ROD   CRANKSHAFT

FIGURE 17–34 Some engines, especially diesel engines, are equipped with oil squirters that spray or stream oil toward the underneath side of the piston head to cool the piston.

In some engines, offset connecting rods provide the most economical distribution of main bearing space and crankshaft cheek clearance.

Many connecting rods are made with **balancing bosses (pads)** so that their weight can be adjusted to specifications. Some have balancing bosses only on the rod cap. Others also have a balancing boss at the small end. Some manufacturers put balancing bosses on the side of the rod, near the center of gravity of the connecting rod. Typical balancing bosses can be seen in ● **FIGURE 17–32.**

Balancing is done on automatic balancing machines as the final machining operation before the rod is installed in an engine.

Some connecting rods have a **spit hole** that bleeds some of the oil from the connecting rod journal. ● **SEE FIGURES 17–33 AND 17–34.**

On inline engines, oil is thrown up from the spit hole into the cylinder in which the rod is located. On V-type engines, it is often thrown into a cylinder in the opposite bank. The oil that is spit from the rod is aimed so that it will splash into the interior of the piston to help lubricate the piston pin. A hole similar to the spit holes may be used, called a **bleed hole,** to control the oil flow through the bearing.

CAST CONNECTING RODS Casting materials and processes have been improved so that they are used in most vehicle engines with high production standards. Cast connecting rods can be identified by their *narrow parting line.* A typical rough connecting rod casting is shown in ● **FIGURE 17–35.**

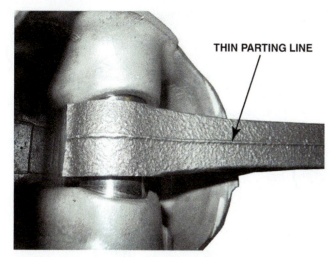

FIGURE 17–35 A cast connecting rod is found on many stock engines and can be identified by the thin parting line.

FORGED CONNECTING RODS Forged connecting rods have been used for years. They are generally used in heavy-duty and high-performance engines. Generally, the forging method produces lighter weight and stronger but more expensive connecting rods. Forged connecting rods can be identified by their *wide parting line*. Many high-performance connecting rods use a bronze bushing in the small end as shown in ● **FIGURE 17–36.**

POWDERED METAL CONNECTING RODS Most new production engines use powdered metal (PM) connecting rods.

Powdered metal connecting rods have many advantages over convention cast or forged rods including precise weight control. Each rod is created using a measured amount of material so that rod balancing, and therefore engine balancing, is now achieved without extra weighting and machining operations.

- Powdered metal connecting rods start as powdered metal, which includes iron, copper, carbon, and other alloying agents.

- This powder is then placed in a die and compacted (forged) under a pressure of 30 to 50 tons per square inch.

- After the part is shaped in the die, it is taken through a sintering operation where the part is heated, without melting, to about 2,000°F. During the sintering process, the ingredients are transformed into metallurgical bonds, giving the part strength.

- Machining is very limited and includes boring the small and big end and drilling the holes for the rod bearing cap retaining bolts.

FIGURE 17–36 This high-performance connecting rod uses a bronze bushing in the small end of the rod and oil hole to allow oil to reach the full-floating piston pin.

FIGURE 17–37 A cast connecting rod is found on many stock engines and can be identified by the thin parting line.

- The big end is then fractured using a large press. The uneven parting line helps ensure a perfect match when the pieces are assembled. ● **SEE FIGURE 17–37.**

FIGURE 17–38 A press used to remove the connecting rod from the piston.

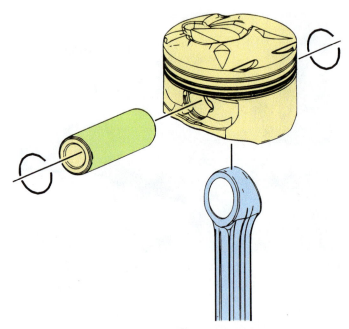

FIGURE 17–39 After removing the retaining rings the pin will push out. (*Courtesy of General Motors*)

CONNECTING ROD SERVICE

REMOVING PISTONS FROM RODS If the pins are an interference fit they can be removed from the rods using a special fixture as shown in ● **FIGURE 17–38.**

Full floating piston pins are removed by first removing the retaining rings and then pushing out the pin. See ● **FIGURE 17–39.**

NOTE: On some engines the piston pin cannot be removed without damaging the rod and/or the piston. The rod and piston come as a complete assembly and cannot be separated. Always refer to GM service information (SI) for the proper procedure.

INSPECTION Before connecting rod reconditioning, the rod should be checked for twist. ● **SEE FIGURE 17–40.**

In other words, the hole at the small end and the hole at the big end of the connecting rod should be parallel. No more than a 0.002 inch (0.05 mm) twist is acceptable. ● **SEE FIGURE 17–41** for the fixture used to check connecting rods for twist.

If measured rod twist is excessive, some specialty shops can remove the twist by bending the rod cold. Both cast and forged rods can be straightened. However, many engine builders replace the connecting rod if it is twisted.

RECONDITIONING PROCEDURE As an engine operates, the forces go through the large end of the connecting rod. This

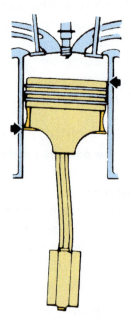

FIGURE 17–40 If the rod is twisted, it will cause diagonal-type wear on the piston skirt.

causes the crankshaft end opening of the rod (eye) to gradually deform. ● **SEE FIGURE 17–42.**

The large eye of the connecting rod is resized during precision engine service.

STEP 1 The parting surfaces of the rod and cap are smoothed to remove all high spots before resizing. A couple of thousandths of an inch of metal is removed from the rod cap parting surface. This is done using the same grinder that is used to remove a slight amount of metal from the parting surface of main bearing caps. The amount

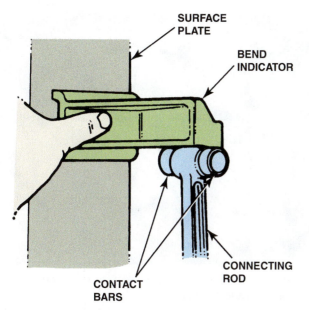

FIGURE 17–41 A rod alignment fixture is used to check a connecting rod for bends or twists.

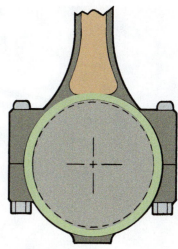

FIGURE 17–42 Rod bearing bores normally stretch from top to bottom, with most wear concentrated on the rod cap.

removed from the rod and rod cap reduces the bore size by only 0.003 to 0.006 inch (0.08 to 0.15 mm).

NOTE: Powdered metal connecting rods cannot be reconditioned using this method. Most manufacturers recommend replacing worn powdered metal connecting rods.

STEP 2   The cap is installed on the rod, and the nuts or cap screws are properly torqued. The hole is then bored or honed to be perfectly round and of the size and finish required to give the correct connecting rod bearing crush. ● FIGURE 17–43 shows the setup for resizing the rod on a typical hone used in engine reconditioning.

Even though material is being removed at the big end of the rod, the compression ratio is changed very little. The inside of the bore at the big end should have a 60 to 90 microinch finish for proper bearing contact and heat transfer.

PISTON AND ROD ASSEMBLY

INTERFERENCE FIT RODS   To assemble the piston and rod, the piston pin is put in one side of the piston. The small end of the connecting rod should be checked for proper size.

The small eye of the connecting rod is heated before the pin is installed. ● SEE FIGURE 17–44.

This causes the rod eye to expand so that the pin can be pushed into place with little force. The pin must be rapidly

FIGURE 17–43 To help ensure that the big ends are honed straight, many experts recommend placing two rods together when performing the honing operation.

pushed into the correct center position. There is only one chance to get it in the right place because the rod will quickly seize on the pin as the rod eye is cooled by the pin.

FULL-FLOATING RODS   Full-floating piston pins operate in a bushing in the small eye of the connecting rod. The bushing can be replaced. The bushing and the piston are honed to the same diameter. This allows the piston pin to slide freely through both. The full-floating piston pin is held in place with a lock ring at each end of the piston pin. The lock ring expands into a small groove in the pin hole of the piston.

NOTE: The original lock rings should always be replaced with new rings.

FIGURE 17–44 The small end of the rod is being heated in an electric heater and the piston is positioned properly so the piston pin can be installed as soon as the rod is removed from the heater.

PISTON RING SERVICE

Each piston ring, one at a time, should be placed backward in the groove in which it is to be run.

STEP 1 **Check side clearance.** As the piston goes rapidly up and down in the cylinder, the rings are pushed to the top and then to the bottom of the ring grooves.

This movement of the ring in its groove gradually increases the piston ring side clearance. Material is worn from both the ring and the groove. Replace the piston if the ring groove is larger than factory specifications. The side clearance in the groove should be checked with a feeler gauge, as shown in ● **FIGURE 17–45.**

STEP 2 **Check ring gap.** After the block and cylinder bores have been reconditioned, invert the piston and push each ring into the lower quarter of the cylinder; then measure the ring gap. ● **SEE FIGURE 17–46.**

FIGURE 17–45 The side clearance of the piston ring is checked with a feeler gauge.

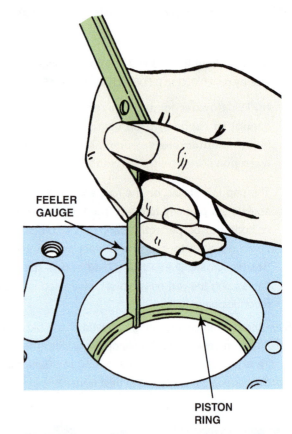

FEELER GAUGE

PISTON RING

FIGURE 17–46 The ring gap is measured using a feeler gauge.

The usual ring gap should be approximately 0.004 inch for each inch of bore diameter (0.004 mm for each centimeter of bore diameter). The second ring also needs to have a similar or even larger end gap.

■ If excessive ring gap is present, the blowby gases can enter the crankcase. Replace the ring(s) if the gap is too large.

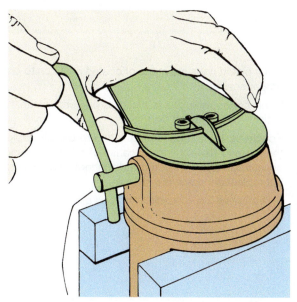

FIGURE 17–47 A hand-operated piston ring end gap grinder being used to increase the end gap of a piston ring so that it is within factory specifications.

FIGURE 17–48 A typical ring expander being used to install a piston ring on a piston.

- If the gap is too narrow, use a file or hand-operated piston ring grinder to achieve the necessary ring gap. ● **SEE FIGURE 17–47.**

STEP 3 **Installing the oil control ring.** The oil rings are installed first. The expander-spacer of the oil ring is placed in the lower ring groove. One oil ring rail is carefully placed above the expander-spacer by winding it into the groove. The other rail is placed below the expander-spacer. The ring should be rotated in the groove to ensure that the expander-spacer ends have not overlapped. If they have, the ring must be removed and reassembled correctly.

STEP 4 **Installing the compression rings.** Installing the compression rings requires the use of a **piston ring expander** tool that will only open the ring gap enough to slip the ring on the piston. ● **SEE FIGURE 17–48.**

Be careful to install the ring with the correct side up. The top of the compression ring is marked with one of the following:

- One dot
- The letter *T*
- The word *top*

● **SEE FIGURE 17–49.**

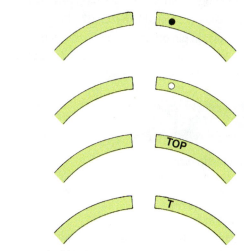

FIGURE 17–49 Identification marks used to indicate the side of the piston ring to be placed toward the head of the piston.

STEP 5 Double-check everything. After the rings are installed they should be rotated in the groove to ensure that they move freely, and checked to ensure that they will go fully into the groove so that the ring face is flush with the surface of the piston ring lands. Usually, the rings are placed on all pistons before any pistons are installed in the cylinders.

SUMMARY

1. Pistons are cam ground so that when operating temperature is reached, the piston will have expanded enough across the piston pin area to become round.

2. Replacement pistons should weigh the same as the original pistons to maintain proper engine balance.

3. Some engines use an offset piston pin to help reduce piston slap when the engine is cold.

4. Piston rings usually include two compression rings at the top of the piston and an oil control ring below the compression rings.

5. If the ring end gap is excessive, blowby gases can travel past the rings and into the crankcase.

6. Many piston rings are made of coated cast iron to provide proper sealing.

7. If the connecting rod is twisted, diagonal wear will be noticed on the piston skirt.

8. Powdered metal connecting rods are usually broken at the big end parting line. Because of this rough junction, powdered metal connecting rods cannot be reconditioned, but replaced if damaged or worn.

9. SIDI engines use a specially shaped piston crown.

REVIEW QUESTIONS

1. List the methods used to control piston heat expansion.

2. Why are some piston skirts tin plated?

3. How does piston pin offset control piston slap?

4. Why are forged pistons recommended for use in high-performance engines?

5. What causes the piston ring groove clearance to widen in service?

6. List the steps needed to recondition connecting rods.

7. How is the piston pin installed in the piston and rod assembly?

CHAPTER QUIZ

1. A hypereutectic piston _____.
   a. Uses about 16% silicon
   b. Is a cast piston
   c. Is a forged piston
   d. Both a and b

2. Many aluminum piston skirts are plated with _____.
   a. Tin or moly graphite
   b. Lead
   c. Antimony
   d. Terneplate

3. A hypereutectic piston has a higher _____.
   a. Weight than an aluminum piston
   b. Silicon content
   c. Tin content
   d. Nickel content

4. The purpose of casting steel struts into an aluminum piston is to _____.
   a. Provide increased strength
   b. Provide increased weight at the top part of the piston where it is needed for stability
   c. Control thermal expansion
   d. Both a and c

5. Full-floating piston pins are retained by _____.
   a. Lock rings
   b. A drilled hole with roll pin
   c. An interference fit between rod and piston pin
   d. An interference fit between piston and piston pin

6. The space behind the ring is called _____.
   a. Side clearance
   b. Forward clearance
   c. Back clearance
   d. Piston ring clearance

7. A misaligned connecting rod causes what type of engine wear?
   a. Cylinder taper
   b. Barrel shape cylinders
   c. Ridge wear
   d. Diagonal wear on the piston skirt

8. Side clearance is a measure taken between the _____ and the _____.
   a. Piston (side skirt); cylinder wall
   b. Piston pin; piston pin retainer (clip)
   c. Piston ring; piston ring groove
   d. Compression ring; oil control ring

9. Piston ring gap should only be measured after _____.
   a. All cylinder work has been performed
   b. Installing the piston in the cylinder
   c. Installing the rings on the piston
   d. Both a and c

10. Which type of connecting rod needs to be heated to install the piston pin
    a. Forged
    b. Interference fit
    c. Floating
    d. PM rods

ENGINE BLOCKS

CONSTRUCTION The engine block, which is the supporting structure for the entire engine, is made from one of the following:

- Gray cast iron
- Cast aluminum
- Die-cast aluminum alloy

Cast iron contains about 3% carbon (graphite), which makes it gray in color. Steel is iron with most of the carbon removed. The carbon in cast iron makes it hard but brittle. Cast iron is used to make engine blocks and cylinder heads for the following reasons.

- The carbon in the cast iron allows for easy machining, often without coolant.
- The graphite in the cast iron also has lubricating properties.
- Cast iron is strong for its weight and usually is magnetic.

The liquid cast iron is poured into a mold made from either sand or Styrofoam. All other engine parts are mounted on or in the block. This large casting supports the crankshaft and camshaft (on OHV engines) and holds all the parts in alignment. Newer blocks use thinner walls to reduce weight. Blocks are often of the **monoblock** design, which means that the cylinder, water jacket, main bearing supports (saddles), and oil passages are all cast as one structure for strength and quietness. Large-diameter holes in the block casting form the cylinders to guide the pistons. The cylinder holes are called **bores** because they are made by a machining process called boring. ● **SEE FIGURE 18–1.**

Combustion pressure loads are carried from the head to the crankshaft bearings through the block structure. The block has webs, walls, and drilled passages to contain the coolant and lubricating oil and to keep them separated from each other.

Mounting pads or lugs on the block transfer the engine torque reaction to the vehicle frame through attached engine mounts. A large mounting surface at the rear of the engine block is used for fastening a bell housing or transmission.

The cylinder head(s) and other components attach to the block. The joints between the components are sealed using gaskets or sealants. Gaskets or sealants are used in the joints to take up differences that are created by machining irregularities and that result from different pressures and temperatures.

BLOCK MANUFACTURING Cast-iron cylinder block sand casting technology continues to be improved. The trend is to make blocks with larger cores, using fewer individual

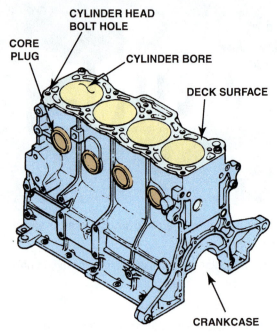

FIGURE 18–1 The cylinder block usually extends from the oil pan rails at the bottom to the deck surface at the top.

pieces. Oil-sand cores are forms that shape the internal openings and passages in the engine block. Before casting, the cores are supported within a core box. The core box also has a liner to shape the outside of the block. Special alloy cast iron is poured into the box. It flows between the cores and the core box liner. As the cast iron cools, the core breaks up. When the cast iron has hardened, it is removed from the core box, and the pieces of sand core are removed through the openings in the block by vigorously shaking the casting. These openings in the block are plugged with **core plugs**. Core plugs are also called **freeze plugs** or **frost plugs**. Although the name seems to mean that the plugs would be pushed outward if the coolant in the passages were to freeze, they seldom work this way. ● **SEE FIGURE 18–2.**

One way to keep the engine weight as low as possible is to make the block with minimum wall thickness. The cast iron used with thin-wall casting techniques has higher nickel content and is harder than the cast iron previously used. Engine designers have used foundry techniques to make engines lightweight by making the cast-iron block walls and bulkheads only as heavy as necessary to support their required loads.

ALUMINUM BLOCKS Aluminum is used for some cylinder blocks and is nonmagnetic and lightweight. Styrofoam is often used as a core when casting an aluminum block. The Styrofoam vaporizes as soon as the molten aluminum comes in contact with the foam leaving behind a cavity where the aluminum flows. ● **SEE FIGURE 18–3.**

FIGURE 18–2 An expansion (core) plug is used to block the opening in the cylinder head or block the holes where the core sand was removed after the part was cast.

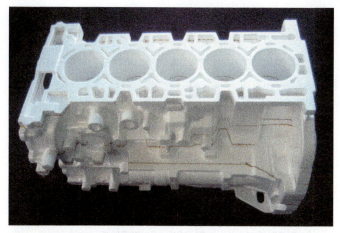

FIGURE 18–3 A Styrofoam casting mold used to make the five cylinder engine blocks for the Chevrolet Colorado and the Hummer H3. The brown lines are glue used to hold the various parts together. Sand is packed around the mold and molten aluminum is poured into the sand which instantly vaporizes the Styrofoam. The aluminum then flows and fills the area of the mold.

? FREQUENTLY ASKED QUESTION

What Is Compacted Graphite Iron?

Compacted graphite iron (CGI) has increased the strength, ductility, toughness, and stiffness compared to gray iron. If no magnesium is added, the iron will form gray iron when cooled, with the graphite present in flake form. If a very small amount of magnesium is added, more and more of the sulfur and oxygen form in the molten solution, and the shape of the graphite begins to change to compacted graphite forms. Compacted graphite iron is used for bedplates and many diesel engine blocks. It has higher strength, stiffness, and toughness than gray iron. The enhanced strength has been shown to permit reduced weight while still reducing noise vibration and harshness. Compacted graphite iron is commonly used in the blocks of diesel and some high-performance engines.

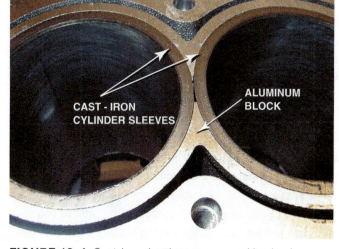

FIGURE 18–4 Cast-iron dry sleeves are used in aluminum blocks to provide a hard surface for the rings.

Aluminum block engines usually require cast-iron cylinder walls for proper wear and longevity. Aluminum blocks may have one of several different types of cylinder walls.

- Most cast-aluminum blocks have cast-iron cylinder sleeves (liners). The cast-iron cylinder sleeves are either cast into the aluminum block during manufacturing or pressed into the aluminum block. These sleeves are not in contact with the coolant passages and are called **dry cylinder sleeves**. ● **SEE FIGURE 18–4.**

- Another aluminum block design has the block die cast from silicon-aluminum alloy with no cylinder liners. Pistons with zinc-copper-hard iron coatings are used in these aluminum bores (in some Porsche engines).

- Some engines have die-cast aluminum blocks with replaceable cast-iron cylinder sleeves. The sleeves are sealed at the block deck and at their base. Coolant flows around the cylinder sleeve, so this type of sleeve is called a **wet cylinder sleeve** (in Cadillac 4.1, 4.5, and 4.9 liter V-8 engines). ● **SEE FIGURE 18–5.**

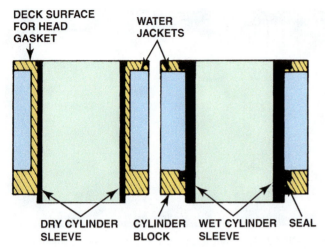

FIGURE 18–5 A dry sleeve is supported by the surrounding cylinder block. A wet sleeve must be thicker to be able to withstand combustion pressures without total support from the block.

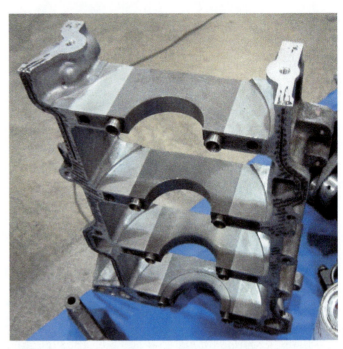

FIGURE 18–6 A bedplate is a structural part of the engine which is attached between the block and the oil pan and supports the crankshaft.

Cast-iron main bearing caps are used with aluminum blocks to give the required strength.

BEDPLATE DESIGN BLOCKS   A **bedplate** is a structural member that attaches to the bottom of the block and supports the crankshaft. The oil pan is mounted under the bedplate which in most cases is also part of the structure and support for the block assembly. ● **SEE FIGURE 18–6.**

CASTING NUMBERS   Whenever an engine part such as a block is cast, a number is put into the mold to identify the casting. These casting numbers can be used to check dimensions, such as the cubic inch displacement, and other information, such as year of manufacture. Sometimes changes are made to the mold, yet the casting number is not changed. Most often the casting number is the best piece of identifying information that the service technician can use. ● **SEE FIGURE 18–7.**

BLOCK DECK   The cylinder head is fastened to the top surface of the block. This surface is called the **block deck**. The deck has a smooth surface to seal *against* the head gasket. Bolt holes are positioned around the cylinders to form an even holding pattern. Four, five, or six head bolts are used around each cylinder in automobile engines. These bolt holes go into reinforced areas within the block that carry the combustion pressure load to the main bearing bulkheads. Additional holes in the block are used to transfer coolant and oil, as seen in ● **SEE FIGURE 18–8.**

COOLING PASSAGES   Cylinders are surrounded by cooling passages. These coolant passages around the cylinders are often called the **cooling jacket.** In most cylinder designs, the cooling passages extend nearly to the bottom of the cylinder. In some engine blocks where the block ends at the centerline of the crankshaft, the cooling passages are limited to the upper portion of the cylinder.

Some engines are built with **Siamese cylinder bores** where the cylinder walls are cast together without a water jacket (passage) between the cylinders. While this design improves the strength of the block and adds stability to the cylinder bores, it can reduce the cooling around the cylinders. ● **SEE FIGURE 18–9** is a typical V-8 engine cutaway that shows the coolant jackets and some of the lubrication holes.

LUBRICATING PASSAGES   An engine block has many oil holes that carry lubricating oil to the required locations. During manufacture, all oil holes, called the **oil gallery**, are drilled from outside the block. When a curved passage is needed, intersecting straight drilled holes are used. In some engines, plugs are placed in the oil holes to direct oil to another point before it comes back to the original hole, on the opposite side of the plug. After oil holes are drilled, the unneeded open ends may be capped by pipe plugs, steel balls, or cup-type soft plugs, often called **oil gallery plugs**. These end plugs in the oil passages can be a source of oil leakage in operating engines. ● **SEE FIGURE 18–10.**

FIGURE 18–7 Casting numbers identify the block.

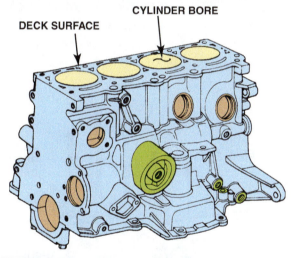

FIGURE 18–8 The deck is the machined top surface of the block.

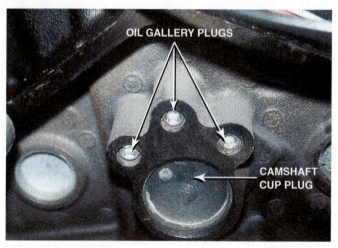

FIGURE 18–10 Typical oil gallery plugs on the rear of a Chevrolet small block V-8 engine.

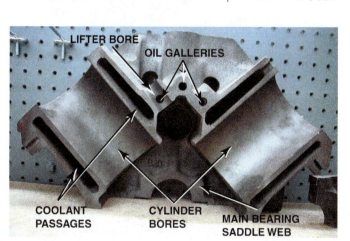

FIGURE 18–9 Cutaway of a Chevrolet V-8 block showing all of the internal passages.

MAIN BEARING CAPS   The main bearing caps are cast or manufactured from sintered or billeted materials, separately from the block.

- They are machined and then installed on the block for a final bore finishing operation.

- With caps installed, the main bearing bores and cam bearing bores (on OHV engines) are machined to the correct size and alignment. On some engines, these bores are honed to a very fine finish and exact size.

- Main bearing caps are not interchangeable or reversible, because they are individually finished in place.

What Does LHD Mean?

The abbreviation LHD means *left-hand dipstick,* which is commonly used by rebuilders and remanufacturers in their literature in describing Chevrolet small block V-8 engines. Before about 1980, most small block Chevrolet V-8s used an oil dipstick pad on the left side (driver's side) of the engine block. Starting in about 1980, when oxygen sensors were first used on this engine, the dipstick was relocated to the right side of the block.

Therefore, to be assured of ordering or delivering the correct engine, knowing the dipstick location is critical. An LHD block cannot be used with the exhaust manifold setup that includes the oxygen sensor without major refitting or the installing of a different style of oil pan that includes a provision for an oil dipstick. Engine blocks with the dipstick pad cast on the right side are, therefore, coded as right-hand dipstick (RHD) engines.

NOTE: Some blocks cast around the year 1980 are cast with both right- and left-hand oil dipstick pads, but only one is drilled for the dipstick tube. ● SEE FIGURE 18–11.

FIGURE 18–11 Small block Chevrolet block. Note the left-hand dipstick hole and a pad cast for a right-hand dipstick.

■ Main bearing caps may have cast numbers indicating their position on the block. If not, they should be marked with numbers and arrows pointing toward the front of the engine.

Standard production engines usually use two bolts to hold the main bearing cap in place. ● SEE FIGURE 18–12.

Heavy-duty and high-performance engines often use additional main bearing support bolts. A four-bolt, and even six-bolt, main cap can be of a cross-bolted design in a deep skirt block or of a parallel design in a shallow skirt block. ● SEE FIGURES 18–13 AND 18–14.

Expansion force of the combustion chamber gases will try to push the head off the top and the crankshaft off the bottom of the block. The engine is held together with the head bolts and main bearing cap bolts screwed into bolt bosses and ribs in the block. The extra bolts on the main bearing cap help to support the crankshaft when there are high combustion pressures and mechanical loads, especially during high engine speed operation. Many engines use a **girdle** which ties all of the main bearing caps together to add strength to the lower part of the block. ● SEE FIGURE 18–15.

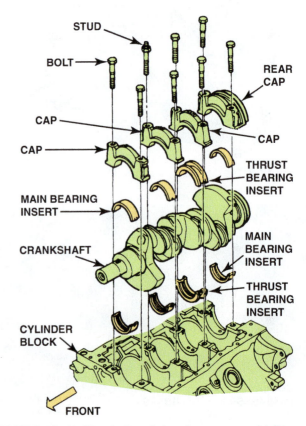

FIGURE 18–12 Two-bolt main bearing caps provide adequate bottom end strength for most engines.

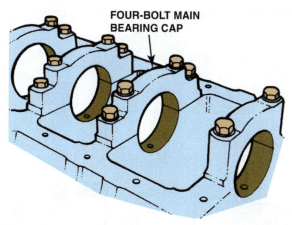

FIGURE 18–13 High-performance and truck engines often use four-bolt main bearing caps for greater durability.

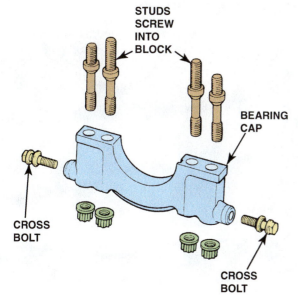

FIGURE 18–14 Some engines add to the strength of a four-bolt main bearing cap by also using cross bolts through the bolt on the sides of the main bearing caps.

ENGINE BLOCK SERVICE

PROCEDURES The engine block is the foundation of the engine. All parts of the block must be of the correct size and they must be aligned. The parts must also have the proper finishes if the engine is to function dependably for a normal service life. Engine blueprinting is the reconditioning of all the critical surfaces and dimensions so that the block is actually like new.

After a thorough cleaning, the block should be inspected for cracks or other flaws before machine work begins. After the block has been cleaned and checked for crack, it should be prepared in the following sequence.

OPERATION 1 Main bearing housing bore alignment, often called "align boring" (or honing)

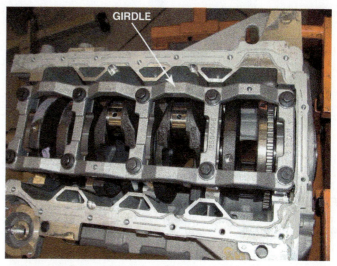

FIGURE 18–15 A girdle is used to tie all of the main bearing caps together.

OPERATION 2 Machining of the block deck surface parallel to the crankshaft

OPERATION 3 Cylinder boring and honing

MAIN BEARING HOUSING BORE ALIGNMENT The main bearing journals of a straight crankshaft are in alignment. If the main bearing housing bores in the block are not in alignment, the crankshaft will bend as it rotates. This condition increases rotational friction of the crankshaft and will lead to premature bearing failure or a broken crankshaft. The original stress in the block casting is gradually relieved as the block is used. Some slight warpage may occur as the stress is relieved. In addition,

---

? FREQUENTLY ASKED QUESTION

What Is a Seasoned Engine?

A new engine is machined and assembled within a few hours after the heads and block are cast from melted iron. Newly cast parts have internal stresses within the metal. The stress results from the different thickness of the metal sections in the head. Forces from combustion in the engine, plus continued heating and cooling, gradually relieve these stresses. By the time the engine has accumulated 20,000 to 30,000 miles (32,000 to 48,000 km), the stresses have been completely relieved. This is why some engine rebuilders prefer to work with used heads and blocks that are stress relieved. Used engines are often called "seasoned" because of the reduced stress and movement these components have as compared with new parts.

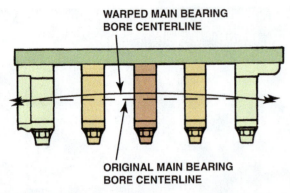

FIGURE 18–16 The main bearing bores of a warped block usually bend into a bowed shape. The greatest distortion is in the center bores.

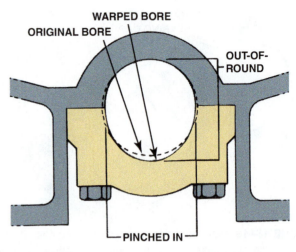

FIGURE 18–17 When the main bearing caps bow downward, they also pinch in at the parting line.

the continued pounding caused by combustion will usually cause some stretch in the main bearing caps. ● SEE FIGURE 18–16.

The main bearing bores gradually bow upward and elongate vertically. This means that the bearing bore becomes smaller at the centerline as the block distorts, pinching the bore inward at the sides. ● SEE FIGURE 18–17.

The procedure includes the following steps.

STEP 1 The first step in determining the condition of the main bearing bores is to determine if the bore alignment in the block is straight. These bores are called the **saddles**. A precision ground straightedge and a feeler gauge are used to determine the amount of warpage. The amount of variation along the entire length of the block should not exceed 0.0015 inch (0.038 mm).

CAUTION: When performing this measurement, be sure that the block is resting on a flat surface. If the engine is mounted to an engine stand, the weight of the block on the unsupported end can cause an error in the measurement of the main bearing bores and saddle alignment.

STEP 2 If the block saddles exceed one-and-a-half thousandth of an inch distortion, then align honing is required to restore the block. If the block saddles are straight, the bores should be measured to be sure that the bearing caps are not distorted. ● SEE FIGURE 18–18.

STEP 3 The bearing caps should be installed and the retaining bolts tightened to the specified torque before measuring the main bearing bores. Using a telescoping gauge, measure each bore in at least two directions. Check the service information for the specified main bearing bore diameter. The bearing bore should not vary by more than one-half of a thousandth of an inch or 0.0005 inch (0.0127 mm). A dial bore gauge is often used to measure the main bearing bore. Set up the dial

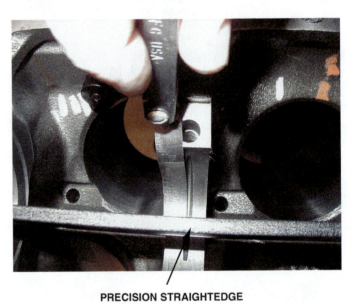

PRECISION STRAIGHTEDGE

FIGURE 18–18 The main bearing bore alignment can be checked using a precision straightedge and a feeler gauge.

bore gauge in the fixture with the necessary extensions to achieve the nominal main bearing bore diameter.

Check the service information for the specified main bearing bore diameter and determine the exact middle of the range.

ARBOR CHECK METHOD The arbor is installed, then all main caps are tightened to specifications. After tightening, the arbor is checked to make sure it rotates freely, indicating a true centerline. ● SEE FIGURE 18–19.

MACHINING THE DECK SURFACE OF THE BLOCK An engine should have the same combustion chamber size in each cylinder. For this to occur, each piston must come up an equal distance from the block deck. The connecting rods are attached to the rod bearing journals of the crankshaft. Pistons

(a)

(b)

FIGURE 18–19 (a) A precision arbor can be used to check the main bearing bore alignment. (b) If the sleeve can be inserted into all of the main bearing bores, then they are aligned.

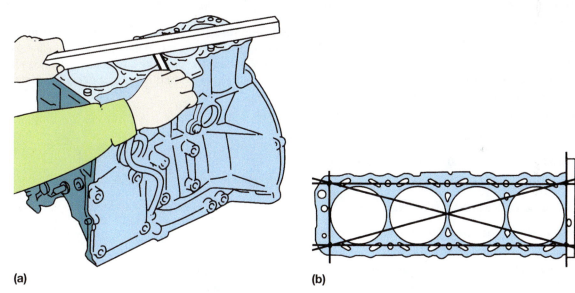
(a)   (b)

FIGURE 18–20 (a) Checking the flatness of the block deck surface using a straightedge and a feeler gauge. (b) To be sure that the top of the block is flat, check the block in six locations as shown.

are attached to the connecting rods. As the crankshaft rotates, the pistons come to the top of the stroke. When all parts are sized equally, all the pistons will come up to the same level. This can only happen if the block deck is parallel to the main bearing bores. Therefore, the flatness of the block deck should be checked. ● **SEE FIGURE 18–20.**

The block deck must be resurfaced in a surfacing machine that can control the amount of metal removed when it is necessary to match the size of the combustion chambers. This procedure is called **decking the block**. The block is set up on a bar located in the main bearing saddles, or set up on the oil pan rails of the block. The bar is parallel to the direction of cutting head movement. The

block is leveled sideways, and then the deck is resurfaced in the same manner as the head is resurfaced. ● **FIGURE 18–21** shows a block deck being resurfaced by grinding.

DECK SURFACE FINISH The surface finish of the block deck should be:

- 60 to 100 Ra (65 to 110 RMS) for cast iron
- 50 to 60 Ra (55 to 65 RMS) for aluminum block decks to be assured of a proper head gasket surface

The surface finish is determined by the type of grinding stone used, as well as the speed and coolant used in the finishing operation. The higher the surface finish number, the rougher the surface.

FIGURE 18–21 Grinding the deck surface of the block.

CYLINDER BORING Cylinders should be measured across the engine (perpendicular to the crankshaft), where the greatest wear occurs. In other words, measure the bores at 90 degrees to the piston pin. Most wear will be found just below the ridge, and the least amount of wear will occur below the lowest ring travel. ● **SEE FIGURE 18–22.**

The cylinder should be checked for out-of-round and taper. ● **SEE FIGURE 18–23.**

Most cylinders are serviceable if they:

- Are a maximum of 0.003 inch (0.076 mm) out-of-round

- Have no more than a 0.005 inch (0.127 mm) taper

- Have no deep scratches in the cylinder wall

NOTE: Always check the specifications for the engine being serviced. For example, the General Motors 4.8, 5.3, 5.7, 6, and 6.2 liter LS series V-8s have a maximum out-of-round of only 0.0003 inch (3/10 of one-thousandths of an inch). This specification is about one-third of the normal dimension of about 0.001 inch.

The most effective way to correct excessive cylinder out-of-round, taper, or scoring is to rebore the cylinder. The rebored cylinder requires the use of a new, oversize piston.

The maximum bore oversize is determined by two factors.

1. Cylinder wall thickness—at least 0.17 inch for street engines and 0.2 inch for high-performance or racing applications

2. Size of the available oversize pistons

If in doubt as to the amount of overbore that is possible without causing structural weakness, an ultrasonic test should be performed on the block to determine the thickness of the cylinder walls. An ultrasonic tester can measure the thickness of the cylinder walls and is used to determine if a cylinder can be bored oversize and, if so, by how much. All cylinders should

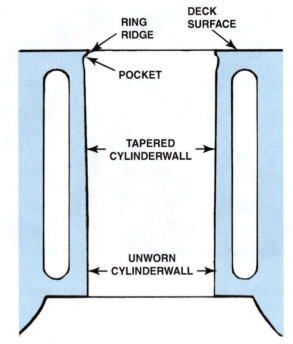

FIGURE 18–22 Cylinders wear in a taper, with most of the wear occurring at the top of the cylinder where the greatest amount of heat and pressure are created. The ridge is formed because the very top part of the cylinder is not contacted by the rings.

FIGURE 18–23 Using a dial bore gauge to measure the bore diameter at the top just below the ridge (maximum wear section) and at the bottom below the ring travel (minimum wear section). The difference between these two measurements is the amount of cylinder taper. Take the measurements in line with the crankshaft and then repeat the measurements at right angles to the centerline of the block in each cylinder to determine out-of-round.

FREQUENTLY ASKED QUESTION

How Do I Determine What Oversize Bore Is Needed?

An easy way to calculate oversize piston size is to determine the amount of taper, double it, and add 0.010 inch (Taper × 2 + 0.010 inch = Oversize piston). Common oversize measurements include:

- 0.020 inch
- 0.030 inch
- 0.040 inch
- 0.060 inch

Use caution when boring for an oversize measurement larger than 0.030 inch due to potential engine damage caused from too thin cylinder walls.

FIGURE 18–24 A cylinder boring machine is used to enlarge cylinder bore diameter so a replacement oversize piston can be used to restore a worn engine to useful service or to increase the displacement of the engine in an attempt to increase power output.

be tested. Variation in cylinder wall thickness occurs because of core shifting (moving) during the casting of the block. For best results, cylinders should be rebored to the smallest size possible.

HINT: The pistons that will be used should always be in hand before the cylinders are rebored. The cylinders are then bored and honed to match the exact size of the pistons.

The cylinder must be perpendicular to the crankshaft for normal bearing and piston life. If the block deck has been aligned with the crankshaft, it can be used to align the cylinders. Portable cylinder boring bars are clamped to the block deck. Heavy-duty production boring machines support the block on the main bearing bores.

Main bearing caps should be torqued in place when cylinders are being rebored. In precision boring, a torque plate is also bolted on in place of the cylinder head while boring cylinders. In this way, distortion is kept to a minimum. The general procedure used for reboring cylinders includes the following steps.

STEP 1 Set the boring bar up so that it is perpendicular to the crankshaft. It must be located over the center of the cylinder.

STEP 2 The cylinder center is found by installing centering pins in the bar.

STEP 3 The bar is lowered so that the centering pins are located near the bottom of the cylinder, where the least wear has occurred. This locates the boring bar over the original cylinder center. Once the boring bar is centered, the boring machine is clamped in place to hold it securely. This will allow the cylinder to be

FREQUENTLY ASKED QUESTION

What Is a Boring Hone?

Many shops now use "boring" hones instead of boring bars. Boring hones have the advantages of being able to resize and finish hone with only one machine setup. Often a diamond hone is used and rough honed to within about 0.003 inch of the finished bore size. Then a finish hone is used to provide the proper surface finish.

rebored on the original centerline, regardless of the amount of cylinder wear.

STEP 4 A sharp, properly ground cutting tool is installed and adjusted to the desired dimension. Rough cuts remove a great deal of metal on each pass of the cutting tool. The rough cut is followed by a fine cut that produces a much smoother and more accurate finish. Different-shaped tool bits are used for rough and finish boring.

STEP 5 The last cut is made to produce a diameter that is at least 0.002 inch (0.05 mm) smaller than the required diameter. ● **SEE FIGURE 18–24.**

SLEEVING THE CYLINDER Sometimes, cylinders have a gouge so deep that it will not clean up when the cylinder is rebored to the maximum size. This could happen if the piston pin moved endways and rubbed on the cylinder wall. Cylinder blocks with deep gouges may be able to be salvaged by **sleeving** the cylinder. The cylinder wall thickness has to be checked to see if sleeving is possible. Sleeving a cylinder

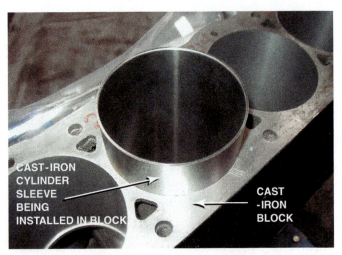

FIGURE 18–25 A dry cylinder sleeve can also be installed in a cast-iron block to repair a worn or cracked cylinder.

FIGURE 18–26 An assortment of ball-type deglazing hones. This type of hone does not straighten wavy cylinder walls.

is done by boring the cylinder to a dimension that is greatly oversize to almost match the outside diameter of the cylinder sleeve. The sleeve is pressed into the rebored block and then the center of the sleeve is bored to the diameter required by the piston. The cylinder can be sized to use a standard-size piston when it is sleeved. ● **SEE FIGURE 18–25.**

CYLINDER HONING It is important to have the proper surface finish on the cylinder wall for the rings to seat against. Honing includes two basic operations depending on the application.

1. When installing new piston rings on a cylinder that is not being bored, some ring manufacturers recommend breaking the hard surface glaze on the cylinder wall with a hone before installing new piston rings. This process is often called "deglazing" the cylinder walls.

2. The cylinder wall should be honed to straighten the cylinder when the wall is wavy or scuffed. If honing is being done with the crankshaft remaining in the block, the crankshaft should be protected to keep honing chips from getting on the shaft.

Two types of hones are used for cylinder service.

- A *deglazing hone* removes the hard surface glaze remaining in the cylinder. It is a flexible hone that follows the shape of the cylinder wall, even when the wall is wavy. It cannot be used to straighten the cylinder. A brush-type (ball-type) deglazing hone is shown in ● **FIGURE 18–26.**

- A *sizing hone* can be used to straighten the cylinder and to provide a suitable surface for the piston rings. Honing the cylinder removes the fractured metal that is created by boring. The cylinders must be honed a minimum of 0.002 inch (0.05 mm) after boring to cut below the rough

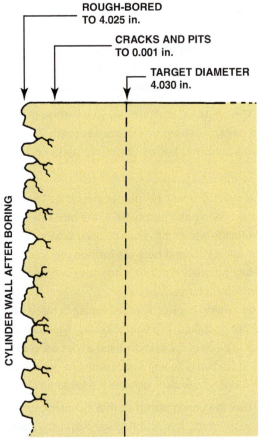

FIGURE 18–27 After boring, the cylinder surface is rough, pitted, and fractured to a depth of about 0.001 inch.

surface and provide an adequate finish. Honing leaves a plateau surface that can support the oil film for the rings and piston skirt. This plateau surface is achieved by first using a coarse stone followed by a smooth stone to achieve the desired surface. The process of using a course and fine stone is called **plateau honing.** ● **SEE FIGURE 18–27.**

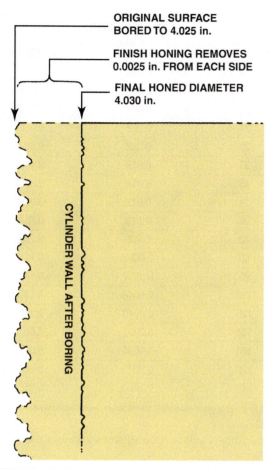

ORIGINAL SURFACE
BORED TO 4.025 in.

FINISH HONING REMOVES
0.0025 in. FROM EACH SIDE

FINAL HONED DIAMETER
4.030 in.

CYLINDER WALL AFTER BORING

FIGURE 18–28 Honing enlarges the cylinder bore to the final size and leaves a plateau surface finish that retains oil.

TECH TIP

Always Use Torque Plates

Torque plates are thick metal plates that are bolted to the cylinder block to duplicate the forces on the block that occur when the cylinder head is installed. Even though not all machine shops use torque plates during the boring operation, the use of torque plates during the final dimensional honing operation is beneficial. Without torque plates, cylinders can become out-of-round (up to 0.003 inch) and distorted when the cylinder heads are installed and torqued down. Even though the use of torque plates does not eliminate all distortion, their use helps to ensure a truer cylinder dimension. ● **SEE FIGURE 18–29.**

Its honing stones are held in a rigid fixture with an expanding mechanism to control the size of the hone. The sizing hone can be used to straighten the cylinder taper by honing the lower cylinder diameter more than the upper

FIGURE 18–29 A torque plate being used during a cylinder honing operation. The thick piece of metal is bolted to the block and simulates the forces exerted on the block by the head bolts when the cylinder head is attached.

diameter. As it rotates, the sizing hone only cuts the high spots so that cylinder out-of-round is also reduced. The cylinder wall surface finish is about the same when the cylinder is refinished with either type of hone. ● **SEE FIGURE 18–28.**

The hone is stroked up and down in the cylinder as it rotates to produce a **crosshatch finish** on the cylinder wall which aides in proper ring break-in. The speed that the operator moves the hone up and down controls the angle. Always check service information for the specified crosshatch angle.

The angle of the crosshatch should be between 20 and 60 degrees. Higher angles are produced when the hone is stroked more rapidly in the cylinder. A typical honed cylinder is pictured in ● **FIGURE 18–30.**

CYLINDER SURFACE FINISH The size of the abrasive particles in the grinding and honing stones controls the surface finish. The size of the abrasive is called the **grit size**. The abrasive is sifted through a screen mesh to sort out the grit size. A coarse-mesh screen has few wires in each square inch, so large pieces can fall through the screen. A fine-mesh screen has many wires in each square inch so that only small pieces can fall through. The screen is used to separate the different grit sizes. The grit size is the number of wires in each square inch of the mesh. A low-numbered grit has large pieces of abrasive material; a high-numbered grit has small pieces of abrasive material. The higher the grit number is, the smoother the surface finish will be. ● **SEE CHART 18–1.**

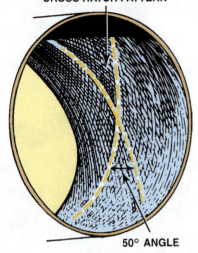

CROSS-HATCH PATTERN

50° ANGLE

FIGURE 18–30 The crosshatched pattern holds oil to keep the rings from wearing excessively, and also keeps the rings against the cylinder wall for a gas-tight fit.

TECH TIP

Bore to Size, Hone for Clearance

Many engine rebuilders and remanufacturers bore the cylinders to the exact size of the oversize pistons that are to be used. After the block is bored to a standard oversize measurement, the cylinder is honed. The rigid hone stones, along with an experienced operator, can increase the bore size by 0.001 to 0.003 inch (one to three thousandths of an inch) for the typical clearance needed between the piston and the cylinder walls.

For example:

Actual piston diameter = 4.028 inch

Bore diameter = 4.028 inch

Diameter after honing = 4.03 inch

Amount removed by honing = 0.002 inch

NOTE: The minimum amount recommended to be removed by honing is 0.002 inch, to remove the fractured metal in the cylinder wall caused by boring.

A given grit size will produce the same finish as long as the cutting pressure is constant. With the same grit size, light cutting pressure produces fine finishes, and heavy cutting pressure produces rough finishes.

The surface finish should match the surface required for the type of piston rings to be used. Typical grit and surface finish standards include the following:

GRIT SIZING CHART		
GRIT/SIEVE SIZE	INCHES	MILLIMETERS
12	0.063	1.600
16	0.043	1.092
20	0.037	0.939
24	0.027	0.685
30	0.022	0.558
36	0.019	0.482
46	0.014	0.355
54	0.012	0.304
60	0.010	0.254
70	0.008	0.203
80	0.0065	0.165
90	0.0057	0.144
100	0.0048	0.121
120	0.0040	0.101
150	0.0035	0.088
180	0.0030	0.076
220	0.0025	0.063
240	0.0020	0.050

CHART 18–1

Grit size numbers and their dimensions in inches and millimeters.

- Chrome rings: 180 grit (25 to 35 microinches)
- Cast-iron rings: 200 grit (20 to 30 microinches)
- Moly rings: 220 grit (18 to 25 microinches)

NOTE: The correct honing oil and coolant are critical to proper operation of the honing equipment and to the quality of the finished cylinders.

CYLINDER HONING PROCEDURE The procedure includes the following steps.

STEP 1 The hone is placed in the cylinder. Before the drive motor is turned on, the hone is moved up and down in the cylinder to get the feel of the stroke length needed. The end of the hone should just break out of the cylinder bore on each end. The hone must *not* be pulled from the top of the cylinder while it is rotating. Also, it must not be pushed so low in the cylinder that it hits the main bearing web or crankshaft.

STEP 2 The sizing hone is adjusted to give a solid drag at the lower end of the stroke.

STEP 3 The hone drive motor is turned on and stroking begins immediately. Stroking continues until the sound of the drag is reduced.

(a)

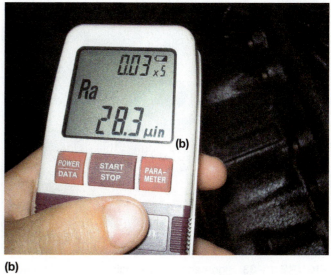

(b)

FIGURE 18–31 (a) The surface finish tool is being held against the cylinder wall. (b) The reading indicates the Ra roughness of the cylinder. More work is needed if moly piston rings are to be used.

FIGURE 18–32 Using a tapered sanding cone to remove the sharp edges at the top of the cylinders created when the block was machined.

STEP 4 The hone drive motor is turned off while it is still stroking. Stroking is stopped as the rotation of the hone stops. After rotation stops, the hone is collapsed and removed from the cylinder.

STEP 5 The cylinder is examined to check the bore size and finish of the wall. If more honing is needed, the cylinder is again coated with honing oil and honed once again. The finished cylinder should be within 0.0005 inch (0.013 mm) on both out-of-round and taper measurements. ● **SEE FIGURE 18–31** for an example of cylinder surface finish reading.

 **TECH TIP**

Install Lifter Bore Bushings

Lifter bores in a block can be out-of-square with the camshaft, resulting in premature camshaft wear and variations in the valve timing from cylinder to cylinder. To correct for this variation, the lifter bores are bored and reamed oversize using a fixture fastened to the block deck to ensure proper alignment. Bronze lifter bushings are then installed and finish-honed to achieve the correct lifter-to-bore clearance. ● **SEE FIGURE 18–33.**

The lifter bores should be "honed" with a ball-type hone. This should be done even if they are "in-line" and do not need bushings. This is often overlooked by technicians and can lead to lifter problems later on, causing lifters to stick on the bores.

CHAMFERING THE CYLINDER BORES Whenever machining is performed on the block such as boring and decking, the top edge of the cylinder bores have sharp edges. These sharp edges must be removed to allow the piston with rings to be installed. The slight chamfer allows the rings to enter the cylinder easily when the pistons are installed. A tapered rubber cone covered in sanding cloth is used to remove the sharp edges. ● **SEE FIGURE 18–32.**

FIGURE 18-33 High-performance engine builders will often install bronze sleeves in the lifter bores.

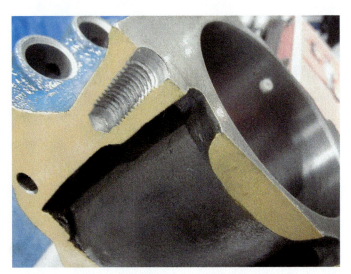

FIGURE 18-34 Notice on this cutaway engine block that some of the head bolt holes do not extend too far into the block and dead end. Debris can accumulate at the bottom of these holes and it must be cleaned out before final assembly.

BLOCK PREPARATION FOR ASSEMBLY

BLOCK CLEANING After the cylinders have been honed and before the block is cleaned, use a sandpaper cone to chamfer the top edge of the cylinder. Cleaning the honed cylinder wall is an important part of the honing process. If any grit remains on the cylinder wall, it will rapidly wear the piston rings. This wear will cause premature failure of the reconditioning job. Degreasing and decarbonizing procedures will only remove the honing oil but will *not* remove the abrasive. The *best* way to clean the honed cylinders is to scrub the cylinder wall with a brush using a mixture of *soap* or *detergent* and *water.* The block is scrubbed until it is absolutely clean. This can be determined by wiping the cylinder wall with a clean lint free cloth. The cloth will pick up no soil when the cylinder wall is clean. Be sure that the cylinders are dried as soon as possible to avoid rust from forming.

BLOCK DETAILING Before the engine block can be assembled, a final detailed cleaning should be performed.

1. All oil passages (galleries) should be cleaned by running a long bottle-type brush through all holes in the block.

FIGURE 18-35 A tread chaser or bottoming tap should be used in all threaded holes before assembling the engine.

2. All tapped holes should have the sharp edges at the top of the holes removed (chamfered) and cleaned with the correct size of thread chaser to remove any dirt and burrs. ● **SEE FIGURES 18-34 AND 18-35.**

3. Coat the newly cleaned block with fogging oil to prevent rust. Cover the block with a large plastic bag to keep out dirt until it is time to assemble the engine.

SUMMARY

1. Engine blocks are made of either cast iron or aluminum.
2. Cores are used inside a mold to form water jackets and cylinder bores. After the cast iron has cooled, the block is shaken, which breaks up the cores so that they fall out of openings in the side of the block. Core plugs are used to fill the holes.
3. The block deck is the surface to which the cylinder head attaches. This surface must be flat, true, and parallel with the centerline of the main bearing journals for proper engine operation.
4. The cylinder should be bored and/or honed to match the size of the pistons to be used.
5. All bolt holes should be chamfered and cleaned with a thread chaser before assembly.

REVIEW QUESTIONS

1. How is Styrofoam used to cast an engine block?
2. What does "decking the block" mean?
3. What is the difference between deglazing and honing a cylinder?
4. What is the best method to use to clean an engine block after honing?

CHAPTER QUIZ

1. The block deck is the _____.
   a. Bottom (pan rail) of the block
   b. Top surface of the block
   c. Valley surface of a V-type engine
   d. Area where the engine mounts are attached to the block

2. The surface finish for the cylinder walls usually depends on _____.
   a. The type of piston rings to be used
   b. The type of engine oil that is going to be used in the engine
   c. The cylinder wall-to-piston clearance
   d. Both b and c

3. What should be installed and torqued to factory specification before machining a block?
   a. Front timing chain cover
   b. Main bearing caps
   c. Oil pan
   d. All of the above

4. Cast iron has about how much carbon content?
   a. Less than 1%   b. 2%
   c. 3%   d. 4% or higher

5. Engine blocks can be manufactured using which method(s)?
   a. Sand cast
   b. Sand cast or die cast
   c. Extruded cylinder
   d. Machined from a solid piece of metal (either cast iron or aluminum)

6. A bedplate is located between the _____ and the _____.
   a. Cylinder bores; water jacket
   b. Cylinder head; block deck
   c. Bottom of the block; oil pan
   d. Block deck; cylinder bore

7. Siamese cylinder bores are _____.
   a. Cylinders that do not have a coolant passage between them
   b. Aluminum cylinders
   c. Another name for cylinder liners
   d. Cast-iron cylinders

8. Ultrasonic testing is used to test _____.
   a. For cracks in the block
   b. Surface finish of the cylinder bores
   c. Cylinder wall thickness
   d. Both b and c

9. An engine block should be machined in which order?
   a. Align honing, cylinder boring, block deck machining
   b. Block decking, align honing, cylinder boring
   c. Cylinder boring, align honing, block decking
   d. Align honing, block decking, cylinder boring

10. After the engine block has been machined, it should be cleaned using _____.
   a. Soap and water
   b. SAE 10W-30 oil and a shop cloth
   c. Sprayed-on brake cleaner to remove the cutting oil
   d. Sprayed-on WD-40

chapter 19

CRANKSHAFTS, BALANCE SHAFTS, AND BEARINGS

LEARNING OBJECTIVES

After studying this chapter, the reader should be able to:

1. Describe the purpose and function of a crankshaft.
2. Discuss how to measure crankshafts.
3. Explain how crankshafts are machined and polished.
4. Discuss the purpose and function of balance shafts.
5. Discuss engine bearing construction and installation procedures.

This chapter will help you prepare for ASE Engine Repair (A1) certification test content area "C" (Engine Block Diagnosis and Repair).

GM STC OBJECTIVES

GM Service Technical College topics covered in this chapter are:

1. Inspect auxiliary (balance, intermediate, idler, counterbalance, or silencer) shaft(s) and support bearings for damage and wear; determine needed repairs; reinstall and time.
2. Measure bearing clearance, journal diameter, out-of-round, run out, and rear flange run out.
3. Inspect crankshaft for surface cracks and journal damage; check oil passage condition; measure journal wear; determine needed repairs.

4. Inspect and measure main and connecting rod bearings for damage, clearances, and end play; determine needed repairs (includes the proper selection of bearings).

KEY TERMS

Aluminum 306
Amplitude 299
Babbitt 305
Bank 296
Bearing crown 305
Bearing shell 305
Billet 295
Case hardening 294
Conformability 307
Copper-lead alloy 305
Corrosion resistance 308
Counterweights 298
Crankpins 294
Crankshaft centerline 293
Crush 309
Elastomer 299
Electroplating 306
Embedability 307
Fatigue life 307
Flying web 298
Frequency 298
Full round bearing 310

Fully counterweighted 298
Half-shell bearing 306
Hub 299
Inertia ring 299
Nitriding 295
Overlay 305
Plain bearing 305
Precision insert-type bearing shells 306
Primary vibration 300
Resonate 298
Score resistance 308
Secondary vibration 300
Sleeve bearing 305
Splay angle 298
Split-type (half-shell) bearing 310
Spread 309
Spun bearing 309
Surface finish 294
Thrust bearing 293
Tuftriding 295
Work hardened 307

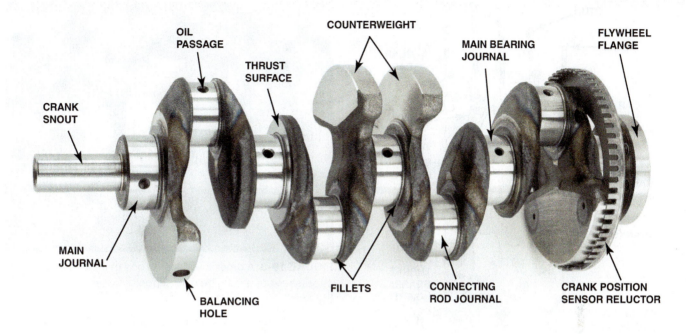

FIGURE 19–1 Typical crankshaft with main journals that are supported by main bearings in the block. Rod journals are offset from the crankshaft centerline. (*Courtesy of General Motors*)

CRANKSHAFT

PURPOSE AND FUNCTION Power from expanding gases in the combustion chamber is delivered to the crankshaft through the piston, piston pin, and connecting rod. The connecting rods and their bearings are attached to a bearing journal on the crank throw. The crank throw is offset from the **crankshaft centerline**. The distance between the centerline of the connecting rod bearing journal and the centerline of the crankshaft main bearing journal determines the stroke of the engine. The engine stroke is calculated by multiplying the distance between the two centerlines by 2. The combustion force is applied to the crank throw after the crankshaft has moved past top center. This produces the turning effort or torque, which rotates the crankshaft. The crankshaft rotates on the main bearings. These bearings are split in half so that they can be assembled around the crankshaft main bearing journals. The crankshaft includes the following parts.

- Main bearing journals
- Rod bearing journals
- Crankshaft throws
- Counterweights
- Front snout
- Flywheel flange

- Keyways
- Oil passages
- Crank position sensor reluctor ring

  ● **SEE FIGURE 19–1.**

MAIN BEARING JOURNALS The crankshaft rotates in the cylinder block supported on main bearings. ● **SEE FIGURE 19–2**.

The main bearings support the crankshaft and allow it to rotate easily without excessive wear. The number of cylinders usually determines the number of main bearings.

- Four-cylinder engines and V-8 engines usually have five main bearings.
- Inline 6-cylinder engines usually have seven main bearings.
- V-6 engines normally have only four main bearings.

The crankshaft also must be able to absorb loads applied longitudinally (end to end) or thrust loads from the clutch on a manual transmission vehicle or the torque converter on a vehicle equipped with an automatic transmission. Thrust loads are forces that push and pull the crankshaft forward and rearward in the engine block. A **thrust bearing** supports these loads and maintains the front-to-rear position of the crankshaft in the block. ● **SEE FIGURE 19–3**.

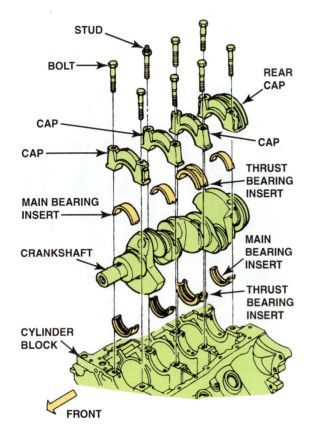

FIGURE 19–2 The crankshaft rotates on main bearings. Longitudinal (end-to-end) movement is controlled by the thrust bearing.

FIGURE 19–3 A ground surface on one of the crankshaft cheeks next to a main bearing supports thrust loads on the crank.

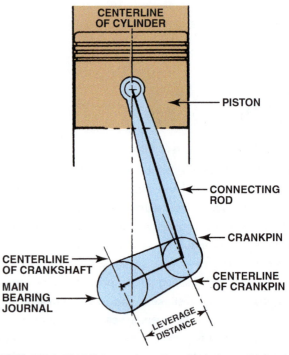

FIGURE 19–4 The distance from the crankpin centerline to the centerline of the crankshaft determines the stroke, which is the leverage available to turn the crankshaft.

The thrust surface on many engines is usually located at the middle or one of the end main bearings. On most engines, the bearing insert for the main bearing is equipped with thrust bearing flanges that ride against the thrust surface.

ROD BEARING JOURNALS
The rod bearing journals, also called **crankpins**, are offset from the centerline of the crank. Insert-type bearings fit between the big end of the connecting rod and the crankpin of the crankshaft. The crankshaft throw distance that measures one-half of the stroke has a direct relationship to the displacement of the engine.

Engine stroke is equal to *twice* the leverage distance or two times the length of the crankshaft throw. ● **SEE FIGURE 19–4.**

SURFACE FINISH
All crankshaft journals are ground to a very smooth finish. **Surface finish** is measured in microinches; and the smaller the number, the smoother the surface. The typical specification for main and rod crankshaft journals is between 10 and 20 roughness average (Ra). This very smooth surface finish is achieved by polishing the crank journals after the grinding operation.

JOURNAL HARDNESS
To improve wear resistance, some manufacturers harden the crankshaft journals. Methods used to harden the crankshaft journals include:

- **Case hardening**, where only the outer portion of the surface is hardened. Case hardening involves heating the crankshaft and adding carbon to the journals where it causes the outer surface to become harder than the rest

FIGURE 19–5 Wide separation lines of a forged crankshaft.

of the crankshaft. If the entire crankshaft was hardened, it would become too brittle to absorb the torsional stresses of normal engine operation.

- **Nitriding**, when the crankshaft is heated to about 1,000°F (540°C) in a furnace filled with ammonia gas, and then allowed to cool. The process adds nitrogen (from the ammonia) into the surface of the metal-forming hard nitrides in the surface of the crankshaft to a depth of about 0.007 inch (0.8 mm).

- **Tuftriding**, another variation of this process, involves heating the crankshaft in a molten cyanide salt bath. Tuftriding is a trade name of General Motors.

CRANKSHAFT CONSTRUCTION

FORGED Crankshafts used in high-production automotive engines may be either forged or cast. Forged crankshafts are stronger than the cast crankshaft, but they are more expensive. Forged crankshafts may have a wide separation line. The wide separation line is the result of a grinding process to remove the metal that was extruded from the forging die during the forging process. ● **SEE FIGURE 19–5**.

Most high-performance forged crankshafts are made from SAE 4340 or a similar type of steel. The crankshaft is formed from a hot steel billet through the use of a series of forging dies. Each die changes the shape of the billet slightly. The crankshaft blank is finally formed with the last die. The blanks

are then machined to finish the crankshaft. Forging makes a very dense, tough crankshaft with the metal's grain structure running parallel to the principal direction of stress.

Two methods are used to forge crankshafts.

- One method is to forge the crankshaft *in place.* This is followed by straightening. The forging in place method is primarily used with forged 4- and 6-cylinder crankshafts.

- A second method is to forge the crankshaft in a *single plane.* It is then twisted in the main bearing journal to index the throws at the desired angles. Most newer crankshafts are not twisted.

CAST CRANKSHAFTS Casting materials and techniques have improved cast crankshaft quality so that cast crankshafts are used in most production automotive engines. Automotive crankshafts may be cast in steel, nodular iron, or malleable iron. Advantages of a cast crankshaft are as follows:

- Crankshaft material and machining costs are less than they are with forging. The reason is that the crankshaft can be made close to the required shape and size, including all complicated counterweights. The only machining required on a carefully designed cast crankshaft is the grinding of bearing journal surfaces and the finishing of front and rear drive ends.

- Metal grain structure in the cast crankshaft is uniform and random throughout; therefore, the shaft is able to handle loads from all directions.

- Counterweights on cast crankshafts are slightly larger than counterweights on a forged crankshaft, because the cast shaft metal is less dense and therefore somewhat lighter.

The narrow mold parting surface lines can be seen on the cast crankshaft in ● **FIGURE 19–6**.

BILLET CRANKSHAFTS A billet crankshaft is machined from a solid piece of forged steel called a **billet**. This solid piece of steel, usually SAE 4340, is then machined through several operations to create a finished crankshaft.

The advantages of a billet crankshaft include:

- Uniform grain structure created by the forging process

- Stiff, strong, and very durable

The disadvantage is the high cost. Billet crankshafts tend to be very expensive because of the large amount of material removal during the machining process and the high material cost and the additional heat treatment required. ● **SEE FIGURE 19–7**.

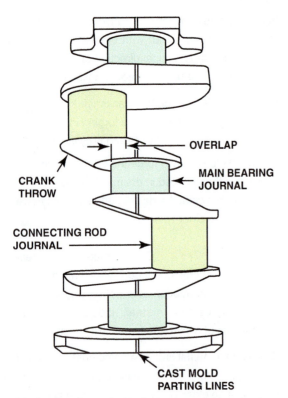

FIGURE 19–6 Cast crankshaft showing the bearing journal overlap and a straight, narrow cast mold parting line. The amount of overlap determines the strength of the crankshaft.

FIGURE 19–7 A billet crankshaft showing how it is machined from a solid chuck of steel, usually 4340 steel, at the right and the finished crankshaft on the left.

CRANKSHAFT OILING HOLES

The crankshaft is drilled to allow oil from the main bearing oil groove to be directed to the connecting rod bearings. ● SEE FIGURE 19–8.

The oil on the bearings forms a hydrodynamic oil film to support bearing loads. Some of the oil may be sprayed out through a spit or bleed hole in the connecting rod. The rest of the oil leaks from the edges of the bearing. It is thrown from the bearing against the inside surfaces of the engine. Some of the oil that is thrown from the crankshaft bearings will land on the camshaft to lubricate the lobes. A part of the throw-off, oil splashes on the cylinder wall to lubricate the piston and rings.

FIGURE 19–8 Crankshaft sawed in half, showing drilled oil passages between the main and rod bearing journals.

Stress tends to concentrate at oil holes drilled through the crankshaft journals. These holes are usually located where the crankshaft loads and stresses are the lowest. The edges of the oil holes are carefully chamfered to relieve as much stress concentration as possible. Chamfered oil holes are shown in ● FIGURE 19–9.

ENGINE CRANKSHAFT TYPES

V-8 ENGINE ARRANGEMENT The V-8 engine has four inline cylinders in each of the two blocks that are placed at a 90 degree angle to each other. Each group of four inline cylinders is called a **bank**. The crankshaft for the V-8 engine has four throws. The connecting rods from two cylinders are connected to each throw, one from each bank. This arrangement results in a condition of being only minimally unbalanced.

The V-8 engine crankshaft has two planes, so there is one throw every 90 degrees. A plane is a flat surface that cuts through the part. These planes could be seen if the crankshaft were cut lengthwise through the center of the main bearing and crankpin journals. Looking at the front of the crankshaft:

- The first throw is at 360 degrees (up).
- The second throw is at 90 degrees (to the right).
- The third throw is at 270 degrees (to the left).
- The fourth throw is at 180 degrees (down).

In operation with this arrangement, one piston reaches top center at each 90 degrees of crankshaft rotation so that the

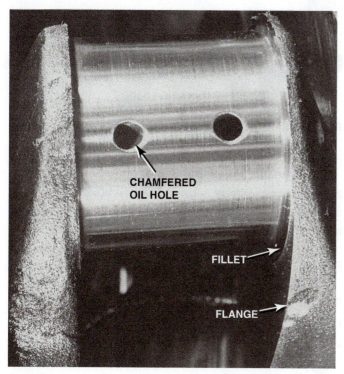

FIGURE 19–9 Typical chamfered hole in a crankshaft bearing journal.

CHAMFERED
OIL HOLE

FILLET

FLANGE

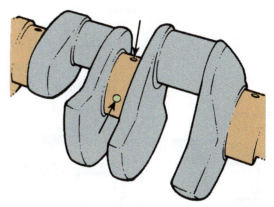

FIGURE 19–10 A cross-drilled crankshaft is used on some production engines and is a common racing modification.

engine operates smoothly with even firing at each 90 degrees of crankshaft rotation.

FOUR-CYLINDER ENGINE CRANKSHAFTS

The crankshaft used on 4-cylinder inline engines has four throws on a single plane. There is usually a main bearing journal between each throw, making it a five main bearing crankshaft. Pistons also move as pairs in this engine.

- Pistons in cylinders 1 and 4 move together, and pistons 2 and 3 move together.
- Each piston in a pair is 360 degrees out-of-phase with the other piston in the 720-degree four-stroke cycle. With this arrangement, the 4-cylinder inline engine fires one cylinder at each 180 degrees of crankshaft rotation.

A 4-cylinder opposed (flat) engine and a 90-degree V-4 engine have crankshafts that look like that of the 4-cylinder inline engine.

FIVE-CYLINDER ENGINE CRANKSHAFTS

The inline 5-cylinder engine has a five-throw crankshaft with one throw at each 72 degrees. Six main bearings are used on this crankshaft. The piston in one cylinder reaches top center at each 144 degrees of crankshaft rotation. Dynamic balancing has been one of the major problems with this engine design,

yet the vibration was satisfactorily dampened and isolated on both the Audi and Acura 5-cylinder engines.

THREE-CYLINDER ENGINE CRANKSHAFTS

A 3-cylinder engine uses a 120-degree three-throw crankshaft with four main bearings. This engine requires a balancing shaft that turns at crankshaft speed, but in the opposite direction, to reduce the vibration to an acceptable level.

INLINE SIX-CYLINDER ENGINE CRANKSHAFT

Inline 6-cylinder engine crankshafts ride on four or seven main bearings and use six crank throws in three planes 120 degrees apart. An inline 6-cylinder engine is in perfect primary and secondary balance.

90-DEGREE V-6 ENGINE CRANKSHAFTS

The crank throws for an even-firing V-6 engine are split, making separate crankpins for each cylinder. The split throw can be seen in ● **FIGURE 19–11.**

FIGURE 19–12 A fully counterweighted 4-cylinder crankshaft.

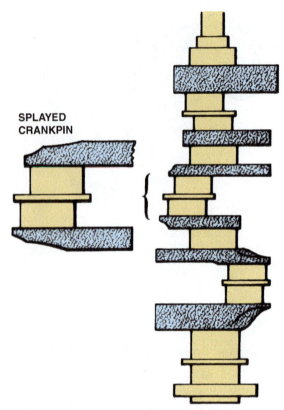

SPLAYED CRANKPIN

FIGURE 19–11 A splayed crankshaft design is used to create an even-firing 90-degree V-6.

This angle between the crankpins on the crankshaft throws is called a **splay angle**. A flange was left between the split crankpin journals. This provides a continuous fillet or edge for machining and grinding operations. It also provides a normal flange for the rod and bearing. This flange between the splayed crankpin journals is sometimes called a **flying web**.

60-DEGREE V-6 ENGINE CRANKSHAFTS The 60-degree V-6 engine is similar to the even-firing 90-degree V-6 engine. The adjacent pairs of crankpins on the crankshaft used in the 60-degree V-6 engine have a splay angle of 60 degrees.

The crankshaft of the 60-degree V-6 engine also uses four main bearings.

COUNTERWEIGHTS

PURPOSE AND FUNCTION Crankshafts are balanced by **counterweights**, which are cast, forged, or machined as part of the crankshaft. A crankshaft that has counterweights on both sides of each connecting rod journal is called **fully counterweighted**. ● **SEE FIGURE 19–12**.

A fully counterweighted crankshaft is the smoothest running and most durable design, but it is also the heaviest and most expensive to manufacture. Most vehicle manufacturers do not use fully counterweighted crankshafts in an effort to lighten the rotating mass of the engine. An engine with a light crankshaft allows the engine to accelerate quicker. Even crankshafts that are not fully counterweighted are still balanced.

VIBRATION DAMAGE Each time combustion occurs, the force deflects the crankshaft as it transfers torque to the output shaft. This deflection occurs in two ways, to bend the shaft sideways and to twist the shaft in torsion. The crankshaft must be rigid enough to keep the deflection forces to a minimum.

Crankshaft deflections are directly related to the operating roughness of an engine. When back-and-forth deflections occur at the same vibration **frequency** (number of vibrations per second) as that of another engine part, the parts will vibrate together. When this happens, the parts are said to **resonate**.

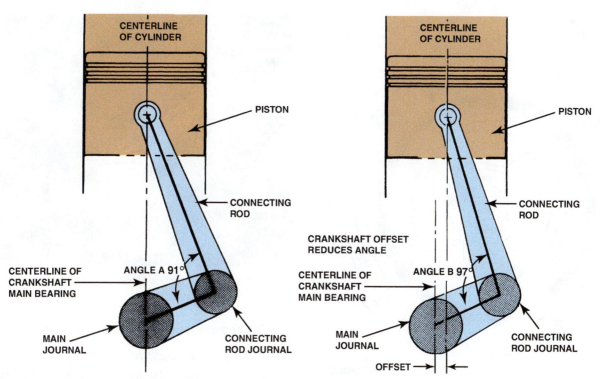

FIGURE 19–13 The crank throw is halfway down on the power stroke. The piston on the left without an offset crankshaft has a sharper angle than the engine on the right with an offset crankshaft.

? **FREQUENTLY ASKED QUESTION**

What Is an Offset Crankshaft?

To reduce side loads, some vehicle manufacturers offset the crankshaft from center. For example, if an engine rotates clockwise as viewed from the front, the crankshaft may be offset to the left to reduce the angle of the connecting rod during the power stroke. ● **SEE FIGURE 19–13**.

The offset usually varies from 1/16 to 1/2 inch, depending on make and model. Many inline 4-cylinder engines used in hybrid electric vehicles use an offset crankshaft.

FIGURE 19–14 A crankshaft broken as a result of using the wrong torsional vibration damper.

These vibrations may become great enough to reach the audible level, producing a thumping sound. If this type of vibration continues, the crankshaft may fail. ● **SEE FIGURE 19–14**.

Harmful crankshaft twisting vibrations are dampened with a torsional vibration damper. It is also called a harmonic balancer. This damper or balancer usually consists of a cast-iron **inertia ring** mounted to a cast-iron **hub** with an **elastomer** sleeve.

HINT: Push on the rubber (elastomer sleeve) of the vibration damper with your fingers or a pencil. *If the rubber does not spring back, replace the damper.*

Elastomers are actually synthetic, rubberlike materials. The inertia ring size is selected to control the **amplitude** of the crankshaft vibrations for each specific engine model. ● **SEE FIGURE 19–15**.

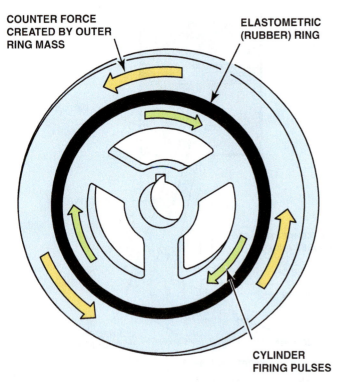

FIGURE 19–15 The hub of the harmonic balancer is attached to the front of the crankshaft. The elastomer (rubber) between the inertia ring and the center hub allows the absorption of crankshaft firing impulses.

COUNTER FORCE CREATED BY OUTER RING MASS

ELASTOMETRIC (RUBBER) RING

CYLINDER FIRING PULSES

TECH TIP

High Engine Speeds Require High-Performance Parts

Do not go racing with stock parts. A stock harmonic balancer can come apart and the resulting vibration can break the crankshaft if the engine is used for racing. Check the Internet or race part suppliers for the recommended balancer to use. ● SEE FIGURE 19–16.

EXTERNALLY AND INTERNALLY BALANCED ENGINES

DEFINITION Most crankshaft balancing is done during manufacture. Holes are drilled in the counterweight to lighten and improve balance. Sometimes these holes are drilled after the crankshaft is installed in the engine. Some manufacturers are able to control casting quality so closely that counterweight machining for balancing is not necessary.

FIGURE 19–16 A General Motors high-performance balancer used on a race engine.

Engine manufacturers balance an engine in one of two ways.

- **Externally balanced.** Weight is added to the harmonic balancer (vibration damper) and flywheel or the flexplate.
- **Internally balanced.** All rotating parts of the engine are individually balanced, including the harmonic balancer and flywheel (flexplate).

For example, the 350-cubic-inch Chevrolet V-8 is internally balanced, whereas the 400-cubic-inch Chevrolet V-8 uses an externally balanced crankshaft. The harmonic balancer used on an externally balanced engine has additional weight.

ENGINE BALANCE

PRIMARY AND SECONDARY BALANCE Anything that rotates will vibrate. This means that an engine will vibrate during operation, although engine designers attempt to reduce the vibration as much as possible.

- **Primary balance.** When pistons move up and down in the cylinders they create a **primary vibration**, which is a strong low-frequency vibration.

A counterweight on the crankshaft opposite the piston/rod assembly helps reduce this vibration. An inline 4-cylinder engine has very little primary vibration, because as two pistons are traveling upward in the cylinders, two are moving downward at the same time, effectively canceling out primary unbalances. ● SEE FIGURE 19–17.

- **Secondary balance.** Four-cylinder engines, however, suffer from a vibration at twice engine speed. This is called a **secondary vibration**, which is a weak

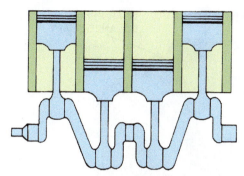

FIGURE 19–17 In a 4-cylinder engine, the two outside pistons move upward at the same time as the inner pistons move downward, which reduces primary unbalance.

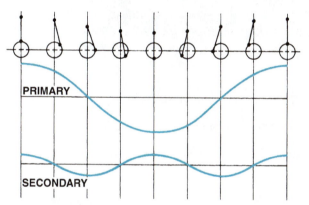

FIGURE 19–18 Primary and secondary vibrations in relation to piston position.

high-frequency vibration caused by a slight difference in the inertia of the pistons at top dead center compared to bottom dead center. This vibration is most noticeable at high engine speeds, especially if the engine size is greater than 2 liters. The larger the displacement of the engine, the larger the bore and the heavier the pistons contribute to the buzzing-type secondary vibration. ● **SEE FIGURE 19–18.**

BALANCE SHAFTS

PURPOSE AND FUNCTION Some engines use balance shafts to dampen normal engine vibrations. *Dampening* is reducing the vibration to an acceptable level. A balance shaft that is turning at crankshaft speed, but in the opposite direction, is used on a 3-cylinder inline engine. Weights on the ends of the balance shaft move in a direction opposite to the direction of the end piston. When the piston goes up, the weight goes down, and when the piston goes down, the weight goes up. This reduces the end-to-end rocking action on the 3-cylinder inline engine.

Another type of balance shaft system is designed to counterbalance vibrations on a four-stroke, 4-cylinder engine. Two shafts are used, and they turn at *twice* the engine speed. In most applications, both shafts rotate in the same direction and

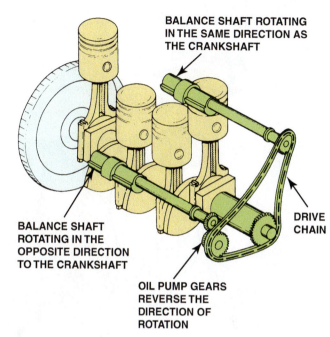

FIGURE 19–19 Two counterrotating balance shafts used to counterbalance the vibrations of a 4-cylinder engine.

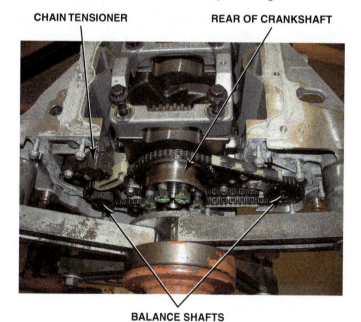

FIGURE 19–20 This General Motors 4-cylinder engine uses two balance shafts driven by a chain at the rear of the crankshaft.

are driven by a chain or gear off the crankshaft. Counterweights on the balance shafts are positioned to oppose the natural rolling action of the engine, as well as the secondary vibrations caused by the piston and rod movements. ● **SEE FIGURE 19–19.**

BALANCE SHAFT APPLICATIONS Balance shafts are commonly found on the larger displacement (over 2 liter) 4-cylinder automotive engines.

- Most 4-cylinder engines larger than 2.2 liters use balance shafts. These are often located underneath the crankshaft. ● **SEE FIGURE 19–20.**

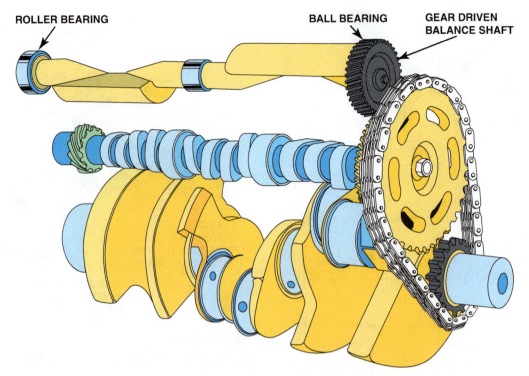

ROLLER BEARING   BALL BEARING   GEAR DRIVEN
BALANCE SHAFT

FIGURE 19–21 Many 90-degree V-6 engines use a balance shaft to reduce vibrations and effectively cancel a rocking motion (rocking couple) that causes the engine to rock front to back.

- Since the late 1980s, General Motors added a balance shaft to many of their V-6 engines. These 90-degree V-6 engines use a split crank journal to create an even-firing arrangement, but these engines suffer from forces that cause the engine to rock back and forth. This motion is called a *rocking couple* and is dampened by the use of a balance shaft. ● **SEE FIGURE 19–21**.

The addition of balance shafts makes a big improvement in the smoothness of the engine. In V-6 engines, the improvement is most evident during idling and low-speed operation, whereas in the 4-cylinder engines, balance shafts are especially helpful at higher engine speeds. The V-6 engines that use a 60-degree design do not create a rocking couple and, therefore, do not need a balance shaft.

CRANKSHAFT SERVICE

CRANKSHAFT VISUAL INSPECTION Crankshaft
damage includes:

- Worn journals
- Scored bearing journals
- Bends or warpage
- Cracks
- Thread damage (flywheel flange or front snout)
- Worn front or rear seal surfaces

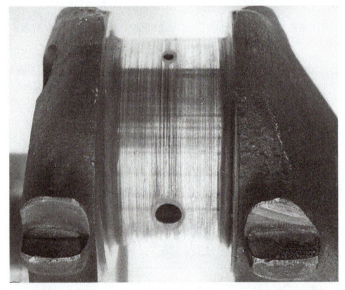

FIGURE 19–22 Scored connecting rod bearing journal.

Damaged shafts must be reconditioned or replaced. The crankshaft is one of the most highly stressed engine parts. *The stress on the crankshaft increases by four times every time the engine speed doubles.* Any sign of a crack is a cause to reject the crankshaft. Most cracks can be seen during a close visual inspection. Crankshafts should also be checked with Magnaflux, which will highlight tiny cracks that would lead to failure.

Bearing journal scoring is a common crankshaft defect. Scoring appears as scratches around the bearing journal surface. Generally, there is more scoring near the center of the bearing journal, as shown in ● **FIGURE 19–22**.

FIGURE 19–23 All crankshaft journals should be measured for diameter as well as taper and out-of-round.

Crankshaft journals should be inspected for nicks, pits, or corrosion. Roughness and slight bends in journals can be corrected by grinding the journals.

HINT: If your fingernail catches on a groove when rubbed across a bearing journal, the journal is too rough to reuse and must be reground. Another test is to rub a copper penny across the journal. If any copper remains on the crankshaft, it must be reground.

MEASURING THE CRANKSHAFT   Crankshafts should be carefully measured to determine the following:

- Size of main and rod bearing journals compared to factory specifications
- Each journal checked for out-of-round condition
- Each journal checked for taper
  - ● **SEE FIGURES 19–23 AND 19–24.**

CRANKSHAFT GRINDING   Crankshaft journals that have excessive scoring, out-of-round, or taper should be reground. The typical procedure includes the following steps.

STEP 1   Crankshafts may require straightening before grinding.

STEP 2   Both crankshaft ends are placed in rotating heads on one style of crankshaft grinder.

STEP 3   The main bearing journals are ground on the centerline of the crankshaft.

STEP 4   The crankshaft is then offset in the two rotating heads just enough to make the crankshaft main bearing journal centerline rotate around the centerline of the

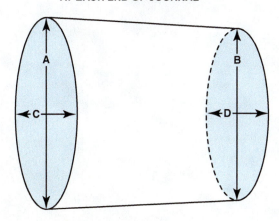

CHECK FOR OUT-OF-ROUNDNESS
AT EACH END OF JOURNAL

A VS. B = VERTICAL TAPER
C VS. D = HORIZONTAL TAPER
A VS. C = OUT OF ROUND
B VS. D = OUT OF ROUND

FIGURE 19–24 Check each journal for taper and out-of-roundness.

crankpin. The crankshaft will then be rotating around the crankpin centerline. The journal on the crankpin is reground in this position.

STEP 5   The crankshaft must be repositioned for each different crankpin center.

In another type of crankshaft grinder, the crankshaft always turns on the main bearing centerline. The grinding head is programmed to move in and out as the crankshaft turns to grind the crankpin bearing journals.

Crankshafts are usually ground to the following undersize.

- 0.010 inch
- 0.020 inch
- 0.030 inch

The finished journal should be accurately ground to size with a smooth surface finish. The radius of the fillet area on the sides of the journal should also be the same as the original.
● **SEE FIGURE 19–25.**

CRANKSHAFT POLISHING   The journal is polished after grinding using a 320-grit polishing cloth and oil to remove the fine metal "fuzz" remaining on the journal. This fuzz feels smooth when the shaft turns in its direction. As the shaft turns in the opposite direction, the fuzz feels like a fine milling cutter. Polishing removes this fuzz. The crankshaft is rotated in its normal direction of rotation so that the polishing cloth can remove the fuzz. This leaves a smooth shaft with the proper

FIGURE 19–25 The rounded fillet area of the crankshaft is formed by the corners of the grinding stone.

FIGURE 19–26 All crankshafts should be polished after grinding. Both the crankshaft and the polishing cloth are being revolved.

FIGURE 19–27 An excessively worn crankshaft can be restored to useful service by welding the journals, and then machining them back to the original size.

surface finish. *Most crankshaft grinders grind in the direction opposite of rotation and then polish in the same direction as rotation.* ● **SEE FIGURE 19–26**.

The crankshaft oil passages should be cleaned and the journals tagged with the undersize dimensions.

WELDING A CRANKSHAFT Sometimes it is desirable to salvage a crankshaft by building up a bearing journal and then grinding it to the original journal size. This is usually done by either electric arc welding or a metal spray. ● **SEE FIGURE 19–27**.

STRESS RELIEVING THE CRANKSHAFT The greatest area of stress on a crankshaft is the fillet area. Stress relief is achieved by *shot peening* the fillet area of the journals with #320 steel shot. This strengthens the fillet area and helps to prevent the development of cracks in this area. Gray duct tape is commonly used to cover the journal to prevent damage to the rest of it. Stress relief procedures are usually performed after the grinding and polishing of the crankshaft.

STORING CRANKSHAFTS All crankshafts should be coated with oil to keep them from rusting, and stored vertically until time for engine assembly. All crankshafts should be placed on the floor vertically to help prevent warping due to gravity. ● **SEE FIGURE 19–28**.

ENGINE BEARINGS

INTRODUCTION Engine bearings are the main supports for the major moving parts of any engine. Engine bearings are important for the following reasons.

1. The clearance between the bearings and the crankshaft is a major factor in maintaining the proper oil pressure throughout the engine. Most engines are designed to provide the maximum protection and lubrication to the engine bearings above all else.

FIGURE 19–28 Crankshafts should be stored vertically to prevent possible damage or warpage. This clever bench-mounted tray for crankshafts not only provides a safe place to store crankshafts but is also out of the way and cannot be accidentally tipped.

2. Engine durability relies on bearing life. Bearing failure usually results in immediate engine failure.

3. Engine bearings are designed to support the operating loads of the engine and, with the lubricant, provide minimum friction. This must be achieved at all designed engine speeds. The bearings must be able to operate for long periods of time, even when small foreign particles are in the lubricant.

TYPES OF BEARINGS
Most engine bearings are one of two types.

- **Plain bearing**
- **Sleeve bearing**

  ● **SEE FIGURE 19–29.**

Most bearing halves, or shells, do not have uniform thickness. The wall thickness of most bearings is largest in the center, called the **bearing crown**. The bearing thickness then tapers to a thinner measurement at each parting line. ● **SEE FIGURE 19–30.**

The tapered wall keeps bearing clearances close at the top and bottom of the bearing, which are the more loaded areas and allow more oil flow at the sides of the bearing. Both need a constant flow of lubricating oil. In automotive engines, the lubricating system supplies oil to each bearing continuously when the engine runs. Bearings and journals *only* wear when the parts come in contact with each other or when foreign particles are present.

Oil enters the bearing through the oil holes and grooves. It spreads into a smooth wedge-shaped oil film that supports the bearing load.

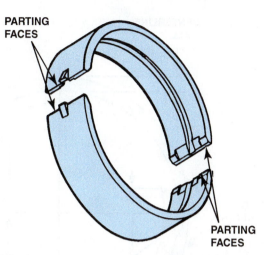

FIGURE 19–29 The two halves of a plain bearing meet at the parting faces.

BEARING MATERIALS
Three materials are used for automobile engine bearings.

- **Babbitt**
- **Copper-lead alloy**
- **Aluminum**

A layer of the bearing materials that is 0.01 to 0.02 inch (0.25 to 0.5 mm) thick is applied over a low carbon steel backing. An engine bearing is called a **bearing shell**, which is a steel backing with a surface coating of bearing material. The steel provides support needed for the shaft load. The bearing material meets the rest of the bearing operating requirements.

- **Babbitt.** Babbitt is the oldest automotive bearing material. Isaac Babbitt (1799 to 1862) first formulated this material in 1839. An excellent bearing material, it was originally made from a combination of lead, tin, and antimony. Lead and tin are alloyed with small quantities of copper and antimony to give it the required strength. Babbitt is still used in applications in which material is required for soft shafts running under moderate loads and speeds. It will work with occasional borderline lubrication and oil starvation without failure.

- **Trimetal. Copper-lead alloy** is a stronger and more expensive bearing material than babbitt. It is used for intermediate- and high-speed applications. Tin, in small quantities, is often alloyed with the copper-lead bearings. This bearing material is most easily damaged by corrosion from acid accumulation in the engine oil. Corrosion results in bearing journal wear as the bearing is eroded by the acids. Many of the copper-lead bearings have an **overlay**, or third layer, of metal. This overlay is usually of babbitt. Babbitt-overlayed bearings have high

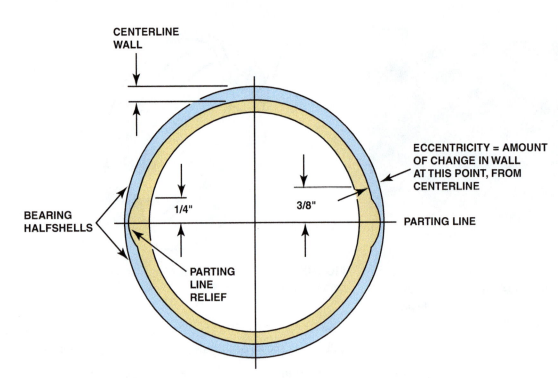

CENTERLINE WALL

ECCENTRICITY = AMOUNT OF CHANGE IN WALL AT THIS POINT, FROM CENTERLINE

BEARING HALFSHELLS

1/4"   3/8"

PARTING LINE

PARTING LINE RELIEF

FIGURE 19–30 Bearing wall thickness is not the same from the center to the parting line. This is called *eccentricity* and is used to help create an oil wedge between the journal and the bearing.

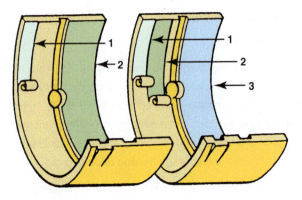

1
2
3

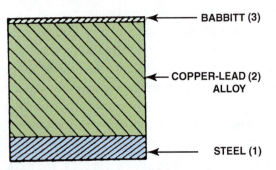

BABBITT (3)

COPPER-LEAD (2) ALLOY

STEEL (1)

FIGURE 19–31 Typical two- and three-layer engine bearing inserts showing the relative thickness of the various materials.

fatigue strength, good conformity, good embedability, and good corrosion resistance. The overplated bearing is a premium bearing. It is also the most expensive because the overplating layer, from 0.0005 to 0.001 inch (0.0125 to 0.025 mm) thick, is put on the bearing with an **electroplating** process. The layers of bearing material on a bearing shell are illustrated in ● **FIGURE 19–31**.

- **Aluminum.** Aluminum was the last of the three materials to be used for automotive bearings. Automotive bearing aluminum has small quantities of tin and silicone alloyed with it. This makes a stronger but more expensive bearing than either babbitt or copper-lead alloy. Most of its bearing characteristics are equal to or better than those of babbitt and copper lead. Aluminum bearings are well suited to high-speed, high-load conditions and do not contain lead, which is a benefit to the environment both at the manufacturing plant and for the technician who may be exposed to the bearings.

BEARING MANUFACTURING Modern automotive engines use **precision insert-type bearing shells**, sometimes called **half-shell bearings**. The bearing is manufactured to very close tolerance so that it will fit correctly in each application. The bearing, therefore, must be made from precisely the correct materials under closely controlled manufacturing conditions. ● **FIGURE 19–32** shows the typical bearing types found in most engines.

BEARING SIZES Bearings are usually available in standard (std.) size, and in measurements 0.010, 0.020, and 0.030 inch *undersize*. ● **SEE FIGURE 19–33**.

Even though the bearing itself is thicker for use on a machined crankshaft, the bearing is referred to as undersize because the crankshaft journals are undersize. Factory bearings may be available in 0.0005 or 0.001 inch undersize for precision fitting of a production crankshaft.

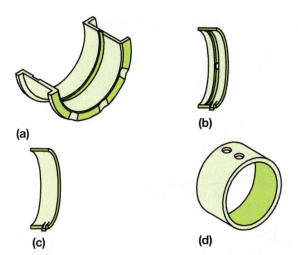

FIGURE 19–32 Typical bearing shell types found in modern engines: (a) half-shell thrust bearing, (b) upper main bearing insert, (c) lower main bearing insert, (d) full round-type camshaft bearing.

Before purchasing bearings, be sure to use a micrometer to measure *all* main and connecting rod journals. Replacement bearings are also available in 0.001, 0.002, and 0.003 inch, to allow the technician to achieve the proper bearing clearance without needing to machine the crankshaft.

BEARING LOADS

The forces on the engine bearings vary with engine speed and load. On the intake stroke, the inertia force is opposed by the force of drawing in the air-fuel mixture. On the compression and power strokes, there is also an opposing force on the rod bearings. On the exhaust stroke, however, there is no opposing force to counteract the inertia force of the piston coming to a stop at TDC. The result is a higher force load on the *bottom* rod bearing due to inertia at TDC of the exhaust stroke. These forces tend to stretch the big end of the rod in the direction of rod movement.

1. As engine speed (RPM) increases, rod bearing loads decrease because of the balancing of inertia and opposing loads.

2. As engine speed (RPM) increases, the main bearing loads increase.

   NOTE: This helps explain why engine blocks with four-bolt main bearing supports are only needed for high-engine speed stability.

3. Because the loads on bearings vary and affect both rod and main bearings, it is generally recommended that *all* engine bearings be replaced at one time.

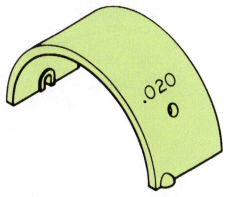

FIGURE 19–33 Bearings are often marked with an undersize dimension. This bearing is used on a crankshaft with a ground journal that is 0.020 inch smaller in diameter than the stock size.

BEARING FATIGUE

Bearings tend to flex or bend slightly under changing loads. This is especially noticeable in reciprocating engine bearings. Bearing metals, like other metals, tend to fatigue and break after being flexed or bent a number of times. Flexing starts fatigue, which shows up as fine cracks in the bearing surface because the bearing material became **work hardened**. These cracks gradually deepen almost to the bond between the bearing metal and the backing metal. The cracks then cross over and intersect with each other. In time, this will allow a piece of bearing material to fall out. The length of time before fatigue will cause failure is called the **fatigue life** of the bearing. ● **SEE FIGURE 19–34.**

BEARING CONFORMABILITY

The ability of bearing materials to creep or flow slightly to match shaft variations is called **conformability**. The bearing conforms to the shaft during the engine break-in period. In modern automobile engines, there is little need for bearing conformability or break-in, because automatic processing has achieved machining tolerances that keep the shaft very close to the designed size.

BEARING EMBEDABILITY

Engine manufacturers have designed engines to produce minimum crankcase deposits. This has been done by providing them with oil filters, air filters, and closed crankcase ventilation systems that minimize contaminants. Still, some foreign particles get into the bearings. The bearings must be capable of embedding these particles into the bearing surface so that they will not score the shaft. To fully embed the particle, the bearing material gradually works across the particle, completely covering it. The bearing property that allows it to do this is called **embedability**. ● **SEE FIGURE 19–35.**

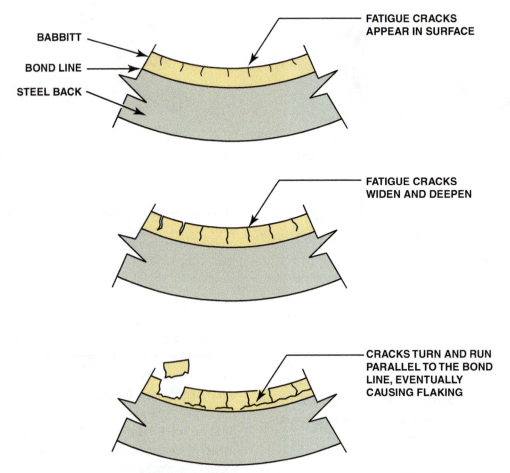

FIGURE 19–34 Work hardened bearing material becomes brittle and cracks, leading to bearing failure.

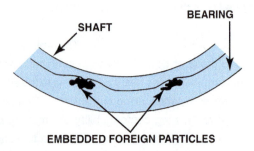

FIGURE 19–35 Bearing material covers foreign material (such as dirt) as it embeds into the bearing.

BEARING DAMAGE RESISTANCE Under some operating conditions, the bearing will be temporarily overloaded. This will cause the oil film to break down and allow the shaft metal to come in contact with the bearing metal. As the rotating crankshaft contacts the bearing high spots, the spots become hot from friction. The friction causes localized hot spots in the bearing material that seize or weld to the crankshaft. The crankshaft then breaks off particles of the bearing material and pulls the particles around with it, scratching or scoring the bearing surface.

Bearings have a characteristic called **score resistance**. It prevents the bearing materials from seizing to the shaft during oil film breakdown.

By-products of combustion form acids in the oil. The bearings' ability to resist attack from these acids is called **corrosion resistance**. Corrosion can occur over the entire surface of the bearing. This will remove material and increase the oil clearance. It can also leach or eat into the bearing material, dissolving some of the bearing material alloys. Either type of corrosion will reduce bearing life.

BEARING CLEARANCE

IMPORTANCE OF PROPER CLEARANCE The bearing-to-journal clearance may be from 0.0005 to 0.0025 inch (0.025 to 0.06 mm), depending on the engine. Doubling the journal clearance will allow more than *four* times more oil to flow from the edges of the bearing. The oil clearance must be large enough to allow an oil film to build up, but small enough to prevent excess oil leakage, which would cause loss of oil

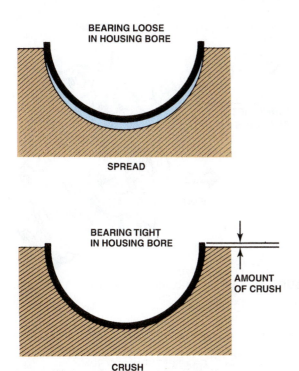

FIGURE 19–36 Bearing spread and crush.

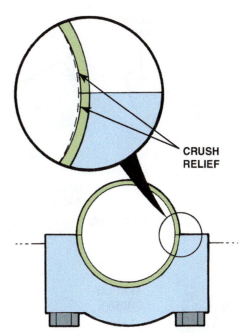

FIGURE 19–37 Bearings are thinner at the parting line faces to provide crush relief.

pressure. A large amount of oil leakage at one of the bearings would starve other bearings farther along in the oil system. This would result in the failure of the oil-starved bearings.

CHECKING BEARING CLEARANCE Bearing oil clearance can be checked in the following ways.

1. Using Plastigage® between the crankshaft journal and the bearing. The thin plasticlike strip material will deform depending on the clearance.

2. Measuring the crankshaft journal diameter and the inside diameter of the bearing as it is installed and subtracting the two measurements. The difference is the bearing clearance.

BEARING SPREAD AND CRUSH The bearing design also includes bearing **spread** and **crush**. ● SEE FIGURE 19–36.

- **Bearing spread.** The bearing shell has a slightly larger arc than the bearing housing. This difference, called bearing spread, makes the shell 0.005 to 0.02 inch (0.125 to 0.5 mm) wider than the housing bore. Spread holds the bearing shell in the housing while the engine is being assembled.

- **Bearing crush.** When the bearing is installed, each end of the bearing shell is slightly above the parting surface. When the bearing cap is tightened, the ends of the two bearing shells touch and are forced together. This force is called bearing crush. Crush holds the bearing in place

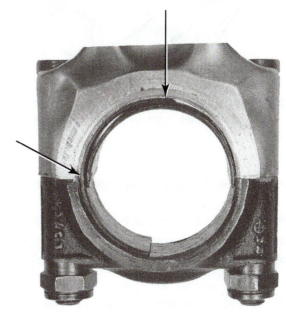

FIGURE 19–38 Spun bearing. The lower cap bearing has rotated under the upper rod bearing.

and keeps the bearing from turning when the engine runs. Crush must exert a force of at least 12,000 PSI (82,740 kPa) at 250°F (121°C) to hold the bearing securely in place. A stress of 40,000 PSI (275,790 kPa) is considered maximum to avoid damaging the bearing or housing. ● SEE FIGURE 19–37.

Bearing shells that do not have enough crush may rotate with the shaft. The result is called a **spun bearing**. ● SEE FIGURE 19–38.

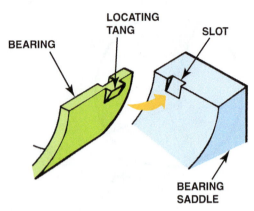

FIGURE 19–39 The tang and slot help index the bearing in the bore.

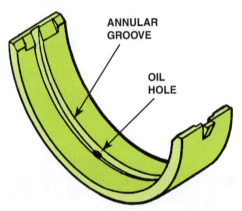

FIGURE 19–40 Many bearings are manufactured with a groove down the middle to improve the oil flow around the main journal.

- **Bearing tang.** A *tang* or lip helps locate the bearing shell in the housing. When the bearing clearance and "crush" have been worn or destroyed, the bearing can "spin," thus creating catastrophic failure. The tang often helps prevent this from occurring. ● **SEE FIGURE 19–39**.

Many newer engines do *not* use a tang on the bearing. Always check service information for the exact bearings and procedures to use for the engine being serviced.

Replacement bearings should be of a quality as good as or better than that of the original bearings. The replacement bearings must also have the same oil holes and grooves.

CAUTION: Some bearings may have oil holes in the top shell only. If these are installed incorrectly, no oil will flow to the connecting or main rods, resulting in instant engine failure. To help the oil spread across the entire bearing, some bearings use an oil groove. ● SEE FIGURE 19–40.

Modified engines have more demanding bearing requirements and therefore usually require a higher quality bearing to provide satisfactory service.

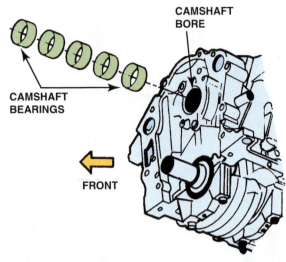

FIGURE 19–41 Cam-in-block engines support the camshaft with sleeve-type bearings.

TECH TIP

Count Your Blessings and Your Pan Bolts!

Replacing cam bearings can be relatively straightforward or can involve keeping count of the number of oil pan bolts. For example, Buick-built V-6 engines use different cam bearings depending on the number of bolts used to hold the oil pan to the block.

- **Fourteen bolts in the oil pan.** The front bearing is special, but the rest of the bearings are the same.
- **Twenty bolts in the oil pan.** Bearings 1 and 4 use two oil feed holes. Bearings 2 and 3 use single oil feed holes.

CAMSHAFT BEARINGS

TYPES OF CAMSHAFT BEARINGS The camshaft in pushrod engines rotates in sleeve bearings that are pressed into bearing bores within the engine block. Overhead camshaft bearings may be one of two sleeve-type bushings, depending on the design of the bearing supports.

- **Full round bearings**
- **Split-type (half-shell) bearings**

The split-type bearing has direct contact with aluminum saddles integral with the head depending on the design of the bearing supports. The integral aluminum head bearing design often requires the replacement of the entire cylinder head in the event of bearing failure from lack of lubrication.

In pushrod engines, the cam bearings are installed in the block. ● **SEE FIGURE 19–41**.

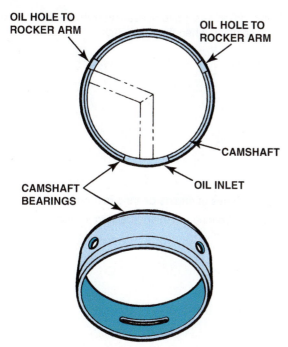

FIGURE 19–42 Camshaft bearings must be installed correctly so that oil passages are not blocked.

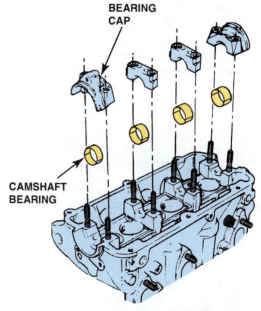

FIGURE 19–43 Some overhead camshaft engines use split bearing inserts.

CAMSHAFT BEARING INSTALLATION

The best rule of thumb to follow is to replace the cam bearings whenever the main bearings are replaced. The replacement cam bearings must have the correct outside diameter to fit snugly in the cam bearing bores of the block. They must have the correct oil holes and be positioned correctly. ● SEE FIGURE 19–42.

Cam bearings must also have the proper inside diameter to fit the camshaft bearing journals. Details regarding cam bearings include the following:

- In many engines, each cam bearing is a different size. The largest is in the front and the smallest is in the rear.

- The cam bearing journal size must be checked and each bearing identified before assembly is begun.

- The location of each new cam bearing can be marked on the outside of the bearing with a felt-tip marker to help avoid mixing up bearings. Marking in this way will not affect the bearing size or damage the bearing in any way.

- Many vehicle manufacturers specify that the cam bearings should be installed "dry" (not oiled) to prevent the cam bearing from moving (spinning) after installation. If the cam bearing were oiled, the rotation of the camshaft could cause the cam bearing to rotate and block oil holes that lubricate the camshaft.

- Many aluminum cylinder heads have "integral" cam bearings that are not replaceable. The entire cylinder head may need to be replaced if a lubrication problem occurs to the cam bearings, because the entire cylinder head may need to be replaced.

- Camshaft bearings used on some older overhead camshaft engines may be either full round or split depending on the engine design. ● SEE FIGURE 19–43.

Always follow the installation tool instructions when installing cam bearings.

SUMMARY

1. Cast crankshafts have a narrow mold parting line, and forged crankshafts have a wide parting line.

2. Even-fire 90-degree V-6 engines require that the crankshaft be splayed to allow for even firing.

3. Oil for the rod bearings comes from holes in the crankshaft drilled between the main journal and the rod journal.

4. A vibration damper, also known as a harmonic balancer, is used to dampen harmful twisting vibrations of the crankshaft.

5. Most engines are internally balanced. This means that the crankshaft and vibration damper are both balanced. Other engines use an offset weight in the vibration damper to balance the crankshaft, called externally balanced engines.

6. Most crankshafts can be reground to be 0.01, 0.02, or 0.03 inch undersize.

7. Most engine bearings are constructed with a steel shell for strength and are covered with a copper-lead alloy. Many bearings also have a thin overlay of babbitt.

8. Bearings should have spread and crush to keep them from spinning when the crankshaft rotates.

REVIEW QUESTIONS

1. How many degrees of crankshaft rotation are there between cylinder firings on an inline 4-cylinder engine, an inline 6-cylinder engine, and a V-8 engine?

2. List the types of engine bearing materials.

3. Describe bearing crush and bearing spread.

CHAPTER QUIZ

1. A forged crankshaft has a _____.
   a. Wide parting line
   b. Thin parting line
   c. Parting line in one plane
   d. Both b and c

2. A typical V-8 engine crankshaft has _____ main bearings.
   a. Three
   b. Four
   c. Five
   d. Seven

3. A 4-cylinder engine fires one cylinder at every _____ degrees of crankshaft rotation.
   a. 27
   b. 180
   c. 120
   d. 90

4. A splayed crankshaft is a crankshaft that _____.
   a. Is externally balanced
   b. Is internally balanced
   c. Has offset main bearing journals
   d. Has offset rod journals

5. The thrust bearing surface is located on one of the main bearings to control thrust loads caused by _____.
   a. Lugging the engine
   b. Torque converter or clutch release forces
   c. Rapid deceleration forces
   d. Both a and c

6. If any crankshaft is ground, it must also be _____.
   a. Shot peened
   b. Chrome plated
   c. Polished
   d. Externally balanced

7. If bearing-to-journal clearance is doubled, how much oil will flow?
   a. One-half as much
   b. The same amount if the pressure is kept constant
   c. Double the amount
   d. Four times the amount

8. Typical journal-to-bearing clearance is _____.
   a. 0.00015 to 0.00018 inch
   b. 0.0005 to 0.0025 inch
   c. 0.15 to 0.25 inch
   d. 0.02 to 0.035 inch

9. A bearing shell has a slightly larger arc than the bearing housing. This difference is called _____.
   a. Bearing crush
   b. Bearing tang
   c. Bearing spread
   d. Bearing saddle

10. Bearing _____ occurs when a bearing shell is slightly above the parting surface of the bearing cap.
    a. Overlap
    b. Crush
    c. Cap lock
    d. Interference fit

chapter 20
GASKETS AND SEALANTS

LEARNING OBJECTIVES

After studying this chapter, the reader should be able to:

1. Describe the various types of gaskets.
2. Explain why the surface finish is important for head gaskets.
3. List the types of sealers and their applications.
4. Explain the use and precautions associated with cover gaskets.

This chapter will help you prepare for ASE Engine Repair (A1) certification test content area "C" (Engine Block Diagnosis and Repair).

KEY TERMS

Anaerobic sealers 320
Armor 316
Fire ring 316
Formed in place gaskets (FIPG) 317
Fretting 318
Multilayered steel (MLS) gaskets 316

No-retorque-type gaskets 315
Room-temperature vulcanization (RTV) 319
Rubber-coated metal (RCM) gaskets 317

STC OBJECTIVES

GM Service Technical College topics covered in this chapter are:

1. Proper use of gaskets and sealants following General Motors service information (SI) procedures.

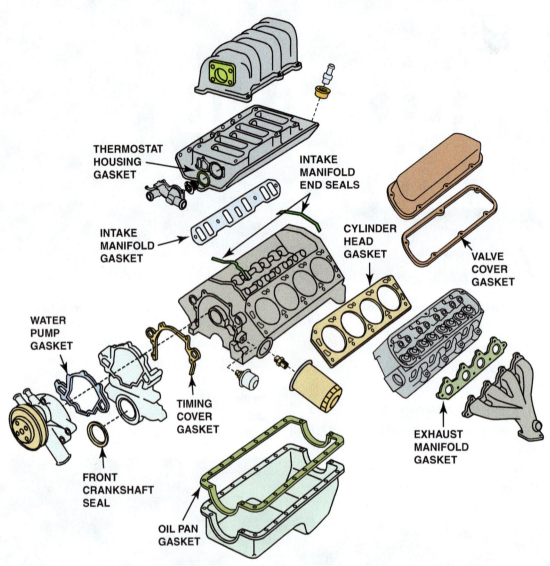

THERMOSTAT HOUSING GASKET

INTAKE MANIFOLD END SEALS

INTAKE MANIFOLD GASKET

CYLINDER HEAD GASKET

VALVE COVER GASKET

WATER PUMP GASKET

TIMING COVER GASKET

FRONT CRANKSHAFT SEAL

OIL PAN GASKET

EXHAUST MANIFOLD GASKET

FIGURE 20–1 Gaskets are used in many locations in the engine.

INTRODUCTION

NEED FOR GASKETS AND SEALANTS Gaskets and sealants are used in engines to seal gaps and potential gaps between two or more parts. Gaskets and sealants must be able to withstand:

- Temperatures to which the engine part may be exposed during normal operation
- Vibrations produced in the engine and the accessories that are attached to the engine
- Acids and other chemicals that are found in and throughout an engine
- Expanding and contracting at different rates (They must be able to seal even though the two parts are expanding and contracting at different rates as the engine is started at low temperature all the way to normal operating temperature and repeating this cycle every time the engine is operated.)

● SEE FIGURE 20–1.

HEAD GASKETS

REQUIREMENTS NEEDED The head gasket is under the highest clamping loads. It must seal passages that carry coolant and often is required to seal a passage that carries hot engine oil. The most demanding job of the head gasket is to seal the combustion chamber. As a rule of thumb, about 75% of the head bolt clamping force is used to seal the combustion chamber. The remaining 25% seals the coolant and oil passages. ● SEE FIGURE 20–2.

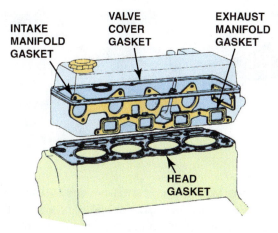

FIGURE 20–2 Gaskets help prevent leaks between two surfaces.

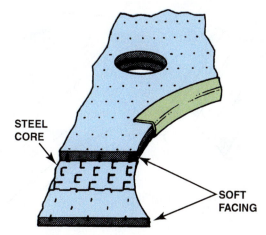

FIGURE 20–3 A typical perforated steel core head gasket with a graphite or composite facing material.

The gasket must seal when the temperature is as low as –40°F (–40°C) and as high as 400°F (204°C). The combustion pressures can get up to 1,000 PSI (6,900 kPa) on gasoline engines.

Cylinder head bolts are tightened to a specified torque, which stretches the bolt. The following forces are applied to a head gasket.

- The combustion pressure tries to push the head upward and the piston downward on the power stroke. This puts additional stress on the head bolts and it reduces the clamping load on the head gasket just when the greatest seal is needed.

- A partial vacuum during the intake stroke tries to pull the head down against the gasket.

- As the crankshaft rotates, the force on the head changes from pressure on the combustion stroke to vacuum on the intake stroke, then back to pressure.

Newer engines have lightweight thin-wall castings. The castings are quite flexible, so they move as the pressure in the combustion chamber changes from high pressure to vacuum. The gasket must be able to compress and recover fast enough to maintain a seal as the pressure in the combustion chamber changes back and forth between pressure and vacuum. As a result, head gaskets are made of several different materials that are assembled in numerous ways, depending on the engine.

NOTE: Older head gasket designs often contained asbestos and required that the head bolts be retorqued after the engine had been run to operating temperature. Head gaskets today are dense and do not compress like those older-style gaskets. Therefore, most head gaskets are called no-retorque-type gaskets, meaning the cylinder

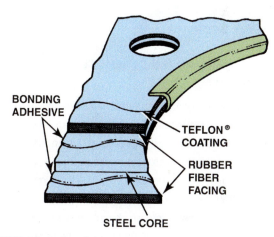

FIGURE 20–4 A solid steel core head gasket with a nonstick coating, which allows some movement between the block and the head, and is especially important on engines that use cast-iron blocks with aluminum cylinder heads.

head bolts do not have to be retorqued after the engine has run. New gaskets do not contain asbestos.

TYPES OF HEAD GASKETS

- **Perforated steel core gaskets.** A perforated steel core gasket uses a wire mesh core with fiber facings. Another design has rubber-fiber facings cemented to a solid steel core with an adhesive. ● SEE FIGURES 20–3 AND 20–4.

  The thickness of the gasket is controlled by the thickness of the metal core. The facing is thick enough to compensate for minor warpage and surface defects. The fiber facing is protected around the combustion

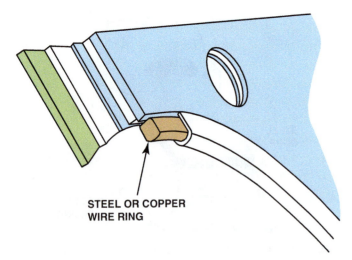

STEEL OR COPPER
WIRE RING

FIGURE 20–5 The armor ring can be made from steel or copper.

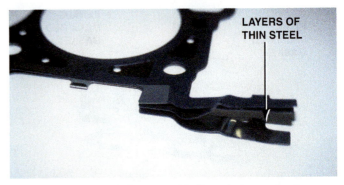
LAYERS OF
THIN STEEL

FIGURE 20–6 Multilayer steel (MLS) gaskets are used on many newer all-aluminum engines as well as on engines that use a cast block with aluminum cylinder heads. This type of gasket allows the aluminum to expand without losing the sealing ability of the gasket.

- The multiple layers of metal provide a springlike effect to the gasket, which allows it to keep the combustion chamber sealed.

The many layers of thin steel reduce bore and overhead camshaft distortion with less clamping force loss than previous designs. ● **SEE FIGURE 20–6**.

The use of multilayered steel gaskets also reduces the torque requirement and, therefore, reduces the stresses on the fastener and engine block. MLS gaskets are used in most engines that use aluminum cylinder heads and cast-iron blocks. The use of MLS head gaskets requires that both the head and the block deck surface have a smooth surface finish of 15 to 30 microinches. This smooth surface finish allows the head to move slightly during operation and not damage the gasket.

chamber with a metal **armor** (also called a **fire ring**). ● **SEE FIGURE 20–5**.

The metal also increases the gasket thickness around the cylinder so that it uses up to 75% of the clamping force and forms a tight combustion seal.

- **Multilayered steel gaskets.** The **multilayered steel (MLS) gaskets** are constructed in the following manner.
  - Three to five layers of stainless steel sheet are separated by elastomer (rubber) material.
  - The elastomer material is between the layers of the sheet metal and on both surfaces.

COVER GASKET MATERIALS

COVER GASKET REQUIREMENTS Cover gaskets are used to seal valve covers, oil pans, timing chain, and other covers. The gasket must be *impermeable* to the fluids it is designed to seal in or out. The gasket must *conform* to the shape of the surface, and it must be *resilient,* or elastic, to maintain the sealing force as it is compressed. Gaskets work best when they are compressed about 30%.

CORK GASKETS Older engines often used gaskets made from cork. Cork is the bark from a Mediterranean cork oak tree. It is made of very small, flexible, 14-sided, air-filled fiber cells, about 0.001 inch (0.025 mm) in size. Disadvantages of cork gaskets include the following:

- Because cork is mostly wood, it expands when it gets wet and shrinks when it dries. This causes cork gaskets

FIGURE 20–7 Left to right: Cork-rubber, paper, composite, and synthetic rubber (elastomer) gaskets.

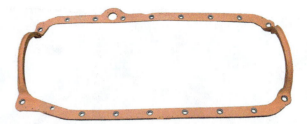

FIGURE 20–8 Rubber-coated steel gaskets have replaced many oil pan gaskets that once had separate side rail gaskets and end seals.

FIGURE 20–9 Formed in place gaskets often use silicone rubber and are applied at the factory using a robot. Check gasket manufacturers for the correct gasket replacement.

to change in size when they are in storage and while installed in the engine.

- Oil gradually wicks through the organic binder of the cork, so a cork gasket often looks like it is leaking.

- Problems with cork gaskets led the gasket industry to develop cork cover gaskets using synthetic rubber as a binder for the cork. This type of gasket is called a *cork-rubber gasket*. These cork-rubber gaskets are easy to use, and they outlast the old cork gaskets.

FIBER GASKETS Some oil pans use fiber gaskets. Covers with higher clamping forces use gaskets with fibers that have greater density. For example, timing covers may have either fiber or paper gaskets.

SYNTHETIC RUBBER GASKETS Molded, oil-resistant synthetic rubber is being used in more applications to seal covers. When it is compounded correctly, it forms a superior cover gasket. It operates at high temperatures for a longer period of time than does a cork-rubber cover gasket. ● **SEE FIGURE 20–7.**

RUBBER-COATED METAL GASKETS The **rubber-coated metal (RCM) gasket** uses a metal core to give strength to the gasket. The metal is coated with a layer on both sides with silicone rubber and molded in sealing beads. RCM gaskets are used in many places, including:

- Water pump gaskets
- Valve cover gaskets
- Oil pan gaskets
  ● **SEE FIGURE 20–8.**

FORMED IN PLACE GASKETS **Formed in place gaskets (FIPG)** are commonly used because they can be applied at the engine plant using a robot. The sealing material is extruded and placed onto the sealing surface and then the two parts being sealed are placed together and the fasteners tightened. When FIPG are being replaced during an engine repair or overhaul, check service information for the exact gasket material to use. ● **SEE FIGURE 20–9.**

PLASTIC/RUBBER GASKETS Most intake manifold gaskets use a nylon (usually nylon 6.6) reinforced body with silicone rubber sealing surfaces.

The nylon is used for two reasons.

1. It provides a thermal barrier to help stop the heat from the cylinder heads to flow to the intake manifold. This helps keep the intake air cooler, resulting in increased engine power.

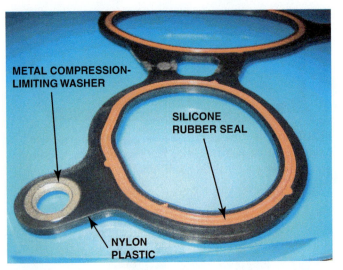

FIGURE 20–10 A typical intake manifold gasket showing the metal washer at each fastener location which keeps the gasket from being compressed too much.

Labels on figure:
METAL COMPRESSION-LIMITING WASHER
SILICONE RUBBER SEAL
NYLON PLASTIC

FIGURE 20–11 This intake manifold gasket was damaged due to fretting. Newer designs allow for more movement between the intake manifold and the cylinder head.

2. The nylon plastic is strong and provides a stable foundation for the silicone rubber seal.

● **SEE FIGURE 20–10.**

GASKET FAILURES

CAUSES OF GASKET FAILURE   Gaskets can fail to seal properly, but the root cause is often a severe condition. A head gasket can fail for the following reasons.

- Detonation (spark knock or ping) may cause extreme pressure to be exerted on the armor of the head gasket, causing it to deform.
- A plugged PCV system can increase crankcase pressure resulting in engine gasket failures such as oil pan, valve cover, timing cover, and main oil seals.
- Improper installation such as incorrect torquing sequence can cause gasket failure.

FRETTING   **Fretting** is a condition that can destroy intake manifold gaskets, caused by the unequal expansion and contraction of two different engine materials. For example, if the intake manifold is constructed of aluminum and the cylinder heads are cast iron, the intake manifold will expand more than the cylinder heads. This causes a shearing effect, which can destroy the gasket. Therefore, before assembling an engine, check for the latest design gaskets that are often different from the type originally used in the engine. ● **SEE FIGURE 20–11.**

TECH TIP

Tips for Gasket Usage

1. **Never reuse an old gasket.** A used gasket or seal has already been compressed, has lost some of its resilience, and has taken a set. If a used gasket does reseal, it will not seal as well as a new gasket or seal.

2. **A gasket should be checked to make sure it is the correct gasket.** Also check the list on the outside of the gasket set to make sure that the set has all the gaskets that may be needed *before* the package is opened.

3. **Read the instruction sheet.** An instruction sheet is included with most gaskets. It includes a review of the things the technician should do to prepare and install the gaskets, to give the best chance of a good seal. The instruction sheet also includes special tips on how to seal spots that are difficult to seal or that require special care to seal on a particular engine.

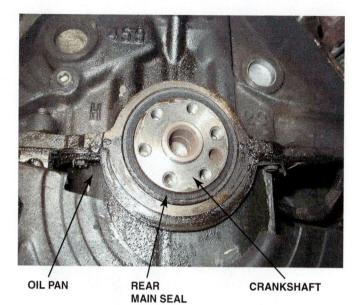

OIL PAN   REAR MAIN SEAL   CRANKSHAFT

FIGURE 20–12 A rear main seal has to be designed to seal oil from leaking around the crankshaft under all temperature conditions.

OIL SEALS

PURPOSE AND FUNCTION Oil seals allow the shaft to rotate and seal the area around the shaft to prevent oil or coolant from leaking. Seals come in varied sizes and styles.

SEAL MATERIALS Most seals use a steel backing for strength and a variety of sealing materials, including:

- Buna-N
- Viton® (fluorocarbon)
- Teflon® (polytetrafluoroethylene, also called PTFE)

● **SEE FIGURE 20–12.**

CAUTION: Do not use oil on a Teflon® seal because this type of seal requires that some of the material be transferred to the rotating shaft to seal properly. If oil is used on the seal, the seal will leak.

ASSEMBLY SEALANTS

RTV SILICONE RTV silicone is used by most technicians in sealing engines. **RTV, or room-temperature vulcanization,** means that the silicone rubber material will cure at room

TECH TIP

Always Check the VIN

There are so many variations in engines that it is important that the correct gasket or seal be used. For example, a similar engine may be used in a front-wheel-drive or a rear-wheel-drive application and this could affect the type or style of gasket or seal used. For best results, the wise technician should know the vehicle identification number (VIN) when ordering any engine part.

temperature. It is not really the temperature that causes RTV silicone to cure, but the moisture in the air. RTV silicone cures to a tack-free state in about 45 minutes. It takes 24 hours to fully cure.

RTV silicone is available in several different colors. The color identifies the special blend within a manufacturer's product line. Equal grades of silicone made by different manufacturers may have different colors. RTV silicone can be used in two ways in engine sealing.

1. It can be used as a gasket substitute between a stamped cover and a cast surface.

2. It is used to fill gaps or potential gaps. A joint between gaskets or between a gasket and a seal is a potential gap.

RTV precautions include:

1. Some RTV silicone sealers use *acetic acid,* and the fumes from this type can be drawn through the engine through

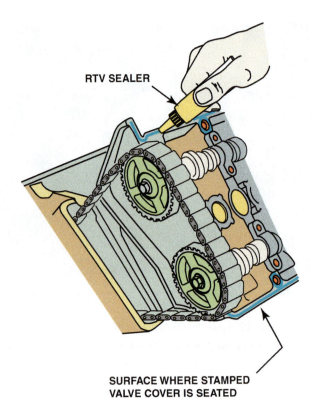

RTV SEALER

SURFACE WHERE STAMPED
VALVE COVER IS SEATED

FIGURE 20–13 Room-temperature vulcanization (RTV) is designed to be a gasket substitute on nonmachined surfaces. Be sure to follow the instructions as printed on the tube for best results.

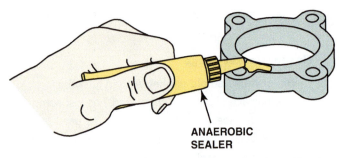

ANAEROBIC
SEALER

FIGURE 20–14 Anaerobic sealer is used to seal machined surfaces. Always follow the instructions on the tube for best results.

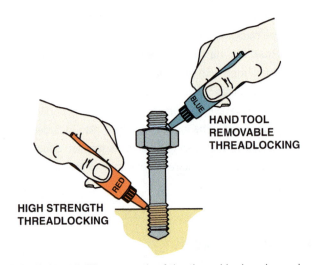

HAND TOOL
REMOVABLE
THREADLOCKING

HIGH STRENGTH
THREADLOCKING

FIGURE 20–15 The strength of the thread locker depends on whether the fastener is to be removed by hand (blue). High-strength thread locker (red) can only be removed if heated.

the PCV system and cause damage to oxygen sensors. Always use an *amine-type* RTV silicone or one that states on the package that it is safe for oxygen sensors.

2. RTV should not be used with a gasket as a sealer because it is slippery and could easily cause the gasket to move out of proper location.

3. RTV silicone should *never* be used around fuel because the fuel will cut through it. Silicone should not be used as a sealer on gaskets. It will squeeze out to leave a bead inside and a bead outside the flange. The inside bead might fall into the engine, plugging passages and causing engine damage. The thin film still remaining on the gasket stays uncured, just as it would be in the original tube. The uncured silicone is likely to let the gasket or seal slip out of place. ● SEE FIGURE 20–13.

ANAEROBIC SEALERS **Anaerobic sealers** cure in the absence of air. They are used as thread lockers (such as Loctite®), and they are used to seal rigid machined joints between cast parts. Anaerobic sealers lose their sealing ability at temperatures above 300°F (149°C). On production lines, the curing process is speeded up by using ultraviolet light.

When the anaerobic sealer is used on threads, air does not get to it so it hardens to form a seal to prevent the fastener from loosening. Anaerobic sealers can be used to seal machined surfaces without a gasket. The surfaces *must* be thoroughly clean to get a good seal. Special primers are recommended for use on the sealing surface to get a better bond with anaerobic sealers. ● SEE FIGURES 20–14 AND 20–15.

NONHARDENING SEALERS Sealers are nonhardening materials. Examples of sealer trade names include:

- Form-A-Gasket 2
- Pli-A-Seal
- Tight Seal 2
- Aviation Form-A-Gasket
- Brush Tack
- Copper Coat
- Spray Tack
- High Tack

Sealers are always used to seal the threads of bolts that break into coolant passages. Sealers for sealing threads may include Teflon. Sealer is often recommended for use on shim-type head gaskets and intake manifold gaskets. These gaskets have a metal surface that does not conform to any small amounts of surface roughness on the sealing surface. The sealer fills the surface variations between the gasket and the sealing surface.

Sealer may be used as a sealing aid on paper and fiber gaskets if the gasket needs help with sealing on a scratched, corroded, or rough surface finish. The sealer may be used on one side or on both sides of the gasket.

CAUTION: Sealer should *never* be used on rubber or cork-rubber gaskets. Instead of holding the rubber gasket or seal, it will help the rubber to slip out of place because the sealer will never harden.

ANTISEIZE COMPOUNDS
Antiseize compounds are used on fasteners in the engine that are subjected to high temperatures to prevent seizing caused by galvanic action between dissimilar metals. These compounds minimize corrosion from moisture. Exhaust manifold bolts or nuts,

FIGURE 20–16 Applying antiseize compound to the threads of a bolt helps prevent the threads from galling or rusting.

and oxygen sensors, keep them from seizing. The antiseize compound minimizes the chance of threads being pulled or breaking as the oxygen sensor is removed. Always follow the vehicle manufacturer's recommendations found in service information. ● **SEE FIGURE 20–16.**

SEALANT SUMMARY ● SEE CHART 20–1.

PRODUCTS	COMMON TRADE NAMES	USES	EXAMPLES
RTV (room-temperature vulcanization)	Silicone	As a gasket substitute or fill gaps	Valve covers, oil pans, intake manifold end seals, timing covers, transmission pans
Anaerobic sealer (threadlocker) medium strength	Loctite® Blue	Keeps fasteners from vibrating loose	For nut and bolt applications 1/4 to 3/4 inch (6–20 mm)
Anaerobic sealer (threadlocker) high temperature, high strength	Loctite® Red	Heavy-duty applications	For larger fasteners 3/8 to 1 inch (9.5–25 mm)
Antiseize (general purpose)	Neverseez™ Kopr Kote™ E-Z Break™	For preventing corrosion seizing	Oxygen sensors, spring bolts, exhaust manifold bolts/nuts
Antiseize (nickel)	Neverseez™ Thred-Gard™	For stainless steel and other metal applications	Harsh chemical environments
Hardening gasket sealant	Permatex® #1	Holds gaskets in place during assembly; also seals paper and cork gaskets	Transmission and engine oil pan gaskets, timing cover (paper gaskets) valve cover gaskets, and intake manifold gaskets
Nonhardening sealant	Permatex® #2	Allows repeated disassembly and reassembly	Thermostat housings, differential coverings, intake manifolds, fuel injectors and fuel pumps, transmission and torque converter seals
Aviation cement/contact cement	Aviation Form-A-Gasket#3™	Holds gaskets in place for assembly	All types of hoses and gaskets

CHART 20–1

Summary chart showing where sealants are used and their common trade names.

SUMMARY

1. Gaskets are used to fill a space or gap between two objects to prevent leakage from occurring.
2. There are many types of gaskets including cylinder head gaskets, valve cover gaskets, and timing cover gaskets.
3. Rubber or contact cement is used to hold a gasket in place.
4. RTV and anaerobic sealers are commonly used to seal engines.
5. Sealers are used to help gaskets seal.

REVIEW QUESTIONS

1. What is the purpose of a gasket?
2. What are the types of cover gaskets?
3. Why is armor used in head gaskets?
4. What is the difference between RTV and anaerobic sealers?

CHAPTER QUIZ

1. What force causes a head gasket to be drawn downward during engine operation?
   a. Intake stroke vacuum
   b. Gravity
   c. Head bolt torque
   d. Exhaust gas pressure

2. Where is a multilayered steel (MLS) gasket most often used in an engine?
   a. Valve cover gasket
   b. Oil pan gasket
   c. Head gasket
   d. Intake manifold gasket

3. A steel or copper wire used in a head gasket around the cylinder is called _____.
   a. Armor
   b. Fire ring
   c. Ridge block
   d. Either a or b

4. A one-piece oil pan gasket often uses _____ in the middle to add strength.
   a. Plastic (nylon)
   c. Hard rubber
   b. Steel
   d. Carbon fiber

5. Some gaskets use a steel washer around each bolt hole. The purpose of this washer is to _____.
   a. Improve the strength of the gasket
   b. Help seal around the bolt hole
   c. Help prevent the gasket from shrinking
   d. Prevent the gasket from being overly compressed

6. A gasket failure caused by the movement of dissimilar materials is called _____.
   a. Fretting
   b. Corrosion
   c. Collapsing
   d. Tearing

7. Which type of oil seal must *not* have oil applied for it to work correctly?
   a. Silicone rubber
   b. Buna-N
   c. Teflon®
   d. Viton®

8. Which type of *sealer* is to be used on nonmachined surfaces?
   a. RTV
   b. Anaerobic sealer
   c. Either a or b
   d. Neither a nor b

9. Which product requires heat to remove?
   a. Red thread locker
   b. Blue thread locker
   c. RTV
   d. Antiseize

10. What precautions should be followed when using gaskets?
    a. Never reuse an old gasket.
    b. A gasket should be checked to make sure it is the correct gasket.
    c. Read the instruction sheet.
    d. All of the above

chapter 21

BALANCING AND BLUEPRINTING

LEARNING OBJECTIVES

After studying this chapter, the reader should be able to:

1. Explain the causes of primary and secondary engine vibration.
2. Describe why balance shafts are used.
3. Explain what parts are rotating weight and what parts are reciprocating weight.
4. List the steps needed to balance an engine.
5. Explain why and how to measure combustion chamber volume.
6. List the steps needed to degree a camshaft.
7. Explain why it may be necessary to determine the valve lifter travel.

This chapter will help you prepare for ASE Engine Repair (A1) certification test content areas "B" (Engine Cylinder Head Diagnosis and Repair) and "C" (Engine Block Diagnosis and Repair).

KEY TERMS

Blueprinting 326
Bob weight 324
Inertial weight 324
Intake lobe centerline method 329
Reciprocating weight 324
Rotating weight 324

BALANCING AN ENGINE

PURPOSE   For any engine to operate with a minimum amount of vibration, all of the reciprocating parts must be close to the same weight. Production engines use parts that are usually within 3 grams of each other and result in a relatively smooth operating engine.

NOTE: A gram is 1/28 of an ounce or the weight of a typical small paper clip.

Custom engine builders attempt to get all reciprocating parts to weigh within 1 gram or less of each other. The reason for such accuracy is that any unbalance is increased greatly by centrifugal force as the engine operates. The force of the unbalance increases by the square of the speed. In other words, if the engine RPM doubles, the force of any unbalance quadruples. An unbalance of 1 ounce that is 1 inch from the center of rotation becomes a force of 7 ounces at 500 RPM. At 5000 RPM, this same 1 ounce of unbalance would be increased to 44 pound. This small amount of imbalance can cause serious vibrations and potential internal engine damage especially at high engine RPM.

ENGINE BALANCING PROCEDURE   Whenever all rotating and reciprocating parts of an engine are to be balanced, the following components are needed to balance inline engines.

- Crankshaft
- Vibration damper (harmonic balancer)
- Flywheel or flexplate
- Pressure plate
- All bolts, lock washers, keys, and spacers needed to assemble the above parts on the crankshaft
- Connecting rods
- Pistons
- Wrist pins

To balance a V-type engine, the following additional parts are needed.

- Rod bearings
- Piston rings
- Wrist pin locks (if full-floating piston pins)

The typical procedure includes the following steps.

STEP 1   The first step is to equalize the **reciprocating weight,** which includes the pistons and rods.

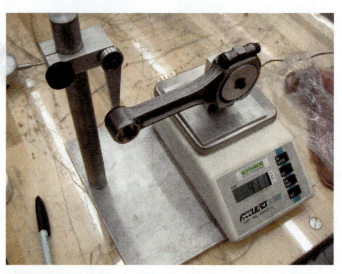

FIGURE 21–1 Weighing the big end of a connecting rod on a scale that keeps it perfectly horizontal so that each end can be weighed separately.

Reciprocating weight is also called **inertial weight.** The pistons should be weighed, including the piston pin and rings, to determine the lightest weight piston. Material should be ground from the heavier pistons until they match the weight of the lightest piston. Material should be removed from the weight balancing pads.

CAUTION: Do not grind or attempt to remove weight from the piston pin. This could weaken a highly stressed part and lead to engine failure.

STEP 2   Connecting rods have a big end and a small end. The big end of the rod is considered to be part of the **rotating weight** and the small end part of the reciprocating weight after the rod has been reconditioned. The two ends should be weighed and matched separately. ● **SEE FIGURE 21–1.**

After both the large and small ends of all the rods have been weighed, then material should be removed from the balancing pads of both the heavier and lighter ends of the rods until they match the lightest rods. ● **SEE FIGURE 21–2.**

BOB WEIGHTS   **Bob weights** are attached to the rod journals on V-type engines to simulate the weight of the rods and pistons. ● **SEE FIGURE 21–3.**

The bob weight must equal the total of the following for each journal.

- Rotating weight
- A percentage of the reciprocating weight
- An amount for the weight of the oil trapped between the journal and the bearing

FIGURE 21–2 Removing material from the balancing pad on the small end of the rod to match it to the weight of the small end of the lightest rod being used in the engine.

FIGURE 21–3 A crankshaft with bob weights attached as well as the flexplate and the harmonic balancer.

The rotating weight includes the big end of the connecting rod and the connecting rod bearings.

NOTE: On V-8 engines, two rods share a crank pin so that the calculations for bob weight, including the weight of both big ends of the connecting rods and bearings, should be taken into consideration.

The reciprocating weight includes the small end of the rod(s) and the piston assemblies, which include the rings, pin, and locks, if equipped.

BALANCING FACTOR A balancing factor is a formula used to determine what percentage (usually 50%) of the reciprocating weight needs to be included in the bob weight. A bob weight is a special fixture that attaches to the rod journal of the V-type crankshaft, where different values of weights are added to usually equal one-half of the total weight of two pistons, two connecting rods, two sets of rings, wrist pins, bearings, and the equivalent amount of oil coating on the parts. When properly assembled, the bob weights allow V-type crankshafts to be rotated at balancing speeds for engine balance adjustments.

BALANCING MACHINES Some machines operate from a stroboscopic light that picks up vibrations in the assembly and a meter indicates the exact location of heaviness to be removed. Other balancing machines use electronics with meter readouts that define the exact amount and location of the metal to be removed. This process usually involves removing metal from the counterweight area of the crankshaft, by drilling a specific sized hole to a calculated depth. Most balancing

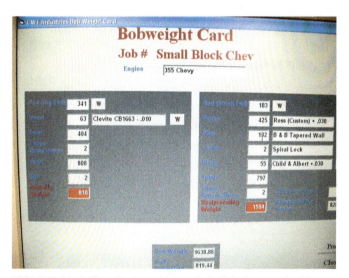

FIGURE 21–4 The display of a crankshaft balancer showing where weight needs to be removed to achieve a balanced assembly.

machines calculate the bob weight automatically after inputting all of the weight information and then display where and how much material needs to be removed to achieve proper balance.
● **SEE FIGURE 21–4.**

A drill is commonly used to remove weight from the counterweight of the crankshaft to achieve proper balance.
● **SEE FIGURE 21–5.**

After the specified material has been removed, the counterweight is checked again by the balance machine. When the procedure has been completed, the rotating assembly is then in balance.

Sometimes weight has to be added to a crankshaft to achieve proper balance. In this case, a hole is drilled parallel to the crankshaft in a counterweight and extra heavy metal is added.

FIGURE 21–5 A drill is often used to remove weight from the crankshaft to achieve proper balance.

FIGURE 21–6 Heavy metal installed and welded in place.

? **FREQUENTLY ASKED QUESTION**

What Is "Heavy Metal"?

Heavy metal, also called mallory metal, is an alloy of tungsten that is 1.5 times heavier than lead. It is used to add weight to a crankshaft if needed, usually on engines that have been stroked using a stroker crankshaft. The heavy metal must be installed parallel to the centerline axis of the crankshaft. ● **SEE FIGURE 21–6.**

BLUEPRINTING PROCESS

GENERAL USE QUESTIONS   **Blueprinting** is the process used to custom fit and select variables to best match a predetermined level of performance. Unless the engine is going to be a stock rebuild or used as intended from the factory, certain decisions have to be made before an engine is built. ● **SEE CHART 21–1** for questions and reasons.

SPECIFIC REQUIREMENT NEEDS   After the overall decisions about general use of the engine have been determined, the individual parts of the engine need to be selected, including:

- **Block.** The higher the cubic inch displacement, the higher the potential torque and horsepower.
- **Rotating assembly.** For a stock rebuild, using the stock parts is all that is needed. Depending on the power level

and RPM needed, parts have to be selected to withstand the forces involved, such as using forged crankshafts, pistons, and connecting rods instead of cast pieces.

- **Breathing system.** The amount of horsepower that any engine produces is directly related to the amount of air-fuel mixture that can enter and exit the engine. This means that the camshaft, cylinder head, and intake manifolds must be correctly sized and matched for optimum performance.

SIZE MATTERS   Almost every part is selected according to the needs of the engine's size. The entire breathing system, such as the heads, camshaft, intake manifold, exhaust system, and fuel delivery system, is selected based on the cubic inch displacement of the engine. Therefore, the first consideration is to determine the size of the engine. Due to engine machining and selection of the crankshaft, the displacement will be changed.

- **Boring the block.** Boring for oversize pistons has a limited effect on the displacement of the engine.
- **Stroking the engine.** Replacing the crankshaft and installing all new pistons and connecting rods makes a big difference in the displacement of the engine. ● **SEE CHART 21–2.**

PARTS MANUFACTURER HELP   Now that the basic parameters for the engine have been determined, parts selection and the recommendation of the parts manufacturer should be followed. Most manufacturers of high-performance parts, such as camshafts, have available specific guidelines for the selection of the best part number to select for the anticipated use of the engine. Before selecting a camshaft or another high-performance part or calling for advice, have the following information determined and available.

QUESTION	REASON
General Use • Street (almost stock?) • High-performance street • Street/strip (daily driver who wants to drag race on weekends) • Drag race (which class, etc.?) • Racing (oval, dirt, 1/2 mile?)	The real use of the engine helps determine the following: • Compression ratio • Knowing the rules of the racing organization regarding parts that can be used • Anticipated maximum engine RPM, which has a huge effect on the short block components needed
Power Adder?	Using nitrous or an add-on turbocharger or supercharger requires great piston-to-cylinder wall clearances, plus the use of forged pistons and connecting rods in most cases.
Type of Fuel	This will affect many factors including the compression ratio and fuel system needs, especially if designed to operate on E85.

CHART 21-1

Knowing exactly how the engine will be used is a necessary first step in the engine building process.

ENGINE	STOCK (CUBIC INCHES)	STOCK BORE (INCHES)	STOCK STROKE (INCHES)	0.030" BORE OVERSIZE (CUBIC INCHES)	AMOUNT OF STROKE CHANGE (INCHES)	NEW STROKE (INCHES)	DISP W/ 0.03 INCH BORE & NEW STROKE (CUBIC INCHES)
CHEVROLET 5.7 L	350	4.000	3.480	354.90 (+ 4.90)	0.270	3.750	382.44 (+ 32.44)
CHEVROLET 7.4 L	454	4.250	4.000	460 (+ 6)	0.250	4.250	489.00 (+ 35)
FORD 5.0 L	302	4.000	3.000	305.95 (+ 2.95)	0.400	3.400	347.33 (+ 45.33)
FORD 4.6 L	281	3.550	3.540	284.93 (+ 3.93)	0.300	3.840	305.78 (+ 24.78)
MOPAR 5.2 L	340	4.040	3.310	344.24 (+ 4.24)	0.690	4.000	416 (+ 76)
HONDA 1.8 L Non-VTEC & VTEC	112 (1834 cc)	3.189 (81 mm)	3.500 (89 mm)	113.95 (+ 1.95)	0.250	3.750	122 (+ 10)

CHART 21-2

Boring an engine increases the engine displacement slightly, whereas stroking an engine has a greater effect on engine displacement.

- Vehicle weight
- Type of transmission (automatic or manual)
- Final drive ratio (helps determine engine RPM needs)
- Type of use (drag racing, street performance, etc.)

FOLLOW PARTS MANUFACTURER'S RECOMMENDATIONS If the above items have been achieved, the parts selected should produce the desired engine performance. For best results, perform the following steps.

STEP 1 Read, understand, and follow all instructions that accompany the parts.

STEP 2 Perform all of the suggested steps including the specified clearances (piston-to-wall, bearings, and end play specifications) that often differs from factory specifications.

STEP 3 Use the specified lubricant on parts such as fasteners and the torque specification which often differs from factory specifications.

FIGURE 21–7 Setup needed to measure the combustion chamber volume in cubic centimeters (cc).

FIGURE 21–8 Cylinder head setup for flow testing. Note the weak valve springs that are strong enough to keep the valves shut, yet weak enough to permit the flow bench operator to vary the intake valve opening amount.

COMBUSTION CHAMBER VOLUME

For best engine performance and smooth operation, make the following a priority.

- All cylinders should have the same compression. This means that all cylinders should have the same combustion chamber volume.

- The technician or engine builder needs to know the combustion chamber volume to accurately calculate the compression ratio.

- To accurately measure the volume of the combustion chamber, a graduated burette is used with mineral spirits (or automatic transmission fluid) to measure the exact volume of the chamber in cubic centimeters (cc). ● **SEE FIGURE 21–7.**

FIGURE 21–9 Modeling clay is installed around the port to duplicate the flow improvement characteristics of an intake manifold.

FLOW TESTING CYLINDER HEADS

PURPOSE Many specialty engines are tested for the amount of air that can flow through the ports and valves of the engine. A flow bench is used to measure the amount of air in cubic feet per minute (cfm) that can flow through the valves at various valve openings.

After completion of the valve job and any port or combustion chamber work, weak valve springs are installed temporarily. ● **SEE FIGURE 21–8.**

Modeling clay is then temporarily applied around the port areas to improve flow characteristics where the intake manifold would normally direct the flow into the port. ● **SEE FIGURE 21–9.**

FIGURE 21–10 A flow bench that can measure and record the airflow through the intake and exhaust ports of each cylinder.

Various thicknesses of metal spacers are placed between the cylinder head holding fixture and the valve stem. Typical thicknesses used are 0.1 inch through 0.7 inch, using 0.1 inch increments. The results are recorded on a worksheet.

FLOW RATE AND HORSEPOWER
Most comprehensive engine machine shops have the equipment to measure the airflow through cylinder head ports and valves. ● **SEE FIGURE 21–10.**

After the airflow through the open intake valve has been determined, a formula can be used to estimate horsepower. The following formula has proven to be a fairly accurate estimate of horsepower when compared with dynamometer testing after the engine is built.

NOTE The first part of the formula is used to convert airflow measurement from a basis of being tested at 28 inch H$_2$O to that of being tested at 20 inch H$_2$O.

$$\text{Horsepower per cylinder} = \text{Airflow at 28 inch H}_2\text{O} \times 0.598 \times 0.43$$

For example, for a V-8 that measures 231 cfm of airflow at 28 inch H$_2$O:

$$\text{Horsepower} = 231 \times 0.598 = 138 \text{ cfm at}$$
$$20 \text{ inch H}_2\text{O} \times 0.43 = 59.4 \text{ hp per cylinder} \times 8 = 475 \text{ hp}$$

CAUTION: Even though this formula has proven to be fairly accurate, there are too many variables in the design of any engine besides the airflow through the head for this formula to be accurate under all conditions.

DEGREEING THE CAMSHAFT

PURPOSE The purpose of degreeing the camshaft in the engine is to locate the valve action exactly as the camshaft manufacturers intended. The reason this should be checked is due to possible variations on the following parts that could affect the designed valve opening and closing events.

- Cam gear locating pin position
- Camshaft grinding variations
- Timing chain or gear variations

PROCEDURE The method most often recommended by camshaft manufacturers is the **intake lobe centerline method.** This method determines the exact centerline of the intake lobe and compares it to the specifications supplied with the replacement camshaft. On an overhead valve engine, the camshaft is usually degreed after the crankshaft, piston, and camshaft are installed and before the cylinder heads are installed.

To determine the centerline of the intake lobe, follow these steps using a degree wheel mounted on the crankshaft.

STEP 1 Locate the exact top dead center. Install a degree wheel and bring the cylinder 1 piston close to TDC. Install a piston stop. (A piston stop is any object attached to the block that can act as a solid mechanical stop to prevent the piston from reaching the top of the cylinder.) By hand, slowly rotate the crankshaft clockwise until the piston *gently* hits the stop. ● **SEE FIGURE 21–11.**

CAUTION Do not use the starter motor to rotate the engine. Use a special wrench on the flywheel or the front of the crankshaft.

Record the reading on the degree wheel, and then turn the engine in the opposite direction until it stops again and record that number. ● **FIGURE 21–12** indicates a reading of 30 degrees ATDC and 26 degrees BTDC. Add the two readings together and divide by two (30 + 26 = 56 ÷ 2 = 28 degrees). Move the degree

FIGURE 21–11 A piston stop is used to help determine top dead center.

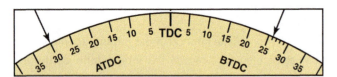

FIGURE 21–12 The degree wheel indicates where the piston stopped near top dead center. By splitting the difference between the two readings, the true TDC (28 degrees) can be located on the degree wheel.

wheel until it is 28 degrees and the engine has stopped rotating in either direction. Now TDC on the degree wheel is exactly at top dead center.

STEP 2 After finding exact TDC (28 degrees in this case), remove the piston stop, then rotate the engine until the degree wheel indicates 28 degrees. Now adjust the degree wheel to read exactly TDC. Place a dial indicator on an intake valve lifter. To accurately locate the point of maximum lift (intake lobe centerline), rotate the engine until the lifter drops 0.05 inch on each side of the maximum lift point. Mark the degree wheel at these points on either side of the maximum lift point. Now count the degrees between these two points and mark the halfway point. This halfway point represents the intake centerline. This point is often located between 100 and 110 degrees. ● **SEE FIGURE 21–13.**

STEP 3 Now that both TDC and intake centerline have been marked, compare the actual intake centerline with the specification. For example, if the actual intake centerline is 106 degrees and the camshaft specification indicates 106 degrees, then the camshaft is installed *straight up.* ● **SEE FIGURE 21–14.** If the actual

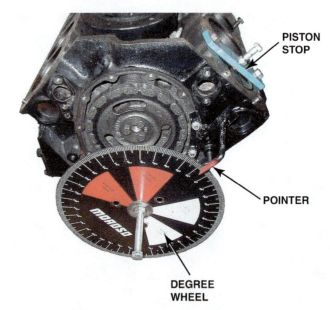

FIGURE 21–13 Note the setup required to degree a camshaft. The pointer, the degree wheel, and the piston stop are used to find exact top dead center.

TECH TIP

Valve-to-Piston Clearance Versus Cam Timing

If the cam timing is *advanced* (relative to the crankshaft), the intake valve-to-piston clearance is *reduced.* If the cam timing is *retarded,* the exhaust valve-to-piston clearance is *reduced.*

This is true because the intake valve lags behind the motion of the piston on the intake stroke, whereas the piston "chases" the exhaust valve on the exhaust stroke.

reading is 104 degrees, the camshaft is advanced by 2 degrees. If the actual reading is 108 degrees, the camshaft is retarded by 2 degrees.

ADVANCED CAM TIMING If the camshaft is slightly ahead of the crankshaft, the camshaft is called *advanced.* An advanced camshaft (maximum of 4 degrees) results in more low-speed torque with a slight decrease in high-speed power. Some aftermarket camshaft manufacturers design about a 4-degree advance into their timing gears or camshaft. This permits the use of a camshaft with more lift and duration, yet still provides the smooth idle and low-speed responses of a milder camshaft.

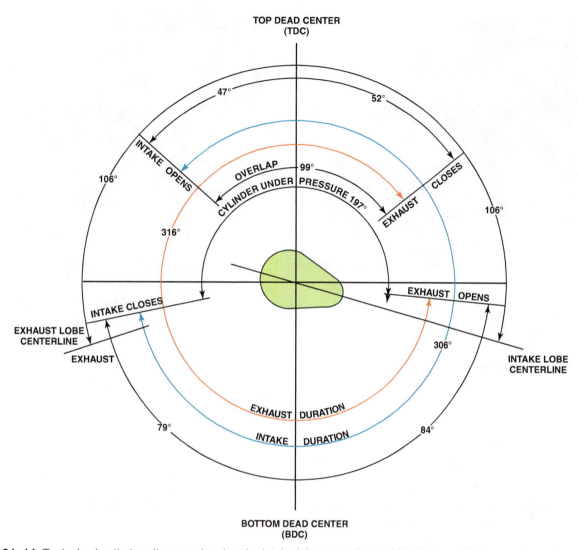

FIGURE 21–14 Typical valve timing diagram showing the intake lobe centerline at 106 degrees ATDC.

RETARDED CAM TIMING

If the camshaft is slightly behind the crankshaft, the camshaft is called *retarded*. A retarded camshaft (maximum of 4 degrees) results in more high-speed power at the expense of low-speed torque.

If the measured values are different from specifications, special offset pins (bushings) or keys are available to relocate the cam gear by the proper amount. Some manufacturers can provide adjustable cam timing sprockets for overhead cam engines.

DETERMINING PROPER PUSHROD LENGTH

PURPOSE

The length of the pushrod is determined by the geometry of the engine when it was originally built. Unless machining was performed, using the stock length pushrods is fine and there is no need to replace the pushrods that are longer or shorter. If, however, machining of the head (OHV engines) or the block deck, then a different length pushrod may be needed to restore the proper valve train geometry. If the pushrod length is correct, then the rocker arm will be contacting the center of the valve stem. ● **SEE FIGURE 21–15.**

WHEN NEEDED

If any of the following operations have been performed, the proper pushrod length *must* be determined.

- Regrinding the camshaft (reduces base circle dimensions)
- Milling or resurfacing cylinder heads
- Milling or resurfacing block deck
- Grinding valves and/or facing valve stems
- Changing to a head gasket thinner or thicker than the original

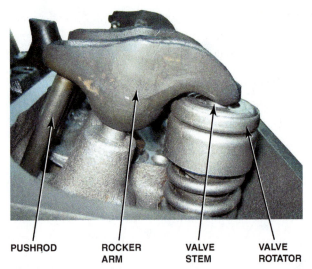

PUSHROD   ROCKER   VALVE   VALVE
           ARM   STEM   ROTATOR

FIGURE 21–15 A side view of a small block Chevrolet engine showing that the rocker arm is contacting the top of the valve stem. A roller-tipped rocker arm will show a more definite line of contact than a stamped steel rocker.

PROCEDURE To determine the pushrod length, assemble the engine and select one cylinder to find out if the pushrod length is okay. Perform the following steps.

STEP 1 Mark the top of the valve tip using a marker or machinist dye. The movement of the rocker arm will wear off the mark where it contacts the tip of the valve.

STEP 2 Install the stock pushrod and adjust the valve as per the vehicle manufacturer's specification.

STEP 3 Rotate the engine several revolutions by hand.

STEP 4 Remove the rocker arm and check where the marker has been worn from the tip of the valve.

- If the marker has been worn off in the center of the valve tip, the pushrod length is correct.

- If the marker has been worn off toward the exhaust outside (exhaust side of the head), the pushrod is too long.

- If the marker has been worn off toward the upper part of the valve stem (toward the intake side of the head), the pushrod is too short. ● **SEE FIGURE 21–16.**

STEP 5 Use an adjustable pushrod and adjust the pushrod length a little at a time until testing results in the correct wear at the center of the valve tip. Measure the adjustable pushrod to determine the length needed. ● **SEE FIGURE 21–17.** Pushrods are often available in length 0.100 inch longer and shorter than stock.

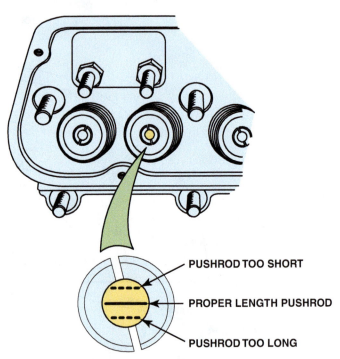

PUSHROD TOO SHORT

PROPER LENGTH PUSHROD

PUSHROD TOO LONG

FIGURE 21–16 Checking where on the valve stem the marker has been worn off by the rocker arm, is the method to use to check for proper pushrod length.

ADJUSTABLE
LENGTH
PUSHROD

STOCK
PUSHROD

FIGURE 21–17 An adjustable pushrod is adjustable for length compared to a conventional stock pushrod.

SHORT BLOCK BLUEPRINTING

DETERMINE ENGINE USE

The short block detailing is similar to any other engine rebuilding except for the following issues.

- Use the clearance specification that is specified for the application.
- Use the torque specification that is recommended by the manufacturer of the crankshaft.
- Always use the specified thread lubricant and/or sealer on fasteners as recommended by the fastener manufacturer.

TRIAL ASSEMBLY

Before the engine is assembled it should be partially assembled to double check all clearances. This is also a good time to verify that the following are correct.

- Cam timing
- Side clearances
- Crankshaft end play
- Piston-to-wall clearance
- Valve-to-piston clearance
- Crankshaft to block clearance
- Camshaft to connecting rod clearance

CRANKSHAFT BALANCING

1 The crankshaft should always be balanced with the flywheel (or flexplate) and harmonic balancer installed.

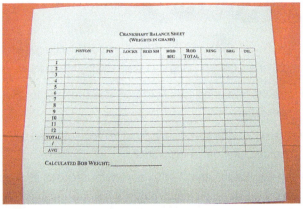

2 Use a worksheet so that all weights can be measured and recorded.

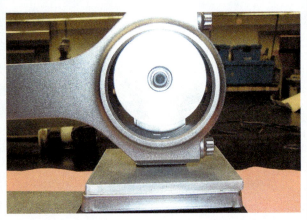

3 Using a fixture to hold the connecting rod horizontally, measure and record the weight of the big end of the rod.

4 Using a fixture to hold the connecting rod horizontally, measure and record the weight of the small end of the rod.

5 Weigh each piston. Remove some metal from the heaviest pistons to match their weight with the lightest.

6 Weigh and record the weight of each piston pin.

7 Weigh and record the weight of each piston pin locks if used.

8 Weigh and record the weight of the piston rings for each piston.

9 Weigh and record the weight of the rod bearings for each connecting rod.

10 Using the worksheet and plugging the measured values into the balancer, adjust the bob weight to the desired weight.

11 Install the bob weights and operate the balancer according to the instructions for the balancer being used.

12 Use a drill and drill the counterweight in the designated location as indicated on the balancer.

SUMMARY

1. Proper balancing of the engine is important for smooth operation.

2. Both rotating weight and reciprocating weight are considered during the balancing procedure.

3. Blueprinting means following the exact procedures and specifications for the parts used.

4. Checking combustion chamber volume is used to ensure that all cylinders have the exact same compression ratio.

5. Degreeing a camshaft is done to ensure that the valve events occur at the correct time.

6. Checking for proper pushrod length is important after the machining operations have changed the height of the cylinder head(s).

REVIEW QUESTIONS

1. What parts are considered to be rotating weights?

2. What parts must be measured when measuring reciprocating weight?

3. What is done to the crankshaft to achieve a balanced rotating engine assembly?

4. What questions should be answered before starting the blueprint process?

5. List the parts and supplies needed to check combustion chamber volume.

6. List the steps needed to degree a camshaft.

CHAPTER QUIZ

1. A gram weighs about the same as a _____.
   a. Paper clip
   b. Chicken feather
   c. Penny
   d. Dime

2. Reciprocating weight is also called _____.
   a. Balance weight
   b. Bob weight
   c. Rotating weight
   d. Inertial weight

3. Connecting rods should be weighed and balanced _____.
   a. Before reconditioning
   b. After reconditioning

4. Pistons and connecting rods can be ground from what area when removing weight?
   a. Balancing pad
   b. Weight bore
   c. Sides
   d. Thrust surface(s)

5. Which of the following is not reciprocating weight?
   a. Piston
   b. Big end of a connecting rod
   c. Small end of a connecting rod
   d. Piston ring

6. How is the crankshaft *usually* balanced?
   a. Material is welded onto the counterweight.
   b. Pistons are replaced until a matched set is achieved.
   c. Material is drilled out of the counterweight.
   d. Heavy metal is used to increase the weight of the counterweight.

7. Blueprinting is a process that _____.
   a. Uses factory-only specification
   b. Uses the parts manufacturer's recommended specification for many of the critical clearances
   c. Includes identifying the use of the engine and the vehicle it is going to be used in
   d. Both b and c

8. Combustion chamber volume is measured using a fluid and what unit of measure?
   a. Cubic inches (inch^3)
   b. Cubic centimeters (cc)
   c. Liters (L)
   d. Ounces (oz.)

9. Why is it recommended that a new camshaft be "degreed"?
   a. Cam gear locating pin position could be different
   b. Because of camshaft grinding variations
   c. Due to timing chain or gear variations
   d. All of the above

10. During flow bench testing cylinders, what is used to hold the valves closed?
    a. Weaker than normal test springs
    b. Normal valve springs
    c. The same valve springs that will be used in the engine
    d. Double counter-wound special high-tension valve springs

chapter 22

ENGINE ASSEMBLY AND DYNAMOMETER TESTING

LEARNING OBJECTIVES

After studying this chapter, the reader should be able to:

1. Describe the steps that should be followed in preparation for assembly.
2. Explain clamping force.
3. Define the torque-to-yield method of fastener tightening.
4. Discuss the advantages of performing a trial assembly of the engine.
5. List the steps needed to assemble an engine.
6. Describe what dynamometer testing can determine about the engine.

This chapter will help you prepare for ASE Engine Repair (A1) certification test content areas "B" (Engine Cylinder Head Diagnosis and Repair) and "C" (Engine Block Diagnosis and Repair).

5. Perform engine piston-to-bore clearance measurement procedures.
6. Inspect, repair, or replace crankshaft vibration damper (harmonic balancer).
7. Inspect flywheel or flex plate and ring gear for cracks and wear; measure run out; determine needed repairs.
8. Inspect auxiliary (balance, intermediate, idler, counterbalance, or silencer) shaft(s) and support bearings for damage and wear; determine needed repairs; reinstall and time.
9. Perform engine crankshaft rear main seal replacement procedures.

GM STC OBJECTIVES

GM Service Technical College topics covered in this chapter are:

1. Remove and install the engine valve timing components.
2. Adjust valves (mechanical or hydraulic lifters).
3. Install an engine cylinder head and gaskets; tighten head bolts according to service manual specifications and procedures.
4. Inspect, measure, and install piston rings.

KEY TERMS

Assembly lube 341
Clamping force 353
Corrected torque 366
Correction factor 366
Dry bulb temperature 365
Expansion plugs 342
Fogging oil 341
Freeze plugs 342

Lash 359
Piston ring compressor 350
Soft core plugs 342
Torque-to-yield (TTY) 355
Transducers 365
Welsh plugs 342

DETAILS, DETAILS, DETAILS

Successful engine assembly depends on getting all of the details right. Where to start? Start when all parts have been purchased or prepared for assembly.

When starting to assemble the engine, be sure to have all of the instructions from all of the parts used.

- **Service Prior to Assembly.** The importance of cleanliness during assembly cannot be overstated. Dirt or debris will cause engine damage. An automobile engine is a combination of many machined, honed, polished, and lapped surfaces with tolerances that are measured in ten thousandths of an inch. When any internal engine parts are serviced, care and cleanliness are important. A liberal coating of engine oil should be applied to friction areas during assembly in order to protect and lubricate the surfaces on initial operation. Throughout this section, it should be understood that proper cleaning and protection of machined surfaces and friction areas are part of the repair procedure. This is considered standard shop practice even if not specifically stated.

    Lubricate all moving parts with engine oil or a specified assembly lubricant. This will provide lubrication for initial start up.[1]

- **Read.** Read *all* instructions that are included with all new parts and gaskets. Often very important information or suggested specifications are included and may be at the end.

- **Get Information.** Use GM service information (SI) as the engine is assembled. The information is listed step-by-step in the order the engine should be assembled. Also included are all torque specifications and methods for tightening critical fasteners.

    NOTE: If you don't have access to GM SI you should not be doing the job.

- **Understand.** Be sure to fully understand everything that is stated in the instructions. If unsure as to what is meant, ask a knowledgeable technician or call the company to be sure that all procedures are clearly understood.

- **Follow.** Be sure to follow *all* of the instructions. Do not pick the easy procedures and skip others.

[1]GM Service Information Doc ID 42592.

FIGURE 22–1 Deburring all sharp edges is an important step to achieve proper engine assembly.

SHORT BLOCK PREPARATION

ITEMS TO CHECK   The following engine block details should be checked.

- All passages should be clean and free of rust and debris.
- All gasket surfaces are properly cleaned and checked for burrs and scratches.
- All cups and plugs should be installed.
- The final bore dimension is correct for the piston.
- The surface finish of the cylinder bore matches with the specified finish required for the piston rings that are going to be used.
- All sharp edges and burrs have been removed. ● **SEE FIGURE 22–1**.
- The main bearing bores (saddles) are straight and inline.
- The lifter bores have been honed and checked for proper dimension.

SURFACE FINISH   The surface finish is important for the proper sealing of any gasket.

- **Surface too rough.** If the surface finish is too rough, the gasket will not be able to seal the deep grooves in the surface.
- **Surface too smooth.** If the surface finish is too smooth, the gasket can move out of proper location, causing leakage.

ENGINE PART MATERIAL	GASKET MATERIAL	ACCEPTABLE SURFACE FINISH (RA) (μinch)
Cast iron/cast iron	Composite	60–80
Aluminum/cast iron	Composite	20–30
Aluminum/cast iron	Rubber-coated multilayered steel (MLS)	15–30

CHART 22–1

The surface finish of the block and cylinder head depends on the type of gasket being used.

🔧 **TECH TIP**

Be Aware of Special Engine Procedures

When rebuilding some aluminum block engines, check service information carefully because some engines require that threaded inserts be installed in all head bolt threads. Performing this operation can increase the cost and time needed. Always follow all recommended service procedures for the engine being serviced. ● **SEE FIGURE 22–2.**

Surface finish is measured in microinches, usually abbreviated by using the Greek letter mu (μ) and the abbreviation for inches together (μin.).

- The higher the microinch finish, the rougher the surface.
- The lower the microinch finish, the smoother the surface. The specification for surface finish is usually specified in roughness average, or Ra.

● **SEE CHART 22–1** for the acceptable roughness for the head gasket surface.

Check the instruction sheet that comes with the gasket for the specified surface finish.

CHECKING SURFACES BEFORE ASSEMBLY

All surfaces of an engine should be clean and straight and have the specified surface finish and flatness. Flatness is a measure of how much the surface varies in any 6 inch span. An industry standard maximum limit for flatness is usually 0.002 inch. If the surface is not flat, the gaskets will not be able to seal properly.

PREPARING THREADED HOLES

STEP 1 All threads in the block should be thoroughly cleaned. Many experts recommend using a thread chaser, because a tap could cut and remove metal. A chaser will restore the threads without removing metal. ● **SEE FIGURE 22–3.**

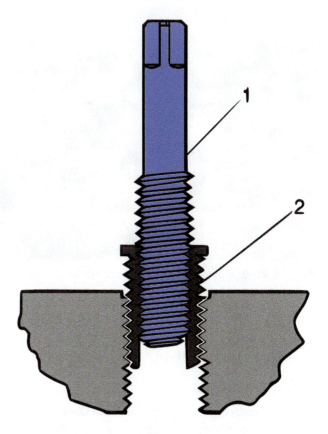

FIGURE 22–2 When rebuilding an aluminum block engine, a threaded insert (2) is installed in the head bolt holes using a special driver tool (1). (*Courtesy of General Motors*)

🔧 **TECH TIP**

Keep the Engine Covered

Using a large plastic trash bag is an excellent way to keep the engine clean when storing it between work sessions. ● **SEE FIGURE 22–4.**

STEP 2 Check that all liquid has been removed from the bolt holes in the block. If liquid is in the bottom of a blind hole, the block can be cracked when the bolt is installed.

CYLINDER HEAD PREPARATION

ITEMS TO CHECK Check the following details on the cylinder head(s).

- The surface finish of the fire deck is as specified for the head gasket type to be used.

FIGURE 22–3 A thread chaser (top) is the preferred tool to clean threaded holes because it cleans without removing metal compared to a tap (bottom).

FIGURE 22–4 Using a plastic trash bag is an excellent way to keep the engine clean during all stages of assembly.

 REAL WORLD FIX

Valve Springs Can Vary

A technician was building a small block Chevrolet V-8 engine at home and was doing the final detailed checks, and found that many of the valve springs did not have the same tension. Using a borrowed valve spring tester, the technician visited a local parts store and measured all of the valve springs that the store had in stock. The technician selected and purchased the 16 valve springs that were within specification and within a very narrow range of tension. Although having all valve springs equal may or may not affect engine operation, the technician was pleased that all of the valve springs were equal.

FIGURE 22–5 A trial assembly showed that some grinding of the block will be needed to provide clearance for the counterweight of the crankshaft. Also, notice that the engine has been equipped with studs for the four-bolt main bearing caps.

- All valves should be checked for leakage by pouring mineral spirits into the intake and exhaust ports and look for leakage past the valves.
- All valve springs should be checked for even spring pressure and installed height.
- Check for proper pushrod length. If the cylinder head(s) has been machined and/or the block deck machined, the pushrods may be too long. If the pushrods are too long, the rocker arm geometry will not be correct. One problem that can occur with incorrect rocker arm geometry is spring bind, which can cause severe engine damage.
- If replacement rocker arms are used, be sure that the geometry and total lift will be okay.

TRIAL ASSEMBLY

SHORT BLOCK Before performing final engine assembly, the wise technician checks that all parts will fit and work. This is especially important if using a different crankshaft that changes the stroke. ● **SEE FIGURE 22–5** for an example of a 400 cu. inch Chevrolet crankshaft being fitted to a 350 cu. inch Chevrolet engine.

VALVE TRAIN Another place where a trial fit is needed is in the valve train. Some timing chain mechanisms require more space than the stock component so some machining may be needed.

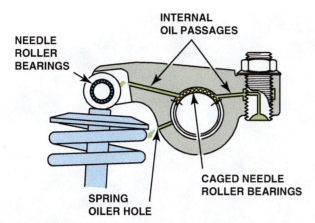

FIGURE 22–6 A typical high-performance aftermarket rocker arm which is equipped with needle roller bearings at the valve stem end and caged needle bearing at the pivot shaft end to reduce friction, which increases engine horsepower and improves fuel economy.

TECH TIP

Fogging Oil and Assembly Lube

When assembling an engine, the parts should be coated with a light oil film to keep them from rusting. This type of oil is commonly referred to as **fogging oil** and is available in spray cans. ● SEE FIGURE 22–7.

During engine assembly, the internal parts should be lubricated. While engine oil or grease could be used, most experts recommend the use of a specific lubricant designed for engine assembly. This lubricant, designed to remain on the parts and not drip or run, is called **assembly lube**. ● SEE FIGURE 22–8.

If the rocker arms have been upgraded to roller rockers, these should be installed and checked that the tip of the roller rests at the center of the valve stem. ● SEE FIGURE 22–6.

If there is a problem, further investigation will be needed because the pushrods may be too long due to machining of the block deck and/or cylinder head. Rotate the engine and check for proper clearance throughout the opening and closing of the valves. Use a feeler gauge between the coils of the valve spring to check for coil bind. If coil bind occurs, a different camshaft or valve spring should be used.

V-ENGINE HEAD ANGLE During the trial assembly, use a gauge to check that the heads are at the correct angle to ensure proper intake manifold gasket sealing. If the angle is not correct, then remachining of the head or block will be needed. ● SEE FIGURE 22–9.

FIGURE 22–7 Fogging oil is used to cover bare metal parts when the engine is being stored to prevent corrosion.

FIGURE 22–8 Engine assembly lube is recommended to be used on engine parts during assembly.

FINAL SHORT BLOCK ASSEMBLY

BLOCK PREPARATION All surfaces should be checked for damage resulting from the machining processes. Items that should be done before assembly begins include the following:

1. The block, including the oil gallery passages, should be thoroughly cleaned. ● SEE FIGURES 22–10 AND 22–11.

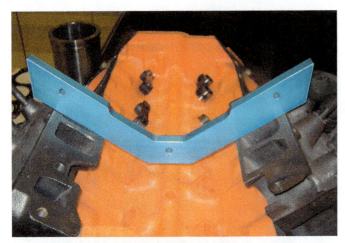

FIGURE 22–9 An angle gauge being used to check the angle between the cylinder heads on this small block Chevrolet V-8 engine.

FIGURE 22–10 The best way to thoroughly clean cylinders is to use soap (detergent), water, and a large washing brush. This method floats the machining particles out of the block and washes them away.

2. All threaded bolt holes should be chamfered.

3. All threaded holes should be cleaned with a thread chaser before final assembly.

INSTALLING CUPS AND PLUGS Oil gallery plugs should be installed using sealant on the threads.

CAUTION: Avoid using Teflon tape on the threads of oil gallery plugs or coolant drain plugs. The tape is often cut by the threads, and thin strips of the tape are then free to flow through the oil galleries where the tape can cause a clog, thereby limiting lubricating engine oil to important parts of the engine.

FIGURE 22–11 All oil galleries should be cleaned using soap (detergent), water, and a long oil gallery cleaning brush.

Core holes left in the external block wall are machined and sealed with **soft core plugs** or **expansion plugs** (also called **freeze plugs** or **Welsh plugs**).

Soft plugs are of two designs.

- **Convex type.** The core hole is counterbored with a shoulder. The convex soft plug is placed in the counterbore, convex side out. It is driven in with a fitted seating tool. This causes the edge of the soft plug to enlarge to hold it in place. A convex plug should be driven in until it reaches the counterbore of the core plug hole.

- **Cup type.** This most common type fits into a smooth, straight hole. The outer edge of the cup is slightly bell mouthed. The bell mouth causes it to tighten when it is driven into the hole to the correct depth with a seating tool. An installed cup-type soft plug is shown in ● **FIGURE 22–12**.

A cup plug is installed about 0.02 to 0.05 inch (0.5 to 1.3 mm) below the surface of the block, using sealant to prevent leaks. ● **SEE FIGURE 22–13**.

CAM BEARINGS A cam bearing installing tool is required to insert the new cam bearing without damaging the bearing. A number of tool manufacturers design and sell cam bearing installation tools. Their common feature is a shoulder on a bushing that fits inside the cam bearing, with a means of keeping the bearing aligned as it is installed.

FIGURE 22–12 This engine uses many cup plugs to block off coolant and oil passages as well as a large plug over the end of the camshaft bore.

FIGURE 22–13 Sealer should be applied to the cup plug before being driven into the block.

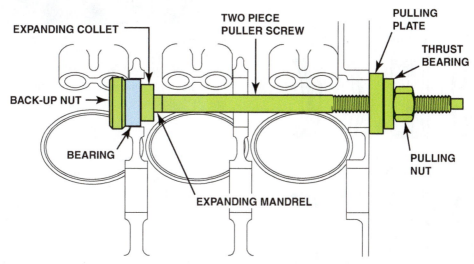

FIGURE 22–14 Screw-type puller being used to install a new cam bearing. Most cam bearings are crush fit. The full round bearing is forced into the cam bearing bore. Most vehicle manufacturers specify that the cam bearings be installed "dry" without lubrication to help prevent them from spinning, which would cause the bearing to block the oil feed hole.

The bearing is placed on the bushing of the tool and rotated to properly align the oil hole. The bearing is then forced into the bearing bore of the block by either a pulling screw or a slide hammer. A pulling screw type of tool is illustrated in ● **FIGURE 22–14**.

The installed bearing must be checked to ensure that it has the correct depth and that the oil hole is indexed with the oil passage in the block. No additional service is required on cam bearings that have been properly installed. The opening at the back of the camshaft is closed with a cup plug.

MEASURING MAIN BEARING CLEARANCE The main bearings are properly fit *before* the crankshaft is lubricated or turned. The oil clearance of both main and connecting rod bearings is set by selectively fitting the bearings. In this way, the oil clearance can be adjusted to within 0.0005 inch of the desired clearance.

CAUTION: Avoid touching bearings with bare hands. The oils on your fingers can start corrosion of the bearing materials. Always wear protective cloth or rubber gloves to avoid the possibility of damage to the bearing surface.

? FREQUENTLY ASKED QUESTION

What Causes Premature Bearing Failure?

According to a major manufacturer of engine bearings, the major causes of premature (shortly after installation) bearing failure include the following:

Dirt (45%)

Misassembly (13%)

Misalignment (13%)

Lack of lubrication (11%)

Overloading or lugging (10%)

Corrosion (4%)

Other (4%)

Many cases of premature bearing failure may result from a combination of several of these items. Therefore, to help prevent bearing failure, *keep everything as clean as possible*.

FIGURE 22–16 The width of the plastic gauging strip determines the oil clearance of the main bearing. An alternate method of determining oil clearance includes careful measurement of the crankshaft journal and bearings after they are installed and the main housing bore caps are torqued to specifications.

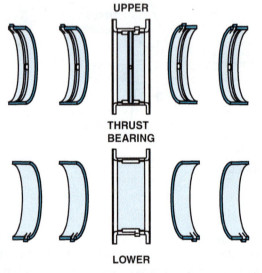

UPPER

THRUST
BEARING

LOWER

FIGURE 22–15 Typical main bearing set. Note that the upper halves are grooved for better oil flow and the lower halves are plain for better load support. This bearing set uses the center main bearing for thrust control. Notice that the upper bearing set has the holes for oil, whereas the lower set does not.

Bearings are usually made in 0.010, 0.020, and 0.030 inch *undersize* for use on reground journals. ● **SEE FIGURE 22–15** for a typical main bearing set.

The crankshaft bearing journals should be measured with a micrometer to select the required bearing size.

- Each of the main bearing caps will only fit one location and the caps must be positioned correctly.

- The correct-size bearings should be placed in the block and cap, making sure that the bearing tang locks into its slot.

- The upper main bearing has an oil feed hole. The lower bearing does not have an oil hole.

- Lower the crankshaft squarely so that it does not damage the thrust bearing. Carefully rest the clean crankshaft in the block on the upper main bearings.

- After making sure that there is no oil on the crank journal of the bearing, place a strip of Plastigage® (gauging plastic) on each main bearing journal. Install the main bearing caps and tighten the bolts to specifications.

- Remove each cap and check the width of the Plastigage® with the markings on the gauge envelope, as shown in ● **FIGURE 22–16**.

- The width of the plastic strip indicates the oil clearance.

CORRECTING BEARING CLEARANCE   Oil clearances normally run from 0.0005 to 0.002 inch (half a thousandth to two thousandths).

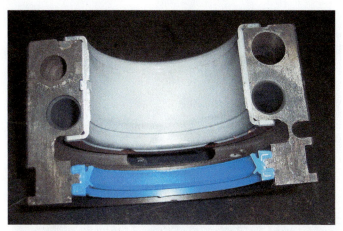

FIGURE 22–17 Lip-type rear main bearing seal in place in the rear main bearing cap. The lip should always be pointing toward the inside of the engine.

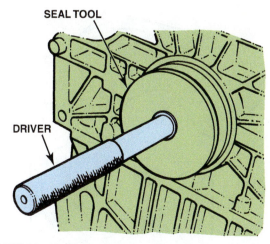

FIGURE 22–18 Always use the proper driver to install a main seal. Never pound directly on the seal.

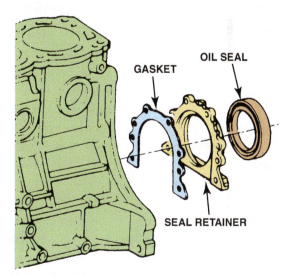

FIGURE 22–19 The rear seal for this engine mounts to a retainer plate. The retainer is then bolted to the engine block.

- The oil clearance can be reduced by 0.001 inch by replacing both bearing shells with bearing shells that are 0.001 inch undersize.

- The clearance can be reduced by 0.0005 inch by replacing only one of the bearing shells with a bearing shell that is 0.001 inch smaller.

- This smaller bearing shell should be placed in the engine block side of the bearing (the upper shell). Oil clearance can be adjusted accurately using this procedure. Try to avoid mismatching the bearing shells by more than a 0.001 inch difference in size.

LIP SEAL INSTALLATION Seals are always used at the front and rear of the crankshaft. Overhead cam engines may also have a seal at the front end of the camshaft and at the front end of an auxiliary accessory shaft. Either a lip seal or a rope seal is used in these locations. ● **SEE FIGURE 22–17.**

The rear crankshaft oil seal is installed after the main bearings have been properly fit. The lip seal may be molded in a steel case or it may be molded around a steel stiffener. The counterbore or guide that supports the seal must be thoroughly clean. In most cases, the back of the lip seal is dry when it is installed. Occasionally, a manufacturer will recommend the use of sealants behind the seal. Check service information for the specified sealing instructions. The lip of the seal should be well lubricated before the shaft and cap are installed. ● **SEE FIGURES 22–18 AND 22–19.**

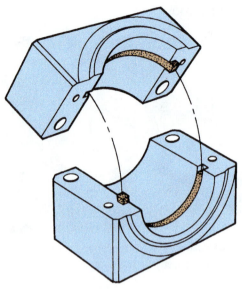

FIGURE 22–20 Many engine builders prefer to stagger the parting lines of a rope-type seal.

FIGURE 22–21 A dial indicator is being used to check the crankshaft end play, known as thrust bearing clearance. Always follow the manufacturer's recommended testing procedures.

CAUTION: Teflon seals should *not* be lubricated. This type of seal should be installed dry. When the engine is first started, some of the Teflon transfers to the crankshaft, to create a Teflon-to-Teflon surface. Even touching the seal with your hands could remove some of the outer coating on the seal and cause a leak. Carefully read, understand, and follow the installation instructions that come with the seal.

ROPE SEAL INSTALLATION Some older engines use rope-type seals at both the front and rear of the crankshaft. Rope-type seals, usually called *braided fabric seals*, are sometimes used as rear crankshaft oil seals. Rope-type oil seals must be compressed tightly into the groove so that no oil can leak behind them. With the crankshaft removed, the upper half of the rope seal is put in a clean groove and compressed by rolling a round object against it to force it tightly into the groove. A piece of pipe, a large socket, or even a hammer handle can be used for this.

When the seal is fully seated in the groove, the ends that extend above the parting surface are cut to be flush with the surface using a sharp single-edge razor blade or a sharp tool specially designed to cut the seal. Some technicians find that leaving a little of the seal higher than the bearing cap creates a better seal, because when the bearing cap is installed and tightened, the extra seal length forces the rope seal further into the groove. ● **SEE FIGURE 22–20.**

CRANKSHAFT INSTALLATION The main bearing caps and crankshaft should be removed after checking for proper bearing clearance. The surface of the bearings should then be given a thin coating of oil or assembly lubricant to provide initial lubrication for engine start-up. Install the crankshaft using the following steps.

STEP 1 The crankshaft should be carefully placed in the bearings to avoid damage to the thrust bearing surfaces.

STEP 2 The bearing caps are installed with their identification numbers correctly positioned. The caps were originally machined in place, so they can only fit correctly in their original position.

STEP 3 The main bearing cap bolts are tightened finger tight, and the crankshaft is rotated. It should rotate freely.

THRUST BEARING CLEARANCE Tighten all main bearing cap bolts to factory specification except for the bearing cap that is used for thrust (usually the center or the rear cap). Pry the crankshaft forward and rearward to align the cap half of the thrust bearing with the block saddle half. Most engine specifications for thrust bearing clearance (also called *crankshaft end play*) can range from 0.002 to 0.012 inch (0.02 to 0.3 mm). This clearance or play can be measured with a:

- Feeler gauge
- Dial indicator ● **SEE FIGURE 22–21.**

If the clearance is too great, oversize main thrust bearings may be available for the engine. Semifinished bearings may have to be purchased and machined to size to restore proper tolerance.

NOTE: Some engines use a separate replaceable thrust bearing. ● SEE FIGURE 22–22.

FIGURE 22–22 A thrust bearing insert being installed before the crankshaft is installed.

FIGURE 22–23 Installing a camshaft is easier if the engine is vertical so gravity can help, and this method reduces the possibility of damaging the cam bearings.

MAIN BEARING TIGHTENING PROCEDURE Tighten the main bearing caps to the specified assembly torque, and in the specified sequence. The procedure specified usually includes tightening the main bearing cap bolts in three stages.

- Torque to one-third of the specified torque.
- Then tighten to two-thirds of the specified torque.
- Finally tighten the bolts to the factory specified torque.

Many manufacturers require that the crankshaft be pried forward or rearward during the main bearing tightening process. The crankshaft should turn freely after all main bearing cap bolts are fully torqued.

CRANKSHAFT ROTATING TORQUE It should never require over 5 pound-feet (lb-ft) (6.75 newton-meters, or N-m) of torque to rotate the crankshaft. An increase in the torque needed to rotate the crankshaft is often caused by a foreign particle that was not removed during cleanup. It may be on the bearing surface, on the crankshaft journal, or between the bearing and saddle.

INSTALLING THE CAMSHAFT

PRELUBRICATION When the camshaft is installed, the lobes must be coated with a special lubricant that contains molydisulfide. This special lube helps to ensure proper initial lubrication to the critical cam lobe sections of the camshaft. Many manufacturers recommend multiviscosity engine oil such

as SAE 5W-30 or SAE 10W-30. Some camshaft manufacturers recommend using straight SAE 30 or SAE 40 engine oil and not a multiviscosity oil for the first oil fill. Some manufacturers also recommend the use of an antiwear additive such as zinc dithiophosphate (ZDP).

CAMSHAFT PRECAUTIONS Whenever repairing an engine, follow these rules regarding the camshaft and lifters.

1. When installing a new camshaft, always install new valve lifters (tappets).

2. When installing new lifters, if the original cam is not excessively worn and if the pushrods all rotate with the original camshaft, the camshaft may be reused.

   NOTE: Some manufacturers recommend that a new camshaft always be installed when replacing valve lifters.

3. *Never* use a hydraulic lifter camshaft with solid lifters or hydraulic lifters with a solid lifter camshaft.

TECH TIP

Installing a New Cam with Flat Bottom Lifters

When installing a new cam that uses flat bottom lifters always install new lifters. The new cam and lifters usually require a break-in lubricant such as one of the following:

1. Oils that contain at least 0.15% or 1,500 parts per million (ppm) of zinc in the form of ZDDP. Oils that contain this much zinc are designed for off-road use only and in a vehicle that does not have a catalytic converter, such as racing oils. If the vehicle is equipped with a catalytic converter, replace the camshaft and lifters to roller type, so that newer oils with lower levels of zinc can be used.

2. Use a newer oil and an additive such as:
   a. GM engine oil supplement (EOS) (Part #1052367 or #88862586)
   b. Comp Cams® camshaft break-in oil additive (Part #159)
   c. Crane Cams® Moly Paste (Part #99002-1)
   d. Crane Cams® Super Lube oil additive (Part #99003-1)
   e. Lumati Assembly lube (Part #99010)
   f. Mell-Lube camshaft tube oil additive (Part # M-10012)
   g. Other available additives designed to protect the camshaft (● **SEE FIGURE 22–24.**)

FIGURE 22–24 The camshaft bores are precision machined and measured. Always use the lubricants recommended in service information (SI) when installing the camshaft. (*Courtesy of General Motors*)

PISTON DIAMETER (INCHES)	RING GAP (INCHES)
2–3	0.007–0.018
3–4	0.01–0.02
4–5	0.013–0.023

CHART 22–2

The approximate ring gap based on the size of the bore in inches. Always check service information for the exact specifications for the engine being assembled.

FIGURE 22–25 A feeler gauge is used to check piston ring gap.

NOTE: If the gap is greater than recommended, some engine performance is lost. However, too small a gap will result in scuffing, because ring ends can be forced together during operation, which forces the rings to scrape the cylinders.

- If the ring gap is too large, the ring should be replaced with one having the next oversize diameter.
- If the ring gap is too small, the ring should be removed and filed to make the gap larger.

PISTON/ROD INSTALLATION

CHECKING PISTON RINGS Before installing the piston assemblies, all piston rings should be checked for proper side clearance and ring gap. ● **SEE FIGURE 22–25.**

Typical ring gap clearances are about 0.004 inch per inch of cylinder bore. ● **SEE CHART 22–2.**

PISTON MARKINGS Care must be taken to ensure that the pistons and rods are in the correct cylinder. They must face in the correct direction. There is usually a *notch* on the piston

FIGURE 22–26 The notch on a piston should always face toward the front of the engine.

FIGURE 22–27 On V-type engines that use paired rod journals, the side of the rod with the large chamfer should face toward the crank throw (outward).

head indicating the *front.* Using this will correctly position the piston pin offset toward the right side of the engine. ● **SEE FIGURE 22–26**.

- The connecting rod *identification marks* on pushrod 4 and 6 cylinder inline engines are normally placed on the camshaft side.
- On V-type engines, the connecting rod cylinder identification marks are on the side of the rods that can be seen from the bottom of the engine when the piston and rod assemblies are installed in the engine. Make sure the connecting rod has been installed on the piston correctly—the chamfer on the side of the big end should face outward (toward the crank throw). ● **SEE FIGURE 22–27**.
- Check service information for any special piston and rod assembly instructions.

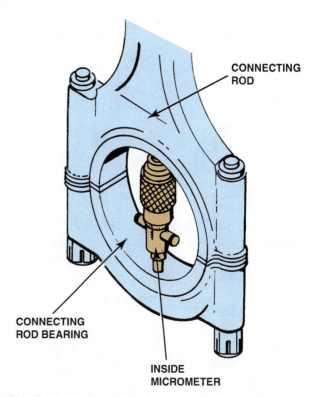

FIGURE 22–28 An inside micrometer can be used to measure the inside diameter of the big end of the connecting rod with the bearings installed. This dimension subtracted from the rod journal diameter is equal to the bearing clearance.

CONNECTING ROD BEARING CLEARANCE   The rod cap, with the bearing in place, is put on the rod. There are two methods that can be used to check for proper connecting rod bearing clearance.

- Use Plastigage® following the same procedure discussed for main bearing clearance.
- Measure the assembled connecting rod big end devices with the bearing installed and the caps torqued to specification. Subtract the diameter of the rod journal to determine the bearing clearance. ● **SEE FIGURE 22–28**.

NOTE: Be certain to check for piston-to-crankshaft counterweight clearance. Most manufacturers specify a minimum 0.06 inch (1.5 mm).

PISTON INSTALLATION   To install a piston, perform the following steps.

STEP 1   Apply a coating of clean engine oil to the cylinder walls. This oil should be spread over the entire cylinder wall surface by hand.

STEP 2   Apply oil or assembly lube to the rod bearings.

STEP 3   Align the piston ring gaps (ring gap stagger) to the locations specified in service information. ● **SEE FIGURE 22–29**.

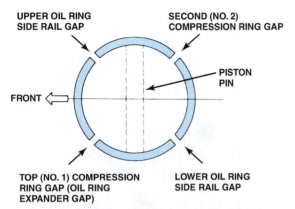

FIGURE 22–29 One method of piston ring installation showing the location of ring gaps. Always follow the manufacturer's recommended method for the location of ring gaps and for ring gap spacing.

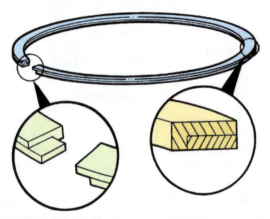

FIGURE 22–30 A gapless ring is made in two pieces that overlap.

STEP 4 Using a squirt-type oil can, squirt oil over the rings and the skirt of the piston.

> **NOTE: Special types of piston rings (overlapping or gapless) are installed dry, without oil.**
> **● SEE FIGURE 22–30. Some manufacturers recommend oiling only the oil control ring. Always check the piston ring instruction sheet for the exact procedure.**

STEP 5 The **piston ring compressor** is then put on the piston to hold the rings in their grooves. ● **SEE FIGURES 22–31 AND 22–32.**

STEP 6 Rotate the crankshaft so the crankshaft journal is at the bottom (BDC) to help prevent the rod from touching the crankshaft when the piston is installed.

STEP 7 Remove the bearing cap from the rod, and install the bearings.

STEP 8 Install protectors over the rod bolts. These help prevent damage to the crankshaft journal when the piston/rod assembly is installed. ● **SEE FIGURE 22–33.**

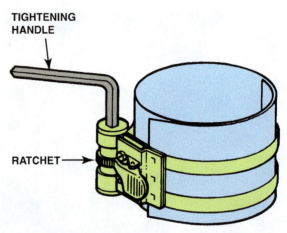

FIGURE 22–31 This style of ring compressor uses a ratchet to contract the spring band and compress the rings into their grooves.

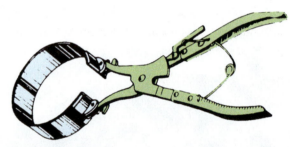

FIGURE 22–32 This pliers-like tool is used to close the metal band around the piston to compress the rings. An assortment of bands is available to service different size pistons.

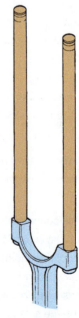

FIGURE 22–33 When threaded onto the rod bolts, these guides not only help align the rod but also protect the threads and hold the bearing shell in place. The soft ends also will not damage the crankshaft journals.

FIGURE 22–34 Installing a piston using a ring compressor to hold the rings into the ring grooves of the piston and then using a hammer handle to drive the piston into the bore. Connecting rod bolt protectors have been installed to help prevent possible damage to the crankshaft during piston installation.

STEP 9 The upper rod bearing should be in the rod and the piston should be turned so that the notch on the piston head is facing the front of the engine.

STEP 10 The piston and rod assembly is placed in the cylinder through the block deck. The ring compressor must be kept tightly against the block deck as the piston is pushed into the cylinder.The ring compressor holds the rings in their grooves so that they will enter the cylinder. ● **SEE FIGURE 22–34**.

STEP 11 The piston is pushed into the cylinder until the rod bearing is fully seated on the journal.

CONNECTING ROD SIDE CLEARANCE The connecting rods should be checked to ensure that they still have the correct side clearance. This is measured by fitting the correct thickness of feeler gauge between the connecting rod and the crankshaft cheek of the bearing journal. ● **SEE FIGURE 22–35**.

- *If the side clearance is too great,* excessive amounts of oil may escape that can cause lower-than-normal oil pressure. To correct excessive clearance:
  1. Weld and regrind or replace the crankshaft.
  2. Carefully measure all connecting rods and replace those that are too thin or mismatched.

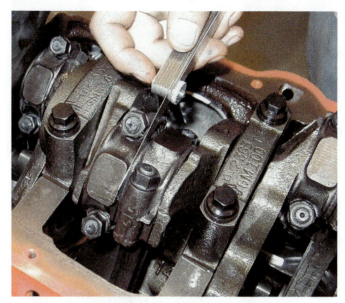

FIGURE 22–35 The connecting rod side clearance is measured with a feeler gauge.

 **TECH TIP**

Tightening Tip for Rod Bearings

Even though the bearing clearances are checked, it is still a good idea to check and record the torque required to rotate the crankshaft with all piston rings dragging on the cylinder walls. The retaining nuts on one bearing should be torqued, and then the torque that is required to rotate the crankshaft should be rechecked and recorded. Follow the same procedure on all rod bearings. If tightening any one of the rod bearing caps causes a large increase in the torque required to rotate the crankshaft, immediately stop the tightening process. Determine the cause of the increased rotating torque using the same method as used on the main bearings. Rotate the crankshaft for several revolutions to ensure that the assembly is turning freely and that there are no tight spots.

The rotating torque of the crankshaft with all connecting rod cap bolts fully torqued should be as follows:

- 4-cylinder engine: 20 pound-feet maximum (88 N-m)
- 6-cylinder engine: 25 pound-feet maximum (110 N-m)
- 8-cylinder engine: 30 pound-feet maximum (132 N-m)

- *If the side clearance is too small,* there may not be enough room for heat expansion. To correct a side clearance that is too small:
  1. Regrind the crankshaft.
  2. Replace the rods.

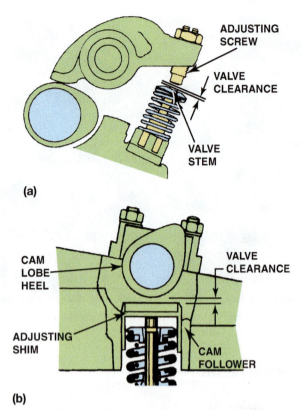

(a)

(b)

FIGURE 22–36 Valve clearance allows the metal parts to expand and maintain proper operation, both when the engine is cold and at normal operating temperature. (a) Adjustment is achieved by turning the adjusting screw. (b) Adjustment is achieved by changing the thickness of the adjusting shim.

CYLINDER HEAD INSTALLATION

INSTALLING THE CAMSHAFT FOR OHC ENGINES
On some overhead camshaft engines, the camshaft is installed before the head is fastened to the block deck. Some engines have the camshaft located directly over the valves. The cam bearings on these engines can be either one piece or split. In other engine types, the camshaft bearings are split to allow the camshaft to be installed without the valves being depressed. The cam bearings and journals are lubricated before assembly. The cam bearing caps must be tightened evenly to avoid bending the camshaft. The valve clearance or lash is checked with the overhead camshaft in place. Some engines use shims under a follower disk, as shown in ● **FIGURE 22–36**.

On these engine types, the camshaft is turned so that the follower is on the base circle of the cam. The clearance of each bucket follower can then be checked with a feeler gauge. The amount of clearance is recorded and compared with the specified clearance, and then a shim of the required

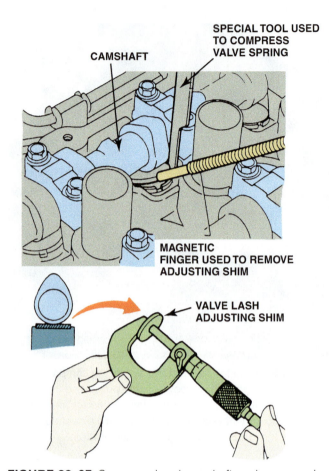

FIGURE 22–37 Some overhead camshaft engines use valve lash adjusting shims to adjust the valve lash. A special tool is usually required to compress the valve spring so that a magnet can remove the shim.

thickness is put in the top of the bucket followers, as shown in ● **FIGURE 22–37**.

Always follow the vehicle manufacturer's recommended procedures.

HEAD BOLT TORQUE SEQUENCE
The torque put on the bolts is used to control the clamping force that is applied to the gasket. The clamping force is correct only when the threads are clean and properly lubricated.

CAUTION: Always use the specified lubricant on the threads. If SAE 30 engine oil is specified, do not use SAE 10W-30 or any other viscosity, because using the incorrect viscosity oil can affect the clamping force exerted on the head gaskets.

In general, the head bolts are tightened in a specified torque sequence in three steps. The procedure starts with the head bolts in the center and then moves to those farther and farther from the center. This procedure helps spread the forces toward the ends of the cylinder.

Watch Out for Wet and Dry Holes

Many engines, such as the small block Chevrolet V-8, use head bolts that extend through the top deck of the block and end in a coolant passage. These bolt holes are called *wet holes.* When installing head bolts into holes that end up in the coolant passage, always use sealer on the threads of the head bolt. Some engines have head bolts that are "wet," whereas others are "dry" because they end in solid cast-iron material. Dry hole bolts do not require sealant, but they still require some oil on the threads of the bolts for lubrication. Do not put oil into a dry hole because the bolt may bottom out in the oil. The liquid oil cannot compress, so the force of the bolt being tightened is transferred to the block by hydraulic force, which can crack the block.

NOTE: Apply oil to a shop cloth and rotate the bolt in the cloth to lubricate the threads. This procedure lubricates the threads without applying too much oil.

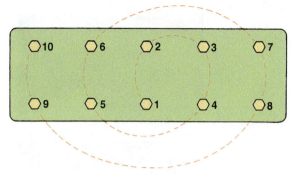

FIGURE 22–38 Typical cylinder head tightening sequence.

Always "Exercise" New Bolts

New bolts and studs are manufactured by rolling the threads and heat treating. Due to this operation, the threads usually have some rough areas, which affect the clamping force on the gasket. Many engine building experts recommend that all new bolts be installed in the engine using a new or used gasket and torqued to specifications at least five times, except for torque-to-yield bolts. This process burnishes the ramps of the threads and makes the fastener provide a more even clamping force. Using the recommended lubricant, the bolts should be torqued and removed and then torqued again.

The Piece of Paper Demonstration

Some students and beginning technicians forget the correct order to tighten head bolts or other fasteners of a component. Try the following demonstration:

- Place a single sheet of paper on a table.
- Place both hands on the paper in the center and then move your hands outward.
- Nothing should have happened and the paper should have not moved.
- Now place your hands on the paper at the ends and move them toward the center.
- The paper will wrinkle as the hands move toward the center.

This demonstration shows that the forces are moved away toward the ends the cylinder head if the fasteners are tightened from the inside toward the outside. However, if the cylinder head bolts were tightened incorrectly, the head would likely crack due to the forces exerted during the tightening.

By tightening the head bolts in three steps, the head gasket has time to compress and conform to the block deck and cylinder head gasket surfaces. Follow that sequence and tighten the bolts in the following manner.

1. Tighten to *one-third* the specified torque.
2. Tighten them a second time following the torque sequence to *two-thirds* the specified torque.
3. Follow the sequence with a final tightening to the specified torque. ● **SEE FIGURES 22–38 AND 22–39.**
4. Also, refer to the section "Torque-to-Yield Head Bolts" later in the chapter.

CLAMPING FORCE   **Clamping force** is the amount of force exerted on a gasket. The clamping force is not the same as the torque applied to the fastener. When tightening a bolt or nut, about 80% of the applied torque is used to overcome friction between the threads. Therefore, it is very important that the threads be clean and lubricated with the proper (specified) lubricant.

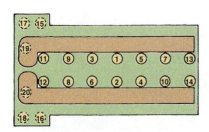
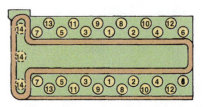

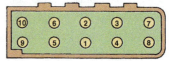

FIGURE 22–39 Examples of cylinder head bolt torquing sequences.

? FREQUENTLY ASKED QUESTION

Why Do Both Head Gaskets Have "Front" Marked?

A common question asked by beginning technicians or students include how to install head gaskets on a V-6 engine that is mounted transversely (sideways) in the vehicle. The technician usually notices that "front" is marked on one gasket and therefore installs that gasket on the block, on top of the forward-facing cylinder bank. Then, the technician notices that the other gasket is also marked with "front." How could both be marked "front"? There must be some mistake. The mistake is in the terminology used. In the case of head gaskets, the "front" means toward the accessory drive belt end of the engine and not on the cylinder bank toward the front of the vehicle. ● **SEE FIGURE 22–40.**

FIGURE 22–40 Typical head gasket markings. The front means that the gasket should be at the accessory drive belt end of the block.

🔧 TECH TIP

Creep Up on the Torque Value

Do not jerk or rapidly rotate a torque wrench. For best results and more even torque, slowly apply force to the torque wrench until it reaches the preset value or the designated torque. Jerky or rapidly moving the torque wrench will often cause the torque to be uneven and not accurate.

FASTENER CONSIDERATION Because most of the torque applied to a fastener is absorbed by friction, it is extremely important that the following steps be performed.

STEP 1 Clean the threads of all fasteners before using.

STEP 2 Check service information for the specified thread lubricant.

THREAD LUBRICANT If using aftermarket bolts or studs, such as ARP (American Racing Products®), use the lubricant and torque that the company specifies. Do not use ARP lubricant and the factory torque specifications or the fasteners will be greatly overtightened. The same applies if using thread sealant to the threads of fasteners being installed in wet holes (holes that extend into the cooling passages). Many vehicle manufacturers recommend the use of 30 weight engine oil (SAE 30).

CAUTION: SAE 5W-30 or SAE 10W-30 is not the same as SAE 30 engine oil. Multiviscosity oil such as SAE 5W-30 is actually SAE 5W oil with additives to provide the protection of SAE 30 oil when it gets hot. Always use the exact oil specified by the vehicle manufacturer.

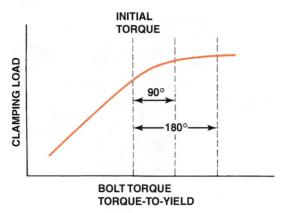

FIGURE 22–41 Due to variations in clamping force with turning force (torque) of head bolts, some engines are specifying the torque-to-yield procedure. The first step is to torque the bolts by an even amount called the initial torque. Final clamping load is achieved by turning the bolt a specified number of degrees. Bolt stretch provides the proper clamping force.

TORQUE-TO-YIELD HEAD BOLTS

DEFINITION AND TERMINOLOGY   Many engines use a tightening procedure called the **torque-to-yield (TTY)** method. The purpose of the TTY procedure is to have a more constant clamping load from bolt to bolt. This aids in head gasket sealing performance and eliminates the need for retorquing.

BOLT CONSTRUCTION   Many torque-to-yield head bolts are made with a narrow section between the head and threads. As the bolts are tightened past their elastic limit, they yield and begin to stretch in this narrow section.

Torque-to-yield head bolts will not become any tighter once they reach this elastic limit, as seen on the graph in ● **FIGURE 22–41**.

The torque angle method also decreases the differences in clamping force that can occur depending on the condition or lubrication of the threads. ● **SEE FIGURE 22–42**.

As a result, many engine manufacturers specify *new* head bolts each time the head is installed. If these bolts are reused, they are likely to break during assembly or fail prematurely as the engine runs. If there is any doubt about the head bolts, replace them.

TORQUE-TO-YIELD PROCEDURE   Torque-to-yield bolts are tightened to a specific initial torque, from 18 to 50 pound-feet (25 to 68 N-m). The bolts are then tightened an additional specified number of degrees, following the tightening sequence. In some cases they are turned a specified number of degrees two or three times. Some specifications limit the maximum torque

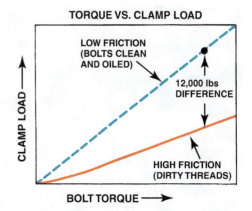

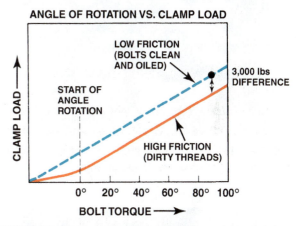

FIGURE 22–42 To ensure consistent clamp force (load), many manufacturers are recommending the torque-angle or torque-to-yield method of tightening head bolts. The torque-angle method specifies tightening fasteners to a low-torque setting and then giving an additional angle of rotation. Notice that the difference in clamping force is much smaller than it would be if just a torque wrench with dirty threads were used.

that can be applied to the bolt while the degree turn is being made. Torque tables in a service manual will show how much initial torque should be applied to the bolt and how many degrees the bolt should be rotated after torquing. Torque-to-yield head bolts should be tightened as per specified in service information.

The procedure includes the following steps.

STEP 1   Tighten the fasteners to an initial torque in the specified sequence.

STEP 2   Turn the fasteners a specific number of degrees using an angle gauge again following the same sequence.

STEP 3   Turn the fasteners another specific number of degrees again following the designated sequence.

For example, a specified head bolt tightening specification may include:

- Initial torque, such as 44 lb-ft
- Rotate 90 degrees
- Rotate head bolts an additional 90 degrees ● **SEE FIGURES 22–43 AND 22–44**.

FIGURE 22–43 The electronic angle meter clips on to the socket extension to measure rotational angle.

FIGURE 22–44 An electronic torque wrench showing the number of degrees of rotation. These very accurate and expensive torque wrenches can be programmed to display torque or number of degrees of rotation.

TORQUE ANGLE METHOD

The *torque angle method*, also called the *torque-turn method*, does not necessarily mean torque-to-yield. Some engine specifications call for a beginning torque and then a specified angle, but the fastener

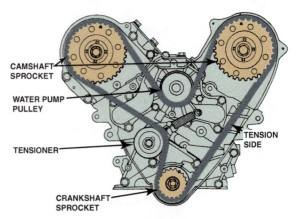

FIGURE 22–45 Both camshafts have to be timed on this engine and the timing belt also drives the water pump.

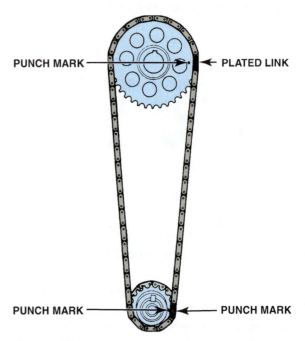

FIGURE 22–46 Some timing chains have plated links that are used to correctly position the chain on the sprockets.

is not designed to yield. These head bolts can often be reused. Always follow the manufacturer's recommended procedures.

VALVE TRAIN ASSEMBLY

TIMING DRIVES FOR OHC ENGINES

After the head bolts have been torqued, the cam drive can be installed on overhead cam (OHC) engines. This is done by aligning the timing marks of the crankshaft and camshaft drive sprockets with their respective timing marks. The location of these marks differs between engines, but the marks can be identified by looking carefully at the sprockets. ● SEE FIGURES 22–45 AND 22–46.

The tensioner may be on either or both sides of the timing belt or chain. After the camshaft drive is engaged, rotate the crankshaft through two full revolutions. On the first full revolution, the exhaust valve will be almost closed and the intake valve will just be starting to open when the *crankshaft* timing mark aligns. At the end of the second revolution, both valves should be closed, and all the timing marks should align on most engines. This is the position the crankshaft should have when cylinder 1 is to fire.

NOTE: Always check the manufacturer's recommended timing chain installation procedure. Engines that use primary and secondary timing chains often require an exact detailed procedure for proper installation.

HYDRAULIC VALVE LIFTER INSTALLATION Most vehicle manufacturers recommend installing lifters *without* filling or pumping the lifter full of oil. If the lifter is filled with oil during engine start-up, the lifter may not be able to bleed down quickly enough and the valves may be kept open. Not only will the engine not operate correctly with the valves held open, but the piston also could hit the open valves, causing serious engine damage. Most manufacturers usually specify that the lifter be lubricated. Roller hydraulic lifters can be lubricated with engine oil, whereas flat lifters require that engine assembly lube or extreme pressure (EP) grease be applied to the base.

BLEEDING HYDRAULIC LIFTERS Air trapped inside a hydraulic valve lifter can be easily bled by simply operating the engine at a fast idle (2500 RPM). Normal oil flow through the lifters will allow all of the air inside the lifter to be bled out.

NOTE: Some engines *must* have the air removed from the lifter before installation. This is accomplished by submerging the lifter in a container of engine oil and using a straightened paper clip to depress the oil passage check ball.

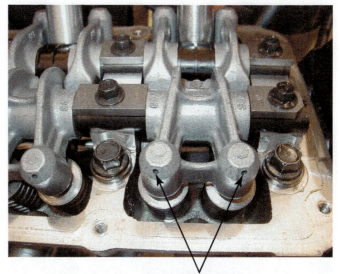

BLEED HOLES FROM HYDRAULIC LASH ADJUSTERS (HLA)

FIGURE 22–47 A special tool may be needed to bleed air from the hydraulic lash adjusters (HLA) through the bleed hole. These lash adjusters are part of the valve end of the rocker arms in this example.

Check service information if in doubt about the bleeding procedure for the vehicle being serviced. ● **SEE FIGURE 22–47.**

TIMING CHAINS AND GEARS INSTALLATION On cam-in-block (OHV) engines, the timing gears or chain and sprocket can be installed after the crankshaft and camshaft. The timing marks should be aligned according to the factory specified marks. ● **SEE FIGURE 22–48.**

When used, the replaceable fuel pump eccentric is installed as the cam sprocket is fastened to the cam. The

TIMING MARK ON CAMSHAFT SPROCKET

TIMING MARK ON CRANKSHAFT SPROCKET

FIGURE 22–48 Timing chain and gears can be installed after the crankshaft and camshaft have been installed and the timing marks are aligned with cylinder 1 at top dead center (TDC).

crankshaft should be rotated several times to see that the camshaft and timing gears or chain rotate freely. The timing mark alignment should be rechecked at this time. If the engine is equipped with a slinger ring, it should also be installed on the crankshaft, in front of the crankshaft gear.

OHV ENGINE LIFTER AND PUSHROD INSTALLATION

The outside of the lifters and the lifter bores in the block should be cleaned and coated with assembly lubricant. The lifters are installed in the lifter bores and the pushrods put in place. There are different length pushrods on some engines. Make sure that the pushrods are installed in the proper location. The rocker arms are then put in place, aligning with the valves and pushrods. Rocker arm shafts should have their retaining bolts tightened a little at a time, alternating between the retaining bolts. This keeps the shaft from bending as the rocker arm pushes some of the valves open.

HYDRAULIC LIFTER ADJUSTMENT

The retaining nut on some rocker arms mounted on studs can be tightened to a

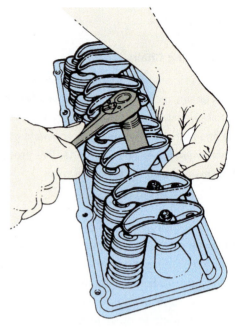

FIGURE 22–49 With the lifter resting on the base circle of the cam, zero lash is achieved by tightening the rocker arm lock nut until the pushrod no longer rotates freely.

specified torque. The rocker arm stud will have a shoulder on this type of rocker assembly. The rocker arm will be adjusted correctly at this torque when the valve tip has the correct height. Other types of rocker arms require tightening the nut to a position that will center the hydraulic lifter. The general procedure includes the following steps.

STEP 1 Rotate the engine until cylinder 1 is at TDC on the compression stroke to be assured that both the intake and exhaust valves are on the base circle of the cam lobes.

STEP 2 Tighten the retaining nut to the point that all free lash is gone and the pushrod cannot be easily rotated.
● **SEE FIGURE 22–49**.

STEP 3 From this point, the retaining nut is tightened by a specified amount, such as three-fourths of a turn or one and one-half turns.

> **HINT: This method usually results in about three threads showing above the adjusting nut on a *stock* small block Chevrolet V-8 equipped with flat-bottom hydraulic lifters.**

STEP 4 Rotate the engine until the next cylinder in the firing order is at top dead center on the compression stroke. The valves on this next cylinder are adjusted in the same manner as those on cylinder 1. This procedure is repeated on each cylinder *following the engine firing order* until all the valves have been adjusted. Always follow the specified procedure found in service information.

FIGURE 22–50 Most adjustable valves use a nut to keep the adjustment from changing. Therefore, to adjust the valves, the nut has to be loosened and the screw rotated until the proper valve clearance is achieved. Then the screw should be held while tightening the lock nut to keep the adjustment from changing. Double-check the valve clearance after tightening the nut.

SOLID LIFTER ADJUSTMENT

The valve clearance or **lash** must be set on a solid lifter engine, so that the valves can positively seat. Check service information for the specified adjustment sequence to follow to set the lash. If this is not available, then the following procedure can be used on all engines requiring valve lash adjustment. The valve lash is adjusted with the valves completely closed.
● **SEE FIGURE 22–50.**

The procedure is similar to that used to adjust hydraulic lifters that are adjustable except that a feeler gauge is used to check the lash. The same valve lash adjustment sequence is used on overhead cam engines. Those engines with rocker arms or with adjustable finger follower pivots are adjusted in the same way as pushrod engines with rocker arms.

FINAL ASSEMBLY

MANIFOLD INSTALLATION

The intake manifold gasket for a V-type engine may be a one-piece gasket or it may have several pieces. V-type engines with open-type manifolds have a cover over the lifter valley. The cover may be a separate part or it may be part of a one-piece intake manifold gasket. Closed-type intake manifolds on V-type engines require gasket

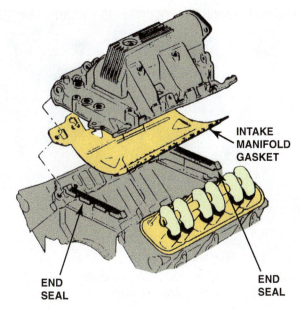

FIGURE 22–51 This intake manifold gasket includes end seals and a full shield cover for the valley to keep hot engine oil from heating the intake manifold.

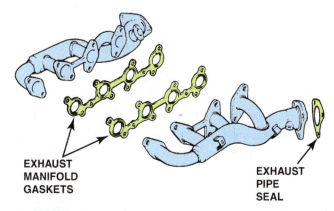

FIGURE 22–52 An exhaust manifold gasket is used on some engines. It seals the exhaust manifold to the cylinder head.

pieces (end seals) at the front and rear of the intake manifold.
● **SEE FIGURE 22–51.**

Inline engines usually have a one-piece intake manifold gasket. The intake manifold is put in place over the gaskets. Use a contact adhesive to hold the gasket and end seal if there is a chance they might slip out of place. Install the bolts and tighten to the specified torque following the correct tightening sequence.

Only some exhaust manifolds use gaskets. The exhaust manifold operates at very high temperatures, so there is usually some expansion and contraction movement in the manifold-to-head joint. It is very important to use attachment bolts, cap screws, and clamps of the correct type and length. ● **SEE FIGURE 22–52.**

FIGURE 22–53 A 1/8 to 3/16 inch (3 to 5 mm) bead of RTV silicon on a parting surface with silicon going around the bolt hole.

They must be properly torqued to avoid both leakage and cracks.

NOTE: If the exhaust manifold gasket has a metal facing on one side, place the metal facing toward the head.

TIMING COVER INSTALLATION

The timing cover with seal installed and gasket are placed over the timing gears and/or chain and sprockets. The attaching bolts are loosely installed to allow the damper hub to align with the cover as it fits in the seal. The damper is installed on the crankshaft. On some engines, it is a press-fit and on others it is held with a large center bolt. After the damper is secured, the attaching bolts on the timing cover can be tightened to the specified torque.

Most timing covers are installed with a gasket, but some use RTV sealer in place of the gasket. A bead of RTV silicon 1/8 to 3/16 inch in diameter is put on the clean sealing surface. ● **SEE FIGURE 22–53**.

Sealing a cover using RTV silicon usually includes the following steps.

STEP 1 Encircle the bolt holes with the sealant.

STEP 2 Install the cover before the silicon begins to cure so that the uncured silicon bonds to both surfaces.

STEP 3 While installing the cover, do not touch the silicon bead, otherwise the bead might be displaced and cause a leak.

STEP 4 Carefully press the cover into place. Do not slide the cover after it is in place.

STEP 5 Install the assembly bolts finger tight, and let the silicon cure for about 30 minutes before tightening the cover bolts.

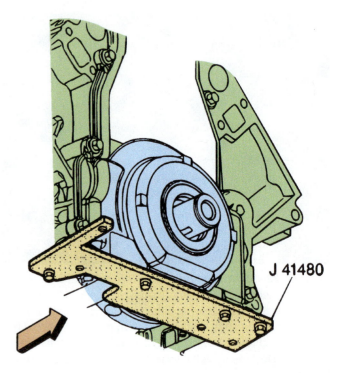

J 41480

FIGURE 22–54 This special tool is used to align the front and rear covers on the 5.3 and 6.0 L engines. (*Courtesy of General Motors*)

Some engines require the use of special tools to properly align the front and rear covers with the engine block. ● **SEE FIGURE 22–54**.

VIBRATION DAMPER INSTALLATION

Vibration dampers are seated in place by one of three methods.

- The damper hub of some engines is pulled into place using the hub attaching bolt.

- The second method uses a special installation tool that screws into the attaching bolt hole to pull the hub into place. The tool is removed and the attaching bolt is installed and torqued. ● **SEE FIGURE 22–55**.

- The last method is used on engines that have no attaching bolt. These hubs depend on a press-fit to hold the hub on the crankshaft. The hub is seated using a special tube-type driver. Check service information for the exact procedure and tool to use.

CAUTION: Driving the balancer on with a hammer instead of using the proper tools will damage the balancer, crankshaft, crankshaft bearings, or all of these. Always use the proper tools as called out in the service information.

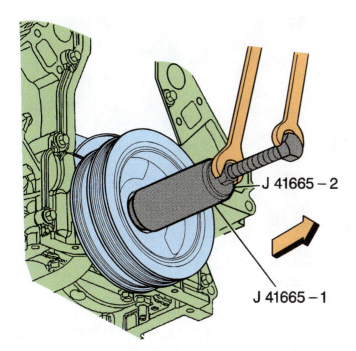

FIGURE 22–55 Special tools are required to install the balancer on many GM engines. (*Courtesy of General Motors*)

FIGURE 22–56 A beam-type torque wrench being used to tighten the oil pump pickup assembly to factory specification.

OIL PUMP INSTALLATION When an engine is rebuilt, the oil pump should be replaced with a new pump and oil pickup screen. Most vehicle manufacturers recommend that the oil pump and screen be replaced rather than cleaned. This ensures positive lubrication and long pump life. Oil pump gears should be coated with assembly lubricant before the cover is put on the pump. This provides initial lubrication, and it primes the pump so that it will draw the oil from the pan when the lubrication system is first operated. Torque the oil pump fasteners to factory specifications. ● **SEE FIGURE 22–56**.

OIL PAN INSTALLATION The oil pan should be checked and straightened as necessary. ● **SEE FIGURE 22–58**.

With the oil pump in place, the oil pan gaskets are properly positioned. The oil pan is carefully placed over the gaskets. All oil pan bolts should be started into their holes before any are tightened. The bolts should be alternately snugged up and then they should be properly tightened to factory specifications. Always follow the instructions that come with the gasket for best results.

WATER PUMP INSTALLATION A reconditioned, rebuilt, or new water pump should be used. Once gaskets are fitted in place, the pump is secured with assembly bolts tightened to the correct torque.

TECH TIP

Check the Oil Pump Pickup to Oil Pan Clearance

Whenever installing the oil pan on a rebuilt engine, it is wise to check the clearance between the oil pump pickup and the bottom of the oil pan. This distance should be 3/16 to 3/8 inch (5 to 9 mm). To check the clearance, two methods can be used.

METHOD 1 With the engine upside down and the oil pump and pickup installed, measure the distance from the oil pan rail to the top (actually the bottom) of the oil pump pickup. Then measure the distance from the oil pan rail to the bottom of the oil pan and subtract the two measurements to get the clearance.

METHOD 2 Place about 1/2 inch (13 mm) of modeling clay on the pickup of the oil pump. Then temporarily install the oil pan with a gasket. Press down on the oil pan to compress the modeling clay. Remove the oil pan and measure the thickness of the clay. This thickness is the oil pan to oil pump pickup clearance. ● **SEE FIGURE 22–57**.

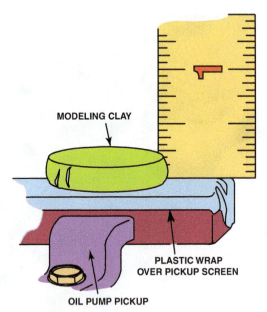

MODELING CLAY

PLASTIC WRAP OVER PICKUP SCREEN

OIL PUMP PICKUP

FIGURE 22–57 Using clay to determine the oil pan to oil pickup clearance, which should be about 1/4 inch.

FIGURE 22–58 Using a hammer to straighten the gasket rail surface of the oil pan before installing a new gasket. When the retaining bolts are tightened, some distortion of sheet metal covers occurs. If the area around the bolt holes is not straightened, leaks can occur with the new gasket.

A new thermostat should be installed, being careful to check that the wax pellet side of the thermostat faces the engine. The thermostat housing with the proper gasket is installed, and the retaining bolts are tightened to the proper torque.

ENGINE PAINTING
Painting an engine helps prevent rust and corrosion and makes the engine look new. Standard engine paints with original colors are usually available at automotive parts stores. Engine paints should be used rather than other types of paints. Engine paints are compounded to stay on the metal as the engine temperatures change. Normal engine fluids will not dissolve or remove them. These paints are usually purchased in pressure cans so that they can be sprayed from the can directly onto the engine.

All parts that should not be painted must be covered before spray painting. This can be done with old parts, such as old spark plugs and old gaskets. This can also be done by taping paper over the areas to be covered. If the intake manifold of an inline engine is to be painted, it can be painted separately. Engine assembly can continue after the paint has dried.

PRELUBRICATING THE ENGINE
With oil in the engine and the distributor, if equipped, out of the engine, oil pressure should be established before the engine is started. This can be done on most engines by rotating the oil pump using an electric drive. This ensures that oil is delivered to all parts of the engine before the engine is started. Adapters are available that allow an electric drill motor to rotate the oil pump. ● **SEE FIGURE 22–59.**

Engines that do not drive the oil pump with a distributor will require the use of a pressurized prelubing tool, such as the General Motor recommended J-45299 or the Goodson PL-40. ● **SEE FIGURE 22–60.**

SETTING IGNITION TIMING
After oil pressure is established, the distributor, if equipped, can be installed. Rotate the crankshaft in its normal direction of rotation until there is compression on cylinder 1. This can be done with the starter

FIGURE 22–59 Oil should be seen flowing to each rocker arm as shown.

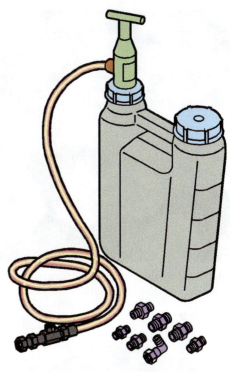

FIGURE 22–60 The prelube tool forces oil under pressure to all parts of the engine. (*Courtesy of General Motors*)

 REAL WORLD FIX

"Oops"

After overhauling a V-8 engine, the technician used an electric drill to rotate the oil pump with a pressure gauge connected to the oil pressure sending unit hole. The oil pressure would start to increase (to about 10 PSI), then drop to zero. In addition, the oil was very aerated (full of air). Replacing the oil pump did not solve the problem. After hours of troubleshooting and disassembly, it was discovered that an oil gallery plug had been left out underneath the intake manifold. The oil pump was working correctly and pumped oil throughout the engine and out of the end of the unplugged oil gallery. It did not take long for the oil pan to empty and the oil pump began drawing in air that aerated the oil which caused the oil pressure to drop. Installing the gallery plug solved the problem. It was smart of the technician to check the oil pressure before starting the engine. This oversight of leaving out one gallery plug could have resulted in a ruined engine shortly after the engine was started.

 TECH TIP

Install Heat Tabs

The wise engine builder should install a heat tab to the back of the cylinder head(s). A heat tab uses a special heat-sensitive metal in the center of a mild steel disc. If the temperature of the cylinder head exceeds 250°F (121°C), the center of the tab will melt and flow out indicating that the engine was overheated. ● **SEE FIGURE 22–61**.

The angle of the distributor gear drive will cause the distributor rotor to turn a few degrees when installed. Before the distributor is installed, the shaft must be positioned to compensate for the gear angle. After installation, the rotor should be pointing to tower 1 of the distributor cap.

The distributor position should be close enough to the basic timing position to start the engine. If the distributor hold-down clamp is slightly loose, the distributor housing can be adjusted to make the engine run smoothly after the engine has been started.

Most vehicles do not require an initial timing setting, since the crankshaft and cam position sensors determine the timing. Some older vehicles may still use a distributor, however, but its

or by using a wrench on the damper bolt. The compression stroke can be determined by covering the opening of spark plug 1 with a finger as the crankshaft is rotated. Continue to rotate the crankshaft slowly as compression is felt, until the timing marks on the damper align with the timing indicator on the timing cover.

FIGURE 22–61 Heat tabs can be purchased from engine supply companies.

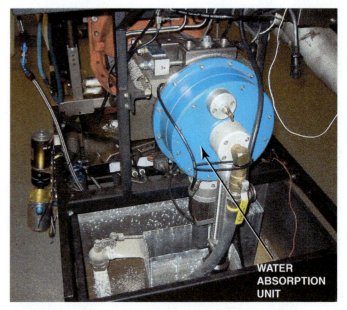

FIGURE 22–63 A dynamometer measures engine torque by applying a resistive force to the engine and measuring the force applied. Water is being used as the resistive load on this dynamometer.

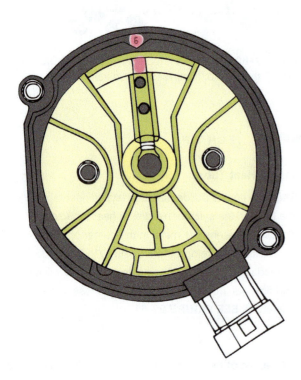

FIGURE 22–62 When the distributor is installed correctly (with engine at TDC, #1 cylinder on compression) the index marks should align. (*Courtesy of General Motors*)

function is to distribute the secondary spark. Turning the distributor housing does not change the ignition timing.

Since the cam position (CMP) sensor is in the distributor, the distributor must be properly timed with the cam drive gear. After installing the distributor, the spark plug towers must be perpendicular to the engine block and the rotor segment aligned with the housing pointer. ● **SEE FIGURE 22–62**.

DYNAMOMETER TESTING

PURPOSES The purposes for using an engine dynamometer after an engine is assembled are varied. The testing:

1. Allows the completed engine to be started and run to operating temperature

2. Permits checking for possible problems or leaks before the engine is installed in a vehicle

3. Allows the piston rings to seat and the engine to be partially broken in before being installed in a vehicle

4. Permits the technician to determine the output of the engine

5. Allows the opportunity to maximize the engine output by changing air-fuel ratios and valve or ignition timing until the best performance has been achieved

TYPES OF DYNAMOMETERS Basic types of dynamometers include:

- *Brake type,* where a variable load is applied to the engine and the computer calculates the power output based on the readings taken from the load cell or strain gauge and engine RPM. Most brake types use a water impeller to create the load on the engine. ● **SEE FIGURE 22–63**.

- *Inertia type,* which measures engine power by using the engine to accelerate a known mass load. An inertia type

FIGURE 22–64 A chassis dynamometer is used to measure torque at the drive wheels. There is a power loss through the drive train so the measured values are about 20% less than when measuring engine output at the flywheel using an engine dynamometer.

dynamometer is most often used to measure the power of an engine at the drive wheels of the vehicle. ● **SEE FIGURE 22–64**.

TERMINOLOGY   Numbers allow values to be assigned to virtually everything being measured or tested. The numbers help identify, quantify, and compare variables and performance. Two types of data include:

1. Basic measured values. Taken directly from the engine using sensors that read the actual data

2. Calculated values. Those found by using basic numbers and a formula to obtain them

MEASURED VALUES   Measured units are those that are obtained directly from sensors and include:

- **Torque.** As the name implies, this is the amount of twisting force that the engine puts out at the crank flange. Typically this is measured in foot-pounds.

   NOTE: Dynamometers only measure torque output of an engine. Horsepower is not measured directly but is instead a calculated value.

- **Fuel flow.** Mass flow rate of fuel is calculated by the number of gallons per hour times pounds per gallon and is measured in pounds per hour. To determine this value, the specific gravity of the fuel has to be measured and entered into the computer prior to the engine tests so the program can calculate the fuel flow. Make sure

there is enough fuel delivery for the engine by checking the gallons per hour prior to running each engine. Proper pressure (PSI) does not mean that there is enough volume being delivered to the engine especially under load conditions.

- **Manifold pressure.** Measured in inches of mercury (in. Hg), this value is called *manifold vacuum* in a normally aspirated engine.

- **Oil pressure.** This should be about 10 PSI per 1000 RPM.

- **Air inlet pressure.** Core value used to calculate the correction factor during the run, also referred to as dry bulb (DB) temperature. **Dry bulb temperature** is the temperature of a room where the thermometer is shielded from moisture. This reduces the effect of evaporation of moisture from the thermometer which could affect the temperature reading.

- **Fuel temperature.** Used to calculate the density of fuel for fuel flow values.

- **Oil temperature.** Very important in run-to-run comparisons. Typically, the hotter the oil, the more horsepower an engine makes (up to a point). Oil that is too hot loses its cooling capability as well as some of its lubricating properties.

- **Engine coolant temperature.** This reading is important to monitor as a safety limit to help prevent possible engine damage if it goes too high.

Transducers are needed to measure the basic values. A transducer is a device that is able to convert various input signals such as pressures and temperature into an electrical signal that a computer can recognize. Typical dynamometer transducers include:

- Magnetic pickups ● **SEE FIGURE 22–65**.

- Load cells

- Strain Gauge Flow meters

- Rotary potentiometers or rheostats

- Thermocouples

- Linear variable displacement transducers (LVDT)

CALCULATED NUMBERS   Calculated numbers are those that are obtained by using the measured values and processing them through software to obtain the following:

- **Corrected torque.** This is a calculated number determined by the actual torque multiplied by the correction factor. This is an important number and the reading should show a wide and flat band of torque over a broad engine speed range.

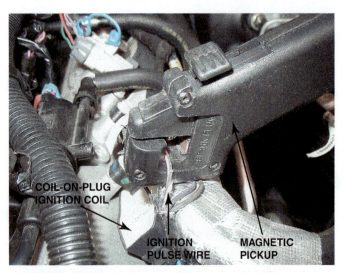

FIGURE 22–65 A magnetic pickup being used to monitor engine speed when the vehicle is being tested on a chassis dynamometer.

- **Corrected horsepower.** This is a calculated number showing the corrected observed horsepower.

- **Frictional horsepower.** This can best be thought of as the power required to rotate the engine over without firing and without pumping losses.

- **Volumetric efficiency.** This is a measure of the engine's cylinder filling efficiency; 100% represents filling a cylinder to its total swept volume. On a race engine, it is quite normal to see over 100% volumetric efficiency.

- **Mechanical efficiency.** This is the ratio of the engine's frictional torque divided by its corrected output torque. A value of 100% would indicate that the engine had no frictional losses.

STANDARDS For best results, perform testing on nice days with low relative humidity and high atmospheric pressure. These factors have a huge effect on the amount of air that the engine can "breathe," which in turn can dramatically affect horsepower readings. Testing on nice days is not always possible, so using corrected data allows the technician to compare test results from day to day and dynamometer to dynamometer. A **correction factor** is a value that is multiplied to the data values so that engine performance can be compared regardless of weather conditions. Over the years there have been many different correction factors specified by the Society of Automotive Engineers (SAE) including:

- SAE J606
- SAE J607 (Using this correction factor results in higher numbers than if using other correction factors mainly due to the higher barometric pressure standard used.)

TECH TIP

Look at the Crossing Point

All dynamometers measure torque of an engine, then calculate the horsepower. Horsepower is torque multiplied by engine speed (RPM) divided by 5,252 (a constant). Therefore, all graphs should show that the two curves for horsepower and torque should be the same at 5252 RPM. ● **SEE FIGURE 22–66.**

TECH TIP

Compare Dyno Results from the Same Dyno Only

There are too many variables between dynamometers to allow a fair comparison when testing an engine. If changes are made to the engine, try to use the same dynamometer and use the same correction factors. Using another dynamometer can result in readings that may not be equivalent when testing on the original tester.

- SAE J1349
- SAE J1739

There are subtle differences between each of the testing standards. The result after the correction factor has been applied is called **corrected torque.** From the corrected torque values, the other units, such as horsepower, can be calculated.

FINAL NOTES

- Corrected numbers are to be applied to wide open throttle (WOT) runs only.

- Corrected numbers only apply to *normally aspirated* engines and are not to be used for turbocharged or supercharged engines.

- Double-check that the spark timing is set relative to top dead center (TDC).

- Double-check that the engine has good electrical grounds and adequate voltage.

- Be sure to have enough *good* fuel before starting to test an engine. Do not use any gasoline older than 90 days.

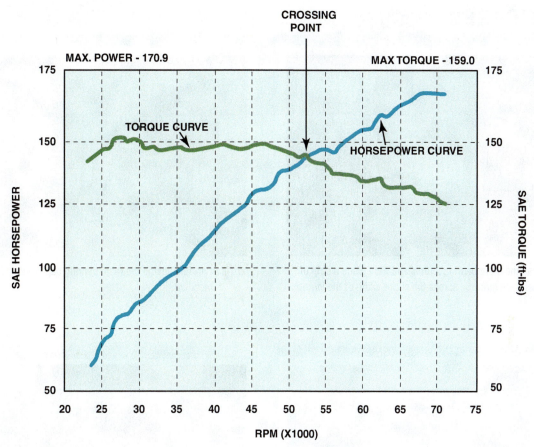

FIGURE 22–66 Because horsepower is calculated from measured torque, the horsepower and torque curves should always cross at exactly 5252 RPM.

PLASTIGAGE

1 Clean the main bearing journal and then place a strip of Plastigage material across the entire width of the journal.

2 Carefully install the main bearing cap with the bearing installed.

3 Torque main bearing cap bolts to factory specifications.

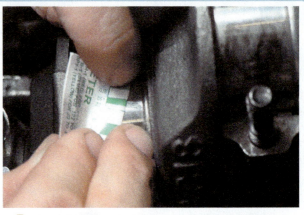

4 Carefully remove the bearing cap and, using the package that contained the Plastigage strips, measure the width of the compressed material. The gauge is calibrated in thousandths of the inch. Repeat for each main bearing.

5 To measure rod bearing oil clearance, start by removing the rod cap.

6 Clean the rod bearing journal and then place a strip of Plastigage across the entire width of the journal.

7 Torque the rod bearing cap nuts to factory specifications.

8 Remove the rod cap and measure the oil clearance using the markings on the Plastigage package. The wider the compressed gauge material, the narrower the bearing oil clearance. Repeat for all rod bearings.

SUMMARY

1. Before assembling an engine, the technician should read, understand, and follow all instructions that came with the parts and gaskets to ensure proper assembly.

2. Assembling the short block includes preparing the block and installing the crankshaft and the piston/rod assemblies.

3. Cylinder head assembly includes checking valve spring tension as well as proper rocker arm and pushrod measurements.

4. A trial assembly should be performed before the final assembly.

5. All bearing oil clearances should be checked using a micrometer and telescoping gauges or Plastigage.

6. Piston ring end gap should be checked before the pistons are installed.

7. Cylinder head bolts should be properly tightened and in the specified sequence.

8. Timing chain or belt and all covers are installed using the specified gaskets or sealers.

9. Testing an engine on a dynamometer allows the engine to be tested before being installed in a vehicle.

REVIEW QUESTIONS

1. List the items that need to be installed as part of the short block assembly.

2. How is crankshaft end play measured?

3. Why should Teflon seals not be oiled prior to being installed?

4. List the measured and calculated values as a result of testing an engine on a dynamometer.

1. About how much of the turning torque applied to a head bolt is lost to friction?
   a. 20%
   c. 60%
   b. 40%
   d. 80%

2. Service information states that SAE 30 engine oil should be used on the threads of the head bolts before installation and torquing. Technician A says that SAE 5W-30 will work. Technician B says that SAE 10W-30 will work. Which technician is correct?
   a. Technician A only
   b. Technician B only
   c. Both Technicians A and B
   d. Neither Technician A nor B

3. Technician A says that the torque applied to the head bolts is the same as the clamping force on the gasket. Technician B says that the clamping force is the force actually applied to the surfaces of the gasket. Which technician is correct?
   a. Technician A only
   b. Technician B only
   c. Both Technicians A and B
   d. Neither Technician A nor B

4. A coating often used to keep an engine from rusting during assembly is called _____.
   a. Engine oil
   c. Fogging oil
   b. Assembly lube
   d. Penetrating oil

5. Head gasket installation is being discussed. Technician A says that the surface finish of the cylinder head or block deck is very important for proper sealing to occur. Technician B says that if "front" is marked on a head gasket, the mark should be installed near the accessory drive belt end of the engine. Which technician is correct?
   a. Technician A only
   b. Technician B only
   c. Both Technicians A and B
   d. Neither Technician A nor B

6. Technician A says that studs should be installed finger tight. Technician B says that studs must be installed using a thread locker such as Loctite®. Which technician is correct?
   a. Technician A only
   b. Technician B only
   c. Both Technicians A and B
   d. Neither Technician A nor B

7. What can be used to check that heads are at the correct angle for the intake manifold on a V-type engine?
   a. Metal rule
   b. Angle gauge
   c. Tape measure
   d. Dial indicator

8. What is true about checking bearing clearance using Plastigage?
   a. The journal should be clean and oil free
   b. The cap should be torqued to factory specifications
   c. The wider the strip means the narrower the oil clearance
   d. all of the above

9. An engine dynamometer measures _____.
   a. Torque
   b. Horsepower
   c. Both horsepower and torque
   d. Fuel economy

10. If the torque and horsepower readings are graphed, where do the curves cross (equal each other)?
    a. Never
    b. At peak horsepower which can vary from engine to engine
    c. At peak torque which can vary from engine to engine
    d. At 5252 RPM

After studying this chapter, the reader should be able to:

1. List the steps necessary to install and start up a rebuilt engine.
2. Discuss the importance of torquing all bolts or fasteners that connect accessories to the engine block.
3. Describe what precautions must be taken to prevent damage to the engine when it is first started.
4. Explain how to break in a newly rebuilt engine.

This chapter will help you prepare for ASE Engine Repair (A1) certification test content area "E" (Fuel, Electrical, Ignition, and Exhaust System Inspection and Service).

Lugging 376
Dressing the engine 373

Normal operating temperature 376

GM Service Technical College topics covered in this chapter are:

1. Inspect, remove, and replace crankshaft pilot bearing or bushing (as applicable).
2. Inspect flywheel or flex plate and ring gear for cracks and wear; measure run out; determine needed repairs.

PREINSTALLATION CHECKLIST

NEED FOR A CHECKLIST Engine installation must be thoroughly checked to ensure that it is in proper condition to give the customer dependable operation for a long time. Using a checklist guarantees that all accessories are correctly reinstalled on the engine.

ENGINE INSTALLATION CHECKLIST Before installing or starting a new or rebuilt engine in a vehicle, be sure all of the following items have been checked.

1. Be sure the battery is fully charged.

2. Prelube the engine and check for proper oil pressure.

3. Check that all electrical wiring connecters and harnesses are properly installed.● **SEE FIGURE 23–1.**

4. Check that all of the vacuum lines are correctly installed and routed.

5. Check that all fuel lines are properly connected and free from leaks.

6. Make sure all engine fluids are at the proper operating level such as coolant, engine oil, and power steering fluid.

7. Know the ignition timing specification and procedure.

8. Check that fresh fuel is in the fuel tank.

9. Be sure that the radiator has been tested, is free from leaks, and flows correctly.

10. Check that all accessory drive belts are routed and tensioned correctly.

CAUTION: Be sure to have a fire extinguisher nearby when the engine is first started.

TRANSMISSION INSTALLATION

MANUAL TRANSMISSION INSTALLATION If the engine was removed with the transmission attached, the transmission should be reinstalled on the engine before other accessories are added. The flywheel is installed on the back of the crankshaft. Often, the attaching bolt holes are unevenly spaced so that the flywheel will fit in only one way to maintain engine balance. The pilot bearing or bushing in the rear of the crankshaft is usually replaced with a new one to minimize the possibility of premature failure of this part.

FIGURE 23–1 A partially melted electrical connector indicates that excessive current flow was present. The cause of the excessive current should be located and corrected before the engine is started.

The clutch is installed next and the installation usually includes the following steps.

STEP 1 Most experts recommend that a new clutch assembly or, at the least, a new clutch friction disc be installed.

STEP 2 The clutch friction disc must be held in position using an alignment tool (sometimes called a dummy shaft) that is secured in the pilot bearing. This holds the disc in position while the pressure plate is being installed.

STEP 3 The engine bell housing is put on the engine, if it is not part of the transmission. Make sure that the alignment dowels are correctly installed. ● **SEE FIGURE 23–2.**

CAUTION: Perfectly round cylinders can be distorted whenever another part of the engine is bolted and torqued to the engine block. For example, it has been determined that after the cylinders are machined, the rear cylinder bore can be distorted to be as much as 0.006 inch (0.15 mm) out-of-round after the bell housing is bolted onto the block! To help prevent this distortion, always apply the specified torque to all fasteners going into the engine block and tighten in the recommended sequence.

STEP 4 The clutch release yoke should be checked for free movement. Usually, the clutch release bearing is replaced to ensure that the new bearing is securely attached to the clutch release yoke.

STEP 5 The transmission is installed by carefully guiding the transmission input (clutch) shaft straight into the clutch disc and pilot bearing. Rotate the

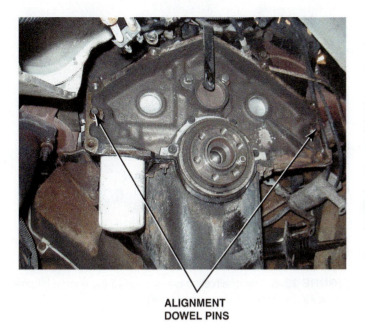

ALIGNMENT
DOWEL PINS

FIGURE 23–2 Bell housing alignment dowel pins are used to ensure proper alignment between the engine block and the transmission.

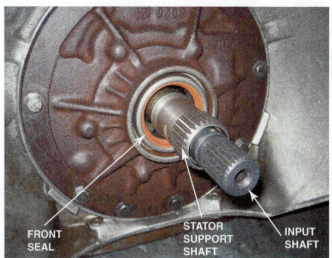

FRONT
SEAL

STATOR
SUPPORT
SHAFT

INPUT
SHAFT

FIGURE 23–3 The internal splines inside the torque converter must be properly aligned with all of the splines of the automatic transmission. Make sure that the TCC O-ring is installed, if used.

transmission output shaft as needed to engage the splines of the clutch disc. The assembly bolts are secured when the transmission fully mates with the bell housing.

CAUTION: Always adjust the clutch free play *before* starting the engine to help prevent engine thrust bearing or clutch release bearing damage.

AUTOMATIC TRANSMISSION INSTALLATION On engines equipped with an automatic transmission, the drive (flex) plate is attached to the back of the crankshaft. Its assembly bolts are tightened to the specified torque. The bell housing is part of the transmission case on most automatic transmissions. Installing an automatic transmission usually includes the following steps.

STEP 1 The torque converter should be installed on the transmission before the transmission is put on the engine.

STEP 2 Rotate the torque converter while it is pushed onto the transmission shafts until the splines of all shafts are engaged in the torque converter. ● **SEE FIGURE 23–3**.

STEP 3 The torque converter is held against the transmission as the transmission is fitted on the back of the engine. The transmission mounting bolts are attached finger tight.

STEP 4 The torque converter should be rotated to make sure that there is no binding. The bell housing is secured to the block and then the torque converter is fastened to the drive plate.

DRESSING THE ENGINE

"**Dressing the engine**" is a term used to describe the process of attaching all of the auxiliary items to the engine. The items include:

- Starter motor
- Fuel rail and related fuel system components
- New oxygen sensor(s), to ensure that the engine will be operating at the correct air-fuel ratio
- Engine/transmission wiring harness
- Ignition components, such the ignition coil(s) and spark plug wires, if equipped
- All belt-driven engine accessories, mounted on the front of the engine (Some engines drive all these accessories with one belt. Other engines use as many as four belts. Check service information or decals under the hood to determine the specific belt routing for the accessories used on the engine.) ● **SEE FIGURE 23–4**.
- Front accessories, such as the power steering pump, alternator, and air-conditioning compressor (These accessories may be installed before the engine is installed in the vehicle. On some vehicles it is easier to put the engine in the chassis before installing the front accessories.)

Always check service information for the exact procedure to follow.

FIGURE 23–4 It is often easier to install all of the accessory drive belts before the engine is installed in the vehicle. Note that this engine uses a "stretch" belt on the AC compressor. (*Courtesy of General Motors*)

FIGURE 23–5 The chain sling is attached to the engine lifting brackets and then lifted with an engine hoist.

ENGINE INSTALLATION

SECURING THE ENGINE   A sling, either a chain or lift cable, is attached to the manifold or head bolts or lifting brackets on the top of the engine. A hoist is attached to the sling and snugged up to take the weight and to make sure that the engine is supported and balanced properly.  **SEE FIGURE 23–5**.

INSTALLING THE ENGINE

- **Rear-wheel drive.** The engine must be tipped as it was during removal to let the transmission go into the engine compartment first. The transmission is worked under the floor pan on rear-wheel-drive vehicles as the engine is lowered into the engine compartment. The front engine mounts are aligned and the rear cross-member and rear engine mount are installed. The engine mount bolts are installed, and the nuts are torqued. Then the hoist is removed.

- **Front-wheel drive.** Many engines for front-wheel-drive vehicles are installed from underneath the vehicle. Often the entire drivetrain package is placed back in the vehicle while it is attached to the cradle. The vehicle is positioned on a hoist and is lowered onto the engine cradle assembly to install. Always check the recommended procedure for the vehicle being serviced.

RECONNECTING COMPONENTS AND CONNECTORS

The following items should be connected to the engine assembly.

- Throttle and cruise control linkages or cables
- Exhaust system to the exhaust manifolds
- If any of the steering linkage was previously disconnected, it can be reattached while work is being done under the vehicle.
- After the engine is in place, the front engine accessories can all be installed, if they were not installed before the engine was put in the chassis.
- The air-conditioning compressor is reattached to the engine, with care being taken to avoid damaging the air-conditioning hoses and lines.

COOLING SYSTEM   The radiator is installed and secured in place, followed by the cooling fan and shroud. The fan and new drive belts are then installed and adjusted. New radiator hoses, including new heater hoses, and new coolant should be installed.

ELECTRICAL SYSTEM   Under the hood the following electrical components will need to be mounted and connected.

- Connect all wiring to the starter and alternator as required.
- Connect the instrument and computer sensor wires to the sensors on the engine.
- Double-check the condition and routing of all wiring, being certain that wires have not been pinched or broken, before installing a fully charged battery.
- Attach the positive cable first and then the ground cable.
- Ensure that the starter will crank the engine.

FREQUENTLY ASKED QUESTION

What Is Break-In Engine Oil?

Many years ago, vehicle manufacturers used straight weight such as SAE 30 nondetergent engine oil as break-in oil. Today, the engine oil recommended for break-in (running in) is the same type of oil that is recommended for use in the engine. No special break-in oil is recommended or used by the factory in new vehicles. Always use the specified viscosity oil as recommended by the vehicle manufacturer.

- Install and time the distributor (if equipped), then connect the ignition cables to the spark plugs, again being sure that they are routed according to service information.

ENGINE START

PRECAUTIONS The engine installation should be given one last inspection to ensure that everything has been put together correctly before the engine is started. If the engine overhaul and installation are done properly, the engine should crank and start on its own fully charged battery without the use of a fast charger or jumper battery. As soon as the engine starts and shows oil pressure, it should be brought up to a fast idle speed and *kept there* to ensure that the engine gets proper lubrication. The fast-running oil pump develops full pressure, and the fast-turning crankshaft throws plenty of oil on the cam and cylinder walls.

NOTE: In camshaft-in-block engines, the only lubrication sent to the contact point between the camshaft lobes and the lifters (tappets) is from the splash off the crankshaft and connecting rods. At idle, engine oil does not splash enough for proper break-in lubrication of the camshaft.

Maintaining engine speed above 1500 RPM for the first 10 minutes of engine operation must be performed to break in a flat-bottom lifter camshaft. If the engine speed is decreased to idle (about 600 RPM), the lifter (tappet) will be in contact with and exerting force *on* the lobe of the cam for a longer period of time than occurs at higher engine speeds. The pressure and volume of oil supplied to the camshaft area are also increased at the higher engine speeds. Therefore, to ensure long camshaft and lifter life, make certain that the engine will

start quickly after reassembly to prevent long cranking periods and subsequent low engine speeds after a new camshaft and lifters have been installed.

NOTE: Many molydisulfide greases used during assembly can start to clog oil filters within 20 minutes after starting the engine. Most engine rebuilders recommend changing the oil and filter after 30 minutes of running time.

After the engine has started, the following items should be checked.

1. Is the valve train quiet? Some engines will require several minutes to quiet down.

2. Record the engine vacuum. It should be 17 to 21 inch Hg (sea level).

3. Check for any gasoline, coolant, or oil leaks. Stop the engine and repair the leaks as soon as possible.

4. Check the charging system for proper operation. The charging voltage should be 13.5 to 15 volts.

As soon the engine is at operating temperature and running well, the vehicle should be driven to a road having minimum traffic. Perform the following during the test drive.

- The vehicle should be accelerated, full throttle, from 30 to 50 mph (48 to 80 km/h).

- Then the throttle is fully closed while the vehicle is allowed to return to 30 mph (48 km/h). This sequence is repeated 10 to 12 times.

- The acceleration sequence puts a high load on the piston rings to properly seat them against the cylinder walls. The piston rings are the only part of the modern engine that needs to be broken in. Good ring seating is indicated by a dry coating inside the tailpipe at the completion of the ring seating drive.

The vehicle is returned to the service area, where the engine is again checked for visible fluid leaks. If the engine is dry, it is ready to be turned over to the customer.

The customer should be instructed to drive the vehicle in a normal fashion, neither babying it at slow speeds nor beating it at high speeds for the first 100 miles (160 km). The oil and filter should be changed at 500 miles (800 km) to remove any dirt that may have been trapped in the engine during assembly and to remove the material that has worn from the surfaces during the break-in period.

A well-designed engine that has been correctly reconditioned and assembled using the techniques described should give reliable service for many miles.

NORMAL OPERATING TEMPERATURE Normal **operating temperature** is the temperature at which the upper radiator hose is hot and pressurized. Another standard method used to determine when normal operating temperature is reached is to observe the operation of the electric cooling fan, when the vehicle is so equipped. Many manufacturers define normal operating temperature as being reached when the cooling fan has cycled on and off at least once after the engine has been started. Some vehicle manufacturers specify that the cooling fan should cycle twice. This method also helps assure the technician that the engine is not being overheated. ● **SEE FIGURE 23–6.**

HOW TO WARM UP A COLD ENGINE The greatest amount of engine wear occurs during start-up. The oil in a cold engine is thick, and it requires several seconds to reach all the moving parts of an engine. After the engine starts, allow the engine to idle until the oil pressure peaks. This will take from 15 to 60 seconds, depending on the outside temperature. *Do not allow the engine to idle for longer than five minutes.* Because an engine warms up faster under load, drive the vehicle in a normal manner until the engine is fully warm. Avoid full-throttle acceleration until the engine is completely up to normal operating temperature. This method of engine warm-up also warms the rest of the powertrain, including transmission and final drive component lubricants.

BREAK-IN PRECAUTIONS

Any engine overhaul represents many hours of work and a large financial investment. Precautions should be taken to protect the investment, including the following:

1. Never add cold water to the cooling system while the engine is running.

FIGURE 23–6 Even though the dash gauge may show normal operating temperature, a scan tool or an infrared pyrometer can also be used to verify proper coolant temperature.

2. Never lug any engine. **Lugging** means increasing the throttle opening without increasing engine speed (RPM). An example where lugging an engine can occur is when the vehicle is driven at a low speed, such as 15 mph, with the manual transmission in third or fourth gear instead of in second gear as per the recommended speed for that gear as published in the owner manual.

3. Applying loads to an engine for *short periods* of time creates higher piston ring pressure against the cylinder walls and assists the breaking-in process by helping to seat the rings.

4. Change the oil and filter at 500 miles (800 km) or after 20 hours of operation.

5. Check for leaks after the engine has gone through several warm-up and cooling down periods.

SUMMARY

1. Carefully install all accessories.
2. When installing the transmission and other components on the engine block, be sure to use a torque wrench and tighten all fasteners to factory specifications.
3. Always adjust the clutch free play before starting the engine.
4. Change the engine oil after 500 miles (800 km) or sooner, and use specified engine oil.

REVIEW QUESTIONS

1. How are the clutch and bell housing installed?

2. What should be done to help prevent rear cylinder distortion when the bell housing is being installed on the engine?

3. Describe the engine break-in procedure.

CHAPTER QUIZ

1. "Dressing the engine" means _____.
   a. Installing all of the exterior engine components
   b. Cleaning the engine
   c. Changing the oil and oil filter
   d. Both b and c

2. If the bell housing is not properly torqued to the engine block, _____.
   a. The bell housing will distort
   b. The engine block will crack
   c. The rear cylinder can be distorted (become out-of-round)
   d. The crankshaft will crack

3. Break-in engine oil is _____.
   a. Of the same viscosity and grade as that specified for normal engine operation
   b. SAE 40
   c. SAE 30
   d. SAE 20W-50

4. Normal operating temperature is reached when _____.
   a. The radiator cap releases coolant into the overflow
   b. The upper radiator hose is hot and pressurized
   c. The electric cooling fan has cycled at least once (if the vehicle is so equipped)
   d. Both b and c

5. Lugging an engine means _____.
   a. Wide-open throttle in low gear above 25 mph
   b. That engine speed does not increase when the throttle is opened wider
   c. Starting a cold engine and allowing it to idle for longer than five minutes
   d. Both b and c

6. Which computer sensor should be replaced to help ensure that the engine will be operating at the correct air-fuel ratio?
   a. Throttle position sensor
   b. Oxygen sensor
   c. Manifold absolute pressure sensor
   d. Engine coolant temperature sensor

7. How should the vehicle be driven to best break in a newly overhauled engine?
   a. At a steady low speed
   b. At varying speeds and loads
   c. At high speed and loads
   d. At idle speed and little or no load

8. Which type of vehicle is the engine most likely to be installed from underneath the vehicle?
   a. Rear-wheel drive (RWD)
   b. Front-wheel drive (FWD)
   c. Four-wheel drive (4WD)
   d. Both a and c

9. Engine vacuum on a normal stock rebuilt engine should be _____.
   a. 10 to 15 inch Hg   c. 17 to 21 inch Hg
   b. 12 to 16 inch Hg   d. 19 to 23 inch Hg

10. Why must flat-bottom camshafts be broken in at a fast idle?
    a. Cam in a cam-in-block engine is only lubricated by splash oil.
    b. The flat-bottom of the lifters must become slightly concave in order to rotate.
    c. Both a and b are correct
    d. Neither a nor b are correct

chapter 24
GASOLINE

LEARNING OBJECTIVES

After studying this chapter, the reader should be able to:

1. Describe how the proper grade of gasoline affects engine performance.
2. List gasoline purchasing hints.
3. Discuss how volatility affects driveability.
4. Explain how oxygenated fuels can reduce CO exhaust emissions.
5. Discuss safety precautions when working with gasoline.

GM STC OBJECTIVES

GM Service Technical College topics covered in this chapter are:

1. Perform a fuel quality test.

KEY TERMS

Air–fuel ratio 382
Antiknock index (AKI) 384
ASTM 381
British thermal unit (BTU) 382
Catalytic cracking 379
Cracking 379
Detonation 383
Distillation 379
Distillation curve 381
Driveability index (DI) 381
E10 386
Ethanol 386
Fungible 379

Gasoline 379
Hydrocracking 379
Octane rating 383
Oxygenated fuels 386
Petroleum 379
Ping 383
Reformulated gasoline (RFG) 388
RVP 380
Spark knock 383
Stoichiometric ratio 383
Tetraethyl lead (TEL) 384
Vapor lock 382
Volatility 380
WWFC 389

GASOLINE

DEFINITION   Gasoline is a term used to describe a complex mixture of various hydrocarbons refined from crude petroleum oil for use as a fuel in engines. Gasoline and air burn in the cylinder of the engine and produce heat and pressure, which is transferred to rotary motion inside the engine and eventually powers the drive wheels of a vehicle. When combustion occurs, carbon dioxide and water are produced if the process is perfect and all of the air and all of the fuel are consumed in the process.

CHEMICAL COMPOSITION

Gasoline is a combination of hydrocarbon molecules that have between five and 12 carbon atoms. The names of these various hydrocarbons are based on the number of carbon atoms and include:

- **Methane**—one carbon atom
- **Ethane**—two carbon atoms
- **Propane**—three carbon atoms
- **Butane**—four carbon atoms
- **Pentane**—five carbon atoms
- **Hexane**—six carbon atoms
- **Heptane**—seven carbon atoms (used to test octane rating—has an octane rating of zero)
- **Octane**—eight carbon atoms (a type of octane is used as a basis for antiknock rating)

REFINING

TYPES OF CRUDE OIL   Refining is a complex combination of interdependent processing units that can separate crude oil into useful products such as gasoline and diesel fuel. As it comes out of the ground, **petroleum** (meaning "rock oil") crude can be as thin and light colored as apple cider or as thick and black as melted tar. A barrel of crude oil is 42 gallons, not 55 gallons as commonly used for industrial barrels. Typical terms used to describe the type of crude oil include:

- Thin crude oil has a high American Petroleum Institute (API) gravity, and therefore, is called *high-gravity* crude. High-gravity-type crude contains more natural gasoline and its lower sulfur and nitrogen content makes it easier to refine.
- Thick crude oil is called *low-gravity* crude.

- Low-sulfur crude oil is also known as "sweet" crude.
- High-sulfur crude oil is also known as "sour" crude.

DISTILLATION   In the late 1800s, crude was separated into different products by boiling, through a process called **distillation**. Distillation works because crude oil is composed of hydrocarbons with a broad range of boiling points.

In a distillation column, the vapors of the lowest-boiling hydrocarbons, propane and butane, rise to the top. The straight-run gasoline (also called naphtha), kerosene, and diesel fuel cuts are drawn off at successively lower positions in the column.

CRACKING   **Cracking** is the process where hydrocarbons with higher boiling points can be broken down (cracked) into lower-boiling hydrocarbons by treating them to very high temperatures. This process, called *thermal cracking*, was used to increase gasoline production starting in 1913.

Instead of high heat, today cracking is performed using a catalyst and is called **catalytic cracking**. A catalyst is a material that speeds up or otherwise facilitates a chemical reaction without undergoing a permanent chemical change itself. Catalytic cracking produces gasoline of higher quality than thermal cracking.

Hydrocracking is similar to catalytic cracking in that it uses a catalyst, but the catalyst is in a hydrogen atmosphere. Hydrocracking can break down hydrocarbons that are resistant to catalytic cracking alone, and it is used to produce diesel fuel rather than gasoline.

Other types of refining processes include:

- Reforming
- Alkylation
- Isomerization
- Hydrotreating
- Desulfurization

● **SEE FIGURE 24–1.**

SHIPPING   The gasoline is transported to regional storage facilities by tank railway car or by pipeline. In the pipeline method, all gasoline from many refiners is often sent through the same pipeline and can get mixed. All gasoline is said to be **fungible**, meaning that it is capable of being interchanged because each grade is created to specification so there is no reason to keep the different gasoline brands separated except for grade. Regular grade, mid-grade, and premium grade

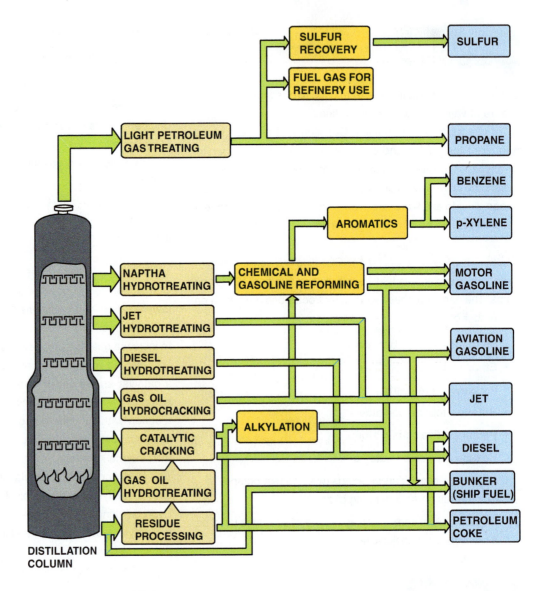

FIGURE 24–1 The crude oil refining process showing most of the major steps and processes.

SULFUR RECOVERY → SULFUR

FUEL GAS FOR REFINERY USE

LIGHT PETROLEUM GAS TREATING → PROPANE

AROMATICS → BENZENE

p-XYLENE

NAPTHA HYDROTREATING → CHEMICAL AND GASOLINE REFORMING → MOTOR GASOLINE

JET HYDROTREATING

DIESEL HYDROTREATING → AVIATION GASOLINE

GAS OIL HYDROCRACKING → JET

CATALYTIC CRACKING → ALKYLATION → DIESEL

GAS OIL HYDROTREATING → BUNKER (SHIP FUEL)

RESIDUE PROCESSING → PETROLEUM COKE

DISTILLATION COLUMN

are separated in the pipeline and the additives are added at the regional storage facilities and then shipped by truck to individual gas stations.

VOLATILITY

DEFINITION OF VOLATILITY **Volatility** describes how easily the gasoline evaporates (forms a vapor). The definition of volatility assumes that the vapors will remain in the fuel tank or fuel line and will cause a certain pressure based on the temperature of the fuel.

REID VAPOR PRESSURE (RVP) **Reid vapor pressure (RVP)** is the pressure of the vapor above the fuel when the fuel is at 100°F (38°C). Increased vapor pressure permits the engine to start in cold weather. Gasoline without air will not burn. Gasoline must be vaporized (mixed with air) to burn in an engine. ● **SEE FIGURE 24–2.**

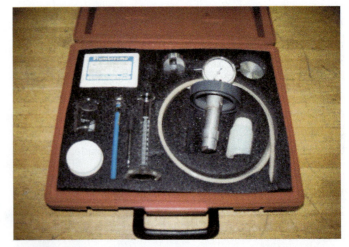

FIGURE 24–2 A gasoline testing kit, including an insulated container where water at 100°F is used to heat a container holding a small sample of gasoline. The reading on the pressure gauge is the Reid vapor pressure (RVP).

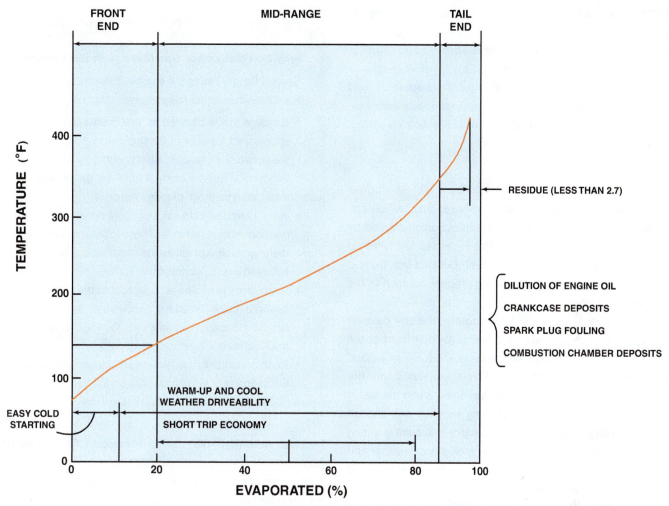

FIGURE 24–3 A typical distillation curve. Heavier molecules evaporate at higher temperatures and contain more heat energy for power, whereas the lighter molecules evaporate easier for starting.

SEASONAL BLENDING   Cold temperatures reduce the normal vaporization of gasoline; therefore, winter-blended gasoline is specially formulated to vaporize at lower temperatures for proper starting and driveability at low ambient temperatures. The **American Society for Testing and Materials (ASTM)** standards for winter-blend gasoline allow volatility of up to 15 pounds per square inch (PSI) RVP.

At warm ambient temperatures, gasoline vaporizes easily. However, the fuel system (fuel pump, carburetor, fuel-injector nozzles, etc.) is designed to operate with liquid gasoline. The volatility of summer-grade gasoline should be about 7.0 PSI RVP. According to ASTM standards, the maximum RVP should be 10.5 PSI for summer-blend gasoline.

DISTILLATION CURVE   Besides Reid vapor pressure, another method of classifying gasoline volatility is the **distillation curve**. A curve on a graph is drawn by plotting the temperature at which the various percentage of the fuel evaporates. A typical distillation curve is shown in ● **FIGURE 24–3.**

DRIVEABILITY INDEX   A distillation curve shows how much of a gasoline evaporates at what temperature range. To predict cold-weather driveability, an index was created called the **driveability index**, also called the *distillation index (DI)*.

The DI was developed using the temperature for the evaporated percentage of 10% (labeled T10), 50% (labeled T50), and 90% (labeled T90). The formula for DI is:

$$DI = 1.5 \times T10 + 3 \times T50 + T90$$

The total DI is a temperature and usually ranges from 1,000°F to 1,200°F. The lower values of DI generally result in good cold-start and warm-up performance. A high DI number is less volatile than a low DI number.

NOTE: Most premium-grade gasoline has a higher (worse) DI than regular-grade or mid-grade gasoline, which could cause poor cold-weather driveability. Vehicles designed to operate on premium-grade gasoline are programmed to handle the higher DI, but engines designed to operate on regular-grade gasoline may not be able to provide acceptable cold-weather driveability.

VOLATILITY-RELATED PROBLEMS At higher temperatures, liquid gasoline can easily vaporize, which can cause **vapor lock**. Vapor lock is a *lean* condition caused by vaporized fuel in the fuel system. This vaporized fuel takes up space normally occupied by liquid fuel. Bubbles that form in the fuel cause vapor lock, preventing proper operation of the fuel-injection system.

Heat causes some fuel to evaporate, thereby causing bubbles. Sharp bends cause the fuel to be restricted at the bend. When the fuel flows past the bend, the fuel can expand to fill the space after the bend. This expansion drops the pressure, and bubbles form in the fuel lines. When the fuel is full of bubbles, the engine is not being supplied with enough fuel and the engine runs lean. A lean engine will stumble during acceleration, will run rough, and may stall. Warm weather and alcohol-blended fuels both tend to increase vapor lock and engine performance problems.

If winter-blend gasoline (or high-RVP fuel) is used in an engine during warm weather, the following problems may occur:

1. Rough idle
2. Stalling
3. Hesitation on acceleration
4. Surging

GASOLINE COMBUSTION PROCESS

CHEMICAL REACTIONS The combustion process involves the chemical combination of oxygen (O_2) from the air (about 21% of the atmosphere) with the hydrogen and carbon from the fuel. In a gasoline engine, a spark starts the combustion process, which takes about 3 ms (0.003 sec) to be completed inside the cylinder of an engine. The chemical reaction that takes place can be summarized as follows: hydrogen (H) plus carbon (C) plus oxygen (O_2) plus nitrogen (N) plus spark equals

heat plus water (H_2O) plus carbon monoxide (CO) (if incomplete combustion) plus carbon dioxide (CO_2) plus hydrocarbons (HC) plus oxides of nitrogen (NO_X) plus many other chemicals. In an equation format it looks like this:

$$H + C + O_2 + N + Spark = Heat + CO_2 + HC + NO_x + H_2O$$

HEAT ENERGY The heat produced by the combustion process is measured in **British thermal units (BTUs)**. One BTU is the amount of heat required to raise one pound of water one Fahrenheit degree. The metric unit of heat is the *calorie* (cal). One calorie is the amount of heat required to raise the temperature of one gram (g) of water one Celsius degree. Gasoline has a heat potential of about 114,000 BTUs per gallon

AIR–FUEL RATIOS Fuel burns best when the intake system turns it into a fine spray and mixes it with air before sending it into the cylinders. In fuel-injected engines, the fuel becomes a spray and mixes with the air in the intake manifold. There is a direct relationship between engine airflow and fuel requirements; this is called the **air–fuel ratio**.

The air–fuel ratio is the proportion by weight of air and gasoline that the injection system mixes as needed for engine combustion. The mixtures, with which a gasoline engine can operate without stalling, range from 8 to 1 to 18.5 to 1. ● **SEE FIGURE 24–4.**

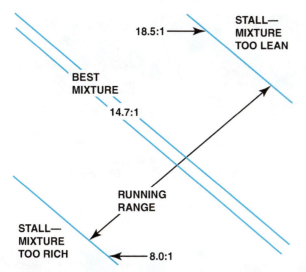

FIGURE 24–4 An engine will not run if the air–fuel mixture is either too rich or too lean.

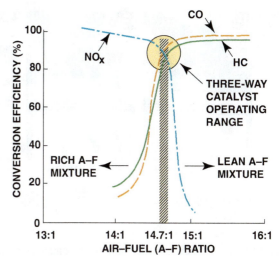

FIGURE 24–5 With a three-way catalytic converter, emission control is most efficient with an air–fuel ratio between 14.65 to 1 and 14.75 to 1.

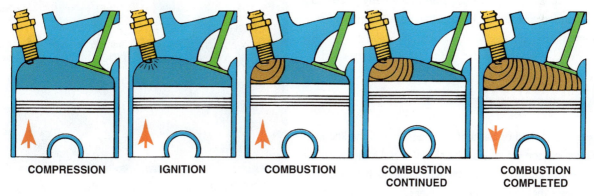

COMPRESSION   IGNITION   COMBUSTION   COMBUSTION CONTINUED   COMBUSTION COMPLETED

FIGURE 24–6 Normal combustion is a smooth, controlled burning of the air–fuel mixture.

These ratios are usually stated by weight, such as:

- 8 parts of air by weight combined with 1 part of gasoline by weight (8:1), which is the richest mixture that an engine can tolerate and still fire reliably.

- 18.5 parts of air mixed with one part of gasoline (18.5:1), which is the leanest practical ratio. Richer or leaner air–fuel ratios cause the engine to misfire badly or not run at all.

STOICHIOMETRIC AIR–FUEL RATIO
The ideal mixture or ratio at which all of the fuel combines with all of the oxygen in the air and burns completely is called the **stoichiometric ratio**, a chemically perfect combination. In theory, this ratio for gasoline is an air–fuel mixture of 14.7 to 1. ● SEE FIGURE 24–5.

In reality, the exact ratio at which perfect mixture and combustion occurs depends on the molecular structure of gasoline, which can vary. The stoichiometric ratio is a compromise between maximum power and maximum economy.

NORMAL AND ABNORMAL COMBUSTION

The **octane rating** of gasoline is the measure of its antiknock properties. *Engine knock* (also called **detonation, spark knock**, or **ping**) is a metallic noise an engine makes, usually during acceleration, resulting from abnormal or uncontrolled combustion inside the cylinder.

Normal combustion occurs smoothly and progresses across the combustion chamber from the point of ignition. ● SEE FIGURE 24–6.

Normal flame-front combustion travels between 45 and 90 mph (72 and 145 km/h). The speed of the flame front depends on air–fuel ratio, combustion chamber design (determining amount of turbulence), and temperature.

During periods of spark knock (detonation), the combustion speed increases by up to 10 times to near the speed of

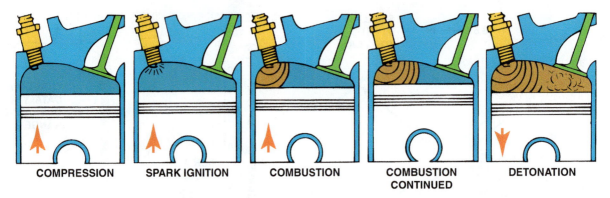

| COMPRESSION | SPARK IGNITION | COMBUSTION | COMBUSTION CONTINUED | DETONATION |

FIGURE 24–7 Detonation is a secondary ignition of the air–fuel mixture. It is also called spark knock or pinging.

sound. The increased combustion speed also causes increased temperatures and pressures, which can damage pistons, gaskets, and cylinder heads. ● **SEE FIGURE 24–7.**

One of the first additives used in gasoline was **tetraethyl lead (TEL)**. TEL was added to gasoline in the early 1920s to reduce the tendency to knock. It was often called ethyl or high-test gasoline.

OCTANE RATING

The antiknock standard or basis of comparison was the knock-resistant hydrocarbon isooctane, chemically called trimethylpentane (C_8H_{18}), also known as 2-2-4 trimethylpentane. If a gasoline tested had the exact same antiknock characteristics as isooctane, it was rated as 100-octane gasoline. If the gasoline tested had only 85% of the antiknock properties of isooctane, it was rated as 85 octane. Remember, octane rating is only a comparison test.

The two basic methods used to rate gasoline for antiknock properties (octane rating) are the *research method* and the *motor method*. Each uses a model of the special cooperative fuel research (CFR) single-cylinder engine. The research method and the motor method vary as to temperature of air, spark advance, and other parameters. The research method typically results in readings that are 6 to 10 points higher than those of the motor method. For example, a fuel with a research octane number (RON) of 93 might have a motor octane number (MON) of 85.

The octane rating posted on pumps in the United States is the average of the two methods and is referred to as $(R + M) \div 2$, therefore, for the fuel used in the previous example, the rating posted on the pumps would be

$$\frac{RON + MON}{2} = \frac{93 + 85}{2} = 89$$

The pump octane is called the **antiknock index (AKI)**.

FIGURE 24–8 A pump showing regular fuel with an octane rating of 87, plus with an octane rating of 89, and premium with an octane rating of 93. These ratings can vary with brand and location in the country.

? **FREQUENTLY ASKED QUESTION**

What Grade of Gasoline Does the EPA Use When Testing Engines?

Due to the various grades and additives used in commercial fuel, the government (EPA) uses a liquid called indolene. Indolene has a research octane number of 96.5 and a motor method octane rating of 88, which results in an $R + M \div 2$ rating of 92.25.

GASOLINE GRADES AND OCTANE NUMBER The posted octane rating on gasoline pumps is the rating achieved by the average of the research and the motor methods. ● **SEE FIGURE 24–8.**

Except for high-altitude areas, the grades and octane ratings are given in ● **CHART 24–1.**

TECH TIP

Horsepower and Fuel Flow

To produce 1 hp, the engine must be supplied with 0.50 pounds of fuel per hour (lb/hr). Fuel injectors are rated in pounds per hour. For example, a V-8 engine equipped with 25 lb/hr fuel injectors could produce 50 hp per cylinder (per injector) or 400 hp. Even if the cylinder head or block is modified to produce more horsepower, the limiting factor may be the injector flow rate.

The following are flow rates and resulting horsepower for a V-8 engine:

30 lb/hr: 60 hp per cylinder or 480 hp
35 lb/hr: 70 hp per cylinder or 560 hp
40 lb/hr: 80 hp per cylinder or 640 hp

Of course, injector flow rate is only one of many variables that affect power output. Installing larger injectors without other major engine modifications could decrease engine output and drastically increase exhaust emissions.

GRADES	OCTANE RATING
Regular	87
Mid-grade (also called Plus)	89
Premium	91 or higher

CHART 24–1

Typical octane ratings for gasoline in most parts of the country.

HIGH-ALTITUDE OCTANE REQUIREMENTS

As the altitude increases, atmospheric pressure drops. The air is less dense because a pound of air takes more volume. The octane rating of fuel does not need to be as high because the engine cannot take in as much air. This process will reduce the combustion (compression) pressures inside the engine. In mountainous areas, gasoline $(R + M)$, 2 octane ratings are two or more numbers lower than normal (according to the SAE, about one octane number lower per 1,000 feet or 300 meter in altitude). ● **SEE FIGURE 24–9.**

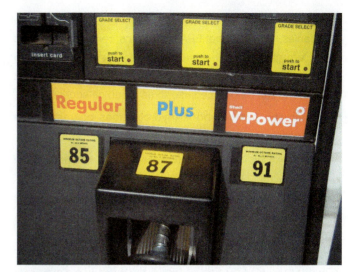

FIGURE 24–9 The posted octane rating in most high-altitude areas shows regular at 85 instead of the usual 87.

A secondary reason for the lowered octane requirement of engines running at higher altitudes is the normal enrichment of the air–fuel ratio and lower engine vacuum with the decreased air density. Some problems, therefore, may occur when driving out of high-altitude areas into lower-altitude areas where the octane rating must be higher. Most computerized engine control systems can compensate for changes in altitude and modify air–fuel ratio and ignition timing for best operation.

Because the combustion rate slows at high altitude, the ignition (spark) timing can be advanced to improve power. The amount of timing advance can be about 1 degree per 1,000 feet over 5,000 feet. Therefore, if driving at 8,000 feet of altitude, the ignition timing can be advanced 3 degrees.

High altitude also allows fuel to evaporate more easily. The volatility of fuel should be reduced at higher altitudes to prevent vapor from forming in sections of the fuel system, which can cause driveability and stalling problems. The extra heat generated in climbing to higher altitudes plus the lower atmospheric pressure at higher altitudes combine to cause possible driveability problems as the vehicle goes to higher altitudes.

GASOLINE ADDITIVES

DYE Dye is usually added to gasoline at the distributor to help identify the grade and/or brand of fuel. In many countries, fuels are required to be colored using a fuel-soluble dye. In the United States and Canada, diesel fuel used for off-road use and not taxed is required to be dyed red for identification. Gasoline sold for off-road use in Canada is dyed purple.

OCTANE IMPROVER ADDITIVES

When gasoline companies, under federal EPA regulations, removed tetraethyl lead from gasoline, other methods were developed to help maintain the antiknock properties of gasoline. Octane improvers (enhancers) can be grouped into three broad categories:

1. Aromatic hydrocarbons (hydrocarbons containing the benzene ring) such as xylene and toluene

2. Alcohols such as ethanol (ethyl alcohol), methanol (methyl alcohol), and tertiary butyl alcohol (TBA)

3. Metallic compounds such as methylcyclopentadienyl manganese tricarbonyl (MMT)

NOTE: MMT has been proven to be harmful to catalytic converters and can cause spark plug fouling. However, MMT is currently one of the active ingredients commonly found in octane improvers available to the public and in some gasoline sold in Canada. If an octane boost additive has been used that contains MMT, the spark plug porcelain will be rust colored around the tip.

Propane and butane, which are volatile by-products of the refinery process, are also often added to gasoline as octane improvers. The increase in volatility caused by the added propane and butane often leads to hot-weather driveability problems.

OXYGENATED FUEL ADDITIVES

Oxygenated fuels contain oxygen in the molecule of the fuel itself. Examples of oxygenated fuels include methanol, ethanol, methyl tertiary butyl ether (MTBE), tertiary-amyl methyl ether (TAME), and ethyl tertiary butyl ether (ETBE).

Oxygenated fuels are commonly used in high-altitude areas to reduce carbon monoxide (CO) emissions. The extra oxygen in the fuel itself is used to convert harmful CO into carbon dioxide (CO_2). The extra oxygen in the fuel helps ensure that there is enough oxygen to convert all CO into CO_2 during the combustion process in the engine or catalytic converter.

METHYL TERTIARY BUTYL ETHER (MTBE). MTBE is manufactured by means of the chemical reaction of methanol and isobutylene. Unlike methanol, MTBE does not increase the volatility of the fuel, and is not as sensitive to water as are other alcohols. The maximum allowable volume level, according to the EPA, is 15% but is currently being phased out due to health concerns, as well as MTBE contamination of drinking water if spilled from storage tanks.

TERTIARY-AMYL METHYL ETHER. Tertiary-amyl methyl ether (TAME) contains an oxygen atom bonded to two carbon atoms

? FREQUENTLY ASKED QUESTION

Can Regular-Grade Gasoline Be Used If Premium Is the Recommended Grade?

Maybe. It is usually possible to use regular-grade or mid-grade (plus) gasoline in most newer vehicles without danger of damage to the engine. Most vehicles built since the 1990s are equipped with at least one knock sensor. If a lower octane gasoline than specified is used, the engine ignition timing setting will usually cause the engine to spark knock, also called detonation or ping. This spark knock is detected by the knock sensor(s), which sends a signal to the computer. The computer then retards the ignition timing until the spark knock stops.

As a result of this spark timing retardation, the engine torque is reduced. While this reduction in power is seldom noticed, it will reduce fuel economy, often by four to five miles per gallon. If premium gasoline is then used, the PCM will gradually permit the engine to operate at the more advanced ignition timing setting. Therefore, it may take several tanks of premium gasoline to restore normal fuel economy. For best overall performance, use the grade of gasoline recommended by the vehicle manufacturer.

and is added to gasoline to provide oxygen to the fuel. It is slightly soluble in water, very soluble in ethers and alcohol, and soluble in most organic solvents including hydrocarbons.

ETHYL TERTIARY BUTYL ETHER. ETBE is derived from ethanol. The maximum allowable volume level is 17.2%. The use of ETBE is the cause of much of the odor from the exhaust of vehicles using reformulated gasoline.

ETHANOL. **Ethanol**, also called *ethyl alcohol*, is usually made from grain. Adding 10% ethanol (ethyl alcohol or grain alcohol) increases the $(R + M) \div 2$ octane rating by three points. The alcohol added to the base gasoline, however, also raises the volatility of the fuel about 0.5 PSI. Most automobile manufacturers permit up to 10% ethanol if driveability problems are not experienced.

The oxygen content of a 10% blend of ethanol in gasoline, called **E10**, is 3.5% oxygen by weight. ● **SEE FIGURE 24–10.**

FIGURE 24–10 This fuel pump indicates that the gasoline is blended with 10% ethanol (ethyl alcohol) and can be used in any gasoline vehicle. E85 contains 85% ethanol and can only be used in vehicles specifically designed to use it.

What Is Meant by "Phase Separation"?

All alcohols absorb water, and the alcohol–water mixture can separate from the gasoline and sink to the bottom of the fuel tank. This process is called *phase separation*. To help avoid engine performance problems, try to keep at least a quarter tank of fuel at all times, especially during seasons when there is a wide temperature span between daytime highs and nighttime lows. These conditions can cause moisture to accumulate in the fuel tank as a result of condensation of the moisture in the air. Keeping the fuel tank full reduces the amount of air and moisture in the tank. ● **SEE FIGURE 24–11.**

GASOLINE BLENDING

Gasoline additives, such as ethanol and dyes, are usually added to the fuel at the distributor. Adding ethanol to gasoline is a way to add oxygen to the fuel itself. Gasoline blended with an additive that has oxygen is called *oxygenated fuel*. There are three basic methods used to blend ethanol with gasoline to create E10 (10% ethanol, 90% gasoline).

1. **Inline blending**—Gasoline and ethanol are mixed in a storage tank or in the tank of a transport truck while it is being filled. Because the quantities of each can be accurately

FIGURE 24–11 A container with gasoline containing alcohol. Notice the separation line where the alcohol–water mixture separated from the gasoline and sank to the bottom.

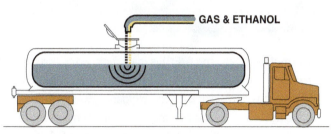

FIGURE 24–12 Inline blending is the most accurate method for blending ethanol with gasoline because computers are used to calculate the correct ratio.

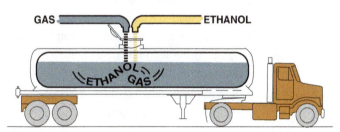

FIGURE 24–13 Sequential blending uses a computer to calculate the correct ratio as well as the prescribed order in which the products are loaded.

measured, this method is most likely to produce a well-mixed blend of ethanol and gasoline. ● **SEE FIGURE 24–12.**

2. **Sequential blending**—This method is usually performed at the wholesale terminal and involves adding a measured amount of ethanol to a tank truck followed by a measured amount of gasoline. ● **SEE FIGURE 24–13.**

3. **Splash blending**—Splash blending can be done at the retail outlet or distributor and involves separate purchases of ethanol and gasoline. In a typical case, a distributor can purchase gasoline, and then drive to another supplier and purchase ethanol. The ethanol is then added (splashed) into the tank of gasoline. This method is the least-accurate method of blending and can result in ethanol concentration for E10 that should be 10% to range from 5% to over 20% in some cases. ● **SEE FIGURE 24–14.**

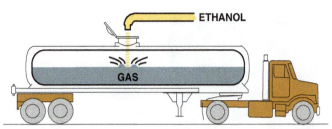

FIGURE 24–14 Splash blending occurs when the ethanol is added to a tanker with gasoline and is mixed as the truck travels to the retail outlet.

REFORMULATED GASOLINE

Reformulated gasoline (RFG) is manufactured to help reduce emissions. The gasoline refiners reformulate gasoline by using additives that contain at least 2% oxygen by weight and reducing the additive benzene to a maximum of 1% by volume. Two other major changes done at the refineries are as follows:

1. **Reduce light compounds.** Refineries eliminate butane, pentane, and propane, which have a low boiling point and evaporate easily. These unburned hydrocarbons are released into the atmosphere during refueling and through the fuel tank vent system, contributing to smog formation. Therefore, reducing the light compounds from gasoline helps reduce evaporative emissions.

2. **Reduce heavy compounds.** Refineries eliminate heavy compounds with high boiling points such as aromatics and olefins. The purpose of this reduction is to reduce the amount of unburned hydrocarbons that enter the catalytic converter, which makes the converter more efficient, thereby reducing emissions.

Because many of the heavy compounds are eliminated, a drop in fuel economy of about 1 mpg has been reported in areas where reformulated gasoline is being used. Formaldehyde is formed when RFG is burned, and the vehicle exhaust has a unique smell when reformulated gasoline is used.

TESTING GASOLINE FOR ALCOHOL CONTENT

Take the following steps when testing gasoline for alcohol content:

1. Pour suspect gasoline into a graduated cylinder.
2. Carefully fill the graduated cylinder to the 90 mL mark.

 WARNING

Do not smoke or run the test around sources of ignition!

3. Add 10 mL of water to the graduated cylinder by counting the number of drops from an eyedropper.
4. Put the stopper in the cylinder and shake vigorously for one minute. Relieve built-up pressure by occasionally removing the stopper. Alcohol dissolves in water and will drop to the bottom of the cylinder.
5. Place the cylinder on a flat surface and let it stand for two minutes.
6. Take a reading near the bottom of the cylinder at the boundary between the two liquids.
7. For percentage of alcohol in gasoline, subtract 10 from the reading and multiply by 10.

For example,

The reading is 20 mL: 20 – 10% = 10 alcohol

If the increase in volume is 0.2% or less, it may be assumed that the test gasoline contains no alcohol. ●**SEE FIGURE 24–15.** Alcohol content can also be checked using an electronic tester. See the step-by-step sequence at the end of the chapter.

GENERAL GASOLINE RECOMMENDATIONS

The fuel used by an engine is a major expense in the operation cost of the vehicle. The proper operation of the engine depends on clean fuel of the proper octane rating and vapor pressure for the atmospheric conditions.

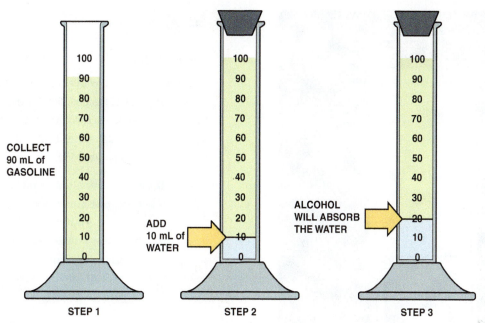

COLLECT 90 mL of GASOLINE

ADD 10 mL of WATER

ALCOHOL WILL ABSORB THE WATER

STEP 1

STEP 2

STEP 3

FIGURE 24–15 Checking gasoline for alcohol involves using a graduated cylinder and adding water to check if the alcohol absorbs the water.

? FREQUENTLY ASKED QUESTION

How Does Alcohol Content in the Gasoline Affect Engine Operation?

In most cases, the use of gasoline containing 10% or less of ethanol (ethyl alcohol) has little or no effect on engine operation. However, because the addition of 10% ethanol raises the volatility of the fuel slightly, occasional rough idle or stalling may be noticed, especially during warm weather. The rough idle and stalling may also be noticeable after the engine is started, driven, and then stopped for a short time. Engine heat can vaporize the alcohol-enhanced fuel causing bubbles to form in the fuel system. These bubbles in the fuel prevent the proper operation of the fuel injection system and result in a hesitation during acceleration, rough idle, or in severe cases repeated stalling until all the bubbles have been forced through the fuel system, replaced by cooler fuel from the fuel tank.

To help ensure proper engine operation and keep fuel costs to a minimum, follow these guidelines:

1. Purchase fuel from a busy station to help ensure that it is fresh and less likely to be contaminated with water or moisture.

? FREQUENTLY ASKED QUESTION

What Is "Top-Tier" Gasoline?

Top-tier gasoline is gasoline that has specific standards for quality, including enough detergent to keep all intake valves clean. Four automobile manufacturers—BMW, General Motors, Honda, and Toyota—developed the standards. Top-tier gasoline exceeds the quality standards developed by the **World Wide Fuel Charter (WWFC)** that was established in 2002 by vehicle and engine manufacturers. The gasoline companies that agreed to make fuel that matches or exceeds the standards as a top-tier fuel include ChevronTexaco, Shell, and ConocoPhillips.

2. Keep the fuel tank above one-quarter full, especially during seasons in which the temperature rises and falls by more than 20°F between daytime highs and nighttime lows. This helps to reduce condensed moisture in the fuel tank and could prevent gas line freeze-up in cold weather.

NOTE: Gas line freeze-up occurs when the water in the gasoline freezes and forms an ice blockage in the fuel line.

3. Do not purchase fuel with a higher octane rating than is necessary. Try using premium high-octane fuel to check for operating differences. Most newer engines are

FIGURE 24–16 Many gasoline service stations have signs posted warning customers to place plastic fuel containers on the ground while filling. If placed in a trunk or pickup truck bed equipped with a plastic liner, static electricity could build up during fueling and discharge from the container to the metal nozzle, creating a spark and possible explosion. Some service stations have warning signs not to use cell phones while fueling to help avoid the possibility of an accidental spark creating a fire hazard.

equipped with a detonation (knock) sensor that signals the vehicle computer to retard the ignition timing when spark knock occurs. Therefore, an operating difference may not be noticeable to the driver when using a low-octane fuel, except for a decrease in power and fuel economy. In other words, the engine with a knock sensor will tend to operate knock free on regular fuel, even if premium, higher-octane fuel is specified. Using premium fuel may result in more power and greater fuel economy. The increase in fuel economy, however, would have to be

substantial to justify the increased cost of high-octane premium fuel. Some drivers find a good compromise by using mid-grade (plus) fuel to benefit from the engine power and fuel economy gains without the cost of using premium fuel all the time.

4. Avoid using gasoline with alcohol in warm weather, even though many alcohol blends do not affect engine driveability. If warm-engine stumble, stalling, or rough idle occurs, change brand of gasoline.

5. Do not purchase fuel from a retail outlet when a tanker truck is filling the underground tanks. During the refilling procedure, dirt, rust, and water may be stirred up in the underground tanks. This undesirable material may be pumped into your vehicle's fuel tank.

6. Do not overfill the gas tank. After the nozzle clicks off, add just enough fuel to round up to the next dime. Adding additional gasoline will cause the excess to be drawn into the charcoal canister. This can lead to engine flooding and excessive exhaust emissions.

7. Be careful when filling gasoline containers. Always fill a gas can on the ground to help prevent the possibility of static electricity buildup during the refueling process. ● **SEE FIGURE 24–16.**

TECH TIP

Do Not Overfill the Fuel Tank

Gasoline fuel tanks have an expansion volume area at the top. The volume of this expansion area is equal to 10% to 15% of the volume of the tank. This area is normally not filled with gasoline, but rather is designed to provide a place for the gasoline to expand into, if the vehicle is parked in the hot sun and the gasoline expands. This prevents raw gasoline from escaping from the fuel system. A small restriction is usually present to control the amount of air and vapors that can escape the tank and flow to the charcoal canister.

This volume area could be filled with gasoline if the fuel is slowly pumped into the tank. Since it can hold an extra 10% (2 gallons in a 20-gallon tank), some people deliberately try to fill the tank completely. When this expansion volume is filled, liquid fuel (rather than vapors) can be drawn into the charcoal canister. When the purge valve opens, liquid fuel can be drawn into the engine, causing an excessively rich air–fuel mixture. Not only can this liquid fuel harm vapor recovery parts, but overfilling the gas tank could also cause the vehicle to fail an exhaust emission test, particularly during an enhanced test when the tank could be purged while on the rollers.

TESTING FOR ALCOHOL CONTENT IN GASOLINE

1 A fuel composition tester (SPX Kent-Moore J-44175) is the General Motors recommended tool to use when testing the alcohol content of gasoline.

2 This battery-powered tester uses light-emitting diodes (LEDs), meter lead terminals, and two small openings for the fuel sample.

3 The first step is to verify the proper operation of the tester by measuring the air frequency by selecting AC hertz on the meter. The air frequency should be between 35 and 48 Hz.

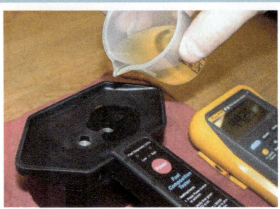

4 After verifying that the tester is capable of correctly reading the air frequency, gasoline is poured into the testing cell of the tool.

5 Record the AC frequency as shown on the meter and subtract 50 from the reading (e.g., 60.50 − 50.00 = 10.5). This number (10.5) is the percentage of alcohol in the gasoline sample.

6 Adding additional amounts of ethyl alcohol (ethanol) increases the frequency reading.

1. Gasoline is a complex blend of hydrocarbons. Gasoline is blended for seasonal usage to achieve the correct volatility for easy starting and maximum fuel economy under all driving conditions.
2. Winter-blend fuel used in a vehicle during warm weather can cause a rough idle and stalling because of its higher Reid vapor pressure (RVP).
3. Abnormal combustion (also called detonation or spark knock) increases both the temperature and the pressure inside the combustion chamber.
4. Most regular-grade gasoline today, using the $(R + M) \div 2$ rating method, is 87 octane; mid-grade (plus) is 89; and premium grade is 91 or higher.
5. Oxygenated fuels contain oxygen to lower CO exhaust emissions.
6. Gasoline should always be purchased from a busy station, and the tank should not be overfilled.

REVIEW QUESTIONS

1. What is the difference between summer-blend and winter-blend gasoline?
2. What is Reid vapor pressure?
3. What is vapor lock?
4. What does the $(R + M) \div 2$ gasoline pump octane rating indicate?
5. What are the octane improvers that may be used during the refining process?
6. What is stoichiometric ratio?

CHAPTER QUIZ

1. Winter-blend gasoline _____.
   a. Vaporizes more easily than summer-blend gasoline
   b. Has a higher RVP
   c. Can cause engine driveability problems if used during warm weather
   d. All of the above

2. Vapor lock can occur _____.
   a. As a result of excessive heat near fuel lines
   b. If a fuel line is restricted
   c. During both a and b
   d. During neither a nor b

3. Technician A says that spark knock, ping, and detonation are different names for abnormal combustion. Technician B says that any abnormal combustion raises the temperature and pressure inside the combustion chamber and can cause severe engine damage. Which technician is correct?
   a. Technician A only
   b. Technician B only
   c. Both Technicians A and B
   d. Neither Technician A nor B

4. Technician A says that the research octane number is higher than the motor octane number. Technician B says that the octane rating posted on fuel pumps is an average of the two ratings. Which technician is correct?
   a. Technician A only
   b. Technician B only
   c. Both Technicians A and B
   d. Neither Technician A nor B

5. Technician A says that in going to high altitudes, engines produce lower power. Technician B says that most engine control systems can compensate the air–fuel mixture for changes in altitude. Which technician is correct?
   a. Technician A only
   b. Technician B only
   c. Both Technicians A and B
   d. Neither Technician A nor B

6. Which method of blending ethanol with gasoline is the most accurate?
   a. In-line
   b. Sequential
   c. Splash
   d. All of the above

7. What can be used to measure the alcohol content in gasoline?
   a. graduated cylinder
   b. electronic tester
   c. scan tool
   d. either a or b

8. To avoid problems with the variation of gasoline, all government testing uses _____ as a fuel during testing procedures.
   a. MTBE (methyl tertiary butyl ether)
   b. Indolene
   c. Xylene
   d. TBA (tertiary butyl alcohol)

9. Avoid topping off the fuel tank because _____.
   a. It can saturate the charcoal canister
   b. The extra fuel simply spills onto the ground
   c. The extra fuel increases vehicle weight and reduces performance
   d. The extra fuel goes into the expansion area of the tank and is not used by the engine

10. Using ethanol-enhanced or reformulated gasoline can result in reduced fuel economy.
    a. True
    b. False

chapter 25

ALTERNATIVE FUELS

LEARNING OBJECTIVES

After studying this chapter, the reader should be able to:

1. List alternatives to gasoline.
2. Discuss how alternative fuels affect driveability.
3. Explain how alternative fuels can reduce CO exhaust emissions.
4. Discuss safety precautions when working with alternative fuels.

This chapter will help you prepare for Engine Repair (A8) ASE certification test content area "A" (General Engine Diagnosis).

GM STC OBJECTIVES

GM Service Technical College topics covered in this chapter are:

1. Describe the compressed natural gas system components and their operation.
2. Identify compressed natural gas vehicles, engines, and diagnostic procedures.
3. Recall compressed natural gas inspection and maintenance procedures.

KEY TERMS

AFV 397
Anhydrous ethanol 395
Biomass 400
Cellulose ethanol 395
Cellulosic biomass 396
Coal to liquid (CTL) 406
Compressed natural gas (CNG) 400
E85 396
Ethanol 395
Ethyl alcohol 395
FFV 397
Fischer-Tropsch 406
Flex Fuels 397
FTD 406
Fuel compensation sensor 397
Gas to liquid (GTL) 406

Grain alcohol 395
liquefied petroleum gas (LPG) 400
LP-gas 400
M85 400
Methanol 399
Methanol to gasoline (MTG) 407
NGV 400
Propane 400
Switchgrass 396
Syncrude 406
Syn-gas 399
Synthetic fuel 406
Underground coal gasification (UCG) 407
V-FFV 398
Variable fuel sensor 397

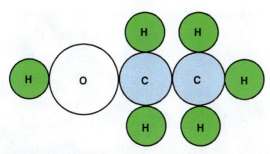

FIGURE 25–1 The ethanol molecule showing two carbon atoms, six hydrogen atoms, and one oxygen atom.

ETHANOL

ETHANOL TERMINOLOGY **Ethanol** is also called **ethyl alcohol** or **grain alcohol**, because it is usually made from grain and is the type of alcohol found in alcoholic drinks such as beer, wine, and distilled spirits like whiskey. Ethanol is composed of two carbon atoms and six hydrogen atoms with one added oxygen atom. ● **SEE FIGURE 25–1.**

ETHANOL PRODUCTION Conventional ethanol is derived from grains, such as corn, wheat, or soybeans. Corn, for example, is converted to ethanol in either a dry or wet milling process. In dry milling operations, liquefied cornstarch is produced by heating cornmeal with water and enzymes. A second enzyme converts the liquefied starch to sugars, which are fermented by yeast into ethanol and carbon dioxide. Wet milling operations separate the fiber, germ (oil), and protein from the starch before it is fermented into ethanol.

The majority of the ethanol in the United States is made from:

- Corn
- Grain
- Sorghum
- Wheat
- Barley
- Potatoes

In Brazil, the world's largest ethanol producer, it is made from sugarcane. Ethanol can be made by the dry mill process in which the starch portion of the corn is fermented into sugar and then distilled into alcohol.

The major steps in the dry mill process include:

1. **Milling.** The feedstock passes through a hammer mill that turns it into a fine powder called *meal*.

2. **Liquefaction.** The meal is mixed with water and then passed through cookers where the starch is liquefied. Heat is applied at this stage to enable liquefaction. Cookers use a high-temperature stage of about 250°F to 300°F (120°C to 150°C) to reduce bacteria levels and then a lower temperature of about 200°F (95°C) for a holding period.

3. **Saccharification.** The mash from the cookers is cooled and a secondary enzyme is added to convert the liquefied starch to fermentable sugars (dextrose).

4. **Fermentation.** Yeast is added to the mash to ferment the sugars to ethanol and carbon dioxide.

5. **Distillation.** The fermented mash, now called beer, contains about 10% alcohol plus all the nonfermentable solids from the corn and yeast cells. The mash is pumped to the continuous-flow, distillation system where the alcohol is removed from the solids and the water. The alcohol leaves the top of the final column at about 96% strength, and the residue mash, called *silage*, is transferred from the base of the column to the co-product processing area.

6. **Dehydration.** The alcohol from the top of the column passes through a dehydration system where the remaining water will be removed. The alcohol product at this stage is called **anhydrous ethanol** (pure, no more than 0.5% water).

7. **Denaturing.** Ethanol that will be used for fuel must be denatured, or made unfit for human consumption, with a small amount of gasoline (2% to 5%), methanol, or denatonium benzoate. This is done at the ethanol plant.

CELLULOSE ETHANOL

TERMINOLOGY **Cellulose ethanol** can be produced from a wide variety of cellulose biomass feedstock, including:

- Agricultural plant wastes (corn stalks, cereal straws)
- Plant wastes from industrial processes (sawdust, paper pulp)
- Energy crops grown specifically for fuel production.

These nongrain products are often referred to as **cellulosic biomass**. Cellulosic biomass is composed of cellulose and lignin, with smaller amounts of proteins, lipids (fats, waxes, and oils), and ash. About two-thirds of cellulosic materials are present as cellulose, with lignin making up the bulk of the remaining dry mass.

REFINING CELLULOSE BIOMASS As with grains, processing cellulose biomass involves extracting fermentable sugars from the feedstock. But the sugars in cellulose are locked in complex carbohydrates called polysaccharides (long chains of simple sugars). Separating these complex structures into fermentable sugars is needed to achieve the efficient and economic production of cellulose ethanol.

Two processing options are employed to produce fermentable sugars from cellulose biomass:

- Acid hydrolysis is used to break down the complex carbohydrates into simple sugars.
- Enzymes are employed to convert the cellulose biomass to fermentable sugars. The final step involves microbial fermentation, yielding ethanol and carbon dioxide.

NOTE: Cellulose ethanol production substitutes biomass for fossil fuels. The greenhouse gases produced by the combustion of biomass are offset by the CO_2 absorbed by the biomass as it grows in the field.

E85

E85 COMPOSITION Vehicle manufacturers have available vehicles that are capable of operating on gasoline plus ethanol or a combination of gasoline and ethanol called **E85**. E85 is composed of 85% ethanol and 15% gasoline.

Pure ethanol has an octane rating of about 113. E85, which contains 35% oxygen by weight, has an octane rating of about 100 to 105. This compares to a regular unleaded gasoline, which has a rating of 87. ● **SEE FIGURE 25–2**.

NOTE: The octane rating of E85 depends on the exact percentage of ethanol used, which can vary from 81% to 85%. It also depends on the octane rating of the gasoline used to make E85.

HEAT ENERGY OF E85 E85 has less heat energy than gasoline.

Gasoline = 114,000 BTUs per gallon

E85 = 87,000 BTUs per gallon

FIGURE 25–2 Some retail stations offer a variety of fuel choices, such as this station in Ohio where E10 and E85 are available.

 FREQUENTLY ASKED QUESTION

What Is Switchgrass?

Switchgrass (Panicum virgatum) can be used to make ethanol and is a summer perennial grass that is native to North America. It is a natural component of the tall-grass prairie, which covered most of the Great Plains, but was also found on the prairie soils in the Black Belt of Alabama and Mississippi. Switchgrass is resistant to many pests and plant diseases, and is capable of producing high yields with very low applications of fertilizer. This means that the need for agricultural chemicals to grow switchgrass is relatively low. Switchgrass is also very tolerant of poor soils, flooding, and drought, which are widespread agricultural problems in the southeast.

There are two main types of switchgrass:

- **Upland types** — usually grow five to six feet tall
- **Lowland types** — grow up to 12 feet tall and are typically found on heavy soils in bottomland sites

Better energy efficiency is gained because less energy is used to produce ethanol from switchgrass.

This means that the fuel economy is reduced by 20% to 30% if E85 is used instead of gasoline.

Example: A Chevrolet Tahoe 5.3-liter V-8 with an automatic transmission has an EPA rating of 15 mpg in the city and 20 mpg on the highway when using gasoline. If this same vehicle was fueled with E85, the EPA fuel economy rating drops to 11 mpg in the city and 15 mpg on the highway.

ALTERNATIVE-FUEL VEHICLES

The 15% gasoline in the E85 blend helps the engine start, especially in cold weather. Vehicles equipped with this capability are commonly referred to as **alternative-fuel vehicles (AFVs)**, **Flex Fuels**, and **flexible fuel vehicles (FFVs)**. Using E85 in a flex-fuel vehicle can result in a power increase of about 5%. For example, an engine rated at 200 hp using gasoline or E10 could produce 210 hp if using E85.

NOTE: E85 may test as containing less than 85% ethanol if tested in cold climates because it is often blended according to outside temperature. A lower percentage of ethanol with a slightly higher percentage of gasoline helps engines start in cold climates.

These vehicles are equipped with an electronic sensor in the fuel supply line that detects the presence and percentage of ethanol. The PCM then adjusts the fuel injector on-time and ignition timing to match the needs of the fuel being used.

E85 contains less heat energy, and therefore will use more fuel, but the benefits include a lower cost of the fuel and the environmental benefit associated with using an oxygenated fuel.

General Motors, Ford, Chrysler, Mazda, and Honda are a few of the manufacturers offering E85 compatible vehicles. E85 vehicles use fuel system parts designed to withstand the additional alcohol content, modified driveability programs that adjust fuel delivery and timing to compensate for the various percentages of ethanol fuel, and a **fuel compensation sensor** that measures both the percentage of ethanol blend and the temperature of the fuel. This sensor is also called a **variable fuel sensor** or **flex fuel sensor**.

FLEX FUEL - SENSOR[1]

The flex fuel sensor measures the ethanol–gasoline ratio of the fuel being used in a flexible fuel vehicle. In order to adjust the ignition timing and the fuel quantity to be injected, the engine management system requires information about the percentage of ethanol in the fuel. The flex fuel sensor measures the fuel alcohol content, and sends an electrical signal to the engine control module (ECM) to indicate the ethanol percentage.

The flex fuel sensor has a three-wire electrical harness connector. The three wires provide a ground circuit, a power source, and a signal output to the ECM. The power source is the battery positive voltage and the ground circuit connects

[1]GM SI Document # 2702265

FIGURE 25–3 The location of the variable fuel sensor (1) can vary, depending on the make and model of vehicle, but it is always in the fuel line between the fuel tank and the fuel injectors. (*Courtesy of General Motors*)

to an engine ground. The signal circuit carries the ethanol percentage via a frequency signal. ● **SEE FIGURE 25–3**.

The flex fuel sensor uses a microprocessor inside the sensor to measure the ethanol percentage and changes the output signal accordingly. The ECM provides an internal pull-up to 5 V on the signal circuit, and the flex-fuel sensor pulls the 5 V to ground in pulses. The normal range of operating frequency is between 50 Hz and 150 Hz, with 50 Hz representing 0% ethanol, and 150 Hz representing 100% ethanol.

NOTE: It is likely that the flex fuel sensor will indicate a slightly lower ethanol percentage than what is advertised at the fueling station. This is not a fault of the sensor. The reason has to do with government requirements for alcohol-based motor fuels. Government regulations require that alcohol intended for use as motor fuel be denatured. This means that 100% pure ethanol is first denatured with approximately 4.5% gasoline, before being mixed with anything else. When an ethanol–gasoline mixture is advertised as E85, the 85% ethanol is denatured before being blended with gasoline, which means that an advertised E85 fuel contains only about 81% ethanol. The flex fuel sensor measures the actual percentage of ethanol in the fuel.

E85 FUEL SYSTEM REQUIREMENTS

Most E85 vehicles are very similar to non-E85 vehicles. Fuel system components may be redesigned to withstand the effects

TECH TIP

Purchase a Flex fuel Vehicle

If purchasing a new or used vehicle, try to find a flex-fuel vehicle. Even though you may not want to use E85, a flex fuel vehicle has a more robust fuel system than a conventional fuel system designed for gasoline or E10. The enhanced fuel system components and materials usually include:

- Stainless steel fuel rail
- Graphite commutator bars instead of copper in the fuel pump motor (ethanol can oxidize into acetic acid, which can corrode copper)
- Diamond-like carbon (DLC) corrosion-resistant fuel injectors
- Alcohol-resistant O-rings and hoses

The cost of a flex fuel vehicle compared with the same vehicle designed to operate on gasoline is a no-cost or a low-cost option.

FIGURE 25–4 A pump for E85 (85% ethanol and 15% gasoline). E85 is available in more locations every year.

? FREQUENTLY ASKED QUESTION

How Does a Sensorless Flex fuel System Work?

Many General Motors flex fuel vehicles do not use a fuel compensation sensor and instead use the oxygen sensor to detect the presence of the lean mixture and the extra oxygen in the fuel.

The Powertrain Control Module (PCM) then adjusts the injector pulse-width and the ignition timing to optimize engine operation to the use of E85. This type of vehicle is called a **virtual flexible fuel vehicle (V-FFV)**. The virtual flexible fuel vehicle can operate on pure gasoline or blends up to 85% ethanol.

of higher concentrations of ethanol. In addition, since the stoichiometric point for ethanol is 9:1 instead of 14.7:1 as for gasoline, the air–fuel mixture has to be adjusted for the percentage of ethanol present in the fuel tank. In order to determine this percentage of ethanol in the fuel tank, a compensation sensor is used. The fuel compensation sensor is the only additional piece of hardware required on some E85 vehicles. The fuel compensation sensor provides both the ethanol percentage and the fuel temperature to the PCM. The PCM uses this information to adjust both the ignition timing and the quantity of fuel delivered to the engine. The fuel compensation sensor uses a microprocessor to measure both the ethanol percentage and the fuel temperature. This information is sent to the PCM on the signal circuit. The compensation sensor produces a square wave frequency and pulse width signal. The normal frequency range of the fuel compensation sensor is 50 hertz, which represents 0% ethanol, to 150 hertz, which represents 100% ethanol. The pulse width of the signal varies from 1 to 5 milliseconds. One millisecond would represent a fuel temperature of –40°F (–40°C), and 5 milliseconds would represent a fuel temperature of 257°F (125°C). Since the PCM knows both the fuel temperature and the ethanol percentage of the fuel, it can adjust fuel quantity and ignition timing for optimum performance and emissions.

The benefits of E85 vehicles are less pollution, less CO_2 production, and less dependence on oil. ● **SEE FIGURE 25–4.**

Ethanol-fueled vehicles generally produce the same pollutants as gasoline vehicles; however, they produce less CO and CO_2 emissions. While CO_2 is not considered a pollutant, it is thought to lead to global warming and is called a greenhouse gas.

FLEX FUEL VEHICLE IDENTIFICATION   Flexible fuel vehicles (FFVs) can be identified by:

- Emblems on the side, front, and/or rear of the vehicle
- Yellow fuel cap showing E85/gasoline (● **SEE FIGURE 25–5**)
- Vehicle emission control information (VECI) label under the hood (● **SEE FIGURE 25–6**)
- Vehicle identification number (VIN)

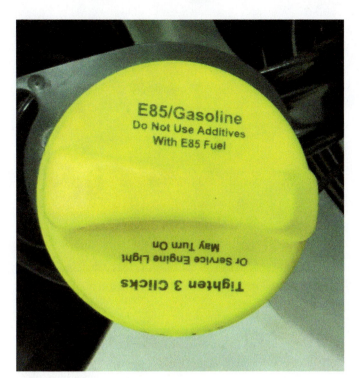

FIGURE 25–5 A flex fuel vehicle often has a yellow gas cap, which is labeled E85/gasoline. (*Courtesy of Tim Wawerczyk*)

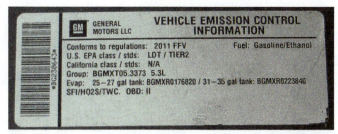

FIGURE 25–6 A vehicle emission control information (VECI) sticker on a flexible fuel vehicle. (*Courtesy of Tim Wawerczyk*)

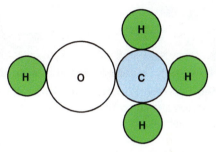

FIGURE 25–7 The molecular structure of methanol showing one carbon atom, four hydrogen atoms, and one oxygen atom.

TECH TIP

Avoid Resetting Fuel Compensation

Starting 2006, many General Motors vehicles designed to operate on E85 did not use a fuel compensation sensor, but instead use the oxygen sensor and refueling information to calculate the percentage of ethanol in the fuel. The PCM uses the fuel level sensor to sense that fuel has been added and starts to determine the resulting ethanol content by using the oxygen sensor. However, if a service technician were to reset fuel compensation by clearing long-term fuel trim, the PCM starts the calculation based on base fuel, which is gasoline with less than or equal to 10% ethanol (E10). If the fuel tank has E85, then the fuel compensation cannot be determined unless the tank is drained and refilled with base fuel. Therefore, avoid resetting the fuel compensation setting unless it is known that the fuel tank contains gasoline or E10 only.

? FREQUENTLY ASKED QUESTION

How Long Can Oxygenated Fuel Be Stored Before All of the Oxygen Escapes?

The oxygen in oxygenated fuels, such as E10 and E85, is not in a gaseous state like the CO_2 in soft drinks. The oxygen is part of the molecule of ethanol or other oxygenates and does not bubble out of the fuel. Oxygenated fuels, just like any fuel, have a shelf life of about 90 days.

Methanol is a light, volatile, colorless, tasteless, flammable, poisonous liquid with a very faint odor. It is used as an antifreeze, a solvent, and a fuel. It is also used to denature ethanol. Methanol burns in air, forming CO_2 (carbon dioxide) and H_2O (water). A methanol flame is almost colorless. Because of its poisonous properties, methanol is also used to denature ethanol. Methanol is often called wood alcohol because it was once produced chiefly as a by-product of the destructive distillation of wood. ● **SEE FIGURE 25–8.**

METHANOL

METHANOL TERMINOLOGY **Methanol,** also known as *methyl alcohol*, *wood alcohol*, or *methyl hydrate,* is a chemical compound that includes one carbon atom, four hydrogen atoms, and one oxygen atom. ● **SEE FIGURE 25–7.**

PRODUCTION OF METHANOL The biggest source of methanol in the United States is coal. Using a simple reaction between coal and steam, a gas mixture called **syn-gas** (*synthesis gas*) is formed. The components of this mixture are carbon monoxide and hydrogen, which, through an additional chemical reaction, are converted to methanol.

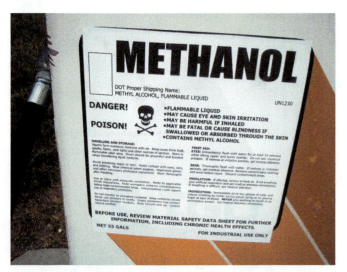

FIGURE 25–8 Sign on methanol pump shows that methyl alcohol is a poison and can cause skin irritation and other personal injury. Methanol is used in industry beside being a fuel.

FIGURE 25–9 Propane fuel storage tank in the trunk of a taxi.

Natural gas can also be used to create methanol and is re-formed or converted to synthesis gas, which is later made into methanol.

Biomass can be converted to synthesis gas by a process called partial oxidation, and later converted to methanol. **Biomass** is organic material, such as:

- Urban wood wastes
- Primary mill residues
- Forest residues
- Agricultural residues
- Dedicated energy crops (e.g., sugarcane and sugar beets) that can be made into fuel

Electricity can be used to convert water into hydrogen, which is then reacted with carbon dioxide to produce methanol.

Methanol is toxic and can cause blindness and death. It can enter the body by ingestion, inhalation, or absorption through the skin. Dangerous doses will build up if a person is regularly exposed to fumes or handles liquid without skin protection. If methanol has been ingested, a doctor should be contacted immediately. The usual fatal dose is 4 fl oz (100 to 125 mL).

M85 Some flexible fuel vehicles are designed to operate on 85% methanol and 15% gasoline called **M85**. Methanol is very corrosive and requires that the fuel system components be constructed of stainless steel and other alcohol-resistant rubber and plastic components. The heat content of M85 is about 60% of that of gasoline.

PROPANE

Propane is the most widely used of all of the alternative fuels. Propane is normally a gas but is easily compressed into a liquid and stored in inexpensive containers. When sold as a fuel, it is also known as **liquefied petroleum gas (LPG)** or **LP-gas** because the propane is often mixed with about 10% of other gases such as butane, propylene, butylenes, and mercaptan to give the colorless and odorless propane a smell. Propane is nontoxic, but if inhaled can cause asphyxiation through lack of oxygen. Propane is heavier than air and lays near the floor if released into the atmosphere. Propane is commonly used in forklifts and other equipment used inside warehouses and factories because the exhaust from the engine using propane is not harmful. Propane is a by-product of petroleum refining of natural gas. In order to liquefy the fuel, it is stored in strong tanks at about 300 PSI (2,000 kPa). The heating value of propane is less than that of gasoline; therefore, more is required, which reduces the fuel economy. ● **SEE FIGURE 25–9.**

COMPRESSED NATURAL GAS (CNG)

CNG VEHICLE DESIGN Another alternative fuel that is often used in fleet vehicles is **compressed natural gas (CNG)**, and vehicles using this fuel are often referred to as **natural gas vehicles (NGVs)**. Look for the blue CNG label on vehicles designed to operate on compressed natural gas. ● **SEE FIGURE 25–10.**

FIGURE 25–10 The blue sticker on the rear of this vehicle indicates that it is designed to use compressed natural gas.

Natural gas has to be compressed to about 3000 PSI (20,000 kPa) or more, so that the weight and the cost of the storage container is a major factor when it comes to preparing a vehicle to run on CNG. The tanks needed for CNG are typically constructed of 0.5 inch-thick (3 mm) aluminum reinforced with fiberglass. The octane rating of CNG is about 130 and the cost per gallon is about half of the cost of gasoline. However, the heat value of CNG is also less, and therefore more is required to produce the same power and the miles per gallon is less.

CNG COMPOSITION

Compressed natural gas is made up of a blend of:

- Methane
- Propane
- Ethane
- N-butane
- Carbon dioxide
- Nitrogen

Once it is processed, it is at least 93% methane. Natural gas is nontoxic, odorless, and colorless in its natural state. It is odorized during processing, using ethyl mercaptan ("skunk"), to allow for easy leak detection. Natural gas is lighter than air and will rise when released into the air. Since CNG is already a vapor, it does not need heat to vaporize before it will burn, which improves cold start-up and results in lower emissions during cold operation. However, because it is already in a gaseous state, it does displace some of the air charge in the intake manifold. This leads to about a 10% reduction in engine power as compared to an engine operating on gasoline. Natural gas also burns slower than gasoline; therefore, the ignition timing must be advanced more when the vehicle operates on natural gas. The stoichiometric ratio, the point at which all the air and fuel are used or burned, is 16.5:1 compared to 14.7:1 for gasoline.

This means that more air is required to burn one pound of natural gas than is required to burn one pound of gasoline.

The CNG engine is designed to include:

- Increased compression ratio
- Strong pistons and connecting rods
- Heat-resistant valves
- Fuel injectors designed for gaseous fuel instead of liquid fuel

CNG FUEL SYSTEMS

When completely filled, the CNG tanks have about 3600 PSI of pressure in the tanks. Fuel flow begins when the ignition is turned on and the high pressure lock-off (HPL) and the high pressure regulator (HPR) solenoids open. The HPR is supplied with fuel at pressures up to 3,600 psi, or 24,821 kPa, at 70°F (21°C). The outlet pressure is regulated to 90-110 psi and delivered through the low pressure lines to the fuel rail and CNG injectors. ● **SEE FIGURES 25-11 AND 25-12.**

The CNG fuel injectors are installed in the base vehicle fuel rail and require spacers between the injector and manifold injector boss. The ECM controls fuel delivery in the same manner as a gasoline vehicle. The CNG fuel system also features the same powertrain diagnostics and use of the Tech 2 scan tool as a gasoline engine. There are not any new DTCs. Follow the standard repair protocol as with a gasoline vehicle. Refer to SI for specific CNG information.

The high pressure CNG fuel system is equipped with a manually operated 1/4 turn isolation valve. The valve can isolate the high pressure side of the fuel system for some service procedures. If the valve is inadvertently left in the Off position, the vehicle will not operate.

The CNG fuel filter a high pressure coalescing media filter, is located forward of the CNG 1/4 turn isolation valve. It requires periodic service intervals.

NOTE: When the fuel supply system needs to be opened, the pressure in the lines must be relieved before attempting repairs. Refer to SI for the low pressure side and high pressure side relief procedures.

CNG vehicles are designed for fleet use that usually have their own refueling capabilities. One of the drawbacks to using CNG is the time that it takes to refuel a vehicle. The ideal method of refueling is the slow fill method. The slow filling method compresses the natural gas as the tank is being fueled. This method ensures that the tank will receive a full charge of CNG; however, this method can take three to five hours to accomplish. If more than one vehicle needs filling, the facility will need multiple CNG compressors to refuel the vehicles.

There are three commonly used CNG refilling station pressures:

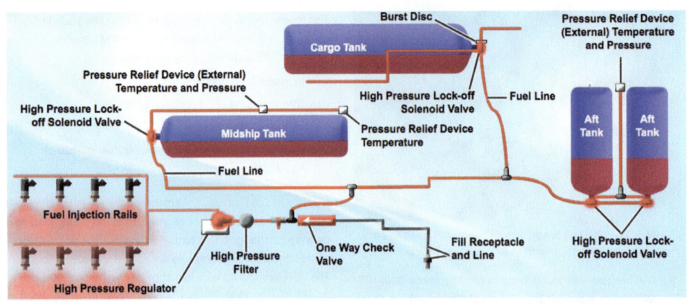

FIGURE 25–11 A delivery van CNG fuel system showing all of the components. (*Courtesy of General Motors*)

FIGURE 25–12 The fuel injectors used on CNG engines are designed to flow gaseous fuel instead of liquid fuel and cannot be interchanged with any other type of injector. (*Courtesy of General Motors*)

What Is the Amount of CNG Equal to in Gasoline?

To achieve the amount of energy of one gallon of gasoline, 122 cubic feet of compressed natural gas (CNG) is needed. While the octane rating of CNG is much higher than gasoline (130 octane), using CNG instead of gasoline in the same engine would result in a reduction 10% to 20% of power due to the lower heat energy that is released when CNG is burned in the engine.

FIGURE 25–13 This CNG pump is capable of supplying compressed natural gas at either 3000 PSI or 3600 PSI. The price per gallon is higher for the higher pressure.

P24 — 2400 PSI

P30 — 3000 PSI

P36 — 3600 PSI

Try to find and use a station with the highest refilling pressure. Filling at lower pressures will result in less compressed natural gas being installed in the storage tank, thereby reducing the driving range. ● **SEE FIGURE 25–13.**

The fast fill method uses CNG that is already compressed. However, as the CNG tank is filled rapidly, the internal temperature of the tank will rise, which causes a rise in tank pressure. Once the temperature drops in the CNG tank, the pressure in the tank also drops, resulting in an incomplete charge in the CNG tank. This refueling method may take only about five minutes; however, it will result in an incomplete charge to the CNG tank, reducing the driving range.

CNG SAFETY PROCEDURES[2]

When indoors, work only in a well-ventilated area and ensure that there are no overhead sources of combustion. Make sure that the indoor heating system is not an open-flame type heating system.

In case of a natural gas fire, the first step is to stop the fuel flow if possible. Extinguish natural gas flames using a carbon dioxide or dry chemical fire extinguisher. If the fire extinguisher cannot quickly extinguish the flames or if the fire is too great to attempt to extinguish, evacuate the area immediately and call the fire department.

PERSONAL SAFETY A full compressed natural gas (CNG) fuel tank holds the fuel at approximately 3,000 to 3,600 pound-force per square inch (207 to 248 bar) and, when released, it will feel extremely cold to the touch. CNG should never be released in a manner where the gas encounters the eyes. It is important to wear safety glasses to protect the eyes and safety gloves to protect the skin. Hearing protection is recommended for venting operations. Always refer to service information for the proper procedures.

BREATHING NATURAL GAS Natural gas is not harmful to anyone breathing low concentrations near minor fuel leaks. However, breathing heavy concentrations, particularly in confined areas with no ventilation, can cause drowsiness and eventual asphyxiation. As a safety measure, an unpleasant odor, similar to propane, is added to ensure that the natural gas is detected in the atmosphere whenever its concentration reaches about 0.5%. This amount is well below the level that causes drowsiness and significantly below the weakest mixture that enables combustion.

CNG FUEL TANKS[3]

Natural gas fuel tanks are required to be more puncture and rupture resistant than standard liquid fuel tanks. If a natural gas tank ruptures, the gas escapes at an extremely high rate, which could cause personal injury. It is normal to smell or detect a slight natural gas odor right after the CNG vehicle is turned off. However, if a strong, persistent natural gas odor is detected, or a hissing sound is heard, the CNG fuel system may have a leak.

---

[2]GM STC Course # 16240.62W
[3]GM STC Course # 16240.62W

TANK TYPES In the CNG industry, the four types of containers, or tanks, are Type 1, 2, 3, and 4.

- Type 1 tanks, which General Motors uses, are steel cylinders with no over-wrap.
- Type 2 tanks are steel cylinders reinforced with a wrap of typically fiberglass or carbon fiber. This adds integrity to the tank.
- Type 3 tanks are aluminum cylinders reinforced with fiberglass overwrap.
- Type 4 tanks are all composite with no metallic liners.

LOW-PRESSURE FUEL SHUT OFF If a low pressure concern occurs while operating the CNG vehicle, the CNG fuel supply should be shut off. To shut off the fuel supply, turn the 1/4 turn isolation valve clockwise to the OFF, or closed, position. This valve is located on the frame rail just below the driver's door. The arrow on the handle will point toward the front of the vehicle.

HIGH-PRESSURE FUEL SHUT OFF If a high pressure concern occurs while operating the CNG vehicle, the CNG fuel supply should be shut off. The manual shut-off valve is located on the high-pressure lock off, which is on each fuel tank. Turn the valve clockwise to shut off the fuel flow.

CNG TANK INSPECTION AND SERVICE LIFE During normal vehicle operation, inspect a CNG fuel tank approximately every three years or 57,900 kilometers (km) or 36,000 miles (mi). Also inspect the tank after a vehicle equipped with a CNG tank or tanks, has caught fire or was in an accident. Record the inspection information in the CNG Fuel Tank Inspection Record in the Owner's Manual supplement. In addition, if exposure to corrosive chemicals, such as acid or alkali has occurred, remove the tank for inspection.

The service life of CNG tanks is 15 years from the date of manufacture as stated on the tank label. Regardless of appearance, replace the tanks when the time limit has been reached. ● **SEE FIGURE 25–14.**

GENERAL MOTORS BI-FUEL SYSTEM[4]

General Motors bi-fuel systems use a combination of CNG fuel and traditional gasoline systems. This system is available on 2500 Heavy Duty (HD) extended cab trucks with 6.0 Liter (L)

---

[4]GM STC Course # 16240.70W

FIGURE 25–14 CNG tanks have a limited life span and must be replaced according to the date on the tank label. (*Courtesy of General Motors*)

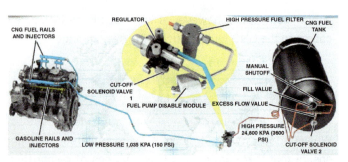

FIGURE 25–15 The Bi-Fuel system includes a normal gas fuel injection system with the CNG system added. (*Courtesy of General Motors*)

🔧 **TECH TIP**

CNG Association Inspection Web site

For additional questions on CNG tank inspection, consult the Compressed Gas Association Web site. Once there, click "Publication Locator," then click on the Title Word Search and search for the document "Methods for External Visual Inspection of Natural Gas Vehicle (NGV) and Hydrogen Vehicle (HV) Fuel Containers and Their Installations." For the latest information on General Motors CNG programs, refer to the General Motors Alternate Fuel web site.

---

engines. For RPO LC8, the VIN code is B. To meet the needs of a broad range of customers, the bi-fuel system trucks are available with long or short beds and either 2-Wheel Drive (2WD) or 4-Wheel Drive (4WD).

Bi-fuel trucks are equipped with the Vortec 6.0L LC8 V-8 engine. This engine contains hardened intake and exhaust valve seat inserts to ensure an excellent seal between the valve and valve seat. The exhaust valve is hardened to resist the higher temperatures and corrosiveness of natural gas.

The bi-fuel system has one CNG tank housed in the bed of the pickup truck. Mounted directly to the frame, the Type 3 CNG tank is made of lightweight composite materials, with an aluminum liner and carbon fiber wrap. The tank's capacity is 66.6L, or 17 Gasoline Gallon Equivalent (GGE).

The tank cover is aluminum with a diamond plate pattern. It has a graphite powdercoat finish for durability. For easy access, the fuel filler door is located on the driver's side of the tank cover, above the bed top rail. This location helps protect the tank from side impact crashes. The manual shutoff valve is also located under the cover. ● **SEE FIGURE 25–15**.

BI-FUEL SYSTEM OPERATION General Motors bi-fuel systems use a combination of CNG fuel and traditional gasoline systems. The bi-fuel system operates on either gasoline or CNG. The vehicle contains a complete gasoline and CNG fuel system. Vehicles equipped with the bi-fuel system always start on gasoline and switch to CNG when conditions are appropriate, usually within 2 minutes. The change over to CNG occurs based on predetermined operating temperatures. The fuel source may also be manually switched to gasoline at any time. The CNG system cannot be turned on manually. The CNG fuel indicator is located on the dash to indicate the CNG level in the tank.

NO START CONDITION Because a bi-fuel vehicle always starts and runs on the gasoline fuel system for a short time, the CNG fuel system cannot be the cause of a no start concern. As with any vehicle, begin diagnosis of the vehicle by performing the Diagnostic System Check.

LIQUEFIED NATURAL GAS (LNG)

Natural gas can be turned into liquid if cooled to below −260°F (−127°C). The natural gas condenses into liquid at normal atmospheric pressure and the volume is reduced by about 600 times. This means that natural gas can be more efficiently transported over long distances where no pipelines are present.

Because the temperature of liquefied natural gas (LNG) must be kept low, it is only practical for use in short haul trucks where they can be refueled from a central location.

P-SERIES FUELS

P-series alternative fuel is patented by Princeton University and is a non-petroleum- or natural gas-based fuel suitable for use in flexible fuel vehicles or any vehicle designed to operate on E85 (85% ethanol, 15% gasoline). P-series fuel is recognized by the U.S. Department of Energy as being an alternative fuel, but is not yet available to the public. P-series fuels are blends of the following:

- Ethanol (ethyl alcohol)
- Methyltetrahydrofuron (MTHF)

COMPOSITION OF P-SERIES FUELS (BY VOLUME)

COMPONENT	REGULAR GRADE (%)	PREMIUM GRADE (%)	COLD WEATHER (%)
Pentanes plus	32.5	27.5	16.0
MTHF	32.5	17.5	26.0
Ethanol	35.0	55.0	47.0
Butane	0.0	0.0	11.0

CHART 25–1

P-series fuel varies in composition, depending on the octane rating and temperature.

- Natural gas liquids, such as pentanes
- Butane

The ethanol and MTHF are produced from renewable feedstocks, such as corn, waste paper, biomass, agricultural waste, and wood waste (scraps and sawdust). The components used in P-type fuel can be varied to produce regular grade, premium grade, or fuel suitable for cold climates. ● **SEE CHART 25–1** for the percentages of the ingredients based on fuel grade.

● **SEE CHART 25–2** for a comparison of the most frequently used alternative fuels.

 FREQUENTLY ASKED QUESTION

What Is a Tri-Fuel Vehicle?

In Brazil, most vehicles are designed to operate on ethanol or gasoline or any combination of the two. In this South American country, ethanol is made from sugarcane, is commonly available, and is lower in price than gasoline. CNG is also being made available so many vehicle manufacturers in Brazil, such as General Motors, are equipping vehicles to be capable of using gasoline, ethanol, or CNG. These vehicles are called tri-fuel vehicles.

ALTERNATIVE FUEL COMPARISON CHART

CHARACTERISTIC	PROPANE	CNG	METHANOL	ETHANOL	REGULAR UNLEADED GAS
Octane	104	130	100	100	87–93
BTU per gallon	91,000	N.A.	70,000	83,000	114,000–125,000
Gallon equivalent	1.15	122 cubic feet—1 gallon of gasoline	1.8	1.5	1
On-board fuel storage	Liquid	Gas	Liquid	Liquid	Liquid
Miles/gallon as compared to gas	85%	N.A.	55%	70%	100%
Relative tank size required to yield driving range equivalent to gas	Tank is 1.25 times larger	Tank is 3.5 times larger	Tank is 1.8 times larger	Tank is 1.5 times larger	
Pressure	200 PSI	3000–3600 PSI	N.A.	N.A.	N.A.
Cold weather capability	Good	Good	Poor	Poor	Good
Vehicle power	5–10% power loss	10–20% power loss	4% power increase	5% power increase	Standard
Toxicity	Nontoxic	Nontoxic	Highly toxic	Toxic	Toxic
Corrosiveness	Noncorrosive	Noncorrosive	Corrosive	Corrosive	Minimally corrosive
Source	Natural gas/petroleum refining	Natural gas/crude oil	Natural gas/coal	Sugar and starch crops/biomass	Crude oil

CHART 25–2

The characteristics of alternative fuels compared to regular unleaded gasoline shows that all have advantages and disadvantages.

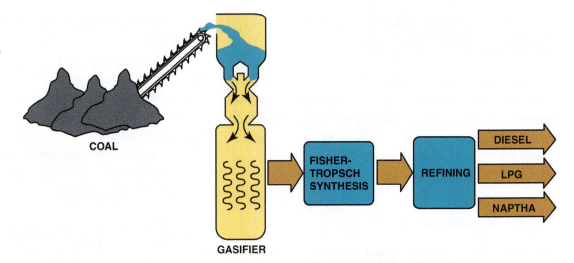

FIGURE 25–16 A Fischer-Tropsch processing plant is able to produce a variety of fuels from coal.

SYNTHETIC FUELS

Synthetic fuels can be made from a variety of products, using several different processes. Synthetic fuel must, however, make these alternatives practical only when conventional petroleum products are either very expensive or not available.

FISCHER-TROPSCH   Synthetic fuels were first developed using the **Fischer-Tropsch** method and have been in use since the 1920s to convert coal, natural gas, and other fossil fuel products into a fuel that is high in quality and clean burning. The process for producing Fischer-Tropsch fuels was patented by two German scientists, Franz Fischer and Hans Tropsch, during World War I. The Fischer-Tropsch method uses carbon monoxide and hydrogen (the same synthesis gas used to produce hydrogen fuel) to convert coal and other hydrocarbons to liquid fuels in a process similar to hydrogenation, another method for hydrocarbon conversion. The process using natural gas, also called **gas-to-liquid (GTL)** technology, uses a catalyst, usually iron or cobalt, and incorporates steam re-forming to give off the by-products of carbon dioxide, hydrogen, and carbon monoxide. ● **SEE FIGURE 25–16**.

Whereas traditional fuels emit environment-harmful particulates and chemicals, namely sulfur compounds, Fischer-Tropsch fuels combust with no soot or odors and emit only low levels of toxins. Fischer-Tropsch fuels can also be blended with traditional transportation fuels with little equipment modification, as they use the same engine and equipment technology as traditional fuels.

The fuels contain a very low sulfur and aromatic content and they produce virtually no particulate emissions. Researchers also expect reductions in hydrocarbon and carbon monoxide emissions. Fischer-Tropsch fuels do not differ in fuel performance from gasoline and diesel. At present, Fischer-Tropsch fuels are very expensive to produce on a large scale, although research is under way to lower processing costs. Diesel fuel created using the Fischer-Tropsch diesel (**FTD**) process is often called *GTL diesel*. GTL diesel can also be combined with petroleum diesel to produce a GTL blend. This fuel product is currently being sold in Europe and plans are in place to introduce it in North America.

COAL TO LIQUID (CTL)   Coal is abundant in the United States and can be converted to a liquid fuel through a process called **coal to liquid (CTL)**. The huge cost is the main obstacle to these plants. The need to invest $1.4 billion per plant before starting production is the reason no one has built a CTL plant yet in the United States. Investors need to be convinced that the cost of oil is going to remain high in order to get them to commit this kind of money.

A large plant might be able to produce 120,000 barrels of liquid fuel a day and would consume about 50,000 tons of coal per day. However, such a plant would create about 6,000 tons of CO_2 per day. These CO_2 emissions, which could contribute to global warming, and the cost involved make CTL a technology that is not likely to expand.

Two procedures can be used to convert coal-to-liquid fuel:

1. **Direct** — In the direct method, coal is broken down to create liquid products. First, the coal is reacted with hydrogen (H_2) at high temperatures and pressure with a catalyst. This process creates a synthetic crude, called **syncrude**, which is then refined to produce gasoline or diesel fuel.

2. **Indirect** — In the indirect method, coal is first turned into gas and the molecules are reassembled to create the desired product. This process involves turning coal into a gas called syn-gas. The syngas is then converted into liquid, using the Fischer-Tropsch (FT) process.

Russia has been using CTL by injecting air into the underground coal seams. Ignition is provided and the resulting gases are trapped and converted to liquid gasoline and diesel fuel through the Fischer-Tropsch process. This underground method is called **underground coal gasification (UCG)**.

METHANOL TO GASOLINE

Exxon Mobil has developed a process for converting methanol (methyl alcohol) into gasoline in a process called **methanol-to-gasoline (MTG)**. The MTG process was discovered by accident when a gasoline additive made from methanol was being created. The process instead created olefins (alkenes), paraffins (alkenes), and aromatic compounds, which in combination are known as gasoline. The process uses a catalyst and is currently being produced in New Zealand.

FUTURE OF SYNTHETIC FUELS

Producing gasoline and diesel fuels by other methods besides refining from crude oil has usually been more expensive. With the increasing cost of crude oil, alternative methods are now becoming economically feasible. Whether or not the diesel fuel or gasoline is created from coal, natural gas, or methanol, or created by refining crude oil, the transportation and service pumps are already in place. Compared to using compressed natural gas or other similar alternative fuels, synthetic fuels represent the lowest cost.

SAFETY PROCEDURES WHEN WORKING WITH ALTERNATIVE FUELS

All fuels are flammable and many are explosive under certain conditions. Whenever working around compressed gases of any kind (CNG, LNG, propane, or LPG), always wear personal protective equipment (PPE), including at least the following items:

1. Safety glasses and/or face shield.
2. Protective gloves.
3. Long-sleeved shirt and pants to help protect bare skin from the freezing effects of gases under pressure in the event that the pressure is lost.
4. If any fuel gets on the skin, the area should be washed immediately.
5. If fuel spills on clothing, change into clean clothing as soon as possible.
6. If fuel spills on a painted surface, flush the surface with water and air dry. If simply wiped off with a dry cloth, the paint surface could be permanently damaged.
7. As with any fuel-burning vehicle, always vent the exhaust to the outside. If methanol fuel is used, the exhaust contains *formaldehyde*, which has a sharp odor and can cause severe burning of the eyes, nose, and throat.

WARNING

Do not smoke or have an open flame in the area when working around or refueling any vehicle.

SUMMARY

1. Flexible fuel vehicles (FFVs) are designed to operate on gasoline or gasoline-ethanol blends up to 85% ethanol (E85).
2. Ethanol can be made from grain, such as corn, or from cellulosic biomass, such as switchgrass.
3. E85 has fewer BTUs of energy per gallon compared with gasoline and will therefore provide lower fuel economy.
4. Flexible fuel vehicles may use a flex-fuel sensor or the oxygen sensor and and the PCM to calculate the percentage of ethanol in the fuel being burned.
5. Methanol is also called methyl alcohol or wood alcohol and, while it can be made from wood, it is mostly made from natural gas.
6. Propane is the most widely used alternative fuel. Propane is also called liquefied petroleum gas (LPG).

7. Compressed natural gas (CNG) is available for refilling at several pressures, including 2400 PSI, 3000 PSI, and 3600 PSI.
8. P-series fuel is recognized by the U.S. Department of Energy as being an alternative fuel. P-series fuel is a non-petroleum-based fuel suitable for use in a flexible fuel vehicle. However, P-series fuel is not commercially available.
9. Synthetic fuels are usually made using the Fischer-Tropsch method to convert coal or natural gas into gasoline and diesel fuel.
10. Safety procedures when working around alternative fuel include wearing the necessary personal protective equipment (PPE), including safety glasses and protective gloves.

REVIEW QUESTIONS

1. Ethanol is also known by what other names?
2. The majority of ethanol in the United States is made from what farm products?
3. How is a flexible fuel vehicle identified?
4. Methanol is also known by what other names?
5. What other gases are often mixed with propane?
6. Why is it desirable to fill a compressed natural gas (CNG) vehicle with the highest pressure available?
7. P-series fuel is made of what products?
8. The Fischer-Tropsch method can be used to change what into gasoline?

CHAPTER QUIZ

1. Ethanol can be produced from what products?
   a. Switchgrass
   b. Corn
   c. Sugarcane
   d. Any of the above

2. E85 means that the fuel is made from _____.
   a. 85% gasoline, 15% ethanol
   b. 85% ethanol, 15% gasoline
   c. Ethanol that has 15% water
   d. Pure ethyl alcohol

3. A flex-fuel vehicle can be identified by _____.
   a. Emblems on the side, front, and/or rear of the vehicle
   b. VECI
   c. VIN
   d. Any of the above

4. Methanol is also called _____.
   a. Methyl alcohol
   b. Wood alcohol
   c. Methyl hydrate
   d. All of the above

5. Which alcohol is dangerous (toxic)?
   a. Methanol
   b. Ethanol
   c. Both ethanol and methanol
   d. Neither ethanol nor methanol

6. Which is the most widely used alternative fuel?
   a. E85
   b. Propane
   c. CNG
   d. M85

7. Liquefied petroleum gas (LPG) is also called _____.
   a. E85
   b. M85
   c. Propane
   d. P-series fuel

8. How much compressed natural gas (CNG) does it require to achieve the energy of one gallon of gasoline?
   a. 130 cubic feet
   b. 122 cubic feet
   c. 105 cubic feet
   d. 91 cubic feet

9. When refueling a CNG vehicle, why is it recommended that the tank be filled to a high pressure?
   a. The range of the vehicle is increased
   b. The cost of the fuel is lower
   c. Less of the fuel is lost to evaporation
   d. Both a and c

10. Producing liquid fuel from coal or natural gas usually uses which process?
    a. Syncrude
    b. P-series
    c. Fischer-Tropsch
    d. Methanol to gasoline (MTG)

chapter 26
DIESEL AND BIODIESEL FUELS

LEARNING OBJECTIVES

After studying this chapter, the reader should be able to:

1. Explain diesel fuel specifications.
2. List the advantages and disadvantages of biodiesel.
3. Discuss API gravity.
4. Explain E-diesel specifications.

This chapter will help you prepare for Engine Repair (A8) ASE certification test content area "A" (General Engine Diagnosis).

KEY TERMS

API gravity 411	E-diesel 414
ASTM 410	Petrodiesel 413
B20 412	PPO 413
Biodiesel 412	SVO 413
Cloud point 410	UCO 413
Diesohol 414	WVO 413

GM STC OBJECTIVES

GM Service Technical College topic covered in this chapter is:

1. Perform a diesel engine fuel quality check.

DIESEL FUEL

FEATURES OF DIESEL FUEL Diesel fuel must meet an entirely different set of standards than gasoline. Diesel fuel contains 12% more heat energy than the same amount of gasoline. The fuel in a diesel engine is not ignited with a spark, but is ignited by the heat generated by high compression. The pressure of compression (400 to 700 PSI or 2,800 to 4,800 kilopascals) generates temperatures of 1200°F to 1600°F (700°C to 900°C), which speeds the preflame reaction to start the ignition of the fuel injected into the cylinder.

DIESEL FUEL REQUIREMENTS All diesel fuels must have the following characteristics:

- **Cleanliness.** It is imperative that the fuel used in a diesel engine be clean and free from water. Unlike the case with gasoline engines, the fuel is the lubricant and coolant for the diesel injector pump and injectors. Good-quality diesel fuel contains additives such as oxidation inhibitors, detergents, dispersants, rust preventatives, and metal deactivators.

- **Low-temperature fluidity.** Diesel fuel must be able to flow freely at all expected ambient temperatures. One specification for diesel fuel is its "pour point," which is the temperature below which the fuel would stop flowing.

- **Cloud point** is another concern with diesel fuel at lower temperatures. Cloud point is the low-temperature point when the waxes present in most diesel fuels tend to form crystals that can clog the fuel filter. Most diesel fuel suppliers distribute fuel with the proper pour point and cloud point for the climate conditions of the area.

CETANE NUMBER The cetane number for diesel fuel is the opposite of the octane number for gasoline. The cetane number is a measure of the ease with which the fuel can be ignited. The cetane rating of the fuel determines, to a great extent, its ability to start the engine at low temperatures and to provide smooth warm-up and even combustion. The cetane rating of diesel fuel should be between 45 and 50. The higher the cetane rating, the more easily the fuel is ignited.

SULFUR CONTENT The sulfur content of diesel fuel is very important to the life of the engine. Sulfur in the fuel creates sulfuric acid during the combustion process, which can damage engine components and cause piston ring wear. Federal regulations are getting extremely tight on sulfur, restricting the content to less than 15 parts per million (PPM). High-sulfur fuel contributes to acid rain.

(a)

(b)

FIGURE 26–1 **(a)** Regular diesel fuel on the left has a clear or greenish tint, whereas fuel for off-road use is tinted red for identification. **(b)** A fuel pump in a farming area that clearly states the red diesel fuel is for off-road use only.

DIESEL FUEL COLOR Diesel fuel intended for use on the streets and highways is clear or green in color. Diesel fuel to be used on farms and off-road use is dyed red. ●**SEE FIGURE 26–1.**

GRADES OF DIESEL FUEL **American Society for Testing Materials (ASTM)** also classifies diesel fuel by volatility (boiling range) into the following grades:

GRADE #1 (TYPE "A" IN CANADA) This grade of diesel fuel has the lowest boiling point and the lowest cloud and pour points, as well as a lower BTU content—less heat per pound of fuel. As a result, grade #1 is suitable for use during low-temperature (winter) operation. Grade #1 produces less heat per pound of fuel compared

FIGURE 26–2 Testing the API viscosity of a diesel fuel sample using a hydrometer.

to grade #2 and may be specified for use in diesel engines involved in frequent changes in load and speed, such as those found in city buses and delivery trucks.

GRADE #2 (TYPE "B" IN CANADA) This grade has a higher boiling point, cloud point, and pour point as compared with grade #1. It is usually specified where constant speed and high loads are encountered, such as in long-haul trucking and automotive diesel applications. Most diesel is Grade #2.

DIESEL FUEL SPECIFIC GRAVITY TESTING
The density of diesel fuel should be tested whenever there is a driveability concern. The density or specific gravity of diesel fuel is measured in units of **API gravity**. API gravity is an arbitrary scale expressing the gravity or density of liquid petroleum products devised jointly by the American Petroleum Institute and the National Bureau of Standards. The measuring scale is calibrated in terms of degrees API. Oil with the least specific gravity has the highest API gravity. The formula for determining API gravity is as follows:

Degrees API gravity = (141.5 ÷ specific gravity at 60°F) − 131.5

The normal API gravity for #1 diesel fuel is 39 to 44 (typically 40). The normal API gravity for #2 diesel fuel is 30 to 39 (typically 35). A hydrometer calibrated in API gravity units should be used to test diesel fuel. ● SEE FIGURE 26–2.

● **SEE CHART 26–1** for a comparison among specific gravity, weight density, pounds per gallon, and API gravity of diesel fuel.

API GRAVITY COMPARISON CHART
Values for API Scale Oil

API GRAVITY SCALE	SPECIFIC GRAVITY	WEIGHT DENSITY, lb/ft	POUNDS PER GALLON
0			
2			
4			
6			
8			
10	1.0000	62.36	8.337
12	0.9861	61.50	8.221
14	0.9725	60.65	8.108
16	0.9593	59.83	7.998
18	0.9465	59.03	7.891
20	0.9340	58.25	7.787
22	0.9218	57.87	7.736
24	0.9100	56.75	7.587
26	0.8984	56.03	7.490
28	0.8871	55.32	7.396
30	0.8762	54.64	7.305
32	0.8654	53.97	7.215
34	0.8550	53.32	7.128
36	0.8448	52.69	7.043
38	0.8348	51.06	6.960
40	0.8251	50.96	6.879
42	0.8155	50.86	6.799
44	0.8030	50.28	6.722
46	0.7972	49.72	6.646
48	0.7883	49.16	6.572
50	0.7796	48.62	6.499
52	0.7711	48.09	6.429
54	0.7628	47.57	6.359
56	0.7547	47.07	6.292
58	0.7467	46.57	6.225
60	0.7389	46.08	6.160
62	0.7313	45.61	6.097
64	0.7238	45.14	6.034
66	0.7165	44.68	5.973
68	0.7093	44.23	5.913
70	0.7022	43.79	5.854
72	0.6953	43.36	5.797
74	0.6886	42.94	5.741
76	0.6819	42.53	5.685
78	0.6754	41.12	5.631
80	0.6690	41.72	5.577
82	0.6628	41.33	5.526
84	0.6566	40.95	5.474
86	0.6506	40.57	5.424
88	0.6446	40.20	5.374
90	0.6388	39.84	5.326
92	0.6331	39.48	5.278
94	0.6275	39.13	5.231
96	0.6220	38.79	5.186
98	0.6116	38.45	5.141
100	0.6112	38.12	5.096

CHART 26–1

The API gravity scale is based on the specific gravity of the fuel.

How Can You Tell If Gasoline Has Been Added to the Diesel Fuel by Mistake?

If gasoline has been accidentally added to diesel fuel and is burned in a diesel engine, the result can be very damaging to the engine. The gasoline can ignite faster than diesel fuel, which would tend to increase the temperature of combustion. This high temperature can harm injectors and glow plugs, as well as pistons, head gaskets, and other major diesel engine components. If contaminated fuel is suspected, first smell the fuel at the filler neck. If the fuel smells like gasoline, then the tank should be drained and refilled with diesel fuel. If the smell test does not indicate a gasoline smell (or any rancid smell), then test a sample for proper API gravity.

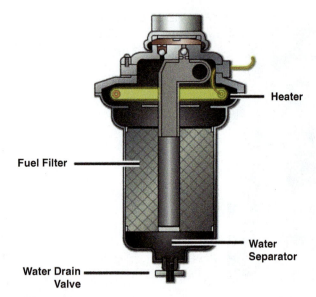

FIGURE 26–3 A Duramax diesel filter assembly, showing the components. (*Courtesy of General Motors*)

DIESEL FUEL HEATERS Diesel fuel heaters, either coolant or electric, help prevent power loss and stalling in cold weather. The heater is placed in the fuel line between the tank and the primary filter. The 100 watt heater is controlled by a thermostat inside the filter assembly. The heater is powered by a 12 volt circuit and turns on at 20°F (–7°C) and turns off at 50°F (10°C). ● SEE FIGURE 26–3.

ULTRA-LOW-SULFUR DIESEL FUEL Diesel fuel is used in diesel engines and is usually readily available throughout the United States, Canada, and Europe, where many more cars are equipped with diesel engines. Diesel engines manufactured to 2007 or newer standards must use ultra-low-sulfur diesel fuel containing less than 15 parts per million (PPM) of sulfur compared to the older, low-sulfur specification of 500 PPM. The purpose of the lower sulfur amount in diesel fuel is to reduce emissions of sulfur oxides (SO_x) and particulate matter (PM) from heavy-duty highway engines and vehicles that use diesel fuel. The emission controls used on 2007 and newer diesel engines require the use of ultra-low-sulfur diesel (ULSD) for reliable operation.

Ultra-low-sulfur diesel (ULSD) has replaced the older highway diesel fuel (low-sulfur diesel), which can have as much as 500 PPM of sulfur. ULSD is required for use in all model year 2007 and newer vehicles equipped with advanced emission control systems. ULSD looks lighter in color and has less smell than other diesel fuel.

BIODIESEL

DEFINITION OF BIODIESEL **Biodiesel** is a domestically produced, renewable fuel that can be manufactured from vegetable oils, animal fats, or recycled restaurant greases. Biodiesel is safe, biodegradable, and reduces serious air pollutants such as particulate matter (PM), carbon monoxide, and hydrocarbons. Biodiesel is defined as mono-alkyl esters of long-chain fatty acids derived from vegetable oils or animal fats that conform to ASTM D6751 specifications for use in diesel engines. Biodiesel refers to the pure fuel before blending with diesel fuel. ● SEE FIGURE 26–4.

BIODIESEL BLENDS Biodiesel blends are denoted as "BXX" with "XX" representing the percentage of biodiesel contained in the blend (i.e., **B20** is 20% biodiesel, 80% petroleum diesel). Blends of 20% biodiesel with 80% petroleum diesel (B20) can generally be used in unmodified diesel engines; however, users should consult their OEM and engine warranty statement. Biodiesel can also be used in its pure form (B100), but it may require certain engine modifications to avoid maintenance and performance problems and may not be suitable for wintertime use. Most manufacturers of diesel engines or manufacturers of diesel vehicles allow the use of B5 (5% biodiesel). For example, some manufacturers allow the use of B20 only if an optional extra fuel filter has been installed. Users should consult their engine warranty statement for more information on fuel blends of greater than 20% biodiesel.

FIGURE 26–4 A pump decal indicating that the biodiesel fuel is ultra-low-sulfur diesel (ULSD) and must be used in 2007 and newer diesel vehicles.

In general, B20 costs 30 to 40 cents more per gallon than conventional diesel. Although biodiesel costs more than regular diesel fuel, often called **petrodiesel**, fleet managers can make the switch to alternative fuels without purchasing new vehicles, acquiring new spare parts inventories, rebuilding refueling stations, or hiring new service technicians.

FEATURES OF BIODIESEL Biodiesel has the following characteristics:

1. Purchasing biodiesel in bulk quantities decreases the cost of fuel.

2. Biodiesel maintains similar horsepower, torque, and fuel economy.

3. Biodiesel has a higher cetane number than conventional diesel, which increases the engine's performance.

4. It is nontoxic, which makes it safe to handle, transport, and store. Maintenance requirements for B20 vehicles and petrodiesel vehicles are the same.

5. Biodiesel acts as a lubricant and this can add to the life of the fuel system components.

NOTE: For additional information on biodiesel and the locations where it can be purchased, visit www. biodiesel.org.

 FREQUENTLY ASKED QUESTION

I Thought Biodiesel Was Vegetable Oil?

Biodiesel is vegetable oil with the glycerin component removed by means of reacting the vegetable oil with a catalyst. The resulting hydrocarbon esters are 16 to 18 carbon atoms in length, almost identical to the petroleum diesel fuel atoms. This allows the use of biodiesel fuel in a diesel engine with no modifications needed. Biodiesel-powered vehicles do not need a second fuel tank, whereas vegetable-oil-powered vehicles do. There are three main types of fuel used in diesel engines. These are:

- Petroleum diesel, a fossil hydrocarbon with a carbon chain length of about 16 carbon atoms.
- Biodiesel, a hydrocarbon with a carbon chain length of 16 to 18 carbon atoms.
- Vegetable oil is a triglyceride with a glycerin component joining three hydrocarbon chains of 16 to 18 carbon atoms each, called straight vegetable oil **(SVO)**. Other terms used when describing vegetable oil include:
  - Pure plant oil **(PPO)**—a term most often used in Europe to describe SVO
  - Waste vegetable oil **(WVO)**—this oil could include animal or fish oils from cooking
  - Used cooking oil **(UCO)**—a term used when the oil may or may not be pure vegetable oil

Vegetable oil is not liquid enough at common ambient temperatures for use in a diesel engine fuel delivery system designed for the lower-viscosity petroleum diesel fuel. Vegetable oil needs to be heated to obtain a similar viscosity to biodiesel and petroleum diesel. This means that a heat source needs to be provided before the fuel can be used in a diesel engine. This is achieved by starting on petroleum diesel or biodiesel fuel until the engine heat can be used to sufficiently warm a tank containing the vegetable oil. It also requires purging the fuel system of vegetable oil with petroleum diesel or biodiesel fuel prior to stopping the engine to avoid the vegetable oil thickening and solidifying in the fuel system away from the heated tank. The use of vegetable oil in its natural state does, however, eliminate the need to remove the glycerin component. Many vehicle and diesel engine fuel system suppliers permit the use of biodiesel fuel that is certified as meeting testing standards. None permit the use of vegetable oil in its natural state.

E-DIESEL FUEL

DEFINITION OF E-DIESEL **E-diesel**, also called **diesohol** outside of the United States, is standard No. 2 diesel fuel that contains up to 15% ethanol. While E-diesel can have up to 15% ethanol by volume, typical blend levels are from 8% to 10%.

CETANE RATING OF E-DIESEL The higher the cetane number, the shorter the delay between injection and ignition. Normal diesel fuel has a cetane number of about 50. Adding 15% ethanol lowers the cetane number. To increase the cetane number back to that of conventional diesel fuel, a cetane-enhancing additive is added to E-diesel. The additive used to increase the cetane rating of E-diesel is ethylhexylnitrate or ditertbutyl peroxide.

E-diesel has better cold-flow properties than conventional diesel. The heat content of E-diesel is about 6% less than conventional diesel, but using E-diesel reduces the particulate matter (PM) emissions by as much as 40%, with 20% less carbon monoxide, and a 5% reduction in oxides of nitrogen (NO_X).

Currently, E-diesel is considered to be experimental and can be used legally in off-road applications or in mass-transit buses with EPA approval. For additional information, visit www.e-diesel.org.

SUMMARY

1. Diesel fuel produces 12% more heat energy than the same amount of gasoline.
2. Diesel fuel requirements include cleanliness, low-temperature fluidity, and proper cetane rating.
3. Emission control devices used on 2007 and newer engines require the use of ultra-low-sulfur diesel (ULSD) that has less than 15 parts per million (PPM) of sulfur.
4. The density of diesel fuel is measured in a unit called API gravity.
5. The cetane rating of diesel fuel is a measure of the ease with which the fuel can be ignited.
6. Biodiesel is the blend of vegetable-based liquid with regular diesel fuel. Most diesel engine manufacturers allow the use of a 5% blend, called B20 without any changes to the fuel system or engine.
7. E-diesel is a blend of ethanol with diesel fuel up to 15% ethanol by volume.

REVIEW QUESTIONS

1. What is meant by the cloud point?
2. What is ultra-low-sulfur diesel?
3. Biodiesel blends are identified by what designation?

CHAPTER QUIZ

1. What color is diesel fuel dyed if it is for off-road use only?
   - **a.** Red
   - **b.** Green
   - **c.** Blue
   - **d.** Yellow

2. What clogs fuel filters when the temperature is low on a vehicle that uses diesel fuel?
   - **a.** Alcohol
   - **b.** Sulfur
   - **c.** Wax
   - **d.** Cetane

3. The specific gravity of diesel fuel is measured in what units?
   - **a.** Hydrometer units
   - **b.** API gravity
   - **c.** Grade number
   - **d.** Cetane number

4. What rating of diesel fuel indicates how well a diesel engine will start?
   - **a.** Specific gravity rating
   - **b.** Sulfur content
   - **c.** Cloud point
   - **d.** Cetane rating

5. Ultra-low-sulfur diesel fuel has how much sulfur content?
   - **a.** 15 PPM
   - **b.** 50 PPM
   - **c.** 500 PPM
   - **d.** 1500 PPM

6. E-diesel is diesel fuel with what additive?
   - **a.** Methanol
   - **b.** Sulfur
   - **c.** Ethanol
   - **d.** Vegetable oil

7. Biodiesel is regular diesel fuel with vegetable oil added.
   - **a.** True
   - **b.** False

8. B20 biodiesel has how much regular diesel fuel?
   - **a.** 20%
   - **b.** 40%
   - **c.** 80%
   - **d.** 100%

9. What grade is most diesel fuel?
   - **a.** Grade #1
   - **b.** Grade #2
   - **c.** Grade #3
   - **d.** Grade #4

10. What type of biodiesel most manufacturers of vehicles equipped with diesel engines allow?
    - **a.** B100
    - **b.** B80
    - **c.** B20
    - **d.** B5

chapter 27
IGNITION SYSTEM COMPONENTS AND OPERATION

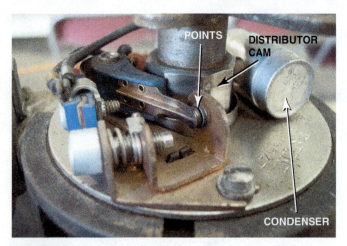

FIGURE 27–1 A point-type ignition system showing the distributor cam which opens the points. The spark occurs when the points open.

IGNITION SYSTEM

PURPOSE AND FUNCTION The ignition system includes components and wiring necessary to create and distribute a high voltage (up to 40,000 volts or more) and send to the spark plug. A high-voltage arc occurs across the gap of a spark plug inside the combustion chamber. The spark raises the temperature of the air–fuel mixture and starts the combustion process inside the cylinder.

BACKGROUND All ignition systems apply battery voltage (close to 12 volts) to the positive side of the ignition coil(s) and pulse the negative side to ground on and off.

EARLY IGNITION SYSTEMS. Before the mid-1970s, ignition systems used a mechanically opened set of contact points to make and break the electrical connection to ground. A cam lobe, located in and driven by the distributor, opened the points. There was one lobe for each cylinder. The points used a rubbing block that was lubricated by applying a thin layer of grease on the cam lobe at each service interval. Each time the points opened, a spark was created in the ignition coil. The high-voltage spark then traveled to each spark plug through the distributor cap and rotor and the spark plug wires. The distributor was used twice in the creation of the spark.

1. It was connected to the camshaft that rotated the distributor cam causing the points to open and close.

2. It used a rotor to direct the high-voltage spark from the coil entering the center of the distributor cap to inserts connected to spark plug wires to each cylinder. ● **SEE FIGURE 27–1.**

ELECTRONIC IGNITION. Since the mid-1970s, ignition systems have used sensors, such as a pickup coil and reluctor (trigger wheel), to trigger or signal an electronic module that switches the primary ground circuit of the ignition coil.

DISTRIBUTOR IGNITION (DI) is the term specified by the Society of Automotive Engineers (SAE) for an ignition system that uses a distributor.

ELECTRONIC IGNITION (EI) is the term specified by the SAE for an ignition system that does not use a distributor. Types of EI systems include:

1. **Waste-spark system.** This type of system uses one ignition coil to fire the spark plugs for two cylinders at the same time.

2. **Coil-on-plug system.** This type of system uses a single ignition coil for each cylinder with the coil placed above or near the spark plug.

IGNITION SYSTEM OPERATION

The ignition system includes components and wiring necessary to create and distribute a high voltage (up to 40,000 volts or more). All ignition systems apply voltage close to battery voltage (12 volts) to the positive side of the ignition coil and pulse the negative side to ground. When the coil negative lead is grounded, the primary (low-voltage) circuit of the coil is complete and a magnetic field is created around the coil windings. When the circuit is opened, the magnetic field collapses and induces a high-voltage spark in the secondary winding of the ignition coil. Early ignition systems used a mechanically opened set of contact points to make and break the electrical connection to ground. Electronic ignition uses a sensor, such as a pickup coil and reluctor (trigger wheel), or trigger to signal an electronic module that makes and breaks the primary connection of the ignition coil.

IGNITION COILS

PURPOSE AND FUNCTION The heart of any ignition system is the **ignition coil.** The coil creates a high-voltage spark by electromagnetic induction. Many ignition coils contain two separate but electrically connected windings of copper wire. Other coils are true transformers in which the primary and secondary windings are not electrically connected. ● **SEE FIGURE 27–2.**

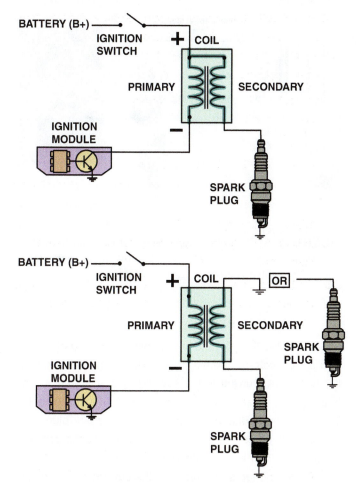

FIGURE 27–2 Some ignition coils are electrically connected, called married (top figure), whereas others use separate primary and secondary windings, called divorced (lower figure). The polarity (positive or negative) of a coil is determined by the direction in which the coil is wound.

COIL CONSTRUCTION
The center of an ignition coil contains a core of laminated soft iron (thin strips of soft iron). This core increases the magnetic strength of the coil. Surrounding the laminated core are approximately 20,000 turns of fine wire (approximately 42 gauge). These windings are called the secondary coil windings. Surrounding the secondary windings are approximately 150 turns of heavy wire (approximately 21 gauge). These windings are called the primary coil windings. The secondary winding has about 100 times the number of turns of the primary winding, referred to as the **turns ratio** (approximately 100:1). The E coil is so named because the laminated, soft-iron core is E-shaped, with the coil wire turns wrapped around the center "finger" of the E and the primary winding wrapped inside the secondary winding. ● SEE FIGURES 27–3 AND 27–4.

The primary windings of the coil extend through the case of the coil and are labeled as positive and negative. The positive terminal of the coil attaches to the ignition switch, which

FIGURE 27–3 The steel lamination used in an E coil helps increase the magnetic field strength, which helps the coil produce higher energy output for a more complete combustion in the cylinders.

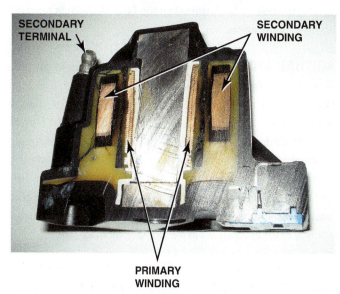

FIGURE 27–4 The primary windings are inside the secondary windings on this General Motors coil.

supplies current from the positive battery terminal. The negative terminal is attached to an **ignition control module (ICM or igniter)**, which opens and closes the primary ignition circuit by opening or closing the ground return path of the circuit. When the ignition switch is on, voltage should be available at *both* the positive terminal and the negative terminal of the coil if the primary windings of the coil have continuity. The labeling of positive (+) and negative (−) of the coil indicates that the positive terminal is *more* positive (closer to the positive terminal of the battery) than the negative terminal of the coil. This condition is called the coil **polarity.** The polarity of the coil must be correct to ensure that electrons will flow from the hot

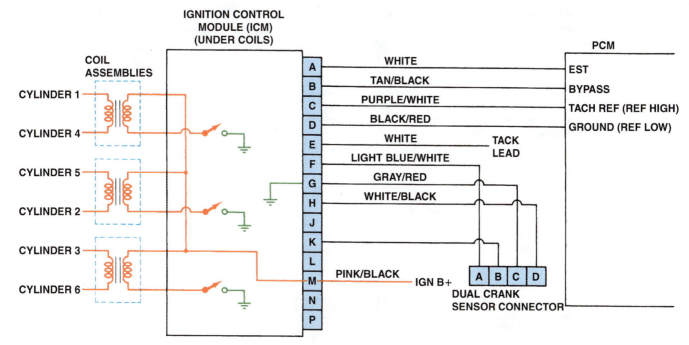

FIGURE 27–22 Typical wiring diagram of a V-6 distributorless (direct fire) ignition system. The powertrain control module (PCM) controls the actual firing time of the spark plugs through the "EST" circuit signal to the ignition control module (ICM).

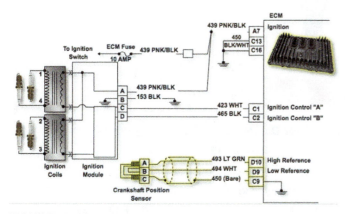

FIGURE 27–23 In an up-integrated ignition system the crank sensor is an input directly to the PCM. (*Courtesy of General Motors*)

interpreted in the PCM, rather than being split between the ignition control module and the PCM. The ignition module, if even used, contains the power transistor for coil switching. The signal as to when the coil fires, is determined and controlled from the PCM. ● **SEE FIGURE 27–23.**

COIL-ON-PLUG IGNITION

Coil-on-plug (COP) ignition uses one ignition coil for each spark plug. This system is also called **coil-by-plug, coil-near-plug,** or **coil-over-plug** ignition. ● **SEE FIGURE 27–24.** The

coil-on-plug system eliminates the spark plug wires, which are often sources of **electromagnetic interference (EMI)** that can cause problems to some computer signals. The vehicle computer controls the timing of the spark. Ignition timing also can be changed (retarded or advanced) on a cylinder-by-cylinder basis for maximum performance and to respond to knock sensor signals. ● **SEE FIGURE 27–25.**

There are two basic types of coil-on-plug ignition including:

- **Two-wire**—This design uses the vehicle computer to control the firing of the ignition coil. The two wires include ignition voltage feed and the pulse ground wire, which is controlled by the computer. All ignition timing and dwell control are handled by the computer.

- **Three-wire**—This design includes an ignition module at each coil. The three wires include:

  - Ignition voltage

  - Ground

  - Pulse from the computer to the built-in module

General Motors vehicles use a variety of coil-on-plug-type ignition systems. Many V-8 engines use a coil-near-plug system with individual coils and modules for each individual cylinder that are placed on the valve covers. Short secondary ignition spark plug wires are used to connect the output terminal of the ignition coil to the spark plug.

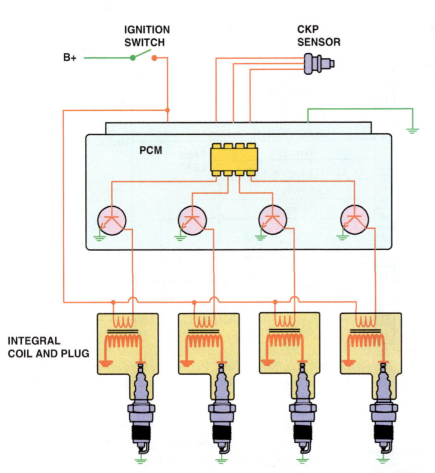

FIGURE 27–24 A typical two-wire coil-on-plug ignition system showing the triggering and the switching being performed by the PCM from input from the crankshaft position sensor.

FIGURE 27–25 This coil-on-plug system integrates the ignition coil, ignition control module, and boot into one assembly. (*Courtesy of General Motors*)

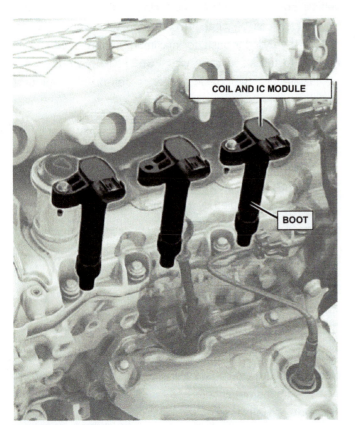

SAFETY TIP

Never Disconnect a Spark Plug Wire When the Engine Is Running!

Ignition systems produce a high-voltage pulse necessary to ignite a lean air–fuel mixture. If you disconnect a spark plug wire when the engine is running, this high-voltage spark could cause personal injury or damage to the ignition coil and/or ignition module.

The majority of current coil-per-plug systems, including coil-at-plug and coil-near-plug, use a 58-tooth reluctor wheel with the crankshaft position sensor as the triggering device. This tooth count leaves a 12 span on the reluctor with a 2-tooth uncut section. The uncut portion of the reluctor provides the ECM with a reference pulse to allow it to determine which cylinders are approaching top dead center (TDC). The crankshaft position sensor only indicates which pairs of cylinders are at TDC, so the ECM must also use the camshaft position sensor to determine which of the pairs of cylinders is in the compression stroke.[1] ● **SEE FIGURE 27–26.**

―――――――――
[1]GM Course # 16044.21W2

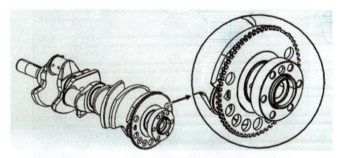

FIGURE 27–26 The reluctor wheel is mounted on the crankshaft. (*Courtesy of General Motors*)

Each coil is controlled by the PCM, which can vary the ignition timing separately for each cylinder based on signals the PCM receives from the knock sensor(s). For example, if the knock sensor detects that a spark knock has occurred after firing cylinder 3, then the PCM will continue to monitor cylinder 3 and retard timing on just this one cylinder if necessary to prevent engine-damaging detonation.

ION-SENSING IGNITION

In an **ion-sensing ignition** system, the spark plug itself becomes a sensor. The ignition control (IC) module applies a voltage of about 100 to 400 volts DC across the spark plug gap after the ignition event to sense the plasma inside the cylinder. ● **SEE FIGURE 27–27.** The coil discharge voltage (10 to 15 kV) is electrically isolated from the ion-sensing circuit. The combustion flame is ionized and will conduct some electricity, which can be accurately measured at the spark plug gap. The purpose of this circuit includes:

- Misfire detection (required by OBD-II regulations)
- Knock detection (eliminates the need for a knock sensor)
- Ignition timing control (to achieve the best spark timing for maximum power with lowest exhaust emissions)
- Exhaust gas recirculation (EGR) control
- Air–fuel ratio control on an individual cylinder basis

Ion-sensing ignition systems still function the same as conventional coil-on-plug designs, but the engine does not need to be equipped with a camshaft position sensor for misfire detection, or a knock sensor because both of these faults are achieved using the electronics inside the ignition control circuits.

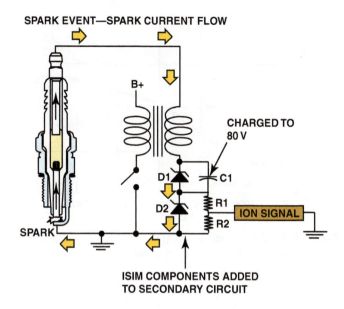

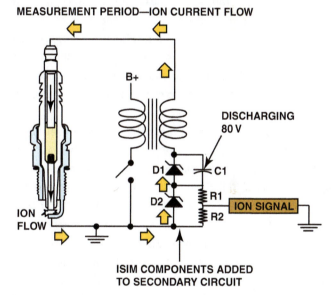

FIGURE 27–27 A DC voltage is applied across the spark plug gap after the plug fires and the circuit can determine if the correct air–fuel ratio was present in the cylinder and if knock occurred.

IGNITION TIMING

THE NEED FOR SPARK ADVANCE
Ignition timing refers to when the spark plug fires in relation to piston position. The time when the spark occurs depends on engine speed, and therefore, must be advanced (spark plugs fire some) as the engine rotates faster. The ignition in the cylinder takes a certain amount of time, usually 30 milliseconds (30/1000 of a second). This burning time is relatively constant throughout

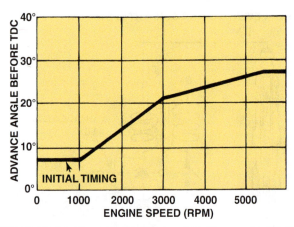

FIGURE 27–28 The initial timing is where the spark plug fires at idle speed. The computer then advances the timing based on engine speed and other factors.

the engine speed range. For maximum efficiency from the expanding gases inside the combustion chamber, the burning of the air–fuel mixture should end by about 10° after top dead center (ATDC). If the burning of the mixture is still occurring after that point, the expanding gases do not exert much force on the piston because it is moving away from the gases (the gases are "chasing" the piston).

Therefore, to achieve the goal of having the air–fuel mixture completely burned by the time the piston reaches 10° after TDC, the spark must be advanced (occur sooner) as the engine speed increases. This timing advance is determined and controlled by the PCM on most vehicles. ● SEE FIGURE 27–28.

INITIAL TIMING If the engine is equipped with a distributor, it may be possible to adjust the base or the **initial timing.** The initial timing is usually set to fire the spark plug between zero degrees (TDC) or slightly before TDC (BTDC). Ignition timing does change as the timing chain or gear wears and readjustment is often necessary on high-mileage engines. ● SEE FIGURE 27–29. Waste-spark and coil-on-plug ignitions cannot be adjusted.

KNOCK SENSORS

Knock sensors are used to detect abnormal combustion, often called **ping, spark knock,** or **detonation.** Whenever abnormal combustion occurs, a rapid pressure increase occurs in the cylinder, creating a vibration in the engine block. It is this vibration that is detected by the knock sensor. The signal from the knock sensor is used by the PCM to retard the ignition timing until the knock is eliminated, thereby reducing the damaging effects of the abnormal combustion on pistons and other engine parts. ● SEE FIGURE 27–30.

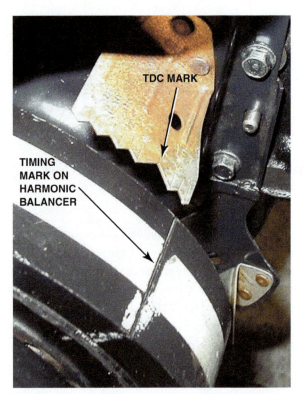

FIGURE 27–29 Older engines with adjustable distributors may have timing marks on the balancer or the flywheel.

FIGURE 27–30 This knock sensor mounts on the side of the engine block, next to the crank sensor.

Inside the knock sensor is a piezoelectric element that generates a voltage when pressure or a vibration is applied to the unit. The knock sensor is tuned to the engine knock frequency, which is a range from 5 to 10 kHz, depending on the engine design. The voltage signal from the **knock sensor (KS)** is sent to the PCM. The PCM retards the ignition timing until the knocking stops.

DIAGNOSING THE KNOCK SENSOR If a knock sensor diagnostic trouble code (DTC) is present, follow the specified testing procedure in the service information. A scan tool can

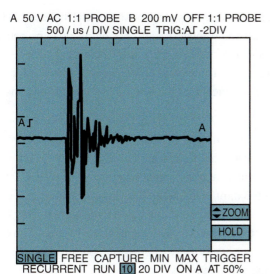

A 50 V AC 1:1 PROBE   B 200 mV OFF 1:1 PROBE
500 / us / DIV SINGLE TRIG:A⌐ -2DIV

ZOOM
HOLD

SINGLE FREE CAPTURE MIN MAX TRIGGER
RECURRENT RUN 10 20 DIV ON A AT 50%

FIGURE 27–31 A typical waveform from a knock sensor during a spark knock event. This signal is sent to the computer which in turn retards the ignition timing. This timing retard is accomplished by an output command from the computer to either a spark advance control unit or directly to the ignition module.

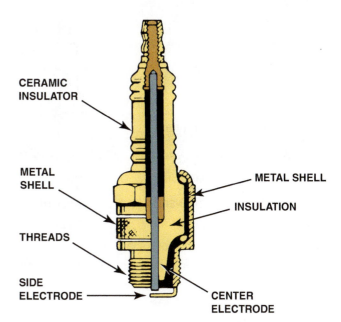

FIGURE 27–32 Parts of a typical spark plug.

be used to check the operation of the knock sensor, using the following procedure:

STEP 1 Start the engine and connect a scan tool to monitor ignition timing and/or knock sensor activity.

STEP 2 Create a simulated engine knocking sound by tapping on the engine block or cylinder head with a soft-faced mallet.

STEP 3 Observe the scan tool display. The vibration from the tapping should have been interpreted by the knock sensor as a knock, resulting in a knock sensor signal and a reduction in the spark advance.

A knock sensor also can be tested using a digital storage oscilloscope. ● **SEE FIGURE 27–31.**

NOTE: Some engine computers are programmed to ignore knock sensor signals when the engine is at idle speed to avoid having the noise from a loose accessory drive belt, or other accessory, interpreted as engine knock. Always follow the vehicle manufacturer's recommended testing procedure.

REPLACING A KNOCK SENSOR If replacing a knock sensor, be sure to purchase the exact replacement needed, because they often look the same, but the frequency range can vary according to engine design, as well as where it is located on the engine. Always tighten the knock sensor using a torque wrench and tighten to the specified torque to avoid causing damage to the piezoelectric element inside the sensor.

SPARK PLUGS

Spark plugs are manufactured from ceramic insulators inside a steel shell. The threads of the shell are rolled and a seat is formed to create a gastight seal with the cylinder head. ● **SEE FIGURE 27–32.** The physical difference in spark plugs includes:

- **Reach.** This is the length of the threaded part of the plug.

- **Heat range.** The heat range of the spark plug refers to how rapidly the heat created at the tip is transferred to the cylinder head. A plug with a long ceramic insulator path will run hotter at the tip than a spark plug that has a shorter path because the heat must travel farther. ● **SEE FIGURE 27–33.**

- **Type of seat.** Some spark plugs use a gasket and others rely on a tapered seat to seal.

RESISTOR SPARK PLUGS Most spark plugs include a resistor in the center electrode, which helps to reduce electromagnetic noise or radiation from the ignition system. The closer the resistor is to the actual spark or arc, the more effective it becomes. The value of the resistor is usually between 2,500 ohms and 7,500 ohms.

PLATINUM SPARK PLUGS **Platinum spark plugs** have a small amount of the precious metal platinum welded onto the end of the center electrode, as well as on the ground or side

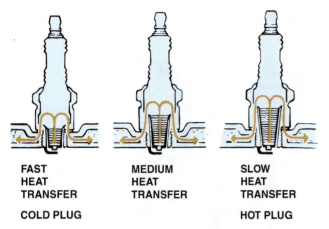

FAST HEAT TRANSFER
COLD PLUG

MEDIUM HEAT TRANSFER

SLOW HEAT TRANSFER
HOT PLUG

FIGURE 27–33 The heat range of a spark plug is determined by the distance the heat has to flow from the tip to the cylinder head.

electrode. Platinum is a grayish-white metal that does not react with oxygen and therefore, will not erode away as can occur with conventional nickel alloy spark plug electrodes. Platinum is also used as a catalyst in catalytic converters where it is able to start a chemical reaction without itself being consumed.

IRIDIUM SPARK PLUGS Iridium is a white precious metal and is the most corrosion-resistant metal known. Most **iridium spark plugs** use a small amount of iridium welded onto the tip of a small center electrode 0.0015 to 0.002 inch (0.4 to 0.6 mm) in diameter. The small diameter reduces the voltage required to jump the gap between the center and the side electrode, thereby reducing possible misfires. The ground or side electrode is usually tipped with platinum to help reduce electrode gap wear.

SUMMARY

1. All inductive ignition systems supply battery voltage to the positive side of the ignition coil and pulse the negative side of the coil on and off to ground to create a high-voltage spark.

2. If an ignition system uses a distributor, it is a distributor ignition (DI) system.

3. If an ignition system does not use a distributor, it is called an electronic ignition (EI) system.

4. A waste-spark ignition system fires two spark plugs at the same time.

5. A coil-on-plug ignition system uses an ignition coil for each spark plug.

REVIEW QUESTIONS

1. How can 12 volts from a battery be changed to 40,000 volts for ignition?

2. How does a magnetic sensor work?

3. How does a Hall-effect sensor work?

4. How does a waste-spark ignition system work?

CHAPTER QUIZ

1. The primary (low-voltage) ignition system must be working correctly before any spark occurs from a coil. Which component is *not* in the primary ignition circuit?
   a. Spark plug wiring
   b. Ignition module (igniter)
   c. Pickup coil (pulse generator)
   d. Ignition switch

2. The ignition module has direct control over the firing of the coil(s) of an EI system. Which component(s) triggers (controls) the module?
   a. Pickup coil
   b. Computer
   c. Crankshaft sensor
   d. All of the above

3. A reluctor is a _____.
   a. Type of sensor used in the secondary circuit.
   b. Notched ring or pointed wheel
   c. Type of optical sensor
   d. Type of Hall effect sensor

4. The CKP sensor sends a signal to the _____ in an up-integrated ignition system.
   a. IC module   c. Ignition switch
   b. PCM   d. Spark plug

5. Coil polarity is determined by the _____.
   a. Direction of rotation of the coil windings
   b. Turns ratio
   c. Direction of laminations
   d. Saturation direction

6. Because of _____, an ignition coil cannot be fully charged (reach magnetic saturation) until after a delay of about 10 milliseconds
   a. Voltage drop across the ignition switch and related wiring
   b. Resistance in the coil windings
   c. Inductive reactance
   d. Saturation

7. The pulse generator _____.
   a. Fires the spark plug directly
   b. Signals the electronic control unit (module)
   c. Signals the computer that fires the spark plug directly
   d. Is used as a tachometer reference signal by the computer and has no other function

8. Two technicians are discussing distributor ignition. Technician A says that the pickup coil or optical sensor in the distributor is used to pulse the ignition module (igniter). Technician B says that some distributor ignition systems have the ignition coil inside the distributor cap. Which technician is correct?
   a. Technician A only
   b. Technician B only
   c. Both Technicians A and B
   d. Neither Technician A nor B

9. A waste-spark-type ignition system _____.
   a. Fires two spark plugs at the same time
   b. Fires one spark plug with reverse polarity
   c. Fires one spark plug with straight polarity
   d. All of the above

10. An ion-sensing ignition system allows the ignition system itself to be able to _____.
   a. Detect misfire
   b. Detect spark knock
   c. Detect rich or lean air–fuel mixture
   d. All of the above

chapter 28

IGNITION SYSTEM DIAGNOSIS AND SERVICE

LEARNING OBJECTIVES

After studying this chapter, the reader should be able to:

1. Describe the procedure used to check for spark.
2. List the steps necessary to check and/or adjust ignition timing on engines equipped with a distributor.
3. Inspect and test ignition coils.
4. Inspect and test ignition system pickup sensor or triggering devices.
5. Discuss what to inspect and look for during a visual inspection of the ignition system.
6. Diagnose ignition system related problems.
7. Inspect and test ignition system secondary circuit wiring and components.

This chapter will help you prepare for Engine Repair (A8) ASE certification test content area "B" (Ignition System Diagnosis and Repair).

GM STC OBJECTIVES

GM Service Technical College topics covered in this chapter are:

1. Diagnose ignition system primary section using triggering device test.
2. Perform a special function test using scan tool.
3. Perform ignition systems service and diagnostics.

KEY TERMS

Base timing 447
Distributor cap 442
Carbon tracks 443
Indexing 442

Remove and replace (R & R) 444
Spark tester 435

FIGURE 28-1 A spark tester looks like a regular spark plug with an alligator clip attached to the shell. This tester has a specified gap that requires at least 25,000 volts (25 kV) to fire.

FIGURE 28-2 A close-up showing the recessed center electrode on a spark tester. It is recessed 3/8 inch into the shell and the spark must then jump another 3/8 inch to the shell for a total gap of 3/4 inch.

CHECKING FOR SPARK

In the event of a no-start condition, the first step should be to check for secondary voltage out of the ignition coil or to the spark plugs. If the engine is equipped with a separate ignition coil, remove the coil wire from the center of the distributor cap, install a **spark tester**, and crank the engine. See the Tech Tip "Always Use a Spark Tester." A good coil and ignition system should produce a blue spark at the spark tester. ● **SEE FIGURES 28-1 AND 28-2.**

If the ignition system being tested does not have a separate ignition coil, disconnect any spark plug wire from a spark plug and, while cranking the engine, test for spark available at the spark plug wire, again using a spark tester.

NOTE: An intermittent spark should be considered a no-spark condition.

Typical causes of a no-spark (intermittent spark) condition include the following:

1. Weak ignition coil
2. Low or no voltage to the primary (positive) side of the coil
3. High resistance or open coil wire, or spark plug wire
4. Negative side of the coil not being pulsed by the ignition module, also called an ignition control module (ICM)
5. Defective pickup coil
6. Defective module

TECH TIP

Always Use a Spark Tester

A spark tester looks like a spark plug except it has a recessed center electrode and no side electrode. The tester commonly has an alligator clip attached to the shell so that it can be clamped on a good ground connection on the engine. A good ignition system should be able to cause a spark to jump this wide gap at atmospheric pressure. Without a spark tester, a technician might assume that the ignition system is okay, because it can spark across a normal, grounded spark plug. The voltage required to fire a standard spark plug when it is out of the engine and not under pressure is about 3,000 volts or less. An electronic ignition spark tester requires a minimum of 25,000 volts to jump the 3/4 inch gap. Therefore, never assume that the ignition system is okay because it fires a spark plug—always use a spark tester. *Remember that an intermittent spark across a spark tester should be interpreted as a no-spark condition.*

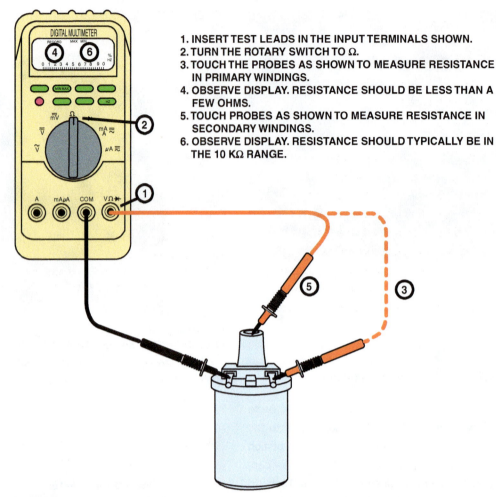

1. INSERT TEST LEADS IN THE INPUT TERMINALS SHOWN.
2. TURN THE ROTARY SWITCH TO Ω.
3. TOUCH THE PROBES AS SHOWN TO MEASURE RESISTANCE IN PRIMARY WINDINGS.
4. OBSERVE DISPLAY. RESISTANCE SHOULD BE LESS THAN A FEW OHMS.
5. TOUCH PROBES AS SHOWN TO MEASURE RESISTANCE IN SECONDARY WINDINGS.
6. OBSERVE DISPLAY. RESISTANCE SHOULD TYPICALLY BE IN THE 10 KΩ RANGE.

FIGURE 28–3 Checking an ignition coil using a multimeter set to read ohms.

IGNITION TROUBLESHOOTING PROCEDURE

When troubleshooting any electronic ignition system for no spark, follow these steps to help pinpoint the exact cause of the problem:

STEP 1 Turn the ignition on (engine off) and, using either a voltmeter or a test light, test for battery voltage available at the positive terminal of the ignition coil. If the voltage is not available, check for an open circuit at the ignition switch or wiring. Also check the condition of the ignition fuse (if used).

STEP 2 Connect the voltmeter or test light to the negative side of the coil and crank the engine. The voltmeter should fluctuate or the test light should blink, indicating that the primary coil current is being turned on and off. If there is no pulsing of the negative side of the coil, then the problem is a defective pickup, electronic control module, or wiring.

IGNITION COIL TESTING USING AN OHMMETER

If an ignition coil is suspected of being defective, a simple ohmmeter check can be performed to test the resistance of the primary and secondary winding inside the coil. For accurate resistance measurements, the wiring to the coil should be removed before testing. To test the primary coil winding resistance, take the following steps (● **SEE FIGURE 28–3**):

STEP 1 Set the meter to read low ohms.

STEP 2 Measure the resistance between the positive terminal and the negative terminal of the ignition coil. Most coils will give a reading between 1 and 3 ohms; however, some coils should indicate less than 1 ohm. Check the manufacturer's specifications for the exact resistance values.

The Weird Running Chevrolet Truck

An older Chevrolet pickup truck equipped with a V-8 engine was towed into a shop because it would not start. A quick check of the ignition system showed that the pickup coil had a broken wire below it and the ignition control module. The distributor was removed from the engine and the distributor shaft was removed, cleaned, and a replacement pickup coil was installed. The engine started but ran rough and hesitated when the accelerator pedal was depressed. After an hour of troubleshooting, a careful inspection of the new pickup coil showed that the time core had six instead of eight points, meaning that the new pickup coil was meant for a V-6 instead of a V-8 engine. Replacing the pickup coil again solved the problem.

To test the secondary coil winding resistance, follow these steps:

STEP 1 Set the meter to read kilohms (kΩ).

STEP 2 Measure the resistance between the primary terminal and the secondary coil tower. The normal resistance of most coils ranges between 6,000 ohms and 30,000 ohms. Check the manufacturer's specifications for the exact resistance values.

NOTE: Older ignition coils use a screw that is inside the secondary tower of the ignition coil. If this screw is loose, an intermittent engine misfire could occur. The secondary coil would also indicate high resistance if this screw was loose.

PICKUP COIL TESTING

The pickup coil, located under the distributor cap on older electronic ignition engines, can cause a no-spark condition if defective. The pickup coil must generate an AC voltage pulse to the ignition module so that the module can pulse the ignition coil.

A pickup coil contains a coil of wire, and the resistance of this coil should be within the range specified by the manufacturer. ● **SEE FIGURE 28–4**. Some common specifications include the following:

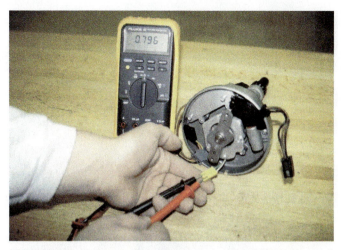

FIGURE 28–4 Measuring the resistance of an HEI pickup coil using a digital multimeter set to the ohms position. The reading on the face of the meter is 0.796 kΩ or 796 ohms in the middle of the 500 to 1,500 ohm specifications.

MANUFACTURER	PICKUP COIL RESISTANCE (OHMS)
General Motors	500–1,500 (white and green leads)
Ford	400–1,000 (orange and purple leads)
Chrysler	150–900 (orange and black leads)

Also check that the pickup coil windings are insulated from ground by checking for continuity using an ohmmeter. With one ohmmeter lead attached to ground, touch the other lead of the ohmmeter to the pickup coil terminal. The ohmmeter should read OL (over limit) with the ohmmeter set on the high scale. If the pickup coil resistance is not within the specified range, or if it has continuity to ground, replace the pickup coil assembly.

The pickup coil also can be tested for proper voltage output. During cranking, most pickup coils should produce a minimum of 0.25 volt AC. This can be tested with the distributor out of the vehicle by rotating the distributor drive gear by hand.

TESTING MAGNETIC SENSORS

The resistance of a magnetic sensor is checked using a multimeter. The sensor can be checked in place or after it is removed. This checks the resistance of the coil in the sensor, however, if the magnet in the sensor is weak, the resulting AC voltage output will also be weak, especially at low RPMs. Switch the meter to AC voltage and read the voltage while cranking the engine. ● **SEE FIGURES 28–5 AND 28–6**.

FIGURE 28–5 Crankshaft position sensor (CKP) resistance is checked using a multimeter set to ohms.

Magnetic sensors can also be tested to see if they will stick to iron or steel, indicating that the magnetic strength of the sensors is okay. If the permanent magnet inside the sensor has cracked, the result is two weak magnets. With the sensor removed from the engine, hold a metal (steel) object against the end of the sensor. It should exert a strong magnetic pull on the steel object. If not, replace the sensor.

TESTING HALL-EFFECT SENSORS

The output of the Hall-effect sensor can be tested using a digital voltmeter. Check for the presence of changing voltage (pulsed on and off or digital DC) when the engine is being cranked. The best test is to use an oscilloscope and observe the waveform. ● **SEE FIGURE 28–7**.

Bad Wire? Replace the Coil!

When performing engine testing (such as a compression test), always ground the coil wire. Never allow the coil to discharge without a path to ground for the spark. High-energy electronic ignition systems can produce 40,000 volts or more of electrical pressure. If the spark cannot spark to ground, the coil energy can (and usually does) arc inside the coil itself, creating a low-resistance path to the primary windings or the steel laminations of the coil. ● **SEE FIGURE 28–8**. This low-resistance path is called a track and could cause an engine misfire under load even though all of the remaining component parts of the ignition system are functioning correctly. Often these tracks do not show up on any coil test, including most scopes. Because the track is a lower-resistance path to ground than normal, it requires that the ignition system be put under a load for it to be detected, and even then, the problem (engine misfire) may be intermittent.

Therefore, when disabling an ignition system, perform one of the following procedures to prevent possible ignition coil damage:

1. Remove the power source wire from the ignition system to prevent any ignition operation.
2. On distributor-equipped engines, remove the secondary coil wire from the center of the distributor cap and connect a jumper wire between the disconnected coil wire and a good engine ground. This ensures that the secondary coil energy will be safely grounded and prevents high-voltage coil damage.

IGNITION SYSTEM DIAGNOSIS USING VISUAL INSPECTION

One of the first steps in the diagnosis process is to perform a thorough visual inspection of the ignition system, including the following items:

- Check all spark plug wires for proper routing. All plug wires should be in the factory wiring separator and be clear of any metallic object that could cause damage to the insulation and cause a short-to-ground fault.

FIGURE 28–6 An AC voltage is produced by a magnetic sensor. Most sensors should produce at least 0.1 volt AC while the engine is cranking and can exceed 100 volts with the engine running if the pickup wheel has many teeth.

PERMANENT MAGNET AC GENERATORS DEVELOP THEIR OWN AC VOLTAGE SIGNAL AS THEY OPERATE. A DIGITAL METER CAN MEASURE THE AC SIGNAL FROM THESE SENSORS, TO CONFIRM THEY'RE WORKING PROPERLY.

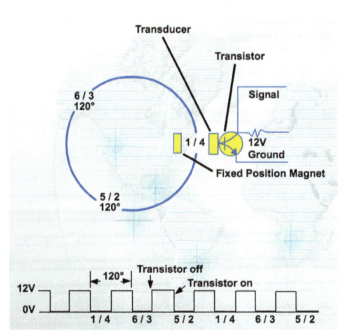

FIGURE 28–7 When tested with a scope, the Hall-effect sensor produces a waveform as shown. (*Courtesy of General Motors*)

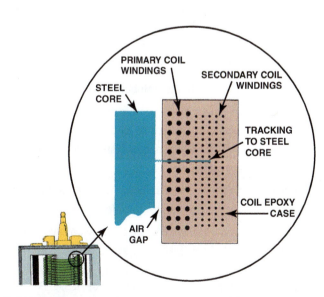

FIGURE 28–8 A track inside an ignition coil is not a short, but rather it is a low-resistance path or hole that has been burned through from the secondary wiring to the steel core.

FIGURE 28–9 If the coil is working, the end of the magnetic pickup tool will move with the changes in the magnetic field around the coil.

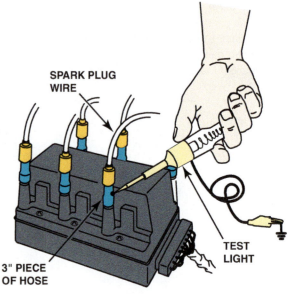

SPARK PLUG WIRE

3" PIECE OF HOSE

TEST LIGHT

FIGURE 28–10 Using a vacuum hose and a grounded test light to ground one cylinder at a time on a DIS. This works on all types of ignition systems and provides a method for grounding out one cylinder at a time without fear of damaging any component.

 TECH TIP

The Magnetic Pickup Tool Test

All ignition coils are pulsed on and off by the ignition control module or PCM. When the coil charges and discharges, the magnetic field around the coil changes. This pulsing of the coil can be observed by holding the magnetic end of a pickup tool near an operating ignition coil. The magnet at the end of the pickup tool will move as the magnetic field around the coil changes. ● **SEE FIGURE 28–9.**

- Check that all spark plug wires are securely attached to the spark plugs and to the distributor cap or ignition coil(s).
- Check that all spark plug wires are clean and free from excessive dirt or oil. Check that all protective covers normally covering the coil and/or distributor cap are in place and not damaged.
- If equipped, remove the distributor cap and carefully check the cap and distributor rotor for faults.
- Remove the spark plugs and check for excessive wear or other visible faults. Replace if needed.

NOTE: According to research conducted by General Motors, about one-fifth (20%) of all faults are detected during a *thorough visual inspection!*

TESTING FOR POOR PERFORMANCE

Many diagnostic equipment manufacturers offer methods for testing distributorless ignition systems on an oscilloscope. If using this type of equipment, follow the manufacturer's recommended procedures and interpretation of the specific test results.

One method of testing distributorless (waste-spark systems) ignition involves removing the spark plug wires (or connectors) from the coils (engine off) and installing short lengths (2 inches) of rubber vacuum hose in series.

NOTE: For best results, use rubber hose that is electrically conductive. Measure the vacuum hose with an ohmmeter. Suitable vacuum hose should give a reading of less than 10,000 ohms (10 kΩ) for a length of about 2 inches. ● SEE FIGURE 28–10.

STEP 1   Start the engine and ground out each cylinder one at a time by touching the tip of a grounded test light to the rubber vacuum hose. Even though the computer will increase idle speed and fuel delivery to compensate for the grounded spark plug wire, a technician should watch for a change in the operation of the engine. If no change is observed or heard, the cylinder being

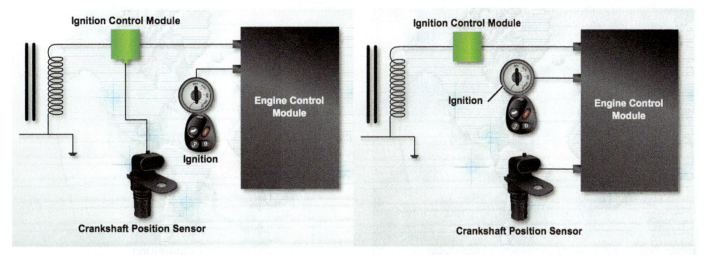

FIGURE 28–11 The CKP sensor sends a signal to the ignition module (older vehicles) or to the PCM (current models), depending on the type of system. (*Courtesy of General Motors*)

grounded is obviously weak or defective. Check the spark plug wire or connector with an ohmmeter to be certain of continuity.

STEP 2 Check all cylinders by grounding them out one at a time. If one weak cylinder is found (very little RPM drop), check the other cylinder using the same ignition coil (except on engines that use an individual coil for each cylinder). If both cylinders are affected, the problem could be an open spark plug wire, defective spark plug, or defective ignition coil.

STEP 3 To help eliminate other possible problems and determine exactly what is wrong, switch the suspected ignition coil to another position (if possible).

- If the problem now affects the other cylinders, the ignition coil is defective and must be replaced.
- If the problem does not "change positions" with changing the position of the ignition coil, the control module affecting the suspected coil or either cylinder's spark plug or spark plug wire could be defective.

TESTING FOR A NO-START CONDITION

A no-start condition (with normal engine cranking speed) can be the result of either no spark or no fuel delivery.

Older engine-control systems used the ignition primary pulses as a signal to inject fuel—a port or throttle-body injection (TBI) style of fuel—injection system. If there is no ignition pulse, then there is no injection of fuel. Newer models use the signals directly from the CKP sensor to trigger both ignition and fuel injection. The CKP signal is the main input that triggers the ignition spark. ● **SEE FIGURE 28–11.**

To determine exactly what is wrong, follow these steps:

STEP 1 Test the output signal from the crankshaft sensor. Most engines use a crankshaft position sensor. These sensors are either the Hall-effect type or the magnetic type. The sensors must be able to produce either a sine or a digital signal. A meter set on AC volts should read a voltage across the sensor leads when the engine is being cranked. If there is no AC voltage output, replace the sensor. For Hall-effect sensors, check the power supply and ground before replacing the sensor.

STEP 2 If the sensor tests okay in step 1, check for a changing AC voltage signal at the ignition module or powertrain control module (PCM), depending on the type of system.

NOTE: Step 2 checks the wiring between the crankshaft position sensor and the ignition control module or PCM.

STEP 3 If the ignition control module is receiving a changing signal from the crankshaft position sensor, it must be capable of switching the power to the ignition coils on and off. Remove a coil or coil pack, and with the ignition switched to on (run), check for voltage at the positive terminal of the coil(s).

STEP 4 Use a test light across the coil positive and the coil negative (trigger) wire and crank the engine. The test light should pulse. If the module is not pulsing the negative side of the coil, replace the ignition control module or check the wiring between the PCM and the coil.

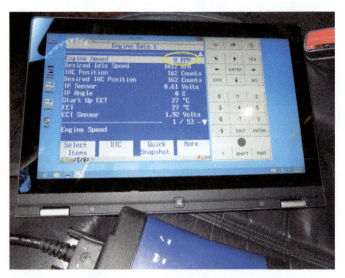

FIGURE 28–12 A scan tool showing zero RPM while cranking (circled) indicates a problem with the CKP sensor or related wiring.

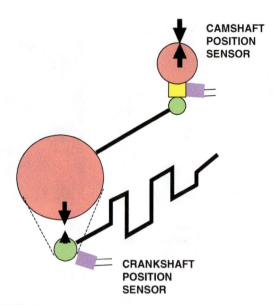

FIGURE 28–13 The relationship between the crankshaft position (CKP) sensor and the camshaft position (CMP) sensor is affected by wear in the timing gear and/or chain.

NOTE: Before replacing the ignition control module, be certain that it is properly grounded (where applicable) and that the module is receiving ignition power from the ignition circuit.

CAUTION: Most ignition systems can produce 40,000 volts or more, with energy levels high enough to cause personal injury. Do not open the circuit of an electronic ignition secondary wire, because damage to the system (or to you) can occur.

DISTRIBUTOR INDEXING

A few engines using a distributor also use it to house a camshaft position (CMP) sensor. One purpose of this sensor is to properly initiate the fuel-injection sequence. Some of these engines use a positive distributor position notch or clamp that allows the distributor to be placed in only one position, while others use a method of **indexing** to verify the distributor position. If a distributor is not indexed correctly, the following symptoms may occur:

- Surging (especially at idle speed)
- Light bucking
- Intermittent engine misfiring

NOTE: This is *not* the same as setting the ignition timing. Indexing the distributor does not affect the ignition timing.

Always use the factory procedure as stated in service information. Most methods require a scan tool. Some GM trucks require indexing. ● **SEE FIGURE 28–13.**

SECONDARY IGNITION INSPECTION

DISTRIBUTOR CAP AND ROTOR Inspect a **distributor cap** for a worn or cracked center carbon insert, excessive side insert wear or corrosion, cracks, or carbon tracks, and check the towers for burning or corrosion by removing spark plug wires from the distributor cap one at a time. A defective distributor cap affects starting and engine performance, especially in high-moisture conditions. If a carbon track is detected, it is

FIGURE 28–14 Corroded terminals on a waste-spark coil can cause misfire diagnostic trouble codes to be set.

most likely the result of a high-resistance or open spark plug wire. Replacement of a distributor cap because of a carbon track without checking and replacing the defective spark plug wire(s) often will result in the new distributor cap failing in a short time. It is recommended that the distributor cap and rotor be inspected every year and replaced if defective. Generally, distributor caps should only need replacement after every three or four years of normal service.

COP AND WASTE SPARK INSPECTION
If a misfire is being diagnosed, perform a thorough visual inspection of the coil-on-lug (COP) assembly and look for evidence of carbon track or heat-related faults to the plug boot.

Check ignition coils of waste spark and coil-on-plug (COP) systems for signs of **carbon tracks** (black lines) or corrosion.

When checking a waste spark-type ignition system, check that the coils are clean and that the spark plug wires are attached to the specified coil and coil terminal. ● **SEE FIGURES 28–14 AND 28–15**.

SPARK PLUG WIRE INSPECTION
Spark plug wires should be visually inspected for cuts or defective insulation and checked for resistance with an ohmmeter. Good spark plug wires should measure less than 10,000 ohms per foot of length. ● **SEE FIGURES 28–16**. Faulty spark plug wire insulation can cause hard starting or no starting in damp weather conditions.

FIGURE 28–15 This spark plug boot on an overhead camshaft engine has been arcing to the valve cover causing a misfire to occur.

 **TECH TIP**

Spark Plug Wire Pliers Are a Good Investment

Spark plug wires are often difficult to remove. Using a good-quality spark plug wire plier, such as shown in ● **FIGURE 28–17**, saves time and reduces the chance of harming the wire during removal.

 **TECH TIP**

Route the Wires Right!

High voltage is present through spark plug wires when the engine is running. Surrounding the spark plugs is a magnetic field that can affect other circuits or components of the vehicle. For example, if a spark plug wire is routed too closely to the signal wire from a mass airflow (MAF) sensor, the induced signal from the ignition wire could create a false MAF signal to the computer. The computer, not able to detect that the signal was false, would act on the MAF signal and command the appropriate amount of fuel based on the false MAF signal.

To prevent any problems associated with high-voltage spark plug wires, be sure to route them as manufactured using all the factory holding brackets and wiring combs. ● **SEE FIGURE 28–18**. If the factory method is unknown, most factory service information shows the correct routing.

FIGURE 28–16 Measuring the resistance of a spark plug wire with a multimeter set to the ohms position. The reading of 0.1603 kΩ (16.030 ohms) is okay because the wire is about 2 feet long. Maximum allowable resistance for a spark plug wire this long would be 20 kΩ (20,000 ohms). High resistance spark plug wires can cause an engine misfire especially during acceleration.

FIGURE 28–17 Spark plug wire boot pliers is a handy addition to any tool box.

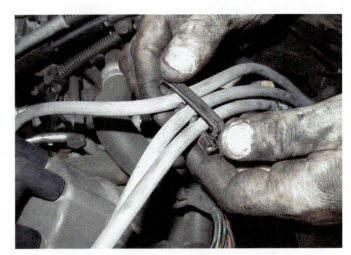

FIGURE 28–18 Always take the time to install spark plug wires back into the original holding brackets (wiring combs).

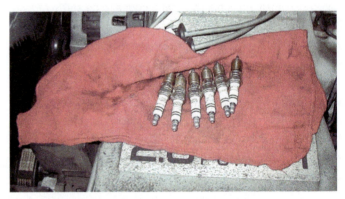

FIGURE 28–19 When removing spark plugs, it is wise to arrange them so that they can be compared and any problem can be identified with a particular cylinder.

SPARK PLUG SERVICE

THE NEED FOR SERVICE Spark plugs should be inspected when an engine performance problem occurs and should be replaced at specified intervals to ensure proper ignition system performance. Most spark plugs have a service life of over 20,000 miles (32,000 km). Platinum-tipped original equipment spark plugs have a typical service life of 60,000 to 100,000 miles (100,000 to 160,000 km). Used spark plugs should *not* be cleaned and reused unless absolutely necessary. The labor required to **remove and replace (R & R)** spark plugs is the same whether the spark plugs are replaced or cleaned. Although cleaning spark plugs often restores proper engine operation, the service life of cleaned spark plugs is definitely shorter than that of new spark plugs. *Platinum-tipped spark plugs should not be regapped!* Using a gapping tool can break the platinum after it has been used in an engine.

Be certain that the engine is cool before removing spark plugs, especially on engines with aluminum cylinder heads. To help prevent dirt from getting into the cylinder of an engine while removing a spark plug, use compressed air or a brush to remove dirt from around the spark plug before removal. ● **SEE FIGURES 28–19 THROUGH 28–21.**

SPARK PLUG INSPECTION Spark plugs are the windows to the inside of the combustion chamber. A thorough visual

FIGURE 28–20 A spark plug thread chaser is a low-cost tool that hopefully will not be used often, but is necessary to use to clean the threads before new spark plugs are installed.

FIGURE 28–21 Since 1991, General Motors engines have been equipped with slightly (1/8 inch or 3 mm) longer spark plugs. This requires that a longer spark plug socket should be used to prevent the possibility of cracking a spark plug during installation. The longer socket is shown next to a normal 5/8 inch spark plug socket.

inspection of the spark plugs often can lead to the root cause of an engine performance problem. Two indications on spark plugs and their possible root causes in engine performance include the following:

1. **Carbon fouling.** If the spark plug(s) has *dry black carbon* (soot), the usual causes include:
   - Excessive idling
   - Slow-speed driving under light loads that keeps the spark plug temperatures too low to burn off the deposits
   - Overrich air–fuel mixture
   - Weak ignition system output

2. **Oil fouling.** If the spark plug has *wet, oily* deposits with little electrode wear, oil may be getting into the combustion chamber from the following:
   - Worn or broken piston rings
   - Defective or missing valve stem seals

NOTE: If the deposits are heavier on the side of the plug facing the intake valve, the cause is usually due to excessive valve stem clearance or defective intake valve stem seals.

When removing spark plugs, place them in order so that they can be inspected to check for engine problems that might affect one or more cylinders. All spark plugs should be in the same condition, and the color of the center insulator should be light tan or gray. If all the spark plugs are black or dark, the engine should be checked for conditions that could cause an overly rich air–fuel mixture or possible oil burning. If only one or a few spark plugs are black, check those cylinders for proper firing (possible defective spark plug wire) or an engine condition affecting only those particular cylinders. ● **SEE FIGURES 28–22 THROUGH 28–25.**

FIGURE 28–22 A normally worn spark plug that has a tapered platinum-tipped center electrode.

If all spark plugs are white, check for possible overadvanced ignition timing or a vacuum leak causing a lean air–fuel mixture. If only one or a few spark plugs are white, check for a vacuum leak affecting the fuel mixture only to those particular cylinders.

NOTE: The engine computer "senses" rich or lean air–fuel ratios by means of input from the oxygen sensor. If one cylinder is lean, the computer may make all other cylinders richer to compensate.

FIGURE 28–23 A worn spark plug showing fuel and/or oil deposits.

FIGURE 28–24 A spark plug from an engine that had a blown head gasket. The white deposits could be from the additives in the coolant.

SPARK PLUG	TORQUE WITH TORQUE WRENCH (lb-ft)		TORQUE WITHOUT TORQUE WRENCH (TURNS)	
	CAST-IRON HEAD	ALUMINUM HEAD	CAST-IRON HEAD	ALUMINUM HEAD
Gasket				
14 mm	26–30	18–22	1/4	1/4
18 mm	32–38	28–34	1/4	1/4
Tapered seat				
14 mm	7–15	7–15	1/16 (snug)	1/16 (snug)
18 mm	15–20	15–20	1/16 (snug)	1/16 (snug)

CHART 28–1

Typical spark plug tightening torque based on type of spark plug and the cylinder head material.

Inspect all spark plugs for wear by first checking the condition of the center electrode. As a spark plug wears, the center electrode becomes rounded. If the center electrode is rounded, higher ignition system voltage is required to fire the spark plug. When installing spark plugs, always use the correct tightening torque to ensure proper heat transfer from the spark plug shell to the cylinder head. ● SEE CHART 28–1.

NOTE: General Motors does not recommend the use of antiseize compound on the threads of spark plugs being installed in an aluminum cylinder head, because the

FIGURE 28–25 A platinum tipped spark plug that is fuel soaked indicating a fault with the fuel system or the ignition system causing the spark plug to not fire.

spark plug will be overtightened. This excessive tightening torque places the threaded portion of the spark plug too far into the combustion chamber where carbon can accumulate and result in the spark plugs being difficult to remove.

QUICK AND EASY SECONDARY IGNITION TESTS

Engine running problems often are caused by defective or out-of-adjustment ignition components. Many ignition problems involve the high-voltage secondary ignition circuit. Following are some quick and easy secondary ignition tests:

TEST 1 If there is a crack in a distributor cap, coil, or spark plug, or if there is a defective spark plug wire, a spark may be visible at night. Because the highest voltage is required during partial throttle acceleration, the

FIGURE 28–26 A water spray bottle is an excellent diagnostic tool to help find an intermittent engine misfire caused by a break in a secondary ignition circuit component.

technician's assistant should accelerate the engine slightly with the gear selector in drive or second gear (if manual transmission) and the brake firmly applied. If any spark is visible or a "snapping" sound is heard, the location should be closely inspected and the defective parts replaced. A blue glow or "corona" around the shell of the spark plug is normal and not an indication of a defective spark plug.

TEST 2 For intermittent problems, use a spray bottle to apply a water mist to the spark plugs, distributor cap, and spark plug wires. ● **SEE FIGURE 28–26**. With the engine running, the water may cause an arc through any weak insulating materials and cause the engine to misfire or stall.

NOTE: Adding a little salt or liquid soap to the water makes the water more conductive and also makes it easier to find those hard-to-diagnose intermittent ignition faults.

IGNITION TIMING

On older vehicles with distributor ignition systems, the ignition timing can be checked and adjusted. Generally, for testing, engines must be at idle with computer engine controls put into **base timing**, the timing of the spark before the computer advances the timing. To be assured of the proper ignition timing, follow exactly the timing procedure indicated on the

FIGURE 28–27 Typical timing marks. The numbers of the degrees are on the stationary plate and the notch is on the harmonic balancer.

underhood emission (VECI) decal. ● **SEE FIGURE 28–27** for a typical ignition timing plate and mark.

If the ignition timing is too far *advanced*, for example, if it is set at 12 degrees before top dead center (BTDC) instead of 8 degrees BTDC, the following symptoms may occur:

1. Engine ping or spark knock may be heard, especially while driving up a hill or during acceleration.

2. Cranking (starting) may be slow and jerky, especially when the engine is warm.

3. The engine may overheat.

If the ignition timing is too far *retarded*, for example, if it is set at 4 degrees BTDC instead of 8 degrees BTDC, the following symptoms may occur:

1. The engine may lack power and performance.

2. The engine may require a long period of starter cranking before starting.

3. Poor fuel economy may result.

4. The engine may overheat.

PRETIMING CHECKS Before the ignition timing is checked or adjusted, the following items should be checked to ensure accurate timing results:

1. The engine should be at normal operating temperature (the upper radiator hose should be hot and pressurized).

2. The engine should be at the correct timing RPM (check the specifications).

3. The vacuum hoses should be removed, and the hose from the vacuum advance unit on the distributor (if the

vehicle is so equipped) should be plugged unless otherwise specified.

4. If the engine is computer equipped, check the timing procedure specified by the manufacturer. This may include disconnecting a "set timing" connector wire, grounding a diagnostic terminal, disconnecting a four-wire connector, or similar procedure.

NOTE: General Motors specifies many different timing procedures depending on the engine, type of fuel system, and type of ignition system. Always consult the emission decal under the hood or service information for the exact procedure to follow.

TIMING LIGHT CONNECTIONS For checking or adjusting ignition timing, make the timing light connections as follows:

1. Connect the timing light battery leads to the vehicle battery: the red to the positive terminal and the black to the negative terminal.

2. Connect the timing light high-tension lead to spark plug cable 1.

NOTE: If cylinder 1 is difficult to reach, such as up against the bulkhead (firewall) or close to an exhaust manifold, simply use the opposite cylinder in the firing order (paired cylinder). The timing light will not detect the difference and will indicate the correct position of the timing mark in relation to the pointer or degree mark.

CHECKING OR ADJUSTING IGNITION TIMING Use the following steps for checking or adjusting ignition timing:

1. Start the engine and adjust the speed to that specified for ignition timing.

2. With the timing light aimed at the stationary timing pointer, observe the position of the timing mark on the vibration damper with the light flashing. Refer to the manufacturer's specifications on underhood decal for the correct setting.

3. To adjust timing, loosen the distributor locking bolt or nut and turn the distributor housing until the timing mark is in correct alignment. Turn the distributor housing in the direction of rotor rotation to retard the timing and against rotor rotation to advance the timing.

4. After adjusting the timing to specifications, carefully tighten the distributor locking bolt. Sometimes it is necessary to readjust the timing after the initial setting because the distributor may rotate slightly when the hold-down bolt is tightened.

Two Marks Are the Key to Success

When a distributor is removed from an engine, always mark the direction the rotor is pointing to ensure that the distributor is reinstalled in the correct position. Because of the helical cut on the distributor drive gear, the rotor rotates as the distributor is being removed from the engine. To help reinstall a distributor without any problems, simply make another mark where the rotor is pointing just as the distributor is lifted out of the engine. Then to reinstall, simply line up the rotor to the second mark and lower the distributor into the engine. The rotor should then line up with the original mark as a double check.

IGNITION SYSTEM SYMPTOM GUIDE

PROBLEM	POSSIBLE CAUSES AND/OR SOLUTIONS
No spark out of the coil	• Possible open in the ignition switch circuit • Possible defective ignition module (if electronic ignition coil) • Possible defective crankshaft position sensor (CKP)
Weak spark out of the coil	• Possible high-resistance coil wire or spark plug wire • Possible poor ground between the distributor or module and the engine block • Ignition coil internally tracked or partially shorted
Engine misfire	• Possible defective (open) spark plug wire • Possible worn or fouled spark plugs • Possible defective CKP sensor • Possible defective module • Possible poor electrical connections at the CKP sensor and/or module

SUMMARY

1. A thorough visual inspection should be performed on all ignition components when diagnosing an engine performance problem.

2. Platinum spark plugs should not be regapped after use in an engine.

3. The crankshaft position sensor is a primary input for the ignition system.

4. A scan tool can be used to check for the proper RPM signal from the crankshaft position sensor.

REVIEW QUESTIONS

1. Why should a spark tester be used to check for spark rather than a standard spark plug?

2. How do you test a magnetic sensor for resistance and AC voltage output?

3. What harm can occur if the engine is cranked or run with an open (defective) spark plug wire?

4. What tests can be performed on a CKP sensor?

5. Explain how to check spark plug wires.

CHAPTER QUIZ

1. A scan tool shows no zero RPM while the engine is cranking. Technician A says that the RPM sender is bad. Technician B says that the crankshaft position sensor could be bad. Which technician is correct?
   a. Technician A only
   b. Technician B only
   c. Both Technicians A and B
   d. Neither Technician A nor B

2. Technician A says that a defective spark plug wire or boot can cause an engine misfire. Technician B says that a tracked ignition coil can cause an engine misfire. Which technician is correct?
   a. Technician A only
   b. Technician B only
   c. Both Technicians A and B
   d. Neither Technician A nor B

3. The _____ sends a pulse signal to an electronic ignition module.
   a. Ballast resistor
   b. Pickup coil
   c. Ignition coil
   d. Condenser

4. Typical primary coil resistance specifications usually range from _____ ohms.
   a. 100 to 450
   b. 500 to 1,500
   c. Less than 1 to 3
   d. 6,000 to 30,000

5. Typical secondary coil resistance specifications usually range from _____ ohms.
   a. 100 to 450
   b. 500 to 1,500
   c. 1 to 3
   d. 6,000 to 30,000

6. Technician A says that an engine will not start and run if the ignition coil is tracked. Technician B says the engine will not start if the crankshaft position sensor fails. Which technician is correct?
   a. Technician A only
   b. Technician B only
   c. Both Technicians A and B
   d. Neither Technician A nor B

7. Technician A says that a tracked distributor cap can cause an engine misfire during acceleration. Technician B says that a defective spark plug wire can cause an engine misfire during acceleration. Which technician is correct?
   a. Technician A only
   b. Technician B only
   c. Both Technicians A and B
   d. Neither Technician A nor B

8. The secondary ignition circuit can be tested using _____.
   a. An ohmmeter
   b. Visual inspection
   c. An ammeter
   d. Both a and b

9. Two technicians are discussing a no-start (no-spark) condition. Technician A says that an open pickup coil could be the cause. Technician B says that a defective ignition control module (ICM) could be the cause. Which technician is correct?
   a. Technician A only
   b. Technician B only
   c. Both Technicians A and B
   d. Neither Technician A nor B

10. Which sensor produces a square wave signal?
    a. Magnetic sensor
    b. Hall-effect sensor
    c. MAP sensor
    d. Coolant sensor

chapter 29
COMPUTER AND NETWORK FUNDAMENTALS

LEARNING OBJECTIVES

After studying this chapter, the reader should be able to:

1. Explain the purpose and function of onboard computers.
2. List the various parts of an automotive computer.
3. List input sensors and output device controlled by the computer.
4. Check for module communication errors using a scan tool.

This chapter will help you prepare for Engine Repair (A6) ASE certification test content area "A" (General Electrical/Electronic Systems Diagnosis).

6. Test GMLAN high/mid-speed using electrical/electronic tools.
7. Perform voltage testing at the DLC on GMLAN.

STC OBJECTIVES

GM Service Technical College topics covered in this chapter are:

1. Diagnose GMLAN low speed using a systematic process.
2. Test GMLAN low speed using Electrical/Electronic tools.
3. Test Class 2 using Electrical/Electronic tools.
4. Test LIN network using electrical/electronic tools.
5. Diagnose GMLAN high/mid-speed using a systematic process.

KEY TERMS

Actuator 453
Analog-to-digital (AD) converter 455
Central processing unit (CPU) 456
Class 2 463
Clock generator 456
Controller 457
Controller area network (CAN) 461
Digital computer 455
Duty cycle 455
EEPROM 453
E^2 PROM 453
Electronic control assembly (ECA) 457
Electronic control module (ECM) 457
Electronic control unit (ECU) 457
Engine mapping 456
Expansion bus 466

GMLAN 464
Input conditioning 452
Keep-alive memory (KAM) 453
Keyword 2000 464
LIN 464
Multiplexing 459
Network 459
Powertrain Control Module (PCM) 452
Programmable read-only memory (PROM) 453
Random-access memory (RAM) 453
Read-only memory (ROM) 452
Serial data 459
Splice pack 459
UART 464
Terminating resistors 462

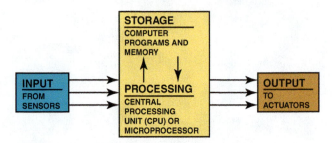

FIGURE 29–1 All computer systems perform four basic functions: input, processing, storage, and output.

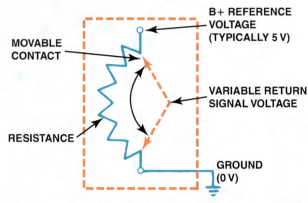

FIGURE 29–2 A potentiometer uses a movable contact to vary resistance and send an analog voltage to the PCM.

COMPUTER CONTROL

Modern automotive control systems consist of a network of electronic sensors, actuators, and computer modules designed to regulate the powertrain and vehicle support systems. The **Powertrain Control Module (PCM)** is the heart of this system. It coordinates engine and transmission operation, processes data, maintains communications, and makes the control decisions needed to keep the vehicle operating.

Automotive computers use voltage to send and receive information. Voltage is electrical pressure and does not flow through circuits, but voltage can be used as a signal. A computer converts input information or data into voltage signal combinations that represent number combinations. The number combinations can represent a variety of information—temperature, speed, or even words and letters. A computer processes the input voltage signals it receives by computing what they represent, and then delivering the data in computed or processed form.

THE FOUR BASIC COMPUTER FUNCTIONS

The operation of every computer can be divided into the following four basic functions: ● **SEE FIGURE 29–1.**

- Input
- Processing
- Storage
- Output

These basic functions are not unique to computers; they can be found in many noncomputer systems. However, we need to know how the computer handles these functions.

INPUT First, the computer receives a voltage signal (input) from an input device. The device can be as simple as a button or a switch on an instrument panel, or a sensor on an automotive engine. ● **SEE FIGURE 29–2** for a typical type of automotive sensor.

Vehicles use various mechanical, electrical, and magnetic sensors to measure factors such as vehicle speed, engine RPM, air pressure, oxygen content of exhaust gas, airflow, and engine coolant temperature. Each sensor transmits its information in the form of voltage signals. The computer receives these voltage signals, but before it can use them, the signals must undergo a process called **input conditioning**. This process includes amplifying voltage signals that are too small for the computer circuitry to handle. Input conditioners generally are located inside the computer, but a few sensors have their own input-conditioning circuitry.

PROCESSING Input voltage signals received by a computer are processed through a series of electronic logic circuits maintained in its programmed instructions. These logic circuits change the input voltage signals, or data, into output voltage signals or commands.

STORAGE The program instructions for a computer are stored in electronic memory. Some programs may require that certain input data be stored for later reference or future processing. In others, output commands may be delayed or stored before they are transmitted to devices elsewhere in the system.

Computers have two types of memory: permanent and temporary. Permanent memory is called **read-only memory (ROM)** because the computer can only read the contents; it cannot change the data stored in it. This data is retained even when power to the computer is shut off. Part of the ROM is built into the computer, and the rest is located in an IC chip called

FIGURE 29–3 A replaceable PROM used in an older General Motors computer. The access panel has been removed to gain access.

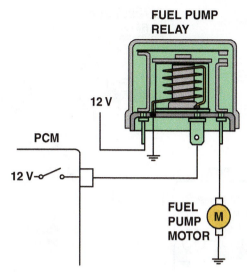

FIGURE 29–4 A typical output driver. In this case, the PCM applies voltage to the fuel pump relay coil to energize the fuel pump.

a **programmable read-only memory (PROM)** or calibration assembly. ● **SEE FIGURE 29–3.** Many chips are erasable, meaning that the program can be changed. These chips are called erasable programmable read-only memory or EPROM. Since the early 1990s most programmable memory has been electronically erasable, meaning that the program in the chip can be reprogrammed by using a scan tool and the proper software. This computer reprogramming is usually called *reflashing*. These chips are electrically erasable programmable read-only memory, abbreviated **EEPROM** or **E² PROM**. All vehicles equipped with onboard diagnosis second generation, called OBD II, are equipped with EEPROMs.

Temporary memory is called **random-access memory (RAM)** because the microprocessor can write or store new data into it as directed by the computer program, as well as read the data already in it. Automotive computers use two types of RAM memory: volatile and nonvolatile. Volatile RAM memory is lost whenever the ignition is turned off. However, a type of volatile RAM called **keep-alive memory (KAM)** can be wired directly to battery power. This prevents its data from being erased when the ignition is turned off. Both RAM and KAM have the disadvantage of losing their memory when disconnected from their power source. One example of RAM and KAM is the loss of station settings in a programmable radio when the battery is disconnected. Since all the settings are stored in RAM, they have to be reset when the battery is reconnected. System trouble codes are commonly stored in RAM and can be erased by disconnecting the battery.

Nonvolatile RAM memory can retain its information even when the battery is disconnected. One use for this type of RAM is the storage of odometer information in an electronic speedometer. The memory chip retains the mileage accumulated by the vehicle. When speedometer replacement is necessary, the odometer chip is removed and installed in the new speedometer unit. KAM is used primarily in conjunction with adaptive strategies.

OUTPUT After the computer has processed the input signals, it sends voltage signals or commands to other devices in the system, such as system actuators. An **actuator** is an electrical or mechanical device that converts electrical energy into heat, light, or motion, such as adjusting engine idle speed, altering suspension height, or regulating fuel metering.

Computers also can communicate with, and control, each other through their output and input functions. This means that the output signal from one computer system can be the input signal for another computer system through a network.

Most outputs work electrically in one of three ways:

- Switched
- Pulse-width modulated
- Digital

A switched output is an output that is either on or off. In many circuits, the PCM uses a relay to switch a device on or off. This is because the relay is a low-current device that can switch a higher-current device. Most computer circuits cannot handle a lot of current. By using a relay circuit as shown in ● **FIGURE 29–4**, the PCM provides the output control to the

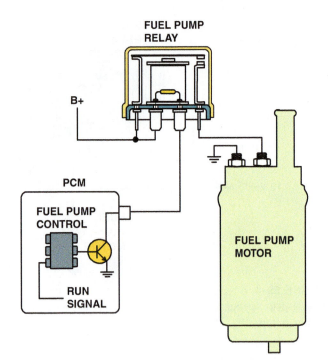

FIGURE 29–5 A typical low-side driver (LSD) which uses a control module to control the ground side of the relay coil.

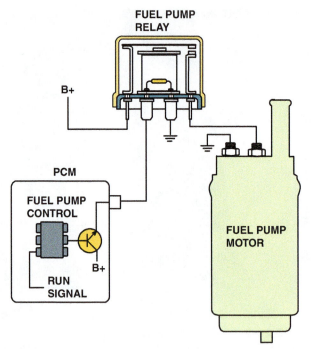

FIGURE 29–6 A typical module-controlled high-side driver (HSD) where the module itself supplies the electrical power to the device. The logic circuit inside the module can detect circuit faults including continuity of the circuit and if there is a short-to-ground in the circuit being controlled.

relay, which in turn provides the output control to the device. The relay coil, which the PCM controls, typically draws less than 0.5 amperes. The device that the relay controls may draw 30 amperes or more. These switches are actually transistors, often called output drivers.

LOW-SIDE DRIVERS Low-side drivers, often abbreviated LSD, are transistors that complete the ground path in the circuit. Ignition voltage is supplied to the relay as well as battery voltage. The computer output is connected to the ground side of the relay coil. The computer energizes the fuel pump relay by turning the transistor on and completing the ground path for the relay coil. A relatively low current flows through the relay coil and transistor that is inside the computer. This causes the relay to switch and provides the fuel pump with battery voltage. The majority of switched outputs have typically been low-side drivers. ● **SEE FIGURE 29–5.** Low-side drivers can often perform a diagnostic circuit check by monitoring the voltage from the relay to check that the control circuit for the relay is complete. A low-side driver, however, cannot detect a short-to-ground.

HIGH-SIDE DRIVERS High-side drivers, often abbreviated HSD, control the power side of the circuit. In these applications when the transistor is switched on, voltage is applied to the device. A ground has been provided to the device so when the high-side driver switches the device will be energized.

In some applications, high-side drivers are used instead of low-side drivers to provide better circuit protection. General Motors vehicles have used a high-side driver to control the fuel pump relay instead of a low-side driver. In the event of an accident, should the circuit to the fuel pump relay become grounded, a high-side driver would cause a short circuit, which would cause the fuel pump relay to de-energize. High-side drivers inside modules can detect electrical faults such as a lack of continuity when the circuit is not energized. ● **SEE FIGURE 29–6.**

PULSE WIDTH MODULATION Pulse width modulation (PWM) is a method of controlling an output using a digital signal. Instead of just turning devices on or off, the computer can control output devices more precisely by using pulse width modulation. For example, a vacuum solenoid could be a pulse-width modulated device. If the vacuum solenoid is controlled by a switched driver, switching either on or off would mean that either full vacuum would flow through the solenoid or no vacuum would flow through the solenoid. However, to control the amount of vacuum that flows through the solenoid, pulse width modulation could be used. A PWM signal is a digital signal, usually 0 and 12 volts, that is cycling at a fixed frequency. Varying the length of time that the signal is on, provides a signal that can vary the on and off time of an

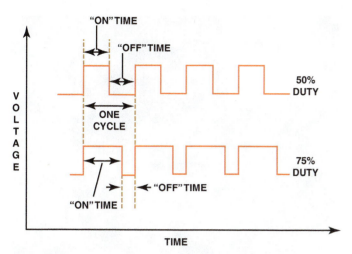

FIGURE 29–7 Both the top and bottom pattern have the same frequency. However, the amount of on-time varies. Duty cycle is the percentage of the time during a cycle that the signal is turned on.

FIGURE 29–8 Many electronic components are used to construct a typical vehicle computer. (*Courtesy of General Motors*)

output. The ratio of on-time relative to the period of the cycle is referred to as **duty cycle**. ● SEE FIGURE 29–7. Depending on the frequency of the signal, which is usually fixed, this signal would turn the device on and off a fixed number of times per second. When, for example, the voltage is high (12 volts) 90% of the time and low (0 volt) the other 10% of the time, the signal has a 90% duty cycle. In other words, if this signal were applied to the vacuum solenoid, the solenoid would be on 90% of the time. This would allow more vacuum to flow through the solenoid. The computer has the ability to vary this on and off time or pulse width modulation at any rate between 0 and 100%.

A good example of pulse width modulation is the cooling fan speed control. The speed of the cooling fan is controlled by varying the amount of on-time that the battery voltage is applied to the cooling fan motor.

100% duty cycle—the fan runs at full speed

75% duty cycle—the fan runs at 3/4 speed

50% duty cycle—the fan runs at 1/2 speed

25% duty cycle—the fan runs at 1/4 speed

The use of PWM, therefore, results in very precise control of an output device to achieve the amount of cooling needed and conserve electrical energy compared to simply timing the cooling fan on high when needed. PWM may be used to control vacuum through a solenoid, the amount of purge of the evaporative purge solenoid, the speed of a fuel pump motor, control of a linear motor, or even the intensity of a lightbulb.

DIGITAL COMPUTERS

In a **digital computer**, the voltage signal or processing function is a simple high/low, yes/no, on/off signal. The digital signal voltage is limited to two voltage levels: high voltage and low voltage. Since there is no stepped range of voltage or current in between, a digital binary signal is a "square wave."

The signal is called "digital" because the on and off signals are processed by the computer as the digits or numbers 0 and 1. The number system containing only these two digits is called the binary system. Any number or letter from any number system or language alphabet can be translated into a combination of binary 0s and 1s for the digital computer.

A digital computer changes the analog input signals (voltage) to digital bits (*bi*nary di*git*s) of information through an **analog-to-digital (AD) converter** circuit. The binary digital number is used by the computer in its calculations or logic networks. Output signals usually are digital signals that turn system actuators on and off.

The digital computer can process thousands of digital signals per second because its circuits are able to switch voltage signals on and off in billionths of a second. ● SEE FIGURE 29–8.

PARTS OF A COMPUTER The software consists of the programs and logic functions stored in the computer's circuitry. The hardware is the mechanical and electronic parts of a computer.

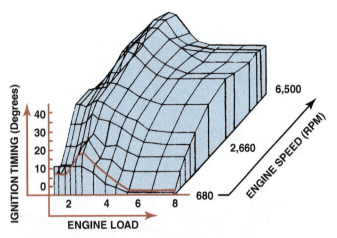

FIGURE 29–9 Typical ignition timing map developed from testing and used by the vehicle computer to provide the optimum ignition timing for all engine speeds and load combinations.

FIGURE 29–10 The clock generator produces a series of pulses that are used by the microprocessor and other components to stay in step with each other at a steady rate.

CENTRAL PROCESSING UNIT (CPU). The microprocessor is the **central processing unit** of a computer. Since it performs the essential mathematical operations and logic decisions that make up its processing function, the CPU can be considered to be the brain of a computer. Some computers use more than one microprocessor, called a coprocessor.

COMPUTER MEMORY. Other IC devices store the computer operating program, system sensor input data, and system actuator output data, information that is necessary for CPU operation.

COMPUTER PROGRAMS
By operating a vehicle on a dynamometer and manually adjusting the variable factors such as speed, load, and spark timing, it is possible to determine the optimum output settings for the best driveability, economy, and emission control. This is called **engine mapping**. ● **SEE FIGURE 29–9.**

Engine mapping creates a three-dimensional performance graph that applies to a given vehicle and powertrain combination. Each combination is mapped in this manner to produce a PROM. This allows an automaker to use one basic computer for all models; a unique PROM individualizes the computer for a particular model. Also, if a driveability problem can be resolved by a change in the program, the manufacturers can release a revised PROM to supersede the earlier part.

Many older vehicle computers used a single PROM that plugged into the computer. Since the mid-1990s the PROM chip is not removable. The computer must be programmed, or flashed before being put into service.

CLOCK RATES AND TIMING
The microprocessor receives sensor input voltage signals, processes them by using information from other memory units, and then sends voltage signals to the appropriate actuators. The microprocessor communicates by transmitting long strings of 0s and 1s in a language called binary code. But the microprocessor must have some way of knowing when one signal ends and another begins. That is the job of a crystal oscillator called a **clock generator**. ● **SEE FIGURE 29–10.** The computer's crystal oscillator generates a steady stream of one-bit-long voltage pulses. Both the microprocessor and the memories monitor the clock pulses while they are communicating. Because they know how long each voltage pulse should be, they can distinguish between a 01 and a 0011. To complete the process, the input and output circuits also watch the clock pulses.

COMPUTER SPEEDS
Not all computers operate at the same speed; some are faster than others. The speed at which a computer operates is specified by the cycle time, or clock speed, required to perform certain measurements. Cycle time or clock speed is measured in megahertz (4.7, 8.0, 15, 18 MHz, etc.).

BAUD RATE
The computer transmits bits of a serial data stream at precise intervals. The computer's processing speed is called the baud rate, or bits per second. Just as mph helps in estimating the length of time required to travel a certain distance, the baud rate is useful in estimating how long a given computer will need to transmit a specified amount of data to

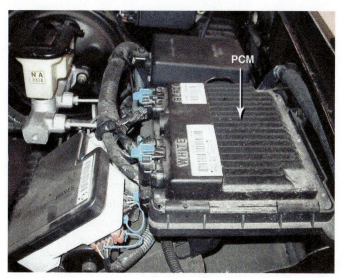

FIGURE 29–11 This powertrain control module (PCM) is located under the hood on this Chevrolet pickup truck.

another computer. Storage of a single character requires eight bits per byte, plus an additional two bits to indicate stop and start. This means that transmission of one character requires 10 bits. Dividing the baud rate by 10 tells us the maximum number of words per second that can be transmitted. For example, if the computer has a baud rate of 600, approximately 60 words can be received or sent per minute.

Automotive computers have evolved from a baud rate of 160 used in the early 1980s to a baud rate as high as 500,000 for some networks. The speed of data transmission is an important factor both in system operation and in system troubleshooting.

CONTROL MODULE LOCATIONS The onboard automotive computer has many names. It may be called an **electronic control unit (ECU)**, **electronic control module (ECM)**, **electronic control assembly (ECA)**, or a **controller**, depending on the manufacturer and the computer application. The Society of Automotive Engineers (SAE) bulletin, J-1930, standardizes the name as a powertrain control module (PCM). The computer hardware is all mounted on one or more circuit boards and installed in a metal case to help shield it from electromagnetic interference (EMI). The wiring harnesses that link the computer to sensors and actuators connect to multipin connectors or edge connectors on the circuit boards.

Onboard computers range from single-function units that control a single operation to multifunction units that manage all of the separate (but linked) electronic systems in the vehicle. They vary in size from a small module to a notebook-sized box. Some engine computers are installed in the passenger compartment either under the instrument panel or in a side kick panel while most GM PCMs are mounted under the hood.
● **SEE FIGURES 29–11 AND 29–12.**

FIGURE 29–12 This engine control module (ECM) measures about 6 × 6 × 1 inches. (*Courtesy of General Motors*)

COMPUTER INPUTS

The vehicle computer uses signals (voltage levels) from a variety of sensors, including the following:

ECT (Engine Coolant Temperature). The engine coolant temperature (ECT) sensor is used to measure the engine coolant temperature to help determine the amount of fuel and spark advance. This is an important sensor, especially when the engine is cold and when the engine is first started.

MAP (Manifold Absolute Pressure). The manifold absolute pressure (MAP) sensor is a strain gauge-type sensor that measures changes in the intake manifold pressure. The ECM uses this information, which indicates engine load, to calculate fuel delivery and spark timing (some vehicles) and for onboard diagnosis of other sensors and systems such as the exhaust gas recirculation (EGR) system. When the engine is not running, the manifold is at atmospheric pressure, and the MAP sensor registers barometric pressure (BARO).

MAF (Mass Air Flow) Sensor. The mass air flow (MAF) sensor is positioned in the intake air duct or manifold. The MAF sensor measures the volume and density of the incoming air. This sensor uses the temperature, density, and humidity of the air to determine the mass of the incoming air. This signal tells the ECM how much airflow there is, so that the ECM can make fuel delivery and spark timing calculations.

TP (Throttle Position) Sensor. The throttle position sensor's signal is used to determine idle, wide open throttle (WOT), deceleration enleanment, and acceleration enrichment. The input is used by the computer to control fuel delivery as well as spark advance and the shift points of the transmission/transaxle.

CKP (Crankshaft Position) Sensor. The crankshaft position sensor is the most critical input to the ignition system. The crankshaft position sensor provides RPM and identifies cylinder pairs at top dead center (TDC).

CMP (Camshaft Position) Sensor. While the crankshaft position sensor identifies cylinder pairs at TDC, the camshaft position sensor identifies cylinder stroke. The camshaft position sensor sends a signal to the ECM, which uses it as a sync pulse to trigger the injectors in the proper sequence. The ECM uses the camshaft position sensor signal to determine the cylinder on the intake stroke. This enables the ECM to synchronize the ignition system and calculate true sequential fuel injection.

Vehicle Speed Sensor. The vehicle speed sensor (VSS) provides vehicle speed information to the ECM.

BARO (Barometric Sensor). Some vehicles use a separate barometric sensor, designed to measure the pressure of the atmosphere, which is affected by altitude and weather conditions.

IAT (Intake Air Temperature) Sensor. The IAT sensor is a two-wire sensor positioned in the engine air intake. Air temperature readings are of particular importance during open loop or cold engine operation. On newer vehicles, the IAT sensor has been incorporated into the MAF sensor.

Intake Air Temperature 2. The IAT 2 sensor is a variable resistor used on supercharged engines to measure the air temperature inside the engine intake manifold.

Fuel Tank Pressure. The fuel tank pressure sensor is used to detect leaks in the evaporative emissions (EVAP) system.

Knock Sensor. The knock sensor system enables the control module to control ignition timing for optimal performance while protecting the engine from potentially damaging detonation. The knock sensor is used to detect engine detonation (knock) and signal the control module to retard ignition timing.

Ceramic Resistor Card Fuel Level Sensor. Starting with 1996 and later enhanced EVAP equipped models, the fuel level sending unit was switched to a ceramic card resistor (40 to 250 Ohm (Ω) potentiometer). This improves fuel level sensing accuracy, which is required when the ECM performs on-board diagnostic tests.

Accelerator Pedal Position Sensor. The accelerator pedal position (APP) sensor is mounted on the accelerator pedal assembly. Newer vehicles have two individual APP sensors within one housing. Older vehicles have three individual APP sensors within one housing. The APP sensor works with the throttle position sensor and the throttle actuator control (TAC) system to provide input to the ECM regarding driver-requested APP and throttle angle at the throttle body.

Oxygen (O2) Sensors. Provide data for fuel trim and catalyst monitor.

COMPUTER OUTPUTS

A vehicle computer can do just two things:

- Turn a device on.
- Turn a device off.

The computer can turn devices such as fuel injectors on and off rapidly or keep them on for a certain amount of time. Typical output devices include the following:

Fuel Pump. Because the fuel pump draws high current, it is not directly controlled by the ECM. Instead, the ECM controls a fuel pump relay that provides system voltage to the fuel pump. When the ignition is turned ON, before the starter is engaged, the ECM energizes the fuel pump relay by providing system voltage. The ECM shuts off the fuel pump relay if an ignition reference pulse is not received within 2 seconds. The ECM powers the relay circuit as long as it receives ignition reference pulses.

Fuel Injector. Fuel is delivered by fuel injectors, which are controlled by the ECM. An electric fuel pump supplies a continuous supply of pressurized fuel from the fuel injector. The ECM controls fuel flow by pulse width modulation (PWM) of the injector, referred to as ON time. Engine temperature, throttle position, manifold pressure or mass airflow, engine load, intake air temperature (IAT), engine RPM, oxygen sensor (O2S), and system voltage determines the fuel injector ON time.

Ignition timing. The computer sends an ignition control (IC) signal to the ignition module or coils to fire the spark plugs based on information from the sensors. The spark is advanced when the engine is cold and/or when the engine is operating under light load conditions.

Transmission shifting. The computer provides a ground to the shift solenoids and torque converter clutch solenoid. The operation of the automatic transmission/transaxle is optimized based on vehicle sensor information.

Malfunction Indicator Lamp. The MIL is located on the dashboard. When illuminated, the MIL indicates an engine status concern.

Idle Speed Control. The idle air control (IAC) valve is used on cable-actuated throttle bodies. The newer throttle actuator control (TAC) system does not use an idle air control valve. This idle air control valve is located in the throttle body of both throttle body injection and multi-port fuel injection systems.

TAC Motor. The throttle actuator control motor controls the throttle opening according to commands from the computer. It also operates as the cruise control system if the vehicle is so equipped.

MODULE COMMUNICATION AND NETWORKS

Since the 1990s, vehicles use modules to control most of the electrical component operation. A typical vehicle will have 10 or more modules and they communicate with each other over data lines or hard wiring, depending on the application.

SERIAL DATA **Serial data** is data that is transmitted by a series of rapidly changing voltage signals pulsed from low to high or from high to low. Most modules are connected together in a network because of the following advantages:

- A decreased number of wires is needed, thereby saving weight, cost, as well as helping with installation at the factory, and decreased complexity, making servicing easier.

- Common sensor data can be shared with those modules that may need the information, such as vehicle speed, outside air temperature, and engine coolant temperature.

MULTIPLEXING **Multiplexing** is the process of sending multiple signals of information at the same time over a signal wire and then separating the signals at the receiving end. This system of intercommunication of computers or processors is

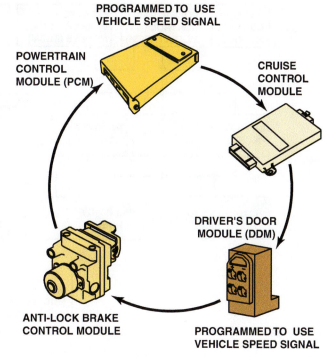

FIGURE 29–13 A network allows all modules to communicate with other modules.

referred to as a **network**. ● **SEE FIGURE 29–13.** By connecting the computers together on a communications network, they can easily share information back and forth. This multiplexing has a number of advantages, including:

- The elimination of redundant sensors and dedicated wiring for these multiple sensors.

- The reduction of the number of wires, connectors, and circuits.

- Addition of more features and option content to new vehicles.

- Weight reduction, increasing fuel economy.

- Allows features to be changed with software upgrades instead of component replacement.

The three most common types of networks used on General Motors vehicles include:

1. Ring link networks. In a ring-type network, all modules are connected to each other by a serial data line in a line until all are connected in a ring. ● **SEE FIGURE 29–14.**

2. Star link. In a star link network, a serial data line attaches to each module and then each is connected to a central point. This central point is called a **splice pack**, abbreviated SP such as in "SP 306." The splice pack uses a bar to splice all of the serial lines together. Some GM vehicles use two or more splice packs to tie the modules together. When more than one splice pack is used, a serial

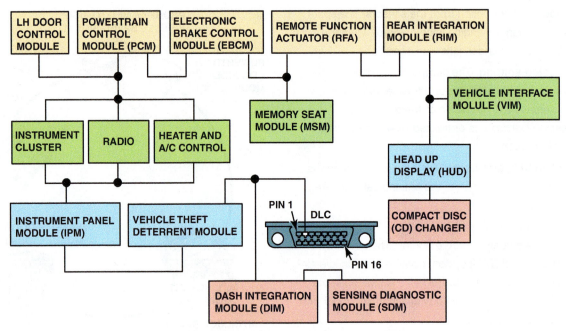

FIGURE 29–14 A ring link network reduces the number of wires it takes to interconnect all of the modules.

data line connects one splice pack to the others. In most applications the bus bar used in each splice pack can be removed. When the bus bar is removed a special tool (J 42236) can be installed in place of the removed bus bar. Using this tool, the serial data line for each module can be isolated and tested for a possible problem. Using the special tool at the splice pack makes diagnosing this type of network easier than many others. ● **SEE FIGURE 29–15** for an example of a star link network system.

3. Ring/Star hybrid. In a ring/star network, the modules are connected using both types of network configuration. Check service information (SI) for details on how this network is connected on the vehicle being diagnosed and always follow the recommended diagnostic steps.

SAE COMMUNICATION CLASSIFICATIONS

The Society of Automotive Engineers (SAE) standards include three categories of in-vehicle network communications, including the following:

CLASS A Low-speed networks (less than 10,000 bits per second [10 kbs]) are generally used for trip computers, entertainment, and other convenience features. Most low-speed Class A communication functions are performed using the following:

- UART (Universal Asynchronous Receive/Transmit) standard used by General Motors (8192 bps).
- CCD (Chrysler Collision Detection) used by Chrysler (7812.5 bps).

  NOTE: The "collision" in CCD-type bus communication refers to the program that avoids conflicts of information exchange within the bus, and does not refer to airbags or other accident-related circuits of the vehicle.

- Chrysler SCI (Serial Communications Interface) is used to communicate between the engine controller and a scan tool (62.5 kbps).
- ACP (Audio Control Protocol) is used for remote control of entertainment equipment (twisted pairs) on Ford vehicles.

CLASS B Medium-speed networks (10,000 to 125,000 bits per second [10 to 125 kbs]) are generally used for information transfer among modules, such as instrument clusters, temperature sensor data, and other general uses.

- General Motors GMLAN, both low- and medium-speed and Class 2, which uses 0 to 7 volt pulses with an available pulse width. Meets SAE 1850 variable pulse width (VPW).

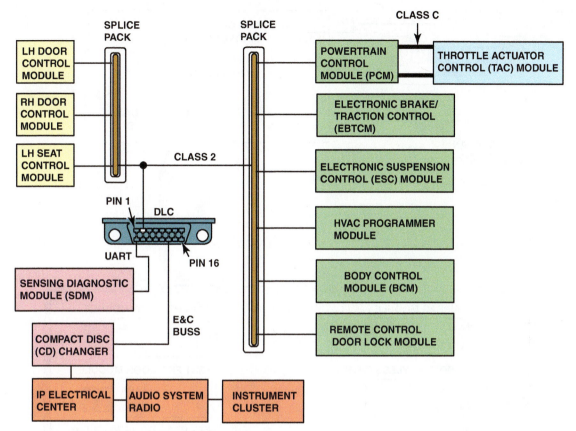

FIGURE 29–15 A star link–type network where all of the modules are connected together using splice packs.

? FREQUENTLY ASKED QUESTION

What Is a Bus?

A "bus" is a term used to describe a communication network. Therefore, there are *connections to the bus and bus communications*, both of which refer to digital messages being transmitted among electronic modules or computers.

- Chrysler Programmable Communication Interface (PCI). Meets SAE standard J-1850 pulse-width modulated (PWM).
- Ford Standard Corporate Protocol (SCP). Meets SAE standard J-1850 pulse-width modulated (PWM).

CLASS C High-speed networks (125,000 to 1,000,000 bits per second [125,000 to 1,000,000 kbs]) are generally used for real-time powertrain and vehicle dynamic control. Most high-speed bus communication is **controller area network** or **CAN**.
● **SEE FIGURE 29–16.**

MODULE COMMUNICATION DIAGNOSIS

Most vehicle manufacturers specify that a scan tool be used to diagnose modules and module communications. Always follow the recommended testing procedures, which usually require the use of a factory scan tool.

Some tests of the communication bus (network) and some of the service procedures require the service technician to attach a DMM, set to DC volts, to monitor communications.

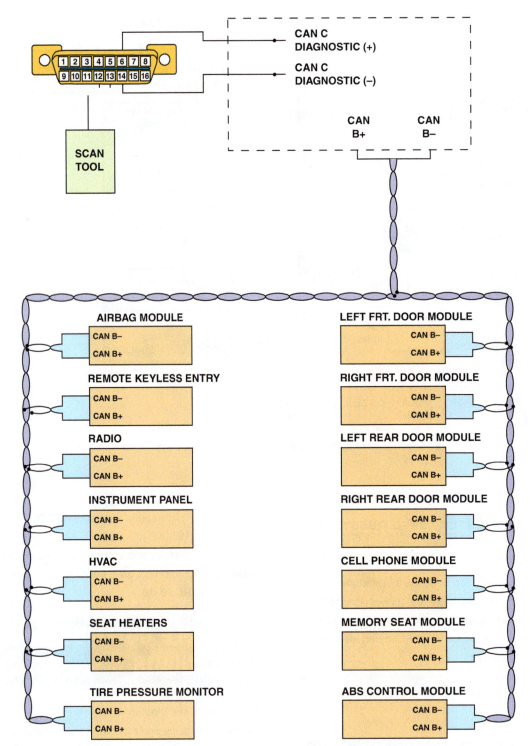

FIGURE 29–16 A typical bus system showing module CAN communications and twisted pairs of wire.

A variable voltage usually indicates that messages are being sent and received.

Most high-speed bus systems use resistors at each end called **terminating resistors**. These resistors are used to help reduce interference into other systems in the vehicle.

Usually two 120-ohm resistors are installed at each end and are therefore connected electrically in parallel. Two 120-ohm resistors connected in parallel would measure 60 ohms if being tested using an ohmmeter. ● **SEE FIGURE 29–17.**

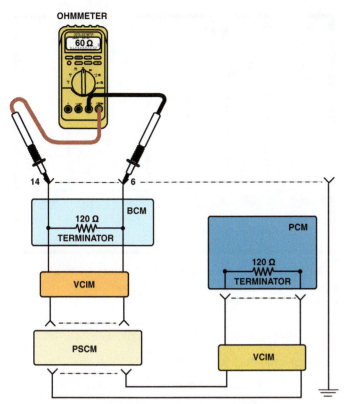

FIGURE 29–17 Checking the terminating resistors using an ohmmeter at the DLC.

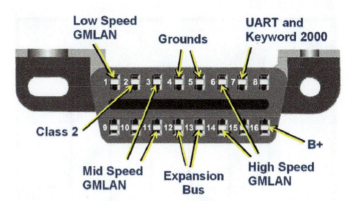

FIGURE 29–18 The data link connector (DLC) showing access points for the various networks. (*Courtesy of General Motors*)

GENERAL MOTORS GLOBAL COMMUNICATION ARCHITECTURE[1]

A Global Communication Architecture incorporates multiple networks, including single wire, dual wire, and LIN. This architecture uses smart components in multiple LIN networks to reduce wiring. It can seem confusing, but by looking at each network individually, diagnosis can be simplified.

We'll be seeing more modules and smart components as GM continues to implement this system. Some advantages of this approach are:

- Combines best features of systems
- Improves serviceability
- Allows component features and systems to be added easily
- Enables common tools and equipment to be used across vehicles

[1] Adapted from GM Course # 18044.20D4

The data link connector (DLC) can be used for diagnosis using a scan tool, oscilloscope, or digital volt/ohmmeter (DVOM) using the terminals shown in ● **FIGURE 29–18.**

SINGLE WIRE COMMUNICATION NETWORKS There are four types of single wire communication networks.

1. Class 2
2. Low-Speed GM Local Area Network (GMLAN)
3. Universal Asynchronous Receiver Transmitter (UART)
4. Keyword 2000

Faults on a single wire data communication circuit cause similar problems, regardless of protocol. When diagnosing faults, look for fluctuating voltage of not less than 1 volt or near B+ voltage

CLASS 2 **Class 2** communication networks have been used in GM vehicles since the mid-1990s. The Class 2 network can transfer data communication messages on a single wire at an average of 10.4 kilobytes per second. This network can only be found in a few GM vehicles currently in production. ● **SEE FIGURE 29–19.**

Characteristics of the Class 2 system are:

- Active at 7 volts (Binary code = 1)
- Inactive at Ground (Binary code = 0)
- Bidirectional Communication

To diagnose Class 2 communication faults:

- Probe the DLC at pin 2
- With 0 to 7 volts used to communicate, a typical voltage reading at pin 2 should be right around 1 to 3 volts and fluctuating

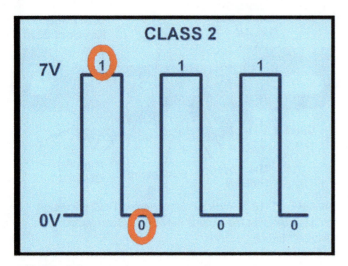

FIGURE 29–19 Class 2 networks use a 0 to 7 volt signal to communicate. (*Courtesy of General Motors*)

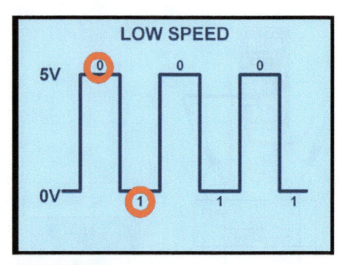

FIGURE 29–20 The low-speed GMLAN uses a 0 to 5 volt signal to communicate. (*Courtesy of General Motors*)

LOW-SPEED GMLAN Low-speed **GMLAN** communication has widely replaced Class 2 communication. This bus operates at 33.33 kilobytes per second, which is triple the speed of Class 2. ● **SEE FIGURE 29–20.**

Characteristics of low-speed GMLAN are:

- Bidirectional
- Code is reversed
- 0 volt = Logic 1
- 5 volts = Logic 0
- Fault prevents communication with modules on this bus ONLY
- Fluctuating voltage is 1–3 volts

This bus is connected together in one of two configurations, star or ring. With a star configuration, a single wire connects each module to one of two splice packs. The splice pack is a good starting point for isolating and troubleshooting the bus. Removing the splice pack comb allows measurements to be taken on each circuit leg to find which one has the fault that is corrupting the entire network. A short-to-voltage or a short-to-ground anywhere on the bus will prevent ALL communication on that bus.

Some low-speed GMLAN buses are connected together in a ring configuration. This means that the modules on a bus are connected together in a loop. These loops are joined together inside each module. Short-to-ground or voltage that occur on one loop will cause a loss of communication on both loops. An open circuit in a ring bus won't cause any concerns because communication occurs in both directions on the loop.

To diagnose low-speed GMLAN communication faults:

- Probe the DLC at pin 1
- With 0 to 5 volts used to communicate, a typical voltage reading at pin 1 should be right around 1 to 3 volts and fluctuating

UART AND KEYWORD 2000 Universal Asynchronous Receive and Transmit (**UART**) and **Keyword 2000** are similar communication protocols. Diagnosing UART is similar to any other protocol. If there is a fault in the wiring, communication will be lost with one or more control modules

- Check to make sure the circuit is not shorted to ground or shorted to power
- A fault within this circuit at pin 7 at the DLC to the splice pack will only cause a communication problem with the scan tool

Keyword 2000 is used only on a small number of vehicles. The protocol uses a single wire bidirectional data line between the module and the scan tool. Message structure is a request and response arrangement. Modules do not exchange data on these systems, so a fault within this the bus will cause an interruption with scan tool diagnostics.

To diagnose UART and Keyword 2000 communication faults, probe the DLC at pin 7.

LOCAL INTERCONNECT NETWORK The local interconnect network (**LIN**) is another type of single wire communication network. It is a UART-based/single-master/multiple-slave networking architecture that was originally developed for

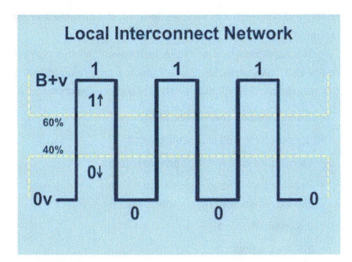

FIGURE 29–21 The LIN voltage pattern ranges from 0 to battery voltage. (*Courtesy of General Motors*)

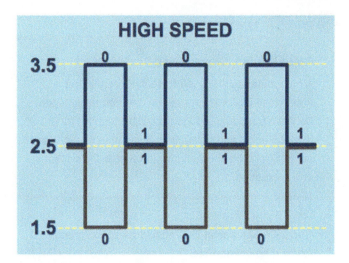

FIGURE 29–22 The voltage signature of 2-wire CAN systems are the same for high-speed GMLAN, mid-speed GMLAN, and expansion bus. One wire is driven high and the other driven low when communicating. (*Courtesy of General Motors*)

automotive sensor and actuator applications. The master node extends communication benefits of in-vehicle networking to individual sensors and actuators. Benefits to the electrical system are reduced wiring, lighter vehicle weight, and cost effective data sharing. More module control allows enhanced diagnostics with expanded trouble codes. The LIN connects with the controller area network (CAN) at the master node. ● **SEE FIGURE 29–21.**

LIN has some unique characteristics:

- Does NOT connect to the DLC
- Only used for communication between a module and a component. In order for communication to take place, voltage and ground must be good at the module and at the component
- Cycles between 0 and B+ volts
- B+ volts = Logic 1
- 0 volt = Logic 0
- Under 40% of battery voltage = Logic 0
- Over 60% of battery voltage = Logic 1

DUAL WIRE COMMUNICATION DATA NETWORKS

There are three types of dual wire communication data buses.

1. High-Speed GM Local Area Network (GMLAN)
2. Expansion Bus
3. Mid-Speed GM Local Area Network (GMLAN)

NOTE: These networks are diagnosed similarly, regardless of protocol.

HIGH-SPEED GMLAN High-speed GMLAN is a dual wire communication network. With dual wire networks, a short-to-power or a short-to-ground has the same effect that it had on the single wire buses, meaning that the entire network will be down. However, since there are two wires, you need to check them both for faults. ● **SEE FIGURE 29–22.**

Characteristics of the high-speed GMLAN are:

- More complex than single wire networks
- Short-to-ground or short-to-power will prevent ALL communication on high-speed bus
- Transmitted on two twisted wires
- Speeds up to 500 kilobytes/second
- Terminated with two 120 ohm resistors
- Positive (pin 6) and negative (pin 14) are driven to opposite extremes from rest or idle level
- 2.5 volts = Logic 1
- 2.5 +/−1 = Logic 0

Dual wire network circuits include two 120 ohm resistors. These resistors are commonly found near each end of the circuit. They help to reduce electrical noise. General diagnosis of GMLAN faults includes the following steps:

- Always refer to service information (SI) first; print out a schematic for reference.
- With the key OFF, begin testing at the DLC. For high-speed GMLAN, you would test at pins 6 and 14.

used on global platform vehicles for both the chassis and the powertrain.

The expansion bus is unique, as it doesn't always connect to the data link connector. Sometimes you may need to test at the specific module. Characteristics of the expansion bus are:

- Transmitted on two twisted wires
- Speeds up to 500 kilobytes/second
- Terminated with two 120 ohm resistors
- Positive (pin 12) and negative (pin 13) are driven to opposite extremes from rest or idle level
- 2.5 volts = Logic 1
- 2.5 +/−1 = Logic 0

To diagnose expansion bus communication faults, check to see if it connected to the DLC.

- If connected, this bus will be at terminals 12 and 13. Otherwise, you may need to test at the specific module
- With 1.5 to 3.5 volts used to communicate, a typical voltage reading at pins 12 and 13 should be right around 1 to 3 volts and fluctuating

- Typical resistance at DLC should be approximately 60 ohms if no open exists.
- Higher resistance suggests an open.
- Lower resistance suggests a short between the wires.
- If there is a measurement of 120 ohms, you are not seeing both terminating resistors but, rather, an open.
- To locate the open, split the circuit and measure in each direction. There should be 120 ohms in one direction and infinite ohms in the other direction.
- Follow the circuit in the direction of the infinite resistance to help to isolate the fault location.
- With the key ON, 1.5 to 3.5 volts is used to communicate; a typical voltage reading at pins 6 and 14 should be right around 1 to 3 volts and fluctuating.

NOTE: Always use the proper terminal adapters when probing at the DLC. DO NOT push the DMM probes into the connector, which can damage the terminal end.

EXPANSION BUS The **expansion bus**, otherwise known as the chassis high-speed GMLAN is similar to high-speed GMLAN in operation. This system addresses a GMLAN bandwidth issue by creating a network for specific modules. The expansion bus is currently used in Two-mode Hybrid trucks and Volt. It's also

MID-SPEED GMLAN The controller area network, or CAN, protocol has been expanded into each of the dual wire networks, including the **mid-speed GMLAN**. It is very similar to the other dual wire networks, with the following characteristics:

- Starts at 2.5 volts
- Moves +/−1 volt to communicate
- Limited to 125 kilobytes per second
- Slower than other high-speed networks
- To diagnose mid-speed GMLAN communication faults, probe the DLC at terminals 3 and 11
- With 1.5 to 3.5 volts used to communicate, a typical voltage reading at pins 3 and 11 should be right around 1 to 3 volts and fluctuating

SUMMARY

1. The Society of Automotive Engineers (SAE) standard J-1930 specifies that the term "Powertrain Control Module" (PCM) be used for the computer that controls the engine and transmission in a vehicle.

2. The four basic computer functions include input, processing, storage, and output.

3. Read-only memory (ROM) can be programmable (PROM), erasable (EPROM), or electrically erasable (EEPROM).

4. Computer input sensors include engine speed (RPM), MAP, MAF, ECT, O2S, TP, and VS.

5. A computer can only turn a device on or turn a device off, but it can do the operation rapidly.

6. A variety of network communication protocols are used to control vehicle systems, including Class 2, low-, mid-, and high-speed GMLAN.

REVIEW QUESTIONS

1. What part of the vehicle computer is considered to be the brain?

2. What is the difference between volatile and nonvolatile RAM?

3. List four input sensors.

4. List four output devices.

5. Explain the difference between a GM Class 2 network and GMLAN.

CHAPTER QUIZ

1. What unit of electricity is used as a signal for a computer?
   a. Volt
   b. Ohm
   c. Ampere
   d. Watt

2. The four basic computer functions include _____.
   a. Writing, processing, printing, and remembering
   b. Input, processing, storage, and output
   c. Data gathering, processing, output, and evaluation
   d. Sensing, calculating, actuating, and processing

3. All OBD II vehicles use what type of read-only memory?
   a. ROM
   b. PROM
   c. EPROM
   d. EEPROM

4. The "brain" of the computer is the _____.
   a. PROM
   b. RAM
   c. CPU
   d. AD converter

5. Computer processing speed is measured in _____.
   a. Baud rate
   b. Clock speed (Hz)
   c. Voltage
   d. Bytes

6. Which item is a computer input sensor?
   a. RPM
   b. Throttle position angle
   c. Engine coolant temperature
   d. All of the above

7. Which item is a computer output device?
   a. Fuel injector
   b. Transmission shift solenoid
   c. Evaporative emission control solenoid
   d. All of the above

8. The SAE term for the vehicle computer is _____.
   a. PCM
   b. ECM
   c. ECA
   d. Controller

9. What two things can a vehicle computer actually perform (output)?
   a. Store and process information
   b. Turn something on or turn something off
   c. Calculate and vary temperature
   d. Control fuel and timing only

10. Through which type of circuit analog signals from sensors are changed to digital signals for processing by the computer?
    a. Digital
    b. Analog
    c. AD converter
    d. PROM

chapter 30

ONBOARD DIAGNOSIS

LEARNING OBJECTIVES

After studying this chapter, the reader should be able to:

1. Explain the purpose and function of onboard diagnosis.
2. List the various duties of the diagnostic executive.
3. List continuous and noncontinuous monitors.
4. Interpret evaporative emission-related diagnostic trouble codes (DTCs).

This chapter will help you prepare for Engine Repair (A6) ASE certification test content area "A" (General Electrical/Electronic Systems Diagnosis).

KEY TERMS

California Air Resources Board (CARB) 469

Comprehensive component monitor (CCM) 470

Diagnostic executive 470

Enable criteria 473

Federal Test Procedure (FTP) 469

Freeze-frame 470

Functionality 471

Malfunction indicator lamp (MIL) 469

On-board diagnostics (OBDs) 469

Parameter identification (PID) 478

Rationality 471

Society of Automotive Engineers (SAE) 473

Task manager 470

Fail records 475

Inspection/Maintenance (I/M) flag 471

Statistical filtering 472

STC OBJECTIVES

GM Service Technical College topics covered in this chapter are:

1. Capture DTC information.
2. Perform emission systems service diagnosis.
3. Perform a road test.

FIGURE 30–1 A typical malfunction indicator lamp (MIL) often labeled "check engine."

FIGURE 30–2 The malfunction indicator lamp might be labeled "service engine soon," which can cause some customer concern if the vehicle had just recently been serviced such as an oil change.

ON-BOARD DIAGNOSTICS GENERATION-II (OBD-II) SYSTEMS

PURPOSE AND FUNCTION OF OBD II During the 1980s, most manufacturers began equipping their vehicles with full-function control systems capable of alerting the driver of a malfunction and of allowing the technician to retrieve codes that identify circuit faults. These early diagnostic systems were meant to reduce emissions and speed up vehicle repair.

The automotive industry calls these systems **on-board diagnostics (OBDs)**. The **California Air Resources Board (CARB)** developed the first regulation requiring manufacturers selling vehicles in that state to install OBD. OBD Generation I (OBD I) applies to all vehicles sold in California beginning with the 1988 model year. It specifies the following requirements:

1. An instrument panel warning lamp able to alert the driver of certain control system failures, now called a **malfunction indicator lamp (MIL)**. ● **SEE FIGURES 30–1 AND 30–2**.

2. The system's ability to record and transmit DTCs for emission-related failures.

3. Electronic system monitoring of the HO2S, EGR valve, and evaporative purge solenoid. Although not U.S. EPA-required, during this time most manufacturers also equipped vehicles sold outside of California with OBD I.

By failing to monitor the catalytic converter, the evaporative system for leaks, and the presence of engine misfire, OBD I did not do enough to lower automotive emissions. This led the CARB and the EPA to develop OBD Generation II (OBD II).

OBD-II OBJECTIVES Generally, the CARB defines an OBD-II-equipped vehicle by its ability to do the following:

1. Detect component degradation or a faulty emission-related system that prevents compliance with federal emission standards.

2. Alert the driver of needed emission-related repair or maintenance.

3. Use standardized DTCs and accept a generic scan tool.

These requirements apply to all 1996 and later model light-duty vehicles. The Clean Air Act of 1990 directed the EPA to develop new regulations for OBD. The primary purpose of OBD II is emission-related, whereas the primary purpose of OBD I (1988) was to detect faults in sensors or sensor circuits. OBD-II regulations require that not only sensors be tested but also all exhaust emission control devices, and that they be verified for proper operation.

All new vehicles must pass the **Federal Test Procedure (FTP)** for exhaust emissions while being tested for 505 seconds on rollers that simulate the urban drive cycle around downtown Los Angeles.

Note: IM 240 is simply a shorter 240-second version of the 505-second federal test procedure.

The regulations for OBD-II vehicles state that the vehicle computer must be capable of testing for, and determining, if the exhaust emissions are within 1.5 times the FTP limits. To achieve this goal, the computer must do the following:

1. Test all exhaust emission system components for correct operation.

2. Actively operate the system and measure the results.

3. Continuously monitor all aspects of the engine operation to be certain that the exhaust emissions do not exceed 1.5 times the FTP.

4. Check engine operation for misfire.

5. Turn on the MIL (check engine) if the computer senses a fault in a circuit or system.

6. Record a **freeze-frame**, which is a snapshot of all of the engine data at the time the DTC was set.

7. Flash the MIL if an engine misfire occurs that could damage the catalytic converter.

DIAGNOSTIC EXECUTIVE AND TASK MANAGER

On OBD-II systems, the PCM incorporates a special segment of software. On Ford and GM systems, this software is called the **diagnostic executive**. On Chrysler systems, it is called the **task manager**. This software program is designed to manage the operation of all OBD-II monitors by controlling the sequence of steps necessary to execute the diagnostic tests and monitors.

MONITORS

A monitor is an organized method of testing a specific part of the system. Monitors are simply tests that the computer performs to evaluate components and systems. If a component or system failure is detected while a monitor is running, a DTC will be stored and the MIL illuminated by the second trip. The two types of monitors are continuous and noncontinuous.

CONTINUOUS MONITORS As required conditions are met, continuous monitors begin to run. These continuous monitors will run for the remainder of the vehicle drive cycle. The three continuous monitors are as follows:

- **Comprehensive component monitor (CCM).** This monitor watches the sensors and actuators in the OBD-II

system. Sensor values are constantly compared with known-good values stored in the PCM's memory.

The CCM is an internal program in the PCM designed to monitor a failure in any electronic component or circuit (including emission-related and nonemission-related circuits) that provides input or output signals to the PCM. The PCM considers that an input or output signal is inoperative when a failure exists due to an open circuit, out-of-range value, or if an onboard rationality check fails. If an emission-related fault is detected, the PCM will set a code and activate the MIL (requires two consecutive trips).

Many PCM sensors and output devices are tested at key-on or immediately after engine start-up. However, some devices, such as the IAC, are only tested by the CCM after the engine meets certain engine conditions. The number of times the CCM must detect a fault before it will activate the MIL depends upon the manufacturer, but most require two consecutive trips to activate the MIL. The components tested by the CCM include:

Four-wheel-drive low switch

Brake switch

Camshaft (CMP) and crankshaft (CKP) sensors

Clutch switch (manual transmissions/transaxles only)

Cruise servo switch

Engine coolant temperature (ECT) sensor

EVAP purge sensor or switch

Fuel composition sensor

Intake air temperature (IAT) sensor

Knock sensor (KS)

Manifold absolute pressure (MAP) sensor

Mass airflow (MAF) sensor

Throttle-position (TP) sensor

Transmission temperature sensor

Transmission turbine speed sensor

Vacuum sensor

Vehicle speed (VS) sensor

EVAP canister purge and EVAP purge vent solenoid

Idle air control (IAC) solenoid

Ignition control system

Transmission torque converter clutch solenoid

Transmission shift solenoids

- **Misfire monitor.** This monitor looks at engine misfire. The PCM uses the information received from the crankshaft position sensor (CKP) to calculate the time between the edges of the reluctor, as well as the rotational speed and acceleration. By comparing the acceleration of each firing event, the PCM can determine if a cylinder is not firing correctly.

Misfire type A. Upon detection of a misfire type A (200 revolutions), which would cause catalyst damage, the MIL will blink once per second during the actual misfire, and a DTC will be stored.

Misfire type B. Upon detection of a misfire type B (1,000 revolutions), which will exceed 1.5 times the EPA federal test procedure (FTP) standard or cause a vehicle to fail an inspection and maintenance tailpipe emissions test, the MIL will illuminate and a DTC will be stored.

The DTC associated with multiple cylinder misfire for a type A or type B misfire is DTC P0300. The DTCs associated with an individual cylinder misfire for a type A or type B misfire are DTCs P0301, P0302, P0303, P0304, P0305, P0306, P0307, P0308, P0309, and P0310.

- **Fuel trim monitor.** The PCM continuously monitors short- and long-term fuel trim. Constantly updated adaptive fuel tables are stored in long-term memory (KAM), and used by the PCM for compensation due to wear and aging of the fuel system components. The MIL will illuminate when the PCM determines the fuel trim values have reached and stayed at their limits for too long a period of time.

NONCONTINUOUS MONITORS Noncontinuous monitors run (at most) once per vehicle drive cycle. The noncontinuous monitors are as follows:

O2S monitor

O2S heater monitor

Catalyst monitor

EGR monitor

EVAP monitor

Secondary AIR monitor

Transmission monitor

PCV system monitor

Thermostat monitor

Once a noncontinuous monitor has run to completion, it will not be run again until the conditions are met during the next vehicle drive cycle. Also, after a noncontinuous monitor has run to completion, the readiness status on your scan tool will show "complete" or "done" for that monitor. Monitors that have not run to completion will show up on your scanner as "incomplete."

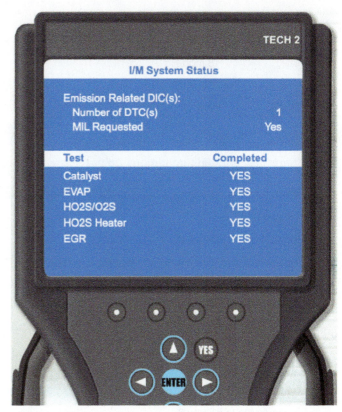

FIGURE 30–3 The scan tool is used to display the status of the I/M flags. (*Courtesy of General Motors*)

I/M FLAGS   The System Status flag or **Inspection/ Maintenance (I/M) flag** stores information about whether a diagnostic test has run and what the results are. If a system diagnostic test has run, the system status flags set a "Yes" or "No" flag. ● **SEE FIGURE 30–3**.

OBD-II MONITOR INFORMATION

COMPREHENSIVE COMPONENT MONITOR   The circuits and components covered by the comprehensive component monitor (CCM) do not include those directly covered by any other monitors.

However, OBD II also requires that inputs from powertrain components to the PCM be tested for **rationality**, and that outputs to powertrain components from the PCM be tested for **functionality**. Both inputs and outputs are to be checked *electrically*. Rationality means that the PCM checks that the input values are plausible and rational based on the readings from all of the other sensors.

Example:

TP	3 Volt
MAP	18 inch Hg
RPM	700 RPM
PRNDL	Park

Note: Comprehensive component monitors are continuous. Therefore, enabling conditions do not apply.

The comprehensive component monitor (CCM) performs the following:

- Monitor runs continuously
- Monitor includes sensors, switches, relays, solenoids, and PCM hardware
- All are checked for opens, shorts-to-ground, and shorts-to-voltage
- Inputs are checked for rationality
- Outputs are checked for functionality
- Most are one-trip DTCs
- Freeze-frame is priority 3
- Three consecutive good trips are used to extinguish the MIL
- Forty warm-up cycles are used to erase DTC and freeze-frame
- Two minutes run time without reoccurrence of the fault constitutes a "good trip"

CONTINUOUS RUNNING MONITORS

- Monitors run continuously, only stop if they fail
- Fuel system: rich/lean
- Misfire: catalyst damaging/FTP (emissions)
- Two-trip faults (except early generation catalyst damaging misfire)
- MIL, DTC, freeze-frame after two consecutive faults
- Freeze-frame is priority 2 on first trip
- Freeze-frame is priority 4 on maturing trip
- Three consecutive good trips in a similar condition window are used to extinguish the MIL
- Forty warm-up cycles are used to erase DTC and freeze-frame (80 to erase one-trip failure if similar conditions cannot be met)

ONCE PER TRIP MONITORS

- Monitor runs once per trip, pass or fail
- O_2 response, O_2 heaters, EGR, purge flow EVAP leak, secondary air, catalyst
- Two-trip DTCs
- MIL, DTC, freeze-frame after two consecutive faults
- Freeze-frame is priority 1 on first trip
- Freeze-frame is priority 3 on maturing trip
- Three consecutive good trips are used to extinguish the MIL
- Forty warm-up cycles are used to erase DTC and freeze-frame

EXPONENTIALLY WEIGHTED MOVING AVERAGE MONITORS
The exponentially weighted moving average (EWMA) monitor is a mathematical method used to determine performance.

- Catalyst monitor
- EGR monitor
- PCM runs six consecutive failed tests; fails in one trip
- Three consecutive failed tests on next trip, then fails
- Freeze-frame is priority 3
- Three consecutive good trips are used to extinguish the MIL
- Forty warm-up cycles are used to erase DTC and freeze-frame

STATISTICAL FILTERING The ECM also has the ability to learn from the results of its diagnostic testing. The ECM internally charts the results of diagnostic testing over a period of time, and creates a baseline of normal test results called statistical filtering. Using **statistical filtering**, the ECM is able to filter out information that may cause a false DTC to set.

ENABLING CRITERIA

With so many different tests (monitors) to run, the PCM needs an internal director to keep track of when each monitor should run. As mentioned, different manufacturers have different names for this director, such as the diagnostic executive or the task manager. Each monitor has enabling criteria. These criteria are a set of conditions that must be met before the task manager will give the go-ahead for each monitor to run. Most enabling criteria follow simple logic, for example:

- The task manager will not authorize the start of the O2S monitor until the engine has reached operating temperature and the system has entered closed loop.
- The task manager will not authorize the start of the EGR monitor when the engine is at idle, because the EGR is always closed at this time.

Because each monitor is responsible for testing a different part of the system, the enabling criteria can differ greatly from one monitor to the next. The task manager must decide when each monitor should run, and in what order, to avoid confusion.

There may be a conflict if two monitors were to run at the same time. The results of one monitor might also be tainted if a second monitor were to run simultaneously. In such cases, the task manager decides which monitor has a higher priority. Some monitors also depend on the results of other monitors before they can run.

A monitor may be classified as pending if a failed sensor or other system fault is keeping it from running on schedule.

The task manager may suspend a monitor if the conditions are not correct to continue. For example, if the catalyst monitor is running during a road test and the PCM detects a misfire, the catalyst monitor will be suspended for the duration of the misfire.

TRIP A trip is defined as a key-on condition that contains the necessary conditions for a particular test to be performed followed by a key-off. These conditions are called the **enable criteria**. For example, for the EGR test to be performed, the engine must be at normal operating temperature and decelerating for a minimum amount of time. Some tests are performed when the engine is cold, whereas others require that the vehicle be cruising at a steady highway speed.

WARM-UP CYCLE Once a MIL is deactivated, the original code will remain in memory until 40 warm-up cycles are completed without the fault reappearing. A warm-up cycle is defined as a trip with an engine temperature increase of at least 40°F and where engine temperature reaches at least 160°F (71°C).

MIL CONDITION: OFF This condition indicates that the PCM has not detected any faults in an emissions-related component or system, or that the MIL circuit is not working.

MIL CONDITION: ON STEADY This condition indicates a fault in an emissions-related component or system that could affect the vehicle emission levels.

MIL CONDITION: FLASHING This condition indicates a misfire or fuel control system fault that could damage the catalytic converter.

Note: In a misfire condition with the MIL on steady, if the driver reaches a vehicle speed and load condition with the engine misfiring at a level that could cause catalyst damage, the MIL would start flashing. It would continue to flash until engine speed and load conditions caused the level of misfire to subside. Then the MIL would go back to the on-steady condition. This situation might result in a customer complaint of a MIL with an intermittent flashing condition.

MIL: OFF The PCM will turn off the MIL if any of the following actions or conditions occurs:

- The codes are cleared with a scan tool.
- Power to the PCM is removed at the battery or with the PCM power fuse for an extended period of time (may be up to several hours or longer).
- A vehicle is driven on three consecutive trips with a warm-up cycle and meets all code set conditions without the PCM detecting any faults.

The PCM will set a code if a fault is detected that could cause tailpipe emissions to exceed 1.5 times the FTP standard; however, the PCM will not deactivate the MIL until the vehicle has been driven on three consecutive trips with vehicle conditions similar to actual conditions present when the fault was detected. This is not merely three vehicle start-ups and trips. It means three trips during which certain engine operating conditions are met so that the OBD-II monitor that found the fault can run again and pass the diagnostic test.

OBD-II DTC NUMBERING DESIGNATION

A scan tool is required to retrieve DTCs from an OBD-II vehicle. Every OBD-II scan tool will be able to read all generic **Society of Automotive Engineers (SAE)** DTCs from any vehicle. ● **SEE FIGURE 30–4** for definitions and explanations of OBD alphanumeric DTCs. The diagnostic trouble codes (DTCs) are grouped into major categories, depending on the location of the fault on the system involved.

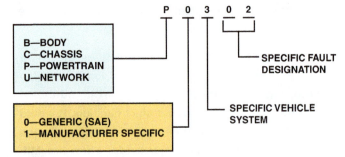

EXAMPLE: P0302 = CYLINDER 2 MISFIRE DETECTED

FIGURE 30–4 OBD-II DTC identification format.

Pxxx codes—powertrain DTCs (engine, transmission-related faults)

Bxxx codes—body DTCs (accessories, interior-related faults)

Cxxx codes—chassis DTCs (suspension and steering-related faults)

Uxxx codes—network DTCs (module communication-related faults)

DTC NUMBERING EXPLANATION The number in the hundredth position indicates the specific vehicle system or subgroup that failed. This position should be consistent for P0xxx and P1xxx type codes. The following numbers and systems were established by SAE:

- P0100—Air metering and fuel system fault
- P0200—Fuel system (fuel injector only) fault
- P0300—Ignition system or misfire fault
- P0400—Emission control system fault
- P0500—Idle speed control, vehicle speed (VS) sensor fault
- P0600—Computer output circuit (relay, solenoid, etc.) fault
- P0700—Transaxle, transmission faults

Note: The tens and ones numbers indicate the part of the system at fault. ˙

TYPES OF DTCS Not all OBD-II DTCs are of the same importance for exhaust emissions. Each type of DTC has different requirements for it to set, and the computer will only turn on the MIL for emissions-related DTCs.

TYPE A CODES A type A DTC is emission-related and will cause the MIL to be turned on the *first trip* if the computer has detected a problem. Engine misfire or a very rich or lean air–fuel ratio, for example, would cause a type A DTC. These codes alert the driver of an emission problem that may cause damage to the catalytic converter.

TYPE B CODES A type B code will be stored and the MIL will be turned on during the *second consecutive trip*, alerting the driver to the fact that a diagnostic test was performed and failed.

Note: Type A and B codes are emission-related codes that will cause the lighting of the malfunction indicator lamp (MIL), usually labeled "check engine" or "service engine soon."

TYPE C AND D CODES. Type C and D codes are for use with non-emission-related diagnostic tests; they will cause the lighting of a "service" lamp (if the vehicle is so equipped). Type C codes are also called type C1 codes and D codes are also called type C0 codes.

DIAGNOSTIC TROUBLE CODE PRIORITY CARB has also mandated that all diagnostic trouble codes (DTCs) be stored according to individual priority. DTCs with a higher priority overwrite those with a lower priority. The OBD-II System DTC Priority is listed below.

Priority 0—Non-emission-related codes

Priority 1—One-trip failure of two-trip fault for non-fuel, non-misfire codes

Priority 2—One-trip failure of two-trip fault for fuel or misfire codes

Priority 3—Two-trip failure or matured fault of non-fuel, non-misfire codes

Priority 4—Two-trip failure or matured fault for fuel or misfire codes

OBD-II FREEZE-FRAME

To assist the service technician, OBD II requires the computer to take a "snapshot" or freeze-frame of all data at the instant an emission-related DTC is set. A scan tool is required to retrieve this data.

Freeze-frame items include:

- Calculated load value
- Engine speed (RPM)
- Short-term and long-term fuel trim percent
- Fuel system pressure (on some vehicles)
- Vehicle speed (mph)
- Engine coolant temperature

MONITOR NAME	MONITOR TYPE (HOW OFTEN IT COMPLETES)	NUMBER OF FAULTS ON SEPARATE TRIPS TO SET A PENDING DTC	NUMBER OF SEPARATE CONSECUTIVE TRIPS TO LIGHT MIL, STORE A DTC	NUMBER OF TRIPS WITH NO FAULTS TO ERASE A MATURING DTC	NUMBER OF TRIPS WITH NO FAULT TO TURN THE MIL OFF	NUMBER OF WARM-UP CYCLES TO ERASE DTC AFTER MIL IS TURNED OFF
CCM	Continuous (when trip conditions allow it)	1	2	1–Trip	3–Trips	40
Catalyst	Once per drive cycle	1	3	1–Trip	3–OBD-II drive cycle	40
Misfire Type A	Continuous		1	1–Trip	3–Similar conditions	80
Misfire Type B	Continuous	1	2	1–Trip	3–Similar conditions	80
Fuel System	Continuous	1	2	1–Trip	3–Similar conditions	80
Oxygen Sensor	Once per trip	1	2	1–Trip	3–Trips	40
EGR	Once per trip	1	2	1–Trip	3–Trips	40
EVAP	Once per trip	1	1	1–Trip	3–Trips	40
AIR	Once per trip	1	2	1–Trip	3–Trips	40

CHART 30–1

PCM determination of faults chart.

- Intake manifold pressure
- Closed–open loop status
- Fault code that triggered the freeze-frame
- If a misfire code is set, identify which cylinder is misfiring

A DTC should not be cleared from the vehicle computer memory unless the fault has been corrected and the technician is so directed by the diagnostic procedure. If the problem that caused the DTC to be set has been corrected, the computer will automatically clear the DTC after 40 consecutive warm-up cycles with no further faults detected (misfire and excessively rich or lean condition codes require 80 warm-up cycles). The codes can also be erased by using a scan tool. **SEE CHART 30–1**.

Note: Disconnecting the battery may not erase OBD-II DTCs or freeze-frame data. Most vehicle manufacturers recommend using a scan tool to erase DTCs rather than disconnecting the battery, because the memory for the radio, seats, and learned engine operating parameters is lost if the battery is disconnected.

FAIL RECORDS   Although OBD II requires that just one freeze frame of data be stored the instant an emission-related DTC is set, vehicle manufacturers usually provide expanded data about the DTC beyond that required. Retrieving this enhanced data usually requires the use of the vehicle-specific scan tool.

Fail records contain a GM enhancement of the OBD II freeze frame. Fail records are stored for any DTC. Unlike freeze frame, the PCM has the ability to store fail records for more than one DTC. The Diagnostic Executive software stores a limited number of fail records, usually five or less. Each fail record is for a different DTC.

? FREQUENTLY ASKED QUESTION

What Are Pending Codes?

Pending codes are set when operating conditions are met and the component or circuit is not within the normal range, yet the conditions have not yet been met to set a DTC. For example, a sensor may require two consecutive faults before a DTC is set. If a scan tool displays a pending code or a failure, a driveability concern could also be present. The pending code can help the technician to determine the root cause before the customer complains of a check engine light indication.

ENABLING CONDITIONS OR CRITERIA

These are the exact engine operating conditions required for a diagnostic monitor to run.

Example:
Specific RPM
Specific ECT, MAP, run time, VSS, etc.

PENDING   Under some situations the PCM will not run a monitor if the MIL is illuminated and a fault is stored from another monitor. In these situations, the PCM postpones monitors pending a resolution of the original fault. The PCM does not run the test until the problem is remedied.

For example, when the MIL is illuminated for an oxygen sensor fault, the PCM does not run the catalyst monitor until the oxygen sensor fault is remedied. Since the catalyst monitor is based on signals from the oxygen sensor, running the test would produce inaccurate results.

CONFLICT There are also situations when the PCM does not run a monitor if another monitor is in progress. In these situations, the effects of another monitor running could result in an erroneous failure. If this conflict is present, the monitor is not run until the conflicting condition passes. Most likely, the monitor will run later after the conflicting monitor has passed.

For example, if the fuel system monitor is in progress, the PCM does not run the EGR monitor. Since both tests monitor changes in air–fuel ratio and adaptive fuel compensation, the monitors conflict with each other.

SUSPEND Occasionally, the PCM may not allow a two-trip fault to mature. The PCM will suspend the maturing fault if a condition exists that may induce erroneous failure. This prevents illuminating the MIL for the wrong fault and allows more precise diagnosis.

For example, if the PCM is storing a one-trip fault for the oxygen sensor and the EGR monitor, the PCM may still run the EGR monitor but will suspend the results until the oxygen sensor monitor either passes or fails. At that point, the PCM can determine if the EGR system is actually failing or if an oxygen sensor is failing.

PCM TESTS

RATIONALITY TEST While input signals to the PCM are constantly being monitored for electrical opens and shorts, they are also tested for rationality. This means that the input signal is compared against other inputs and information to see if it makes sense under the current conditions.

PCM sensor inputs that are checked for rationality include:

- MAP sensor
- O_2 sensor
- ECT
- Camshaft position sensor (CMP)
- VS sensor
- Crankshaft position sensor (CKP)
- IAT sensor
- TP sensor
- Ambient air temperature sensor

- Power steering switch
- O_2 sensor heater
- Engine controller
- Brake switch
- P/N switch
- Transmission controls

FUNCTIONALITY TEST A functionality test refers to PCM inputs checking the operation of the outputs.

Example:

PCM commands the IAC open; expected change in engine RPM is not seen
IAC 60 counts
RPM 700 RPM

PCM outputs that are checked for functionality include:

- EVAP canister purge solenoid
- EVAP purge vent solenoid
- Cooling fan
- Idle air control solenoid
- Ignition control system
- Transmission torque converter clutch solenoid
- Transmission shift solenoids (A,B,1–2, etc.)

ELECTRICAL TEST Refers to the PCM check of both input and outputs for the following:

- Open
- Shorts
- Ground

Example:

ECT
Shorted high (input to PCM) above capable voltage, that is, 5 volt sensor with 12 volt input to PCM would indicate a short to voltage or a short high.

MONITOR TYPE	CONDITIONS TO SET DTC AND ILLUMINATE MIL	EXTINGUISH MIL	CLEAR DTC CRITERIA	APPLICABLE DTC
Compre-hensive Monitor	Conti-nuous 1-trip monitor	(See note below) Input and output failure— rationally, functionally, electrically	3 consecu-tive pass trips	40 warm-up cycles	P0123

NOTE: The number of times the comprehensive component monitor must detect a fault depends on the vehicle manufacturer. On some vehicles, the comprehensive component monitor will activate the MIL as soon as it detects a fault. On other vehicles, the comprehensive component monitor must fail two times in a row.

- Freeze-frame captured on first-trip failure
- Enabling conditions: Many PCM sensors and output devices are tested at key-on or immediately after engine start-up. However, some devices (ECT, idle speed control) are only tested by the comprehensive component monitor after the engine meets particular engine conditions
- Pending: No pending condition
- Conflict: No conflict conditions
- Suspend: No suspend conditions

SYSTEM INSPECTION

The OBD II system inspection includes a visual check of the MIL operation and an electronic check of the OBD II system. The MIL performs a self-test by illuminating at start-up. The self-test may be observed, and the scan tool is used to trigger the MIL while the engine is running. Results of the test may be either pass, fail, or rejected.

Pass. The OBD II system passes if:

- The MIL operates correctly
- The MIL illuminates when diagnostic trouble codes (DTCs) are present
- The inspection and maintenance monitors (I/M flags) are complete

Fail. The OBD II system fails when:

- The MIL operates incorrectly.
- One or more MIL illuminating DTCs are present
- The data link connector (DLC) is missing, tampered with, or inoperable

Rejected. The OBD II system is rejected if:

- The inspection and maintenance monitors are not completed
- the DLC cannot be located and/or is inaccessible.

OBD-II DRIVE CYCLE[1]

The typical OBD-II drive cycle begins with a cold start, and has a number of requirements or preconditions. These requirements are that the:

- Barometric pressure (BARO) is greater than 75 kilopascals (kPa)
- Engine coolant temperature (ECT) is below 30°C (86°F)
- Intake air temperature (IAT) is below 30°C (86°F)
- IAT and ECT temperature have a difference of less than 5°C (7°F)
- Battery voltage is between 10.5 and 16 volts (V)
- Fuel tank level is between one-half and three-quarters full

Always refer to service information (SI) for vehicle specific applications. The purpose of the OBD-II drive cycle is to run all of the emissions-related OBD monitors. When all diagnostics have run, the system status (I/M) flags are set to Yes. Use the scan tool to determine if the OBD-II monitors are complete.

1. First, preprogram the scan tool with the vehicle information before turning the ignition ON.

2. Then, turn off all accessories, such as the A/C, blower fan, and radio.

3. Apply the parking brake. An automatic transmission needs to be in Park (P), and a manual transmission needs to be in Neutral (N).

4. Then, start the engine and allow the vehicle to idle for 2 minutes. During this step, diagnostics run for the heated oxygen sensors (HO2S) and the EVAP system.

5. Next, accelerate to 88 kilometers per hour (kph), or 55 miles per hour (mph), and maintain this speed until the engine reaches operating temperature. This may take 8 to 10 minutes. Continue operation for an additional 6 minutes. During this time, EVAP, air injection reaction, O2S, and catalyst tests operate on some vehicles.

6. After the acceleration cycle is complete, decelerate to 72 kph (45 mph) and maintain speed for 1 minute, followed by four decelerations of 25 seconds each from 72 kph (45 mph) while the throttle is closed. During these decelerations, the brake or clutch is not applied, there is

---

[1]Adapted from GM Training Course #16044.21W3

not a manual downshift, and the vehicle speed remains above 40 kph (25 mph). After each deceleration period, accelerate to 72 kph (45 mph) and maintain speed for 15 seconds while the EGR test runs.

7. Finally, after the EGR test runs, accelerate to between 72 kph and 88 kph (45 mph and 55 mph) while maintaining speed for 2 minutes, then decelerate to 0 kph (0 mph). Let the engine idle for 2 minutes while depressing the brake. Automatic transmissions need to be in Drive (D), and manual transmissions need to be in Neutral (N) with the clutch pedal depressed. This step operates the catalyst test, oxygen sensor, and/or EVAP test, depending on the vehicle.

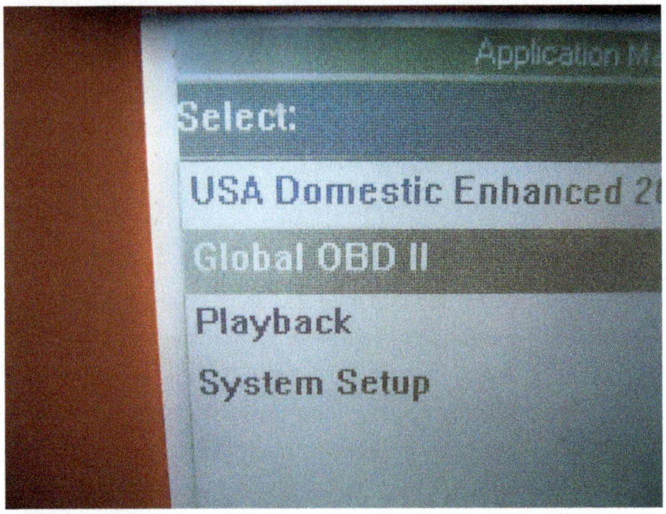

FIGURE 30–5 Global OBD II can be accessed from the main menu on all aftermarket and some original equipment scan tools.

GLOBAL OBD-II

All OBD-II vehicles must be able to display data on a global (also called *generic*) scan tool under nine different modes of operation. These modes include:

Mode One	Current powertrain data (**parameter identification or PID**)
Mode Two	Freeze-frame data
Mode Three	Diagnostic trouble codes
Mode Four	Clear and reset diagnostic trouble codes (DTCs), freeze-frame data, and readiness status monitors for noncontinuous monitors only
Mode Five	Oxygen sensor monitor test results
Mode Six	Onboard monitoring of test results for non-continuously monitored systems
Mode Seven	Onboard monitoring of test results for continuously monitored systems
Mode Eight	Bidirectional control of onboard systems
Mode Nine	Module identification

The global (generic) data is used by most state emission programs.

ACCESSING GLOBAL OBD II

Global (generic) OBD II is used by inspectors where emission testing is performed. Aftermarket scan tools are designed to retrieve global OBD II; however, some original equipment scan tools, such as the Tech 2 used on General Motors vehicles, are not able to retrieve the information without special software.

? **FREQUENTLY ASKED QUESTION**

How Can You Tell Generic from Factory?

When using a scan tool on an OBD II–equipped vehicle, if the display asks for make, model, and year, then the factory or enhanced part of the PCM is being accessed. If the generic or global part of the PCM is being scanned, then there is no need to know the vehicle details.

Global OBD II is accessible using ISO-9141-2, KWP 2000, J1850 PWM, J1850 VPW, and CAN.

SNAP-ON SOLUS From the main menu select "Generic OBD II/EOBD" and then follow the on-screen instructions to select the desired test.

SNAP-ON MODIS Select the scanner using the down arrow key and then select "Global OBD II." Follow on-screen instructions to get to "start communication" and then to the list of options to view.

OTC GENISYS From the main menu select "Global OBD II" and then follow the on-screen instructions. Select "special tests" to get access to mode $06 information and parameters.

MASTER TECH From the main menu, select "Global OBD II." At the next screen, select "OBD II functions," then "system tests," and then "other results" to obtain mode $06 data. ● **SEE FIGURE 30–5**.

SUMMARY

1. If the MIL is on, retrieve the DTC and follow the manufacturer's recommended procedure to find the root cause of the problem.

2. All monitors must have the enable criteria achieved before a test is performed.

3. OBD-II vehicles use common generic DTCs.

4. OBD II includes generic (SAE), as well as vehicle manufacturer-specific DTCs, and data display.

REVIEW QUESTIONS

1. What does the PCM do during a trip to test emission-related components?

2. What is the difference between a type A and type B OBD-II DTC?

3. What is the difference between a trip and a warm-up cycle?

4. What could cause the MIL to flash?

CHAPTER QUIZ

1. A freeze-frame is generated on an OBD-II vehicle _____.
   a. When a type C or D diagnostic trouble code is set
   b. When a type A or B diagnostic trouble code is set
   c. Every other trip
   d. When the PCM detects a problem with the O2S

2. An ignition misfire or fuel mixture problem is an example of what type of DTC?
   a. Type A
   b. Type B
   c. Type C
   d. Type D

3. The comprehensive component monitor checks computer-controlled devices for_____.
   a. opens
   b. shorts-to-ground
   c. rationality
   d. All of the above

4. OBD II has been on all passenger vehicles in the United States since _____.
   a. 1986
   b. 1991
   c. 1996
   d. 2000

5. Which is a continuous monitor?
   a. Fuel system monitor
   b. EGR monitor
   c. Oxygen sensor monitor
   d. Catalyst monitor

6. DTC P0302 is a _____.
   a. Generic DTC
   b. Vehicle manufacturer-specific DTC
   c. Idle speed-related DTC
   d. Transmission/transaxle-related DTC

7. Global (generic) OBD II contains some data in what format?
   a. Plain English
   b. Hexadecimal
   c. Roman numerals
   d. All of the above

8. By looking at the way diagnostic trouble codes are formatted, which DTC could indicate that the gas cap is loose or defective?
   a. P0221
   b. P1301
   c. P0442
   d. P1603

9. The computer will automatically clear a DTC if there are no additional detected faults after _____.
   a. Forty consecutive warm-up cycles
   b. Eighty warm-up cycles
   c. Two consecutive trips
   d. Four key-on/key-off cycles

10. A pending code is set when a fault is detected on _____.
    a. A one-trip fault item
    b. The first fault of a two-trip failure
    c. The catalytic converter efficiency
    d. Thermostat problem (too long to closed-loop status)

SENSORS

LEARNING OBJECTIVES

After studying this chapter, the reader should be able to:

1. Describe the purpose and function of engine coolant temperature sensors.
2. Describe how to inspect and test temperature sensors.
3. Diagnose emissions and drivability problems resulting from malfunctions in the intake air temperature control systems.
4. Discuss how automatic fluid temperature sensor values can affect transmission operation.

This chapter will help you prepare for Engine Repair (A8) ASE certification test content area "E" (Computerized Engine Controls Diagnosis and Repair).

KEY TERMS

Engine coolant temperature (ECT) 481

Engine fuel temperature (EFT) 489

Negative temperature coefficient (NTC) 481

Throttle-body temperature (TBT) 487

Transmission fluid temperature (TFT) 489

GM STC OBJECTIVES

GM Service Technical College topics covered in this chapter are:

1. Diagnose signal circuit using a systematic process.
2. Test signal circuit (two wire) using electrical/electronic tools.

FIGURE 31–1 The engine coolant temperature (ECT) sensor sensing element is enclosed in a metal body. (*Courtesy of General Motors*)

FIGURE 31–2 The engine coolant temperature (ECT) sensor (1) is located in the engine water jacket near the thermostat, cylinder head, or engine block. (*Courtesy of General Motors*)

ENGINE COOLANT TEMPERATURE SENSORS

PURPOSE AND FUNCTION Computer-equipped vehicles use an **engine coolant temperature (ECT)** sensor. When the engine is cold, the fuel mixture must be richer to prevent stalling and engine stumble. When the engine is warm, the fuel mixture can be leaner to provide maximum fuel economy with the lowest possible exhaust emissions. Because the computer controls spark timing and fuel mixture, it will need to know the engine temperature. **SEE FIGURE 31–1**.

An engine coolant temperature sensor screwed into the engine coolant passage will provide the computer with this information. ● **SEE FIGURE 31–2**. This will be the most important (high-authority) sensor while the engine is cold. The ignition timing can also be tailored to engine (coolant) temperature. A hot engine cannot have the spark timing as far advanced as can a cold engine. The ECT sensor is also used as an important input for the following:

- Idle air control (IAC) position
- Oxygen sensor closed-loop status
- Canister purge on/off times
- Idle speed

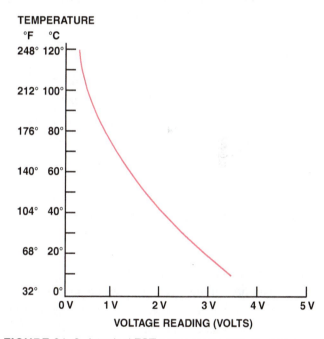

FIGURE 31–3 A typical ECT sensor temperature versus voltage curve.

ECT SENSOR CONSTRUCTION Engine coolant temperature sensors are constructed of a semiconductor material that decreases in resistance as the temperature of the sensor increases. Coolant sensors have very high resistance when the coolant is cold and low resistance when the coolant is hot. This is referred to as having a **negative temperature coefficient (NTC)**, which is opposite to the situation with most other electrical components. ● **SEE FIGURE 31–3**. Therefore, if the coolant sensor has a poor connection (high resistance) at the

FIGURE 31–4 A typical two-step ECT circuit showing that when the coolant temperature is low, the PCM applies a 5 volt reference voltage to the ECT sensor through a higher resistance compared to when the temperature is higher.

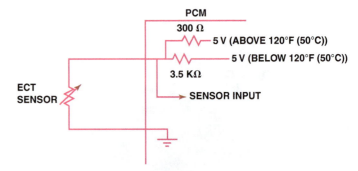

FIGURE 31–5 The transition between steps usually occurs at a temperature that would not interfere with cold engine starts or the cooling fan operation. In this example, the transition occurs when the sensor voltage is about 1 volt and rises to about 3.6 volts.

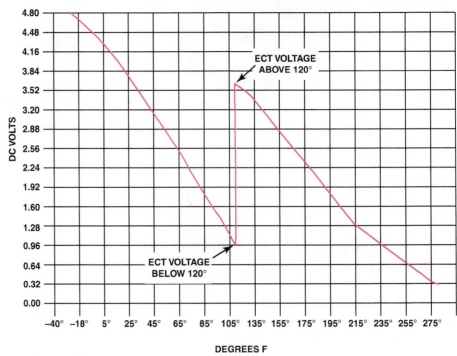

wiring connector, the computer will supply a richer-than-normal fuel mixture based on the resistance of the coolant sensor. Poor fuel economy and a possible-rich code can be caused by a defective sensor or high resistance in the sensor wiring. If the sensor was shorted or defective and had too low a resistance, a leaner-than-normal fuel mixture would be supplied to the engine. A too-lean fuel mixture can cause driveability problems and a possible-lean computer code.

STEPPED ECT CIRCUITS
Some vehicle manufacturers use a step-up resistor to effectively broaden the range of the ECT sensor. Chrysler and General Motors vehicles use the same sensor as a non-stepped ECT circuit, but instead apply the sensor voltage through two different resistors.

- When the temperature is cold, usually below 120°F (50°C), the ECT sensor voltage is applied through a high-value resistor inside the PCM.
- When the temperature is warm, usually above 120°F (50°C), the ECT sensor voltage is applied through a much lower resistance value inside the PCM. ● **SEE FIGURE 31–4.**

The purpose of this extra circuit is to give the PCM a more accurate reading of the engine coolant temperature compared to the same sensor with only one circuit. ● **SEE FIGURE 31–5.**

TESTING THE ENGINE COOLANT TEMPERATURE SENSOR

TESTING THE ENGINE COOLANT TEMPERATURE BY VISUAL INSPECTION
The correct functioning of the engine coolant temperature sensor depends on the following points that should be checked or inspected:

- **Properly filled cooling system.** Check that the radiator reservoir bottle is full and that the radiator itself is filled to the top.

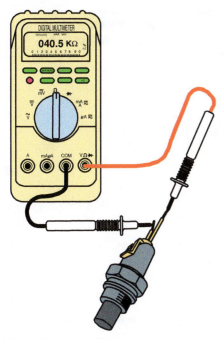

FIGURE 31–6 Measuring the resistance of the ECT sensor. The resistance measurement can then be compared with specifications. (*Courtesy of Fluke Corporation*)

CAUTION: Be sure that the radiator is cool before removing the radiator cap to avoid being scalded by hot coolant.

The ECT sensor must be submerged in coolant to be able to indicate the proper coolant temperature.

- **Proper pressure maintained by the radiator cap.** If the radiator cap is defective and cannot allow the cooling system to become pressurized, air pockets could develop. These air pockets could cause the engine to operate at a hotter-than-normal temperature and prevent proper temperature measurement, especially if the air pockets occur around the sensor.

- **Proper antifreeze–water mixture.** Most vehicle manufacturers recommend a 50–50 mixture of antifreeze and water as the best compromise between freezing protection and heat transfer ability.

- **Proper operation of the cooling fan.** If the cooling fan does not operate correctly, the engine may overheat.

TESTING THE ECT USING A MULTIMETER
Both the resistance (in ohms) and the voltage drop across the sensor can be measured and compared with specifications. ● **SEE FIGURE 31–6.** See the following charts showing examples of typical engine coolant temperature sensor specifications.

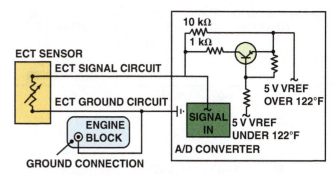

FIGURE 31–7 When the voltage drop reaches approximately 1.20 volts, the PCM turns on a transistor. The transistor connects a 1 kΩ resistor in parallel with the 10 kΩ resistor. Total circuit resistance now drops to around 909 ohms. This function allows the PCM to have full binary control at cold temperatures up to approximately 122°F, and a second full binary control at temperatures greater than 122°F.

Some vehicles use the PCM to attach another resistor in the ECT circuit to provide a more accurate measure of the engine temperature. ● **SEE FIGURE 31–7.**

If resistance values match the approximate coolant temperature and there is still a coolant sensor trouble code, the problem is generally in the wiring between the sensor and the computer. Always consult the manufacturers' recommended procedures for checking this wiring. If the resistance values do not match, the sensor may need to be replaced.

GENERAL MOTORS ECT SENSOR WITH PULL-UP RESISTOR			
°F	°C	OHMS	VOLTAGE DROP ACROSS SENSOR
−40	−40	100,000 +	4.95
18	−8	14,628	4.68
32	0	9,420	4.52
50	10	5,670	4.25
68	20	3,520	3.89
86	30	2,238	3.46
104	40	1,459	2.97
122	50	973	2.47
140	60	667	2.00
158	70	467	1.59
176	80	332	1.25
194	90	241	0.97
212	100	177	0.75

GENERAL MOTORS ECT SENSOR WITHOUT PULL-UP RESISTOR

°F	°C	OHMS	VOLTAGE DROP ACROSS SENSOR
−40	−40	100,000	5
−22	−30	53,000	4.78
−4	−20	29,000	4.34
14	−10	16,000	3.89
32	0	9,400	3.45
50	10	5,700	3.01
68	20	3,500	2.56
86	30	2,200	1.80
104	40	1,500	1.10
122	50	970	3.25
140	60	670	2.88
158	70	470	2.56
176	80	330	2.24
194	90	240	1.70
212	100	177	1.42
230	110	132	1.15
248	120	100	0.87

FORD ECT SENSOR

°F	°C	RESISTANCE (Ω)	VOLTAGE (V)
50	10	58,750	3.52
68	20	37,300	3.06
86	30	24,270	2.26
104	40	16,150	2.16
122	50	10,970	1.72
140	60	7,600	1.35
158	70	5,370	1.04
176	80	3,840	0.80
194	90	2,800	0.61
212	100	2,070	0.47
230	110	1,550	0.36
248	120	1,180	0.28

NOTE: Non-GM values are included for reference and comparison.

CHRYSLER ECT SENSOR WITHOUT PULL-UP RESISTOR

°F	°C	VOLTAGE (V)
130	54	3.77
140	60	3.60
150	66	3.40
160	71	3.20
170	77	3.02
180	82	2.80
190	88	2.60
200	93	2.40
210	99	2.20
220	104	2.00
230	110	1.80
240	116	1.62
250	121	1.45

CHRYSLER ECT SENSOR WITH PULL-UP RESISTOR

°F	°C	VOLTS
−20	−29	4.70
−10	−23	4.57
0	−18	4.45
10	−12	4.30
20	−7	4.10
30	−1	3.90
40	4	3.60
50	10	3.30
60	16	3.00
70	21	2.75
80	27	2.44
90	32	2.15
100	38	1.83
		PULL-UP RESISTOR SWITCHED BY PCM
110	43	4.20
120	49	4.10
130	54	4.00
140	60	3.60
150	66	3.40
160	71	3.20
170	77	3.02
180	82	2.80
190	88	2.60
200	93	2.40
210	99	2.20
220	104	2.00
230	110	1.80
240	116	1.62
250	121	1.45

NISSAN ECT SENSOR		
°F	°C	RESISTANCE (Ω)
14	−10	7,000–11,400
68	20	2,100–2,900
122	50	680–1,000
176	80	260–390
212	100	180–200

HONDA ECT SENSOR (RESISTANCE CHART)		
°F	°C	RESISTANCE (Ω)
0	−18	15,000
32	0	5,000
68	20	3,000
104	40	1,000
140	60	500
176	80	400
212	100	250

MERCEDES ECT		
°F	°C	VOLTAGE (DCV)
60	20	3.5
86	30	3.1
104	40	2.7
122	50	2.3
140	60	1.9
158	70	1.5
176	80	1.2
194	90	1.0
212	100	0.8

HONDA ECT SENSOR (VOLTAGE CHART)		
°F	°C	VOLTAGE (V)
0	−18	4.70
10	−12	4.50
20	−7	4.29
30	−1	4.10
40	4	3.86
50	10	3.61
60	16	3.35
70	21	3.08
80	27	2.81
90	32	2.50
100	38	2.26
110	43	2.00
120	49	1.74
130	54	1.52
140	60	1.33
150	66	1.15
160	71	1.00
170	77	0.88
180	82	0.74
190	88	0.64
200	93	0.55
210	99	0.47

EUROPEAN BOSCH ECT SENSOR		
°F	°C	RESISTANCE (Ω)
32	0	6,500
50	10	4,000
68	20	3,000
86	30	2,000
104	40	1,500
122	50	900
140	60	650
158	70	500
176	80	375
194	90	295
212	100	230

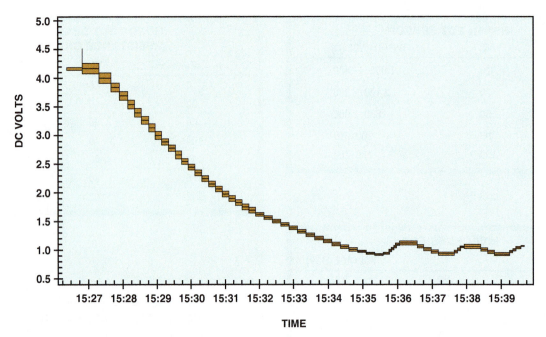

FIGURE 31–8 An ECT sensor being tested using a digital meter set to DC volts. A chart showing the voltage decrease of the ECT sensor as the temperature increases from a cold start. The bumps at the bottom of the waveform represent temperature decreases when the thermostat opens and is controlling coolant temperature.

Normal operating temperature varies with vehicle make and model. Some vehicles are equipped with a thermostat with an operating temperature of 180°F (82°C), whereas other vehicles use a thermostat that is 195°F (90°C) or higher. Before replacing the ECT sensor, be sure that the engine is operating at the temperature specified by the manufacturer. Most manufacturers recommend checking the ECT sensor after the cooling fan has cycled twice, indicating a fully warmed engine. To test for voltage at the ECT sensor, select DC volts on a digital meter and carefully back probe the sensor wire and read the voltage. ● **SEE FIGURE 31–8.**

NOTE: Many manufacturers install another resistor in parallel inside the computer to change the voltage drop across the ECT sensor. This is done to expand the scale of the ECT sensor and to make the sensor more sensitive. Therefore, if measuring *voltage* at the ECT sensor, check with the service manual for the proper voltage at each temperature.

TESTING THE ECT SENSOR USING A SCAN TOOL
Follow the scan tool manufacturer's instructions and connect a scan tool to the data link connector (DLC) of the vehicle. Comparing the temperature of the engine coolant as displayed on a scan tool with the actual temperature of the engine is an excellent method to test an engine coolant temperature sensor.

1. Record the scan tool temperature of the coolant (ECT).
2. Measure the actual temperature of the coolant using an infrared pyrometer or contact-type temperature probe.

NOTE: Often the coolant temperature gauge in the dash of the vehicle can be used to compare with the scan tool temperature. Although not necessarily accurate, it may help to diagnose a faulty sensor, especially if the temperature shown on the scan tool varies greatly from the temperature indicated on the dash gauge.

The maximum difference between the two readings should be 10°F (5°C). If the actual temperature varies by more than 10°F from the temperature indicated on the scan tool, check the ECT sensor wiring and connector for damage or corrosion. If the connector and wiring are okay, check the sensor with a DVOM for resistance and compare with the actual engine temperature chart. If that checks out okay, check the computer.

NOTE: Some manufacturers use two coolant sensors, one for the dash gauge and another one for the computer.

INTAKE AIR TEMPERATURE SENSOR

PURPOSE AND FUNCTION The intake air temperature (IAT) sensor is a negative temperature coefficient (NTC) thermistor that decreases in resistance as the temperature of

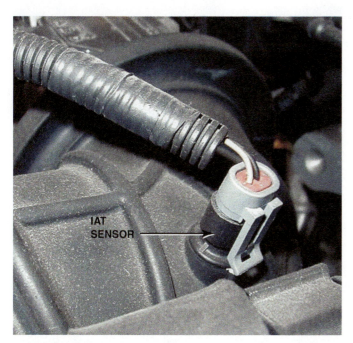

FIGURE 31–9 The IAT sensor on this General Motors 3800 V-6 engine is in the air passage duct between the air cleaner housing and the throttle body.

TECH TIP

Quick and Easy ECT Test

To check that the wiring and the computer are functioning, regarding the ECT sensor, connect a scan tool and look at the ECT temperature display.

STEP 1   Unplug the connector from the ECT sensor. The temperature displayed on the scan tool should read about –40°C.

   NOTE: –40° Celsius is also –40° Fahrenheit. This is the point where both temperature scales meet.

STEP 2   With the connector still removed from the ECT sensor, use a fused jumper lead and connect the two terminals of the connector together. The scan tool should display about 285°F (140°C).

This same test procedure will work for the IAT and most other temperature sensors.

the sensor increases. The IAT sensor can be located in one of the following locations:

- In the air cleaner housing
- In the air duct between the air filter and the throttle body, as shown in ● **FIGURE 31–9**
- Built into the mass air flow (MAF) or airflow sensor
- Screwed into the intake manifold where it senses the temperature of the air entering the cylinders

NOTE: An IAT installed in the intake manifold is the most likely to suffer damage due to an engine backfire, which can often destroy the sensor.

The purpose and function of the intake air temperature sensor is to provide the engine computer (PCM) the temperature of the air entering the engine. The IAT sensor information is used for fuel control (adding or subtracting fuel) and spark timing, depending on the temperature of incoming air.

The IAT sensor is used as an input sensor by the PCM to control many functions including:

- If the air temperature is cold, the PCM will modify the amount of fuel delivery and add fuel.
- If the air temperature is hot, the PCM will subtract the calculated amount of fuel.
- Spark timing is also changed, depending on the temperature of the air entering the engine. The timing is

advanced if the temperature is cold and retarded from the base-programmed timing if the temperature is hot.

- Cold air is more dense, contains more oxygen, and therefore requires a richer mixture to achieve the proper air–fuel mixture. Air at 32°F (0°C) is 14% denser than air at 100°F (38°C).
- Hot air is less dense, contains less oxygen, and therefore requires less fuel to achieve the proper air–fuel mixture.

The IAT sensor is a low-authority sensor and is used by the computer to modify the amount of fuel and ignition timing as determined by the engine coolant temperature sensor.

The IAT sensor is used by the PCM as a backup in the event that the ECT sensor is determined to be inoperative.

NOTE: Some older engines use a throttle-body temperature (TBT) sensor to sense the temperature of the air entering the engine, instead of an intake air temperature sensor.

Engine temperature is most accurately determined by looking at the engine coolant temperature sensor. In certain conditions, the IAT has an effect on performance and driveability. One such condition is a warm engine being stopped in very cold weather. In this case, when the engine is restarted, the ECT may be near normal operating temperature such as 200°F (93°C), yet the air temperature could be –20°F (–30°C).

Poor Fuel Economy? Black Exhaust Smoke? Look at the IAT

If the intake air temperature sensor is defective, it may be signaling the computer that the intake air temperature is extremely cold when in fact it is warm. In such a case, the computer will supply a mixture that is much richer than normal.

If a sensor is physically damaged or electrically open, the computer will often set a diagnostic trouble code (DTC). This DTC is based on the fact that the sensor temperature did not change for a certain amount of time, usually about nine minutes. If, however, the wiring or the sensor itself has excessive resistance, a DTC will not be set and the result will be lower-than-normal fuel economy, and in serious cases, black exhaust smoke from the tailpipe during acceleration.

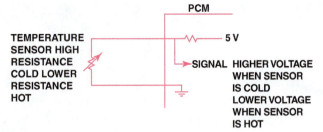

FIGURE 31–10 A typical temperature sensor circuit.

In this case, the engine requires a richer mixture due to the cold air than the ECT would seem to indicate.

TESTING THE INTAKE AIR TEMPERATURE SENSOR

If the intake air temperature sensor circuit is damaged or faulty, a diagnostic trouble code is set and the malfunction indicator lamp (MIL) may or may not turn on depending on the condition and the type and model of the vehicle. To diagnose the IAT sensor follow these steps:

STEP 1 After the vehicle has been allowed to cool for several hours, use a scan tool, observe the IAT, and compare it to the engine coolant temperature. The two temperatures should be within 5°F of each other.

STEP 2 Perform a thorough visual inspection of the sensor and the wiring. If the IAT is screwed into the intake manifold, remove the sensor and check for damage.

STEP 3 Check the voltage and compare with the following chart.

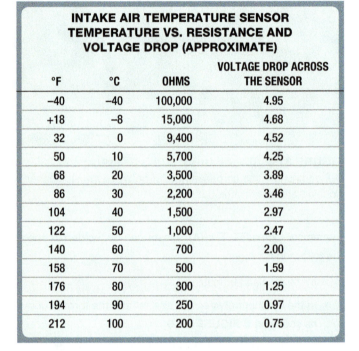

INTAKE AIR TEMPERATURE SENSOR TEMPERATURE VS. RESISTANCE AND VOLTAGE DROP (APPROXIMATE)

°F	°C	OHMS	VOLTAGE DROP ACROSS THE SENSOR
−40	−40	100,000	4.95
+18	−8	15,000	4.68
32	0	9,400	4.52
50	10	5,700	4.25
68	20	3,500	3.89
86	30	2,200	3.46
104	40	1,500	2.97
122	50	1,000	2.47
140	60	700	2.00
158	70	500	1.59
176	80	300	1.25
194	90	250	0.97
212	100	200	0.75

? FREQUENTLY ASKED QUESTION

What Exactly Is an NTC Sensor?

A negative temperature coefficient (NTC) thermistor is a semiconductor whose resistance decreases as the temperature increases. In other words, the sensor becomes more electrically conductive as the temperature increases. Therefore, when a voltage is applied, typically 5 volts, the signal voltage is high when the sensor is cold because the sensor has a high resistance and little current flows through to ground.
● **SEE FIGURE 31–10.**

However, when the temperature increases, the sensor becomes more electrically conductive and takes more of the 5 volts to ground, resulting in a lower signal voltage as the sensor warms.

TRANSMISSION FLUID TEMPERATURE SENSOR

The **transmission fluid temperature (TFT)**, also called *transmission oil temperature (TOT)*, sensor is an important sensor for the proper operation of the automatic transmission. A TFT sensor is a negative temperature coefficient (NTC) thermistor that decreases in resistance as the temperature of the sensor increases.

GENERAL MOTORS
Transaxle Sensor—Temperature to Resistance (approximate)

°F	°C	RESISTANCE (Ω)
32	0	7,987–10,859
50	10	4,934–6,407
68	20	3,106–3,923
86	30	1,991–2,483
104	40	1,307–1,611
122	50	878–1,067
140	60	605–728
158	70	425–507
176	80	304–359
194	90	221–259
212	100	163–190

CHRYSLER
Sensor Resistance (Ohms)—Transmission Temperature Sensor

°F	°C	RESISTANCE (Ω)
−40	−40	291,490–381,710
−4	−20	85,850–108,390
14	−10	49,250–61,430
32	0	29,330–35,990
50	10	17,990–21,810
68	20	11,370–13,610
77	25	9,120–10,880
86	30	7,370–8,750
104	40	4,900–5,750
122	50	3,330–3,880
140	60	2,310–2,670
158	70	1,630–1,870
176	80	1,170–1,340
194	90	860–970
212	100	640–720
230	110	480–540
248	120	370–410

FORD
Transmission Fluid Temperature

°F	°C	RESISTANCE (Ω)
−40 to −4	−40 to −20	967–284 K
−3 to 31	−19 to −1	284–100 K
32 to 68	0 to 20	100–37 K
69 to 104	21 to 40	37–16 K
105 to 158	41 to 70	16–5 K
159 to 194	71 to 90	5–2.7 K
195 to 230	91 to 110	2.7–1.5 K
231 to 266	111 to 130	1.5–0.8 K
267 to 302	131 to 150	0.8–0.54 K

The transmission fluid temperature signal is used by the powertrain control module (PCM) to perform certain strategies based on the temperature of the automatic transmission fluid. For example:

- If the temperature of the automatic transmission fluid is low (typically below 32°F [0°C]), the shift points may be delayed and overdrive disabled. The torque converter clutch also may not be applied to assist in the heating of the fluid.

- If the temperature of the automatic transmission fluid is high (typically above 260°F [130°C]), the overdrive is disabled and the torque converter clutch is applied to help reduce the temperature of the fluid.

NOTE: Check service information for the exact shift strategy based on high and low transmission fluid temperatures for the vehicle being serviced.

ENGINE FUEL TEMPERATURE (EFT) SENSOR

Vehicles that are equipped with an electronic returnless type of fuel injection may include an **engine fuel temperature (EFT)** sensor to give the PCM information regarding the temperature and, therefore, the density of the fuel.

DIAGNOSTIC TROUBLE CODE	DESCRIPTION	POSSIBLE CAUSES
P0112	IAT sensor low voltage	• IAT sensor internally shorted-to-ground • IAT sensor wiring shorted-to-ground • IAT sensor damaged by backfire (usually associated with IAT sensors that are mounted in the intake manifold) • Possible defective PCM
P0113	IAT sensor high voltage	• IAT sensor internally (electrically) open • IAT sensor signal, circuit, or ground circuit open • Possible defective PCM
P0117	ECT sensor low voltage	• ECT sensor internally shorted-to-ground • The ECT sensor circuit wiring shorted-to-ground • Possible defective PCM
P0118	ECT sensor high voltage	• ECT sensor internally (electrically) open • ECT sensor signal, circuit, or ground circuit open • Engine operating in an overheated condition • Possible defective PCM

CHART 31–1

Selected temperature sensor-related diagnostic trouble codes.

EXHAUST GAS RECIRCULATION (EGR) TEMPERATURE SENSOR

Some engines are equipped with exhaust gas recirculation (EGR) temperature sensors. EGR is a well-established method for reduction of NO_X emissions in internal combustion engines. The exhaust gas contains unburned hydrocarbons, which are recirculated in the combustion process. Recirculation is controlled by valves, which operate as a function of exhaust gas speed, load, and temperature. The gas reaches a temperature of about 850°F (450°C) for which a special heavy-duty glass-encapsulated NTC sensor is available.

The PCM monitors the temperature in the exhaust passage between the EGR valve and the intake manifold. If the temperature increases when the EGR is commanded on, the PCM can determine that the valve or related components are functioning.

ENGINE OIL TEMPERATURE SENSOR

Engine oil temperature sensors are used on many General Motors vehicles and are used as an input to the oil life monitoring system. The computer program inside the PCM calculates engine oil life based on run time, engine RPM, and oil temperature.

TEMPERATURE SENSOR DIAGNOSTIC TROUBLE CODES

The OBD-II diagnostic trouble codes that relate to temperature sensors include both high- and low-voltage codes, as well as intermittent codes. ● **SEE CHART 31–1.**

SUMMARY

1. The ECT sensor is a high-authority sensor at engine start-up and is used for closed-loop control, as well as idle speed.

2. All temperature sensors decrease in resistance as the temperature increases. This is called negative temperature coefficient (NTC).

FIGURE 33–2 A plastic MAP sensor used for training purposes showing the electronic circuit board and electrical connections.

FIGURE 33–3 A General Motors MAP sensor. (*Courtesy of General Motors*)

same as atmospheric pressure. On deceleration or at idle, manifold pressure is below atmospheric pressure, thus creating a vacuum. In cases where turbo- or supercharging is used, under part- or full-load condition, intake manifold pressure rises above atmospheric pressure. Also, oxygen content and barometric pressure change with differences in altitude, and the computer must be able to compensate by making changes in the flow of fuel entering the engine. To provide the computer with changing airflow information, a fuel-injection system may use the following:

- Manifold absolute pressure (MAP) sensor
- Manifold absolute pressure sensor plus barometric absolute pressure (BARO) sensor
- Barometric and manifold absolute pressure sensors combined (BMAP)

The **manifold absolute pressure (MAP) sensor** may be a ceramic capacitor diaphragm, an aneroid bellows, or a piezoresistive crystal. It has a sealed vacuum reference input on one side; the other side is connected (vented) to the intake manifold. This sensor housing also contains signal conditioning circuitry. ● **SEE FIGURE 33–2.** Pressure changes in the manifold cause the sensor to deflect, varying its analog or digital return signal to the computer. As the air pressure increases, the MAP sensor generates a higher voltage or frequency return signal to the computer.

CONSTRUCTION OF MANIFOLD ABSOLUTE PRESSURE SENSORS

The manifold absolute pressure sensor is used by the engine computer to sense engine load. The typical MAP sensor consists of a ceramic or silicon wafer sealed on one side with a perfect vacuum and exposed to intake manifold vacuum on the other side. As the engine vacuum changes, the pressure difference on the wafer changes the output voltage or frequency of the MAP sensor.

A manifold absolute pressure sensor is used on many engines for the PCM to determine the load on the engine. The relationship among barometer pressure, engine vacuum, and MAP sensor voltage includes:

- Absolute pressure is equal to barometric pressure minus intake manifold vacuum.
- A decrease in manifold vacuum means an increase in manifold pressure.
- The MAP sensor compares manifold vacuum to a perfect vacuum.
- Barometric pressure minus MAP sensor reading equals intake manifold vacuum. Normal engine vacuum is 17 to 21 inch Hg.
- Supercharged and turbocharged engines require a MAP sensor that is calibrated for pressures above atmospheric, as well as for vacuum.

SILICON-DIAPHRAGM STRAIN GAUGE MAP SENSOR This is the most commonly used design for a MAP sensor and the output is a DC analog (variable) voltage. One side of a silicon wafer is exposed to engine vacuum and the other side is exposed to a perfect vacuum.

There are four resistors attached to the silicon wafer, which changes in resistance when strain is applied to the wafer. This change in resistance due to strain is called **piezoresistivity**. The resistors are electrically connected to a Wheatstone bridge circuit and then to a differential amplifier, which creates a voltage in proportion to the vacuum applied.

A typical General Motors MAP sensor voltage varies from 0.88 to 1.62 at engine idle. ● **SEE FIGURE 33–3.**

- 17 inch Hg is equal to about 1.62 volts
- 21 inch Hg is equal to about 0.88 volt

Therefore, a good reading should be about 1.0 volt from the MAP sensor on a sound engine at idle speed. See the

ENGINE LOAD	MANIFOLD VACUUM	MANIFOLD ABSOLUTE PRESSURE	MAP SENSOR VOLT SIGNAL
Heavy (WOT)	Low (almost 0 in. Hg)	High (almost atmospheric)	High (4.6–4.8 V)
Light (idle)	High (17–21 in. Hg)	Low (lower than atmospheric)	Low (0.8–1.6 V)

CHART 33–1

Engine load and how it is related to engine vacuum, and MAP sensor reading.

chart that shows engine load, engine vacuum, and MAP.
● SEE CHART 33–1.

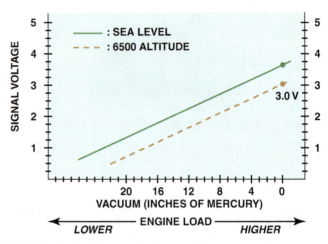

FIGURE 33–4 Altitude affects the MAP sensor voltage.

PCM USES OF THE MAP SENSOR

The PCM uses the MAP sensor to determine the following:

- **The load on the engine.** The MAP sensor is used on a **speed density**–type fuel-injection system to determine the load on the engine, and therefore the amount of fuel needed. On engines equipped with a mass air flow (MAF) sensor, the MAP is used as a backup to the MAF, for diagnosis of other sensors, and systems such as the EGR system.

- **Altitude, fuel, and spark control calculations.** At key on, the MAP sensor determines the altitude (acts as a BARO sensor) and adjusts the fuel delivery and spark timing accordingly.

  - If the altitude is high, generally over 5,000 feet (1,500 m), the PCM will reduce fuel delivery and advance the ignition timing.

  - The altitude is also reset when the engine is accelerated to wide-open throttle and the MAP sensor is used to reset the altitude reading. ● SEE FIGURE 33–4.

- **EGR system operation.** As part of the OBD-II standards, the exhaust gas recirculation (EGR) system must be checked for proper operation. One method used by many vehicle manufacturers is to command the EGR valve on and then watch the MAP sensor signal. The opening of the EGR pintle should decrease engine vacuum. If the MAP sensor does not react with the specified drop in manifold vacuum (increase in manifold pressure), an EGR flow rate problem diagnostic trouble code is set.

- **Detect deceleration (vacuum increases).** The engine vacuum rises when the accelerator is released, which changes the MAP sensor voltage. When deceleration is detected by the PCM, fuel is either stopped or greatly reduced to improve exhaust emissions.

- **Monitor engine condition.** As an engine wears, the intake manifold vacuum usually decreases. The PCM is programmed to detect the gradual change in vacuum and is able to keep the air–fuel mixture in the correct range. If the PCM were not capable of making adjustments for engine wear, the lower vacuum could be interpreted as increased load on the engine, resulting in too much fuel being injected, thereby reducing fuel economy and increasing exhaust emissions.

- **Load detection for returnless-type fuel injection.** On fuel delivery systems that do not use a return line back to the fuel tank, the engine load calculation for the fuel needed is determined by the signals from the MAP sensor.

- **Altitude and MAP sensor values.** On an engine equipped with a speed-density-type fuel injection, the MAP sensor is the most important sensor needed to determine injection pulse width. Changes in altitude change the air density as well as weather conditions. Barometric pressure and altitude are inversely related:

  - As altitude increases—barometric pressure decreases

  - As altitude decreases—barometric pressure increases

As the ignition switch is turned from off to the start position, the PCM reads the MAP sensor value to determine atmospheric and air pressure conditions. This barometric pressure reading is updated every time the engine is started and whenever wide-open throttle is detected. The barometric pressure reading at that time is updated.
● SEE CHART 33–2.

Use the MAP Sensor as a Vacuum Gauge

A MAP sensor measures the pressure inside the intake manifold compared with absolute zero (perfect vacuum). For example, an idling engine that has 20 inch Hg of vacuum has a lower pressure inside the intake manifold than when the engine is under a load and the vacuum is at 10 inch Hg. A decrease in engine vacuum results in an increase in manifold pressure. A normal engine should produce between 17 inch Hg and 21 inch Hg at idle. Comparing the vacuum reading with the voltage reading output of the MAP sensor indicates that the reading should be between 1.62 and 0.88 volts. Therefore, a digital multimeter (DMM), scan tool, or scope can be used to measure the MAP sensor voltage and be used instead of a vacuum gauge.

NOTE: This chart was developed by testing a MAP sensor at a location about 600 feet above sea level. For best results, a chart based on your altitude should be made by applying a known vacuum, and reading the voltage of a known-good MAP sensor. Vacuum usually drops about 1 inch per 1,000 feet of altitude.

VACUUM (in. Hg)	GM (DC VOLTS)
0	4.80
1	4.52
2	4.46
3	4.26
4	4.06
5	3.88
6	3.66
7	3.50
8	3.30
9	3.10
10	2.94
11	2.76
12	2.54
13	2.36
14	2.20
15	2.00
16	1.80
17	1.62
18	1.42
19	1.20
20	1.10
21	0.88
22	0.66

ALTITUDE AND MAP SENSOR VOLTAGE	
Altitude	MAP Sensor Voltage (key on, engine off)(V)
Sea level	4.6–4.8
2,500 (760 m)	4.0
5,000 (1,520 m)	3.7
7,500 (2,300 m)	3.35
10,000 (3,050 m)	3.05
12,500 (3,800 m)	2.80
15,000 (4,600 m)	2.45

CHART 33–2

Comparison between MAP sensor voltage and altitude.

BAROMETRIC PRESSURE SENSOR

A **barometric pressure (BARO) sensor** is similar in design, but senses more subtle changes in barometric absolute pressure (atmospheric air pressure). It is vented directly to the atmosphere. The **barometric manifold absolute pressure (BMAP) sensor** is actually a combination of a BARO and MAP sensor in the same housing. The BMAP sensor has individual circuits to measure barometric and manifold pressure. This input not only allows the computer to adjust for changes in atmospheric pressure due to weather, but also is the primary sensor used to determine altitude.

NOTE: A MAP sensor and a BARO sensor are usually the same sensor, but the MAP sensor is connected to the manifold and a BARO sensor is open to the atmosphere. The MAP sensor is capable of reading barometric pressure just as the ignition switch is turned to the on position before the engine starts. Therefore, altitude and weather changes are available to the computer. During mountainous driving, it may be an advantage to stop and then restart the engine so that the engine computer can take another barometric pressure reading and recalibrate fuel delivery based on the new altitude.

TESTING THE MAP SENSOR

Most pressure sensors operate on 5 volts from the computer and return a signal (voltage or frequency) based on the pressure (vacuum) applied to the sensor. If a MAP sensor is being tested,

The Cavalier Convertible Story

The owner of a Cavalier convertible stated to a service technician that the "check engine" (MIL) was on. The technician found a diagnostic trouble code (DTC) for a MAP sensor. The technician removed the hose at the MAP sensor and discovered that gasoline had accumulated in the sensor and dripped out of the hose as it was being removed. The technician replaced the MAP sensor and test drove the vehicle to confirm the repair. Almost at once the check engine light came on with the same MAP sensor code. After several hours of troubleshooting without success in determining the cause, the technician decided to start over again. Almost at once, the technician discovered that no vacuum was getting to the MAP sensor where a vacuum gauge was connected with a T-fitting in the vacuum line to the MAP sensor. The vacuum port in the base of the throttle body was clogged with carbon. After a thorough cleaning, and clearing the DTC, the Cavalier again performed properly and the check engine light did not come on again. The technician had assumed that if gasoline was able to reach the sensor through the vacuum hose, surely vacuum could reach the sensor. The technician learned to stop assuming when diagnosing a vehicle and concentrate more on testing the simple things first.

Visual Check of the MAP Sensor

A defective vacuum hose to a MAP sensor can cause a variety of driveability problems including poor fuel economy, hesitation, stalling, and rough idle. A small air leak (vacuum leak) around the hose can cause these symptoms and often set a trouble code in the vehicle computer. When working on a vehicle that uses a MAP sensor, make certain that the vacuum hose travels consistently *downward* on its route from the sensor to the source of manifold vacuum. Inspect the hose, especially if another technician has previously replaced the factory-original hose. It should not be so long that it sags down at any point. Condensed fuel and/or moisture can become trapped in this low spot in the hose and cause all types of driveability problems and MAP sensor codes.

When checking the MAP sensor, if anything comes out of the sensor itself, it should be replaced. This includes water, gasoline, or any other substance.

make certain that the vacuum hose and hose fittings are sound and making a good, tight connection to a manifold vacuum source on the engine.

Three different types of test instruments can be used to test a pressure sensor:

1. A digital voltmeter with three test leads connected in series between the sensor and the wiring harness connector or back-probe the terminals.

2. A scope connected to the sensor output, power, and ground.

3. A scan tool or a specific tool recommended by the vehicle manufacturer.

NOTE: Always check service information for the exact testing procedures and specifications for the vehicle being tested.

TESTING THE MAP SENSOR USING A DMM OR SCOPE
Use jumper wires, T-pins to back-probe the connector, or a breakout box to gain electrical access to the wiring to the pressure sensor. Most pressure sensors use three wires:

1. A 5 volt wire from the computer

2. A variable-signal wire back to the computer

3. A ground or reference low wire

The procedure for testing the sensor is as follows:

1. Turn the ignition on (engine off)

2. Measure the voltage (or frequency) of the sensor output

3. Using a hand-operated vacuum pump (or other variable vacuum source), apply vacuum to the sensor

A good pressure sensor should change voltage (or frequency) in relation to the applied vacuum. If the signal does not change or the values are out of range according to the manufacturers' specifications, the sensor must be replaced.

TESTING THE MAP SENSOR USING A SCAN TOOL
A scan tool can be used to test a MAP sensor by monitoring the injector pulse width (in milliseconds) when vacuum is being applied to the MAP sensor using a hand-operated vacuum pump. ● **SEE FIGURE 33–5.**

FIGURE 33–5 A typical hand-operated vacuum pump.

FIGURE 33–6 The SIDI fuel-rail pressure sensor is a 3-wire strain gauge-type with a stainless steel housing. (*Courtesy of General Motors*)

STEP 1 Apply about 20 inch Hg of vacuum to the MAP sensor and start the engine.

STEP 2 Observe the injector pulse width. On a warm engine, the injector pulse width will normally be 1.5 to 3.5 milliseconds.

STEP 3 Slowly reduce the vacuum to the MAP sensor and observe the pulse width. A lower vacuum to the MAP sensor indicates a heavier load on the engine and the injector pulse width should increase.

NOTE: If 23 inch Hg or more vacuum is applied to the MAP sensor with the engine running, this high vacuum will often stall the engine. The engine stalls because the high vacuum is interpreted by the PCM to indicate that the engine is being decelerated, which shuts off the fuel. During engine deceleration, the PCM shuts off the fuel injectors to reduce exhaust emissions and increase fuel economy.

FUEL PRESSURE SENSOR

A fuel-rail pressure (FRP) sensor is used on some vehicles that are equipped with electronic returnless fuel injection. This sensor provides fuel pressure information to the PCM for fuel injection pulse width calculations.

On some electronic returnless fuel systems the desired fuel pressure is commanded by the engine control module (ECM), and transmitted to the fuel-pump flow control module via a GMLAN serial data message. A liquid fuel pressure sensor provides the feedback the fuel-pump flow control module requires for closed-loop fuel pressure control.

The fuel pressure sensor is a 5-V, 3-pin device. It is located on the fuel feed line ahead of the fuel tank, and receives power and ground from the fuel-pump flow control module through a vehicle wiring harness.

Vehicles equipped with spark ignited direct injection (SIDI) have a fuel pressure sensor mounted on the high-pressure fuel rail. ● SEE FIGURE 33–6.

FUEL TANK PRESSURE SENSOR

The **fuel tank pressure (FTP)** sensor is used to detect leaks in the evaporative emissions (EVAP) system. The FTP sensor measures the difference between the pressure or vacuum in the fuel tank and outside air pressure. The sensor is a three-wire strain gauge sensor and is similar in appearance to a MAP sensor. The ECM provides a 5 volt reference and a ground to the FTP sensor. Depending on the vehicle, the sensor can be located in the vapor space on top of the fuel tank, in the vapor tube between the canister and the tank, or on the EVAP canister.

The FTP sensor provides a signal voltage back to the ECM that can vary between 0.1 and 4.9 volts. A high FTP sensor voltage indicates a low fuel tank pressure or vacuum. A low FTP sensor voltage indicates a high fuel tank pressure.

MAP/BARO DIAGNOSTIC TROUBLE CODES

The diagnostic trouble codes (DTCs) associated with the MAP and BARO sensors include:

DIAGNOSTIC TROUBLE CODE	DESCRIPTION	POSSIBLE CAUSES
P0106	BARO sensor out-of-range at key on	▪ MAP sensor fault ▪ MAP sensor O-ring damaged or missing
P0107	MAP sensor low voltage	▪ MAP sensor fault ▪ MAP sensor signal circuit shorted-to-ground ▪ MAP sensor 5 volt supply circuit open
P0108	Map sensor high voltage	▪ MAP sensor fault ▪ MAP sensor O-ring damaged or missing ▪ MAP sensor signal circuit shorted-to-voltage

SUMMARY

1. Pressure below atmospheric pressure is called vacuum and is measured in inches of mercury.

2. A manifold absolute pressure sensor uses a perfect vacuum (zero absolute pressure) in the sensor to determine the pressure.

3. The most common type of MAP sensor is the silicon-diaphragm strain gauge.

4. A heavy engine load results in low intake manifold vacuum and a high MAP sensor signal voltage.

5. A light engine load results in high intake manifold vacuum and a low MAP sensor signal voltage.

6. A MAP sensor is used to detect changes in altitude, as well as check other sensors and engine systems.

7. A MAP sensor can be tested by visual inspection, testing the output using a digital meter, or scan tool.

8. Three wire-pressure sensors may be found on the fuel rail (SIDI) or in the fuel feed lines on electronic returnless fuel systems.

REVIEW QUESTIONS

1. What is the relationship among atmospheric pressure, vacuum, and boost pressure in PSI?

2. What pressure sensors may be found on a typical vehicle?

3. What is the MAP sensor signal voltage at idle on a typical General Motors engine?

4. What are three uses of a MAP sensor by the PCM?

CHAPTER QUIZ

1. As the load on an engine increases, the manifold vacuum decreases and the manifold absolute pressure _____.
   a. Increases
   b. Decreases
   c. Changes with barometric pressure only (altitude or weather)
   d. Remains constant (absolute)

2. A typical MAP sensor compares the vacuum in the intake manifold to _____.
   a. Atmospheric pressure
   b. A perfect vacuum
   c. Barometric pressure
   d. The value of the IAT sensor

3. Which statement is *false?*
   a. Absolute pressure is equal to barometric pressure plus intake manifold vacuum.
   b. A decrease in manifold vacuum means an increase in manifold pressure.
   c. The MAP sensor compares manifold vacuum to a perfect vacuum.
   d. Barometric pressure minus the MAP sensor reading equals intake manifold vacuum.

4. Where would a fuel pressure sensor be found?
   a. On the fuel rail
   b. On the fuel delivery pipe
   c. Either a or b
   d. Neither a nor b

5. What is the purpose of the fuel tank pressure sensor?
   a. To detect EVAP system leaks
   b. To detect fuel level reference pressure
   c. Controls evaporative vapor purging
   d. Measures the weight of the remaining fuel

6. Which is *not* a purpose or function of the MAP sensor?
   a. Measures the load on the engine
   b. Measures engine speed
   c. Calculates fuel delivery based on altitude
   d. Helps diagnose the EGR system

7. When measuring the output signal of a MAP sensor on a General Motors vehicle, the digital multimeter should be set to read _____.
   a. DC V
   b. AC V
   c. Hz
   d. DC A

8. Two technicians are discussing testing MAP sensors. Technician A says that the MAP sensor voltage on a General Motors vehicle at idle should be about 1.0 volt. Technician B says that manifold vacuum at idle is about 18 inch Hg. Which technician is correct?
   a. Technician A only
   b. Technician B only
   c. Both Technicians A and B
   d. Neither Technician A nor B

9. Technician A says that MAP sensors use a 5 volt reference voltage from the PCM. Technician B says that the MAP sensor voltage will be higher at idle at high altitudes compared to when the engine is operating at near sea level. Which technician is correct?
   a. Technician A only
   b. Technician B only
   c. Both Technicians A and B
   d. Neither Technician A nor B

10. A P0107 DTC is being discussed. Technician A says that a defective MAP sensor could be the cause. Technician B says that a MAP sensor signal wire shorted-to-ground could be the cause. Which technician is correct?
   a. Technician A only
   b. Technician B only
   c. Both Technicians A and B
   d. Neither Technician A nor B

chapter 34

MASS AIR FLOW SENSORS

LEARNING OBJECTIVES

After studying this chapter, the reader should be able to:

1. Discuss how MAF sensors work.
2. List the methods that can be used to test MAF sensors.
3. Describe the symptoms of a failed MAF sensor.

This chapter will help you prepare for Engine Repair (A8) ASE certification test content area "E" (Computerized Engine Controls Diagnosis and Repair).

KEY TERMS

False air 512
High-authority sensor 512
Mass airflow (MAF) sensor 510
Speed density 509
Tap test 512

 ## STC OBJECTIVES

GM Service Technical College topics covered in this chapter are:

1. Diagnose signal circuit using a systematic process.
2. Test signal circuit (three-wire) using electrical/electronic tools.

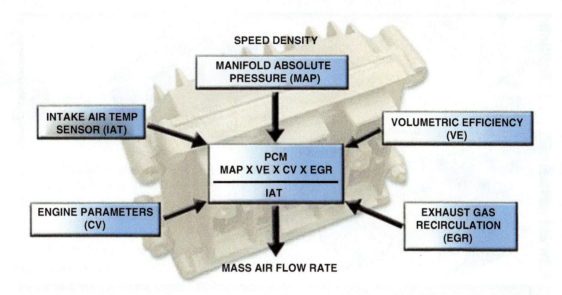

SPEED DENSITY

FIGURE 34–1 A speed/density system uses these sensors and a calculation to determine the fuel injection quantity. (*Courtesy of General Motors*)

INTRODUCTION

The powertrain control module (PCM) must use intake airflow measurement information to program various operations and perform diagnostics. There are two methods of sensing incoming engine air flow, speed density, and mass air flow.

SPEED DENSITY
Speed density is an older system of measuring intake airflow by sensing changes in intake manifold pressures, which result from engine load and speed changes. The PCM combines the manifold absolute pressure with other values, such as engine speed, throttle position, and incoming air temperature, to calculate mass airflow. As manifold pressure increases, air density and flow increases. Additional fuel is required, and the PCM increases injector pulse width to meet this requirement. The speed density system may be used as a backup strategy in case of a MAF sensor failure. ● **SEE FIGURE 34–1.**

MASS AIR FLOW
On most vehicles since 1996, mass air flow values are not calculated based on other sensor inputs. The air going into the engine is measured with a **mass air flow sensor (MAF)**. The MAF sensor converts the air temperature difference or temperature sensors in the airstream into a frequency signal that the PCM monitors. The PCM calculates the air flow based on the signal and adjusts the air–fuel ratio accordingly. ● **SEE FIGURE 34–2.**

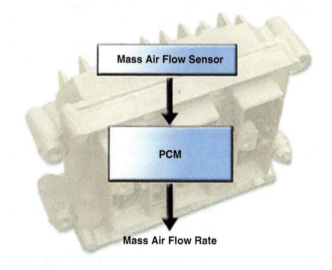

FIGURE 34–2 Mass air flow systems directly measure the air going into the engine. (*Courtesy of General Motors*)

MASS AIRFLOW SENSOR TYPES

There are several types of mass airflow sensors.

HOT FILM SENSOR
The hot film sensor uses a temperature-sensing resistor (thermistor) to measure the temperature of the incoming air. Through the electronics within the sensor,

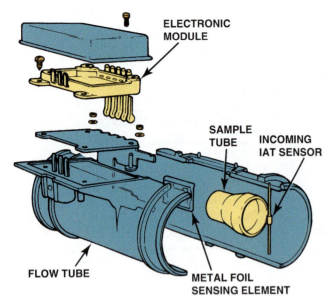

FIGURE 34–3 This five-wire mass air flow sensor consists of a metal foil sensing unit, an intake air temperature (IAT) sensor, and the electronic module.

FIGURE 34–4 The MAF sensor protrudes into the air inlet duct to measure air flow. (*Courtesy of General Motors*)

a conductive film is kept at a temperature 70°C above the temperature of the incoming air. ● **SEE FIGURE 34–3.**

Because the amount and density of the air both tend to contribute to the cooling effect as the air passes through the sensor, this type of sensor can actually produce an output based on the *mass* of the airflow. *Mass equals volume times density*. For example, cold air is denser than warm air so a small amount of cold air may have the same mass as a larger amount of warm air. Therefore, a mass airflow sensor is designed to measure the mass, not the volume, of the air entering the engine.

The output of this type of sensor is usually a frequency based on the amount of air entering the sensor. The greater the mass of air that enters the sensor, the more the hot film is cooled. The electronics inside the sensor, therefore, increase the current flow through the hot film to maintain the 70°C temperature differential between the air temperature and the temperature of the hot film. This change in current flow is converted to a frequency output that the computer can use as a measurement of airflow. Most of these types of sensors are referred to as **mass airflow (MAF) sensors** because, unlike the air vane sensor, the MAF sensor takes into account relative humidity, altitude, and temperature of the air. The denser the air, the greater the cooling effect on the hot film sensor and the greater the amount of fuel required for proper combustion.

HOT WIRE SENSOR The hot wire sensor is similar to the hot film type, but uses a hot wire to sense the mass airflow instead of the hot film. Like the hot film sensor, the hot wire sensor uses a temperature-sensing resistor (thermistor) to

measure the temperature of the air entering the sensor. The electronic circuitry within the sensor keeps the temperature of the wire at 70°C above the temperature of the incoming air.

CURRENT MODEL MAF SENSORS On most of today's vehicles the MAF sensor is located in the ductwork before the throttle body assembly, rather than being a separate assembly. Modern MAF sensors also have the IAT sensor integrated into the MAF sensor. ● **SEE FIGURE 34–4.**

The air flow through the MAF sensor passes over a temperature sensor, a heated sensing element, and then over another temperature sensor. As the air flow increases, the difference in temperature between the two sensors increases. The air flow is directly proportional to the difference in temperatures. ● **SEE FIGURE 34–5.**

These designs operate in essentially the same way. A resistor wire or screen installed in the path of intake airflow is heated to a constant temperature by electric current provided by the computer. ● **SEE FIGURE 34–6.** Air flowing past the screen or wire cools it. The degree of cooling varies with air velocity, temperature, density, and humidity. These factors combine to indicate the mass of air entering the engine. As the screen or wire cools, more current is required to maintain the specified temperature. As the screen or wire heats up, less current is required. The operating principle can be summarized as follows:

- More intake air volume = cooler sensor, more current.
- Less intake air volume = warmer sensor, less current.

The computer constantly monitors the change in current and translates it into a voltage signal that is used to determine injector pulse width.

BURN-OFF CIRCUIT. Some MAF sensors use a burn-off circuit to keep the sensing wire clean of dust and dirt. A high current is passed through the sensing wire for a short time, but long enough to cause the wire to glow due to the heat. The burn-off

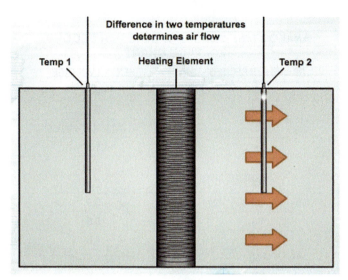

FIGURE 34–5 The MAF sensing components include two temperature sensors and a small heating element. (*Courtesy of General Motors*)

FIGURE 34–6 The MAF sensor is inserted into the incoming air stream. This intake duct has a venturi in the measuring area to increase accuracy.

circuit is turned on when the ignition switch is switched off after the engine has been operating long enough to achieve normal operating temperature.

PCM USES FOR AIRFLOW SENSORS

The PCM uses the information from the airflow sensor for the following purposes:

- Airflow sensors are used mostly to determine the amount of fuel needed and base pulse-width numbers. The greater the mass of the incoming air, the longer the injectors are pulsed on.

- Airflow sensors back up the TP sensor in the event of a loss of signal or an inaccurate throttle position sensor signal. If the MAF sensor fails, then the PCM will calculate the fuel delivery needs of the engine based on throttle position and engine speed (RPM).

TESTING MASS AIRFLOW SENSORS

VISUAL INSPECTION Start the testing of a MAF sensor by performing a thorough visual inspection. Look at all the hoses that direct and send air, especially between the MAF sensor and the throttle body. Also check the electrical connector for:

 REAL WORLD FIX

The Dirty MAF Sensor Story

The owner of a Buick Park Avenue equipped with a 3,800 V-6 engine complained that the engine would hesitate during acceleration, showed lack of power, and seemed to surge or miss at times. A visual inspection found everything to be like new, including a new air filter. There were no stored diagnostic trouble codes (DTCs). A look at the scan data showed airflow to be within the recommended 3 to 7 grams per second. A check of the frequency output showed the problem.

Idle frequency = 2.177 kHz (2,177 Hz)

Normal frequency at idle speed should be 2.37 to 2.52 kHz. Cleaning the hot wire of the MAF sensor restored proper operation. The sensor wire was covered with what looked like fine fibers, possibly from the replacement air filter.

NOTE: Older GM MAF sensors operated at a lower frequency of 32 to 150 Hz, with 32 Hz being the average reading at idle and 150 Hz for wide-open throttle.

- Corrosion
- Terminals that are bent or pushed out of the plastic connector
- Frayed wiring

What Is Meant by a "High-Authority Sensor"?

A **high-authority sensor** is a sensor that has a major influence over the amount of fuel being delivered to the engine. For example, at engine start-up, the engine coolant temperature (ECT) sensor is a high-authority sensor and the oxygen sensor (O2S) is a low-authority sensor. However, as the engine reaches operating temperature, the oxygen sensor becomes a high-authority sensor and can greatly affect the amount of fuel being supplied to the engine. See the chart.

High-Authority Sensors	Low-Authority Sensors
ECT (especially when the engine starts and is warming up)	IAT (intake air temperature) sensors modify and back up the ECT
O2S (after the engine reaches closed-loop operation)	TFT (transmission fluid temperature)
MAP	PRNDL (shift position sensor)
MAF	KS (knock sensor)
TP (high authority during acceleration and deceleration)	EFT (engine fuel temperature)

ANALOG MAF SENSOR GRAMS PER SECOND/ VOLTAGE CHART	
GRAMS PER SECOND	SENSOR VOLTAGE
0	0.2
2	0.7
4	1.0 (typical idle value)
8	1.5
15	2.0
30	2.5
50	3.0
80	3.5
110	4.0
150	4.5
175	4.8

CHART 34–1

Chart showing the amount of air entering the engine in grams per second compared to the sensor output voltage.

What Is False Air?

Airflow sensors and mass airflow (MAF) sensors are designed to measure all the air entering the engine. If an air inlet hose was loose or had a hole, extra air could enter the engine without being measured. This extra air is often called **false air**. **SEE FIGURE 34–7.** Because this extra air is unmeasured, the computer does not provide enough fuel delivery and the engine operates too lean, especially at idle. A small hole in the air inlet hose would represent a fairly large percentage of false air at idle, but would represent a very small percentage of extra air at highway speeds.

To diagnose for false air, look at long-term fuel trim numbers at idle and at 3000 RPM.

NOTE: If the engine runs well in reverse, yet runs terrible in any forward gear, carefully look at the inlet hose for air leaks that would open when the engine torque moves the engine slightly on its mounts.

MAF SENSOR OUTPUT TEST A digital multimeter, set to read DC volts, can be used to check the MAF sensor. See the chart that shows the voltage output compared with the grams per second of airflow through the sensor. Normal airflow is three to seven grams per second. ● **SEE CHART 34–1.**

TAP TEST With the engine running at idle speed, *gently* tap the MAF sensor with the fingers of an open hand. If the engine stumbles or stalls, the MAF sensor is defective. This test is commonly called the **tap test**.

DIGITAL METER TEST OF A MAF SENSOR A digital multimeter can be used to measure the frequency (Hz) output of the sensor and compare the reading with specifications.

The frequency output and engine speed in RPM can also be plotted on a graph to check to see if the frequency and RPM are proportional, resulting in a straight line on the graph.

SCAN TOOL TESTING A MAF SENSOR As always, refer to service information for the specific vehicle being diagnosed. When using the scan tool to diagnose or verify MAF sensor operation, some typical procedures are:

- Observe the DTC information with a scan tool. Verify that DTC P0641 or P0651 is not set. If these DTCs are set, refer to the DTC List for further diagnosis.

- With the engine idling, observe the scan tool MAF sensor parameter. The reading should be between 2,000 Hz

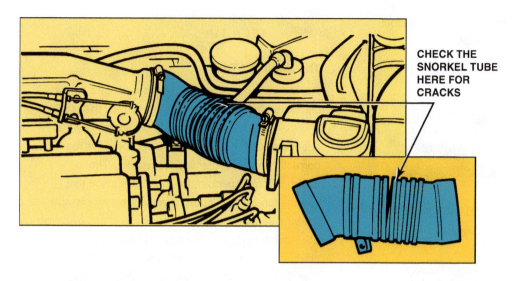

CHECK THE SNORKEL TUBE HERE FOR CRACKS

FIGURE 34–7 Carefully check the hose between the MAF sensor and the throttle plate for cracks or splits that could create extra (false) air into the engine that is not measured by the MAF sensor.

and 3,900 Hz depending on the engine temperature as reported by the ECT sensor.

- A WOT (wide-open throttle) acceleration from a stop should cause the MAF Sensor parameter on the scan tool to increase rapidly. This increase should be from 4 g/s to 9 g/s at idle to greater than 180 g/s at the time of the 1-2 shift. Normal g/s will be less for smaller engines and higher for larger engines.

MAF SENSOR INSPECTION A good visual inspection can often locate problems with the MAF sensor, especially if a do-it-yourself mechanic has been working on the vehicle. Here are some areas to check, from GM service information:

- Inspect the wiring harness of the MAF sensor to verify that it is not routed too close to the ignition coil module, any solenoids, any relays, or any motors. These can be the source of inductive "noise" that can affect the MAF signal.

- Any type of contamination on the MAF sensor heating elements will degrade the proper operation of the sensor. Certain types of contaminants act as a heat insulator, which will impair the response of the sensor to airflow changes. Water or snow can create the opposite effect, and cause the signal to increase rapidly. Inspect for any contamination, water intrusion, or debris on the sensing elements of the MAF sensor. If debris is present, clean the sensor. If the sensor cannot be cleaned, replace it.

- A high resistance in the wiring or connectors may cause a driveability concern that is noticed before any DTC sets.

- Certain aftermarket air filters may cause DTCs to set.

- Certain aftermarket air induction systems may cause DTCs to set.

- Modifications to the air induction system may cause DTCs to set.

- A steady or intermittent high resistance of 15 Ω or greater on the ignition voltage circuit (power supply to the MAF sensor) will cause the MAF sensor signal to be increased by as much as 60 g/s. To pinpoint this condition perform a voltage drop test on the circuit.

- A skewed or stuck ECT or IAT sensor will cause the calculated models to be inaccurate and may cause MAF DTCs to run when they should not. This can set a DTC for a MAF concern when the actual problem is in the ECT or IAT sensor.

MAF SENSOR CONTAMINATION

Dirt, oil, silicon, or even spider webs can coat the sensing wire. Because contamination tends to insulate the sensing wire at low airflow rates, the sensor often overestimates the amount of air entering the engine at idle, and therefore causes the fuel system to go rich. At higher engine speeds near wide-open throttle (WOT), the contamination can cause the sensor to underestimate the amount of air entering the engine. As a result, the fuel system will go lean, causing spark knock and lack of power concerns. To check for contamination, check the fuel trim numbers.

If the fuel trim is negative (removing fuel) at idle, yet is positive (adding fuel) at higher engine speeds, a contaminated MAF sensor is a likely cause. Other tests for a contaminated MAF sensor include:

- At WOT, the grams per second, as read on a scan tool, should exceed 100.

- At WOT, the voltage, as read on a digital voltmeter, should exceed 4 volts for an analog sensor.

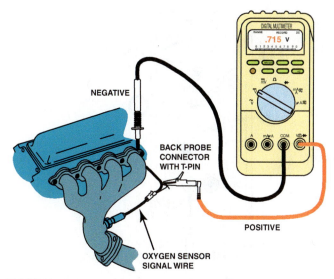

NEGATIVE

BACK PROBE
CONNECTOR
WITH T-PIN

POSITIVE

OXYGEN SENSOR
SIGNAL WIRE

FIGURE 35–8 Testing an oxygen sensor using a DMM set on DC volts. With the engine operating in closed loop, the oxygen voltage should read over 800 mV and lower than 200 mV and be constantly fluctuating.

 FREQUENTLY ASKED QUESTION

What Happens to the Bias Voltage?

Some vehicle manufacturers such as General Motors Corporation have the computer apply 450 mV (0.450 V) to the O2S signal wire. This voltage is called the **bias voltage** and represents the threshold voltage for the transition from rich to lean.

This bias voltage is displayed on a scan tool when the ignition switch is turned on with the engine off. When the engine is started, the O2S becomes warm enough to produce a usable voltage and bias voltage "disappears" as the O2S responds to a rich and lean mixture. What happened to the bias voltage that the computer applied to the O2S? The voltage from the O2S simply overcame the very weak voltage signal from the computer. This bias voltage is so weak that even a 20-megohm impedance DMM will affect the strength enough to cause the voltage to drop to 426 mV. Other meters with only 10 megohms of impedance will cause the bias voltage to read less than 400 mV.

Therefore, even though the O2S voltage is relatively low powered, it is more than strong enough to override the very weak bias voltage the computer sends to the O2S.

 REAL WORLD FIX

The Oxygen Sensor Is Lying to You

A technician was trying to solve a driveability problem with an older V-6 passenger car. The car idled roughly, hesitated, and accelerated poorly. A thorough visual inspection did not indicate any possible problems and there were no diagnostic trouble codes stored.

A check was made on the oxygen sensor activity using a DMM. The voltage stayed above 600 mV most of the time. If a large vacuum hose was removed, the oxygen sensor voltage would temporarily drop to below 450 mV and then return to a reading of over 600 mV. Remember:

- High O2S readings = rich exhaust (low O_2 content in the exhaust)
- Low O2S readings = lean exhaust (high O_2 content in the exhaust)

As part of a thorough visual inspection, the technician removed and inspected the spark plugs. All the spark plugs were white, indicating a lean mixture, not the rich mixture that the oxygen sensor was indicating. The high O2S reading signaled the computer to reduce the amount of fuel, resulting in an excessively lean operation.

After replacing the oxygen sensor, the engine ran great. But what killed the oxygen sensor? The technician finally learned from the owner that the head gasket had been replaced over a year ago. The phosphate and silicate additives in the antifreeze coolant had coated the oxygen sensor. Because the oxygen sensor was coated, the oxygen content of the exhaust could not be detected—the result: a false rich signal from the oxygen sensor.

- If the oxygen sensor voltage remains low (below 350 mV), the fuel system could be supplying too lean a fuel mixture. Check for a vacuum leak or partially clogged fuel injector(s). Before replacing the oxygen sensor, check the manufacturer's recommended procedures.

TESTING THE OXYGEN SENSOR USING THE MIN/ MAX METHOD A digital meter set on DC volts can be used to record the minimum and maximum voltage with the engine running. A good oxygen sensor should be able to produce a value of less than 300 millivolts and a maximum voltage above

WATCH ANALOG POINTER SWEEP AS O$_2$ VOLTAGE CHANGES.
DEPENDING ON THE DRIVING CONDITIONS, THE O$_2$ V
WILL RISE AND FALL, BUT IT USUALLY AVERAGES AROUND 0.45 V

1. SHUT THE ENGINE OFF AND INSERT TEST LEAD IN THE INPUT
   TERMINALS SHOWN.
2. SET THE ROTARY SWITCH TO VOLTS DC.
3. MANUALLY SELECT THE 4 V RANGE BY DEPRESSING THE RANGE
   BUTTON THREE TIMES.
4. CONNECT THE TEST LEADS AS SHOWN.
5. START THE ENGINE. IF THE O$_2$ SENSOR IS UNHEATED, FAST IDLE
   THE CAR FOR A FEW MINUTES. THEN PRESS MIN/MAX TO SELECT
   MIN/MAX RECORDING.
6. PRESS MIN/MAX BUTTON TO DISPLAY MAXIMUM (MAX)
   02 V; PRESS AGAIN TO DISPLAY MINIMUM (MIN)
   VOLTAGE; PRESS AGAIN TO DISPLAY AVERAGE (AVG) VOLTAGE;
   PRESS AND HOLD DOWN MIN/MAX FOR 2 SECONDS TO EXIT.

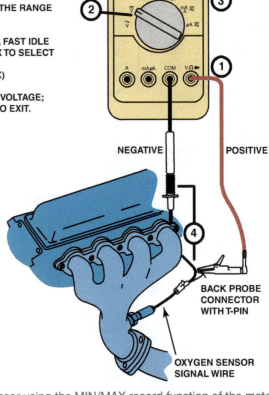

NEGATIVE   POSITIVE

BACK PROBE
CONNECTOR
WITH T-PIN

OXYGEN SENSOR
SIGNAL WIRE

FIGURE 35–9 Using a digital multimeter to test an oxygen sensor using the MIN/MAX record function of the meter.

800 mV. Replace any oxygen sensor that fails to go above 700 mV or lower than 300 mV. ● **SEE FIGURE 35– 9.** See the MIN/MAX oxygen sensor test chart.

TESTING AN OXYGEN SENSOR USING A SCAN TOOL
A good oxygen sensor should be able to sense the oxygen content and change voltage outputs rapidly. How fast an oxygen sensor switches from high (above 450 mV) to low (below 350 mV) is measured in oxygen sensor **cross counts**. Cross counts are the number of times an oxygen sensor changes voltage from high to low (from low to high voltage is not counted) in 1 second (or 1.25 second, depending on scan tool and computer speed).

NOTE: On a fuel-injected engine at 2000 engine RPM, 8 to 10 cross counts is normal.

Oxygen sensor cross counts can only be determined using a scan tool or other suitable tester that reads computer data. ● **SEE CHART 35–1.**

If the cross counts are low (or zero), the oxygen sensor may be contaminated, or the fuel delivery system is delivering a constant rich or lean air–fuel mixture. To test an engine using a scan tool, follow these steps:

1. Connect the scan tool to the DLC and start the engine.

2. Operate the engine at a fast idle (2500 RPM) for two minutes to allow time for the oxygen sensor to warm to operating temperature.

3. Observe the oxygen sensor activity on the scan tool to verify closed-loop operation. Select "snapshot" mode and hold the engine speed steady and start recording.

4. Play back snapshot and place a mark beside each range of oxygen sensor voltage for each frame of the snapshot.

A good oxygen sensor and computer system should result in most snapshot values at both ends (0 to 300 and 600 to 1,000 mV). If most of the readings are in the middle, the oxygen sensor is not working correctly.

MIN/MAX OXYGEN SENSOR TEST CHART			
MINIMUM VOLTAGE	MAXIMUM VOLTAGE	AVERAGE VOLTAGE (mV)	TEST RESULTS
Below 200 mV	Above 800 mV	400 to 500	Oxygen sensor is okay.
Above 200 mV	Any reading	400 to 500	Oxygen sensor is defective.
Any reading	Below 800 mV	400 to 500	Oxygen sensor is defective.
Below 200 mV	Above 800 mV	Below 400	System is operating lean.*
Below 200 mV	Below 800 mV	Below 400	System is operating lean. (Add propane to the intake air to see if the oxygen sensor reacts. If not, the sensor is defective.)
Below 200 mV	Above 800 mV	Above 500	System is operating rich.
Above 200 mV	Above 800 mV	Above 500	System is operating rich. (Remove a vacuum hose to see if the oxygen sensor reacts. If not, the sensor is defective.)

* Check for an exhaust leak upstream from the O2S or ignition misfire that can cause a false lean indication before further diagnosis.

CHART 35–1

Use this chart to check for proper operation of the oxygen sensors and fuel system after checking them using a multimeter set to read Min/Max.

TESTING AN OXYGEN SENSOR USING A SCOPE A
scope can also be used to test an oxygen sensor. Connect the scope to the signal wire and ground for the sensor (if it is so equipped). ● **SEE FIGURE 35–10.** With the engine operating in closed loop, the voltage signal of the sensor should be constantly changing. ● **SEE FIGURE 35–11.** Check for rapid switching from rich to lean and lean to rich and change between once every two seconds and five times per second (0.5 to 5.0 Hz). ● **SEE FIGURES 35–12 THROUGH 35–14.**

NOTE: General Motors warns not to base the diagnosis of an oxygen sensor problem solely on its scope pattern. The varying voltage output of an oxygen sensor can easily be mistaken for a fault in the sensor itself, rather than a fault in the fuel delivery system.

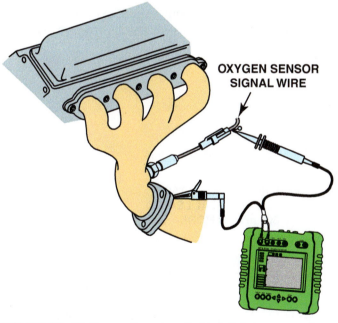

OXYGEN SENSOR
SIGNAL WIRE

FIGURE 35–10 Connecting a handheld digital storage oscilloscope to an oxygen sensor signal wire. The use of the low-pass filter helps eliminate any low-frequency interference from affecting the scope display.

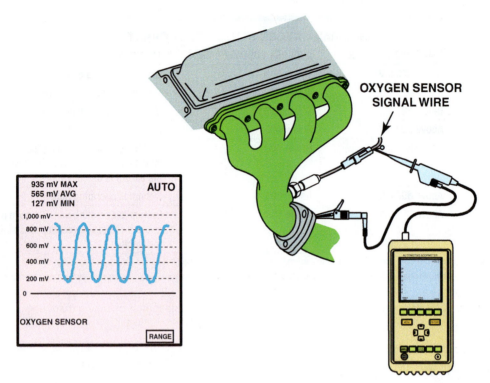

OXYGEN SENSOR
SIGNAL WIRE

935 mV MAX
565 mV AVG
127 mV MIN

AUTO

1,000 mV
800 mV
600 mV
400 mV
200 mV
0

OXYGEN SENSOR

RANGE

FIGURE 35–11 The waveform of a good oxygen sensor as displayed on a digital storage oscilloscope (DSO). Note that the maximum reading is above 800 mV and the minimum reading is less than 200 mV.

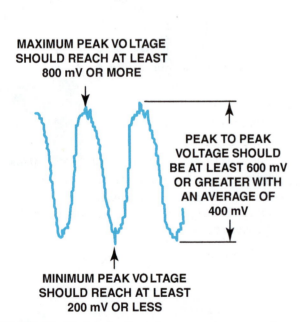

MAXIMUM PEAK VOLTAGE
SHOULD REACH AT LEAST
800 mV OR MORE

PEAK TO PEAK
VOLTAGE SHOULD
BE AT LEAST 600 mV
OR GREATER WITH
AN AVERAGE OF
400 mV

MINIMUM PEAK VOLTAGE
SHOULD REACH AT LEAST
200 mV OR LESS

FIGURE 35–12 A typical good oxygen sensor waveform as displayed on a digital storage oscilloscope. Look for transitions that occur between once every two seconds at idle and five times per second at higher engine speeds (0.5 and 5 Hz).

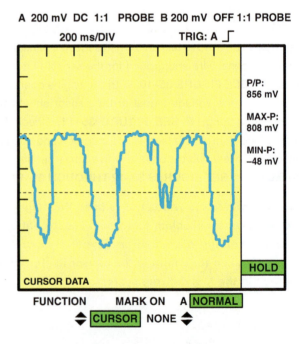

A 200 mV DC 1:1 PROBE B 200 mV OFF 1:1 PROBE

200 ms/DIV   TRIG: A

P/P:
856 mV

MAX-P:
808 mV

MIN-P:
–48 mV

HOLD

CURSOR DATA

FUNCTION   MARK ON   A NORMAL

CURSOR NONE

ONCE YOU'VE ACTIVATED "PEAK-TO-PEAK,"
"MAX-PEAK," AND "MIN-PEAK," FRAME THE
WAVEFORM WITH CURSORS–LOOK FOR
THE MINIMUM AND MAXIMUM VOLTAGES
AND THE DIFFERENT BETWEEN THEM IN
THE RIGHT DISPLAY.

FIGURE 35–13 Using the cursors on the oscilloscope, the high- and low-oxygen sensor values can be displayed on the screen.

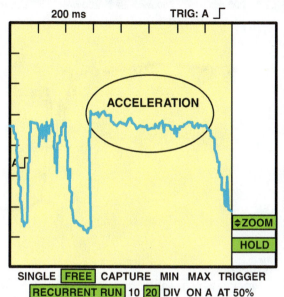

A 200 mV DC 1:1 PROBE B 200 mV OFF 1:1 PROBE
200 ms   TRIG: A ⌐

A ⌐

ACCELERATION

⬍ZOOM
HOLD

SINGLE FREE CAPTURE MIN MAX TRIGGER
RECURRENT RUN 10 20 DIV ON A AT 50%

UNDER HARD ACCELERATION, THE AIR–FUEL MIXTURE SHOULD BECOME RICH—THE VOLTAGE SHOULD STAY FAIRLY HIGH

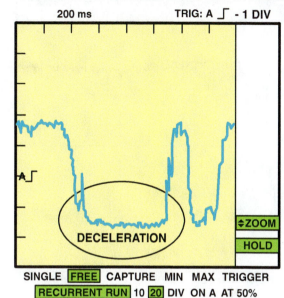

A 200 mV DC 1:1 PROBE B 200 mV OFF 1:1 PROBE
200 ms   TRIG: A ⌐ - 1 DIV

A ⌐

⬍ZOOM
HOLD

DECELERATION

SINGLE FREE CAPTURE MIN MAX TRIGGER
RECURRENT RUN 10 20 DIV ON A AT 50%

WHILE DECELERATING, MIXTURE BECOMES LEAN. LOOK FOR LOW VOLTAGE LEVELS.

FIGURE 35–14 When the air–fuel mixture rapidly changes such as during a rapid acceleration, look for a rapid response. The transition from low to high should be less than 100 ms.

🔧 TECH TIP

The Key On, Engine Off Oxygen Sensor Test

This test works on General Motors vehicles and may work on others if the PCM applies a bias voltage to the oxygen sensors if the heater is commanded "ON". Zirconia oxygen sensors become more electrically conductive as they get hot. To perform this test, be sure that the vehicle has not run for several hours.

STEP 1 Connect a scan tool and get the display ready to show oxygen sensor data.

STEP 2 Key the engine on *without* starting the engine. The heater in the oxygen sensor will start heating the sensor.

STEP 3 Observe the voltage of the oxygen sensor. The applied bias voltage of 450 mV should slowly decrease for all oxygen sensors as they become more electrically conductive and other bias voltage is flowing to ground.

STEP 4 A good oxygen sensor should indicate a voltage of less than 100 mV after three minutes. Any sensor that displays a higher-than-usual voltage or seems to stay higher longer than the others could be defective or skewed high.

🔧 TECH TIP

The Propane Oxygen Sensor Test

Adding propane to the air inlet of a running engine is an excellent way to check if the oxygen sensor is able to react to changes in air–fuel mixture. Follow these steps in performing the propane trick:

1. Connect a digital storage oscilloscope to the oxygen sensor signal wire.

2. Start and operate the engine until up to operating temperature and in closed-loop fuel control.

3. While watching the scope display, add some propane to the air inlet. The scope display should read full rich (over 800 mV), as shown in
   ● **FIGURE 35–15.**

4. Shut off the propane. The waveform should drop to less than 200 mV (0.200 V), as shown in
   ● **FIGURE 35–16.**

5. Quickly add some propane while the oxygen sensor is reading low and watch for a rapid transition to rich. The transition should occur in less than 100 milliseconds (ms).

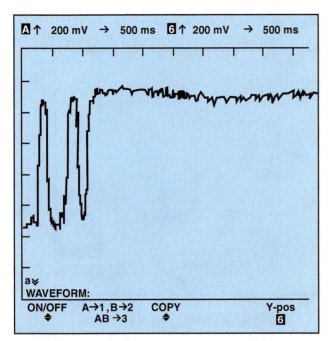

FIGURE 35–15 Adding propane to the air inlet of an engine operating in closed loop with a working oxygen sensor causes the oxygen sensor voltage to read high.

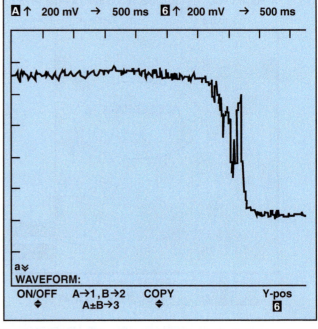

FIGURE 35–16 When the propane is shut off, the oxygen sensor should read below 200 mV.

OXYGEN SENSOR WAVEFORM ANALYSIS

As the O_2 sensor warms up, the sensor voltage begins to rise. When the sensor voltage rises above 450 mV, the PCM determines that the sensor is up to operating temperature, takes control of the fuel mixture, and begins to cycle rich and lean. At this point, the system is considered to be in closed loop. ● **SEE FIGURE 35–17.**

FREQUENCY The frequency of the O_2 sensor is important in determining the condition of the fuel control system. The higher the frequency the better, but the frequency must not exceed 6 Hz. For its OBD-II standards, the government has stated that a frequency greater than 6 Hz represents a misfire.

THROTTLE-BODY FUEL-INJECTION SYSTEMS. Normal TBI system rich/lean switching frequencies are from about 0.5 Hz at idle to about 3 Hz at 2500 RPM. Additionally, due to the TBI design limitations, fuel distribution to individual cylinders may not always be equal (due to unequal intake runner length, etc.). This may be normal unless certain other conditions are present at the same time.

PORT FUEL-INJECTION SYSTEMS. Specification for port fuel-injection systems is 0.5 Hz at idle to 5 Hz at 2500 RPM. ● **SEE**

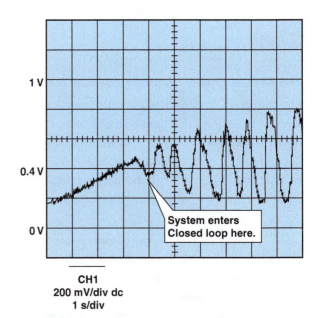

CH1
200 mV/div dc
1 s/div

FIGURE 35–17 When the O2S voltage rises above 450 mV, the PCM starts to control the fuel mixture based on oxygen sensor activity.

FIGURE 35–18. Port fuel-injection systems have more rich–lean O2S voltage transitions (cross counts) for a given amount of time than any other type of system, due to the greatly improved system design compared to TBI units.

Port fuel-injection systems take the least amount of time to react to the fuel adaptive command (e.g., changing injector pulse width).

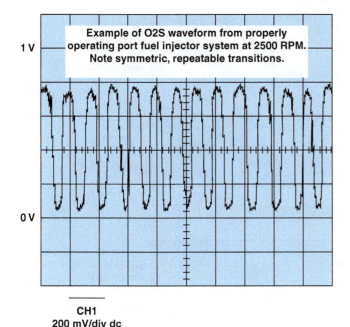

1 V

0 V

CH1
200 mV/div dc
1 s/div

FIGURE 35–18 Normal oxygen sensor frequency is from about one to five times per second.

 **TECH TIP**

Sensor or Wiring?

When troubleshooting a diagnostic trouble code, it is sometimes difficult to determine if the sensor itself is defective or its wiring and ground connections are defective. For example, when diagnosing an O2S code, perform the following to check the wiring:

1. Connect a scan tool and observe the O2S voltage with the ignition on (engine off).
2. Disconnect the O2S pigtail to open the circuit between the computer and the O2S. The scan tool should read 450 mV if the wiring is okay and the scan tool is showing the bias voltage.

   NOTE: Some vehicle manufacturers do not apply a bias voltage to the O2S and the reading on the scan tool may indicate zero and be okay.

3. Ground the O2S wire from the computer. The scan tool should read 0 volt if the wiring is okay.

NEGATIVE O2S VOLTAGE

When testing O2S waveforms, some O_2 sensors will exhibit some negative voltage. The acceptable amount of negative O2S voltage is –0.75 mV, providing that the maximum voltage peak exceeds 850 mV. Testing has shown that negative voltage signals from an O_2 sensor have usually been caused by the following:

1. Chemical poisoning of sensing element (silicon, oil, etc.).
2. Overheated engines.
3. Mishandling of new O_2 sensors (dropped and banged around, resulting in a cracked insulator).
4. Poor O_2 sensor ground.

LOW O2S READINGS

An oxygen sensor reading that is low could be due to other things besides a lean air–fuel mixture. Remember, an oxygen sensor senses oxygen, not unburned gas, even though a high reading generally indicates a rich exhaust (lack of oxygen) and a low reading indicates a lean mixture (excess oxygen).

FALSE LEAN If an oxygen sensor reads low as a result of a factor besides a lean mixture, it is often called a **false lean indication**.

False lean indications (low O2S readings) can be attributed to the following:

1. Ignition misfire. An ignition misfire due to a defective spark plug wire, fouled spark plug, and so forth, causes no burned air and fuel to be exhausted past the O2S. The O2S "sees" the oxygen (not the unburned gasoline) and the O2S voltage is low.
2. Exhaust leak in front of the O2S. An exhaust leak between the engine and the oxygen sensor causes outside oxygen to be drawn into the exhaust and past the O2S. This oxygen is "read" by the O2S and produces a lower-than-normal voltage. The computer interprets the lower-than-normal voltage signal from the O2S as meaning that the air–fuel mixture is lean. The computer will cause the fuel system to deliver a richer air–fuel mixture.
3. A spark plug misfire represents a false lean signal to the oxygen sensor. The computer does not know that the extra oxygen going past the oxygen sensor is not due to a lean air–fuel mixture. The computer commands a richer mixture, which could cause the spark plugs to foul, increasing the rate of misfirings.

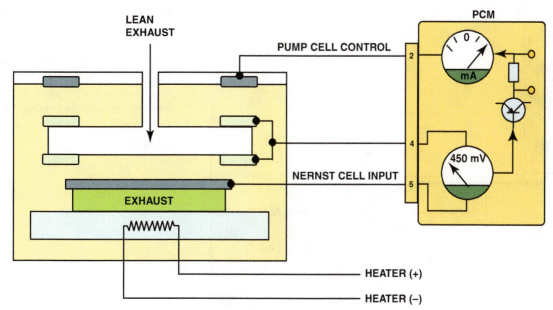

FIGURE 36–9 When the exhaust is lean, the PCM applies a positive current into the pump cell.

SCAN TOOL DATA (PID)
The following information will be displayed on a scan tool when looking at data for a wide-band oxygen sensor:

HO2S = _____ mA	If the current is positive, this means that the PCM is pumping current in the diffusion gap due to a rich exhaust.
	If the current is negative, the PCM is pumping current out of the diffusion gap due to a lean exhaust.
Air–fuel ratio =	Usually expressed in lambda. One means that the exhaust is at stoichiometric (14.7:1 air–fuel ratio) and numbers higher than 1 indicate a lean exhaust and numbers lower than 1 indicate a rich exhaust.

The diagnostic routine will flow as follows:

- Use the scan tool to store and clear DTCs and operate the vehicle to see if the condition reoccurs.
- Inspect the exhaust system for leaks and ensure that the HO2S is not damaged.
- Perform HO2S circuit tests.

The HO2S is replaced only after all other concerns are eliminated. The ECM is able to compensate for some sensor contamination.

It is very important to note that when viewing the sensor data on the Tech 2 display, wide-band oxygen sensors

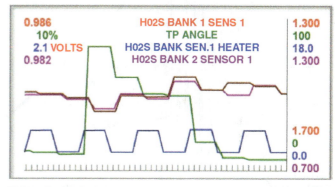

FIGURE 36–10 The wide-band oxygen sensor does not switch like a conventional O2 sensor. (Courtesy of General Motors)

DO NOT switch like conventional sensors. It is normal to see a steady, slightly oscillating signal. ● **SEE FIGURE 36–10.**

DIGITAL MULTIMETER TESTING

When testing a wide-band oxygen sensor for proper operation, perform the following steps:

STEP 1 Check service information and determine the circuit and connector terminal identification.

STEP 2 Measure the calibration resistor. While the value of this resistor can vary widely, depending on the type of sensor, the calibrating resistor should still be checked for opens and shorts.

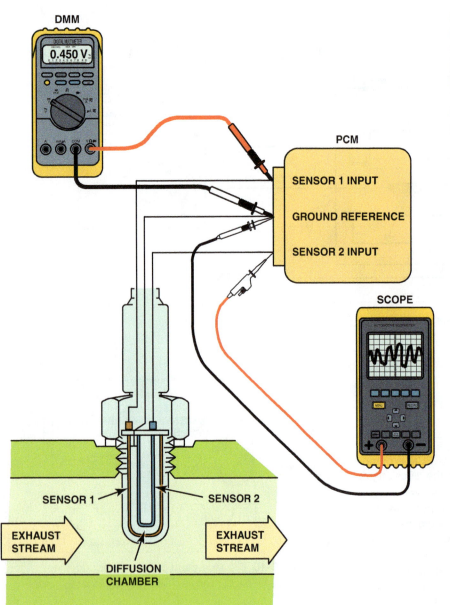

DMM

0.450 V

PCM

SENSOR 1 INPUT

GROUND REFERENCE

SENSOR 2 INPUT

SCOPE

SENSOR 1   SENSOR 2

EXHAUST STREAM   EXHAUST STREAM

DIFFUSION CHAMBER

FIGURE 36–11 Testing a dual cell wideband oxygen sensor can be done using a voltmeter or a scope. The meter reading is attached to the Nernst cell and should read stoichiometric (450 mV) at all times. The scope is showing activity to the pump cell with commands from the PCM to keep the Nernst cell at 14.7:1 air–fuel ratio.

NOTE: The calibration resistor is usually located within the connector itself.

- If open, the ohmmeter will read OL (infinity ohms).
- If shorted, the ohmmeter will read zero or close to zero.

STEP 3 Measure the heater circuit for proper resistance or current flow.

STEP 4 Measure the reference voltage relative to ground. This can vary but is generally 2.4 to 2.6 volts.

STEP 5 Using jumper wires, connect an ammeter and measure the current in the pump cell control wire.

NOTE: ● SEE FIGURE 36–11 for an alternative testing method.

 **TECH TIP**

Replacing a Wide-Band Oxygen Sensor

When replacing a wide-band HO2S, perform the following:

- A code clear with a scan tool, regardless of whether or not a DTC, is set
- HO2S resistance learn reset with a scan tool, where available

Performing these steps will lead to resetting the HO2S resistance learned value and avoiding possible HO2S failure.

SINGLE CELL WIDE-BAND OXYGEN SENSORS

CONSTRUCTION   A typical **single cell** wide-band oxygen sensor looks similar to a conventional four-wire zirconia oxygen sensor. The typical single cell wide-band oxygen sensor, usually called an **air–fuel ratio sensor**, has the following construction features:

- Can be made using the cup or planar design
- Oxygen (O_2) is pumped into the diffusion layer similar to the operation of a dual cell wide-band oxygen sensor.
  ● **SEE FIGURE 36–12.**
- Current flow reverses positive and negative
- Consists of two cell wires and two heater wires (power and ground)
- The heater usually requires 6 amperes and the ground side is pulse-width modulated.

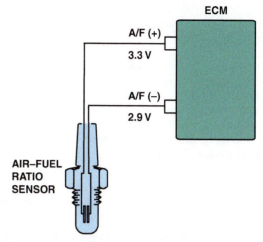

FIGURE 36–12 A single cell wide-band oxygen sensor has four wires with two for the heater and two for the sensor itself. The voltage applied to the sensor is 0.4 volt (3.3 - 2.9 = 0.4) across the two leads of the sensor.

WIDE-BAND OXYGEN SENSOR PATTERN FAILURES

Wide-band oxygen sensors have a long life but can fail. Most of the failures will cause a diagnostic trouble code (DTC) to set, usually causing the malfunction indicator (check engine) lamp to light.

However, one type of failure may not set a DTC when the following occurs:

1. Voltage from the heater circuit bleeds into the Nernst cell.
2. This voltage will cause the engine to operate extremely lean and may or may not set a diagnostic trouble code.
3. When testing indicates an extremely lean condition, unplug the connector to the oxygen sensor. If the engine starts to operate correctly with the sensor unplugged, this is confirmation that the wide-band oxygen sensor has failed and requires replacement.

TESTING WITH A MILLIAMMETER   The PCM controls the single cell wide-band oxygen sensor by maintaining a voltage difference of 300 mV (0.3 V) between the two sensor leads. The PCM keeps the voltage difference constant under all operating conditions by increasing or decreasing current between the element of the cell.

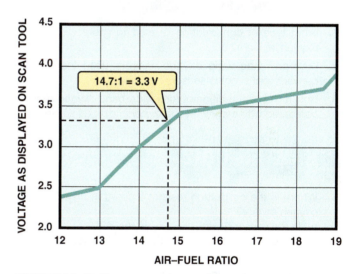

FIGURE 36–13 The scan tool can display various voltage but will often show 3.3 volts because the PCM is controlling the sensor by applying a low current to the sensor to achieve balance.

- Zero (0 mA) represents lambda or stoichiometric air–fuel ratio of 14.7:1
- +10 mA indicates a lean condition
- –10 mA indicates a rich condition

TESTING USING A SCAN TOOL   A scan tool will display a voltage reading but can vary depending on the type and maker of scan tool. ● **SEE FIGURE 36–13.**

1. Wide-band oxygen sensors are known by many different terms, including:
   - Broadband oxygen sensor
   - Wide-range oxygen sensor
   - Air–fuel ratio (AFR) sensor
   - Wide-range air–fuel (WRAF) sensor
   - Lean air–fuel (LAF) sensor
   - Air–fuel (AF) sensor

2. A wide-band oxygen sensor is capable of furnishing the PCM with exhaust air–fuel ratios as rich as 10:1 and as lean as 23:1.

3. The use of a wide-band oxygen sensor allows the engine to achieve more stringent exhaust emission standards.

4. The heater used on a conventional zirconia oxygen sensor uses up to 2 amperes and heats the sensor to about 600°F (315°C). A broadband sensor heater has to heat the sensor to 1,200–1,400°F (650°C to 760°C) and requires up to 8 to 10 amperes.

5. A typical dual cell wide-band oxygen sensor uses the PCM to apply a current to the pump cell to keep the Nernst cell at 14.7:1.
   - When the exhaust is rich, the PCM applies a negative current to the pump cell.
   - When the exhaust is lean, the PCM applies a positive current to the pump cell.

6. Wide-band oxygen sensors can also be made using a single cell design.

7. Wide-band oxygen sensors can be best tested using a scan tool, but dual cell sensors can be checked with a voltmeter or scope. Single cell sensors can be checked using a milliammeter.

REVIEW QUESTIONS

1. What type of construction is used to make wide-band oxygen sensors?

2. Why are wide-band oxygen sensors used instead of conventional zirconia sensors?

3. How is the heater different for a wide-band oxygen sensor compared with a conventional zirconia oxygen sensor?

4. How does a wide-range oxygen sensor work?

5. How can a wide-band oxygen sensor be tested?

CHAPTER QUIZ

1. Where is the calibration resistor located in a wide-band oxygen sensor?
   - **a.** In the sensor heater
   - **b.** In the connector
   - **c.** In the PCM
   - **d.** In the diffusion chamber

2. A wide-band oxygen sensor is capable of detecting the air–fuel mixture in the exhaust from _____ (rich) to _____ (lean).
   - **a.** 12:1 to 15:1
   - **b.** 13:1 to 16.7:1
   - **c.** 10:1 to 23:1
   - **d.** 8:1 to 18:1

3. A conventional zirconia oxygen sensor can be made with what designs?
   - **a.** Cup and thimble
   - **b.** Cup and planar
   - **c.** Finger and thimble
   - **d.** Dual cell and single cell

4. What is the purpose of the heater in a wide-band oxygen sensor?
   - **a.** Keeps sensor from freezing
   - **b.** Helps to warm the catalytic converter
   - **c.** Allows faster closed loop operation
   - **d.** Drains excessive battery amperage

5. A wide-band oxygen sensor heater could draw how much current (amperes)?
   - **a.** 0.8 to 2.0 A
   - **b.** 2 to 4 A
   - **c.** 6 to 8 A
   - **d.** 8 to 10 A

6. A wide-band oxygen sensor needs to be heated to what operating temperature?
   - **a.** 600°F (315°C)
   - **b.** 800°F (427°C)
   - **c.** 1,400°F (760°C)
   - **d.** 2,000°F (1,093°C)

7. The two internal chambers of a dual cell wide-band oxygen sensor include _____.
   - **a.** Single and dual
   - **b.** Nernst and pump
   - **c.** Air reference and diffusion
   - **d.** Inside and outside

8. When the exhaust is rich, the PCM applies a _____ current into the pump cell.
   - **a.** Positive
   - **b.** Negative

9. When the exhaust is lean, the PCM applies a _____ current into the pump cell.
   - **a.** Positive
   - **b.** Negative

10. A dual cell wide-band oxygen sensor can be tested using a _____.
    - **a.** Scan tool
    - **b.** Voltmeter
    - **c.** Scope
    - **d.** All of the above

chapter 37

FUEL PUMPS, LINES, AND FILTERS

LEARNING OBJECTIVES

After studying this chapter, the reader should be able to:

1. Describe how to check an electric fuel pump for proper pressure and volume delivery.
2. Explain how to check a fuel-pressure regulator.
3. Describe how to test and replace fuel filters.

This chapter will help you prepare for Engine Repair (A8) ASE certification test content area "C" (Fuel, Air Induction, and Exhaust Systems Diagnosis and Repair).

STC OBJECTIVES

GM Service Technical College topics covered in this chapter are:

1. Interpret electrical schematic diagrams to determine most probable faults with components.
2. Perform a fuel system pressure test.

KEY TERMS

Baffle 542
Gerotor 547
Hydrokinetic pump 547
Onboard refueling vapor recovery (ORVR) 543
Residual or rest pressure 547
Roller cell 547
Rotary vane pump 547
Side-channel 547
Turbine pump 547
Vapor lock 544
Volatile organic compound (VOC) 546

FUEL DELIVERY SYSTEM

Creating and maintaining a correct air–fuel mixture requires a properly functioning fuel and air delivery system. Fuel delivery (and return) systems use many if not all of the following components to make certain that fuel is available under the right conditions to the fuel-injection system:

- Fuel storage tank, filler neck, and gas cap
- Fuel tank pressure sensor
- Fuel pump
- Fuel filter(s)
- Fuel delivery lines and fuel rail
- Fuel-pressure regulator
- Fuel return line (if equipped with a return-type fuel delivery system)

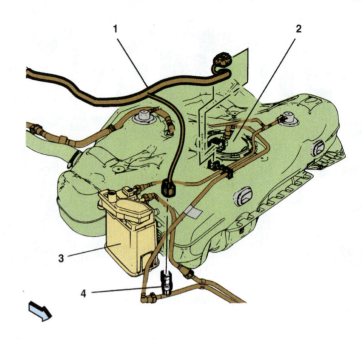

FIGURE 37–1 A fuel tank showing the sensor harness (1), fuel pump module (2), vapor canister (3), and the fuel pressure sensor (4). (*Courtesy of General Motors*)

FUEL TANKS

A vehicle fuel tank is made of corrosion-resistant steel or polyethylene plastic. Some models, such as sport utility vehicles (SUVs) and light trucks, may have an auxiliary fuel tank.

Tank design and capacity are a compromise between available space, filler location, fuel expansion room, and fuel movement. Fuel tank designs deliberately limit tank capacity by extending the filler tube neck into the tank low enough to prevent complete filling, or by providing for expansion room. ● **SEE FIGURE 37–1.** A vertical **baffle** in this same tank limits fuel sloshing as the vehicle moves.

Regardless of size and shape, all fuel tanks incorporate most if not all of the following features:

- Inlet or filler tube through which fuel enters the tank
- Filler cap with pressure holding and relief features
- An outlet to the fuel line leading to the fuel pump or fuel injector
- Fuel pump mounted within the tank
- Tank vent system
- Fuel pickup tube and fuel level sending unit

TANK LOCATION AND MOUNTING Most vehicles use a horizontally suspended fuel tank, usually mounted below the rear of the floor pan, just ahead of or behind the rear axle. Fuel tanks are located there so that frame rails and body

components protect the tank in the event of a crash. To prevent squeaks, some models have insulated strips cemented on the top or sides of the tank wherever it contacts the underbody.

Fuel inlet location depends on the tank design and filler tube placement. It is located behind a filler cap and is often a hinged door in the outer side of either rear fender panel.

Generally, a pair of metal retaining straps holds a fuel tank in place. Underbody brackets or support panels hold the strap ends using bolts. The free ends are drawn underneath the tank to hold it in place, then bolted to other support brackets or to a frame member on the opposite side of the tank. ● **SEE FIGURE 37–2.**

FILLER TUBES Fuel enters the tank through a large tube extending from the tank to an opening on the outside of the vehicle.

Effective 1993, federal regulations require manufacturers to install a device to prevent fuel from being siphoned through the filler neck. Federal authorities recognized methanol as a poison, and methanol used in gasoline is a definite health hazard. Additionally, gasoline is a suspected carcinogen (cancer-causing agent). To prevent siphoning, manufacturers welded a filler-neck check-ball tube in fuel tanks. To drain check ball–equipped fuel tanks, a technician must disconnect the check-ball tube at the tank and attach a siphon directly to the tank. ● **SEE FIGURE 37–3.**

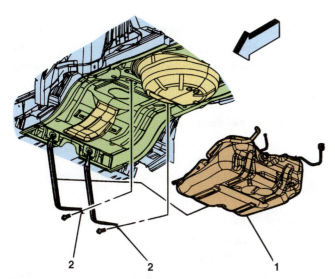

FIGURE 37–2 The tank (1) is usually held in place under the vehicle with metal straps (2). (*Courtesy of General Motors*)

FIGURE 37–3 A view of a typical filler tube with the fuel tank removed. Notice the ground strap used to help prevent the buildup of static electricity as the fuel flows into the plastic tank. The check ball looks exactly like a ping-pong ball.

Onboard refueling vapor recovery (ORVR) systems have been developed to reduce evaporative emissions during refueling. ● **SEE FIGURE 37–4.** These systems add components to the filler neck and the tank. One ORVR system utilizes a tapered filler neck with a smaller diameter tube and a check valve. When fuel flows down the neck, it opens the normally closed check valve. The vapor passage to the charcoal canister is opened. The decreased size neck and the opened air passage allow fuel and vapor to flow rapidly into the tank and the canister, respectively. When the fuel has reached a predetermined level, the check valve closes, and the fuel tank pressure increases. This forces the nozzle to shut off, thereby preventing the tank from being overfilled.

PRESSURE-VACUUM FILLER CAP

Fuel and vapors are sealed in the tank by the safety filler cap. The safety cap must release excess pressure or excess vacuum. Either condition could cause fuel tank damage, fuel spills, and vapor escape. Typically, the cap will release if the pressure is over 1.5 to 2.0 PSI (10 to 14 kPa) or if the vacuum is 0.15 to 0.30 PSI (1 to 2 kPa).

FUEL PICKUP TUBE

The fuel pickup tube is usually a part of the fuel sender assembly or the electric fuel pump assembly. Since dirt and sediment eventually gather on the bottom of a fuel tank, the fuel pickup tube is fitted with a filter sock or strainer to prevent contamination from entering the fuel lines. The woven plastic strainer also acts as a water separator by preventing water from being drawn up with the fuel. The filter sock usually

FIGURE 37–4 Vehicles equipped with onboard refueling vapor recovery usually have a reduced-size fill tube.

is designed to filter out particles that are larger than 70 to 100 microns, or 30 microns if a gerotor-type fuel pump is used. One micron is 0.000039 inch. ● **SEE FIGURE 37–5.**

NOTE: The human eye cannot see anything smaller than about 40 microns.

The filter is made from woven Saran resin (copolymer of vinylidene chloride and vinyl chloride). The filter blocks any water that may be in the fuel tank, unless it is completely submerged in water. In that case, it will allow water through the filter. This filter should be replaced whenever the fuel pump is replaced.

TANK VENTING REQUIREMENTS

Fuel tanks must be vented to prevent a vacuum lock as fuel is drawn from the tank. As fuel is used and its level drops in the tank, the space above the fuel increases. As the air in the tank expands to fill this greater space, its pressure drops. Without a vent, the air pressure inside the tank would drop below atmospheric

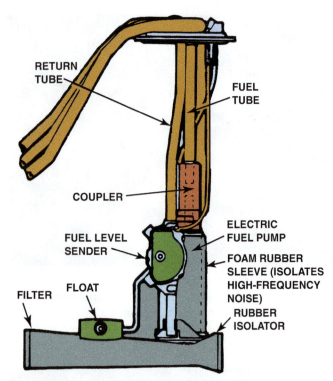

FIGURE 37–5 The fuel pickup tube is part of the fuel sender and pump assembly.

RETURN TUBE

FUEL TUBE

COUPLER

FUEL LEVEL SENDER

ELECTRIC FUEL PUMP

FOAM RUBBER SLEEVE (ISOLATES HIGH-FREQUENCY NOISE)

RUBBER ISOLATOR

FILTER

FLOAT

pressure, developing a vacuum, which prevents the flow of fuel. Under extreme pressure variance, the tank could collapse. Venting the tank allows outside air to enter as the fuel level drops, preventing a vacuum from developing.

An EVAP system vents gasoline vapors from the fuel tank directly to a charcoal-filled vapor storage canister, and uses an unvented filler cap. Many filler caps contain valves that open to relieve pressure or vacuum above specified safety levels. Systems that use completely sealed caps have separate pressure and vacuum relief valves for venting.

Because fuel tanks are not vented directly to the atmosphere, the tank must allow for fuel expansion, contraction, and overflow that can result from changes in temperature or overfilling. One way is to use a dome in the top of the tank. Many General Motors vehicles use a design that includes a vertical slosh baffle which reserves up to 12% of the total tank capacity for fuel expansion.

ROLLOVER LEAKAGE PROTECTION

All vehicles have one or more devices to prevent fuel leaks in case of vehicle rollover or a collision in which fuel may spill.

Variations of the basic one-way check valve may be installed in any number of places between the fuel tank and the engine. The valve may be installed in the fuel return line, vapor vent line, or fuel tank filler cap.

In addition to the rollover protection devices, some vehicles use devices to ensure that the fuel pump shuts off when an accident occurs. Some pumps depend upon an oil pressure or an engine speed signal to continue operating; these pumps turn off whenever the engine dies. Loss of an RPM signal will also turn off the fuel pump.

FUEL LINES

Fuel and vapor lines made of steel, nylon tubing, or fuel-resistant rubber hoses connect the parts of the fuel system. Fuel lines supply fuel to the throttle body or fuel rail. They also return excess fuel and vapors to the tank. Depending on their function, fuel and vapor lines may be either rigid or flexible.

Fuel lines must remain as cool as possible. If any part of the line is located near too much heat, the gasoline passing through it vaporizes and **vapor lock** occurs. When this happens, the fuel pump supplies only vapor that passes into the injectors. Without liquid gasoline, the engine stalls and a hot restart problem develops.

The fuel delivery system supplies 10 to 15 PSI (69 to 103 kPa) or up to 35 PSI (241 kPa) to many throttle-body injection units and up to 50 PSI (345 kPa) or more for multiport fuel-injection systems. Fuel-injection systems retain residual or rest pressure in the lines for a half hour or longer when the engine is turned off to prevent hot engine restart problems. Higher-pressure systems such as these require special fuel lines.

RIGID LINES   All fuel lines fastened to the body, frame, or engine are made of seamless steel tubing. Steel springs may be wound around the tubing at certain points to protect against impact damage.

Only steel tubing, or that recommended by the manufacturer, should be used when replacing rigid fuel lines. *Never substitute copper or aluminum tubing for steel tubing.* These materials do not withstand normal vehicle vibration and could combine with the fuel to cause a chemical reaction.

FLEXIBLE LINES   Most fuel systems use synthetic rubber hose sections where flexibility is needed. Short hose sections often connect steel fuel lines to other system components. The fuel delivery hose inside diameter (ID) is generally larger (3/16 to 3/8 inches or 8 to 10 millimeters) than the fuel return hose ID (1/4 inches or 6 millimeters).

Fuel-injection systems require special-composition reinforced hoses specifically made for these higher-pressure systems. Similarly, vapor vent lines must be made of materials that resist fuel vapors. Replacement vent hoses are usually marked with the designation "EVAP" to indicate their intended use.

FUEL LINE MOUNTING
Fuel supply lines from the tank to a throttle body or fuel rail are routed to follow the frame along the underbody of the vehicle. Vapor and return lines may be routed with the fuel supply line. All rigid lines are fastened to the frame rail or underbody with screws and clamps, or clips. ● **SEE FIGURE 37–6.**

FUEL-INJECTION LINES AND CLAMPS
Hoses used for fuel-injection systems are made of materials with high resistance to oxidation and deterioration. Replacement hoses for injection systems should always be equivalent to original equipment manufacturer (OEM) hoses.

CAUTION: *Do not use spring-type clamps on fuel-injected engines—they cannot withstand the fuel pressures involved.*

FUEL-INJECTION FITTINGS AND NYLON LINES
Because of their operating pressures, fuel-injection systems often use special kinds of fittings to ensure leakproof connections. Some high-pressure fittings on GM vehicles with port fuel-injection systems use O-ring seals instead of the traditional flare connections. When disconnecting such a fitting, inspect the O-ring for damage and replace it if necessary. *Always* tighten O-ring fittings to the specified torque value to prevent damage.

Other manufacturers also use O-ring seals on fuel line connections. In all cases, the O-rings are made of special materials that withstand contact with gasoline and oxygenated fuel blends. Some manufacturers specify that the O-rings be replaced every time the fuel system connection is opened. When replacing one of these O-rings, a new part specifically designed for fuel system service must be used.

General Motors has used nylon fuel lines with quick-connect fittings at the fuel tank and fuel filter since the early 1990s. Like the GM threaded couplings used with steel lines, nylon line couplings use internal O-ring seals. Unlocking the metal connectors requires a special quick-connector separator tool; plastic connectors can be released without the tool. ● **SEE FIGURES 37–7 AND 37–8.**

FUEL LINE LAYOUT
Fuel pressures have tended to become higher to prevent vapor lock, and a major portion of the fuel routed to the fuel-injection system returns to the tank

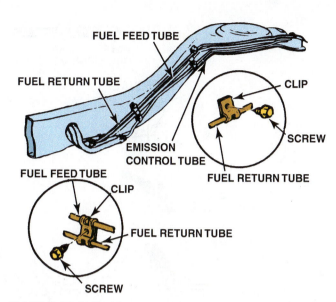

FIGURE 37–6 Fuel lines are routed along the frame or body and secured with clips.

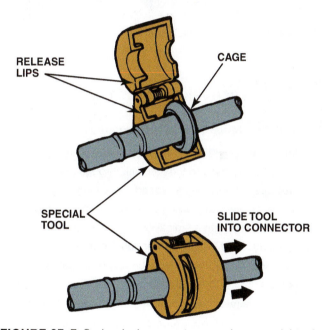

FIGURE 37–7 Spring-lock connectors require a special tool for disassembly.

by way of a fuel return line or return-type systems. This allows better control, within limits, of heat absorbed by the gasoline as it is routed through the engine compartment. Throttle-body and multiport injection systems have typically used a pressure regulator to control fuel pressure in the throttle body or fuel rail, and also allow excess fuel not used by the injectors to return to the tank. However, the warmer fuel in the tank may create problems, such as an excessive rise in fuel vapor pressures in the tank.

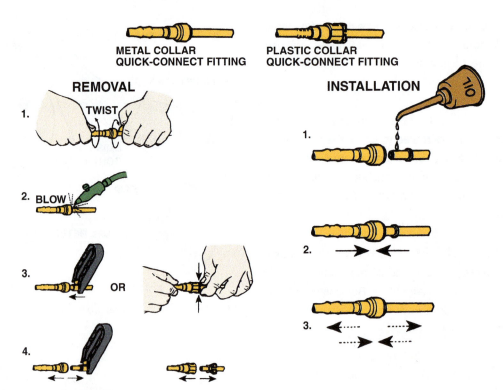

METAL COLLAR
QUICK-CONNECT FITTING

PLASTIC COLLAR
QUICK-CONNECT FITTING

REMOVAL

INSTALLATION

1. TWIST

2. BLOW

3.   OR

4.

1.

2.

3.

FIGURE 37–8 Typical quick-connect steps.

? **FREQUENTLY ASKED QUESTION**

Just How Much Fuel Is Recirculated?

Approximately 80% of the available fuel-pump volume is released to the fuel tank through the fuel-pressure regulator at idle speed. For example, a passenger vehicle cruising down the road at 60 mph gets 30 mpg. With a typical return-style fuel system pumping about 30 gallons per hour from the tank, it would burn 2 gallons per hour, and return about 28 gallons per hour to the tank!

? **FREQUENTLY ASKED QUESTION**

How Can an Electric Pump Work Inside a Gas Tank and Not Cause a Fire?

Even though fuel fills the entire pump, no burnable mixture exists inside the pump because there is no air and no danger of commutator brush arcing, igniting the fuel.

With late-model vehicles, there has been some concern about too much heat being sent back to the fuel tank, causing rising in-tank temperatures and increases in fuel vaporization and **volatile organic compound (VOC)** (hydrocarbon) emissions. To combat this problem, manufacturers have placed the pressure regulator back by the tank instead of under the hood on mechanical returnless systems. In this way, returned fuel is not subjected to the heat generated by the engine and the underhood environment. To prevent vapor lock in these systems, pressures have been raised in the fuel rail, and injectors tend to have smaller openings to maintain control of the fuel spray under pressure.

Not only must the fuel be filtered and supplied under adequate pressure, but there must also be a consistent *volume* of fuel to assure smooth engine performance even under the heaviest of loads.

ELECTRIC FUEL PUMPS

The electric fuel pump is a pusher unit. When the pump is mounted in the tank, the entire fuel supply line to the engine can be pressurized. Because the fuel, when pressurized, has a higher boiling point, it is unlikely that vapor will form to interfere with fuel flow.

Most vehicles use the impeller or turbine pumps. ● **SEE FIGURE 37–9.** All electrical pumps are driven by a small

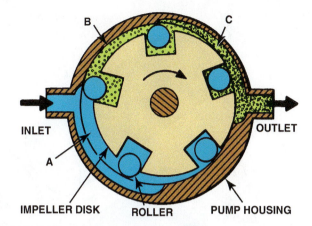

FIGURE 37–10 The pumping action of an impeller or rotary vane pump.

FIGURE 37–10 The pumping action of an impeller or rotary vane pump.

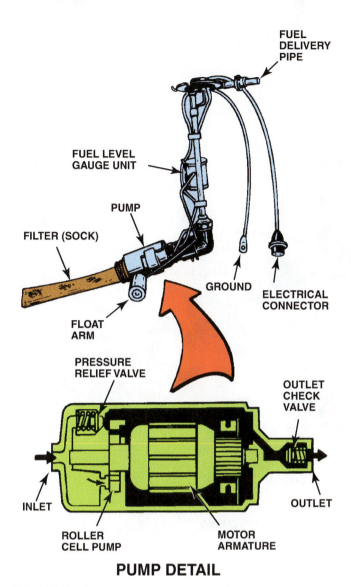

PUMP DETAIL

FIGURE 37–9 A roller cell-type electric fuel pump.

electric motor, but the turbine pump turns at higher speeds and is quieter than the others.

POSITIVE DISPLACEMENT PUMP A positive displacement pump is a design that forces everything that enters the pump to leave the pump.

In the **roller cell** or vane pump, the impeller draws fuel into the pump, and then pushes it out through the fuel line to the injection system. All designs of pumps use a variable-sized chamber to draw in fuel. When the maximum volume has been reached, the supply port closes and the discharge opens. Fuel is then forced out the discharge as this volume decreases. The chambers are formed by rollers or gears in a rotor plate. Since this type of pump uses no valves to move the fuel, the fuel flows steadily through the pump housing. Since fuel flows steadily through the entire pump, including the electrical portion, the pump stays cool. Usually, only when a vehicle runs out of fuel is there a risk of pump damage.

Most electric fuel pumps are equipped with a fuel outlet check valve that closes to maintain fuel pressure when the pump shuts off. **Residual or rest pressure** prevents vapor lock and hot-start problems on these systems.

● **FIGURE 37–10** shows the pumping action of a **rotary vane pump**. The pump consists of a central impeller disk, several rollers or vanes that ride in notches in the impeller, and a pump housing that is offset from the impeller centerline. The impeller is mounted on the end of the motor armature and spins whenever the motor is running. The rollers are free to slide in and out within the notches in the impeller to maintain sealing contact. Unpressurized fuel enters the pump, fills the spaces between the rollers, and is trapped between the impeller, the housing, and two rollers. An internal gear pump, called a **gerotor**, is another type of positive displacement pump that is often used in engine oil pumps. It uses the meshing of internal and external gear teeth to pressurize the fuel. ● **SEE FIGURE 37–11** for an example of a gerotor-type fuel pump that uses an impeller as the first stage and is used to move the fuel gerotor section where it is pressurized.

HYDROKINETIC FLOW PUMP DESIGN The word *hydro* means liquid and the term *kinetic* refers to motion, so the term **hydrokinetic pump** means that this design of pump rapidly moves the fuel to create pressure. This design of pump is a nonpositive displacement pump design.

A **turbine pump** is the most common because it tends to be less noisy. Also called **turbine**, **peripheral**, and **side-channel**, this unit uses an impeller that accelerates the fuel particles before actually discharging them into a tract where they generate pressure via pulse exchange. Actual pump volume is controlled by using a different number of impeller

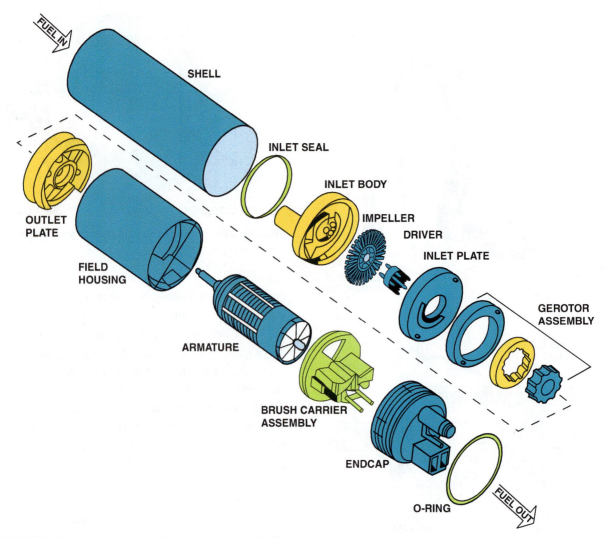

FIGURE 37–11 An exploded view of a gerotor electric fuel pump.

blades, and in some cases a higher number of impellers, or different shapes along the side discharge channels. These units are fitted more toward lower operating pressures of less than 60 PSI. ● **SEE FIGURE 37–12** for an example of a two-stage turbine pump. The turbine impeller has a staggered blade design to minimize pump harmonic noise and to separate vapor from the liquid fuel. The end cap assembly contains a pressure relief valve and a radio-frequency interference (RFI) suppression module. The check valve is usually located in the upper fuel pipe connector assembly.

After it passes through the strainer, fuel is drawn into the lower housing inlet port by the impellers. It is pressurized and delivered to the convoluted fuel tube for transfer through a check valve into the fuel feed pipe. A typical electric fuel pump used on a fuel-injection system delivers about 40 to 50 gallons per hour or 0.6 to 0.8 gallons per minute at a pressure of 70 to 90 PSI.

MODULAR FUEL SENDER ASSEMBLY The modular fuel sender consists of a fuel level sensor, a turbine pump, and a jet pump. The reservoir housing is attached to the cover containing fuel pipes and the electrical connector. Fuel is transferred from the pump to the fuel pipe through a convoluted (flexible) fuel pipe. The convoluted fuel pipe eliminates the need for rubber hoses, nylon pipes, and clamps. The reservoir dampens fuel slosh to maintain a constant fuel level available to the roller vane pump; it also reduces noise.

Some of the flow, however, is returned to the jet pump for recirculation. Excess fuel is returned to the reservoir through one of the three hollow support pipes. The hot fuel quickly mixes with the cooler fuel in the reservoir; this minimizes the possibility of vapor lock. In these modules, the reservoir is filled by the jet pump. Some of the fuel from the pump is sent through the jet pump to lift fuel from the tank into the reservoir.

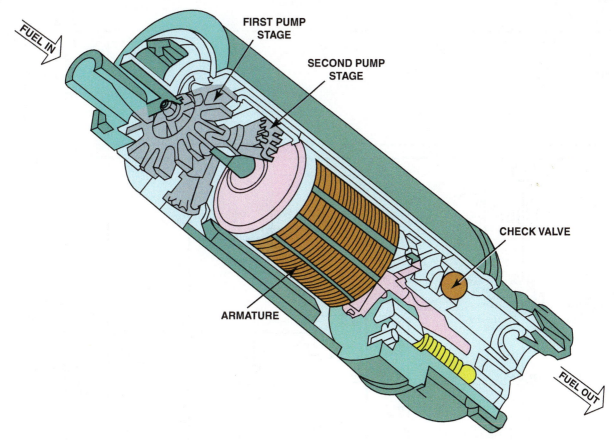

FIGURE 37–12 A cutaway view of a typical two-stage turbine electric fuel pump.

ELECTRIC PUMP CONTROL CIRCUITS Fuel-pump circuits are controlled by the fuel-pump relay. Fuel-pump relays are activated initially by turning the ignition key to on, which allows the pump to pressurize the fuel system. As a safety precaution, the relay de-energizes after a few seconds until the key is moved to the crank position. On some systems, once an ignition coil signal, or "tach" signal, is received by the engine control computer, indicating the engine is rotating, the relay remains energized even with the key released to the run position.

 FREQUENTLY ASKED QUESTION

Why Are Many Fuel-Pump Modules Spring-Loaded?

Fuel modules that contain the fuel pickup sock, fuel pump, and fuel level sensor are often spring-loaded when fitted to a plastic fuel tank. The plastic material shrinks when cold and expands when hot, so having the fuel module spring-loaded ensures that the fuel pickup sock will always be the same distance from the bottom of the tank. ● **SEE FIGURE 37–13.**

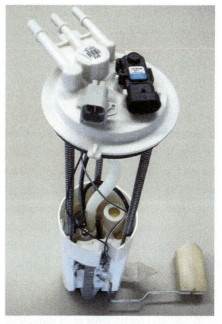

FIGURE 37–13 A typical fuel-pump module assembly, which includes the pickup strainer and fuel pump, as well as the fuel-pressure sensor and fuel level sensing unit. The three pipes on top are the fuel feed, fuel return, and the vapor line.

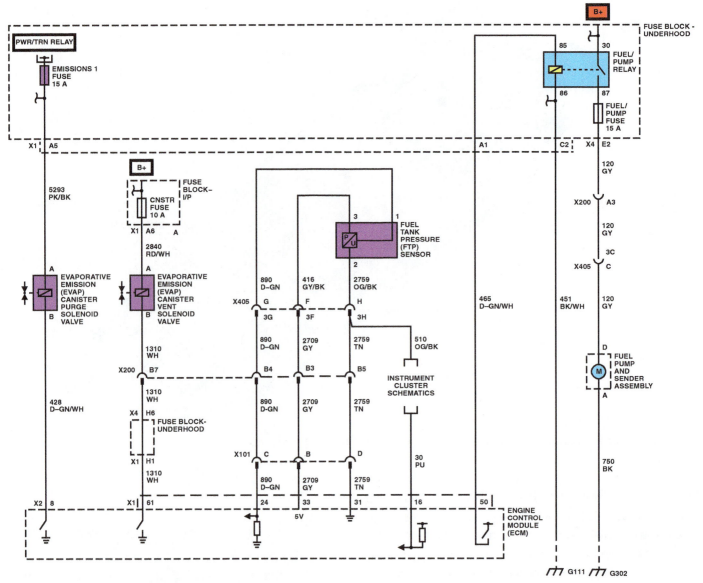

FIGURE 37-14 A schematic showing the fuel pump relay and motor (blue). Also shown are components of the EVAP system (purple). (*Courtesy of General Motors*)

General Motors systems energize the pump with the ignition switch to initially pressurize the fuel lines, but then deactivate the pump if an RPM signal is not received within one or two seconds. The pump is reactivated as soon as engine cranking is detected. The oil pressure sending unit serves as a backup to the fuel-pump relay on older vehicles. In case of pump relay failure, the oil pressure switch will operate the fuel pump once oil pressure reaches about 4 PSI (28 kPa).

VARIABLE SPEED PUMPS Another way to help reduce noise, current draw, and pump wear is to reduce the speed of the pump when less than maximum output is required. Pump speed and pressure can be regulated by controlling the voltage supplied to the pump with a resistor switched into the circuit,

or by using a separate fuel pump driver module to supply a pulse-width modulated (PWM) voltage to the pump. With slower pump speed and pressure, less noise is produced.

ELECTRONIC RETURNLESS FUEL SYSTEM[1]

Newer model vehicles are using an electronic returnless fuel system, which is a microprocessor-controlled fuel delivery system that delivers fuel from the tank to the fuel rail. It functions as an electronic replacement for a traditional, mechanical fuel

[1]Adapted from General Motors Service Information

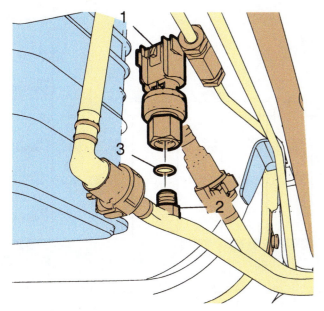

FIGURE 37–15 The fuel pressure sensor (1) is threaded onto the fuel outlet line (2) with an O-ring (3). Relieve fuel pressure before removing the sensor. (*Courtesy of General Motors*)

FIGURE 37–16 The fuel pump flow control module (1) is located in the rear of this vehicle. (*Courtesy of General Motors*)

pressure regulator. A pressure relief regulator valve within the fuel tank is used for over-pressure protection.

Desired fuel pressure is commanded by the engine control module (ECM), and transmitted to the fuel pump flow control module via a GMLAN serial data message. A liquid fuel pressure sensor provides the feedback the fuel pump flow control module requires for closed loop fuel pressure control.

FUEL PRESSURE SENSOR   The fuel pressure sensor is a serviceable 5-V, 3-pin device. It is located on the fuel feed line forward of the fuel tank, and receives power and ground from the fuel pump flow control module through a vehicle wiring harness. The sensor provides a fuel pressure signal to the fuel pump flow control module. ● **SEE FIGURE 37–15.**

FUEL PUMP FLOW CONTROL MODULE   The fuel pump flow control module is a serviceable GMLAN module. The fuel pump flow control module receives the desired fuel pressure message from the engine control module (ECM) and controls the fuel pump located within the fuel tank to achieve the desired fuel pressure. The fuel pump flow control module sends a 25 kHz PWM (pulse width modulated) signal to the fuel pump, and pump speed is changed by varying the duty cycle

of this signal. Maximum current supplied to the fuel pump is 15 A. ● **SEE FIGURES 37–16 AND 37–17.**

FUEL FILTERS

Despite the care generally taken in refining, storing, and delivering gasoline, some impurities get into the automotive fuel system. Fuel filters remove dirt, rust, water, and other contamination from the gasoline before it can reach the fuel injectors. Most fuel filters are designed to filter particles that are 10 to 20 microns or larger in size.

The useful life of many filters is limited, but vehicles that use a returnless-type fuel-injection system usually use filters that are part of the fuel pump assembly and do not have any specified interval. This means that they should last the life of the vehicle. If fuel filters are not replaced according to the manufacturer's recommendations, they can become clogged and restrict fuel flow.

In addition to using several different types of fuel filters, a single fuel system may contain two or more filters. The inline filter is located in the line between the fuel pump and

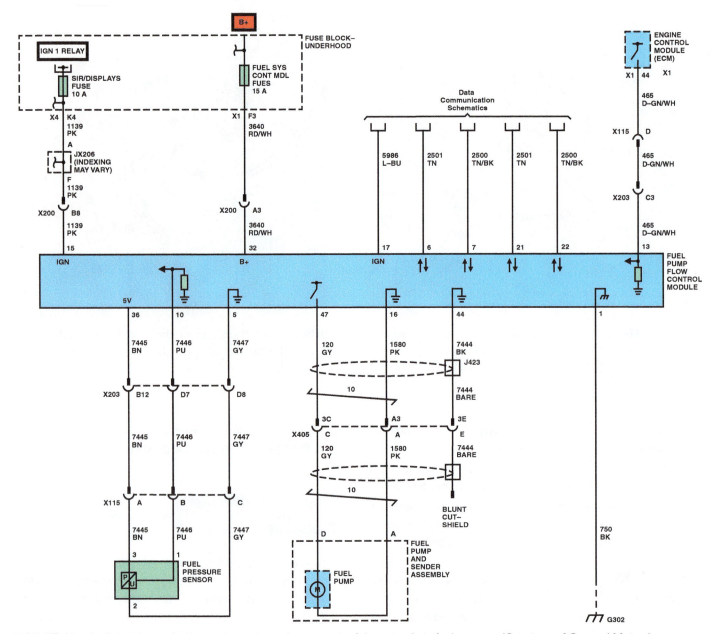

FIGURE 37–17 This schematic shows the various components of the returnless fuel system. (*Courtesy of General Motors*)

the throttle body or fuel rail. ● **SEE FIGURE 37–18.** This filter protects the system from contamination, but does not protect the fuel pump.

The inline filter usually is a metal or plastic container with a pleated paper element sealed inside.

Fuel filters may be mounted on a bracket on the fender panel, a shock tower, or another convenient place in the engine compartment. They may also be installed under the vehicle near the fuel tank. Fuel filters should be replaced according to the vehicle manufacturer's recommendations, which range

from every 30,000 miles (48,000 km) to 100,000 miles (160,000 km) or longer. Fuel filters that are part of the fuel-pump module assemblies usually do not have any specified service interval.

If the fuel filter becomes partially clogged, the following problems are likely to occur:

1. There will be low power at higher engine speeds. The vehicle usually will not go faster than a certain speed (engine acts as if it has a built-in speed governor).

2. The engine will cut out or miss on acceleration, especially when climbing hills or during heavy-load acceleration.

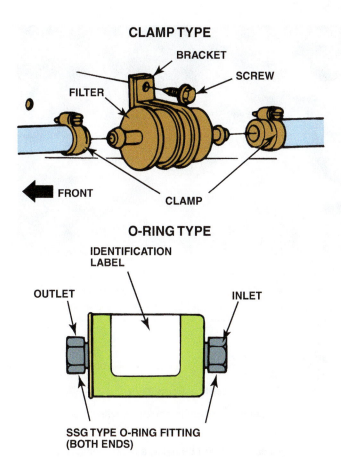

CLAMP TYPE

BRACKET

SCREW

FILTER

FRONT

CLAMP

O-RING TYPE

IDENTIFICATION
LABEL

OUTLET

INLET

SSG TYPE O-RING FITTING
(BOTH ENDS)

FIGURE 37–18 Inline fuel filters are usually attached to the fuel line with screw clamps or threaded connections. The fuel filter must be installed in the proper direction or a restricted fuel flow can result.

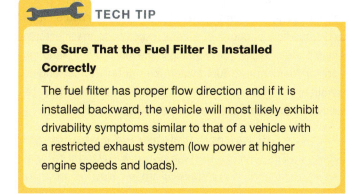

🔧 **TECH TIP**

Be Sure That the Fuel Filter Is Installed Correctly

The fuel filter has proper flow direction and if it is installed backward, the vehicle will most likely exhibit drivability symptoms similar to that of a vehicle with a restricted exhaust system (low power at higher engine speeds and loads).

All injectors, throttle body or port, are fitted with one or more filter screens or strainers to remove any particles (generally 10 microns or 0.00039 inch) that might have passed through the other filters. These screens, which surround the fuel inlet, are on the side of throttle-body injectors and are inserted in the top of port injectors. ● **SEE FIGURE 37–19.**

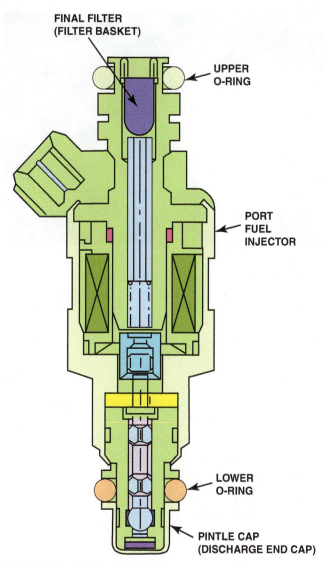

FINAL FILTER
(FILTER BASKET)

UPPER
O-RING

PORT
FUEL
INJECTOR

LOWER
O-RING

PINTLE CAP
(DISCHARGE END CAP)

FIGURE 37–19 The final filter, also called a **filter basket**, is the last filter in the fuel system.

FUEL-PUMP TESTING

Fuel-pump testing includes many different tests and procedures. Even though a fuel pump can pass one test, it does not mean that there is not a fuel-pump problem. For example, if the pump motor is rotating slower than normal, it may be able to produce the specified pressure, but not enough volume to meet the needs of the engine while operating under a heavy load.

TESTING FUEL-PUMP PRESSURE Fuel pump–regulated pressure has become more important than ever with a more exact fuel control. Although an increase in fuel

(a)

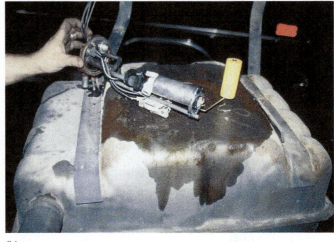

(b)

FIGURE 37–20 (a) A funnel helps in hearing if the electric fuel pump inside the gas tank is working. (b) If the pump is not running, check the wiring and current flow before going through the process of dropping the fuel tank to remove the pump.

🔧 **TECH TIP**

The Ear Test

No, this is not a test of your hearing, but rather using your ear to check that the electric fuel pump is operating. The electric fuel pump inside the fuel tank is often difficult to hear running, especially in a noisy shop environment. A commonly used trick to better hear the pump is to use a funnel in the fuel filter neck. ● **SEE FIGURE 37–20.**

🔧 **TECH TIP**

Read Pressure with a Scan Tool

If the vehicle fuel system is equipped with a fuel pressure sensor (many late models are), the fuel pressure can be found by using a scan tool to read the engine data list. Ideally the scan tool pressure and the digital gauge pressure should be the same.

pressure does increase fuel volume to the engine, this is *not* the preferred method to add additional fuel as some units will not open correctly at the increased fuel pressure. On the other side of the discussion, many newer engines will not start when fuel pressure is just a few PSI low. Correct fuel pressure is very important for proper engine operation. Most fuel-injection systems operate at either a low pressure of about 10 PSI or a high pressure of between 35 and 65 PSI.

CAUTION: Do not apply power to the fuel pump outside of the fuel tank. It can cause a fire or small explosion. Also, running a new pump without having fuel to cool and lubricate the brushes can damage the pump.

Normal Operating Pressure	(PSI)	Maximum Pump Pressure (PSI)
Low-pressure TBI units	9–13	18–20
Electronic returnless	50–94	100–110
Port fuel-injection systems	35–45	70–90
Central port fuel injection (GM)	55–64	90–110

In most types of systems, maximum fuel-pump pressure is about double the normal operating pressure to ensure that a continuous flow of cool fuel is being supplied to the injector(s) to help prevent vapor from forming in the fuel system. Although vapor or foaming in a fuel system can greatly affect engine operation, the cooling and lubricating flow of the fuel must be maintained to ensure the durability of injector nozzles.

NOTE: The TBI and port fuel injected pressures will remain steady within a narrow range. Electronic returnless systems will vary depending on engine operating conditions. For example, normal pressure at idle is 43 to 58 PSI with higher pressures possible as the vehicle accelerates.

The recommended pressure gauge for General Motors vehicles is the CH-48027 digital pressure/vacuum gauge. Accurate measurement and recording of minimum, maximum, and operating fuel pressures is critical to making a correct diagnosis of fuel system condition and function. ● **SEE FIGURE 37–21.**

To measure fuel-pump pressure, locate the Schrader valve and attach a fuel-pressure gauge. ● **SEE FIGURE 37–22.**

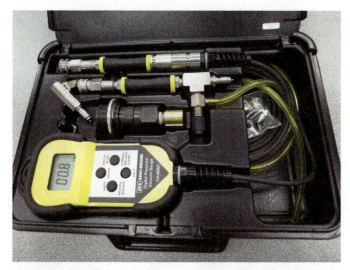

FIGURE 37–21 The CH-48027 digital pressure/vacuum gauge is recommended for testing of GM fuel systems.

FIGURE 37–22 The Schrader valve on this engine is located next to the fuel-pressure regulator.

TECH TIP

The Rubber Mallet Trick

Often a no-start condition is due to an inoperative electric fuel pump. A common trick is to tap on the bottom of the fuel tank with a rubber mallet in an attempt to jar the pump motor enough to work. Instead of pushing a vehicle into the shop, simply tap on the fuel tank and attempt to start the engine. This is not a repair, but rather a confirmation that the fuel pump does indeed require replacement.

NOTE: Some vehicles, such as those with General Motors TBI fuel-injection systems, require a specific fuel-pressure gauge that connects to the fuel system. Always follow the manufacturers' recommendations and procedures.

REST PRESSURE TEST If the fuel pressure is acceptable, then check the system for leakdown. Observe the pressure gauge after five minutes. ● **SEE FIGURE 37–23.** The pressure should be the same as the initial reading. If not, then the pressure regulator, fuel-pump check valve, or the injectors are leaking.

DYNAMIC PRESSURE TEST To test the pressure dynamically, start the engine. If the pressure is vacuum referenced, then the pressure should change when the throttle is cycled. If it does not, then check the vacuum supply circuit. Remove the vacuum line from the regulator and inspect for any presence of fuel. ● **SEE FIGURE 37–24.** There should never be any fuel present on the vacuum side of the regulator

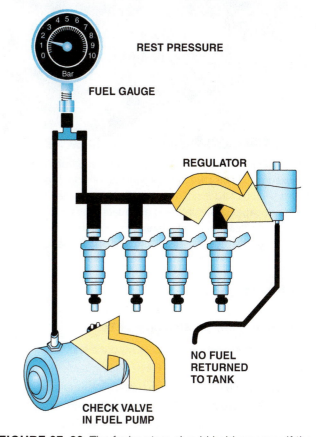

FIGURE 37–23 The fuel system should hold pressure if the system is leak free.

diaphragm. When the engine speed is increased, the pressure reading should remain within the specifications.

Some engines do not use a vacuum-referenced regulator. The running pressure remains constant, which is typical for a mechanical returnless-type fuel system. On these systems, the pressure is higher than on return-type systems to help reduce the formation of fuel vapors in the system.

FIGURE 37–24 If the vacuum hose is removed from the fuel-pressure regulator when the engine is running, the fuel pressure should increase. If it does not increase, then the fuel pump is not capable of supplying adequate pressure or the fuel-pressure regulator is defective. If gasoline is visible in the vacuum hose, the regulator is leaking and should be replaced.

🔧 TECH TIP

The Fuel-Pressure Stethoscope Test

When the fuel pump is energized and the engine is not running, fuel should be heard flowing back to the fuel tank at the outlet of the fuel-pressure regulator.
● **SEE FIGURE 37–25.** If fuel is heard flowing through the return line, the fuel-pump pressure is higher than the regulator pressure. If no sound of fuel is heard, either the fuel pump or the fuel-pressure regulator is at fault.

TESTING FUEL-PUMP VOLUME
Fuel pressure alone is not enough for proper engine operation. ● **SEE FIGURE 37–26.** Sufficient fuel capacity (flow) should be at least 2 pints (1 liter) every 30 seconds or 1 pint in 15 seconds. Fuel flow

FIGURE 37–25 Fuel should be heard returning to the fuel tank at the fuel return line if the fuel pump and fuel-pressure regulator are functioning correctly.

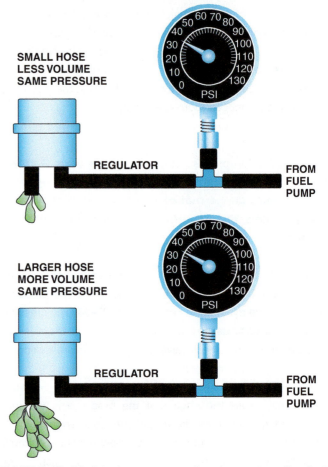

FIGURE 37–26 A fuel-pressure reading does not confirm that there is enough fuel volume for the engine to operate correctly.

Quick and Easy Fuel Volume Test

Testing for pump volume involves using a specialized tester or a fuel-pressure gauge equipped with a hose to allow the fuel to be drawn from the system into a container with volume markings to allow for a volume measurement. This test can be hazardous because of expanding gasoline. An alternative test involves connecting a fuel-pressure gauge to the system with the following steps:

STEP 1   Start the engine and observe the fuel-pressure gauge. The reading should be within factory specifications (typically between 35 and 45 PSI).

STEP 2   Remove the hose from the fuel-pressure regulator. The pressure should increase if the system uses a demand-type regulator.

STEP 3   Rapidly accelerate the engine while watching the fuel-pressure gauge. If the fuel volume is okay, the fuel pressure should not drop more than 2 PSI. If the fuel pressure drops more than 2 PSI, replace the fuel filter and retest.

STEP 4   After replacing the fuel filter, accelerate the engine and observe the pressure gauge. If the pressure drops more than 2 PSI, replace the fuel pump.

NOTE: The fuel pump could still be delivering less than the specified volume of fuel, but as long as the volume needed by the engine is met, the pressure will not drop. If, however, the vehicle is pulling a heavy load, the demand for fuel volume may exceed the capacity of the pump.

FIGURE 37–27 A fuel system tester connected in series in the fuel system so all of the fuel used flows through the meter, which displays the rate of flow and the fuel pressure.

Remove the Bed to Save Time?

The electric fuel pump is easier to replace on many General Motors pickup trucks if the bed is removed. Access to the top of the fuel tank, where the access hole is located, for the removal of the fuel tank sender unit and pump is restricted by the bottom of the pickup truck bed. It would take several people (usually other technicians in the shop) to lift the truck bed from the frame after removing only a few fasteners. ● **SEE FIGURE 37–28.**

CAUTION: Be sure to clean around the fuel pump opening so that dirt or debris does not enter the tank when the fuel pump is removed.

specifications are usually expressed in gallons per minute. A typical specification would be 0.5 gallons per minute or more. Volume testing is shown in ● **FIGURE 37–27.**

A weak or defective fuel pump can also be the cause of the symptoms just listed. If an electric fuel pump for a fuel-injected engine becomes weak, additional problems include the following:

1. The engine may be hard to start.
2. There may be a rough idle and stalling.
3. There may be erratic shifting of the automatic transmission as a result of engine missing due to lack of fuel-pump pressure and/or volume.

CAUTION: Be certain to consult the vehicle manufacturers' recommended service and testing procedures before attempting to test or replace any component of a high-pressure electronic fuel-injection system.

FIGURE 37–28 Removing the bed from a pickup truck makes gaining access to the fuel pump a lot easier.

FUEL-PUMP CURRENT DRAW TEST

Another test that can be performed on a fuel pump is to measure the current draw in amperes. This test is most often performed by connecting a digital multimeter set to read DC amperes and test the current draw. ● **SEE FIGURE 37–29** for the hookup for vehicles equipped with a fuel-pump relay. Compare the reading to factory specifications. ● **SEE CHART 37–1** for an example of typical fuel-pump current draw readings.

NOTE: Testing the current draw of an electric fuel pump may not indicate whether the pump is good. A pump that is not rotating may draw normal current.

FUEL-PUMP REPLACEMENT

The following recommendations should be followed whenever replacing an electric fuel pump:

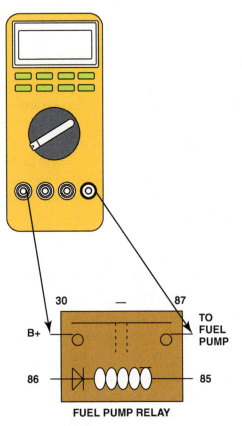

FIGURE 37–29 Hookup for testing fuel-pump current draw on any vehicle equipped with a fuel-pump relay.

- The fuel-pump strainer (sock) should be replaced with the new pump.
- If the original pump had a defector shield, it should always be used to prevent fuel return bubbles from blocking the inlet to the pump.
- Always check the interior of the fuel tank for evidence of contamination or dirt.
- Double-check that the replacement pump is correct for the application.
- Check that the wiring and electrical connectors are clean and tight.

FUEL-PUMP CURRENT DRAW TABLE

AMPERAGE READING	EXPECTED VALUE	AMPERAGE TOO HIGH	AMPERAGE TOO LOW
Throttle-Body Fuel-Injection Engines	2–5 A	• Check the fuel filter. • Check for restrictions in other fuel line areas. • Replace the fuel pump.	• Check for a high-resistance connection. • Check for a high-resistance ground fault. • Replace the fuel pump.
Port Fuel-Injection Engines	4–8 A	• Check the fuel filter. • Check for restrictions in other fuel line areas. • Replace the fuel pump.	• Check for a high-resistance connection. • Check for a high-resistance ground fault. • Replace the fuel pump.
Turbo Engines	6–10 A	• Check the fuel filter. • Check for restrictions in other fuel line areas. • Replace the fuel pump.	• Check for a high-resistance connection. • Check for a high-resistance ground fault. • Replace the fuel pump.
GM CPI Truck Engines	8–12 A	• Check the fuel filter. • Check for restrictions in other fuel line areas. • Replace the fuel pump.	• Check for a high-resistance connection. • Check for a high-resistance ground fault. • Replace the fuel pump.

CHART 37–1

FUEL SUPPLY–RELATED SYMPTOM GUIDE

PROBLEM	POSSIBLE CAUSES
Pressure too high after engine start-up.	1. Defective fuel-pressure regulator 2. Restricted fuel return line 3. Excessive system voltage 4. Restricted return line 5. Wrong fuel pump
Pressure too low after engine start-up.	1. Stuck-open pressure regulator 2. Low voltage 3. Poor ground 4. Plugged fuel filter 5. Faulty inline fuel pump 6. Faulty in-tank fuel pump 7. Partially clogged filter sock 8. Faulty hose coupling 9. Leaking fuel line 10. Wrong fuel pump 11. Leaking pulsator 12. Restricted accumulator 13. Faulty pump check valves 14. Faulty pump installation
Pressure drops off with key on/engine off. With key off, the pressure does not hold.	1. Leaky pulsator 2. Leaking fuel-pump coupling hose 3. Faulty fuel pump (check valves) 4. Faulty pressure regulator 5. Leaking fuel injector 6. Leaking cold-start fuel injector 7. Faulty installation 8. Lines leaking

FUEL-PUMP RELAY CIRCUIT DIAGNOSIS

1 The tools needed to diagnose a circuit containing a relay include a digital multimeter (DMM), a fused jumper wire, and an assortment of wiring terminals.

2 Start the diagnosis by locating the relay center. It is under the hood on this General Motors vehicle, so access is easy. Not all vehicles are this easy.

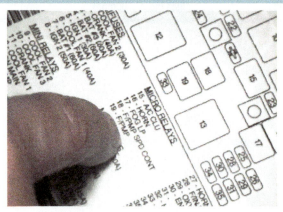

3 The chart under the cover for the relay center indicates the location of the relay that controls the electric fuel pump.

4 Locate the fuel-pump relay and remove by using a puller if necessary. Try to avoid rocking or twisting the relay to prevent causing damage to the relay terminals or the relay itself.

5 Terminals 85 and 86 represent the coil inside the relay. Terminal 30 is the power terminal, 87a is the normally closed contact, and 87 is the normally open contact.

6 The terminals are also labeled on most relays.

7 To help make good electrical contact with the terminals without doing any harm, select the proper-size terminal from the terminal assortment.

8 Insert the terminals into the relay socket in 30 and 87.

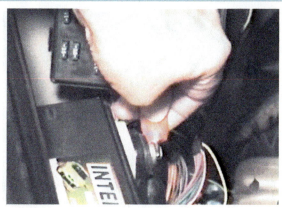

9 To check for voltage at terminal 30, use a test light or a voltmeter. Start by connecting the alligator clip of the test light to the positive (+) terminal of the battery.

10 Touch the test light to the negative (–) terminal of the battery or a good engine ground to check the test light.

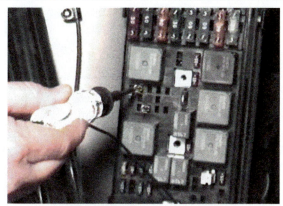

11 Use the test light to check for voltage at terminal 30 of the relay. The ignition may have to be in the on (run) position.

12 To check to see if the electric fuel pump can be operated from the relay contacts, use a fused jumper wire and touch the relay contacts that correspond to terminals 30 and 87 of the relay.

CONTINUED ▶

13 Connect the leads of the meter to contacts 30 and 87 of the relay socket. The reading of 4.7 amperes is okay because the specification is 4 to 8 amperes.

14 Set the meter to read ohms (Ω) and measure the resistance of the relay coil. The usual reading for most relays is between 60 and 100 ohms.

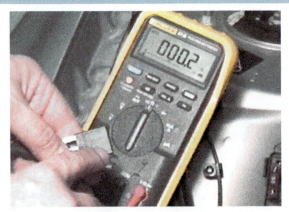

15 Measure between terminal 30 and 87a. Terminal 87a is the normally closed contact, and there should be little, if any, resistance between these two terminals, as shown.

16 To test the normally open contacts, connect one meter lead to terminal 30 and the other lead to terminal 87. The ohmmeter should show an open circuit by displaying OL.

17 Connect a fused jumper wire to supply 12 volts to terminal 86 and a ground to terminal 85 of the relay. If the relay clicks, then the relay coil is able to move the armature (movable arm) of the relay.

18 After testing, be sure to reinstall the relay and the relay cover.

SUMMARY

1. The fuel delivery system includes the following items:
   - Fuel tank
   - Fuel pump
   - Fuel filter(s)
   - Fuel lines
2. A fuel tank is either constructed of steel with a tin plating for corrosion resistance or polyethylene plastic.
3. Fuel tank filler tubes contain an anti-siphoning device.
4. Accident and rollover protection devices include check valves and pressure switches.
5. Most fuel lines are made of nylon plastic.
6. Electric fuel-pump types include roller cell, gerotor, and turbine.
7. Fuel filters remove particles that are 10 to 20 microns or larger in size and should be replaced regularly.
8. Fuel pumps can be tested by checking:
   - Pressure
   - Volume`
   - Specified current draw

REVIEW QUESTIONS

1. What are the two materials used to construct fuel tanks?
2. What are the three most commonly used pump designs?
3. What is the proper way to disconnect and connect plastic fuel line connections?
4. Where are the fuel filters located in the fuel system?
5. What accident and rollover devices are installed in a fuel delivery system?
6. What three methods can be used to test a fuel pump?

CHAPTER QUIZ

1. The first fuel filter in the sock inside the fuel tank normally filters particles larger than _____.
   - **a.** 0.001 to 0.003 inches
   - **b.** 0.010 to 0.030 inches
   - **c.** 10 to 20 microns
   - **d.** 70 to 100 microns

2. On an electronic returnless fuel system the fuel pump is controlled by _____.
   - **a.** A relay
   - **b.** A ground switch
   - **c.** A fuel pump control module
   - **d.** A vacuum control module

3. Fuel lines are constructed from _____.
   - **a.** Seamless steel tubing
   - **b.** Nylon plastic
   - **c.** Copper and/or aluminum tubing
   - **d.** Both a and b

4. What prevents the fuel pump inside the fuel tank from catching the gasoline on fire?
   - **a.** Electricity is not used to power the pump
   - **b.** No air is around the motor brushes
   - **c.** Gasoline is hard to ignite in a closed space
   - **d.** All of the above

5. A good fuel pump should be able to supply how much fuel per minute?
   - **a.** 1/4 pint
   - **b.** 1/2 pint
   - **c.** 1 pint
   - **d.** 0.6 to 0.8 gallons

6. Technician A says that fuel pump modules are spring-loaded so that they can be compressed to fit into the opening. Technician B says that they are spring-loaded to allow for expansion and contraction of plastic fuel tanks. Which technician is correct?
   - **a.** Technician A only
   - **b.** Technician B only
   - **c.** Both Technicians A and B
   - **d.** Neither Technician A nor B

7. Most fuel filters are designed to remove particles larger than _____.
   - **a.** 10 microns
   - **b.** 20 microns
   - **c.** 70 microns
   - **d.** 100 microns

8. The amperage draw of an electric fuel pump is higher than specified. All of the following are possible causes *except:*
   - **a.** Corroded electrical connections at the pump motor
   - **b.** Clogged fuel filter
   - **c.** Restriction in the fuel line
   - **d.** Defective fuel pump

9. A fuel pump is being replaced for the third time. Technician A says that the gasoline could be contaminated. Technician B says that wiring to the pump could be corroded. Which technician is correct?
   - **a.** Technician A only
   - **b.** Technician B only
   - **c.** Both Technicians A and B
   - **d.** Neither Technician A nor B

10. A fuel filter has been accidentally installed backwards. What is the most likely result?
    - **a.** Nothing will be noticed
    - **b.** Reduced fuel economy
    - **c.** Lower power at higher engine speeds and loads
    - **d.** Fuel system pulsation noises may be heard

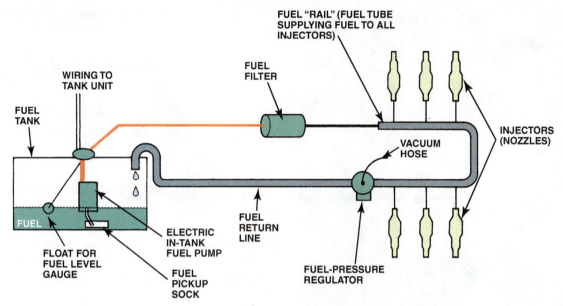

FIGURE 38–1 Typical port fuel-injection system, indicating the location of various components. Notice that the fuel-pressure regulator is located on the fuel return side of the system. The computer does not control fuel pressure, but does control the operation of the electric fuel pump (on most systems) and the pulsing on and off of the injectors.

ELECTRONIC FUEL-INJECTION OPERATION

Electronic fuel-injection systems use the computer to control the following operations of fuel injectors and other functions based on information sent to the computer from the various sensors. Most electronic fuel-injection systems share the following:

1. Electric fuel pump (usually located inside the fuel tank)
2. Fuel-pump relay (usually controlled by the computer)
3. Fuel-pressure regulator (mechanically operated spring-loaded rubber diaphragm maintains proper fuel pressure)
4. Fuel-injector nozzle or nozzles

● **SEE FIGURE 38–1**. Most electronic fuel-injection systems use the computer to control the following aspects of their operation:

1. Pulsing the fuel injectors on and off. The longer the injectors are held open, the greater the amount of fuel injected into the cylinder.
2. Operating the fuel-pump relay circuit. The computer usually controls the operation of the electric fuel pump located inside (or near) the fuel tank. The computer uses signals from the ignition switch and RPM signals from the ignition module or system to energize the fuel-pump relay circuit.

NOTE: This is a safety feature, because if the engine stalls and the tachometer (engine speed) signal is lost, the computer will shut off (de-energize) the fuel-pump relay and stop the fuel pump.

Computer-controlled fuel-injection systems are normally reliable systems if the proper service procedures are followed. Fuel-injection systems use the gasoline flowing through the injectors to lubricate and cool the injector electrical windings and pintle valves.

NOTE: The fuel does not actually make contact with the electrical windings because the injectors have O-rings at the top and bottom of the winding spool to keep fuel out.

 **TECH TIP**

"Two Must-Do's"

For long service life of the fuel system always do the following:
1. Avoid operating the vehicle on a near-empty tank of fuel. The water or alcohol becomes more concentrated when the fuel level is low. Dirt that settles near the bottom of the fuel tank can be drawn through the fuel system and cause damage to the pump and injector nozzles.
2. Replace the fuel filter at regular service intervals.

FIGURE 38–2 A dual-nozzle TBI unit on a Chevrolet 5.0 L V-8 engine. The fuel is sprayed above the throttle plate where the fuel mixes with air before entering the intake manifold.

The two types of electronic fuel injection systems covered in this chapter are:

- **Throttle-body-injection (TBI)** type. A TBI system delivers fuel from a nozzle(s) into the air above the throttle plate. ● **SEE FIGURE 38–2.**
- **Port fuel-injection** type. A port fuel-injection design uses a nozzle for each cylinder and the fuel is sprayed into the intake manifold about 2 to 3 inches (70 to 100 mm) from the intake valve. ● **SEE FIGURE 38–3.**

NOTE: Spark-ignited direct injection (SIDI) fuel-injection systems will be covered in the next chapter.

SPEED-DENSITY FUEL-INJECTION SYSTEMS

Fuel-injection computer systems require a method for measuring the amount of air the engine is breathing in, in order to match the correct fuel delivery. There are two basic methods used:

1. Speed density
2. Mass airflow

The speed-density method does not require an air quantity sensor, but rather calculates the amount of fuel required by the engine. The computer uses information from sensors such as the MAP and TP to calculate the needed amount of fuel.

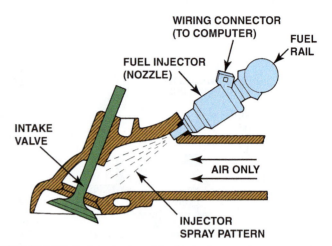

FIGURE 38–3 A typical port fuel-injection system sprayed fuel into the low pressure (vacuum) of the intake manifold, about 3 inch (70 to 100 mm) from the intake valve.

- **MAP sensor.** The value of the intake (inlet) manifold pressure (vacuum) is a direct indication of engine load.
- **TP sensor.** The position of the throttle plate and its rate of change are used as part of the equation to calculate the proper amount of fuel to inject.
- **Temperature sensors.** Both engine coolant temperature (ECT) and intake air temperature (IAT) are used to calculate the density of the air and the need of the engine for fuel. A cold engine (low-coolant temperature) requires a richer air–fuel mixture than a warm engine.

On speed-density systems, the computer calculates the amount of air in each cylinder by using manifold pressure and engine RPM. The amount of air in each cylinder is the major factor in determining the amount of fuel needed. Other sensors provide information to modify the fuel requirements. The formula used to determine the injector pulse width (PW) in milliseconds (ms) is:

Injector pulse width = MAP/BARO × RPM/maximum RPM

The formula is modified by values from other sensors, including:

- Throttle position (TP)
- Engine coolant temperature (ECT)
- Intake air temperature (IAT)
- Oxygen sensor voltage (O2S)
- Adaptive memory

A fuel injector delivers atomized fuel into the airstream where it is instantly vaporized. All throttle-body (TB) fuel-injection systems and many older multipoint (port) injection systems use the speed-density method of fuel calculation.

MASS AIRFLOW FUEL-INJECTION SYSTEMS

The formula used by fuel-injection systems that use a mass airflow (MAF) sensor to calculate the injection base pulse width is:

Injector pulse width = airflow/RPM

The formula is modified by other sensor values such as:

- Throttle position
- Engine coolant temperature
- Barometric pressure
- Adaptive memory

THROTTLE-BODY INJECTION

The computer controls injector pulses in one of two ways:

- Synchronized
- Nonsynchronized

If the system uses a synchronized mode, the injector pulses once for each distributor reference pulse. In some vehicles, when dual injectors are used in a synchronized system, the injectors pulse alternately. In a nonsynchronized system, the injectors are pulsed once during a given period (which varies according to calibration) completely independent of distributor reference pulses.

The injector always opens the same distance, and the fuel pressure is maintained at a controlled value by the pressure regulator. The strength of the spring inside the regulator determines at what pressure the valve is unseated, sending unneeded fuel back to the tank and lowering the pressure. ● **SEE FIGURE 38–4.** The amount of fuel delivered by the injector depends on the amount of time (on-time) that the nozzle is open. This is the injector pulse width—the on-time in milliseconds that the nozzle is open.

The PCM commands a variety of pulse widths to supply the amount of fuel that an engine needs at any specific moment.

- A long pulse width delivers more fuel.
- A short pulse width delivers less fuel.

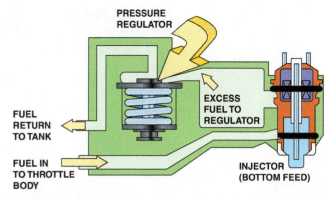

FIGURE 38–4 The tension of the spring in the fuel-pressure regulator determines the operating pressure on a throttle-body fuel-injection unit.

? FREQUENTLY ASKED QUESTION

How Do the Sensors Affect the Pulse Width?

The base pulse width of a fuel-injection system is primarily determined by the value of the MAF or MAP sensor and engine speed (RPM). However, the PCM relies on the input from many other sensors, such as the following, to modify the base pulse width as needed:

- **TP Sensor.** This sensor causes the PCM to command up to 500% (five times) the base pulse width if the accelerator pedal is depressed rapidly to the floor. It can also reduce the pulse width by about 70% if the throttle is rapidly closed.
- **ECT.** The value of this sensor determines the temperature of the engine coolant, helps determine the base pulse width, and can account for up to 60% of the determining factors.
- **BARO.** The BARO sensor compensates for altitude and adds up to about 10% under high-pressure conditions and subtracts as much as 50% from the base pulse width at high altitudes.
- **IAT.** The intake air temperature is used to modify the base pulse width based on the temperature of the air entering the engine. It is usually capable of adding as much as 20% if very cold air is entering the engine or reducing the pulse width by up to 20% if very hot air is entering the engine.
- **O2S.** This is one of the main modifiers to the base pulse width and can add or subtract up to about 20 to 25% or more, depending on the oxygen sensor activity.

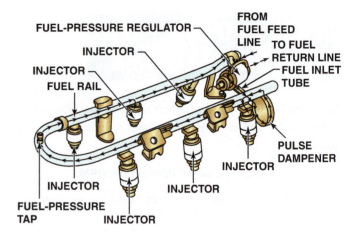

FIGURE 38–5 The injectors receive fuel and are supported by the fuel rail.

FROM FUEL FEED LINE
TO FUEL RETURN LINE
FUEL INLET TUBE
FUEL-PRESSURE REGULATOR
INJECTOR
INJECTOR
FUEL RAIL
PULSE DAMPENER
INJECTOR
INJECTOR
INJECTOR
FUEL-PRESSURE TAP
INJECTOR

FIGURE 38–6 Cross section of a typical port fuel-injection nozzle assembly. These injectors are serviced as an assembly only; no part replacement or service is possible except for replacement of external O-ring seals.

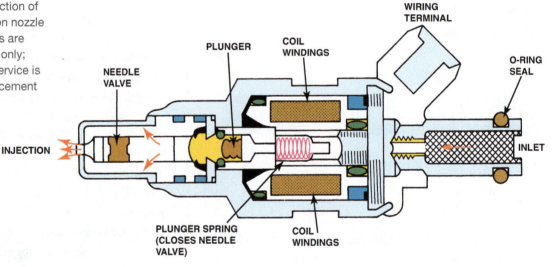

WIRING TERMINAL
PLUNGER
COIL WINDINGS
O-RING SEAL
NEEDLE VALVE
INJECTION
INLET
PLUNGER SPRING (CLOSES NEEDLE VALVE)
COIL WINDINGS

PORT FUEL-INJECTION

The advantages of port fuel-injection design also are related to characteristics of intake manifolds:

- Fuel distribution is equal to all cylinders because each cylinder has its own injector. ● **SEE FIGURE 38–5**.

- The fuel is injected almost directly into the combustion chamber, so there is no chance for it to condense on the walls of a cold intake manifold.

- Because the intake manifold does not have to carry fuel to properly position a TBI unit, it can be shaped and sized to tune the intake airflow to achieve specific engine performance characteristics.

An EFI injector is a specialized solenoid. ● **SEE FIGURE 38–6**. It has an armature winding to create a magnetic field, and a needle (pintle), a disc, or a ball valve. A spring holds the needle, disc, or ball closed against the valve seat, and when energized, the armature winding pulls open the valve when it receives a current pulse from the powertrain control module (PCM). When the solenoid is energized, it unseats the valve to inject fuel.

Electronic fuel-injection systems use a solenoid-operated injector to spray atomized fuel in timed pulses into the manifold or near the intake valve. ● **SEE FIGURE 38–7**. Injectors may be sequenced and fired in one of several ways, but their pulse width is determined and controlled by the engine computer.

Port systems have an injector for each cylinder, but they do not all fire the injectors in the same way. Domestic systems use one of three ways to trigger the injectors:

- Grouped double-fire
- Simultaneous double-fire
- Sequential

GROUPED/SIMULTANEOUS TRIGGERING Used on early electronic fuel injected vehicles, the grouped double-fire or simultaneous double-fire designs fire the injectors in groups

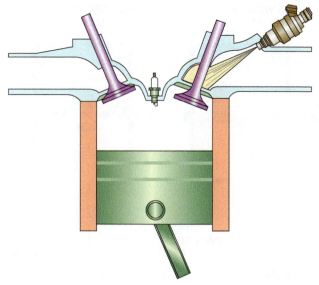

FIGURE 38–7 Port fuel injectors spray atomized fuel into the intake manifold about 3 inches (75 mm) from the intake valve.

FIGURE 38–8 Port fuel injection allows the use of long, tuned intake runners. (*6.2L V8 LS3, Courtesy of General Motors*)

 FREQUENTLY ASKED QUESTION

How Can It Be Determined If the Injection System Is Sequential?

Look at the color of the wires at the injectors. If a sequentially fired injector is used, then one wire color (the pulse wire) will be a different color for each injector. The other wire is usually the same color because all injectors receive voltage from some source. If a group- or batch-fired injection system is being used, the wire colors will be the same for the injectors that are group fired. For example, a V-6 group-fired engine will have three injectors with a pink and blue wire (power and pulse) and the other three will have pink and green wires.

of two, three, or four (depending on number of cylinders) or all at the same time, twice per four-stroke cycle. This method of pulsing injectors in groups is sometimes called **gang fired**.

SEQUENTIAL   Sequential firing of the injectors according to engine firing order is the most accurate and desirable method of regulating port fuel injection. In this system, the injectors are timed and pulsed individually, much like the spark plugs are sequentially operated in firing order of the engine. This system is often called **sequential fuel injection** or **SFI**. Each cylinder receives one charge every two crankshaft revolutions, just before the intake valve opens. This means that the mixture is never static in the intake manifold and mixture adjustments can be made almost instantaneously between the firing of one injector and the next. A camshaft position sensor (CMP) signal or a special distributor reference pulse informs the PCM when the No. 1 cylinder is on its compression stroke. If the sensor fails or the reference pulse is interrupted, some injection systems shut down, while others revert to pulsing the injectors simultaneously.

The major advantage of using port injection instead of the simpler throttle-body injection is that the intake manifolds on port fuel-injected engines only contain air, not a mixture of air and fuel. This allows the engine design engineer the opportunity to design long, "tuned" intake-manifold runners that help the engine produce increased torque at low engine speeds. ● **SEE FIGURE 38–8**.

NOTE: Some port fuel-injection systems used on engines with four or more valves per cylinder may use two injectors per cylinder. One injector is used all the time, and the second injector is operated by the computer when high-engine speed and high-load conditions are detected by the computer. Typically, the second injector injects fuel into the high-speed intake ports of the manifold. This system permits good low-speed power and throttle responses as well as superior high-speed power.

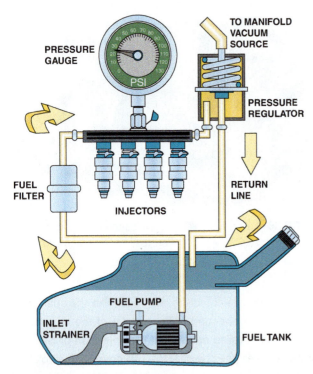

FIGURE 38–9 A typical port fuel-injected system showing a vacuum-controlled fuel-pressure regulator.

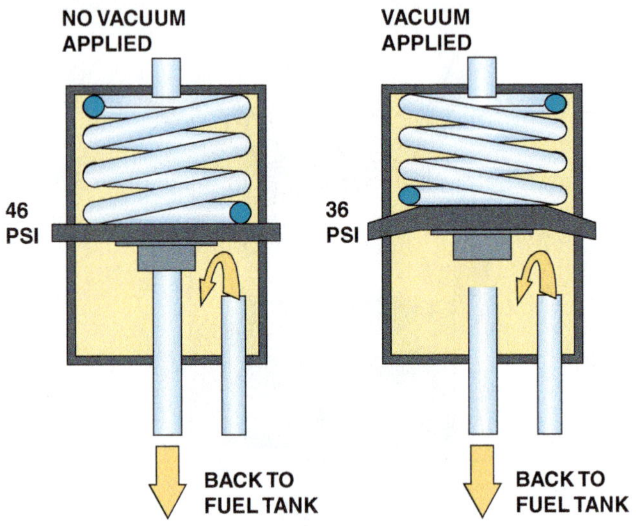

FIGURE 38–10 A typical fuel-pressure regulator that has a spring that exerts 46 pounds of force against the fuel. If 20 inches of vacuum are applied above the spring, the vacuum reduces the force exerted by the spring on the fuel, allowing the fuel to return to the tank at a lower pressure.

FUEL-PRESSURE REGULATOR

The pressure regulator and fuel pump work together to maintain the required pressure drop at the injector tips. The fuel-pressure regulator typically consists of a spring-loaded, diaphragm-operated valve in a metal housing.

Fuel-pressure regulators on fuel-return-type fuel-injection systems are installed on the return (downstream) side of the injectors at the end of the fuel rail, or are built into or mounted upon the throttle-body housing. Downstream regulation minimizes fuel-pressure pulsations caused by pressure drop across the injectors as the nozzles open. It also ensures positive fuel pressure at the injectors at all times and holds residual pressure in the lines when the engine is off. On mechanical returnless systems, the regulator is located back at the tank with the fuel filter.

In order for excess fuel (about 80 to 90% of the fuel delivered) to return to the tank, fuel pressure must overcome spring pressure on the spring-loaded diaphragm to uncover the return line to the tank. This happens when system pressure exceeds operating requirements. With TBI, the regulator is

close to the injector tip, so the regulator senses essentially the same air pressure as the injector.

The pressure regulator used in a port fuel-injection system has an intake manifold vacuum line connection on the regulator vacuum chamber. This allows fuel pressure to be modulated by a combination of spring pressure and manifold vacuum acting on the diaphragm. ● **SEE FIGURES 38–9 AND 38–10.**

In both TBI and port fuel-injection systems, the regulator shuts off the return line when the fuel pump is not running. This maintains pressure at the injectors for easy restarting after hot soak as well as reducing vapor lock.

NOTE: Some General Motors throttle-body units do not hold pressure and are called nonchecking.

Port fuel-injection systems generally operate with pressures at the injector of about 30 to 55 PSI (207 to 379 kPa), while TBI systems work with injector pressures of about 10 to 20 PSI (69 to 138 kPa). The difference in system pressures results from the difference in how the systems operate. Since injectors in a TBI system inject the fuel into the airflow at the manifold inlet (above the throttle), there is more time for atomization in the manifold before the air–fuel charge reaches the intake valve. This allows TBI injectors to work at lower pressures than injectors used in a port system.

FIGURE 38–11 A lack of fuel flow could be due to a restricted fuel-pressure regulator. Notice the fine screen filter. If this filter were to become clogged, higher than normal fuel pressure would occur.

TECH TIP

Don't Forget the Regulator

Some fuel-pressure regulators contain a 10 micron filter. If this filter becomes clogged, fuel will be unable to return to the tank, resulting in excessive fuel pressure in the fuel rail. ● **SEE FIGURE 38–11**.

VACUUM-BIASED FUEL-PRESSURE REGULATOR

The primary reason why many port fuel-injected systems use a vacuum-controlled fuel-pressure regulator is to ensure that there is a constant pressure drop across the injectors. In a throttle-body fuel-injection system, the injector squirts into the atmospheric pressure regardless of the load on the engine. In a port fuel-injected engine, however, the pressure inside the intake manifold changes as the load on the engine increases.

ENGINE OPERATING CONDITION	INTAKE MANIFOLD VACUUM	FUEL PRESSURE
Idle or cruise	High	Lower
Heavy load	Low	Higher

The computer can best calculate injector pulse width based on all sensors if the pressure drop across the injector is the same under all operating conditions. A vacuum-controlled fuel-pressure regulator allows the equal pressure drop by reducing the force exerted by the regulator spring at high vacuum (low-load condition), yet allowing the full force of the regulator spring to be exerted when the vacuum is low (high-engine-load condition).

ELECTRONIC RETURNLESS FUEL SYSTEM

This system is unique because it does not use a mechanical valve to regulate rail pressure. Fuel pressure at the rail is sensed by a pressure transducer, which sends a low-level signal to a controller. The controller contains logic to calculate a signal to the pump power driver. The power driver contains a high-current transistor that controls the pump speed using pulse width modulation (PWM). This system is called the **electronic returnless fuel system (ERFS)**. ● **SEE FIGURE 38–12**. This transducer can be differentially referenced to manifold pressure for closed-loop feedback, correcting and maintaining the output of the pump to a desired rail setting. This system is capable of continuously varying rail pressure as a result of engine vacuum, engine fuel demand, and fuel temperature (as sensed by an external temperature transducer, if necessary). A **pressure vent valve (PVV)** is employed at the tank to relieve overpressure due to thermal expansion of fuel. In addition, a supply-side bleed, by means of an in-tank reservoir using a supply-side jet pump, is necessary for proper pump operation.

MECHANICAL RETURNLESS FUEL SYSTEM

The first production returnless systems employed the **mechanical returnless fuel system (MRFS)** approach. This system has a bypass regulator to control rail pressure that is located in close proximity to the fuel tank. Fuel is sent by the in-tank pump to a chassis-mounted inline filter with excess fuel returning to the tank through a short return line. ● **SEE FIGURE 38–13**. The inline filter may be mounted directly to the tank, thereby eliminating the shortened return line. Supply pressure is regulated on the downstream side of the inline filter to accommodate changing restrictions throughout the filter's service life. This system is limited to constant rail pressure (*CRP) system calibrations, whereas with ERFS, the pressure transducer can be referenced to atmospheric pressure for CRP systems or differentially referenced to intake manifold pressure for constant differential injector pressure (**CIP) systems.

NOTE: *CRP is referenced to atmospheric pressure, has lower operating pressure, and is desirable for calibrations using speed/air density sensing. **CIP is referenced to manifold pressure, varies rail pressure, and is desirable in engines that use mass airflow sensing.

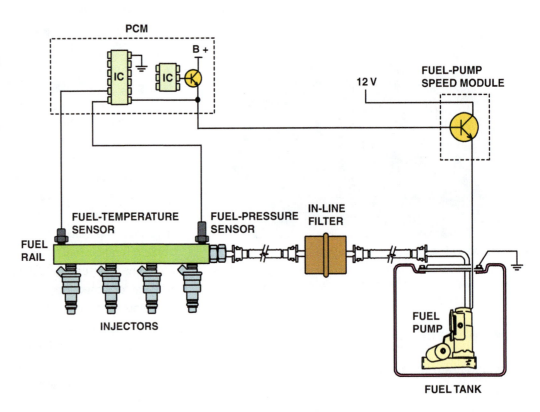

FIGURE 38–12 The fuel-pressure sensor and fuel-temperature sensor are often constructed together in one assembly to help give the PCM the needed data to control the fuel-pump speed.

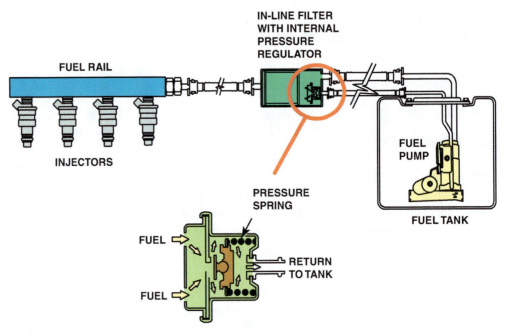

FIGURE 38–13 A mechanical returnless fuel system. The bypass regulator in the fuel tank controls fuel line pressure.

DEMAND DELIVERY SYSTEM (DDS)

Given the experience with both ERFS and MRFS, a need was recognized to develop new returnless technologies that could combine the speed control and constant injector pressure attributes of ERFS together with the cost savings, simplicity, and reliability of MRFS. This new technology also needed to address pulsation dampening/hammering and fuel transient response. Therefore, the **demand delivery system (DDS)** technology was developed. A different form of demand pressure regulator has been applied to the fuel rail. It mounts at the head or port entry and regulates the pressure downstream at the injectors by admitting the precise quantity of fuel into the rail as consumed by the engine. Having demand regulation at the rail improves pressure response to flow transients and

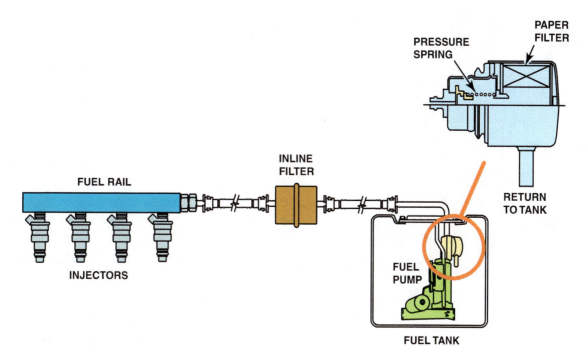

FIGURE 38–14 A demand delivery system uses a fuel-pressure regulator attached to the fuel pump assembly inside the fuel tank.

FIGURE 38–15 A rectangular-shaped fuel rail is used to help dampen fuel system pulsations and noise caused by the injectors opening and closing.

? FREQUENTLY ASKED QUESTION

Why Are Some Fuel Rails Rectangular Shaped?

A port fuel-injection system uses a pipe or tubes to deliver fuel from the fuel line to the intended fuel injectors. This pipe or tube is called the **fuel rail**. Some vehicle manufacturers construct the fuel rail in a rectangular cross section. ● **SEE FIGURE 38–15**. The sides of the fuel rail are able to move in and out slightly, thereby acting as a fuel pulsator evening out the pressure pulses created by the opening and closing of the injectors to reduce underhood noise. A round cross-sectional fuel rail is not able to deform and, as a result, some manufacturers have had to use a separate dampener.

provides rail pulsation dampening. A fuel pump and a low-cost, high-performance bypass regulator are used within the appropriate fuel sender. ● **SEE FIGURE 38–14**. They supply a pressure somewhat higher than the required rail set pressure to accommodate dynamic line and filter pressure losses. Electronic pump speed control is accomplished using a smart regulator as an integral flow sensor. A **pressure control valve (PCV)** may also be used and can readily reconfigure an existing design fuel sender into a returnless sender.

FUEL INJECTORS

EFI systems use solenoid-operated injectors. ● **SEE FIGURE 38–16**. This electromagnetic device contains an armature and a spring-loaded needle valve or ball valve assembly. When the computer energizes the solenoid, voltage is applied to the solenoid coil until the current reaches a specified level. This permits a quick pull-in of the armature during turn-on. The armature is pulled off of its seat against spring force, allowing fuel to

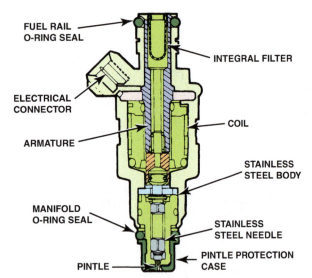

FIGURE 38–16 A multiport fuel injector. Notice that the fuel flows straight through and does not come in contact with the coil windings.

Labels on figure:
FUEL RAIL O-RING SEAL
INTEGRAL FILTER
ELECTRICAL CONNECTOR
ARMATURE
COIL
STAINLESS STEEL BODY
MANIFOLD O-RING SEAL
STAINLESS STEEL NEEDLE
PINTLE
PINTLE PROTECTION CASE

FIGURE 38–17 Each of the eight injectors shown are producing a correct spray pattern for the applications. While all throttle-body injectors spray a conical pattern, most port fuel injections do not.

FREQUENTLY ASKED QUESTION

How Can the Proper Injector Size Be Determined?

Most people want to increase the output of fuel to increase engine performance. Injector sizing can sometimes be a challenge, especially if the size of injector is not known. In most cases, manufacturers publish the rating of injectors, in pounds of fuel per hour (lb/hr). The rate is figured with the injector held open at 3 bars (43.5 PSI). An important consideration is that larger flow injectors have a higher minimum flow rating. Here is a formula to calculate injector sizing when changing the mechanical characteristics of an engine.

Flow rate = hp × BSFC/number of cylinders × maximum duty cycle (% of on-time of the injectors)

- **hp** is the projected horsepower. Be realistic!
- **BSFC** is brake-specific fuel consumption in pounds per horsepower-hour. Calculated values are used for this, 0.4 to 0.8 pound. In most cases, start on the low side for naturally aspirated engines and the high side for engines with forced induction.
- **Number of cylinders** is actually the number of injectors being used.
- **Maximum duty cycle** is considered at 0.8 (80%). Above this, the injector may overheat, lose consistency, or not work at all.

For example:

5.7 liter V-8 = 240 hp × 0.65/8 cylinders × 8
= 24.37 lb/hr injectors required

flow through the inlet filter screen to the spray nozzle, where it is sprayed in a pattern that varies with application. ● **SEE FIGURE 38–17**. The injector opens the same amount each time it is energized, so the amount of fuel injected depends on the length of time the injector remains open. By angling the director hole plates, the injector sprays fuel more directly at the intake valves, which further atomizes and vaporizes the fuel before it enters the combustion chamber. PFI injectors typically are a top-feed design in which fuel enters the top of the injector and

passes through its entire length to keep it cool before being injected.

Two basic designs of deposit-resistant injectors are used on some engines. One design, manufactured by Bosch, uses a four-hole director/metering plate similar to that used by Multec injectors. Another design, manufactured by Nippondenso, uses an internal upstream orifice in the adjusting tube. It also has a redesigned pintle/seat containing a wider tip opening that tolerates deposit buildup without affecting injector performance.

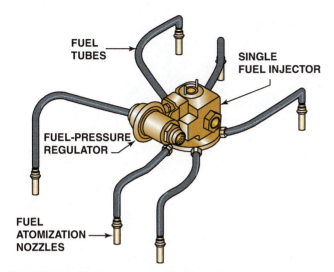

FIGURE 38–18 A central port fuel-injection system.

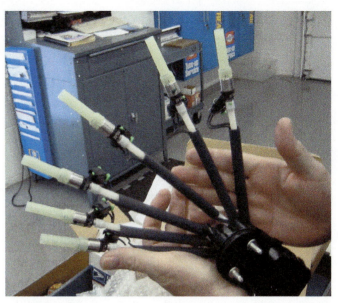

FIGURE 38–19 A factory replacement unit for a CSFI unit that has individual injectors at the ends that go into the intake manifold instead of poppet valves.

CENTRAL PORT INJECTION

A cross between port fuel injection and throttle-body injection, CPI, was introduced in the early 1990s by General Motors. The CPI assembly consists of a single fuel injector, a pressure regulator, and six poppet nozzle assemblies with nozzle tubes. ● SEE FIGURE 38–18. The central sequential fuel injection (CSFI) system has six injectors in place of just one used on the CPI unit.

When the injector is energized, its armature lifts off of the six fuel tube seats and pressurized fuel flows through the nozzle tubes to each poppet nozzle. The increased pressure causes each poppet nozzle ball to also lift from its seat, allowing fuel to flow from the nozzle. This hybrid injection system combines the single injector of a TBI system with the equalized fuel distribution of a PFI system. It eliminates the individual fuel rail while allowing more efficient manifold tuning than is otherwise possible with a TBI system. Newer versions use six individual solenoids to fire one for each cylinder. ● SEE FIGURE 38–19.

FUEL-INJECTION MODES OF OPERATION

All fuel-injection systems are designed to supply the correct amount of fuel under a wide range of engine operating conditions. These modes of operation include:

Starting (cranking)	Acceleration enrichment
Clear flood	Deceleration enleanment
Idle (run)	Fuel shutoff

STARTING MODE   When the ignition is turned to the start (on) position, the engine cranks and the PCM energizes the fuel-pump relay. The PCM also pulses the injectors on, basing the pulse width on engine speed and engine coolant temperature. The colder the engine, the greater the pulse width. Cranking mode air–fuel ratio varies from about 1.5:1 at –40°F (–40°C) to 14.7:1 at 200°F (93°C).

CLEAR FLOOD MODE   If the engine becomes flooded with too much fuel, the driver can depress the accelerator pedal to greater than 80% to enter the clear flood mode. When the PCM detects that the engine speed is low (usually below 600 RPM) and the throttle-position (TP) sensor voltage is high (WOT), the injector pulse width is greatly reduced or even shut off entirely, depending on the vehicle.

OPEN-LOOP MODE   Open-loop operation occurs during warm-up before the oxygen sensor can supply accurate information to the PCM. The PCM determines injector pulse width based on values from the MAF, MAP, TP, ECT, and IAT sensors.

CLOSED-LOOP MODE   Closed-loop operation is used to modify the base injector pulse width as determined by feedback from the oxygen sensor to achieve proper fuel control.

ACCELERATION ENRICHMENT MODE   During acceleration, the throttle-position (TP) voltage increases, indicating that a richer air–fuel mixture is required. The PCM

What Is Battery Voltage Correction?

Battery voltage correction is a program built into the PCM that causes the injector pulse width to increase if there is a drop in electrical system voltage. Lower battery voltage would cause the fuel injectors to open slower than normal and the fuel pump to run slower. Both of these conditions can cause the engine to run leaner than normal if the battery voltage is low. Because a lean air–fuel mixture can cause the engine to overheat, the PCM compensates for the lower voltage by adding a percentage to the injector pulse width. This richer condition will help prevent serious engine damage. The idle speed is also increased to turn the generator (alternator) faster if low battery voltage is detected.

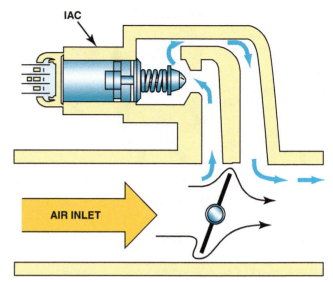

FIGURE 38–20 The small arrows indicate the air bypassing the throttle plate in the closed throttle position. This air is called minimum air. The air flowing through the IAC is the airflow that determines the idle speed.

then supplies a longer injector pulse width and may even supply extra pulses to supply the needed fuel for acceleration.

DECELERATION ENLEANMENT MODE When the engine decelerates, a leaner air–fuel mixture is required to help reduce emissions and to prevent deceleration backfire. If the deceleration is rapid, the injector may be shut off entirely for a short time and then pulsed on enough to keep the engine running.

FUEL SHUTOFF MODE Besides shutting off fuel entirely during periods of rapid deceleration, PCM also shuts off the injector when the ignition is turned off to prevent the engine from continuing to run.

IDLE CONTROL

Older Port fuel-injection systems use an auxiliary air bypass.
● **SEE FIGURE 38–20**. The system is calibrated to maintain engine idle speed at a specified value regardless of engine temperature.

These PFI systems use an **idle air control (IAC)** motor to regulate idle bypass air. The IAC is computer-controlled, and is a stepper motor that regulates the airflow around the throttle.

When the engine stops, most IAC units will retract outward to get ready for the next engine start. When the engine starts, the engine speed is high to provide for proper operation when the engine is cold. Then, as the engine gets warmer, the computer reduces engine idle speed gradually by reducing the number of counts or steps commanded by the IAC.

When the engine is warm and restarted, the idle speed should momentarily increase, then decrease to normal idle speed. This increase and then decrease in engine speed is often called an engine **flare**. If the engine speed does not flare, then the IAC may not be working (it may be stuck in one position).

NOTE: Engines using a throttle actuator control system, or electronic throttle control (no throttle cable) use the throttle actuator to control idle speed; refer to Chapter 40.

STEPPER MOTOR OPERATION A digital output is used to control stepper motors. Stepper motors are DC motors that move in fixed steps or increments from de-energized (no voltage) to fully energized (full voltage). A stepper motor often has as many as 120 steps of motion.

A common use for stepper motors is as an idle air control (IAC) valve, which controls engine idle speeds and prevents stalls due to changes in engine load. When used as an IAC, the stepper motor is usually a reversible DC motor that moves in increments, or steps. The motor moves a shaft back and forth to operate a conical valve. When the conical valve is moved back, more air bypasses the throttle plates and enters the engine, increasing idle speed. As the conical valve moves inward, the idle speed decreases.

When using a stepper motor that is controlled by the PCM, it is very easy for the PCM to keep track of the position of the stepper motor. By counting the number of steps that have been sent to the stepper motor, the PCM can determine the relative position of the stepper motor. While the PCM does not actually receive a feedback signal from the stepper motor, it does know how many steps forward or backward the motor should have moved.

A typical stepper motor uses a permanent magnet and two electromagnets. Each of the two electromagnetic windings is controlled by the computer. The computer pulses the windings and changes the polarity of the windings to cause the armature of the stepper motor to rotate 90 degrees at a time. Each 90-degree pulse is recorded by the computer as a "count" or "step"; therefore, the name given to this type of motor. ● **SEE FIGURE 38–21**.

Idle airflow in a TBI system travels through a passage around the throttle and is controlled by a stepper motor. In some applications, an externally mounted permanent magnet motor called the **idle speed control (ISC) motor** mechanically advances the throttle linkage to advance the throttle opening.

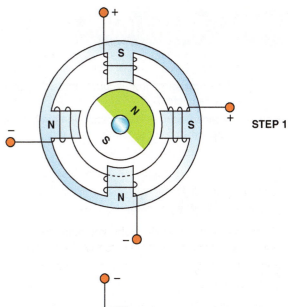

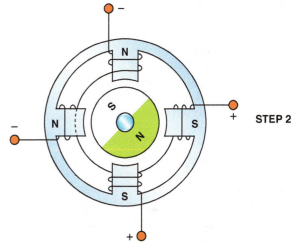

FIGURE 38–21 Most stepper motors use four wires, which are pulsed by the computer to rotate the armature in steps.

SUMMARY

1. A fuel-injection system includes the electric fuel pump and fuel-pump relay, fuel-pressure regulator, and fuel injectors (nozzles).

2. The two types of fuel-injection systems are the throttle-body design and the port fuel-injection design.

3. The two methods of fuel-injection control are the speed-density system, which uses the MAP to measure the load on the engine, and the mass airflow, which uses the MAF sensor to directly measure the amount of air entering the engine.

4. The amount of fuel supplied by fuel injectors is determined by how long they are kept open. This opening time is called the pulse width and is measured in milliseconds.

5. The fuel-pressure regulator is usually located on the fuel return on return-type fuel-injection systems.

6. TBI-type fuel-injection systems do not use a vacuum-controlled fuel-pressure regulator, whereas many port fuel-injection systems use a vacuum-controlled regulator to monitor equal pressure drop across the injectors.

7. Other fuel designs include the electronic returnless, the mechanical returnless, and the demand delivery systems.

REVIEW QUESTIONS

1. What are the two basic types of fuel-injection systems?
2. What is the purpose of the vacuum-controlled (biased) fuel-pressure regulator?
3. How many sensors are used to determine the base pulse width on a speed-density system?
4. How many sensors are used to determine the base pulse width on a mass airflow system?
5. What are the three types of returnless fuel-injection systems?

CHAPTER QUIZ

1. Technician A says that the fuel-pump relay is usually controlled by the PCM. Technician B says that a TBI injector squirts fuel above the throttle plate. Which technician is correct?
   a. Technician A only
   b. Technician B only
   c. Both Technicians A and B
   d. Neither Technician A nor B

2. Why are some fuel rails rectangular in shape?
   a. Increases fuel pressure
   b. Helps keep air out of the injectors
   c. Reduces noise
   d. Increases the speed of the fuel through the fuel rail

3. Which fuel-injection system uses the MAP sensor as the primary sensor to determine the base pulse width?
   a. Speed density
   b. Mass airflow
   c. Demand delivery
   d. Mechanical returnless

4. Why is a vacuum line attached to a fuel-pressure regulator on many port fuel-injected engines?
   a. To draw fuel back into the intake manifold through the vacuum hose
   b. To create an equal pressure drop across the injectors
   c. To raise the fuel pressure at idle
   d. To lower the fuel pressure under heavy engine load conditions to help improve fuel economy

5. Which sensor has the greatest influence on injector pulse width besides the MAF sensor?
   a. IAT
   b. BARO
   c. ECT
   d. TP

6. Technician A says that the port fuel-injection injectors operate using 5 volts from the computer. Technician B says that sequential fuel injectors all use a different wire color on the injectors. Which technician is correct?
   a. Technician A only
   b. Technician B only
   c. Both Technicians A and B
   d. Neither Technician A nor B

7. Which type of port fuel-injection system uses a fuel-temperature and/or fuel-pressure sensor?
   a. All port fuel-injected engines
   b. TBI units only
   c. Electronic returnless systems
   d. Demand delivery systems

8. Dampeners are used on some fuel rails to _____.
   a. Increase the fuel pressure in the rail
   b. Reduce (decrease) the fuel pressure in the rail
   c. Reduce noise
   d. Trap dirt and keep it away from the injectors

9. Where is the fuel-pressure regulator located on a vacuum-biased port fuel-injection system?
   a. In the tank
   b. At the inlet of the fuel rail
   c. At the outlet of the fuel rail
   d. Near or on the fuel filter

10. What type of device is used in a typical idle air control?
    a. DC motor
    b. Stepper motor
    c. Pulsator-type actuator
    d. Solenoid

After studying this chapter, the reader should be able to:

1. Explain how a gasoline direct-injection system works.

2. Describe the differences between port fuel-injection and gasoline direct-injection systems.

3. List the various modes of operation of a gasoline direct-injection system.

This chapter will help you prepare for Engine Repair (A8) ASE certification test content area "C" (Fuel, Air Induction, and Exhaust Systems Diagnosis and Repair).

Gasoline direct injection (GDI) 580

Homogeneous mode 583

Spark ignition direct injection (SIDI) 580

Stratified mode 583

GM Service Technical College topics covered in this chapter are:

1. Identify and describe the characteristics and features of the SIDI fuel-injection system. (16044.20D)

2. Identify and describe the operation of the SIDI fuel-injection system.

3. Identify and describe service procedures for the SIDI fuel-injection system.

4. Perform spark-ignited direct injection (SIDI) system diagnostics.

DIRECT FUEL INJECTION

Several vehicle manufacturers including General Motors are using **gasoline direct injection (GDI)** systems, which General Motors refers to as a **spark ignition direct injection (SIDI)** system. A direct-injection system sprays high-pressure fuel, up to 2900 PSI, into the combustion chamber as the piston approaches the top of the compression stroke. With the combination of high-pressure swirl injectors and modified combustion chamber, almost instantaneous vaporization occurs. This combined with a higher compression ratio allows a direct-injected engine to operate using a leaner-than-normal air–fuel ratio, which results in improved fuel economy with higher power output and reduced exhaust emissions. ● **SEE FIGURE 39–1.**

ADVANTAGES OF GASOLINE DIRECT INJECTION
The use of direct injection compared to port fuel injection has many advantages including the following:

- Improved fuel economy due to reduced pumping losses and heat loss
- Allows a higher compression ratio for higher engine efficiency
- Allows the use of lower-octane gasoline
- The volumetric efficiency is higher
- Less need for extra fuel for acceleration
- Improved cold starting and throttle response
- Allows the use of greater percentage of EGR to reduce exhaust emissions
- Up to 25% improvement in fuel economy
- 12 to 15% reduction in exhaust emissions

DISADVANTAGES OF GASOLINE DIRECT INJECTION

- Higher cost due to high-pressure pump and injectors
- More components compared with port fuel injection
- Due to the high compression, a NO_x storage catalyst is sometimes required to meet emission standards, especially in Europe.
- Uses up to six operating modes depending on engine load and speed, which requires more calculations to be performed by the powertrain control module (PCM).

FIGURE 39–1 A gasoline direct-injection system places the injectors in the cylinder head and injects fuel under high pressure directly into the combustion chamber. (*Corvette LT1, Courtesy of General Motors*)

FIGURE 39–2 A gasoline direct-injection system uses a specially shaped piston and a high pressure fuel injector (*2.0L VVT DI Turbo LHU, Courtesy of General Motors*)

DIRECT-INJECTION FUEL DELIVERY SYSTEM

LOW-PRESSURE SUPPLY PUMP The fuel pump in the fuel tank supplies fuel to the high-pressure fuel pump at a pressure of approximately 60 PSI. The fuel filter is located in the fuel tank and is part of the fuel pump assembly. It is not usually serviceable as a separate component; the engine control

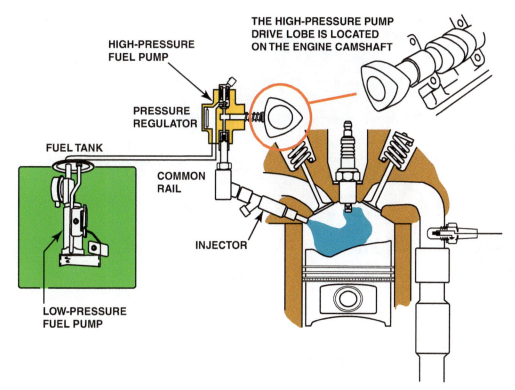

FIGURE 39–3 A typical direct-injection system uses two pumps—one low-pressure electric pump in the fuel tank and the other a high-pressure pump driven by the camshaft. The high pressure fuel system operates at a pressure as low as 500 PSI during light load conditions and as high as 2900 PSI under heavy loads.

module (ECM) controls the output of the high-pressure pump, which has a range between 500 PSI (3,440 kPa) and 2900 PSI (15,200 kPa) during engine operation. ● **SEE FIGURE 39–3.** A fuel pulse dampener is used to dampen fuel-pump pressure pulsations.

NOTE: There may be an audible clicking noise from the fuel pulse dampener during idle.

HIGH-PRESSURE PUMP In a General Motors system, the engine control module (ECM) controls the output of the high-pressure pump, which has a range between 500 PSI (3,440 kPa) and 2900 PSI (15,200 kPa) during engine operation. The high-pressure fuel pump connects to the pump in the fuel tank through the low-pressure fuel line. The pump consists of a single-barrel piston pump, which is driven by the engine camshaft. The pump plunger rides on a three-lobed cam on the camshaft. The high-pressure pump is cooled and lubricated by the fuel itself. ● SEE FIGURE 39–4.

HIGH PRESSURE FUEL LINE There is a high-pressure fuel line that runs from the high-pressure pump to the fuel rail. This line is made of stainless steel and must be replaced whenever it is removed. In addition, when installing the fuel

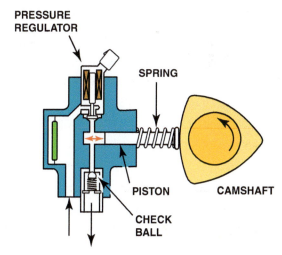

FIGURE 39–4 A typical camshaft-driven high-pressure pump used to increase fuel pressure to 2000 PSI or higher.

line, a silicone-free lubricant, such as motor oil, must be used to lubricate the fittings before installation.

CAUTION: Do NOT "crack" open the high-pressure fuel line with the engine cranking or running. Any fuel that flows out will be at high pressure, which can cause serious injury to skin and eyes. Always depressurize the fuel system before removing components that are under high fuel pressure.

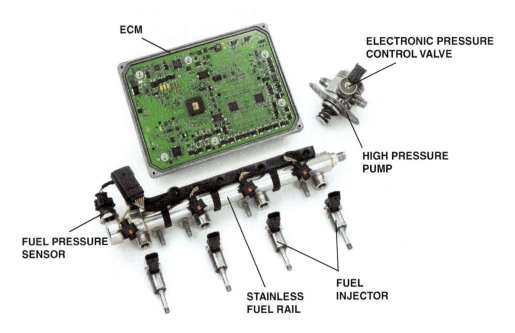

ECM

ELECTRONIC PRESSURE
CONTROL VALVE

HIGH PRESSURE
PUMP

FUEL PRESSURE
SENSOR

FUEL
INJECTOR

STAINLESS
FUEL RAIL

FIGURE 39–5 The main components of a spark-ignited direct injection (SIDI) fuel injection system. (*Courtesy of General Motors*)

FUEL RAIL   The fuel rail stores the fuel from the high-pressure pump and stores high-pressure fuel for use to each injector. All injectors get the same pressure fuel from the fuel rail.

FUEL PRESSURE REGULATOR   An electric pressure-control valve is installed between the pump inlet and outlet valves. The fuel rail pressure sensor connects to the PCM with three wires:

- 5 volt reference
- Ground
- Signal

The sensor signal provides an analog signal to the PCM that varies in voltage as fuel rail pressure changes. Low pressure results in a low-voltage signal and high pressure results in a high-voltage signal.

The PCM uses internal drivers to control the power feed and ground for the pressure control valve. When both PCM drivers are deactivated, the inlet valve is held open by spring pressure. This causes the high-pressure fuel pump to default to low-pressure mode. The fuel from the high-pressure fuel pump flows through a line to the fuel rail and injectors. ● **SEE FIGURE 39–5.**

GASOLINE DIRECT-INJECTION FUEL INJECTORS

Each high-pressure fuel injector assembly is an electrically magnetic injector mounted in the cylinder head. In the GDI system, the PCM controls each fuel injector with 50 to 90 volts (usually 60 to 70 volts), depending on the system, which is created by a boost capacitor in the PCM. During the high-voltage boost phase, the capacitor is discharged through an injector, allowing for initial injector opening. The injector is then held open with 12 volts. The high-pressure fuel injector has a small slit or six precision-machined holes that generate the desired spray pattern. The injector also has an extended tip to allow for cooling from a water jacket in the cylinder head. **SEE FIGURE 39–6.**

● **SEE CHART 39–1** for an overview of the differences between a port fuel-injection system and a gasoline direct-injection system.

FIGURE 39–6 Close-up view of a SIDI fuel injector. (*Courtesy of General Motors*)

PORT FUEL-INJECTION SYSTEM COMPARED WITH GDI SYSTEM		
	PORT FUEL INJECTION	GASOLINE DIRECT INJECTION
Fuel pressure	35–60 PSI	Lift pump—50–60 PSI High-pressure pump— 500–2900 PSI
Injection pulse width at idle	1.5–3.5 ms	About 0.4 ms (400 µs)
Injector resistance	12–16 ohms	1–3 ohms
Injector voltage	6 V for low-resistance injectors, 12 V for most injectors	50–90 V
Number of injections per event	One	1–3
Engine compression ratio	8:1–11:1	11:1–13:1

CHART 39–1

A comparison chart showing the major differences between a port fuel-injection system and a gasoline direct-injection system.

MODES OF OPERATION

The two basic modes of operation include:

1. **Stratified mode**. In this mode of operation, the air–fuel mixture is richer around the spark plug than it is in the rest of the cylinder.

2. **Homogeneous mode**. In this mode of operation, the air–fuel mixture is the same throughout the cylinder.

There are variations of these modes that can be used to fine-tune the air–fuel mixture inside the cylinder. For example, Bosch, a supplier to many vehicle manufacturers, uses six modes of operation including:

- **Homogeneous mode.** In this mode, the injector is pulsed one time to create an even air–fuel mixture in the cylinder. The injection occurs during the intake stroke. This mode is used during high-speed and/or high-torque conditions.

- **Homogeneous lean mode.** Similar to the homogeneous mode except that the overall air–fuel mixture is slightly lean for better fuel economy. The injection occurs during the intake stroke. This mode is used under steady, light-load conditions.

- **Stratified mode.** In this mode of operation, the injection occurs just before the spark occurs resulting in lean combustion, reducing fuel consumption.

- **Homogeneous stratified mode.** In this mode, there are two injections of fuel:

  - The first injection is during the intake stroke.

  - The second injection is during the compression stroke.

  As a result of these double injections, the rich air–fuel mixture around the spark plug is ignited first. Then, the rich mixture ignites the leaner mixture. The advantages of this mode include lower exhaust emissions than the stratified mode and less fuel consumption than the homogeneous lean mode.

- **Homogeneous knock protection mode.** The purpose of this mode is to reduce the possibility of spark knock from occurring under heavy loads at low engine speeds. There are two injections of fuel:

  - The first injection occurs on the intake stroke.

  - The second injection occurs during the compression stroke with the overall mixture being stoichiometric.

  As a result of this mode, the PCM does not need to retard ignition timing as much to operate knock-free.

- **Stratified catalyst heating mode.** In this mode, there are two injections:

  - The first injection is on the compression stroke just before combustion.

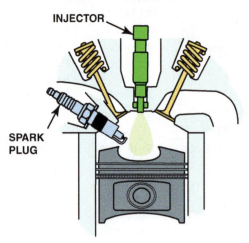

FIGURE 39–7 In this design, the fuel injector is at the top of the cylinder and sprays fuel into the cavity of the piston.

- The second injection is after combustion occurs to heat the exhaust. This mode is used to quickly warm the catalytic converter and to burn the sulfur from the NO_x catalyst.

PISTON TOP DESIGNS

Gasoline direct-injection (GDI) systems use a variety of shapes of piston and injector locations depending on make and model of engine. Three of the most commonly used designs include:

- **Spray-guided combustion.** In this design, the injector is placed in the center of the combustion chamber and injects fuel into the dished-out portion of the piston. The shape of the piston helps guide and direct the mist of fuel in the combustion chamber. ● **SEE FIGURE 39–7.**

- **Swirl combustion.** This design uses the shape of the piston and the position of the injector at the side of the combustion chamber to create turbulence and swirl of the air–fuel mixture. ● **SEE FIGURE 39–8.**

- **Tumble combustion.** Depending on when the fuel is injected into the combustion chamber helps determine how the air–fuel mixture is moved or tumbled. ● **SEE FIGURE 39–9.**

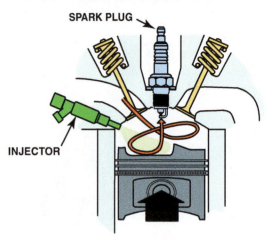

FIGURE 39–8 The side injector combines with the shape of the piston to create a swirl as the piston moves up on the compression stroke.

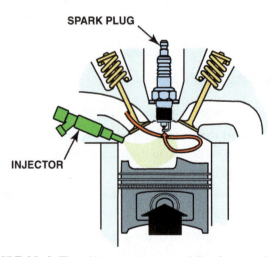

FIGURE 39–9 The piston creates a tumbling force as it moves upward.

GASOLINE DIRECT-INJECTION SERVICE

NOISE ISSUES Gasoline direct-injection systems operate at high pressure and the injectors can often be heard with the engine running and the hood open. This noise can be a customer concern because the clicking sound is similar to noisy valves. If a noise issue is the customer concern, check the following:

- Check a similar vehicle to determine if the sound is louder or more noticeable than normal.

- Check that nothing under the hood is touching the fuel rail. If another line or hose is in contact with the fuel rail, the sound of the injectors clicking can be transmitted throughout the engine, making the sound more noticeable.

- Check for any technical service bulletins (TSBs) that may include new clips or sound insulators to help reduce the noise.

CARBON ISSUES   Carbon is often an issue in engines equipped with gasoline direct-injection systems. Carbon can affect engine operation by accumulating in two places:

- **On the injector itself.** Because the injector tip is in the combustion chamber, fuel residue can accumulate on the injector, reducing its ability to provide the proper spray pattern and amount of fuel. ● **SEE FIGURE 39–10.**

- **The backside of the intake valve.** This is a common place for fuel residue and carbon to accumulate on engines equipped with gasoline direct injection. The accumulation of carbon on the intake valve can become so severe that the engine will start and idle, but lack power to accelerate the vehicle. The carbon deposits restrict the airflow into the cylinder enough to decrease engine power.

CARBON CLEANING.   Most experts recommend the use of Techron®, a fuel system dispersant, to help keep carbon from accumulating. The use of a dispersant every six months or every 6,000 miles has proven to help prevent injector and intake valve deposits.

If the lack of power is discovered and there are no stored diagnostic trouble codes, a conventional carbon cleaning procedure will likely restore power if the intake valves are coated.

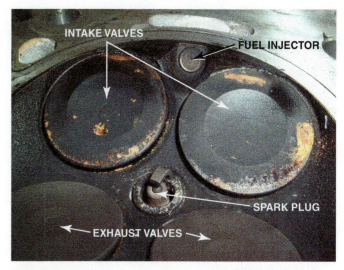

FIGURE 39–10 There may be a driveability issue because the gasoline direct-injection injector is exposed to combustion carbon and fuel residue.

LOW PRESSURE SIDE SERVICE   System service and the fuel-pressure relief procedure for the low-pressure side of the SIDI system is the same as with standard fuel-injection systems.

HIGH PRESSURE SIDE SERVICE   Before servicing any component on the high-pressure side of the system, the pressure must be relieved. There are two methods for relieving high pressure side fuel pressure:

Scan tool available

- Using Tech 2 or GDS 2, command the fuel pump relay OFF, allowing the low pressure fuel pump to shut off.

- Start the vehicle and allow the engine to idle until the engine stops. The engine will stop in approximately 20 to 30 seconds.

- Turn the ignition OFF.

- Using the scan tool, verify that there is little to no fuel pressure, if there is still fuel pressure, repeat step 2.

Scan tool unavailable

- Wait at least two hours after the engine has been run.

- Cover the high-pressure fitting with a shop towel and loosen the fitting.

1. A gasoline direct-injection system uses a fuel injector that delivers a short squirt of fuel directly into the combustion chamber rather than in the intake manifold, near the intake valve on a port fuel-injection system.

2. The advantages of using gasoline direct injection instead of port fuel injection include:
   • Improved fuel economy
   • Reduced exhaust emissions
   • Greater engine power

3. Some of the disadvantages of gasoline direct-injection systems compared with a port fuel-injection system include:
   • Higher cost
   • The need for NO_x storage catalyst in some applications
   • More components

4. The operating pressure can vary from as low as 500 PSI during some low-demand conditions to as high as 2900 PSI.

5. The fuel injectors are open for a very short period of time and are pulsed using a 50 to 90 volt pulse from a capacitor circuit.

6. GDI systems can operate in many modes, which are separated into the two basic modes:
   • Stratified mode
   • Homogeneous mode

7. GDI does create a louder clicking noise from the fuel injectors than port fuel-injection injectors.

8. Carbon deposits on the injector and the backside of the intake valve are a common problem with engines equipped with gasoline direct-injection systems.

9. Relieve fuel pressure before disconnecting any GDI fuel system components.

REVIEW QUESTIONS

1. What are two advantages of gasoline direct injection compared with port fuel injection?

2. What are two disadvantages of gasoline direct injection compared with port fuel injection?

3. How is the fuel delivery system different from a port fuel-injection system?

4. What are the basic modes of operation of a GDI system?

CHAPTER QUIZ

1. Where is the fuel injected in an engine equipped with gasoline direct injection?
   a. Into the intake manifold near the intake valve
   b. Directly into the combustion chamber
   c. Above the intake port
   d. In the exhaust port

2. The fuel pump inside the fuel tank on a vehicle equipped with gasoline direct injection produces about what fuel pressure?
   a. 5 to 10 PSI
   b. 10 to 20 PSI
   c. 20 to 40 PSI
   d. 50 to 60 PSI

3. The high-pressure fuel pumps used in gasoline direct-injection (GDI) systems are powered by _____.
   a. Electricity (DC motor)
   b. Electricity (AC motor)
   c. The camshaft
   d. The crankshaft

4. The high-pressure fuel pump pressure is regulated by using _____.
   a. An electric pressure-control valve
   b. A vacuum-biased regulator
   c. A mechanical regulator at the inlet to the fuel rail
   d. A non-vacuum biased regulator

5. The fuel injectors operate under a fuel pressure of about _____.
   a. 35 to 45 PSI
   b. 90 to 150 PSI
   c. 500 to 2900 PSI
   d. 2000 to 5000 PSI

6. The fuel injectors used on a gasoline direct-injection system are pulsed on using what voltage?
   a. 12 to 14 volt
   b. 50 to 90 volt
   c. 100 to 110 volt
   d. 200 to 220 volt

7. Which mode of operation results in a richer air–fuel mixture near the spark plug?
   a. Stoichiometric
   b. Homogeneous
   c. Stratified
   d. Knock protection

8. After removing the high-pressure fuel line, it must be _____ before being reinstalled.
   a. Polished
   b. Cleaned with oil
   c. Replaced with a new line
   d. Re-flared

9. The fuel pressure dampener is located in the _____ portion of the fuel system.
   a. Low pressure
   b. High pressure
   c. Mid-pressure
   d. Regulator

10. A lack of power from an engine equipped with gasoline direct injection could be due to _____.
    a. Noisy injectors
    b. Carbon on the injectors
    c. Carbon on the intake valves
    d. Both b and c

chapter 40

THROTTLE ACTUATOR CONTROL SYSTEM

LEARNING OBJECTIVES

After studying this chapter, the reader should be able to:

1. Describe the purpose and function of the throttle actuator control (TAC) system.
2. Explain how a throttle actuator control system works.
3. List the parts of a typical throttle actuator control system.
4. Describe how to diagnose faults in a throttle actuator control system.
5. Explain how to service a throttle actuator system.

This chapter will help you prepare for ASE content area "E" (Computerized Engine Controls Diagnosis and Repair).

KEY TERMS

Accelerator pedal position (APP) sensor 588
Coast-down stall 594
Default position 589
Drive-by-wire 588
Fail safe position 589
Neutral position 589
Servomotor 589
Throttle position (TP) sensor 588
Throttle actuator control (TAC) 588

GM STC OBJECTIVES

GM Service Technical College topics covered in this chapter are:

1. Identify air management system types. (16044.21W1)
2. Diagnose air management system (electronic throttle actuator control) electronic control using Tech 2 and DMM.

THROTTLE ACTUATOR CONTROL (TAC) SYSTEM

ADVANTAGES OF TAC The absence of any mechanical linkage between the throttle pedal and the throttle body requires the use of an electric actuator motor. The throttle actuator control system has the following advantages over the conventional cable:

- Eliminates the mechanical throttle cable, thereby reducing the number of moving parts.

- Eliminates the need for cruise control actuators and controllers.

- Helps reduce engine power for traction control (TC and electronic stability control [ESC] systems).

- Used to delay rapid applications of torque to the transmission/transaxle to help improve driveability and to smooth shifts.

- Helps reduce pumping losses by using the throttle actuator to open at highway speeds with greater fuel economy. The throttle actuator control (TAC) opens the throttle to maintain engine and vehicle speed as the powertrain control module (PCM) leans the air–fuel ratio, retards ignition timing, and introduces additional exhaust gas recirculation (EGR) to reducing pumping losses.

- Used to provide smooth engine operation, especially during rapid acceleration.

- Eliminates the need for an idle air control valve.

The throttle actuator can be called **drive-by-wire,** but most vehicle manufacturers use the term **throttle actuator control (TAC)** or **electronic throttle control (ETC)** to describe the system that opens the throttle valve electrically.

PARTS INVOLVED The typical TAC system includes the following components:

1. **Accelerator pedal position (APP) sensor**, also called *accelerator pedal sensor (APS)*
2. The throttle actuator (servomotor), which is part of the throttle actuator body
3. A **throttle position (TP) sensor**
4. An electronic control unit, which is usually the PCM

● **SEE FIGURE 40–1.**

FIGURE 40–1 The throttle pedal is connected to the accelerator pedal position (APP) sensor. The throttle actuator body includes a throttle position sensor to provide throttle angle feedback to the vehicle computer. Early systems used a throttle actuator control (TAC) module to operate the throttle blade (plate). (*Courtesy of General Motors*)

NORMAL OPERATION OF THE TAC SYSTEM

Driving a vehicle equipped with a throttle actuator control system is about the same as driving a vehicle with a conventional mechanical throttle cable and throttle valve. However, the driver may notice some differences, which are to be considered normal. These normal conditions include:

- The engine may not increase above idle speed when depressing the accelerator pedal when the gear selector is in PARK.

- If the engine speed does increase when the accelerator is depressed with the transmission in PARK or NEUTRAL, the engine speed will likely be limited to less than 2000 RPM.

- While accelerating rapidly, there is often a slight delay before the engine responds. ● **SEE FIGURE 40–2.**

- While at cruise speed, the accelerator pedal may or may not cause the engine speed to increase if the accelerator pedal is moved slightly.

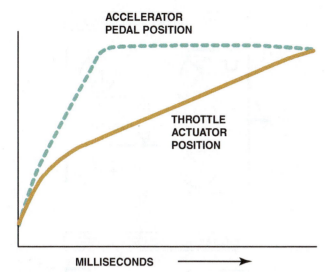

FIGURE 40–2 The opening of the throttle plate can be delayed as long as 30 milliseconds (0.030 sec) to allow time for the amount of fuel needed to catch up to the opening of the throttle plate.

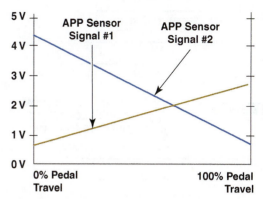

FIGURE 40–3 A typical accelerator pedal position (APP) sensor, showing two different output voltage signals that are used by the PCM to determine accelerator pedal position. Two (or three in some applications) are used as a double check because this is a safety-related sensor. (*Courtesy of General Motors*)

ACCELERATOR PEDAL POSITION SENSOR

The accelerator pedal position sensor uses two and sometimes three separate sensors, which act together to give accurate accelerator pedal position information to the controller, but also are used to check that the sensor is working properly. They function just like a throttle position sensor, and two are needed for proper system function. One APP sensor output signal increases as the pedal is depressed and the other signal decreases. The controller compares the signals with a look-up table to determine the pedal position. Using two or three signals improves redundancy should one sensor fail, and allows the PCM to quickly detect a malfunction. When three sensors are used, the third signal can either decrease or increase with pedal position, but its voltage range will still be different from the other two. ● **SEE FIGURE 40–3.**

THROTTLE BODY ASSEMBLY

The throttle body assembly contains the following components:

- Throttle plate
- Electric actuator DC motor

- Dual throttle position (TP) sensors
- Gears used to multiply the torque of the DC motor
- Springs used to hold the throttle plate in the default location

THROTTLE PLATE AND SPRING The throttle plate is held slightly open by a concentric clock spring. The spring applies a force that will close the throttle plate if power is lost to the actuator motor. The spring is also used to open the throttle plate slightly from the fully closed position.

THROTTLE ACTUATOR MOTOR The actuator is a DC electric motor and is often called a **servomotor.** The throttle plate is held in a **default position** by a spring inside the throttle body assembly. This partially open position, also called the **neutral position** or the **fail safe position,** is about 16% to 20% open. This default position varies depending on the vehicle and usually results in an engine speed of 1200 to 1500 RPM.

- The throttle plate is driven closed to achieve speeds lower than the default position, such as idle speed.
- The throttle plate is driven open to achieve speeds higher than the default position, such as during acceleration. ● **SEE FIGURE 40–4.**

The throttle plate motor is driven by a bidirectional pulse-width modulated (PWM) signal from the PCM or throttle actuator control module using an H-bridge circuit. ● **SEE FIGURE 40–5.**

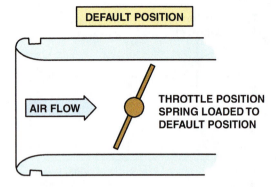

DEFAULT POSITION

AIR FLOW

THROTTLE POSITION SPRING LOADED TO DEFAULT POSITION

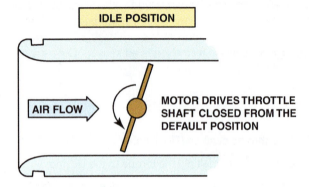

IDLE POSITION

AIR FLOW

MOTOR DRIVES THROTTLE SHAFT CLOSED FROM THE DEFAULT POSITION

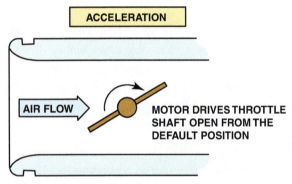

ACCELERATION

AIR FLOW

MOTOR DRIVES THROTTLE SHAFT OPEN FROM THE DEFAULT POSITION

FIGURE 40–4 The default position for the throttle plate is in slightly open position. The servomotor then is used to close it for idle and open it during acceleration.

The H-bridge circuit is controlled by the PCM by:

- Reversing the polarity of power and ground brushes to the DC motor
- Pulse-width modulating (PWM) the current through the motor

The PCM monitors the position of the throttle from the two throttle position (TP) sensors. The PCM then commands the throttle plate to the desired position. ● **SEE FIGURE 40–6.**

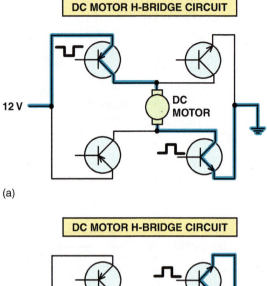

DC MOTOR H-BRIDGE CIRCUIT

12 V

DC MOTOR

(a)

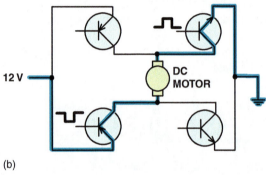

DC MOTOR H-BRIDGE CIRCUIT

12 V

DC MOTOR

(b)

FIGURE 40–5 (a) An H-bridge circuit is used to control the direction of the DC electric motor of the throttle actuator control unit. (b) To reverse the direction of operation, the polarity of the current through the motor is reversed.

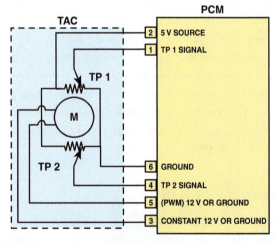

FIGURE 40–6 Schematic of a typical throttle actuator control (TAC) system. Note that terminal #5 is always pulse-width modulated and that terminal #3 is always constant, but both power and ground are switched to change the direction of the motor.

THROTTLE POSITION (TP) SENSOR

Two throttle position sensors are used in the throttle body assembly to provide throttle position signals to the PCM. Two sensors are used as a fail-safe measure and for diagnosis. There are two types of TP sensors used in throttle actuator control systems: potentiometers and Hall-effect.

THREE-WIRE POTENTIOMETER SENSORS These sensors use a 5 volt reference from the PCM and produce an analog (variable) voltage signal that is proportional to the

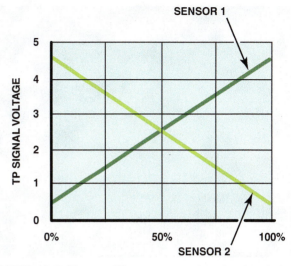

FIGURE 40–7 The two TP sensors used on the throttle body of a throttle actuator body assembly produce opposite voltage signals as the throttle is opened. The total voltage of both combined at any throttle plate position is 5 volts.

throttle plate position. The two sensors produce opposite signals as the throttle plate opens:

- One sensor starts at low voltage (about 0.5 volt) and increases as the throttle plate is opened.
- The second sensor starts at a higher voltage (about 4.5 volt) and produces a lower voltage as the throttle plate is opened. ● **SEE FIGURE 40–7.**

HALL-EFFECT TP SENSORS Some vehicle manufacturers use a non-contact Hall-effect throttle position sensor. Because there is no physical contact, this type of sensor is less likely to fail due to wear.

DIAGNOSIS OF THROTTLE ACTUATOR CONTROL SYSTEMS

FAULT MODE Throttle actuator control systems can have faults like any other automatic system. Due to the redundant sensors in accelerator pedal position sensors and throttle position sensor, many faults result in a "limp home" situation instead of a total failure. The limp home mode is also called the "fail-safe mode" and indicates the following actions performed by the PCM.

- Engine speed is limited to the default speed (about 1200 to 1600 RPM).
- There is slow or no response when the accelerator pedal is depressed.

(a)

(b)

FIGURE 40–8 (a) A "reduced power" warning light indicates a fault with the throttle actuator control system on some General Motors vehicles. (b) A symbol showing an engine with an arrow pointing down is used on some General Motors vehicles to indicate a fault with the throttle actuator control system.

? FREQUENTLY ASKED QUESTION

How Do You Calibrate a New APP Sensor?

Whenever an accelerator pedal position (APP) sensor is replaced, it should be calibrated before it will work correctly. Always check service information for the exact procedure to follow after APP sensor replacement. Here is a typical example of the procedure:

STEP 1 Make sure accelerator pedal is fully released.

STEP 2 Turn the ignition switch on (engine off) and wait at least 2 seconds.

STEP 3 Turn the ignition switch off and wait at least 10 seconds.

STEP 4 Turn the ignition switch on (engine on) and wait at least 2 seconds.

STEP 5 Turn the ignition switch off and wait at least 10 seconds.

- The cruise control system is disabled.
- A diagnostic trouble code (DTC) is set.
- A TAC warning lamp on the dash will light. The warning lamp may be labeled differently, depending on the vehicle manufacturer. For example:

- **General Motors vehicle**—Reduced power lamp
  (● **SEE FIGURE 40–8**)
- **Ford**—Wrench symbol (amber or green)
  (● **SEE FIGURE 40–9**)
- **Chrysler**—Red lightning bolt symbol
  (● **SEE FIGURE 40–10**)

- The engine will run and can be driven slowly. This limp-in mode operation allows the vehicle to be driven off of the road and to a safe location.

The TAC may enter the limp-in mode if any of the following has occurred:

- Low battery voltage has been detected
- PCM failure
- One TP and the MAP sensor have failed
- Both TP sensors have failed
- The TAC actuator motor has failed
- The TAC throttle spring has failed

VACUUM LEAKS The throttle actuator control system is able to compensate for many vacuum leaks. A vacuum leak at the intake manifold, for example, will allow air into the engine that is not measured by the mass airflow sensor. The TAC system will simply move the throttle as needed to achieve the proper idle speed to compensate for the leak.

FIGURE 40–9 A wrench symbol warning lamp on a Ford vehicle. The symbol can also be green.

FIGURE 40–10 A symbol used on a Chrysler vehicle indicating a fault with the throttle actuator control.

DIAGNOSTIC PROCEDURE If a fault occurs in the TAC system, check service information for the specified procedure to follow for the vehicle being checked. Most vehicle service information includes the following steps:

STEP 1 Verify the customer concern.

STEP 2 Use a factory scan tool or an aftermarket scan tool with original equipment capability and check for diagnostic trouble codes (DTCs).

STEP 3 If there are stored diagnostic trouble codes, follow service information instructions for diagnosing the system.

STEP 4 If there are no stored diagnostic trouble codes, check scan tool data for possible fault areas in the system.

SCAN TOOL DATA Scan data related to the throttle actuator control system can be confusing. Typical data and their meaning include:

- **APP indicated angle.** The scan tool will display a percentage ranging from 0% to 100%. When the throttle is released, the indicated angle should be 0%. When the throttle is depressed to wide open, the reading should indicate 100%.

- **TP desired angle.** The scan tool will display a percentage ranging from 0% to 100%. This represents the desired throttle angle as commanded by the driver of the vehicle.

- **TP indicated angle.** The TP indicated angle is the angle of the measured throttle opening and it should agree with the TP desired angle.

- **TP sensors 1 and 2.** The scan tool will display "agree" or "disagree." If the PCM or throttle actuator control (TAC) module receives a voltage signal from one of the TP sensors that is not in proper relationship with the other TP sensor, the scan tool will display *disagree*.

TAC THROTTLE SWEEP TEST

On some vehicles, the operation of the throttle actuator control can be tested using a factory or factory-level scan tool. To perform this test, use the "throttle sweep test" procedure as shown on the scan tool. An assistant is needed to check that the throttle plate is moving as the accelerator pedal is depressed. This test cannot be done without a scan tool because the PCM does not normally allow the throttle plate to be moved unless the engine is running.

SERVICING THROTTLE ACTUATOR SYSTEMS

TAC-RELATED PERFORMANCE ISSUES The only service that a throttle actuator control system may require is a cleaning of the throttle body. Throttle body cleaning is a routine service procedure on port fuel-injected engines and is still needed when the throttle is being opened by an electric motor

A High Idle Problem

The owner of a TAC equipped vehicle complained that the engine would idle at over 1200 RPM compared with a normal 600 to 700 RPM. The vehicle would also not accelerate. Using a scan tool, a check for diagnostic trouble codes showed one code: P2101—"TAC motor position performance."

Checking service information led to the inspection of the throttle actuator control throttle body assembly. With the ignition key out of the ignition and the inlet air duct off the throttle body, the technician used a screwdriver to see if the throttle plate would move.

Normal operation—The throttle plate should move and then spring back quickly to the default position.

Abnormal operation—If the throttle plate stays where it is moved or does not return to the default position, there is a fault with the throttle body assembly.
- **SEE FIGURE 40–11.**

Solution: The technician replaced the throttle body assembly with an updated version and proper engine operation was restored. The technician disassembled the old throttle body and found it was corroded inside due to moisture entering the unit through the vent hose. **SEE FIGURE 40–12.**

FIGURE 40–11 The throttle plate stayed where it was moved, which indicates that there is a problem with the throttle actuator body control assembly.

FIGURE 40–12 A corroded throttle actuator control assembly shown with the cover removed.

rather than a throttle cable tied to a mechanical accelerator pedal. The throttle body may need cleaning if one or more of the following symptoms are present:

- Lower than normal idle speed
- Rough idle
- Engine stalls when coming to a stop (called a **coast-down stall**)

If any of the above conditions exists, a throttle body cleaning will often correct these faults.

CAUTION: Some vehicle manufacturers add a nonstick coating to the throttle assembly and warn that cleaning could remove this protective coating. Always follow the vehicle manufacturer's recommended procedures.

THROTTLE BODY CLEANING PROCEDURE Before attempting to clean a throttle body on an engine equipped with a throttle actuator control system, be sure that the ignition key is out of the vehicle and the ready light is off if working on a hybrid electric vehicle to avoid the possibility of personal injury.

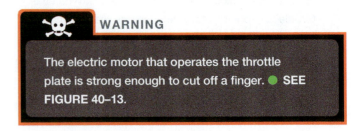

WARNING

The electric motor that operates the throttle plate is strong enough to cut off a finger. **SEE FIGURE 40–13.**

To clean the throttle, perform the following steps:

STEP 1 With the ignition off and the key removed from the ignition, remove the air inlet hose from the throttle body.

STEP 2 Spray throttle body cleaner onto a shop cloth.

STEP 3 Open the throttle body and use the shop cloth to remove the varnish and carbon deposits from the throttle body housing and throttle plate.

CAUTION: Do not spray cleaner into the throttle body assembly. The liquid cleaner could flow into and damage the throttle position (TP) sensors.

STEP 4 Reinstall the inlet hose being sure that there are no air leaks between the hose and the throttle body assembly.

STEP 5 Start the engine and allow the PCM to learn the correct idle. If the idle is not correct, check service information for the specified procedures to follow to perform a throttle relearn.

THROTTLE BODY RELEARN PROCEDURE

The engine control module (ECM) learns the airflow through the throttle body to ensure the correct idle. The learned airflow values are stored within the ECM. These values will continuously change during the life of the vehicle to compensate for reduced airflow in case of throttle body coking. The idle may be unstable or a DTC may set if the learned values do not match the actual airflow.

Anytime the throttle body airflow rate changes, for example due to cleaning or replacing, the values must be relearned. To accelerate the process, the scan tool has the ability to reset all learned values back to zero. A new ECM will also have values set to zero.

SCAN TOOL IDLE LEARN OR IDLE LEARN RESET PROCEDURE

1. With the ignition ON, engine OFF, use the scan tool to perform the Idle Learn or Idle Learn Reset in Configuration/Reset or Module Setup.

2. With the engine idling, observe the scan tool Throttle Body (TB) Idle Airflow Compensation parameter. The TB Idle

FIGURE 40–13 Notice the small motor gear on the left drives a larger plastic gear (black), which then drives the small gear in mesh with the section of a gear attached to the throttle plate. This results in a huge torque increase from the small motor and helps explain why it could be dangerous to insert a finger into the throttle body assembly.

Airflow Compensation value should equal 0 % and the engine should be idling at a normal idle speed.

SERVICE BAY/ON ROAD IDLE LEARN

1. Start and idle the engine in PARK for 3 minutes. The ECM will start to learn the new idle cells and desired RPM (on scan tool) should start to decrease.

2. Turn the ignition OFF for 60 seconds.

3. Start and idle the engine in PARK for 3 minutes.

4. After the 3 minute run time the engine should be idling normally. If the engine idle speed has not been learned the vehicle will need to be driven at speeds above 70 km/h (44 mph) with several decelerations and extended idles.

5. After the drive cycle, the engine should be idling normally. If the engine idle speed has not been learned, turn OFF the ignition for 60 seconds and repeat step 4.

6. Once the engine idle speed has returned to normal, clear DTCs.

SUMMARY

1. Using a throttle actuator control (TAC) system on an engine has many advantages over a conventional method that uses a mechanical cable between the accelerator pedal and the throttle valve.

2. The major components of a throttle actuator control system include:
   - Accelerator pedal position (APP) sensor
   - Throttle actuator control motor and spring
   - Throttle position (TP) sensor
   - Electronic control unit

3. The throttle position (TP) sensor is actually two sensors that share the 5 volt reference from the PCM and produce opposite signals as a redundant check.

4. Limp-in mode is commanded if there is a major fault in the system, which can allow the vehicle to be driven enough to be pulled off the road to safety.

5. The diagnostic procedure for the TAC system includes verifying the customer concern, using a scan tool to check for diagnostic trouble codes, and checking the value of the TP and APP sensors.

6. Servicing the TAC system includes cleaning the throttle body and throttle plate.

7. After replacing the ECM, throttle body, or cleaning the of throttle body, an idle relearn procedure must be performed.

REVIEW QUESTIONS

1. What parts can be deleted if an engine uses a throttle actuator control (TAC) system instead of a conventional accelerator pedal and cable to operate the throttle valve?

2. How can the use of a TAC system improve fuel economy?

3. How is the operation of the throttle different on a system that uses a TAC system compared with a conventional mechanical system?

4. What component parts are included in a TAC system?

5. What is the default or limp-in position of the throttle plate?

6. What dash warning light indicates a fault with the TAC system?

CHAPTER QUIZ

1. The use of a TAC system allows the elimination of all except _____.
   a. Accelerator pedal
   b. Mechanical throttle cable (most systems)
   c. Cruise control actuator
   d. Idle air control

2. To what extent is the throttle plate spring loaded to hold the throttle slightly open?
   a. 3% to 5%   **c.** 16% to 20%
   b. 8% to 10%   **d.** 22% to 28%

3. What type of electric motor is the throttle plate actuator motor?
   a. Stepper motor   **c.** AC motor
   b. DC motor   **d.** Brushless motor

4. The actuator motor is controlled by the PCM through what type of circuit?
   a. Series   **c.** H-bridge
   b. Parallel   **d.** Series-parallel

5. When does the PCM perform a self-test of the TAC system?
   a. During cruise speed when the throttle is steady
   b. During deceleration
   c. During acceleration
   d. When the ignition switch is first rotated to the on position before the engine starts

6. What type is the throttle position sensor used in the throttle body assembly of a TAC system?
   a. A single potentiometer
   b. Two potentiometers that read in the opposite direction
   c. A Hall-effect sensor
   d. Either b or c

7. A green wrench symbol is displayed on the dash. What does this mean?
   a. A fault in the TAC in a Ford vehicle has been detected
   b. A fault in the TAC in a Honda vehicle has been detected

   c. A fault in the TAC in a Chrysler vehicle has been detected
   d. A fault in the TAC in a General Motors vehicle has been detected

8. A technician is checking the operation of the throttle actuator control system by depressing the accelerator pedal with the ignition in the on (run) position (engine off). What is the most likely result if the system is functioning correctly?
   a. The throttle goes to wide open when the accelerator pedal is depressed all the way
   b. No throttle movement
   c. The throttle will open partially but not all of the way
   d. The throttle will perform a self-test by closing and then opening to the default position

9. With the ignition off and the key out of the ignition, what should happen if a technician uses a screwdriver and pushes on the throttle plate in an attempt to open the valve?
   a. Nothing. The throttle should be kept from moving by the motor, which is not energized with the key off.
   b. The throttle should move and stay where it is moved and not go back unless moved back.
   c. The throttle should move, and then spring back to the home position when released.
   d. The throttle should move closed, but not open further than the default position.

10. The throttle body may be cleaned (if recommended by the vehicle manufacturer) if what conditions are occurring?
   a. Coast-down stall
   b. Rough idle
   c. Lower-than-normal idle speed
   d. Any of the above

chapter 41
FUEL-INJECTION SYSTEM DIAGNOSIS AND SERVICE

LEARNING OBJECTIVES

After studying this chapter, the reader should be able to:

1. Explain how to check a fuel-pressure regulator.
2. Describe how to test fuel injectors.
3. Explain how to diagnose electronic fuel-injection problems.
4. Describe how to service the fuel-injection system.

This chapter will help you prepare for Engine Repair (A8) ASE certification test content area "C" (Fuel, Air Induction, and Exhaust Systems Diagnosis and Repair).

KEY TERMS

Active Fuel Injector Tester (AFIT) 606
Graphing multimeter (GMM) 598
IAC counts 600
Idle air control (IAC) 609
Noid light 602
Peak-and-hold injector 608
Pressure transducer 598
Saturation 608

STC OBJECTIVES

GM Service Technical College topics covered in this chapter are:

1. Perform the fuel injector balance test.
2. Perform the fuel injector coil test
3. Describe fuel injector diagnosis and service using General Motors prescribed procedures.

PRESSURE REGULATOR DIAGNOSIS

Many port fuel-injected engines use a vacuum hose connected to the fuel-pressure regulator. At idle, the pressure inside the intake manifold is low (high vacuum). Manifold vacuum is applied above the diaphragm inside the fuel-pressure regulator. This reduces the pressure exerted on the diaphragm and results in a lower, about 10 PSI (69 kPa), fuel pressure applied to the injectors. To test a vacuum-controlled fuel-pressure regulator, follow these steps:

1. Connect a fuel-pressure gauge to monitor the fuel pressure.

2. Locate the fuel-pressure regulator and disconnect the vacuum hose from the regulator.

   NOTE: If gasoline drips out of the vacuum hose when removed from the fuel-pressure regulator, the regulator is defective and will require replacement.

3. With the engine running at idle speed, reconnect the vacuum hose to the fuel-pressure regulator while watching the fuel-pressure gauge. The fuel pressure should drop (about 10 PSI or 69 kPa) when the hose is reattached to the regulator.

4. Using a hand-operated vacuum pump, apply vacuum (20 inches Hg) to the regulator. The regulator should hold vacuum. If the vacuum drops, replace the fuel-pressure regulator. ● **SEE FIGURE 41–1.**

NOTE: Some vehicles do not use a vacuum-regulated fuel-pressure regulator. Many of these vehicles use a regulator located inside the fuel tank that supplies a constant fuel pressure to the fuel injectors.

FUEL-PRESSURE REGULATOR

FIGURE 41–1 If the vacuum hose is removed from the fuel-pressure regulator when the engine is running, the fuel pressure should increase. If it does not increase, then the fuel pump is not capable of supplying adequate pressure or the fuel-pressure regulator is defective. If gasoline is visible in the vacuum hose, the regulator is leaking and should be replaced.

 **TECH TIP**

Pressure Transducer Fuel Pressure Test

Using a **pressure transducer** and a **graphing multimeter (GMM)** or digital storage oscilloscope (DSO) allows the service technician to view the fuel pressure over time. ● **SEE FIGURE 41–2(a).** Note that the fuel pressure dropped from 15 PSI down to 6 PSI on a TBI-equipped vehicle after just one minute. A normal pressure holding capability is shown in ● **FIGURE 41–2(b)** when the pressure dropped only about 10% after 10 minutes on a port fuel-injection system.

DIAGNOSING ELECTRONIC FUEL-INJECTION PROBLEMS USING VISUAL INSPECTION

All fuel-injection systems require the proper amount of clean fuel delivered to the system at the proper pressure and the correct amount of filtered air. The following items should be carefully inspected before proceeding to more detailed tests:

- Check the air filter and replace as needed.
- Check the air induction system for obstructions.
- Check the conditions of all vacuum hoses. Replace any hose that is split, soft (mushy), or brittle.

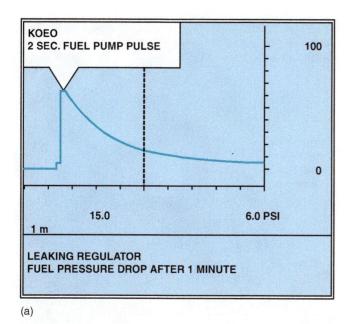

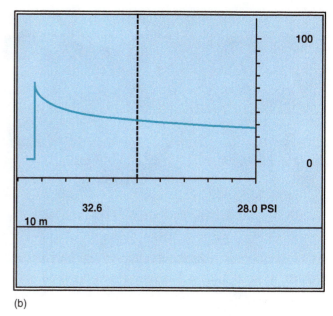

(a)   (b)

FIGURE 41–2 (a) A fuel-pressure graph after key on, engine off (KOEO) on a TBI system. (b) Pressure drop after 10 minutes on a normal port fuel-injection system.

FIGURE 41–3 A clogged PCV system caused the engine oil fumes to be drawn into the air cleaner assembly. This is what the technician discovered during a visual inspection.

 **TECH TIP**

Stethoscope Fuel-Injection Test

A commonly used test for injector operation is to listen to the injector using a stethoscope with the engine operating at idle speed. ● **SEE FIGURE 41–4.** All injectors should produce the same clicking sound. If any injector makes a clunking or rattling sound, it should be tested further or replaced. With the engine still running, place the end of the stethoscope probe to the return line from the fuel-pressure regulator. ● **SEE FIGURE 41–5.** Fuel should be heard flowing back to the fuel tank if the fuel-pump pressure is higher than the fuel-regulator pressure. If no sound of fuel is heard, then either the fuel pump or the fuel-pressure regulator is at fault.

- Check the positive crankcase ventilation (PCV) valve for proper operation or replacement as needed. ● **SEE FIGURE 41–3.**

  NOTE: The use of an incorrect PCV valve can cause a rough idle or stalling.

- Check all fuel-injection electrical connections for corrosion or damage.

- Check for gasoline at the vacuum port of the fuel-pressure regulator if the vehicle is so equipped. Gasoline in the vacuum hose at the fuel-pressure regulator indicates that the regulator is defective and requires replacement.

FIGURE 41–4 All fuel injectors should make the same sound with the engine running at idle speed. A lack of sound indicates a possible electrically open injector or a break in the wiring. A defective computer could also be the cause of a lack of clicking (pulsing) of the injectors.

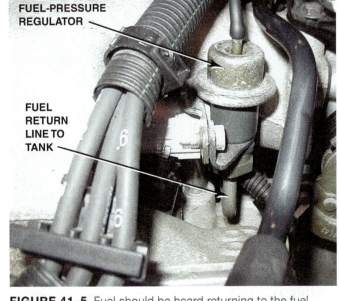

FUEL-PRESSURE REGULATOR

FUEL RETURN LINE TO TANK

FIGURE 41–5 Fuel should be heard returning to the fuel tank at the fuel return line if the fuel-pump and fuel-pressure regulator are functioning correctly.

SCAN TOOL VACUUM LEAK DIAGNOSIS

If a vacuum (air) leak occurs on an engine equipped with a speed-density-type of fuel injection, the extra air would cause the following to occur:

- The idle speed increases due to the extra air just as if the throttle pedal was depressed.
- The MAP sensor reacts to the increased air from the vacuum leak as an additional load on the engine.
- The computer increases the injector pulse width slightly longer due to the signal from the MAP sensor.
- The air–fuel mixture remains unchanged.

- The idle air control (IAC) counts will decrease, thereby attempting to reduce the engine speed to the target idle speed stored in the computer memory. ● SEE FIGURE 41–6.

Therefore, one of the best indicators of a vacuum leak on a speed-density fuel-injection system is to look at the IAC counts or percentage. Normal **IAC counts** or percentage is usually 15 to 25. A reading of less than 5 indicates a vacuum leak.

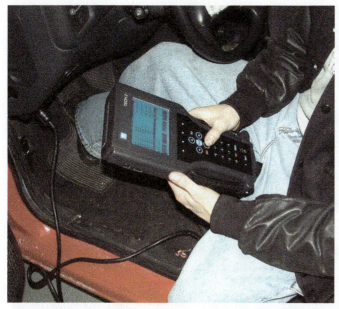

FIGURE 41–6 Using a scan tool to check for IAC counts or percentage as part of a diagnostic routine.

FIGURE 41–7 Checking the fuel pressure using a fuel-pressure gauge connected to the Schrader valve.

If a vacuum leak occurs on an engine equipped with a mass airflow-type fuel-injection system, the extra air causes the following to occur:

- The engine will operate leaner than normal because the extra air has not been measured by the MAF sensor.

- The idle speed will likely be lower due to the leaner-than-normal air–fuel mixture.

- The idle air control (IAC) counts or percentage will often increase in an attempt to return the engine speed to the target speed stored in the computer.

- Short- and long-term fuel trims will be incorrect.

INJECTION SYSTEM DIAGNOSIS

To determine if a port fuel-injection system—including the fuel pump, injectors, and fuel-pressure regulator—is operating correctly, take the following steps:

1. Attach a fuel-pressure gauge to the Schrader valve on the fuel rail. ● **SEE FIGURE 41–7.**

2. Turn the ignition key on or start the engine to build up the fuel-pump pressure (to about 35 PSI to 45 PSI).

3. Wait 20 minutes and observe the fuel pressure retained in the fuel rail and note the PSI reading. The fuel pressure should not drop more than 20 PSI (140 kPa) in 20 minutes. If the drop is less than 20 PSI in 20 minutes, everything is okay; if the drop is *greater,* then there is a possible problem with:

- The check valve in the fuel pump

- Injectors, lines, or fittings

- A fuel-pressure regulator

To determine which unit is defective, perform the following:

- Reenergize the electric fuel pump.

- Clamp the fuel *supply* line, and wait 10 minutes (see CAUTION). If the pressure drop does not occur, replace the fuel pump. If the pressure drop still occurs, continue with the next step.

- Repeat the pressure buildup of the electric pump and clamp the fuel return line. If the pressure drop time is now okay, replace the fuel-pressure regulator.

- If the pressure drop still occurs, one or more of the injectors is leaking. Remove the injectors with the fuel rail and hold over paper. Replace those injectors that drip one or more drops after 10 minutes with pressurized fuel.

CAUTION: Do not clamp plastic fuel lines. Connect shutoff valves to the fuel system to shut off supply and return lines. ● **SEE FIGURE 41–8.**

FIGURE 41–8 Shutoff valves must be used on vehicles equipped with plastic fuel lines to isolate the cause of a pressure drop in the fuel system.

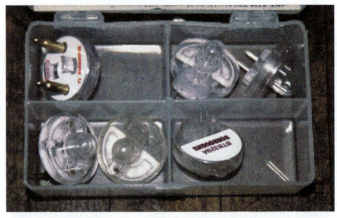

(a)

(b)

FIGURE 41–9 (a) Noid lights are usually purchased as an assortment so that one is available for any type or size of injector wiring connector. (b) The connector is unplugged from the injector and a noid light is plugged into the injector connector. The noid light should flash when the engine is being cranked if the power circuit and the pulsing to ground by the computer are functioning okay.

TESTING FOR AN INJECTOR PULSE

One of the first checks that should be performed when diagnosing a no-start condition is whether the fuel injectors are being pulsed by the computer. Checking for proper pulsing of the injector is also important in diagnosing a weak or dead cylinder.

A **noid light** is designed to electrically replace the injector in the circuit and to flash if the injector circuit is working correctly. ● **SEE FIGURE 41–9.** To use a noid light, disconnect the electrical connector at the fuel injector and plug the noid light into the injector harness connections. Crank or start the engine. The noid light should flash regularly.

NOTE: The term *noid* **is simply an abbreviation of the word sole***noid***. Injectors use a movable iron core and are therefore solenoids. Therefore, a noid light is a replacement for the solenoid (injector).**

Possible noid light problems and causes include the following:

1. **The light is off and does not flash.** The problem is an "open" in either the power side or ground side (or both) of the injector circuit.

2. **The noid light flashes dimly.** A dim noid light indicates excessive resistance or low voltage available to the injector. Both the power and ground side must be checked.

3. **The noid light is on and does not flash.** If the noid light is on, then both a power and a ground are present. Because the light does not flash (blink) when the engine is being cranked or started, a short-to-ground fault exists either in the computer itself or in the wiring between the injector and the computer.

CAUTION: A noid lamp must be used with caution. The computer may show a good noid light operation and have low supply voltage. ● **SEE FIGURE 41–10.**

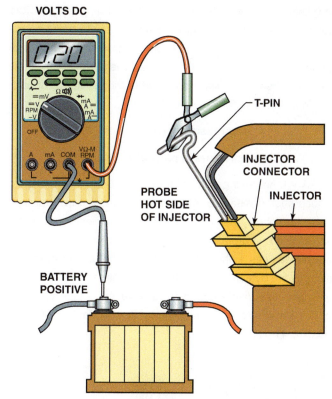

VOLTS DC

T-PIN

INJECTOR CONNECTOR

INJECTOR

PROBE HOT SIDE OF INJECTOR

BATTERY POSITIVE

FIGURE 41–10 Use a DMM set to read DC volts to check the voltage drop of the positive circuit to the fuel injector. A reading of 0.5 volt or less is generally considered to be acceptable.

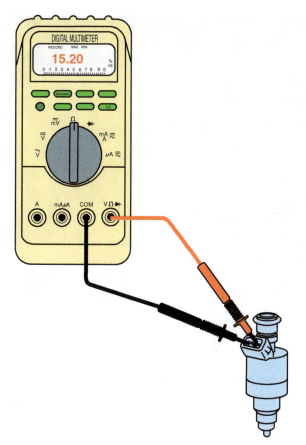

DIGITAL MULTIMETER

15.20

FIGURE 41–11 Connections and settings necessary to measure fuel-injector resistance.

CHECKING FUEL-INJECTOR RESISTANCE

Each port fuel injector must deliver an equal amount of fuel or the engine will idle roughly or perform poorly.

MEASURING THE RESISTANCE OF INDIVIDUAL INJECTORS

While there are many ways to check injectors, the first test is to measure the resistance of the coil inside and compare it to factory specifications. If the injectors are not accessible, check service information for the location of the electrical connector for the injectors. Unplug the connector and measure the resistance of each injector at the injector side of the connector. Use service information to determine the wire colors for the power side and the pulse side of each injector. For best engine operation, all injectors should have the same electrical resistance. To measure the resistance, carefully release the locking feature of the connector and remove the connector from the injector.

NOTE: Some engines require specific procedures to gain access to the injectors. Always follow the manufacturers' recommended procedures.

With an ohmmeter, measure the resistance across the injector terminals. Be sure to use the low-ohms feature of the digital ohmmeter to read in tenths (0.1) of an ohm. ● **SEE FIGURES 41–11 AND 41–12.** Check service information for the resistance specification of the injectors. Measure the resistance of all of the injectors. Replace any injector that does not fall within the resistance range of the specification. The resistance of the injectors should be measured twice—once when the engine (and injectors) is cold and once after the engine has reached normal operating temperature. If any injector measures close to specification, make certain that the terminals of the injector are electrically sound, and perform other tests to confirm an injector problem before replacement.

TYPICAL RESISTANCE VALUES

There are two basic types of injectors that have an effect on their resistance.

FIGURE 41–12 To measure fuel-injector resistance, a technician constructed a short wiring harness with a double banana plug that fits into the V and COM terminals of the meter and an injector connector at the other end. This setup makes checking resistance of fuel injectors quick and easy.

1. **Low-resistance injectors.** The features of a low-resistance injector include:
   - Uses a "peak and hold" type firing where a high current, usually about 4 amperes, is used to open the injector, then it is held open by using a lower current, which is usually about 1 ampere.
   - All throttle body injection (TBI) injectors and some port fuel injectors are low-resistance injectors and are fired using a peak-and-hold circuit by the PCM.
   - The resistance value of a peak-and-hold-type injector is usually 1.5 to 4.0 ohms.

2. **Higher-resistance injectors.** The features of a higher-resistance injector include:
   - Uses a constant low current, usually 1 ampere, to open the injector.
   - Is called a "saturated" type of injector because the current flows until the magnetic field is strong enough to open the injector.
   - Most port fuel injectors are of the saturated type.
   - The resistance value of a saturated injector is usually 12 to 16 ohms.

MEASURING RESISTANCE OF GROUPED INJECTORS Some older vehicles are equipped with a port fuel-injection system that "fires" two or more injectors at a time. For example, a V-6 may group all three injectors on one bank

to pulse on at the same time. Then the other three injectors will be pulsed on. This sequence alternates. To measure the resistance of these injectors, it is often easiest to measure each group of three that is wired in parallel. The resistance of three injectors wired in parallel is one-third of the resistance of each individual injector. For example,

Injector resistance = 12 ohms (Ω)

Three injectors in parallel = 4 ohms (Ω)

A V-6 has two groups of three injectors. Therefore, both groups should measure the same resistance. If both groups measure 4 ohms, then it is likely that all six injectors are okay. However, if one group measures only 2.9 ohms and the other group measures 4 ohms, then it is likely that one or more fuel injectors are defective (shorted). This means that the technician now has reasonable cause to remove the intake manifold to get access to each injector for further testing. ● **SEE FIGURE 41–13.**

PRESSURE-DROP BALANCE TEST

The pressure balance test involves using an electrical timing device to pulse the fuel injectors on for a given amount of time, usually 500 milliseconds or 0.5 seconds, and observing the drop in pressure that accompanies the pulse. If the *fuel flow* through each injector is equal, the drop in pressure in the system will be equal. Most manufacturers recommend that the pressures be within about 1.5 PSI (10 kPa) of each other for satisfactory engine performance. This test method not only tests the electrical functioning of the injector (for definite time and current pulse), but also tests for mechanical defects that could affect fuel flow amounts.

The purpose of running this injector balance test is to determine which injector is restricted, inoperative, or delivering fuel differently than the other injectors. Replacing a complete set of injectors can be expensive. The basic tools needed are:

- Accurate pressure gauge with pressure relief
- Injector pulser with time control (J39021 or equivalent)
- Necessary injector connection adapters
- Safe receptacle for catching and disposing of any fuel released

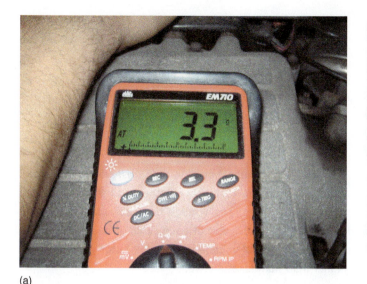
(a)

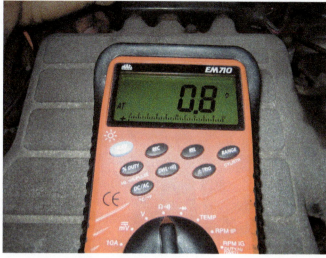
(b)

FIGURE 41–13 (a) The meter is connected to read one group of three 12 ohm injectors. The result should be 4 ohms and this reading is a little low indicating that at least one injector is shorted (low resistance). (b) This meter is connected to the other group of three injectors and indicates that most, if not all three, injectors are shorted. The technician replaced all six injectors and the engine ran great.

TECH TIP

Equal Resistance Test

All fuel injectors should measure the specified resistance. However, the specification often indicates the temperature of the injectors be at room temperature and of course will vary according to the temperature. Rather than waiting for all of the injectors to achieve room temperature, measure the resistance and check that they are all within 0.4 ohm of each other. To determine the difference, record the resistance of each injector and then subtract the lowest resistance reading from the highest resistance reading to get the difference. If more than 0.4 ohm then further testing will be needed to verify defective injector(s).

FIGURE 41–14 Connect a fuel-pressure gauge to the fuel rail at the Schrader valve.

STEP 1 Attach the pressure gauge to the fuel delivery rail on the supply side. Make sure the connections are safe and leakproof.

STEP 2 Attach the injector pulser to the first injector to be tested.

STEP 3 Turn the ignition key to the on position to prime the fuel rail. Note the static fuel-pressure reading. ● **SEE FIGURE 41–14.**

STEP 4 Activate the pulser for the timed firing pulses.

STEP 5 Note and record the new static rail pressure after the injector has been pulsed.

STEP 6 Reenergize the fuel pump and repeat this procedure for all of the engine injectors.

STEP 7 Compare the two pressure readings and compute the pressure drop for each injector. Compare the pressure drops of the injectors to each other. Any variation in pressure drops will indicate an uneven fuel delivery rate between the injectors.

FIGURE 41–15 An injector tester (EL-39021 or J-39021) being used to check the voltage drop through the injector while the tester is sending current through the injectors. This test is used to check the coil inside the injector. This same tester can be used to check for equal pressure drop of each injector by pulsing the injector on for 500 ms.

For example:

INJECTOR	1	2	3		4	5	6
Initial pressure	40	40	40		40	40	40
Second pressure	30	30	35		30	20	30
Pressure drop	10	10	5		10	20	10
Possible problem	OK	OK	Restriction		OK	Leak	OK

NOTE: Depending on the vehicle being tested, the scan tool software may have an injector balance test feature that replaces the stand-alone pulse tester. The injector balance test is listed under the Special Functions menu.

INJECTOR VOLTAGE-DROP TESTS

Another test of injectors involves pulsing the injector and measuring the voltage drop across the windings as current is flowing. A typical voltage-drop tester is shown in ● **FIGURE 41–15.** The tester, which is recommended for use by General Motors, pulses the injector while a digital multimeter is connected to the unit, which will display the voltage drop as the current flows through the winding.

CAUTION: Do not test an injector using a pulse-type tester more than one time without starting the engine to help avoid a hydrostatic lock caused by the flow of fuel into the cylinder during the pulse test.

Record the highest voltage drop observed on the meter display during the test. Repeat the voltage-drop test for all of the injectors. The voltage drop across each injector should be within 0.1 volt of each other. If an injector has a higher-than-normal voltage drop, the injector windings have higher-than-normal resistance.

ACTIVE FUEL INJECTOR TESTER[1]

The CH-47976 **active fuel injector tester (AFIT)** was developed to address important issues concerning diagnosing today's gasoline fuel-injection systems. On some vehicles, Tech 2 output control for the Fuel Injector Balance Test does not work if equipped with a Theft Immobilizer system. ● **SEE FIGURE 41–16.**

Existing service information (SI) procedures using a pressure gauge and Tech 2 are not reliable enough to determine the root cause of certain driveability issues. Needless replacement of injectors can occur if not diagnosed correctly. The AFIT can perform multiple fuel system tests, including the Fuel Injector Coil Test, Fuel Pump Pressure Leakdown Test, and the Fuel Injector Balance Test.

AFIT OPERATION The AFIT uses a microprocessor and software program to completely automate the test procedure. It eliminates variations in test results due to individual testing methods or physical property changes of the fuel. All measurements and calculations are performed by the AFIT software, which reduces the possibility of human error.

The AFIT connects to the DLC with a cable. Certain applications with the Theft Immobilizer system or some other

---

[1]Adapted from GM Techlink, June 2006

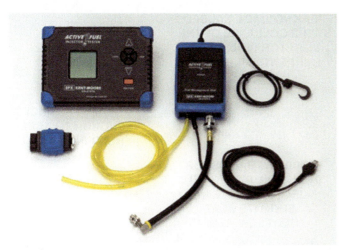

FIGURE 41–16 The CH-47976 active fuel injector tester (AFIT) includes these components and other adapter harnesses, depending on the engine. (*Courtesy of General Motors*)

engines may also require an adapter harness. These harnesses connect directly to the injectors or to the vehicle injector harness connector.

Inside the AFIT is a reference injector with a known standard flow rate. This reference injector is used to monitor changes within the fuel system during the balance test.

The AFIT will determine if the injectors are within the GM design and operating specifications for each specific engine. Each injector is identified as GOOD or BAD, using the balance graph.

USING THE AFIT If test results show injector clogging, injectors are to be cleaned or replaced. Refer to SI for the proper cleaning or replacement procedure for the vehicle you are working on. Run the test again to verify that the cleaning or replacement has been successful. A comparison of the before and after test results can be used to document that the repair was successful.

NOTE: Not all injectors can be cleaned. Refer to SI or GM Bulletin 03-06-04-030A to determine which injectors can be cleaned.

During the retest, the AFIT again pinpoints any faulty injector(s) that were not improved. If cleaning was performed, these injector(s) will now need to be replaced. If all of the injectors now test good, the condition has likely been repaired. It is recommended that the vehicle be operated to fully verify the repair. Complete test results, including balance percentages and flow

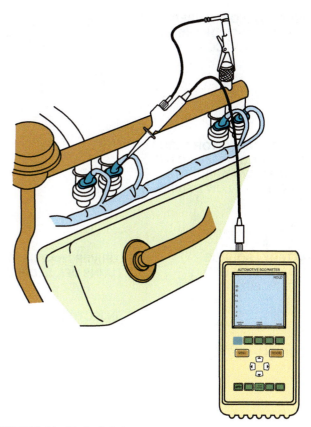

FIGURE 41–17 A digital storage oscilloscope can be connected to an injector by carefully back probing the electrical connector.

rates, can be downloaded to the Techline PC for printing and attachment to the repair order for repair verification purposes.

SCOPE-TESTING FUEL INJECTORS

A scope (analog or digital storage) can be connected into each injector circuit. There are three types of injector drive circuits and each type of circuit has its own characteristic pattern.
● **SEE FIGURE 41–17** for an example of how to connect a scope to read a fuel-injector waveform.

SATURATED SWITCH TYPE In a saturated switch-type injector-driven circuit, voltage (usually a full 12 volts) is applied to the injector. The ground for the injector is provided by the vehicle computer. When the ground connection is completed,

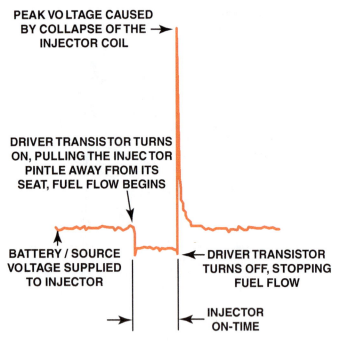

FIGURE 41–18 The injector on-time is called the pulse width.

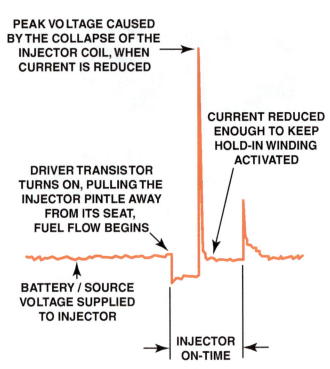

FIGURE 41–19 A typical peak-and-hold fuel-injector waveform. Most fuel injectors that measure less than 6 ohms will usually display a similar waveform.

current flows through the injector windings. Due to the resistance and inductive reactance of the coil itself, it requires a fraction of a second (about 3 milliseconds or 0.003 seconds) for the coil to reach **saturation** or maximum current flow. Most saturated switch-type fuel injectors have 12 to 16 ohms of resistance. This resistance, as well as the computer switching circuit, control and limit the current flow through the injector. A voltage spike occurs when the computer shuts off (opens the injector ground-side circuit) the injectors. ● **SEE FIGURE 41–18.**

PEAK-AND-HOLD TYPE

A **peak-and-hold** type is typically used for TBI and some port low-resistance injectors. Full battery voltage is applied to the injector and the ground side is controlled through the computer. The computer provides a high initial current flow (about 4 amperes) to flow through the injector windings to open the injector core. Then the computer reduces the current to a lower level (about 1 ampere). The hold current is enough to keep the injector open, yet conserves energy and reduces the heat buildup that would occur if the full

current flow remains on as long as the injector is commanded on. Typical peak-and-hold-type injector resistance ranges from 2 to 4 ohms.

The scope pattern of a typical peak-and-hold-type injector shows the initial closing of the ground circuit, then a voltage spike as the current flow is reduced. Another voltage spike occurs when the lower level current is turned off (opened) by the computer. ● **SEE FIGURE 41–19.**

PULSE-WIDTH MODULATED TYPE

A pulse-width modulated type of injector drive circuit uses lower-resistance coil injectors. Battery voltage is available at the positive terminal of the injector and the computer provides a variable-duration connection to ground on the negative side of the injector. The computer can vary the time intervals that the injector is grounded for very precise fuel control.

Each time the injector circuit is turned off (ground circuit opened), a small voltage spike occurs. It is normal to see multiple voltage spikes on a scope connected to a pulse-width modulated type of fuel injector.

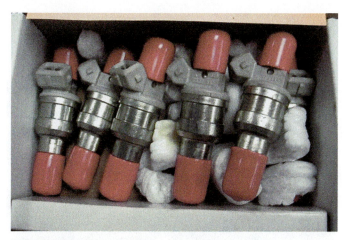

FIGURE 41–20 A set of six reconditioned injectors. The sixth injector is barely visible at the far right.

If Three of Six Injectors Are Defective, Should I Also Replace the Other Three?

This is a good question. Many service technicians "recommend" that the three good injectors be replaced along with the other three that tested as being defective. The reasons given by these technicians include:

- All six injectors have been operating under the same fuel, engine, and weather conditions.
- The labor required to replace all six is just about the same as replacing only the three defective injectors.
- Replacing all six at the same time helps ensure that all of the injectors are flowing the same amount of fuel so that the engine is operating most efficiently.

With these ideas in mind, the customer should be informed and offered the choice. Complete sets of injectors such as those in ● **FIGURE 41–20** can be purchased at a reasonable cost.

IDLE AIR SPEED CONTROL DIAGNOSIS

On an engine equipped with fuel injection (TBI or port injection), the idle speed is controlled by increasing or decreasing the amount of air bypassing the throttle plate. An electronic stepper motor is used to maintain the correct idle speed. This control is often called the **idle air control (IAC)**. ● **SEE FIGURES 41–21 AND 41–22.**

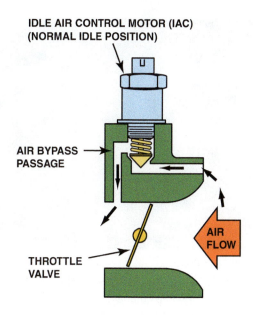

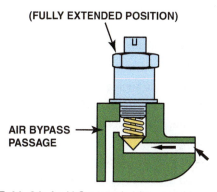

FIGURE 41–21 An IAC controls idle speed by controlling the amount of air that passes around the throttle plate. More airflow results in a higher idle speed.

FIGURE 41–22 A typical IAC.

When the engine stops, most IAC units will retract outward to get ready for the next engine start. When the engine starts, the engine speed is high to provide for proper operation when the engine is cold. Then, as the engine gets warmer, the computer reduces engine idle speed gradually by reducing the number of counts or steps commanded by the IAC.

(a)

(b)

FIGURE 41–23 (a) Nothing looks unusual when the hood is first opened. (b) When the cover is removed from the top of the engine, a mouse or some other animal nest is visible. The animal had already eaten through a couple of injector wires. At least the cause of the intermittent misfire was discovered.

 REAL WORLD FIX

There Is No Substitute for a Thorough Visual Inspection

An intermittent "check engine" light and a random-misfire diagnostic trouble code (DTC) P0300 was being diagnosed. A scan tool did not provide any help because all systems seemed to be functioning normally. Finally, the technician removed the engine cover and discovered a mouse nest. ● **SEE FIGURE 41–23.**

When the engine is warm and restarted, the idle speed should momentarily increase, then decrease to normal idle speed. This increase and then decrease in engine speed is often called an engine-flare. If the engine speed does not flare, then the IAC may not be working (it may be stuck in one position).

FUEL-INJECTION SERVICE

All engines using fuel injection do require some type of fuel-system maintenance. Normal wear and tear with today's underhood temperatures and changes in gasoline quality contribute to the buildup of olefin wax, dirt, water, and many other additives.

Fuel-injection system service should include the following operation:

Check fuel-pump operating pressure and volume. Many technicians assume that if the pressure is correct, the

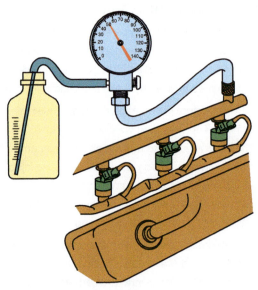

FIGURE 41–24 Testing fuel-pump volume using a fuel-pressure gauge with a bleed hose inserted into a suitable container. The engine is running during this test.

volume is also okay. Hook up a fuel-pressure tester to the fuel rail test port to test the fuel pressure with the engine running. At the same time, test the volume of the pump by sending fuel into a holding tank. (One ounce per second is the usual specification.)

- Good pressure does not mean proper volume. For example, a clogged filter may test okay on pressure but the restriction may not allow proper volume under load. ● **SEE FIGURE 41–24.**

CLEANING FUEL INJECTORS[2]

CONDITION OR CONCERN   A vehicle that has any of the following driveability symptoms may benefit from an injector cleaning procedure:

- Extended crank time
- Hard to start
- MIL/SES illuminated with stored DTCs
- Hesitation
- Lack of power
- Surge or chuggle
- Rough idle
- Light or intermittent misfire

CAUSE   Due to various factors, the fuel injectors may become restricted. Extensive testing has demonstrated that fuel related issues are the cause of clogged injectors. At this point, no specific fuel, fuel constituent, or engine condition has been identified as causing the restriction. The restriction causes the engine to operate at a lean air–fuel ratio. This may either trigger the MIL to illuminate or the engine to develop various driveability symptoms.

CORRECTION   Fuel injector restrictions or deposits can be cleaned on the vehicle using the following procedure. Under NO circumstances should this procedure be modified, changed, or shortened. As a long-term solution, and to prevent reoccurrence, customers should be encouraged to use **Top Tier Detergent Gasoline.** For further information on Top Tier detergent gasoline and fuel retailers, please refer to the latest version of the following Corporate Bulletin Numbers:

- 04-06-04-047 (United States only)
- 05-06-04-022 (Canada only)

GM does not support cleaning injectors on any engines that are not listed in **CHART 41–1**. Engines other than the ones listed that diagnosis indicates as having restricted injectors should have those injectors replaced.

NOTE: GM UPPER ENGINE AND FUEL INJECTOR CLEANER is the only injector cleaning agent approved for use with General Motors fuel system components.

---

[2]Adapted from GM TSB #03-06-04-030H

MODEL YEAR	ENGINE RPO
2005	LH6, LS2, LQ4, LM7, LR4, L33, LQ9, L31, LU3, LL8, LK5, L52, L18
2006	LH6, LS2, LQ4, LM7, LR4, L33, LQ9, L31, LU3, LL8, LK5, L52, L18
2007	LH6, LS2, LQ4, LM7, LR4, LY2, LY5, L76, L92, LU3, LLR, LLV, LL8, L18
2008	LH8, LS2, L92, LY2, LY5, LY6, LH6, LFA, LU3, L18
2009	LH8, LS2, LH6, LY2, LFA, LY5, LU3, L18
2010	LU3
2011	LU3
2012	LU3
2013	LU3

CHART 41–1

2005–2013 GM passenger cars and light-duty trucks equipped with the engine RPOs listed and MULTEC® 2 Fuel Injectors can be cleaned. (*Courtesy of General Motors*)

Other injector cleaners may cause damage to plastics, plated metals, or bearings. General Motors has completed extensive laboratory testing of GM Upper Engine and Fuel Injector Cleaner, and can assure its compatibility with General Motors fuel system components, as long as the cleaning procedure is followed correctly. Under NO circumstances should the GM Upper Engine and Fuel Injector Cleaner be added to the vehicle fuel tank.

INJECTOR CLEANING PROCEDURE

1. Before starting, have on hand the proper cleaning and treatment chemicals. Always refer to service information for the specific procedure for the vehicle being serviced.
   - One bottle of GM Upper Engine and Fuel Injector Cleaner, P/N 88861803 (in Canada, P/N 88861804)
   - One bottle of GM Fuel System Treatment Plus, P/N 88861013 (in Canada, P/N 88861012)

Do not exceed the recommended cleaning solution concentration. Testing has demonstrated that exceeding the recommended cleaning solution concentration does not improve the effectiveness of this procedure.

2. Empty two of the 30 ml (1 oz.) reservoirs of the GM Upper Engine and Fuel Injector Cleaner container into a J 35800-A—injector cleaning tank. Then add 420 ml (14 oz) of regular unleaded gasoline. If you are using any other brand of cleaning tank, you will need a total of 60 ml (2 oz.) mixed with 420 ml (14 oz) of regular unleaded gasoline.

Check the Injectors at the "Bends and the Ends"

Injectors that are most likely to become restricted due to clogging of the filter basket screen are the injectors at the ends of the rail, especially on returnless systems where dirt can accumulate. Moreover, the injectors that are located at the bends of the fuel rail are also subject to possible clogging due to the dirt being deposited where the fuel makes a turn in the rail.

Be Sure to Clean the Fuel Rail

Whenever you service the fuel injectors, or if you suspect that there may be a fuel-injector problem, remove the entire fuel rail assembly and check the passages for contamination. Always thoroughly clean the rail when replacing fuel injectors.

NOTE: This procedure will need to be repeated for a second time for an 8-cylinder engine (8-cylinder engines receive 960 ml total fluid—120 ml (4 oz.) of Upper Engine and Fuel Injector Cleaner and 840 ml (28 oz.) of gasoline.

3. Be sure to follow all additional instructions provided with the tool.

4. Electrically disable the vehicle fuel pump by either removing the fuel pump fuse or the fuel pump relay and disconnect the oil pressure switch connector, if equipped.

5. Relieve fuel pressure and disconnect the fuel feed and return lines at the fuel rail. Plug the fuel feed and return lines coming off the fuel rail with J 37287, J 42873, or J 42964 as appropriate for the fuel system.

6. Connect the J 35800-A to the vehicle fuel rail.

7. Pressurize the J 35800-A to 510 kPa (75 PSI).

8. Start and idle the engine until it stalls, due to lack of fuel. This should take approximately 15–20 minutes.

9. Turn the ignition to the OFF position.

10. Disconnect the J 35800-A from the fuel rail.

11. Reconnect the vehicle fuel pump relay and oil pressure switch connector, if equipped.

12. Remove the J 37287, J 42873, or J 42964 and reconnect the vehicle fuel feed and return lines.

FUEL-INJECTION SYMPTOM CHART

SYMPTOM	POSSIBLE CAUSES
Hard cold starts	• Low fuel pressure
	• Leaking fuel injectors
	• Contaminated fuel
	• Low-volatility fuel
	• Dirty throttle plate
Garage stalls	• Low fuel pressure
	• Insufficient fuel volume
	• Restricted fuel injector
	• Contaminated fuel
	• Low-volatility fuel
Poor cold performance	• Low fuel pressure
	• Insufficient fuel volume
	• Contaminated fuel
	• Low-volatility fuel
Tip-in hesitation (hesitation just as the accelerator pedal is depressed)	• Low fuel pressure
	• Insufficient fuel volume
	• Intake valve deposits
	• Contaminated fuel
	• Low-volatility fuel

13. Start and idle the vehicle for an additional two minutes to ensure residual injector cleaner is flushed from the fuel rail and fuel lines.

14. Pour the entire content of GM Fuel System Treatment Plus into the tank and advise the customer to fill the tank.

15. Road test the vehicle to verify that the customer concern has been corrected.

FUEL-SYSTEM SCAN TOOL DIAGNOSTICS

Diagnosing a faulty fuel system can be a difficult task. However, it can be made easier by utilizing the information available via the serial data stream. By observing the long-term fuel trim and the short-term fuel trim, it can be determined how the fuel system is performing. Short-term fuel trim and long-term fuel trim can help zero in on specific areas of trouble. Readings should be taken at idle and at 3000 RPM.

CONDITION	LONG-TERM FUEL TRIM AT IDLE	LONG-TERM FUEL TRIM AT 3000 RPM
System normal	0% ± 10%	0% ± 10%
Vacuum leak	HIGH	OK
Fuel flow problem	OK	HIGH
Low fuel pressure	HIGH	HIGH
High fuel pressure	*OK or LOW	*OK or LOW

*High fuel pressure will affect trim at idle, at 3000 RPM, or both.

1 Start the fuel injector cleaning process by bringing the vehicle's engine up to operating temperature. Shut off the engine, remove the cap from the fuel rail test port, and install the appropriate adapter.

2 The vehicle's fuel pump is disabled by removing its relay or fuse. In some cases, it may be necessary to disconnect the fuel pump at the tank if the relay or fuse powers more than just the pump.

3 Turn the outlet valve of the canister to the OFF or CLOSED position.

4 Remove the fuel injector cleaning canister's top and regulator assembly. Note that there is an O-ring seal located here that must be in place for the canister's top to seal properly.

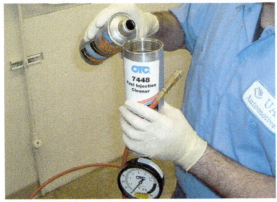

5 Pour the injection system cleaning fluid into the open canister. Rubber gloves are highly recommended for this step as the fluid is toxic.

6 Replace the canister's top (making sure it is tight) and connect its hose to the fuel rail adapter. Be sure that the hose is routed away from exhaust manifolds and other hazards.

7 Hang the canister from the vehicle's hood and adjust the air pressure regulator to full OPEN position (CCW).

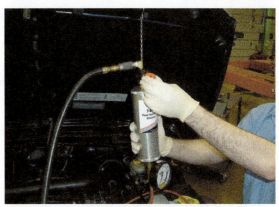

8 Connect shop air to the canister and adjust the air pressure regulator to the desired setting. Canister pressure can be read directly from the gauge.

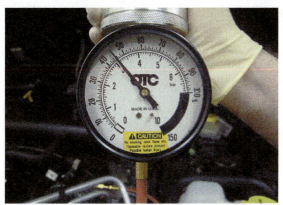

9 Canister pressure should be adjusted to 5 PSI below system fuel pressure. An alternative for return-type systems is to block the fuel return line to the tank.

10 Open the outlet valve on the canister.

11 Start the vehicle's engine and let run at 1000–1500 RPM. The engine is now running on fuel injector cleaning fluid provided by the canister.

12 Continue the process until the canister is empty and the engine stalls. Remove the cleaning equipment, enable the vehicle's fuel pump, and run the engine to check for leaks.

SUMMARY

1. A typical throttle-body fuel injector uses a computer-controlled injector solenoid to spray fuel into the throttle-body unit above the throttle plates.

2. A typical port fuel-injection system uses an individual fuel injector for each cylinder and squirts fuel directly into the intake manifold about 3 inches (80 mm) from the intake valve.

3. A typical fuel-injection system fuel pressure should not drop more than 20 PSI in 20 minutes.

4. A noid light can be used to check for the presence of an injector pulse.

5. Injectors can be tested for resistance and should be within 0.3 to 0.4 ohms of each other.

6. Different designs of injectors have a different scope waveform depending on how the computer pulses the injector on and off.

REVIEW QUESTIONS

1. List the ways fuel injectors can be tested.
2. List the steps necessary to test a fuel-pressure regulator.
3. Describe why it may be necessary to clean the fuel injectors of a port fuel-injected engine.

CHAPTER QUIZ

1. Most port fuel-injected engines operate on how much fuel pressure?
   a. 3 to 5 PSI (21 to 35 kPa)
   b. 9 to 13 PSI (62 to 90 kPa)
   c. 35 to 45 PSI (240 to 310 kPa)
   d. 55 to 65 PSI (380 to 450 kPa)

2. Fuel injectors can be tested using _____.
   a. An ohmmeter
   b. A stethoscope
   c. A scope
   d. All of the above

3. Throttle-body fuel-injection systems use what type of injector driver?
   a. Peak and hold
   b. Saturated switch
   c. Pulse-width modulated
   d. Pulsed

4. Port fuel-injection systems generally use what type of injector driver?
   a. Peak and hold
   b. Saturated switch
   c. Pulse-width modulated
   d. Pulsed

5. The vacuum hose from the fuel-pressure regulator was removed from the regulator and gasoline dripped out of the hose. Technician A says that is normal and that everything is okay. Technician B says that one or more of the injectors may be defective, causing the fuel to get into the hose. Which technician is correct?
   a. Technician A only
   b. Both Technicians A and B
   c. Technician B only
   d. Neither Technician A nor B

6. The fuel pressure drops rapidly when the engine is turned off. Technician A says that one or more injectors could be leaking. Technician B says that a defective check valve in the fuel pump could be the cause. Which technician is correct?
   a. Technician A only
   b. Technician B only
   c. Both Technicians A and B
   d. Neither Technician A nor B

7. In a typical port fuel-injection system, which injectors are most subject to becoming restricted?
   a. Any of them equally
   b. The injectors at the end of the rail on a returnless system
   c. The injectors at the bends in the rail
   d. Either b or c

8. What component pulses the fuel injector on most vehicles?
   a. Electronic control unit (computer)
   b. Ignition module
   c. Crankshaft sensor
   d. Both b and c

9. Fuel-injection service is being discussed. Technician A says that all fuel injectors on GM vehicles can be cleaned. Technician B says that the AFIT tool can be used to clean injectors. Which technician is correct?
   a. Technician A only
   b. Technician B only
   c. Both Technicians A and B
   d. Neither Technician A nor B

10. If the fuel injectors need to be cleaned, what symptoms will be present regarding the operation of the engine?
    a. Stalls
    b. Rough idle
    c. Hesitation
    d. All of the above

chapter 42

VEHICLE EMISSION STANDARDS AND TESTING

LEARNING OBJECTIVES

After studying this chapter, the reader should be able to:

1. Discuss emissions standards.
2. Identify the reasons why excessive amounts of HC, CO, and NO_x exhaust emissions are created.
3. Diagnose driveability and emissions problems resulting from malfunctions of interrelated systems.
4. Describe how to test for various emissions products.

This chapter will help you prepare for ASE A8 certification test content area "D" (Emissions Control Systems Diagnosis and Repair) and ASE L1 certification test content area "F" (I/M Failure Diagnosis).

KEY TERMS

Acceleration simulation mode (ASM) 621
ASM 25/25 test 621
ASM 50/15 test 621
Federal Test Procedure (FTP) 620
I/M 240 test 621
Lean indicator 625
Non-methane hydrocarbon (NMHC) 623
Rich indicator 625
State Implementation Plan (SIP) 620

STC OBJECTIVES

GM Service Technical College topic covered in this chapter is:

1. Explain the emission standards that apply to all General Motors vehicles.

EMISSION STANDARDS IN THE UNITED STATES

In the United States, emissions standards are managed by the Environmental Protection Agency (EPA) as well as some U.S. state governments. Some of the strictest standards in the world are formulated in California by the California Air Resources Board (CARB).

TIER 1 AND TIER 2 Federal emission standards are set by the Clean Air Act Amendments (CAAA) of 1990 grouped by tier. All vehicles sold in the United States must meet Tier 1 standards that went into effect in 1994 and are the least stringent. Additional Tier 2 standards have been optional since 2001, and are currently being phased-in to be fully adopted by 2009. The current Tier 1 standards are different for automobiles and light trucks (SUVs, pickup trucks, and minivans), but Tier 2 standards will be the same for both types.

There are several ratings that can be given to vehicles, and a certain percentage of a manufacturer's vehicles must meet different levels in order for the company to sell its products in affected regions. Beyond Tier 1 standards, and in order by stringency, are the following levels:

- **TLEV: Transitional Low-Emission Vehicle.** More stringent for HC than Tier 1.
- **LEV** (also known as **LEV I**): **Low-Emission Vehicle.** An intermediate California standard about twice as stringent as Tier 1 for HC and NO_x.
- **ULEV** (also known as **ULEV I**): **Ultra-Low-Emission Vehicle.** A stronger California standard emphasizing very low HC emissions.
- **ULEV II: Ultra-Low-Emission Vehicle.** A cleaner-than-average vehicle certified under the Phase II LEV standard. Hydrocarbon and carbon monoxide emissions levels are nearly 50% lower than those of a LEV II-certified vehicle. ● **SEE FIGURE 42–1.**
- **SULEV: Super-Ultra-Low-Emission Vehicle.** A California standard even tighter than ULEV, including much lower HC and NO_x emissions; roughly equivalent to Tier 2 Bin 2 vehicles.
- **ZEV: Zero-Emission Vehicle.** A California standard prohibiting any tailpipe emissions. The ZEV category is largely restricted to electric vehicles and hydrogen-fueled vehicles. In these cases, any emissions that are created

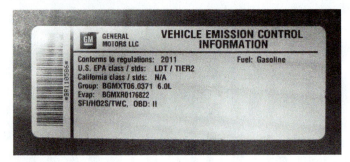

FIGURE 42–1 The underhood decal showing that this vehicle meets Tier 2 standards for light-duty trucks (LDT).

are produced at another site, such as a power plant or hydrogen reforming center, unless such sites run on renewable energy.

NOTE: A battery-powered electric vehicle charged from the power grid will still be up to 10 times cleaner than even the cleanest gasoline vehicles over their respective lifetimes.

- **PZEV: Partial Zero-Emission Vehicle.** Compliant with the SULEV standard; additionally has near-zero evaporative emissions and a 15-year/150,000-mile warranty on its emission control equipment.

Tier 2 standards are even more stringent. Tier 2 variations are appended with "II," such as LEV II or SULEV II. Other categories have also been created:

- **ILEV: Inherently Low-Emission Vehicle**
- **AT-PZEV: Advanced Technology Partial Zero-Emission Vehicle.** If a vehicle meets the PZEV standards and is using high-technology features, such as an electric motor or high-pressure gaseous fuel tanks for compressed natural gas, it qualifies as an AT-PZEV. Hybrid electric vehicles can qualify, as can internal combustion engine vehicles that run on natural gas (CNG). These vehicles are classified as "partial" ZEV because they receive partial credit for the number of ZEV vehicles that automakers would otherwise be required to sell in California.
- **NLEV: National Low-Emission Vehicle.** All vehicles nationwide must meet this standard, which started in 2001.

FEDERAL EPA BIN NUMBER The higher the tier number, the newer the regulation; the lower the bin number, the cleaner the vehicle. ● **SEE CHARTS 42–1 TO 42–3.**

CERTIFICATION LEVEL (BIN)*	NMOG (G/MI)	CO (G/MI)	NO$_x$ (G/MI)
1	0.0	0.0	0.0
2	0.010	2.1	0.02
3	0.055	2.1	0.03
4	0.070	2.1	0.04
5	0.090	4.2	0.07
6	0.090	4.2	0.10
7	0.090	4.2	0.15
8a	0.125	4.2	0.20
8b	0.156	4.2	0.20
9a	0.090	4.2	0.30
9b	0.130	4.2	0.30
9c	0.180	4.2	0.30
10a	0.156	4.2	0.60
10b	0.230	6.4	0.60
10c	0.230	6.4	0.60
11	0.230	7.3	0.90

CHART 42–1

EPA Tier 2—120,000 mile tailpipe emission limits. After January 2007, the highest allowable Bin is 8.
Source: Data compiled from the Environmental Protection Agency (EPA).
*The bin number is determined by the type and weight of the vehicle.

U.S. EPA VEHICLE INFORMATION PROGRAM (THE HIGHER THE SCORE, THE LOWER THE EMISSIONS)	
SELECTED EMISSIONS STANDARDS	SCORE
BIN 1 AND ZEV	10
PZEV	9.5
BIN 2	9
BIN 3	8
BIN 4	7
BIN 5 AND LEV II CARS	6
BIN 6	5
BIN 7	4
BIN 8	3
BIN 9A AND LEV I CARS	2
BIN 9B	2
Bin 10a	1
BIN 10B AND TIER 1 CARS	1
BIN 11	0

CHART 42–2

Air pollution score.
Source: Courtesy of the Environmental Protection Agency (EPA).

MINIMUM FUEL ECONOMY (MPG) COMBINED CITY-HIGHWAY LABEL VALUE					
SCORE	GASOLINE	DIESEL	E-85	LPG	CNG*
10	44	50	31	28	33
9	36	41	26	23	27
8	30	35	22	20	23
7	26	30	19	17	20
6	23	27	17	15	18
5	21	24	15	14	16
4	19	22	14	12	14
3	17	20	12	11	13
2	16	18	—	—	12
1	15	17	11	10	11
0	14	16	10	9	10

CHART 42–3

Greenhouse gas score.
Source: Courtesy of the Environmental Protection Agency (EPA).
*CNG assumes a gallon equivalent of 121.5 cubic feet.

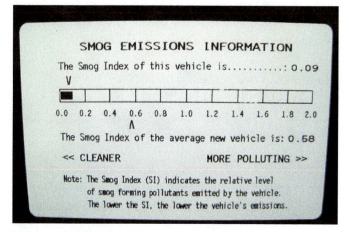

FIGURE 42–2 This label on a hybrid vehicle shows the relative smog-producing emissions, but this does not include carbon dioxide (CO_2), which may increase global warming.

SMOG EMISSION INFORMATION

New vehicles are equipped with a sticker that shows the relative level of smog-causing emissions created by the vehicle compared to others on the market. Smog-causing emissions include unburned hydrocarbons (HC) and oxides of nitrogen (NO$_x$). ● **SEE FIGURE 42–2.**

CALIFORNIA STANDARDS

The pre-2004 California Air Resources Board (CARB) standards as a whole were known as LEV I. Within that, there were four possible ratings: Tier 1,

TLEV, LEV, and ULEV. The newest CARB rating system (since January 1, 2004) is known as LEV II. Within that rating system there are three primary ratings: LEV, ULEV, and SULEV. States other than California are given the option to use the federal EPA standards, or they can adopt California's standards.

EUROPEAN STANDARDS

Europe has its own set of standards that vehicles must meet, which includes the following tiers:

- Euro I (1992–1995)
- Euro II (1995–1999)
- Euro III (1999–2005)
- Euro IV (2005–2008)
- Euro V (2008+)

Vehicle emission standards and technological advancements have successfully reduced pollution from cars and trucks by about 90% since the 1970s. Unfortunately, there currently are more vehicles on the road and they are being driven more miles each year, partially offsetting the environmental benefits of individual vehicle emissions reductions.

EXHAUST ANALYSIS TESTING

The Clean Air Act Amendments require enhanced I/M programs in areas of the country that have the worst air quality and the Northeast Ozone Transport region. The states must submit to the EPA a **State Implementation Plan (SIP)** for their programs. Each enhanced I/M program is required to include as a minimum the following items:

- Computerized emission analyzers
- Visual inspection of emission control items
- Minimum waiver limit (to be increased based on the inflation index)
- Remote on-road testing of one-half of 1% of the vehicle population
- Registration denial for vehicles not passing an I/M test
- Denial of waiver for vehicles that are under warranty or that have been tampered with
- Annual inspections
- OBD-II systems check for 1996 and newer vehicles

FEDERAL TEST PROCEDURE (FTP) The **Federal Test Procedure (FTP)** is the test used to certify all new vehicles before they can be sold. Once a vehicle meets these standards, it is certified by the EPA for sale in the United States. The FTP test procedure is a loaded-mode test lasting for a total duration of 505 seconds and is designed to simulate an urban driving trip. A cold start-up representing a morning start and a hot start after a soak period is part of the test. In addition to this drive cycle, a vehicle must undergo evaporative testing. Evaporative emissions are determined using the Sealed Housing for Evaporative Determination (SHED) test, which measures the evaporative emissions from the vehicle after a heat-up period representing a vehicle sitting in the sun. In addition, the vehicle is driven and then tested during the hot soak period.

NOTE: A SHED is constructed entirely of stainless steel. The walls, floors, and ceiling, plus the door, are all constructed of stainless steel because it does not absorb hydrocarbons, which could offset test results.

The FTP is a much more stringent test of vehicle emissions than is any test type that uses equipment that measures percentages of exhaust gases. The federal emission standards for each model year vehicle are the same for that model regardless of what size engine the vehicle is equipped with. This is why larger V-8 engines often are equipped with more emission control devices than smaller four- and six-cylinder engines.

I/M TEST PROGRAMS There are a variety of I/M testing programs that have been implemented by the various states. These programs may be centralized testing programs or decentralized testing programs. Each state is free to develop a testing program suitable to their needs as long as they can demonstrate to the EPA that their plan will achieve the attainment levels set by the EPA. This approach has led to a variety of different testing programs. ● SEE FIGURE 42–3.

VISUAL TAMPERING CHECKS Visual tampering checks may be part of an I/M testing program and usually include checking for the following items:

- Catalytic converter
- Fuel tank inlet restrictor
- Exhaust gas recirculation (EGR)
- Evaporative emission system
- Air-injection reaction system (AIR)
- Positive crankcase ventilation (PCV)

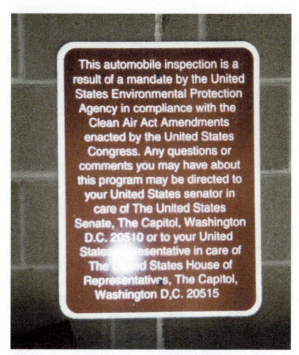

FIGURE 42–3 Photo of a sign taken at an emissions test facility.

If any of these systems are missing, not connected, or tampered with, the vehicle will fail the emissions test and will have to be repaired/replaced by the vehicle owner. Any cost associated with repairing or replacing these components may not be used toward the waiver amount required for the vehicle.

ONE-SPEED AND TWO-SPEED IDLE TEST

The one-speed and two-speed idle test measures the exhaust emissions from the tailpipe of the vehicle at idle and/or at 2500 RPM. This uses stand-alone exhaust gas sampling equipment that measures the emissions in percentages. Each state chooses the standards that the vehicle has to meet in order to pass the test. The advantage to using this type of testing is that the equipment is relatively cheap and allows states to have decentralized testing programs because many facilities can afford the necessary equipment required to perform this test.

LOADED MODE TEST

The loaded mode test uses a dynamometer that places a "single weight" load on the vehicle. The load applied to the vehicle varies with the speed of the vehicle. Typically, a four-cylinder vehicle speed would be 24 mph, a six-cylinder vehicle speed would be 30 mph, and an eight-cylinder vehicle speed would be 34 mph. Conventional stand-alone sampling equipment is used to measure HC and CO emissions. This type of test is classified as a Basic I/M test by the EPA. ● **SEE FIGURE 42–4.**

FIGURE 42–4 A vehicle being tested during an enhanced emissions test.

ACCELERATION SIMULATION MODE (ASM)

The **ASM-type** of test uses a dynamometer that applies a heavy load on the vehicle at a steady-state speed. The load applied to the vehicle is based on the acceleration rate on the second simulated hill of the FTP. This acceleration rate is 3.3 mph/sec/sec (read as 3.3 mph per second per second, which is the unit of acceleration). There are different ASM tests used by different states.

The **ASM 50/15 test** places a load of 50% on the vehicle at a steady 15 mph. This load represents 50% of the horsepower required to simulate the FTP acceleration rate of 3.3 mph/sec. This type of test produces relatively high levels of NO_x emissions; therefore, it is useful in detecting vehicles that are emitting excessive NO_x.

The **ASM 25/25 test** places a 25% load on the vehicle while it is driven at a steady 25 mph. This represents 25% of the load required to simulate the FTP acceleration rate of 3.3 mph/sec. Because this applies a smaller load on the vehicle at a higher speed, it will produce a higher level of HC and CO emissions than the ASM 50/15. NO_x emissions will tend to be lower with this type of test.

I/M 240 TEST

The **I/M 240 test** is the EPA's enhanced test. It is actually a portion of the 505-second FTP test used by the manufacturers to certify their new vehicles. The "240" stands for 240 seconds of drive time on a dynamometer. This is a loaded-mode transient test that uses constant volume sampling equipment to measure the exhaust emissions in mass just as is done during the FTP. The I/M 240 test simulates the first two hills of the FTP drive cycle. ● **SEE FIGURE 42–5** shows the I/M 240 drive trace.

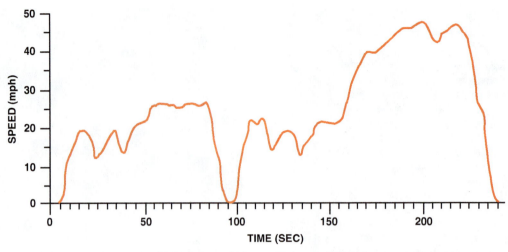

FIGURE 42–5 Trace showing the Inspection/Maintenance 240 test. The test duplicates an urban test loop around Los Angeles, California. The first "hump" in the curve represents the vehicle being accelerated to about 20 mph, then driving up a small hill to about 30 mph and coming to a stop. At about 94 seconds, the vehicle stops and again accelerates while climbing a hill and speeding up to about 50 mph during this second phase of the test.

OBD-II TESTING In 1999, the EPA requested that states adopt OBD-II systems testing for 1996 and newer vehicles. The OBD-II system is designed to illuminate the MIL light and store trouble codes any time a malfunction exists that would cause the vehicle emissions to exceed 1 1/2 times the FTP limits. If the OBD-II system is working correctly, the system should be able to detect a vehicle failure that would cause emissions to increase to an unacceptable level. The EPA has determined that the OBD-II system should detect emission failures of a vehicle even before that vehicle would fail an emissions test of the type that most states are employing. Furthermore, the EPA has determined that, as the population of OBD-II-equipped vehicles increases and the population of older non-OBD-II-equipped vehicles decreases, tailpipe testing will no longer be necessary.

The OBD-II testing program consists of a computer that can scan the vehicle OBD-II system using the DLC connector. The technician first performs a visual check of the vehicle MIL light to determine if it is working correctly. Next, the computer is connected to the vehicle's DLC connector. The computer will scan the vehicle OBD-II system and determine if there are any codes stored that are commanding the MIL light on. In addition, it will scan the status of the readiness monitors and determine if they have all run and passed. If the readiness monitors have all run and passed, it indicates that the OBD-II system has tested all the components of the emission control system. An OBD-II vehicle would fail this OBD-II test if:

- The MIL light does not come on with the key on, engine off
- The MIL is commanded on
- A number (varies by state) of the readiness monitors has not been run

If none of these conditions are present, the vehicle will pass the emissions test.

REMOTE SENSING The EPA requires that in high-enhanced areas states perform on-the-road testing of vehicle emissions. The state must sample 0.5% of the vehicle population base in high-enhanced areas. This may be accomplished by using a remote sensing device. This type of sensing may be done through equipment that projects an infrared light through the exhaust stream of a passing vehicle. The reflected beam can then be analyzed to determine the pollutant levels coming from the vehicle. If a vehicle fails this type of test, the vehicle owner will receive notification in the mail that he or she must take the vehicle to a test facility to have the emissions tested.

RANDOM ROADSIDE TESTING Some states may implement random roadside testing that would usually involve visual checks of the emission control devices to detect tampering. Obviously, this method is not very popular as it can lead to traffic tie-ups and delays on the part of commuters.

Exhaust analysis is an excellent tool to use for the diagnosis of engine performance concerns. In areas of the country that require exhaust testing to be able to get license plates, exhaust analysis must be able to:

- Establish a baseline for failure diagnosis and service.
- Identify areas of engine performance that are and are not functioning correctly.
- Determine that the service and repair of the vehicle have been accomplished and are complete.

FIGURE 42–6 A partial stream sampling exhaust probe being used to measure exhaust gases in parts per million (PPM) or percent (%).

EXHAUST ANALYSIS AND COMBUSTION EFFICIENCY

A popular method of engine analysis, as well as emissions testing, involves the use of five-gas exhaust analysis equipment. ● **SEE FIGURE 42–6.** The five gases analyzed and their significance include:

- **Hydrocarbons** Hydrocarbons (HC) are unburned gasoline and are measured in parts per million (PPM). A correctly operating engine should burn (oxidize) almost all the gasoline; therefore, very little unburned gasoline should be present in the exhaust. Acceptable levels of HC are 50 PPM or less. High levels of HC could be due to excessive oil consumption caused by weak piston rings or worn valve guides. The most common cause of excessive HC emissions is a fault in the ignition system. Items that should be checked include:

  - Spark plugs
  - Spark plug wires
  - Distributor cap and rotor (if the vehicle is so equipped)
  - Ignition timing (if possible)
  - Ignition coil

- **Carbon Monoxide** Carbon monoxide (CO) is unstable and will easily combine with any oxygen to form stable carbon dioxide (CO_2). The fact that CO combines with oxygen is the reason that CO is a poisonous gas (in the lungs, it combines with oxygen to form CO_2 and deprives the brain of oxygen). CO levels of a properly operating engine should be less than 0.5%. High levels of CO can be caused by clogged or restricted crankcase ventilation devices such as the PCV valve, hose(s), and tubes. Other items that might cause excessive CO include:

  - Clogged air filter
  - Incorrect idle speed
  - Too-high fuel-pump pressure
  - Any other items that can cause a rich condition

- **Carbon Dioxide (CO_2)** Carbon dioxide (CO_2) is the result of oxygen in the engine combining with the carbon of the gasoline. An acceptable level of CO_2 is between 12% and 15%. A high reading indicates an efficiently operating engine. If the CO_2 level is low, the mixture may be either too rich or too lean.

- **Oxygen** The next gas is oxygen (O_2). There is about 21% oxygen in the atmosphere, and most of this oxygen should be "used up" during the combustion process to oxidize all the hydrogen and carbon (hydrocarbons) in the gasoline. Levels of O_2 should be very low (about 0.5%). High levels of O_2, especially at idle, could be due to an exhaust system leak.

NOTE: Adding 10% alcohol to gasoline provides additional oxygen to the fuel and will result in lower levels of CO and higher levels of O_2 in the exhaust.

- **Oxides of Nitrogen (NO_x)** An oxide of nitrogen (NO) is a colorless, tasteless, and odorless gas when it leaves the engine, but as soon as it reaches the atmosphere and mixes with more oxygen, nitrogen oxides (NO_2) are formed. NO_2 is reddish-brown and has an acid and pungent smell. NO and NO_2 are grouped together and referred to as NO_x, where *x* represents any number of oxygen atoms. NO_x, the symbol used to represent all oxides of nitrogen, is the fifth gas commonly tested using a five-gas analyzer. The exhaust gas recirculation (EGR) system is the major controlling device limiting the formation of NO_x. ● **SEE FIGURE 42–7 AND CHART 42–4.**

HC TOO HIGH

High hydrocarbon exhaust emissions are usually caused by an engine misfire. What burns the fuel in an engine? The ignition system ignites a spark at the spark plug to ignite the *proper* mixture inside the combustion chamber. If a spark plug does not ignite the mixture, the resulting unburned fuel is pushed out of the cylinder on the exhaust stroke by the piston through the exhaust valves and into the exhaust system. Therefore, if any of the following ignition components or adjustments are not correct, excessive HC emission is likely.

1. Defective or worn spark plugs

2. Defective or loose spark plug wires

3. Defective distributor cap and/or rotor

4. Incorrect ignition timing (either too far advanced or too far retarded)

5. A lean air–fuel mixture can also cause a misfire. This condition is referred to as a lean misfire. A lean air–fuel mixture can be caused by low fuel pump pressure, a clogged fuel filter, or a restricted fuel injector.

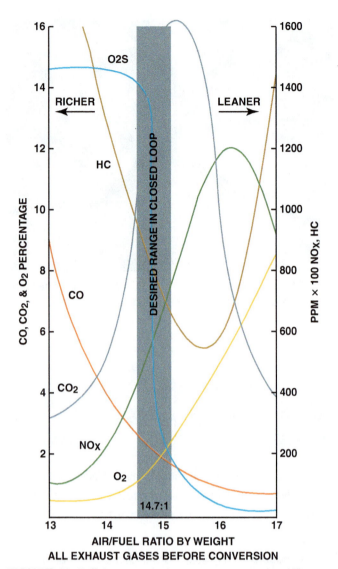

FIGURE 42–7 Exhaust emissions are very complex. When the air–fuel mixture becomes richer, some exhaust emissions are reduced, while others increase.

	WITHOUT CATALYTIC CONVERTER	WITH CATALYTIC CONVERTER
HC	300 PPM or less	30–50 PPM or less
CO	3% or less	0.3%–0.5% or less
O_2	0%–2%	0%–2%
CO_2	12%–15% or higher	12%–15% or higher
NO_x	Less than 100 PPM at idle and less than 1000 PPM at WOT	Less than 100 PPM at idle and less than 1000 PPM at WOT

CHART 42–4

Typical specifications for gasses with and without a catalytic converter. If the readings are about right for a vehicle that does not have a converter yet it is equipped with one, then the catalytic converter is likely not functioning.

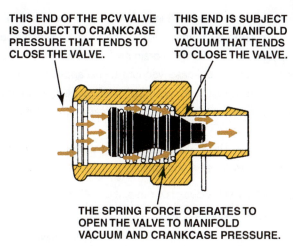

THIS END OF THE PCV VALVE IS SUBJECT TO CRANKCASE PRESSURE THAT TENDS TO CLOSE THE VALVE.

THIS END IS SUBJECT TO INTAKE MANIFOLD VACUUM THAT TENDS TO CLOSE THE VALVE.

THE SPRING FORCE OPERATES TO OPEN THE VALVE TO MANIFOLD VACUUM AND CRANKCASE PRESSURE.

FIGURE 43–8 Spring force, crankcase pressure, and intake manifold vacuum work together to regulate the flow rate through the PCV valve.

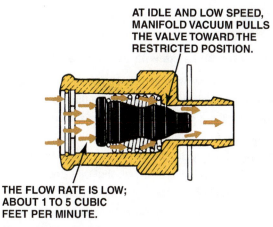

AT IDLE AND LOW SPEED, MANIFOLD VACUUM PULLS THE VALVE TOWARD THE RESTRICTED POSITION.

THE FLOW RATE IS LOW; ABOUT 1 TO 5 CUBIC FEET PER MINUTE.

FIGURE 43–9 Air flows through the PCV valve during idle, cruising, and light-load conditions.

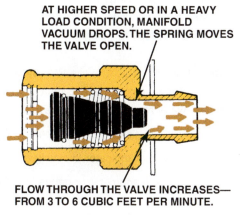

AT HIGHER SPEED OR IN A HEAVY LOAD CONDITION, MANIFOLD VACUUM DROPS. THE SPRING MOVES THE VALVE OPEN.

FLOW THROUGH THE VALVE INCREASES— FROM 3 TO 6 CUBIC FEET PER MINUTE.

FIGURE 43–10 Air flows through the PCV valve during acceleration and when the engine is under a heavy load.

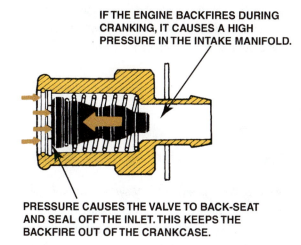

IF THE ENGINE BACKFIRES DURING CRANKING, IT CAUSES A HIGH PRESSURE IN THE INTAKE MANIFOLD.

PRESSURE CAUSES THE VALVE TO BACK-SEAT AND SEAL OFF THE INLET. THIS KEEPS THE BACKFIRE OUT OF THE CRANKCASE.

FIGURE 43–11 PCV valve operation in the event of a backfire.

 REAL WORLD FIX

The Whistling Engine

An older vehicle was being diagnosed for a whistling sound whenever the engine was running, especially at idle. It was finally discovered that the breather in the valve cover was plugged and caused high vacuum in the crankcase. The engine was sucking air from what was likely the rear main seal lip, making the "whistle" noise. After replacing the breather and PCV, the noise stopped.

ORIFICE-CONTROLLED SYSTEMS

The closed PCV system used on some four-cylinder engines contains a calibrated orifice instead of a PCV valve. The orifice may be located in the valve cover or intake manifold, or in a hose connected between the valve cover, air cleaner, and intake manifold.

While most orifice flow control systems work the same as a PCV valve system, they may not use fresh air scavenging of the crankcase. Crankcase vapors are drawn into the intake manifold in calibrated amounts depending on manifold pressure and the orifice size. If vapor availability is low, as during idle, air is drawn in with the vapors. During off-idle operation, excess vapors are sent to the air cleaner.

At idle, PCV flow is controlled by a 0.050 inch (1.3 mm) orifice. As the engine moves off-idle, ported vacuum pulls a spring-loaded valve off of its seat, allowing PCV flow to pass through a 0.090 inch (2.3 mm) orifice.

SEPARATOR SYSTEMS

Turbocharged and many fuel-injected engines use an oil/vapor or oil/water separator and a calibrated orifice instead of a PCV valve. In the most common applications, the air intake throttle body acts as the source for crankcase ventilation vacuum and a calibrated orifice acts as the metering device.

Check for Oil Leaks with the Engine Off

The owner of an older vehicle equipped with a V-6 engine complained to his technician that he smelled burning oil, but only *after* shutting off the engine. The technician found that the rocker cover gaskets were leaking. But why did the owner only notice the smell of hot oil when the engine was shut off? Because of the positive crankcase ventilation (PCV) system, engine vacuum tends to draw oil away from gasket surfaces. But when the engine stops, engine vacuum disappears and the oil remaining in the upper regions of the engine will tend to flow down and out through any opening. Therefore, a good technician should check an engine for oil leaks not only with the engine running but also shortly after shutdown.

PCV SYSTEM DIAGNOSIS

When intake air flows freely, the PCV system functions properly, as long as the PCV valve or orifice is not clogged. Modern engine design includes the air and vapor flow as a calibrated part of the air–fuel mixture. In fact, some engines receive as much as 30% of their idle air through the PCV system. For this reason, a flow problem in the PCV system results in driveability problems.

A blocked or plugged PCV system is a major cause of high oil consumption, and contributes to many oil leaks. Before expensive engine repairs are attempted, check the condition of the PCV system.

PCV SYSTEM PERFORMANCE CHECK
A properly operating positive crankcase ventilation system should be able to draw vapors from the crankcase and into the intake manifold. If the pipes, hoses, and PCV valve itself are not restricted, vacuum is applied to the crankcase. A slight vacuum is created in the crankcase (usually less than 1 inch Hg if measured at the dipstick) and is also applied to other areas of the engine. Oil drain-back holes provide a path for oil to drain back into the oil pan. These holes also allow crankcase vacuum to be applied under the rocker covers and in the valley area of most V-type engines. There are several methods that can be used to test a PCV system.

THE RATTLE TEST
The rattle test is performed by simply removing the PCV valve and shaking it in your hand.

- If the PCV valve does *not* rattle, it is definitely defective and must be replaced.

- If the PCV valve *does* rattle, it does not necessarily mean that the PCV valve is good. All PCV valves contain springs that can become weaker with age and heating and cooling cycles. Replace any PCV valve with the *exact* replacement according to vehicle manufacturers' recommended intervals (usually every three years or 36,000 miles, or 60,000 kilometer).

CRANKCASE VACUUM TEST
The PCV system can be checked by testing for a weak vacuum at the oil dipstick tube using an inches-of-water manometer or gauge as follows:

STEP 1 Remove the oil-filler cap and cover the opening.

STEP 2 Remove the oil-level indicator (dipstick).

STEP 3 Connect a water manometer or gauge to the dipstick tube.

STEP 4 Start the engine and observe the gauge at idle and at 2500 RPM. ● SEE FIGURE 43–12.

The gauge should show some vacuum, especially at 2500 RPM. If not, carefully inspect the PCV system for blockages or other faults.

PCV MONITOR
Starting with 2004 and newer vehicles, all vehicles must be checked for proper operation of the PCV system. The PCV monitor will fail if the PCM detects an opening between the crankcase and the PCV valve or between the PCV valve and the intake manifold. ● SEE FIGURE 43–13.

DTCs related to the PCV system include the one shown in ● CHART 43–2.

FIGURE 43–12 Using a gauge that measures vacuum in units of inches of water to test the vacuum at the dipstick tube, checking that the PCV system is capable of drawing a vacuum on the crankcase (28 inches of water equals 1 PSI or about 2 inch Hg of vacuum).

PCV-RELATED DIAGNOSTIC TROUBLE CODE		
DIAGNOSTIC TROUBLE CODE	**DESCRIPTION**	**POSSIBLE CAUSES**
P1480	PCV solenoid circuit fault	• Defective PCV solenoid • Loose or corroded electrical connection • Loose defective vacuum hoses/connections

CHART 43–2

SECONDARY AIR INJECTION SYSTEM

An air pump provides the air necessary for the oxidizing process inside the catalytic converter. The system of adding air to the exhaust is commonly called secondary air injection (SAI).

NOTE: This system is commonly called AIR, meaning air injection reaction. Therefore, an AIR pump does pump air.

The AIR pump, sometimes referred to as a smog pump *or* thermactor pump, is mounted at the front of the engine and driven by a belt from the crankshaft pulley. It pulls fresh air in through an external filter and pumps the air under slight pressure to each exhaust port through connecting hoses or a manifold.

BELT-DRIVEN AIR PUMPS
Found on older vehicles, the belt-driven air pump uses a centrifugal filter just behind the drive pulley. ● **SEE FIGURE 43–14.** As the pump rotates,

FIGURE 43–13 Most PCV valves used on newer vehicles are secured with fasteners, which makes it more difficult to disconnect and thereby less likely to increase emissions.

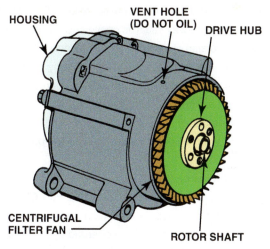

FIGURE 43–14 A typical belt-driven AIR pump (in older vehicles). Air enters through the revolving fins behind the drive pulley. The fins act as an air filter because dirt is heavier than air and therefore the dirt is deflected off of the fins at the same time air is being drawn into the pump.

underhood air is drawn into the pump and slightly compressed. The air is then directed to:

- The exhaust manifold when the engine is cold to help oxidize CO and HC into carbon dioxide (CO_2) and water vapor (H_2O)

- The catalytic converter on many models to help provide the extra oxygen needed for the efficient conversion of CO and HC into CO_2 and H_2O

- The air cleaner during deceleration or wide-open throttle (WOT) engine operation

ELECTRIC MOTOR-DRIVEN AIR PUMPS
This style of pump is generally used only during cold engine operation and is

FIGURE 43–15 A typical electric motor-driven AIR pump. This unit is on a Chevrolet Corvette and only works when the engine is cold.

computer controlled. The air injection reaction (AIR) system helps reduce hydrocarbon (HC) and carbon monoxide (CO). It also helps to warm up the three-way catalytic converters quickly on engine start-up so conversion of exhaust gases may occur sooner.

The AIR pump and solenoid is controlled by the PCM. The PCM turns on the AIR pump by providing the ground to complete the circuit which energizes the AIR pump solenoid relay. When air to the exhaust ports is desired, the PCM energizes the relay in order to turn on the solenoid and the AIR pump. ● SEE FIGURE 43–15.

The PCM turns on the AIR pump during start-up any time the engine coolant temperature is above 32°F (0°C). A typical electric AIR pump operates for a maximum of 240 seconds, or until the system enters closed-loop operation. The AIR system is disabled under the following conditions:

- The PCM recognizes a problem and sets a diagnostic trouble code.
- The AIR pump has been on for 240 seconds.
- The engine speed is more than 2825 RPM.
- The manifold absolute pressure (MAP) is less than 6 inch Hg (20 kPa).
- Increased temperature detected in three-way catalytic converter during warm-up.
- The short- and long-term fuel trim are not in their normal ranges.
- Power enrichment is detected.

If no air (oxygen) enters the exhaust stream at the exhaust ports, the HC and CO emission levels will be higher than normal. Air flowing to the exhaust ports at all times could increase temperature of the three-way catalytic converter (TWC).

The diagnostic trouble codes P0410 and/or P0418 set if there is a malfunction in the following components:

- The AIR pump
- The AIR solenoid
- The AIR pump solenoid relay
- Leaking hoses or pipes
- Leaking check valves
- The circuits going to the AIR pump and the AIR pump solenoid relay

The AIR pump is an electric-type pump that requires no periodic maintenance. To check the operation of the AIR pump, the engine should be at normal operating temperature in neutral at idle. Using a scan tool, enable the AIR pump system and watch the heated oxygen sensor (HO2S) voltages for both bank 1 and bank 2 HO2S. The HO2S voltages for both sensors should remain under 350 mV because air is being directed to the exhaust ports. If the HO2S voltages remain low during this test, the AIR pump, solenoid, and shut-off valve are operating satisfactorily. If the HO2S voltage does not remain low when the AIR pump is enabled, inspect for the following:

- Voltage at the AIR pump when energized
- A seized AIR pump
- The hoses, vacuum lines, pipes, and all connections for leaks and proper routing
- Airflow going to the exhaust ports
- AIR pump for proper mounting
- Hoses and pipes for deterioration or holes

If a leak is suspected on the pressure side of the system, or if a hose or pipe has been disconnected on the pressure side, the connections should be checked for leaks with a soapy water solution. With the AIR pump running, bubbles form if a leak exists.

● **CHART 43–3** lists some AIR system DTCs.

SAI-RELATED DIAGNOSTIC TROUBLE CODES		
DIAGNOSTIC TROUBLE CODE	DESCRIPTION	POSSIBLE CAUSES
P0411	SAI incorrect airflow detected	• Defective AIR solenoid • Loose or corroded electrical connections • Loose, missing, or defective rubber hose(s)
P0418	SAI pump relay control circuit fault	• Relay control circuit open, shorted to ground, or shorted to voltage

CHART 43–3

FIGURE 43–16 Most catalytic converters are located as close to the exhaust manifold as possible as seen in this display of a Chevrolet Corvette.

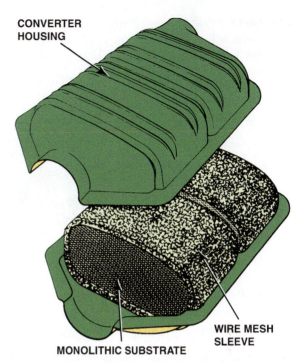

CONVERTER HOUSING

WIRE MESH SLEEVE

MONOLITHIC SUBSTRATE

FIGURE 43–17 A typical catalytic converter with a monolithic substrate.

CATALYTIC CONVERTERS

A **catalytic converter** is an after-treatment device used to reduce exhaust emissions outside of the engine. This device is installed in the exhaust system between the exhaust manifold and the muffler, and usually is positioned beneath the passenger compartment. The location of the converter is important, since as much of the exhaust heat as possible must be retained for effective operation. The nearer it is to the engine, the better. ● **SEE FIGURE 43–16.**

CERAMIC MONOLITH CATALYTIC CONVERTER

Most catalytic converters are constructed of a ceramic material in a honeycomb shape with square openings for the exhaust gases. There are approximately 400 openings per square inch (62 per sq cm) and the wall thickness is about 0.006 inch (1.5 mm). The substrate is then coated with a porous aluminum material called the **washcoat**, which makes the surface rough. The catalytic materials are then applied on top of the washcoat. The substrate is contained within a shell made by welding together two stamped pieces of stainless steel. ● **SEE FIGURE 43–17.**

The ceramic substrate in monolithic converters is not restrictive, but the converter breaks easily when subject to shock or severe jolts and is more expensive to manufacture. Monolithic converters can be serviced only as a unit.

An exhaust pipe is connected to the manifold or header to carry gases through a catalytic converter and then to the muffler or silencer. V-type engines usually route the exhaust into one catalytic converter.

CATALYTIC CONVERTER OPERATION The converter contains small amounts of **rhodium**, **palladium**, and **platinum**. These elements act as catalysts. A **catalyst** is an element that starts a chemical reaction without becoming a part of, or being consumed in, the process. In a **three-way catalytic converter (TWC)** all three exhaust emissions (NO_x, HC, and CO) are converted to carbon dioxide (CO_2) and water (H_2O). As the exhaust gas passes through the catalyst, oxides of nitrogen (NO_x) are chemically reduced (i.e., nitrogen and oxygen are separated) in the first section of the catalytic converter. In the second section of the catalytic converter, most of the hydrocarbons and carbon monoxide remaining in the exhaust gas are oxidized to form harmless carbon dioxide (CO_2) and water vapor (H_2O). ● **SEE FIGURE 43–18.**

Since the early 1990s, many converters also contain **cerium**, an element that can store oxygen. The purpose of the cerium is to provide oxygen to the oxidation bed of the converter when the exhaust is rich and lacks enough oxygen for proper oxidation. When the exhaust is lean, the cerium absorbs the extra oxygen. The converter must have a varying rich-to-lean exhaust for proper operation:

- A rich exhaust is required for reduction—stripping the oxygen (O_2) from the nitrogen in NO_x

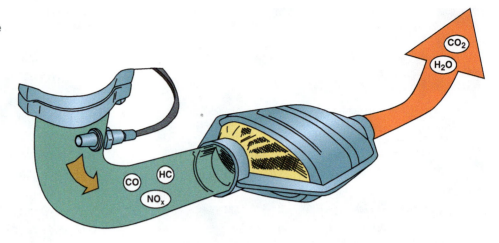

FIGURE 43–18 The three-way catalytic converter first separates the NO_X into nitrogen and oxygen and then converts the HC and CO into harmless water (H_2O) and carbon dioxide (CO_2).

- A lean exhaust is required to provide the oxygen necessary to oxidize HC and CO (combining oxygen with HC and CO to form H_2O and CO_2)

If the catalytic converter is not functioning correctly, check to see that the air–fuel mixture being supplied to the engine is correct and that the ignition system is free of defects.

CONVERTER LIGHT-OFF The catalytic converter does not work when cold and it must be heated to its light-off temperature of close to 500°F (260°C) before it starts working at 50% effectiveness. When fully effective, the converter reaches a temperature range of 900° to 1,600°F (482° to 871°C). In spite of the intense heat, however, catalytic reactions do not generate a flame associated with a simple burning reaction. Because of the extreme heat (almost as hot as combustion chamber temperatures), a converter remains hot long after the engine is shut off. Most vehicles use a series of heat shields to protect the passenger compartment and other parts of the chassis from excessive heat.

CONVERTER USAGE A catalytic converter must be located as close as possible to the exhaust manifold to work effectively. The farther back the converter is positioned in the exhaust system, the more gases cool before they reach the converter. Since positioning in the exhaust system affects the oxidation process, cars that use only an oxidation converter generally locate it underneath the front of the passenger compartment.

Some vehicles have used a small, quick-heating oxidation converter called a **preconverter**, **pup**, or mini-converter that connects directly to the exhaust manifold outlet. These have a small catalyst surface area close to the engine that heats up rapidly to start the oxidation process more quickly during cold

engine warm-up. For this reason, they were often called light-off converters, or LOC. The oxidation reaction started in the LOC is completed by the larger main converter under the passenger compartment.

OBD-II CATALYTIC CONVERTER MONITOR

With OBD-II-equipped vehicles, catalytic converter performance is monitored by heated oxygen sensors (HO2Ss), both before and after the converter. The converters used on these vehicles have what is known as **OSC** or **oxygen storage capacity**. OSC is due mostly to the cerium coating in the catalyst rather than the precious metals used. When the TWC is operating as it should, the postconverter HO2S is far less active than the preconverter sensor. The converter stores, then releases the oxygen during normal reduction and oxidation of the exhaust gases, smoothing out the variations in O_2 being released.

Where a cycling sensor voltage output is expected before the converter, because of the converter action, the postconverter HO2S should read a steady signal without much fluctuation. ● **SEE FIGURE 43–19.**

Engineers established a correlation between the amount of oxygen absorbed and converter efficiency. The OBD-II system monitors how much oxygen the catalyst retains.

A voltage waveform from the downstream HO2S of a good catalyst should have little or no activity. A voltage waveform from the downstream HO2S of a degraded catalyst shows a lot of activity.

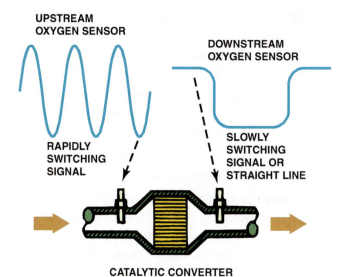

FIGURE 43–19 The OBD-II catalytic converter monitor compares the signals of the upstream and downstream O2Ss to determine converter efficiency.

In other words, the closer the activity of the downstream HO2S matches that of the upstream HO2S, the greater the degree of converter degradation. In operation, the OBD-II monitor compares activities between the two exhaust oxygen sensors.

CONVERTER-DAMAGING CONDITIONS

Since converters have no moving parts, they require no periodic service. Under federal law, catalyst effectiveness is warranted for 80,000 miles or eight years.

The three main causes of premature converter failure are:

- **Contamination.** Substances that can destroy the converter include exhaust that contains excess engine oil, antifreeze, sulfur (from poor fuel), and various other chemical substances.

- **Excessive temperatures.** Although a converter operates at high temperature, it can be destroyed by excessive temperatures. This most often occurs either when too much unburned fuel enters the converter, or with excessively lean mixtures. Excessive temperatures may be caused by long idling periods on some vehicles, since more heat develops at those times than when driving at normal highway speeds. Severe high temperatures can cause the converter to melt down, leading to the internal parts breaking apart and either clogging the converter or moving downstream to plug the muffler. In either case, the restricted exhaust flow severely reduces engine power.

 FREQUENTLY ASKED QUESTION

Can a Catalytic Converter Be Defective Without Being Clogged?

Yes. Catalytic converters can fail by being chemically damaged or poisoned without being mechanically clogged. Therefore, the catalytic converter should not only be tested for physical damage (clogging) by performing a backpressure or vacuum test and a rattle test but also a test for temperature rise, usually with a pyrometer, or propane test, to check the efficiency of the converter.

- **Improper air–fuel mixtures.** Rich mixtures or raw fuel in the exhaust can be caused by engine misfiring, or an excessively rich air–fuel mixture resulting from a defective coolant temperature sensor or defective fuel injectors. Lean mixtures are commonly caused by intake manifold leaks. When either of these circumstances occurs, the converter can become a catalytic furnace, causing the previously described damage.

To avoid excessive catalyst temperatures and the possibility of fuel vapors reaching the converter, follow these rules:

1. Do not try to start the engine by pushing the vehicle. Use jumper cables or a jump box to start the engine.

2. Do not crank an engine for more than 40 seconds when it is flooded or firing intermittently.

3. Do not turn off the ignition switch when the vehicle is in motion.

4. Do not disconnect a spark plug wire for more than 30 seconds.

5. Repair engine problems such as dieseling, misfiring, or stumbling as soon as possible.

DIAGNOSING CATALYTIC CONVERTERS

THE TAP TEST   The simple tap test involves tapping (not pounding) on the catalytic converter using a rubber mallet. If the substrate inside the converter is broken, the converter will rattle when hit. If the converter rattles, a replacement converter is required.

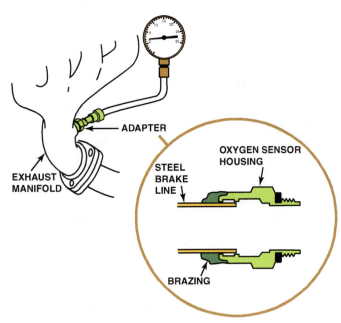

FIGURE 43–20 A backpressure tool can be made by using an oxygen sensor housing and using epoxy or braze to hold the tube to the housing.

TESTING BACKPRESSURE WITH A VACUUM GAUGE

A vacuum gauge can be used to measure manifold vacuum at a high idle (2000 RPM to 2500 RPM). If the exhaust system is restricted, pressure increases in the exhaust system. This pressure is called **backpressure**. Manifold vacuum will drop gradually if the engine is kept at a constant speed if the exhaust is restricted.

The reason the vacuum will drop is that all the exhaust leaving the engine at the higher engine speed cannot get through the restriction. After a short time (within one minute), the exhaust tends to "pile up" above the restriction and eventually remains in the cylinder of the engine at the end of the exhaust stroke. Therefore, at the beginning of the intake stroke, when the piston traveling downward should be lowering the pressure (raising the vacuum) in the intake manifold, the extra exhaust in the cylinder *lowers* the normal vacuum. If the exhaust restriction is severe enough, the vehicle can become undriveable because cylinder filling cannot occur except at idle.

TESTING BACKPRESSURE WITH A PRESSURE GAUGE

Exhaust system backpressure can be measured directly by installing a pressure gauge in an exhaust opening. This can be accomplished in one of the following ways:

1. To test an oxygen sensor, remove the inside of an old, discarded oxygen sensor and thread in an adapter to convert it to a vacuum or pressure gauge.

NOTE: An adapter can be easily made by inserting a metal tube or pipe. A short section of brake line works great. The pipe can be brazed to the oxygen sensor housing or it can be glued with epoxy. An 18-millimeter compression gauge adapter can also be adapted to fit into the oxygen sensor opening.
● **SEE FIGURE 43–20.**

2. To test an exhaust gas recirculation (EGR) valve, remove the EGR valve and fabricate a plate.

3. To test an air injection reaction (AIR) check valve, remove the check valve from the exhaust tubes leading to the exhaust manifold. Use a rubber cone with a tube inside to seal against the exhaust tube. Connect the tube to a pressure gauge.

At idle the maximum backpressure should be less than 1.5 PSI (10 kPa), and it should be less than 2.5 PSI (15 kPa) at 2500 RPM.

TESTING A CATALYTIC CONVERTER FOR TEMPERATURE RISE

A properly working catalytic converter should be able to reduce NO_x exhaust emissions into nitrogen (N) and oxygen (O_2) and oxidize unburned hydrocarbon (HC) and carbon monoxide (CO) into harmless carbon dioxide (CO_2) and water vapor (H_2O). During these chemical processes, the catalytic converter should increase in temperature at least 10% if the converter is working properly. To test the converter, operate the engine at 2500 RPM for at least 2 minutes to fully warm up the converter. Measure the inlet and the outlet temperatures using an infrared pyrometer as shown in ● **FIGURE 43–21.**

NOTE: If the engine is extremely efficient, the converter may not have any excessive unburned hydrocarbons or carbon monoxide to convert! In this case, a spark plug wire could be grounded out using a vacuum hose and a test light to create some unburned hydrocarbon in the exhaust. Do not ground out a cylinder for longer than 10 seconds or the excessive amount of unburned hydrocarbon could overheat and damage the converter.

CATALYTIC CONVERTER EFFICIENCY TESTS

The efficiency of a catalytic converter can be determined using an exhaust gas analyzer.

OXYGEN LEVEL TEST. With the engine warm and in closed-loop, check the oxygen (O_2) and carbon monoxide (CO) levels.

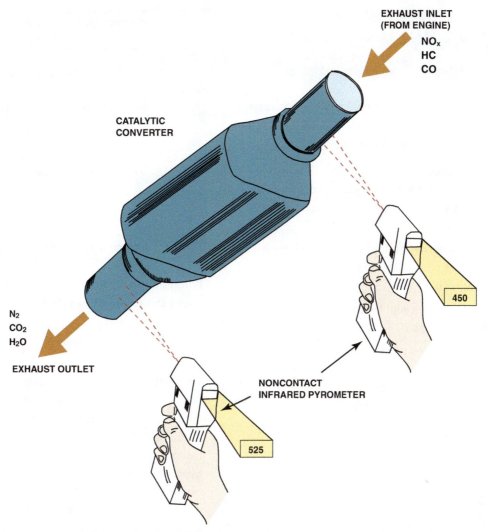

EXHAUST INLET
(FROM ENGINE)
NO_x
HC
CO

CATALYTIC
CONVERTER

N_2
CO_2
H_2O

EXHAUST OUTLET

NONCONTACT
INFRARED PYROMETER

450

525

FIGURE 43–21 The temperature of the outlet should be at least 10% hotter than the temperature of the inlet. If a converter is not working, the inlet temperature will be hotter than the outlet temperature.

- If O_2 is zero, go to the snap-throttle test.
- If O_2 is greater than zero, check the CO level.
- If CO is greater than zero, the converter is *not* functioning correctly.

SNAP-THROTTLE TEST. With the engine warm and in closed-loop, snap the throttle to wide open (WOT) in park or neutral and observe the oxygen reading.

- O_2 reading should not exceed 1.2%; if it does, the converter is *not* working.
- If the O_2 rises to 1.2%, the converter may have low efficiency.
- If the O_2 remains below 1.2%, then the converter is okay.

 **TECH TIP**

Aftermarket Catalytic Converters

Some replacement aftermarket (nonfactory) catalytic converters do not contain the same amount of cerium as the original part. Cerium is the element that is used in catalytic converters to store oxygen. As a result of the lack of cerium, the correlation between the oxygen storage and the conversion efficiency may be affected enough to set a false diagnostic trouble code (P0422).

CATALYTIC CONVERTER REPLACEMENT GUIDELINES

Because a catalytic converter is a major exhaust gas emission control device, the Environmental Protection Agency (EPA) has strict guidelines for its replacement, including:

- If a converter is replaced on a vehicle with less than 80,000 miles/8 years, depending on the year of the vehicle, an original equipment catalytic converter *must* be used as a replacement.

- The replacement converter must be of the same design as the original. If the original had an air pump fitting, so must the replacement.

- The old converter must be kept for possible inspection by the authorities for 60 days.

- A form must be completed and signed by both the vehicle owner and a representative from the service facility. This form must state the cause of the converter failure and must remain on file for two years.

● **SEE CHART 43–4.**

CATALYTIC CONVERTER-RELATED DIAGNOSTIC TROUBLE CODE		
DIAGNOSTIC TROUBLE CODE	**DESCRIPTION**	**POSSIBLE CAUSES**
P0420	Catalytic converter efficiency failure	• Engine mechanical fault • Exhaust leaks • Fuel contaminants, such as engine oil, coolant, or sulfur

CHART 43–4

TECH TIP

Catalytic Converters Are Murdered

Catalytic converters start a chemical reaction but do not enter into the chemical reaction. Therefore, catalytic converters do not wear out and they do not die of old age. If a catalytic converter is found to be defective (nonfunctioning or clogged), look for the *root* cause. Remember this:

"Catalytic converters do not commit suicide—they're murdered."

Items that should be checked when a defective catalytic converter is discovered include all components of the ignition and fuel systems. Excessive unburned fuel can cause the catalytic converter to overheat and fail. The oxygen sensor must be working and fluctuating from 0.5 Hz to 5 Hz (times per second) to provide the necessary air–fuel mixture variations for maximum catalytic converter efficiency.

 FREQUENTLY ASKED QUESTION

When Filling My Fuel Tank, Why Should I Stop When the Pump Clicks Off?

Every fuel tank has an upper volume chamber that allows for expansion of the fuel when hot. The volume of the chamber is between 10% and 20% of the volume of the tank. For example, if a fuel tank had a capacity of 20 gallons, the expansion chamber volume would be from 2 gallons to 4 gallons. A hose is attached at the top of the chamber and vented to the charcoal canister. If extra fuel is forced into this expansion volume, liquid gasoline can be drawn into the charcoal canister. This liquid fuel can saturate the canister and create an overly rich air–fuel mixture when the canister purge valve is opened during normal vehicle operation. This extra-rich air–fuel mixture can cause the vehicle to fail an exhaust emissions test, reduce fuel economy, and possibly damage the catalytic converter. To avoid problems, simply add fuel to the next dime's worth after the nozzle clicks off. This will ensure that the tank is full, yet not overfilled.

EVAPORATIVE EMISSION CONTROL SYSTEM

The purpose of the evaporative (EVAP) emission control system is to trap and hold gasoline vapors also called volatile organic compounds, or VOCs. The charcoal canister is part of an entire system of hoses and valves called the evaporative control system. These vapors are instead routed into a charcoal canister, from where they go to the intake airflow so they are burned in the engine.

COMMON COMPONENTS The fuel tank filler caps used on vehicles with modern EVAP systems are a special design. Most EVAP fuel tank filler caps have pressure-vacuum relief built into them. When pressure or vacuum exceeds a calibrated value, the valve opens. Once the pressure or vacuum has been relieved, the valve closes. If a sealed cap is used on an EVAP system that requires a pressure-vacuum relief design, a vacuum lock may develop in the fuel system, or the fuel tank may be damaged by fuel expansion or contraction.

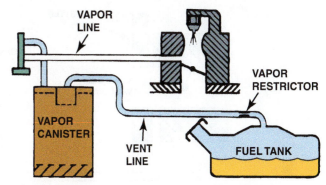

FIGURE 43–22 The evaporative emission control system includes all of the lines, hoses, and valves, plus the charcoal canister.

● **CHART 43–5** may be useful when discussing the pressures that may be found in the EVAP system.

HOW THE EVAPORATIVE CONTROL SYSTEM WORKS

The canister is located under the hood or underneath the vehicle, and is filled with activated charcoal granules that can hold up to one-third of their own weight in fuel vapors. A vent line connects the canister to the fuel tank.

NOTE: Some vehicles with large or dual fuel tanks may have dual canisters.

Activated charcoal is an effective vapor trap because of its great surface area. Each gram of activated charcoal has a surface area of 1,100 square meters, or more than a quarter acre. Typical canisters hold either 300 or 625 grams of charcoal *with a surface area equivalent to 80 or 165 football fields*. **Adsorption** attaches the fuel vapor molecules to the carbon surface. This attaching force is not strong, so the system purges the vapor molecules by sending a fresh airflow through the charcoal. ● **SEE FIGURE 43–22.**

VAPOR PURGING During engine operation, stored vapors are drawn from the canister into the engine through a hose connected to the throttle body or the air cleaner. This "purging" process mixes HC vapors from the canister with the existing air–fuel charge.

COMPUTER-CONTROLLED PURGE Canister purging is regulated by the powertrain control module (PCM). This is done by a microprocessor-controlled vacuum solenoid, and one or more purge valves. ● **SEE FIGURE 43–23.** Under normal conditions, most engine control systems permit purging only during closed-loop operation at cruising speeds. During other engine operation conditions, such as open-loop mode, idle, deceleration, or wide-open throttle, the PCM prevents canister purging.

PRESSURE CONVERSIONS		
PSI	INCH Hg	INCH H₂O
14.7	29.93	407.19
1.0	2.036	27.7
0.9	1.8	24.93
0.8	1.63	22.16
0.7	1.43	19.39
0.6	1.22	16.62
0.5	1.018	13.85
0.4	0.814	11.08
0.3	0.611	8.31
0.2	0.407	5.54
0.1	0.204	2.77
0.09	0.183	2.49
0.08	0.163	2.22
0.07	0.143	1.94
0.06	0.122	1.66
0.05	0.102	1.385

1 PSI = 28 inches of water; 1/4 PSI = 7 inches of water.

CHART 43–5

NONENHANCED EVAPORATIVE CONTROL SYSTEMS

Prior to 1996, evaporative systems were referred to as evaporative (EVAP) control systems. This term refers to evaporative systems that had limited diagnostic capabilities. While they are often PCM controlled, their diagnostic capability is usually limited to their ability to detect if purge has occurred.

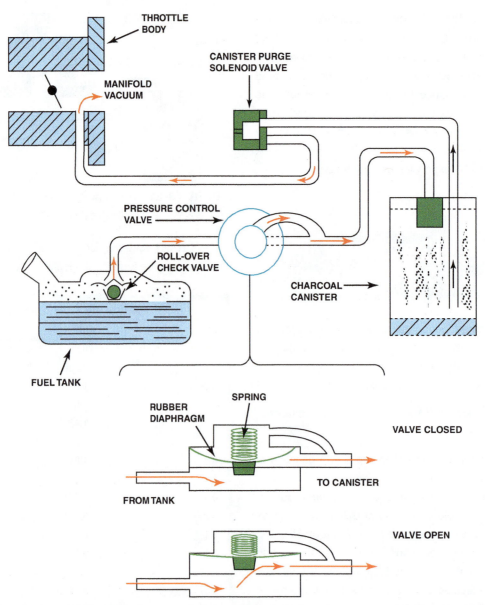

FIGURE 43–23 A typical evaporative emission control system. Note that when the computer turns on the canister purge solenoid valve, manifold vacuum draws any stored vapors from the canister into the engine. Manifold vacuum also is applied to the pressure control valve. When this valve opens, fumes from the fuel tank are drawn into the charcoal canister and eventually into the engine. When the solenoid valve is turned off (or the engine stops and there is no manifold vacuum), the pressure control valve is spring-loaded shut to keep vapors inside the fuel tank from escaping to the atmosphere.

Many systems have a diagnostic switch that could sense if purge is occurring and set a code if no purge is detected. This system does not check for leaks. On some vehicles, the PCM also has the capability of monitoring the integrity of the purge solenoid and circuit. These systems' limitations are their ability to check the integrity of the evaporative system on the vehicle. They could not detect leaks or missing or loose gas caps that could lead to excessive evaporative emissions from the vehicle. Nonenhanced evaporative systems use either a canister purge solenoid or a vapor management valve to control purge vapor.

ENHANCED EVAPORATIVE CONTROL SYSTEM

Beginning in 1996 with OBD-II vehicles, manufacturers were required to install systems that are able to detect both purge flow and evaporative system leakage. The systems on models produced between 1996 and 2000 have to be able to detect a leak as small as 0.040 inch diameter. Beginning in the model year 2000, the enhanced systems started a phase-in of 0.020 inch-diameter leak detection.

All vehicles built after 1995 have enhanced evaporative systems that have the ability to detect purge flow and system leakage. If either of these two functions fails, the system is required to set a diagnostic trouble code and turn on the MIL light to warn the driver of the failure.

ENHANCED EVAP SYSTEM COMPONENTS AND OPERATION[2]

The evaporative emission (EVAP) control system limits fuel vapors from escaping into the atmosphere. Fuel tank vapors are allowed to move from the fuel tank, due to pressure in the tank, through the EVAP vapor tube, into the EVAP canister. Carbon in the canister absorbs and stores the fuel vapors. Excess pressure is vented through the vent hose and EVAP vent solenoid valve to the atmosphere. ● **SEE FIGURE 43–24.**

The EVAP canister stores the fuel vapors until the engine is able to use them. At an appropriate time, the engine control module (ECM) will command the EVAP purge solenoid valve ON, allowing engine vacuum to be applied to the EVAP canister. With the normally open EVAP vent solenoid valve off, fresh air is drawn through the vent solenoid valve and the vent hose to the EVAP canister. Fresh air is drawn through the canister, pulling fuel vapors from the carbon. The air–fuel vapor mixture continues through the EVAP purge tube and EVAP purge solenoid valve into the intake manifold to be consumed during normal combustion. The ECM uses several tests to determine if the EVAP system is leaking or restricted.

PURGE SOLENOID VALVE LEAK TEST If the EVAP purge solenoid valve does not seal properly, fuel vapors could enter the engine at an undesired time, causing driveability concerns. The ECM tests for this by commanding the EVAP purge solenoid valve OFF and the vent solenoid valve ON which seals the system. With the engine running, the ECM monitors the fuel tank pressure (FTP) sensor for an increase in vacuum. The ECM will log a fault if a vacuum develops in the tank under these test conditions.

LARGE LEAK TEST This diagnostic test creates a vacuum condition in the EVAP system. When the enabling criteria has been met, the ECM commands the normally open EVAP vent solenoid valve closed and the EVAP purge solenoid valve open, creating a vacuum in the EVAP system. The ECM then monitors

---
[2]GM Service Information Document # 2201718

TECH TIP

Problems After Refueling? Check the Purge Valve

The purge valve is normally closed and open only when the PCM is commanding the system to purge. If the purge solenoid were to become stuck in the open position, gasoline fumes would be allowed to flow directly from the gas tank to the intake manifold. When refueling, this would result in a lot of fumes being forced into the intake manifold and as a result would cause a hard-to-start condition after refueling. This would also result in a rich exhaust and likely black exhaust when first starting the engine after refueling. While the purge solenoid is usually located under the hood of most vehicles and is less subject to rust and corrosion than the vent valve, it can still fail.

the FTP sensor voltage to verify that the system is able to reach a predetermined level of vacuum within a set amount of time. Failure to achieve the expected level of vacuum indicates the presence of a large leak in the EVAP system or a restriction in the purge path. The ECM will log a fault if it detects a weaker than expected vacuum level under these test conditions.

CANISTER VENT RESTRICTION TEST If the EVAP vent system is restricted, fuel vapors will not be properly purged from the EVAP canister. The ECM tests this by commanding the EVAP purge solenoid valve ON while commanding the EVAP vent solenoid valve OFF, and then monitoring the FTP sensor for an increase in vacuum. If the vacuum increases more than the expected amount, in a set amount of time, a fault will be logged by the ECM.

SMALL LEAK TEST The engine off natural vacuum diagnostic is the small-leak detection diagnostic for the EVAP system. The test is designed to detect leaks as small as 0.51 mm (0.020 inch). The engine off natural vacuum diagnostic monitors the EVAP system pressure with the ignition off.

NOTE: It may be normal for the ECM to remain active for up to 40 min after the ignition is turned off. This is important to remember when performing a parasitic draw test on vehicles equipped with engine off natural vacuum.

When the vehicle is driven, the temperature rises in the tank due to heat transfer from the exhaust system. After the

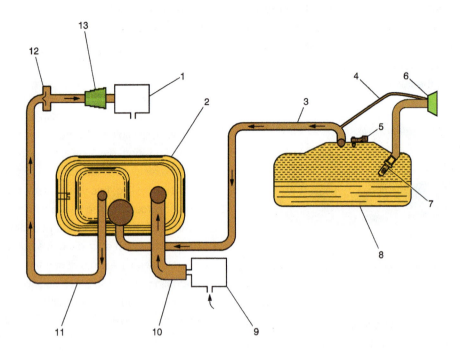

FIGURE 43-24 EVAP system components. (1) Evaporative Emissions (EVAP) Purge Solenoid Valve; (2) EVAP Canister; (3) EVAP Vapor Tube; (4) Vapor Recirculation Tube; (5) Fuel Tank Pressure Sensor; (6) Fuel Filler Cap (some vehicles may have a capless design); (7) Fuel Fill Pipe Inlet Check Valve; (8) Fuel Tank; (9) EVAP Canister Vent Solenoid Valve; (10) Vent hose; (11) EVAP Purge Tube; (12) Purge Tube Check Valve (turbo-charged applications only); (13) EVAP Canister Purge Tube Connector. (*Courtesy of General Motors*)

vehicle is parked, the temperature in the tank continues to rise for a period of time, and then starts to drop. The engine off natural vacuum diagnostic relies on this temperature change, and the corresponding pressure change in a sealed system, to determine if an EVAP system leak is present.

EVAP SYSTEM COMPONENTS
The EVAP system consists of the following components:

- **EVAP Purge Solenoid Valve.** The EVAP purge solenoid valve controls the flow of vapors from the EVAP system to the intake manifold. The purge solenoid valve opens when commanded ON by the ECM. This normally closed valve is pulse-width modulated by the ECM to precisely control the flow of fuel vapor to the engine. The valve will also be opened during some portions of the EVAP testing when the engine is running, allowing engine vacuum to enter the EVAP system.

- **Purge Tube Check Valve.** Turbocharged vehicles have a check valve in the purge tube between the EVAP purge solenoid valve and the EVAP canister to prevent pressurization of the EVAP system under boost conditions.

- **EVAP Canister.** The canister is filled with carbon pellets used to absorb and store fuel vapors. Fuel vapor is

stored in the canister until the ECM determines that the vapor can be consumed in the normal combustion process.

- **Vapor Recirculation Tube.** A vapor path between the fuel fill pipe and the vapor tube to the carbon canister is necessary for Vehicle Onboard Diagnostics to fully diagnose the EVAP system. It also accommodates service diagnostic procedures by allowing the entire EVAP system to be diagnosed from either end of the system.

- **Fuel Tank Pressure Sensor.** The FTP sensor measures the difference between the pressure or vacuum in the fuel tank and outside air pressure. The ECM provides a 5 volt reference and a ground to the FTP sensor. Depending on the vehicle, the sensor can be located in the vapor space on top of the fuel tank, in the vapor tube between the canister and the tank, or on the EVAP canister. The FTP sensor provides a signal voltage back to the ECM that can vary between 0.1 and 4.9 volts. A high FTP sensor voltage indicates a low fuel tank pressure or vacuum. A low FTP sensor voltage indicates a high fuel tank pressure.

- **Fuel Fill Pipe Check Valve.** The check valve on the fuel fill pipe is there to prevent spit-back during refueling.

- **EVAP Vent Solenoid Valve.** The EVAP vent solenoid valve controls fresh airflow into the EVAP canister. The valve is normally open. The canister vent solenoid valve is closed only during EVAP system tests performed by the ECM.
- **Fuel Fill Cap.** The fuel fill cap is equipped with a seal and a vacuum relief valve.
- **Capless Fuel Fill.** Some vehicles may have a capless fuel fill design behind a locking fuel door. There is no fuel fill cap to remove. One just fully inserts the fuel nozzle into the fill neck, making sure it latches before refueling. Flapper valves close to seal this interface once the fill nozzle is removed.

ONBOARD REFUELING VAPOR RECOVERY

The onboard refueling vapor recovery (ORVR) system was first introduced on some 1998 vehicles. Previously designed EVAP systems allowed fuel vapor to escape to the atmosphere during refueling.

The primary feature of most ORVR systems is the restricted tank filler tube, which is about 1 inch (25 mm) in diameter. This reduced-size filler tube creates an aspiration effect, which tends to draw outside air into the filler tube. During refueling, the fuel tank is vented to the charcoal canister, which captures the gas fumes, and with air flowing into the filler tube, no vapors can escape to the atmosphere.

STATE INSPECTION EVAP TESTS

In some states, a periodic inspection and test of the fuel system are mandated along with a dynamometer test. The emissions inspection includes tests on the vehicle before and during the dynamometer test. Before the running test, the fuel tank and cap, fuel lines, canister, and other fuel system components must be inspected and tested to ensure that they are not leaking gasoline vapors into the atmosphere.

First, the fuel tank cap is tested to ensure that it is sealing properly and holds pressure within specs. Next, the cap is installed on the vehicle, and using a special adapter, the EVAP system is pressurized to approximately 0.5 PSI and monitored for 2 minutes. Pressure in the tank and lines should not drop below approximately 0.3 PSI.

If the cap or system leaks, hydrocarbon emissions are likely being released, and the vehicle fails the test. If the system leaks, an ultrasonic leak detector may be used to find the leak.

Finally, with the engine warmed up and running at a moderate speed, the canister purge line is tested for adequate flow using a special flow meter inserted into the system. In one example, if the flow from the canister to the intake system, when the system is activated, is at least one liter per minute, then the vehicle passes the canister purge test.

DIAGNOSING THE EVAP SYSTEM

Before vehicle emissions testing began in many parts of the country, little service work was done on the evaporative emission system. Common engine-performance problems that can be caused by a fault in this system include:

- **Poor fuel economy.** A leak in a vacuum-valve diaphragm can result in engine vacuum drawing in a constant flow of gasoline vapors from the fuel tank. This usually results in a drop in fuel economy of 2 to 4 miles per gallon (mpg). Use a hand-operated vacuum pump to check that the vacuum diaphragm can hold vacuum.
- **Poor performance.** A vacuum leak in the manifold or ported vacuum section of vacuum hose in the system can cause the engine to run rough. Age, heat, and time all contribute to the deterioration of rubber hoses.

Enhanced exhaust emissions (I/M-240) testing tests the evaporative emission system. A leak in the system is tested by pressurizing the entire fuel system to a level below 1 pound per square inch or 1 PSI (about 14 inches of water). The system is typically pressurized with nitrogen, a nonflammable gas that makes up 78% of our atmosphere. The pressure in the system is then shut off and the pressure monitored. If the pressure drops below a set standard, then the vehicle fails the test. This test determines if there is a leak in the system.

NOTE: To help pass the evaporative section of an enhanced emissions test, arrive at the test site with less than a half-tank of fuel. This means that the rest of the volume of the fuel tank is filled with air. It takes longer for the pressure to drop from a small leak when the volume of the air is greater compared to when the tank is full and the volume of air remaining in the tank is small.

FIGURE 43–25 Some vehicles will display a message if an evaporative control system leak is detected that could be the result of a loose gas cap.

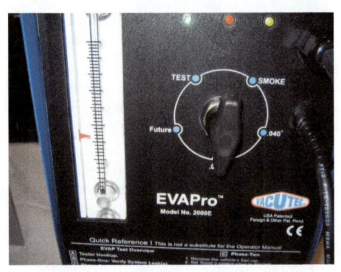

FIGURE 43–26 To test for a leak, this tester was set to the 0.020 inch hole and turned on. The ball rose in the scale on the left and the red arrow was moved to that location. If when testing the system for leaks, the ball rises higher than the arrow, then the leak is larger than 0.020 inch. If the ball does not rise to the level of the arrow, the leak is smaller than 0.020 inch.

LOCATING LEAKS IN THE SYSTEM Leaks in the evaporative emission control system will cause the "check engine" (malfunction indictor light (MIL)) to light on most vehicles. ● **SEE FIGURE 43–25.** A leak will also cause a gas smell, which would be most noticeable if the vehicle were parked in an enclosed garage. The first step is to determine if there is leak in the system by setting the EVAP tester to either a 0.040 inch or a 0.020 inch hole size leak. ● **SEE FIGURE 43–26.** After it has been determined that a leak exists and that it is larger than specified, there are two methods that can be used to check for leaks in the evaporative system.

- **Smoke machine testing.** The most efficient method of leak detection is to introduce smoke under low pressure from a machine specifically designed for this purpose. ● **SEE FIGURE 43–27.**

FIGURE 43–27 This unit is applying smoke to the fuel tank through an adapter and the leak was easily found to be the gas cap seal.

FIGURE 43–28 An emission tester that uses nitrogen to pressurize the fuel system.

- **Nitrogen gas pressurization.** This method uses nitrogen gas under a very low pressure (lower than 1 PSI) in the fuel system. The service technician then listens for the escaping air, using amplified headphones. ● **SEE FIGURE 43–28.**

EVAPORATIVE SYSTEM MONITOR

OBD-II computer programs not only detect faults, but also *periodically test various systems* and alert the driver before emissions-related components are harmed by system faults. Serious faults cause a blinking malfunction indicator lamp (MIL) or even an engine shutdown; less serious faults may simply store a code but not illuminate the MIL.

The OBD-II requirements did not radically affect fuel system design. However, one new component, a fuel evaporative canister purge line pressure sensor, was added for monitoring purge line pressure during tests. The OBD-II requirements state that vehicle fuel systems are to be routinely tested *while underway* by the PCM management system.

All OBD-II vehicles—during normal driving cycles and under specific conditions—experience a canister purge system pressure test, as commanded by the PCM. While the vehicle is being driven, the vapor line between the canister and the purge valve is monitored for pressure changes. When the canister purge solenoid is open, the line should be under a vacuum since vapors must be drawn from the canister into the intake system. However, when the purge solenoid is closed, there should be no vacuum in the line. The pressure sensor detects if a vacuum is present or not, and the information is compared to the command given to the solenoid. If, during the canister purge cycle, no vacuum exists in the canister purge line, a code is set indicating a possible fault, which could be caused by an inoperative or clogged solenoid or a blocked or leaking canister purge fuel line. Likewise, if vacuum exists when no command for purge is given, a stuck solenoid is evident, and a code is set.

The EVAP system monitor tests for purge volume and leaks. Most applications purge the charcoal canister by venting the vapors into the intake manifold during cruise. To do this, the PCM typically opens a solenoid-operated purge valve installed in the purge line leading to the intake manifold.

A typical EVAP monitor first closes off the system to atmospheric pressure and opens the purge valve during cruise operation. A fuel tank pressure (FTP) sensor then monitors the rate with which vacuum increases in the system. The monitor uses this information to determine the purge volume flow rate. To test for leaks, the EVAP monitor closes the purge valve, creating a completely closed system. The fuel tank pressure sensor then monitors the leak down rate. If the rate exceeds PCM-stored values, a leak greater than or equal to the OBD-II standard of 0.040 inch (1.0 mm) or 0.020 inch (0.5 mm) exists. After two consecutive failed trips testing either purge volume or the presence of a leak, the PCM lights the MIL and sets a DTC.

The fuel tank pressure sensor is often the same part as the MAP sensor, and instead of monitoring intake manifold absolute pressure, it is used to monitor fuel tank pressure. ● SEE FIGURE 43–29.

ENGINE OFF NATURAL VACUUM System integrity (leakage) can also be checked after the engine is shut off. The premise is that a warm evaporative system will cool down after

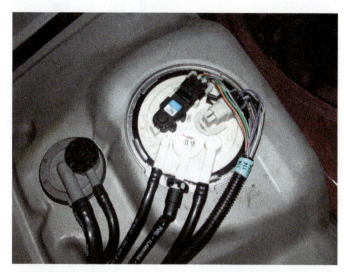

FIGURE 43–29 The fuel tank pressure sensor (black unit with three wires) looks like a MAP sensor and is usually located on top of the fuel pump module (white unit).

 **TECH TIP**

Always Tighten the Cap Correctly

Many diagnostic trouble codes (DTCs) are set because the gas cap has not been properly installed. To be sure that a screw-type gas cap is properly sealed, tighten the cap until it clicks three times. The clicking is a ratchet device and the clicking does not harm the cap. Therefore, if a P0440 or similar DTC is set, check the cap. ● SEE FIGURE 43–29.

the engine is shut off and the vehicle is stable. A slight vacuum will be created in the gas tank during this cool down period. If a specific level of vacuum is reached and maintained, the system is said to have integrity (no leakage).

TYPICAL EVAP MONITOR

The PCM will run the EVAP monitor when the following enable criteria are met. Typical enable criteria include:

- Cold start
- BARO greater than 70 kPa (20.7 inch Hg or 10.2 PSI)
- IAT between 39°F and 86°F at engine start-up
- ECT between 39°F and 86°F at engine start-up
- ECT and IAT within 39°F of each other at engine start-up
- Fuel level within 15% to 85%
- TP sensor between 9% and 35%

FIGURE 43–30 This filler cap has a warning—the check engine light will come on if not tightened until one click.

FIGURE 43–31 The fuel level must be above 15% and below 85% before the EVAP monitor will run on most vehicles.

RUNNING THE EVAP MONITOR The following four tests are performed during a typical GM EVAP monitor. A DTC is assigned to each test.

1. **Weak Vacuum Test (P0440—large leak).** This test identifies gross leaks. During the monitor, the vent solenoid is closed and the purge solenoid is duty cycled. The FTP should indicate a vacuum of approximately 6 to 10 inch H_2O.

2. **Small Leak Test (P0442—small leak).** After the large leak test passes, the PCM checks for a small leak by keeping the vent solenoid closed and closing the purge solenoid. The system is now sealed. The PCM measures the change in FTP voltage over time.

3. **Excess Vacuum Test (P0446).** This test checks for vent path restrictions. With the vent solenoid open and purge commanded, the PCM should not see excessive vacuum in the EVAP system. Typical EVAP system vacuum with the vent solenoid open is about 5 to 6 inch H_2O.

4. **Purge Solenoid Leak Test (P1442).** With the purge solenoid and vent solenoid closed, no vacuum should be present in the system. If there is vacuum present, the purge solenoid may be leaking.
   ● **SEE CHART 43–6** for some EVAP related DTCs.

🔧 **TECH TIP**

Keep the Fuel Tank Properly Filled

Most evaporative system monitors will not run unless the fuel level is between 15% and 85%. In other words, if a driver always runs with close to an empty tank or always tries to keep the tank full, the EVAP monitor may not run. ● **SEE FIGURE 43–31.**

EVAP SYSTEM-RELATED DIAGNOSTIC TROUBLE CODES		
DIAGNOSTIC TROUBLE CODE	**DESCRIPTION**	**POSSIBLE CAUSES**
P0440	Evaporative system fault	• Loose gas cap • Defective EVAP vent • Cracked charcoal canister • EVAP vent or purge vapor line problems
P0442	Small leak detected	• Loose gas cap • Defective EVAP vent or purge solenoid • EVAP vent or purge line problems
P0446	EVAP canister vent blocked	• EVAP vent or purge solenoid electrical problems • Restricted EVAP canister vent line

CHART 43–6

SUMMARY

1. Recirculating 6% to 10% inert exhaust gases back into the intake system reduces peak temperature inside the combustion chamber and reduces NO_x exhaust emissions.

2. EGR is usually not needed at idle, at wide-open throttle, or when the engine is cold.

3. Most EGR systems use a feedback potentiometer to signal the PCM the position of the EGR valve pintle.

4. OBD-II regulation requires that the flow rate be tested and then is achieved by opening the EGR valve and observing the reaction of the MAP sensor.

5. Positive crankcase ventilation (PCV) systems use a valve or a fixed orifice to transfer and control the fumes from the crankcase back into the intake system.

6. A PCV valve regulates the flow of fumes depending on engine vacuum and seals the crankcase vent in the event of a backfire.

7. As much as 30% of the air needed by the engine at idle speed flows through the PCV system.

8. The AIR system forces air at low pressure into the exhaust to reduce CO and HC exhaust emissions.

9. A catalytic converter is an after-treatment device that reduces exhaust emissions outside of the engine. A catalyst is an element that starts a chemical reaction but is not consumed in the process.

10. The catalyst material used in a catalytic converter includes rhodium, palladium, and platinum.

11. The OBD-II system monitor compares the relative activity of a rear oxygen sensor to the precatalytic oxygen sensor to determine catalytic converter efficiency.

12. The purpose of the evaporative emission (EVAP) control system is to reduce the release of volatile organic compounds (VOCs) into the atmosphere.

13. A carbon (charcoal) canister is used to trap and hold gasoline vapors until they can be purged and run into the engine to be burned.

14. OBD-II regulation requires that the evaporative emission control system be checked for leakage and proper purge flow rates.

15. External leaks can best be located by pressurizing the fuel system with low-pressure smoke.

REVIEW QUESTIONS

1. How does the use of exhaust gas reduce NO_x exhaust emission?

2. What exhaust emissions does the SAI system control?

3. How does a catalytic converter reduce NO_x to nitrogen and oxygen?

4. How does the computer monitor catalytic converter performance?

5. What components are used in a typical evaporative emission control system?

6. How does the computer control the purging of the vapor canister?

CHAPTER QUIZ

1. Two technicians are discussing clogged EGR passages. Technician A says clogged EGR passages can cause excessive NO_x exhaust emission. Technician B says that clogged EGR passages can cause the engine to ping (spark knock or detonation). Which technician is correct?
   a. Technician A only
   b. Technician B only
   c. Both Technicians A and B
   d. Neither Technician A nor B

2. An EGR valve that is partially stuck open would *most likely* cause what condition?
   a. Rough idle/stalling
   b. Excessive NO_x exhaust emissions
   c. Ping (spark knock or detonation)
   d. Missing at highway speed

3. How much air flows through the PCV system when the engine is at idle speed?
   a. 1% to 3%
   b. 5% to 10%
   c. 10% to 20%
   d. Up to 30%

4. Technician A says that if a PCV valve rattles, then it is okay and does not need to be replaced. Technician B says that if a PCV valve does not rattle, it should be replaced. Which technician is correct?
   a. Technician A only
   b. Technician B only
   c. Both Technicians A and B
   d. Neither Technician A nor B

5. The EVAP system small-leak test can detect a leak as small as _____.
   a. 1 inch
   b. 0.020 inch
   c. 0.002 inch
   d. 0.51 inch

6. Two technicians are discussing testing a catalytic converter. Technician A says that a vacuum gauge can be used and observed to see if the vacuum drops with the engine at idle for 30 seconds. Technician B says that a pressure gauge can be used to check for backpressure. Which technician is correct?
   a. Technician A only
   b. Technician B only
   c. Both Technicians A and B
   d. Neither Technician A nor B

7. At about what temperature does oxygen combine with the nitrogen in the air to form NO$_x$?
   a. 500°F (260°C)
   b. 750°F (400°C)
   c. 1,500°F (815°C)
   d. 2,500°F (1,370°C)

8. A P0401 is being discussed. Technician A says that a stuck-closed EGR valve could be the cause. Technician B says that clogged EGR ports could be the cause. Which technician is correct?
   a. Technician A only
   b. Technician B only
   c. Both Technicians A and B
   d. Neither Technician A nor B

9. Which EVAP valve(s) is (are) normally closed?
   a. Canister purge valve
   b. Canister vent valve
   c. Both canister purge and canister vent valve
   d. Neither canister purge nor canister vent valve

10. What must be the fuel level before an evaporative emission monitor will run?
    a. At least 75% full
    b. Over 25%
    c. Between 15% and 85%
    d. The level of the fuel in the tank is not needed to run the monitor test

chapter 44
DIESEL ENGINE EMISSIONS AND DIAGNOSIS

LEARNING OBJECTIVES

After studying this chapter, the reader should be able to:

1. List emission control systems used on diesel engines.
2. Discuss how the EGR systems operate on a diesel engine.
3. Explain how the diesel particulate filter and oxidation catalyst reduce exhaust emissions.
4. Discuss the operation of the selective catalytic reduction system (diesel exhaust fluid).
5. List diesel diagnostic tests.

This chapter will help you prepare for Light Duty Diesel Engines (A9) ASE certification test content area "F" (Fuel System Diagnosis and Repair).

KEY TERMS

aftermarket Power-Up Kits 666
calibration verification number (CVN) 666
diesel exhaust fluid (DEF) 660
Diesel exhaust particulate filters (DPFs) 657
Diesel oxidation catalysts (DOC) 657
differential pressure sensor (DPS) 658

hydrocarbon injector (HCI) 659
injection quantity adjustment (IQA) 664
Opacity 665
Particulate matter (PM) 656
pop tester 663
regeneration 657
Selective catalytic reduction (SCR) 660
soot 656
Urea 660

STC OBJECTIVES

GM Service Technical College topics covered in this chapter are:

1. Characteristics of the engine emission control system. (16410.00W3)
2. Characteristics of the engine exhaust after-treatment system.
3. Characteristics of the selective catalytic reduction process.
4. Characteristics of the diesel particulate regeneration process.

FIGURE 44–1 A cutaway showing the exhaust cooler. The cooler the exhaust is, the more effective it is in controlling NO$_x$ emissions.

FIGURE 44–2 The EGR valve assembly used on the 6.6 L Duramax engine. (*Courtesy of General Motors*)

EXHAUST GAS RECIRCULATION

The EGR system recycles some exhaust gas back into the intake stream to cool combustion, which reduces oxides of nitrogen (NO$_x$) emissions. The EGR system includes:

- Plumbing that carries some exhaust gas from the turbocharger exhaust inlet to the intake ports
- EGR control valve
- Stainless steel cooling element used to cool the exhaust gases (● **SEE FIGURE 44–1.**)

The EGR valve is PCM controlled and often uses a DC stepper motor and worm gear to move the valve stem open. The gear is not attached to the valve and can only force it open. Return spring force closes the valve. The EGR valve and sensor assembly is a five-wire design. The PCM uses the position sensor to verify that valve action is as commanded. ● **SEE FIGURE 44–2.**

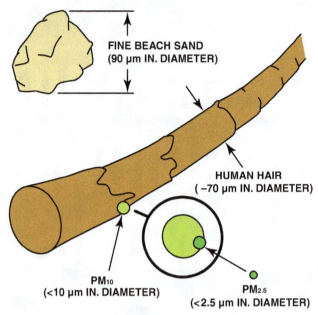

FIGURE 44–3 Relative size of particulate matter to a human hair.

DIESEL PARTICULATE MATTER

PARTICULATE MATTER STANDARDS **Particulate matter (PM)**, also called **soot**, refers to tiny particles of solid or semisolid material suspended in the atmosphere. This includes particles between 0.1 micron and 50 microns in diameter. The heavier particles, larger than 50 microns, typically tend to settle out quickly due to gravity. Particulates are generally categorized as follows:

- **Total suspended particulate (TSP).** Refers to all particles between 0.1 microns and 50 microns. Up until 1987, the Environmental Protection Agency (EPA) standard for particulates was based on levels of TSP.
- **PM10.** Refers to particulate matter of 10 microns or less (approximately 1/6 the diameter of a human hair). EPA has a standard for particles based on levels of PM10.
- **PM2.5.** Refers to particulate matter of 2.5 microns or less (approximately 1/20 the diameter of a human hair), also called "fine" particles. In July 1997, the EPA approved a standard for PM2.5. ● **SEE FIGURE 44–3.**

SOOT CATEGORIES In general, soot particles produced by diesel combustion fall into the following categories.

- **Fine.** Less than 2.5 microns
- **Ultrafine.** Less than 0.1 micron, and make up 80% to 95% of soot

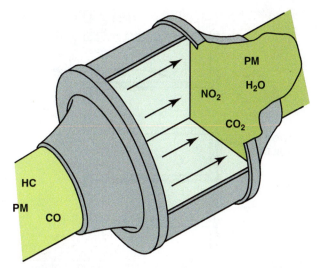

FIGURE 44–4 Chemical reaction within the DOC.

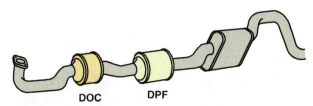

FIGURE 44–5 Aftertreatment of diesel exhaust is handled by the DOC and DPF.

FREQUENTLY ASKED QUESTION

What Is the Big Deal for the Need to Control Very Small Soot Particles?

For many years soot or particulate matter (PM) was thought to be less of a health concern than exhaust emissions from gasoline engines. It was felt that the soot could simply fall to the ground without causing any noticeable harm to people or the environment. However, it was discovered that the small soot particulates when breathed in are not expelled from the lungs like larger particles but instead get trapped in the deep areas of the lungs where they accumulate.

DIESEL OXIDATION CATALYST

PURPOSE AND FUNCTION   Diesel oxidation catalysts **(DOC)** are used in all light-duty diesel engines, since 2007. They consist of a flow-through honeycomb-style substrate structure that is wash coated with a layer of catalyst materials, similar to those used in a gasoline engine catalytic converter. These materials include the precious metals platinum and palladium, as well as other base metal catalysts.

Catalysts chemically react with exhaust gas to convert harmful nitrogen oxide into nitrogen dioxide, and to oxidize absorbed hydrocarbons. The chemical reaction acts as a combustor for the unburned fuel that is characteristic of diesel compression ignition. The main function of the DOC is to start a regeneration event by converting the fuel-rich exhaust gases to heat.

The DOC also reduces:

- Carbon monoxide (CO)
- Hydrocarbons (HC)
- Odor-causing compounds such as aldehydes and sulfur
  ● **SEE FIGURE 44–4.**

DIESEL EXHAUST PARTICULATE FILTER

PURPOSE AND FUNCTION   Diesel exhaust particulate filters **(DPFs)** are used in all light-duty diesel vehicles, since 2007, to meet the exhaust emissions standards. The heated exhaust gas from the DOC flows into the DPF, which captures diesel exhaust gas particulates (soot) to prevent them from being released into the atmosphere. This is done by forcing the exhaust through a porous cell which has a silicon carbide substrate with honeycomb-cell-type channels that trap the soot. The main difference between the DPF and a typical catalyst filter is that the entrance to every other cell channel in the DPF substrate is blocked at one end. So instead of flowing directly through the channels, the exhaust gas is forced through the porous walls of the blocked channels and exits through the adjacent open-ended channels. This type of filter is also referred to as a "wall-flow" filter. ● **SEE FIGURE 44–5.**

OPERATION   Soot particulates in the gas remain trapped on the DPF channel walls where, over time, the trapped particulate matter will begin to clog the filter. The filter must therefore be purged periodically to remove accumulated soot particles. The process of purging soot from the DPF is described as **regeneration.** When the temperature of the exhaust gas is increased, the heat incinerates the soot particles trapped in the filter and is effectively renewed. ● **SEE FIGURE 44–6.**

EXHAUST GAS TEMPERATURE SENSORS   The following two exhaust gas temperature sensors are used to help the PCM control the DPF.

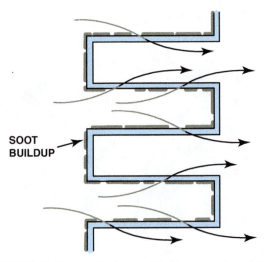

FIGURE 44–6 The soot is trapped in the passages of the DPF. The exhaust has to flow through the sides of the trap and exit.

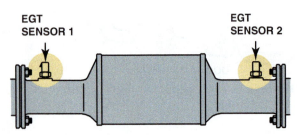

FIGURE 44–7 EGT 1 and EGT 2 are used by the PCM to help control after treatment.

- EGT sensor 1 is positioned between the DOC and the DPF where it can measure the temperature of the exhaust gas entering the DPF.
- EGT sensor 2 measures the temperature of the exhaust gas stream immediately after it exits the DPF.

The powertrain control module (PCM) monitors the signals from the EGT sensors as part of its calibrations to control DPF regeneration. Proper exhaust gas temperatures at the inlet of the DPF are crucial for proper operation and for starting the regeneration process. Too high a temperature at the DPF will cause the DPF substrate to melt or crack. Regeneration will be terminated at temperatures above 1,470°F (800°C). With too low a temperature, self-regeneration will not fully complete the soot-burning process. ● SEE FIGURE 44–7.

DPF DIFFERENTIAL PRESSURE SENSOR
The DPF **differential pressure sensor (DPS)** has two pressure sample lines.

- One line is attached before the DPF.
- The other is located after the DPF.

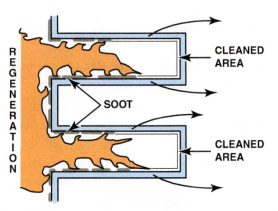

FIGURE 44–8 Regeneration burns the soot and renews the DPF.

The exact location of the DPS varies by vehicle model type such as medium duty, pickup, or van. By measuring the exhaust supply (upstream) pressure from the DOC, and the postDPF (downstream) pressure, the PCM can determine differential pressure, also called "delta" pressure, across the DPF. Data from the DPF differential pressure sensor is used by the PCM to calibrate for controlling DPF exhaust system operation.

DIESEL PARTICULATE FILTER REGENERATION
The primary reason for soot removal is to prevent the buildup of exhaust back pressure. Excessive back pressure increases fuel consumption, reduces power output, and can potentially cause engine damage. Several factors can trigger the diesel PCM to perform regeneration, including:

- Distance since last DPF regeneration
- Fuel used since last DPF regeneration
- Engine run time since last DPF regeneration
- Exhaust differential pressure across the DPF

DPF REGENERATION PROCESS
A number of engine components are required to function together for the regeneration process to be performed, as follows:

1. PCM controls that impact DPF regeneration include late postinjections, engine speed, and adjusting fuel pressure.
2. Adding late postinjection pulses provides the engine with additional fuel to be oxidized in the DOC, which increases exhaust temperatures entering the DPF to 900°F (500°C) or higher. ● SEE FIGURE 44–8.
3. The intake air valve acts as a restrictor that reduces air entry to the engine, which increases engine operating temperature.
4. The intake air heater may also be activated to warm intake air during regeneration.

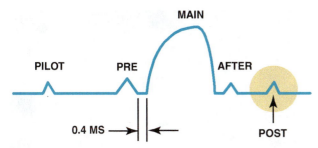

FIGURE 44–9 The postinjection pulse occurs to create the heat needed for regeneration.

? FREQUENTLY ASKED QUESTION

Will the Postinjection Pulses Reduce Fuel Economy?

Maybe. Due to the added fuel-injection pulses and late fuel-injection timing, an increase in fuel consumption may be noticed on the driver information center (DIC) during the regeneration time period. A drop in overall fuel economy should not be noticeable. ● **SEE FIGURE 44–9.**

HYDROCARBON INJECTOR The **hydrocarbon injector (HCI)** injects fuel into the exhaust system prior to the DOC. This is done in place of late post injections to raise the temperature of the exhaust for diesel particulate filter (DPF) regeneration. This helps to minimize oil dilution in the crankcase.

The pressure line taps into the fuel injection pump between the supply pump and the high-pressure pump supplying a pressure of 310 to 696 kiloPascals (kPa), or 45 to 101 pounds per square inch (psi). The pressure comes from the pressure side of the supply pump.

The HCI is located on the right side of the engine and is plumbed into the exhaust downpipe between the turbocharger and the DOC. The HCI is triggered when ECM data inputs indicate that the conditions for regeneration have been met. The ECM can command late post injections if there is a failure of the valve, or if there is a related DTC for the HCI. ● **SEE FIGURE 44–10.**

TYPES OF DPF REGENERATION DPF regeneration can be initiated in a number of ways, depending on the vehicle application and operating circumstances. The two main regeneration types are as follows:

FIGURE 44–10 The hydrocarbon injector solenoid (upper right) injects fuel for regeneration into the exhaust manifold (lower left). (*Courtesy of General Motors*)

- **Passive regeneration.** During normal vehicle operation when driving conditions produce sufficient load and exhaust temperatures, passive DPF regeneration may occur. This passive regeneration occurs without input from the PCM or the driver. A passive regeneration may typically occur while the vehicle is being driven at highway speed or towing a trailer.

- **Active regeneration.** Active regeneration is commanded by the PCM when it determines that the DPF requires it to remove excess soot buildup and conditions for filter regeneration have been met. Active regeneration is usually not noticeable to the driver. The vehicle needs to be driven at speeds above 30 mph for approximately 20 to 30 minutes to complete a full regeneration. During regeneration, the exhaust gases reach temperatures above 1000°F (550°C). Active regeneration is usually not noticeable to the driver.

ASH LOADING Regeneration will not burn off ash. Only the particulate matter (PM) is burned off during regeneration. Ash is a noncombustible by-product from normal oil consumption. Ash accumulation in the DPF will eventually cause a restriction in the particulate filter. To service an ash-loaded DPF, the DPF will need to be removed from the vehicle and cleaned or replaced. Low ash content engine oil (API CJ-4) is required for vehicles with the DPF system. The CJ-4 rated oil is limited to 1% ash content.

FIGURE 44–11 The exhaust pipe has a venturi sleeve attached that draws in fresh air as the exhaust leaves the tailpipe. The end result is cooler exhaust gases exiting the tailpipe.

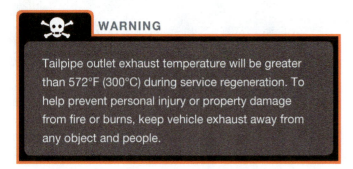

☠ **WARNING**

Tailpipe outlet exhaust temperature will be greater than 572°F (300°C) during service regeneration. To help prevent personal injury or property damage from fire or burns, keep vehicle exhaust away from any object and people.

❓ FREQUENTLY ASKED QUESTION

What Is an Exhaust Air Cooler?

An exhaust air cooler is a section of tailpipe narrowed into a venturi with a gap for air to enter. As hot exhaust rushes past the gap, outside air is drawn into the area which reduces the exhaust discharge temperature. The cooler significantly lowers exhaust temperature at the tailpipe from about 800°F (430°C) to approximately 500°F (270°C). ● **SEE FIGURE 44–11.**

SELECTIVE CATALYTIC REDUCTION

PURPOSE AND FUNCTION   Selective catalytic reduction **(SCR)** is a method used to reduce NO_x emissions by injecting urea into the exhaust stream. Instead of using large amounts of exhaust gas recirculation (EGR), the SCR system uses a urea. **Urea** is used as a nitrogen fertilizer. It is colorless, odorless, and nontoxic. Urea is called **diesel exhaust fluid (DEF)** in North America and AdBlue in Europe: ● **SEE FIGURE 44–12.**

The urea is injected into the catalyst where it sets off a chemical reaction which converts nitrogen oxides (NO_x) into

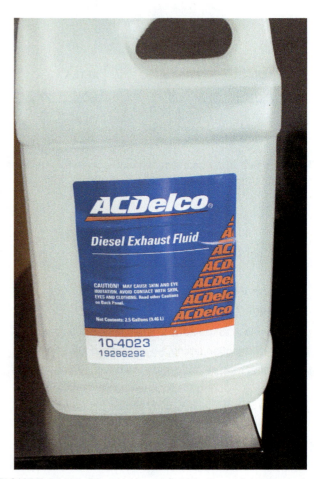

FIGURE 44–12 Diesel exhaust fluid is stored in a reservoir on the vehicle that contains from 5 to 10 gallons, or enough to last until the next scheduled oil change in most diesel vehicles that use SCR.

nitrogen (N_2) and water (H_2O). Vehicle manufacturers size the onboard urea storage tank so that it needs to be refilled at about each scheduled oil change or every 7,500 miles (12,000 km). A warning light alerts the driver when the urea level needs to be refilled. If the warning light is ignored and the diesel exhaust fluid is not refilled, current EPA regulations require that the operation of the engine be restricted and may not start unless the fluid is refilled. This regulation is designed to prevent the engine from being operated without the fluid, which, if not, would greatly increase exhaust emissions. ● **SEE FIGURE 44–13.**

ADVANTAGES OF SCR   Using urea injection instead of large amounts of EGR results in the following advantages.

- Potential higher engine power output for the same size engine
- Reduced NO_x emissions up to 90%
- Reduced HC and CO emissions up to 50%
- Reduced particulate matter (PM) by 50%

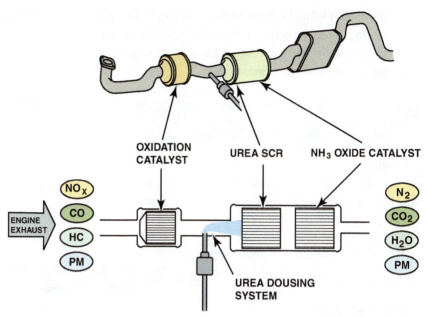

OXIDATION CATALYST   UREA SCR   NH₃ OXIDE CATALYST

NOₓ / CO / HC / PM

ENGINE EXHAUST

N₂ / CO₂ / H₂O / PM

UREA DOUSING SYSTEM

FIGURE 44–13 Urea (diesel exhaust fluid) injection is used to reduce NOₓ exhaust emissions. It is injected after the diesel oxidation catalyst (DOC) and before the diesel particulate filter (DPF).

DISADVANTAGES OF SCR   Using urea injection instead of large amounts of EGR results in the following disadvantages.

- Onboard storage tank required for the urea
- Difficult to find local sources of urea
- Increased costs to the vehicle owner due to having to refill the urea storage tank

DIESEL EXHAUST SMOKE DIAGNOSIS

Although some exhaust smoke is considered normal operation for many diesel engines, especially older units, the cause of excessive exhaust smoke should be diagnosed and repaired.

BLACK SMOKE   Black exhaust smoke is caused by incomplete combustion because of a lack of air or a fault in the injection system that could cause an excessive amount of fuel in the cylinders. Items that should be checked include the following:

- Fuel specific gravity (API gravity)
- Injector balance test to locate faulty injectors using a scan tool
- Proper operation of the engine coolant temperature (ECT) sensor
- Proper operation of the fuel rail pressure (FRP) sensor
- Restrictions in the intake or turbocharger
- Engine oil usage

WHITE SMOKE   White exhaust smoke occurs most often during cold engine starts because the smoke is usually condensed fuel droplets. White exhaust smoke is also an indication of cylinder misfire on a warm engine. The most common causes of white exhaust smoke include:

- Inoperative glow plugs
- Low engine compression
- Incorrect injector spray pattern
- Coolant leak into the combustion chamber

GRAY OR BLUE SMOKE   Blue exhaust smoke is usually due to oil consumption caused by worn piston rings, scored cylinder walls, or defective valve stem seals. Gray or blue smoke can also be caused by a defective injector(s).

DIESEL PERFORMANCE DIAGNOSIS

Always start the diagnosis of an diesel engine concern by checking the oil. Higher than normal oil level can indicate that diesel fuel has leaked into the oil. Diesel engines can be diagnosed using a scan tool in most cases, because most of the pressure sensors values can be displayed. Common faults include:

- Hard starting
- No start
- Extended cranking before starting
- Low power

Using a scan tool, check the sensor values in ● **CHART 44-1.** to help pin down the source of the problem. Also check the minimum pressures that are required to start the engine if a no-start condition is being diagnosed.

COMPRESSION TESTING

A compression test is fundamental for determining the mechanical condition of a diesel engine. Worn piston rings can cause low power and excessive exhaust smoke. To test the compression on a diesel engine, the following will have to be done.

- Remove the glow plug (if equipped) or the injector.
- Use a diesel compression gauge, as the compression is too high to use a gasoline engine compression gauge.

A diesel engine should produce at least 300 PSI (2068 kPa) of compression pressure and all cylinders should be within 50 PSI (345 kPa) of each other. ● **SEE FIGURE 44-14.**

DIESEL TROUBLESHOOTING CHART	
5.9 Dodge Cummins	
Low-pressure pump	8–12 PSI
Pump amperes	4 A
Pump volume	45 oz. in 30 sec.
High-pressure pump	5000–23,000 PSI
Idle PSI	5600–5,700 PSI
Electronic Fuel Control (EFC) maximum fuel pressure	Disconnect EFC to achieve maximum pressure
Injector volts	90 V
Injector amperes	20 A
Glow plug amperes	60–80 A × 2 (120–160 A)
Minimum PSI to start	**5000 PSI**
GM Duramax	
Low-pressure pump vacuum	2–10 inch Hg
Pump amperes	NA
Pump volume	NA
High-pressure pump	5 K to 29 K PSI
Idle PSI	5000–6000 PSI (30–40 MPa)
Fuel Rail Pressure Regulator (FRPR) maximum fuel pressure	Disconnect to achieve maximum pressure
Injector volts	48 V or 93 V or up to 250 V (depending on year)
Injector amperes	20 A
Glow plug amperes	160 A
Minimum to start	**1,500 PSI (10 MPa)**
6.0 Powerstroke	
Low-pressure pump	50–60 PSI
High-pressure pump	500–4000 PSI
Idle PSI	500 PSI+
Injection Pressure Regulator (IPR) maximum fuel pressure	Apply power and ground to IPR
Injector volts	48 V
Injector amperes	20 A
Glow plug amperes	20–25 A each (160–200 A total)
Minimum to start	**500 PSI (0.85 V)**

CHART 44-1

The values can be obtained by using a scan tool and basic test equipment. Always follow the vehicle manufacturer's recommended procedures.

FIGURE 44–14 A compression gauge that is designed for the higher compression rate of a diesel engine should be used when checking the compression.

GLOW PLUG RESISTANCE BALANCE TEST

Glow plugs increase in resistance as their temperature increases. All glow plugs should have about the same resistance when checked with an ohmmeter. A similar test of the resistance of the glow plugs can be used to detect a weak cylinder. This test is particularly helpful on a diesel engine that is not computer controlled. To test for even cylinder balance using glow plug resistance, perform the following on a warm engine.

1. Unplug, measure, and record the resistance of all glow plugs.
2. With the wires still removed from the glow plugs, start the engine.
3. Allow the engine to run for several minutes to allow the combustion inside the cylinder to warm the glow plugs.
4. Measure the plugs and record the resistance of all glow plugs.
5. The resistance of all glow plugs should be higher than at the beginning of the test. A glow plug that is in a cylinder that is not firing correctly will not increase in resistance as much as the others.
6. Another test is to measure exhaust manifold temperature at each exhaust port using an infrared thermometer or a pyrometer. Misfiring cylinders will run cold.

FIGURE 44–15 A typical pop tester used to check the spray pattern of a diesel engine injector.

INJECTOR POP TESTING

A **pop tester** is a device used for checking a diesel injector nozzle for proper spray pattern. The handle is depressed and pop-off pressure is displayed on the gauge. ● SEE FIGURE 44–15.

The spray pattern should be a hollow cone, but will vary depending on design. The nozzle should also be tested for leakage (dripping of the nozzle) while under pressure. If the spray pattern is not correct, then cleaning, repairing, or replacing the injector nozzle may be necessary.

FUEL INJECTOR FLOW RATE PROGRAMMING[1]

CIRCUIT/SYSTEM DESCRIPTION   The control functions for the fuel injection system are integrated in the engine control module (ECM). Each injector's flow rate information and cylinder position are stored in the memory of both the glow

[1] GM Service Information Document #2425838

Always Use Cardboard to Check for High-Pressure Leaks

If diesel fuel is found on the engine, a high-pressure leak could be present. When checking for such a leak, wear protective clothing including safety glasses, a face shield, gloves, and a long-sleeved shirt. Then use a piece of cardboard to locate the high-pressure leak. When a Duramax diesel is running, the pressure in the common rail and injector tubes can reach over 20,000 PSI. At these pressures, the diesel fuel is atomized and cannot be seen but can penetrate the skin and cause personal injury. A leak will be shown as a dark area on the cardboard. When a leak is found, shut off the engine and find the exact location of the leak without the engine running.

CAUTION: Sometimes a leak can actually cut through the cardboard, so use extreme care.

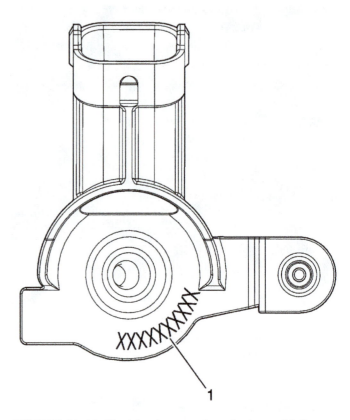

FIGURE 44–16 The injection quantity adjustment (IQA) flow rate number (1) is etched onto the fuel injector housing. (*Courtesy of General Motors*)

plug control module (GPCM) and the ECM. The fuel injector flow rate programming must be done when any of the following procedures are performed:

- The ECM is replaced
- The GPCM is replaced
- Any fuel injectors are replaced

If the ECM does not communicate, the flow rate information can be retrieved from the GPCM. If both control modules fail to communicate, the fuel injector flow rate information, or **injection quantity adjustment (IQA)** flow rate numbers, will need to be retrieved from each individual injector. ● **SEE FIGURE 44–16.**

CIRCUIT/SYSTEM VERIFICATION Review the "Display ECM & GPCM Inj. Flow Rates" parameter with a scan tool. All cylinders should be programmed with a flow rate number. Both the GPCM and the ECM should be programmed with the same flow rate numbers for the corresponding cylinders.

With a scan tool installed, enter the vehicle information and select the following options:

- Engine Control Module
- Module Setup
- Injector Flow Rate Programming
- Display ECM & GPCM Inj. Flow Rates

Record all flow rate numbers with the corresponding cylinders from the control modules.

NOTE: When installing a new fuel injector, ensure that the IQA data number from the yellow IQA Data Tag, shipped with the new injector, is programmed to the correct cylinder.

If any injectors have been replaced, go to "Reprogram Injector Flow Rates" parameter and enter the flow rate number of the new injector to the corresponding cylinder. The flow rate numbers will automatically update both control modules.

NOTE: The ECM and the GPCM must be allowed to completely power down after programming is complete.

FUEL INJECTOR CORRECTION RESET[2]

DESCRIPTION The ECM has the ability to learn injector timing performance. With the engine at operating temperature and in closed throttle decel mode, the ECM will pulse each injector individually and measure the changes in rotational

---

[2]GM Service Information Document #2791362

speed of the crankshaft using the input from the crankshaft position sensor (CPS). The ECM will run this diagnostic under three different fuel rail pressures for each injector. The ECM will adjust the timing of fuel delivered by each injector to obtain the desired RPM increase. The ECM stores the injector timing value required to increase the crankshaft speed by the desired RPM. If the ECM cannot control an increase in RPM for a given injector, the appropriate code will set for that injector. The Fuel Injector Correction Reset must be performed anytime a fuel injector is replaced or an ECM is replaced and the values cannot be transferred from the old ECM.

RESET PROCEDURE This procedure will reset the ECM so that it will re-learn the timing correction data.

- With the ignition on, engine off, use the scan tool to navigate to Module Setup.
- Follow the instructions to perform the Fuel Injector Correction Reset in Module Setup for each fuel injector that was replaced.
- If all fuel injectors were replaced, select "Reset Injection Value—All Cylinders" to reset all the fuel injectors at the same time.

DIESEL EMISSION TESTING

OPACITY TEST The most common diesel exhaust emission test used in state or local testing programs is called the opacity test. **Opacity** means the percentage of light that is blocked by the exhaust smoke.

- A 0% opacity means that the exhaust has no visible smoke and does not block light from a beam projected through the exhaust smoke.
- A 100% opacity means that the exhaust is so dark that it completely blocks light from a beam projected through the exhaust smoke.
- A 50% opacity means that the exhaust blocks half of the light from a beam projected through the exhaust smoke. ● SEE CHART 44–2.

SNAP ACCELERATION TEST In a snap acceleration test, the vehicle is held stationary, with wheel chocks in place and brakes released as the engine is rapidly accelerated to high idle, with the transmission in neutral while smoke emissions are measured. This test is conducted a minimum of six times and the three most consistent measurements are averaged for a final score.

FIGURE 44–17 The letters on the side of this injector indicate the calibration number for the injector.

	20% opacity
	40% opacity
	60% opacity
	80% opacity
	100% opacity

CHART 44–2

An opacity test is sometimes used during a state emission test on diesel engines.

TECH TIP

Do Not Switch Injectors

In the past, it was common practice to switch diesel fuel injectors from one cylinder to another when diagnosing a dead cylinder problem. However, most high-pressure common rail systems used in new diesels utilize precisely calibrated injectors that should not be mixed up during service. Each injector has its own calibration number. ● SEE FIGURE 44–17.

ROLLING ACCELERATION TEST Vehicles with a manual transmission are rapidly accelerated in low gear from an idle speed to a maximum governed RPM while the smoke emissions are measured.

STALL ACCELERATION TEST Vehicles with automatic transmissions are held in a stationary position with the parking brake and service brakes applied while the transmission is placed in "drive." The accelerator is depressed and held momentarily while smoke emissions are measured.

The standards for diesels vary according to the type of vehicle and other factors, but usually include a 40% opacity or less.

DIESEL POWER-UP KITS[3]

Aftermarket power-up kits have become a very popular add-on for performance-minded customers. These devices can add horsepower and torque and can add additional stress to the engine. These aftermarket calibrations take the Duramax™ powertrain outside of its design torque and horsepower rating. They do this by altering air–fuel ratios and injector timing, resulting in excessive cylinder pressure and temperature. When these calibrated parameters are altered, it will upset the design balance and can lead to a reduction of engine life expectancy. Generally, in an inspection of a Duramax™ engine failure due to power-up failures, two or more cylinders will be affected.

IDENTIFYING NON-GM ECM CALIBRATIONS[4]

General Motors has identified an increasing number of engine, transmission, diesel oxidation catalyst (DOC), and exhaust particulate filter failures that are the result of non-GM **(aftermarket Power-Up Kits)** engine and transmission control calibrations being used. When alteration to the GM-released engine or transmission control calibrations occurs, it subjects powertrain and driveline components, such as the engine, transmission, transfer case, driveshaft, universal joints, and the rear axle to stresses that were not tested by General Motors.

NOTE: GM has adopted a policy that prevents any unauthorized Service Agent warranty claim submissions to any remaining warranty coverage to the powertrain and driveline components whenever the presence of a non-GM calibration is confirmed, even if the non-GM control module calibration is subsequently removed.

GM testing and validation matches the calibration to a host of criteria that is essential to assure reliability, durability, and emissions performance over the life of the warranty coverage and beyond. Stresses resulting from calibrations different

than those tested and released by GM can damage or weaken components, leading to poor performance and/or shortened life. Additionally, non-GM-issued engine control modifications do not meet the same emissions performance standards as GM-issued calibrations. Depending on state statutes, individuals who install ECM calibrations that put the vehicle outside the parameters of emissions certification standards may be subject to fines and/or penalties.

SYMPTOMS CAUSED BY AN AFTERMARKET POWER-UP KIT Some customers may have reprogrammed the ECM with a non-GM-released calibration. The power-up kit engine calibration changes fueling and timing parameters and likely contributes to the following vehicle conditions:

- Poor performance.
- Driveability concerns.
- Increased emissions.
- Black smoke from the exhaust. This symptom is not valid for the Duramax™ diesel engine RPO LGH, LML, or LMM equipped with the diesel particulate filter (DPF). The DPF will trap black exhaust smoke unless it is cracked, melted, or has been removed from the exhaust system.
- Knocking noise.
- Engine damage.

CALIBRATION VERIFICATION The calibration verification procedure is used to identify the presence of non-GM (aftermarket) calibrations. GM recommends performing this check whenever a hard part failure is seen on internal engine, transmission, transfer case, or rear-axle components, and **before** disassembly, repair, or replacement of an engine, transmission, transfer case, or rear-axle assembly under warranty. It is also recommended that the engine calibration verification procedure be performed whenever diagnostics indicate that an exhaust aftertreatment system component replacement is necessary.

NOTE: Refer to General Motors service information (SI) and technical service bulletins (TSBs) for the specific procedure used to verify calibrations.

For 2007–2013 applications, an ECM algorithm was implemented that records the engine calibration part number and **calibration verification number (CVN)** for the last 10 flash programming events. The ECM records the engine calibration part number because it contains the parameters for increasing torque and fueling rates.

---

[3]Adapted from GM TSB # 06-06-01-007G

[4]Adapted from GM TSB # 08-06-04-006L

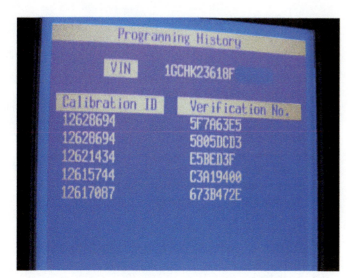

FIGURE 44–18 The programming history records the last 10 programming events. If an aftermarket calibration has been used, the verification number will not match the information found in the TIS2WEB database. (*Courtesy of General Motors*)

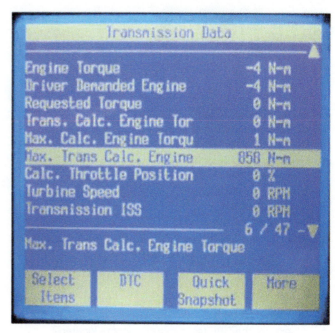

FIGURE 44–19 On some trucks the transmission input maximum torque is saved in the ECM. (*Courtesy of General Motors*)

If a vehicle comes in for service for a driveability/powertrain concern as a result of a power-up kit installation, the technician can read the last 10 engine calibration part numbers and CVN history using a Tech 2. The technician can input each ECM calibration part number into the TIS2WEB/SPS CVN database to confirm the CVN history information. ● **SEE FIGURE 44–18.**

TRANSMISSION MAXIMUM INPUT TORQUE One example of available power-up hardware is a propane injection system. This causes an increase of engine torque beyond the maximum torque value specified for the engine. On some vehicles a transmission control module (TCM) algorithm has been implemented that records a maximum calculated input torque.

This information can be read using the Tech 2® and the following procedure:

- Build the vehicle with the Tech 2
- Select F3: Transmission Control Module
- Select F1: Data Display
- Select F0: Transmission Data

If the Max Transmission Calc Engine Torque is higher than the maximum specified torque, it is likely that some sort of power-up device has been used on the vehicle. ● **SEE FIGURE 44–19**

NOTE: Transmission data are available ONLY with GMC Sierra, TopKick, Chevrolet Kodiak, and Silverado.

SUMMARY

1. Emissions are controlled on newer diesel engines by using a diesel oxidation catalytic converter, a diesel exhaust particulate filter, exhaust gas recirculation, and a selective catalytic reduction system.

2. Diesel engines can be tested using a scan tool, as well as measuring the glow plug resistance or compression reading, to determine a weak or nonfunctioning cylinder.

3. Diesel injectors must be programmed into the vehicle control modules when replaced.

REVIEW QUESTIONS

1. What exhaust aftertreatment is needed to achieve exhaust emission standards for vehicles 2007 and newer?

2. What are the advantages and disadvantages of SCR?

1. What is the purpose of the EGR system on a diesel engine?
   a. To reduce nitrogen emissions
   b. To reduce oxygen emissions
   c. To increase oxygen emissions
   d. To decrease oxides of nitrogen emissions

2. Which of these is NOT part of the EGR system?
   a. Cooler
   b. Stepper motor
   c. Vacuum servo
   d. Position sensor

3. The diesel exhaust particulate filter captures _____ from the exhaust.
   a. Soot
   b. Ice crystals
   c. Oxides of nitrogen
   d. Unburned fuel

4. Where are the DPF temperature sensors located?
   a. One in each cylinder head
   b. One before and one after the DPF
   c. At the inlet and outlet of the turbocharger
   d. None of these

5. The DPF regeneration process cleans _____ out of the DPF.
   a. Ash
   b. Particulate matter
   c. Both ash and particulate matter
   d. Oxides of nitrogen

6. What will happen if the DEF tank becomes empty?
   a. Warning light will come on
   b. Engine operation may be restricted
   c. Engine may not start
   d. All of the above

7. What procedure should be performed if an injector has been replaced?
   a. Program the new IQA number into the ECM
   b. Injector correction rate reset
   c. Both a and b
   d. Neither a nor b

8. The calibration verification number can be found by using a(an) _____.
   a. Scan tool
   b. Voltmeter
   c. Pressure gauge
   d. Reading the number in the injector

9. If the cylinder is firing correctly, the resistance of the glow plug will _____ as the engine warms up.
   a. Remain stable
   b. Decrease
   c. Increase
   d. Stop

10. A diesel engine is exhausting black smoke. What could be the cause?
    a. Too much fuel
    b. Not enough intake air
    c. Both a and b
    d. Neither a nor b

chapter 45
ENGINE PERFORMANCE DIAGNOSIS

LEARNING OBJECTIVES

After studying this chapter, the reader will be able to:

1. List the steps of the diagnostic process.
2. Discuss the types of scan tools that are used to assess vehicle components.
3. Explain the troubleshooting procedures to follow if no diagnostic trouble code has been set.
4. Explain the troubleshooting procedures to follow if a diagnostic trouble code has been set.
5. Describe the methods that can be used to reprogram (reflash) a vehicle computer.

This chapter will help you prepare for the ASE computerized engine controls diagnosis (A8) certification test content area "E."

KEY TERMS

Data link connector (DLC) 674
Drive cycle 689
Paper test 673
Pending code 674
Smoke machine 673
Strategy-Based Diagnosis 686
Technical service bulletins (TSBs) 674
Trip 682

 ## STC OBJECTIVES

GM Service Technical College topics covered in this chapter are:

1. Make diagnostic data parameter snapshot.
2. Verify the customer concern.
3. Make quick checks.
4. Perform a diagnostic system check.

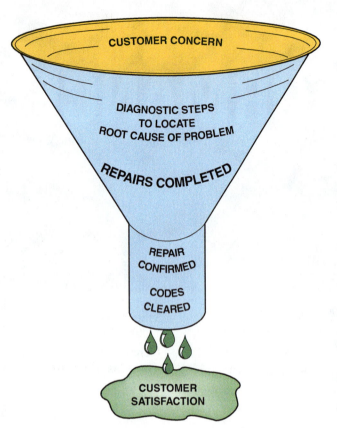

FIGURE 45–1 A funnel is one way to visualize the diagnostic process. The purpose is to narrow the possible causes of a concern until the root cause is determined and corrected.

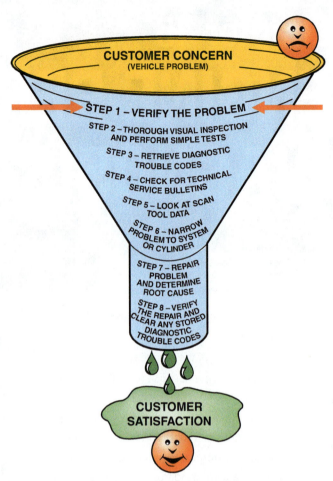

FIGURE 45–2 Step 1 is to verify the customer concern or problem. If the problem cannot be verified, then the repair cannot be performed.

THE EIGHT-STEP DIAGNOSTIC PROCEDURE

It is important that all automotive service technicians know how to diagnose and troubleshoot engine computer systems. The diagnostic process is a strategy that eliminates known-good components or systems in order to find the root cause of automotive engine performance problems. All vehicle manufacturers recommend a diagnostic procedure, and the plan suggested in this chapter combines most of the features of these plans plus additional steps developed over years of real-world problem solving.

Many different things can cause an engine performance problem or concern. The service technician has to narrow the possibilities to find the cause of the problem and correct it. A funnel is a way of visualizing a diagnostic procedure. ● **SEE FIGURE 45–1**. At the wide top are the symptoms of the problem; the funnel narrows as possible causes are eliminated until the root cause is found and corrected at the bottom of the funnel.

All problem diagnoses deal with symptoms that could be the result of many different causes. The wide range of possible solutions must be narrowed to the most likely and these must eventually be further narrowed to the actual cause. The following section describes eight steps the service technician can take to narrow the possibilities to one cause.

STEP 1 VERIFY THE PROBLEM (CONCERN) Before a minute is spent on diagnosis, be certain that a problem exists. If the problem cannot be verified, it cannot be solved or tested to verify that the repair was complete. ● **SEE FIGURE 45–2**.

The driver of the vehicle knows much about the vehicle and how it is driven. *Before* diagnosis, always ask the following questions:

- Is the malfunction indicator light (check engine) on?
- What was the temperature outside?
- Was the engine warm or cold?
- Was the problem during starting, acceleration, cruise, or some other condition?

ENGINE PERFORMANCE DIAGNOSIS WORKSHEET

(To Be Filled Out By the Vehicle Owner)

Name: _____ Mileage: _____ Date: _____

Make: _____ Model: _____ Year: _____ Engine: _____

(Please Circle All That Apply in All Categories)	
Describe Problem:	
When Did the Problem First Occur?	• Just Started • Last Week • Last Month • Other _____
List Previous Repairs in the Last 6 Months:	
Starting Problems	• Will Not Crank • Cranks, but Will Not Start • Starts, but Takes a Long Time
Engine Quits or Stalls	• Right after Starting • When Put into Gear • During Steady Speed Driving • Right after Vehicle Comes to a Stop • While Idling • During Acceleration • When Parking
Poor Idling Conditions	• Is Too Slow at All Times • Is Too Fast • Intermittently Too Fast or Too Slow • Is Rough or Uneven • Fluctuates Up and Down
Poor Running Conditions	• Runs Rough • Lacks Power • Bucks and Jerks • Poor Fuel Economy • Hesitates or Stumbles on Acceleration • Backfires • Misfires or Cuts Out • Engine Knocks, Pings, Rattles • Surges • Dieseling or Run-On
Auto. Transmission Problems	• Improper Shifting (Early/Late) • Changes Gear Incorrectly • Vehicle Does Not Move when in Gear • Jerks or Bucks
Usually Occurs	• Morning • Afternoon • Anytime
Engine Temperature	• Cold • Warm • Hot
Driving Conditions During Occurrence	• Short—Less Than 2 Miles • 2–10 Miles • Long—More Than 10 Miles • Stop and Go • While Turning • While Braking • At Gear Engagement • With A/C Operating • With Headlights On • During Acceleration • During Deceleration • Mostly Downhill • Mostly Uphill • Mostly Level • Mostly Curvy • Rough Road
Driving Habits	• Mostly City Driving • Highway • Park Vehicle Inside • Park Vehicle Outside **Drive Per Day:** • Less Than 10 Miles • 10–50 • More Than 50
Gasoline Used	**Fuel Octane:** • 87 • 89 • 91 • More Than 91 **Brand:** _____
Temperature when Problem Occurs	• 32–55°F • Below Freezing (32°F) • Above 55°F
Check Engine Light/ Dash Warning Light	• Light on Sometimes • Light on Always • Light Never On
Smells	• "Hot" • Gasoline • Oil Burning • Electrical
Noises	• Rattle • Knock • Squeak • Other

FIGURE 45–3 A form that the customer should fill out if there is a driveablilty concern to help the service technician more quickly find the root cause.

- How far had the vehicle been driven?
- Were any dash warning lights on? If so, which one(s)?
- Has there been any service or repair work performed on the vehicle lately?

NOTE: This last question is very important. Many engine performance faults are often the result of something being knocked loose or a hose falling off during repair work. Knowing that the vehicle was just serviced before the problem began may be an indicator as to where to look for the solution to a problem.

After the nature and scope of the problem are determined, the complaint should be verified before further diagnostic tests are performed. A sample form that customers could fill out with details of the problem is shown in ● **FIGURE 45–3**.

NOTE: Because drivers differ, it is sometimes the best policy to take the customer on the test-drive to verify the concern.

STEP 2 PERFORM A THOROUGH VISUAL INSPECTION AND BASIC TESTS
The visual inspection is the most important aspect of diagnosis! Most experts agree that between 10% and 30% of all engine performance problems can be

FIGURE 45–4 This is what was found when removing an air filter from a vehicle that had a lack-of-power concern. Obviously the nuts were deposited by squirrels or some other animal, blocking a lot of the airflow into the engine.

found simply by performing a *thorough* visual inspection. The inspection should include the following:

- **Check for obvious problems (basics, basics, basics).**
  Fuel leaks

  Vacuum hoses that are disconnected or split

  Corroded connectors

  Unusual noises, smoke, or smell

  Check the air cleaner and air duct (squirrels and other small animals can build nests or store dog food in them). ● **SEE FIGURE 45–4**.

- **Check everything that does and does not work.** This step involves turning things on and observing that everything is working properly.

- **Look for evidence of previous repairs.** Any time work is performed on a vehicle, there is always a risk that something will be disturbed, knocked off, or left disconnected.

- **Check oil level and condition.** Another area for visual inspection is oil level and condition.

  Oil level. Oil should be to the proper level.

  Oil condition. Using a match or lighter, try to light the oil on the dipstick; if the oil flames up, gasoline is present in the engine oil. Drip some engine oil from the dipstick onto the hot exhaust manifold. If the oil bubbles or boils, coolant (water) is present in the oil. Check for grittiness by rubbing the oil between your fingers.

NOTE: Gasoline in the oil will cause the engine to run rich by drawing fuel through the positive crankcase ventilation (PCV) system.

TECH TIP

"Original Equipment" Is Not a Four-Letter Word

To many service technicians, an original-equipment part is considered to be only marginal and to get the really "good stuff" an aftermarket (renewal market) part has to be purchased. However, many problems can be traced to the use of an aftermarket part that has failed early in its service life. Technicians who work at dealerships usually go immediately to an aftermarket part that is observed during a visual inspection. It has been their experience that simply replacing the aftermarket part with the factory original-equipment (OE) part often solves the problem.

Original equipment parts are *required* to pass quality and durability standards and tests at a level not required of aftermarket parts. The technician should be aware that the presence of a new part does not necessarily mean that the part is good.

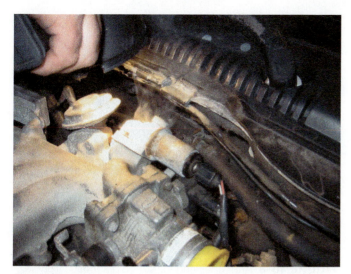

FIGURE 45–5 Using a bright light makes seeing where the smoke is coming from easier. In this case, smoke was added to the intake manifold with the inlet blocked with a yellow plastic cap and smoke was seen escaping past a gasket at the idle air control.

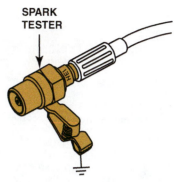

SPARK TESTER

FIGURE 45–6 A spark tester connected to a spark plug wire or coil output. A typical spark tester will only fire if at least 25,000 volts is available from the coil, making a spark tester a useful tool. Do not use one that just lights when a spark is present, because it does not require more than about 2000 volts to light.

TECH TIP

Smoke Machine Testing

Vacuum (air) leaks can cause a variety of driveability problems and are often difficult to locate. One good method is to use a machine that generates a stream of smoke. Connecting the outlet of the **smoke machine** to the hose that was removed from the vacuum brake booster allows smoke to enter the intake manifold. Any vacuum leaks will be spotted by observing smoke coming out of the leak. ● **SEE FIGURE 45–5**.

■ **Check coolant level and condition.** Many mechanical engine problems are caused by overheating. The proper operation of the cooling system is critical to the life of any engine.

NOTE: **Check the coolant level in the radiator only if the radiator is cool. If the radiator is hot and the radiator cap is removed, the drop in pressure above the coolant will cause the coolant to boil immediately, which can cause severe burns because the coolant expands explosively upward and outward from the radiator opening.**

■ **Use the paper test.** A soundly running engine should produce even and steady exhaust at the tailpipe. For the **paper test**, hold a piece of paper (even a dollar bill works) or a 3-by-5 inch card within 1 inch (2.5 cm) of the tailpipe with the engine running at idle. The paper should blow evenly away from the end of the tailpipe without "puffing" or being drawn inward toward the end of the tailpipe. If the paper is at times drawn *toward* the tailpipe, the valves in one or more cylinders could be burned. Other reasons why the paper might be drawn toward the tailpipe include the following:

1. The engine could be misfiring because of a lean condition that could occur normally when the engine is cold.

2. Pulsing of the paper toward the tailpipe could also be caused by a hole in the exhaust system. If exhaust escapes through a hole in the exhaust system, air could be drawn—in the intervals between the exhaust puffs—from the tailpipe to the hole in the exhaust, causing the paper to be drawn toward the tailpipe.

■ **Ensure adequate fuel level.** Make certain that the fuel tank is at least one-fourth to one-half full; if the fuel level is low it is possible that any water or alcohol at the bottom of the fuel tank is more concentrated and can be drawn into the fuel system.

■ **Check the battery voltage.** The voltage of the battery should be at least 12.4 volts and the charging voltage (engine running) should be 13.5 to 15.0 volts at 2,000 RPM. Low battery voltage can cause a variety of problems including reduced fuel economy and incorrect (usually too high) idle speed. Higher-than-normal battery voltage can also cause the PCM problems and could cause damage to electronic modules.

■ **Check the spark using a spark tester.** Remove one spark plug wire and attach the removed plug wire to the spark tester. Attach the grounding clip of the spark tester to a good clean engine ground, start or crank the engine, and observe the spark tester. ● **SEE FIGURE 45–6**.

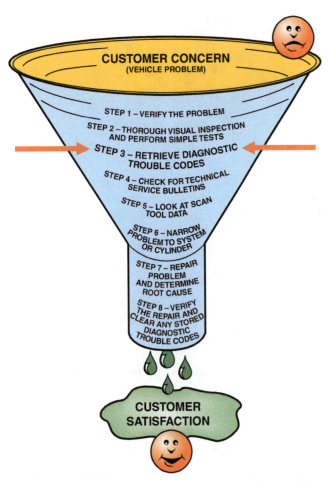

FIGURE 45–7 Step 3 in the diagnostic process is to retrieve any stored diagnostic trouble codes.

The spark at the spark tester should be steady and consistent. If an intermittent spark occurs, then this condition should be treated as a no-spark condition. If this test does not show satisfactory spark, carefully inspect and test all components of the primary and secondary ignition systems.

NOTE: Do not use a standard spark plug to check for proper ignition system voltage. An electronic ignition spark tester is designed to force the spark to jump about 0.75 inch (19 mm). This amount of gap requires between 25,000 and 30,000 volts (25 to 30 kV) at atmospheric pressure, which is enough voltage to ensure that a spark can occur under compression inside an engine.

- **Check the fuel-pump pressure.** Checking the fuel-pump pressure is relatively easy on many port fuel-injected engines. Often the cause of intermittent engine performance is due to a weak electric fuel pump or clogged fuel filter. Checking fuel pump pressure early in the diagnostic process eliminates low fuel pressure as a possibility.

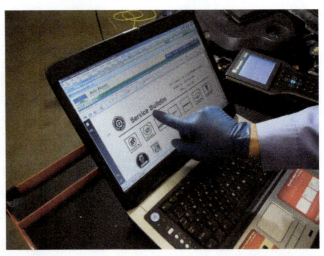

FIGURE 45–8 After checking for stored diagnostic trouble codes (DTCs), the wise technician checks service information for any technical service bulletins that may relate to the vehicle being serviced.

STEP 3 RETRIEVE THE DIAGNOSTIC TROUBLE CODES (DTCS)

If a diagnostic trouble code (DTC) is present in the computer memory, it may be signaled by illuminating a malfunction indicator lamp (MIL), commonly labeled "check engine" or "service engine soon." ● SEE FIGURE 45–7. Any code(s) that is displayed when the MIL is *not* on is called a **pending code**. Because the MIL is not on, this indicates that the fault has not repeated to cause the PCM to turn on the MIL. Although this pending code is helpful to the technician to know that a fault has, in the past, been detected, further testing will be needed to find the root cause of the problem.

STEP 4 CHECK FOR TECHNICAL SERVICE BULLETINS (TSBS)

Check for corrections in **technical service bulletins (TSBs)** that match the symptoms. ● SEE FIGURE 45–8. According to studies performed by automobile manufacturers, as many as 30% of vehicles can be repaired following the information, suggestions, or replacement parts found in a service bulletin. DTCs must be known before searching for service bulletins, because bulletins often include information on solving problems that involve a stored diagnostic trouble code.

STEP 5 LOOK CAREFULLY AT SCAN TOOL DATA

Vehicle manufacturers have been giving the technician more and more data on a scan tool connected to the **data link connector (DLC)**. ● SEE FIGURE 45–9. Beginning technicians are often observed scrolling through scan data without a real clue about what they are looking for. When asked, they usually reply that they are looking for something unusual, as if the screen will flash a big message "LOOK HERE—THIS IS NOT CORRECT."

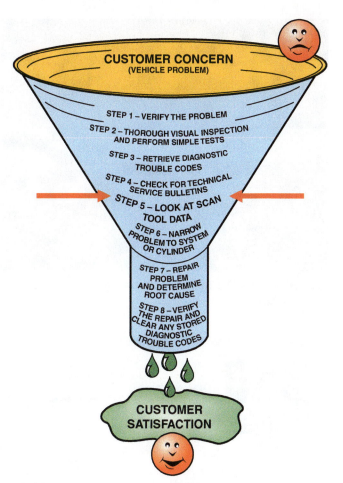

FIGURE 45–9 Looking carefully at the scan tool data is very helpful in locating the source of a problem.

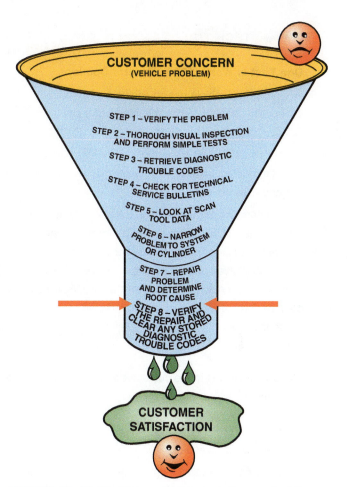

FIGURE 45–10 Step 8 is very important. Be sure that the customer's concern has been corrected.

That statement does not appear on scan tool displays. The best way to look at scan data is in a definite sequence and with specific, selected bits of data that can tell the most about the operation of the engine, such as the following:

- Engine coolant temperature (ECT) is the same as intake air temperature (IAT) after the vehicle sits for several hours.
- Idle air control (IAC) valve is being commanded to an acceptable range.
- Oxygen sensor (O2S) is operating properly:

  1. Readings below 200 mV at times
  2. Readings above 800 mV at times
  3. Rapid transitions between rich and lean

STEP 6 NARROW THE PROBLEM TO A SYSTEM OR CYLINDER
Narrowing the focus to a system or individual cylinder is the hardest part of the entire diagnostic process.

- Perform a cylinder power balance test.
- If a weak cylinder is detected, perform a compression and a cylinder leakage test to determine the probable cause.

STEP 7 REPAIR THE PROBLEM AND DETERMINE THE ROOT CAUSE
The repair or part replacement must be performed following vehicle manufacturer's recommendations and be certain that the root cause of the problem has been found. Also follow the manufacturer's recommended repair procedures and methods.

STEP 8 VERIFY THE REPAIR AND CLEAR ANY STORED DTCS ● SEE FIGURE 45–10.

- Test-drive to verify that the original problem (concern) is fixed.
- Verify that no additional problems have occurred during the repair process.
- Check for and then clear all diagnostic trouble codes. (This step ensures that the computer will not make any changes based on a stored DTC, but should not be performed if the vehicle is going to be tested for emissions because all of the monitors will need to be run and pass.)

One Test Is Worth 1000 "Expert" Opinions

Whenever any vehicle has an engine performance or driveability concern, certain people always say:

"Sounds like it's a bad injector."

"I'll bet you it's a bad computer."

"I had a problem just like yours yesterday and it was a bad EGR valve."

Regardless of the skills and talents of those people, it is still more accurate to perform tests on the vehicle than to rely on feelings or opinions of others who have not even seen the vehicle. Even your own opinion should not sway your thinking. Follow a plan, perform tests, and the test results will lead to the root cause.

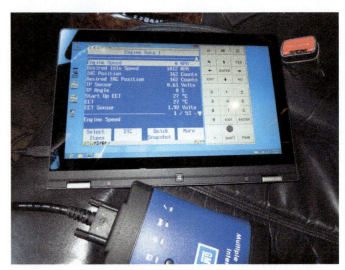

FIGURE 45–11 The Tech2Win program runs on a laptop using the MDI as an interface.

- Return the vehicle to the customer and double-check the following:

1. The vehicle is clean.
2. The radio is turned off.
3. The clock is set to the right time and the radio stations have been restored if the battery was disconnected during the repair procedure.

SCAN TOOLS

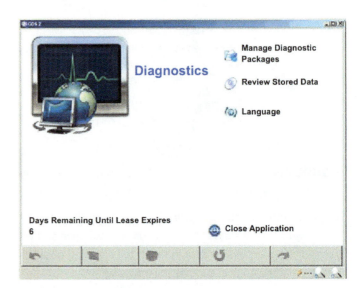

FIGURE 45–12 Global Diagnostic System 2 is required for the latest GM vehicles. (*Courtesy of General Motors*)

Scan tools are the workhorses for any diagnostic work on all vehicles. All factory scan tools are designed to provide bidirectional capability, which allows the service technician the opportunity to operate components using the scan tool, thereby confirming that the component is able to work when commanded. Also, all factory scan tools are capable of displaying all factory parameters.

1. On General Motors vehicles the required scan tools are as follows:
   - Tech 2 (1996 to 2010, depends on model).
   - Tech 2 and CANdi module (2005 to 2012, depending on model).
   - Tech2Win and multiple diagnostic interface (MDI) ● **SEE FIGURE 45–11**.
   - Global Diagnostic System 2 (GDS2) and multiple diagnostic interface (MDI) (2009 and later, depending on model) ● **SEE FIGURE 45–12**.

All factory scan tools are designed to provide bidirectional capability which allows the service technician the opportunity to operate components using the scan tool thereby confirming that the component is able to work when commanded. Also all factory scan tools are capable of displaying all factory parameters.

2. **Aftermarket scan tools.** These scan tools are designed to function on more than one brand of vehicle. Examples of aftermarket scan tools include:
   - **Snap-on** (various models including Ethos®, Solus®, and Verus®
   - **OTC** (various models including Genisys® and Pegisys®)
   - **AutoEnginuity** and other programs that use a laptop or handheld computer for the display

FIGURE 45–13 All scan tools plug in the data link connector (DLC) usually located under the dash on most vehicles.

While many aftermarket scan tools can display most if not all of the parameters of the factory scan tool, there can be a difference when trying to troubleshoot some faults.

RETRIEVAL OF DIAGNOSTIC INFORMATION

To retrieve diagnostic information from the powertrain control module (PCM), a scan tool is needed. If a factory or factory-level scan tool is used, then all of the data can be retrieved. If a global-only type scan tool (generic) is used, only the emissions-related data can be retrieved. ● **SEE CHART 45–1** for a typical data list. To retrieve diagnostic information from the PCM, use the following steps:

STEP 1 Locate and gain access to the data link connector (DLC). ● **SEE FIGURE 45–13**.

STEP 2 Connect the scan tool to the DLC and establish communication.

> **NOTE:** If no communication is established, follow the vehicle manufacturer's specified instructions.

STEP 3 Follow the on-screen instructions of the scan tool to correctly identify the vehicle.

STEP 4 Observe the scan data, as well as any diagnostic trouble codes.

STEP 5 Follow vehicle manufacturer's instructions if any DTCs are stored. If no DTCs are stored, compare all sensor values with a factory acceptable range chart to see if any sensor values are out-of-range.

PARAMETER IDENTIFICATION (PID)

SCAN TOOL PARAMETER	UNITS DISPLAYED	TYPICAL DATA VALUE
Engine Idling/Radiator Hose Hot/Closed Throttle/Park or Neutral/ Closed Loop/Accessories Off/Brake Pedal Released		
3X Crank Sensor	RPM	Varies
24X Crank Sensor	RPM	Varies
Actual EGR Position	Percent	0
BARO	kPa/Volts	65–110 kPa/ 3.5–4.5 volts
CMP Sensor Signal Present	Yes/No	Yes
Commanded Fuel Pump	On/Off	On
Cycles of Misfire Data	Counts	0–99
Desired EGR Position	Percent	0
ECT	°C/°F	Varies
EGR Duty Cycle	Percent	0
Engine Run Time	Hr: Min: Sec	Varies
EVAP Canister Purge	Percent	Low and Varying
EVAP Fault History	No Fault/Excess Vacuum/Purge Valve Leak/ Small Leak/ Weak Vacuum	No Fault
Fuel Tank Pressure	Inches of H$_2$O/ Volts	Varies
HO2S Sensor 1	Ready/Not Ready	Ready
HO2S Sensor 1	Millivolts	0–1000 and Varying
HO2S Sensor 2	Millivolts	0–1000 and Varying
HO2S X Counts	Counts	Varies
IAC Position	Counts	15–25 preferred
IAT	°C/°F	Varies
Knock Retard	Degrees	0
Long Term FT	Percent	0–10
MAF	Grams per second	3–7
MAF Frequency	Hz	1200–3000 (depends on altitude and engine load)
MAP	kPa/Volts	20–48 kPa/0.75–2 Volts (depends on altitude)
Misfire Current Cyl. 1–10	Counts	0

CHART 45–1 *(CONTINUED)*

SCAN TOOL PARAMETER	UNITS DISPLAYED	TYPICAL DATA VALUE
Misfire History Cyl. 1–10	Counts	0
Short Term FT	Percent	0–10
Start-Up ECT	°C/°F	Varies
Start-Up IAT	°C/°F	Varies
Total Misfire Current Count	Counts	0
Total Misfire Failures	Counts	0
Total Misfire Passes	Counts	0
TP Angle	Percent	0
TP Sensor	Volts	0.20–0.74
Vehicle Speed	Mph/Km/h	0

Note: Viewing the PID screen on the scanner is useful in determining if a problem is occurring at the present time.

CHART 45–1 (CONTINUED)

TROUBLESHOOTING USING DIAGNOSTIC TROUBLE CODES

Pinning down causes of the actual problem can be accomplished by trying to set the opposite code. For example, if a code indicates an open throttle position (TP) sensor (high resistance), clear the code and create a shorted (low-resistance) condition. This can be accomplished by using a jumper wire and connecting the signal terminal to the 5-volt reference terminal. This should set a diagnostic trouble code.

- **If the opposite code sets,** this indicates that the wiring and connector for the sensor is okay and the sensor itself is defective (open).
- **If the same code sets,** this indicates that the wiring or electrical connection is open (has high resistance) and is the cause of the setting of the DTC.

METHODS FOR CLEARING DIAGNOSTIC TROUBLE CODES

Clearing diagnostic trouble codes from a vehicle computer sometimes needs to be performed. There are three methods that can be used to clear stored diagnostic trouble codes.

CAUTION: Clearing diagnostic trouble codes (DTCs) also will clear all of the noncontinuous monitors.

- **Clearing codes—Method 1.** The preferred method of clearing codes is by using a scan tool. This is the method recommended by most vehicle manufacturers if the procedure can be performed on the vehicle. The computer of some vehicles cannot be cleared with a scan tool.

- **Clearing codes—Method 2.** If a scan tool is not available or a scan tool cannot be used on the vehicle being serviced, the power to the computer can be disconnected.

  1. Disconnect the fusible link (if so equipped) that feeds the computer.
  2. Disconnect the fuse or fuses that powers the computer.

- **Clearing codes—Method 3.** If the other two methods cannot be used, the negative (–) battery cable can be disconnected to clear stored diagnostic trouble codes.

NOTE: Because of the adaptive learning capacity of the computer, a vehicle may fail an exhaust emissions test if the vehicle is not driven enough to allow the computer to run all of the I/M monitors.

CAUTION: By disconnecting the battery, the radio presets and clock information will be lost. They should be reset before returning the vehicle to the customer. If the radio has a security code, the code must be entered before the radio will function. Before disconnecting the battery, always check with the vehicle owner to be sure that the code is available.

FLASH CODE RETRIEVAL ON OBD-I GENERAL MOTORS VEHICLES

Early GM computer systems (1981–1995) use a "check engine" or "check engine soon" MIL to notify the driver of possible system failure. Under the dash is a data link connector (DLC) previously called an assembly line communications link (ALCL) or assembly line diagnostic link (ALDL).

On these older General Motors vehicles diagnostic trouble codes can be retrieved by using a metal tool and contacting terminals A and B of the 12-pin DLC. ● **SEE FIGURE 45–14.** This method is called flash code retrieval because the MIL will flash to indicate diagnostic trouble codes. The steps are as follows:

1. Turn the ignition switch to on (engine off). The "check engine" light or "service engine soon" light should be on. If the amber malfunction indicator light (MIL) is not on, a problem exists within the light circuit.

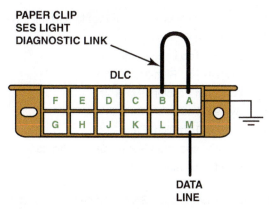

**PAPER CLIP
SES LIGHT
DIAGNOSTIC LINK**

DLC

F E D C B A
G H J K L M

**DATA
LINE**

FIGURE 45–14 To retrieve flash codes from an OBD-I General Motors vehicle, connect terminals A and B with the ignition on–engine off. The M terminal is used to retrieve data from the sensors to a scan tool (Tech I).

2. Connect terminals A and B at the DLC.

3. Observe the MIL. A code 12 (one flash, then a pause, then two flashes) reveals that there is no engine speed indication to the computer. Because the engine is not running, this simply indicates that the computer diagnostic system is working correctly.

   NOTE: Refer to service manual diagnostic procedures if the MIL is on and does not flash a code 12 when terminals A and B are connected.

4. After code 12 is displayed three times, the MIL will flash any other stored DTCs in numeric order starting with the lowest-number code. If only code 12 is displayed another three times, the computer has not detected any other faults.

NOTE: Trouble codes can vary according to year, make, model, and engine. Always consult the service literature or service manual for the exact vehicle being serviced. Check service information for the meaning and recommended steps to follow if a diagnostic trouble code is retrieved.

OBD-II DIAGNOSIS

Starting with the 1996 model year, all vehicles sold in the United States must use the same type of 16-pin data link connector (DLC) and must monitor emissions-related components.

RETRIEVING OBD-II CODES A scan tool is required to retrieve diagnostic trouble codes from most OBD-II vehicles. Every OBD-II scan tool will be able to read all generic Society of Automotive Engineers (SAE) DTCs from any vehicle.

Fuel and Air Metering System

P0100	Mass or Volume Airflow Circuit Problem
P0101	Mass or Volume Airflow Circuit Range or Performance Problem
P0102	Mass or Volume Airflow Circuit Low Input
P0103	Mass or Volume Airflow Circuit High Input
P0105	Manifold Absolute Pressure or Barometric Pressure Circuit Problem
P0106	Manifold Absolute Pressure or Barometric Pressure Circuit Range or Performance Problem
P0107	Manifold Absolute Pressure or Barometric Pressure Circuit Low Input
P0108	Manifold Absolute Pressure or Barometric Pressure Circuit High Input
P0110	Intake Air Temperature Circuit Problem
P0111	Intake Air Temperature Circuit Range or Performance Problem
P0112	Intake Air Temperature Circuit Low Input
P0113	Intake Air Temperature Circuit High Input
P0115	Engine Coolant Temperature Circuit Problem
P0116	Engine Coolant Temperature Circuit Range or Performance Problem
P0117	Engine Coolant Temperature Circuit Low Input
P0118	Engine Coolant Temperature Circuit High Input

P0120	Throttle Position Circuit Problem
P0121	Throttle Position Circuit Range or Performance Problem
P0122	Throttle Position Circuit Low Input
P0123	Throttle Position Circuit High Input
P0125	Excessive Time to Enter Closed-Loop Fuel Control
P0128	Coolant Temperature Below Thermostat Regulating Temperature
P0130	O2 Sensor Circuit Problem (Bank 1* Sensor 1)
P0131	O2 Sensor Circuit Low Voltage (Bank 1* Sensor 1)
P0132	O2 Sensor Circuit High Voltage (Bank 1* Sensor 1)
P0133	O2 Sensor Circuit Slow Response (Bank 1* Sensor 1)
P0134	O2 Sensor Circuit No Activity Detected (Bank 1* Sensor 1)
P0135	O2 Sensor Heater Circuit Problem (Bank 1* Sensor 1)
P0136	O2 Sensor Circuit Problem (Bank 1* Sensor 2)
P0137	O2 Sensor Circuit Low Voltage (Bank 1* Sensor 2)
P0138	O2 Sensor Circuit High Voltage (Bank 1* Sensor 2)
P0139	O2 Sensor Circuit Slow Response (Bank 1* Sensor 2)
P0140	O2 Sensor Circuit No Activity Detected (Bank 1* Sensor 2)
P0141	O2 Sensor Heater Circuit Problem (Bank 1* Sensor 2)
P0142	O2 Sensor Circuit Problem (Bank 1* Sensor 3)
P0143	O2 Sensor Circuit Low Voltage (Bank 1* Sensor 3)
P0144	O2 Sensor Circuit High Voltage (Bank 1* Sensor 3)
P0145	O2 Sensor Circuit Slow Response (Bank 1* Sensor 3)
P0146	O2 Sensor Circuit No Activity Detected (Bank 1* Sensor 3)
P0147	O2 Sensor Heater Circuit Problem (Bank 1* Sensor 3)
P0150	O2 Sensor Circuit Problem (Bank 2 Sensor 1)
P0151	O2 Sensor Circuit Low Voltage (Bank 2 Sensor 1)
P0152	O2 Sensor Circuit High Voltage (Bank 2 Sensor 1)
P0153	O2 Sensor Circuit Slow Response (Bank 2 Sensor 1)
P0154	O2 Sensor Circuit No Activity Detected (Bank 2 Sensor 1)
P0155	O2 Sensor Heater Circuit Problem (Bank 2 Sensor 1)
P0156	O2 Sensor Circuit Problem (Bank 2 Sensor 2)
P0157	O2 Sensor Circuit Low Voltage (Bank 2 Sensor 2)
P0158	O2 Sensor Circuit High Voltage (Bank 2 Sensor 2)
P0159	O2 Sensor Circuit Slow Response (Bank 2 Sensor 2)
P0160	O2 Sensor Circuit No Activity Detected (Bank 2 Sensor 2)
P0161	O2 Sensor Heater Circuit Problem (Bank 2 Sensor 2)
P0162	O2 Sensor Circuit Problem (Bank 2 Sensor 3)
P0163	O2 Sensor Circuit Low Voltage (Bank 2 Sensor 3)
P0164	O2 Sensor Circuit High Voltage (Bank 2 Sensor 3)
P0165	O2 Sensor Circuit Slow Response (Bank 2 Sensor 3)
P0166	O2 Sensor Circuit No Activity Detected (Bank 2 Sensor 3)
P0167	O2 Sensor Heater Circuit Problem (Bank 2 Sensor 3)
P0170	Fuel Trim Problem (Bank 1*)
P0171	System Too Lean (Bank 1*)
P0172	System Too Rich (Bank 1*)
P0173	Fuel Trim Problem (Bank 2)
P0174	System Too Lean (Bank 2)
P0175	System Too Rich (Bank 2)
P0176	Fuel Composition Sensor Circuit Problem
P0177	Fuel Composition Sensor Circuit Range or Performance
P0178	Fuel Composition Sensor Circuit Low Input
P0179	Fuel Composition Sensor Circuit High Input
P0180	Fuel Temperature Sensor Problem
P0181	Fuel Temperature Sensor Circuit Range or Performance
P0182	Fuel Temperature Sensor Circuit Low Input
P0183	Fuel Temperature Sensor Circuit High Input

Fuel and Air Metering (Injector Circuit)

P0201	Injector Circuit Problem—Cylinder 1
P0202	Injector Circuit Problem—Cylinder 2
P0203	Injector Circuit Problem—Cylinder 3
P0204	Injector Circuit Problem—Cylinder 4
P0205	Injector Circuit Problem—Cylinder 5
P0206	Injector Circuit Problem—Cylinder 6
P0207	Injector Circuit Problem—Cylinder 7
P0208	Injector Circuit Problem—Cylinder 8
P0209	Injector Circuit Problem—Cylinder 9
P0210	Injector Circuit Problem—Cylinder 10
P0211	Injector Circuit Problem—Cylinder 11
P0212	Injector Circuit Problem—Cylinder 12
P0213	Cold Start Injector 1 Problem
P0214	Cold Start Injector 2 Problem

Ignition System or Misfire

P0300	Random Misfire Detected
P0301	Cylinder 1 Misfire Detected
P0302	Cylinder 2 Misfire Detected
P0303	Cylinder 3 Misfire Detected
P0304	Cylinder 4 Misfire Detected
P0305	Cylinder 5 Misfire Detected
P0306	Cylinder 6 Misfire Detected
P0307	Cylinder 7 Misfire Detected
P0308	Cylinder 8 Misfire Detected
P0309	Cylinder 9 Misfire Detected
P0310	Cylinder 10 Misfire Detected
P0311	Cylinder 11 Misfire Detected
P0312	Cylinder 12 Misfire Detected
P0320	Ignition or Distributor Engine Speed Input Circuit Problem

P0321	Ignition or Distributor Engine Speed Input Circuit Range or Performance
P0322	Ignition or Distributor Engine Speed Input Circuit No Signal
P0325	Knock Sensor 1 Circuit Problem
P0326	Knock Sensor 1 Circuit Range or Performance
P0327	Knock Sensor 1 Circuit Low Input
P0328	Knock Sensor 1 Circuit High Input
P0330	Knock Sensor 2 Circuit Problem
P0331	Knock Sensor 2 Circuit Range or Performance
P0332	Knock Sensor 2 Circuit Low Input
P0333	Knock Sensor 2 Circuit High Input
P0335	Crankshaft Position Sensor Circuit Problem
P0336	Crankshaft Position Sensor Circuit Range or Performance
P0337	Crankshaft Position Sensor Circuit Low Input
P0338	Crankshaft Position Sensor Circuit High Input

Auxiliary Emissions Control

P0400	Exhaust Gas Recirculation Flow Problem
P0401	Exhaust Gas Recirculation Flow Insufficient Detected
P0402	Exhaust Gas Recirculation Flow Excessive Detected
P0405	Air Conditioner Refrigerant Charge Loss
P0410	Secondary Air Injection System Problem
P0411	Secondary Air Injection System Insufficient Flow Detected
P0412	Secondary Air Injection System Switching Valve or Circuit Problem
P0413	Secondary Air Injection System Switching Valve or Circuit Open
P0414	Secondary Air Injection System Switching Valve or Circuit Shorted
P0420	Catalyst System Efficiency below Threshold (Bank 1*)
P0421	Warm Up Catalyst Efficiency below Threshold (Bank 1*)
P0422	Main Catalyst Efficiency below Threshold (Bank 1*)
P0423	Heated Catalyst Efficiency below Threshold (Bank 1*)
P0424	Heated Catalyst Temperature below Threshold (Bank 1*)
P0430	Catalyst System Efficiency below Threshold (Bank 2)
P0431	Warm Up Catalyst Efficiency below Threshold (Bank 2)
P0432	Main Catalyst Efficiency below Threshold (Bank 2)
P0433	Heated Catalyst Efficiency below Threshold (Bank 2)
P0434	Heated Catalyst Temperature below Threshold (Bank 2)
P0440	Evaporative Emission Control System Problem
P0441	Evaporative Emission Control System Insufficient Purge Flow
P0442	Evaporative Emission Control System Leak Detected
P0443	Evaporative Emission Control System Purge Control Valve Circuit Problem
P0444	Evaporative Emission Control System Purge Control Valve Circuit Open
P0445	Evaporative Emission Control System Purge Control Valve Circuit Shorted
P0446	Evaporative Emission Control System Vent Control Problem
P0447	Evaporative Emission Control System Vent Control Open
P0448	Evaporative Emission Control System Vent Control Shorted
P0450	Evaporative Emission Control System Pressure Sensor Problem
P0451	Evaporative Emission Control System Pressure Sensor Range or Performance
P0452	Evaporative Emission Control System Pressure Sensor Low Input
P0453	Evaporative Emission Control System Pressure Sensor High Input

Vehicle Speed Control and Idle Control

P0500	Vehicle Speed Sensor Problem
P0501	Vehicle Speed Sensor Range or Performance
P0502	Vehicle Speed Sensor Low Input
P0505	Idle Control System Problem
P0506	Idle Control System RPM Lower Than Expected
P0507	Idle Control System RPM Higher Than Expected
P0510	Closed Throttle Position Switch Problem

Computer Output Circuit

| P0600 | Serial Communication Link Problem |
| P0605 | Internal Control Module (Module Identification Defined by J1979) |

Transmission

P0703	Brake Switch Input Problem
P0705	Transmission Range Sensor Circuit Problem (PRNDL Input)
P0706	Transmission Range Sensor Circuit Range or Performance
P0707	Transmission Range Sensor Circuit Low Input
P0708	Transmission Range Sensor Circuit High Input
P0710	Transmission Fluid Temperature Sensor Problem
P0711	Transmission Fluid Temperature Sensor Range or Performance
P0712	Transmission Fluid Temperature Sensor Low Input
P0713	Transmission Fluid Temperature Sensor High Input
P0715	Input or Turbine Speed Sensor Circuit Problem
P0716	Input or Turbine Speed Sensor Circuit Range or Performance

P0717	Input or Turbine Speed Sensor Circuit No Signal
P0720	Output Speed Sensor Circuit Problem
P0721	Output Speed Sensor Circuit Range or Performance
P0722	Output Speed Sensor Circuit No Signal
P0725	Engine Speed Input Circuit Problem
P0726	Engine Speed Input Circuit Range or Performance
P0727	Engine Speed Input Circuit No Signal
P0730	Incorrect Gear Ratio
P0731	Gear 1 Incorrect Ratio
P0732	Gear 2 Incorrect Ratio
P0733	Gear 3 Incorrect Ratio
P0734	Gear 4 Incorrect Ratio
P0735	Gear 5 Incorrect Ratio
P0736	Reverse Incorrect Ratio
P0740	Torque Converter Clutch System Problem
P0741	Torque Converter Clutch System Performance or Stuck Off
P0742	Torque Converter Clutch System Stuck On
P0743	Torque Converter Clutch System Electrical
P0745	Pressure Control Solenoid Problem
P0746	Pressure Control Solenoid Performance or Stuck Off
P0747	Pressure Control Solenoid Stuck On
P0748	Pressure Control Solenoid Electrical
P0750	Shift Solenoid A Problem
P0751	Shift Solenoid A Performance or Stuck Off
P0752	Shift Solenoid A Stuck On
P0753	Shift Solenoid A Electrical
P0755	Shift Solenoid B Problem
P0756	Shift Solenoid B Performance or Stuck Off
P0757	Shift Solenoid B Stuck On
P0758	Shift Solenoid B Electrical
P0760	Shift Solenoid C Problem
P0761	Shift Solenoid C Performance or Stuck Off
P0762	Shift Solenoid C Stuck On
P0763	Shift Solenoid C Electrical
P0765	Shift Solenoid D Problem
P0766	Shift Solenoid D Performance or Stuck Off
P0767	Shift Solenoid D Stuck On
P0768	Shift Solenoid D Electrical
P0770	Shift Solenoid E Problem
P0771	Shift Solenoid E Performance or Stuck Off
P0772	Shift Solenoid E Stuck On
P0773	Shift Solenoid E Electrical

* The side of the engine where number one cylinder is located.

OBD-II ACTIVE TESTS

The vehicle computer must run tests on the various emission-related components and turn on the malfunction indicator lamp (MIL) if faults are detected. OBD II is an *active* computer analysis system because it actually tests the operation of the oxygen sensors, exhaust gas recirculation system, and so forth whenever conditions permit. It is the purpose and function of the PCM to monitor these components and perform these active tests.

For example, the PCM may open the EGR valve momentarily to check its operation while the vehicle is decelerating. A change in the manifold absolute pressure (MAP) sensor signal will indicate to the computer that the exhaust gas is, in fact, being introduced into the engine. Because these tests are active and certain conditions must be present before these tests can be run, the computer uses its internal diagnostic program to keep track of all the various conditions and to schedule active tests so that they will not interfere with each other.

OBD-II DRIVE CYCLE The vehicle must be driven under a variety of operating conditions for all active tests to be performed. A **trip** is defined as an engine-operating drive cycle that contains the necessary conditions for a particular test to be performed. For example, for the EGR test to be performed, the engine has to be at normal operating temperature and decelerating for a minimum amount of time. Some tests are performed when the engine is cold, whereas others require that the vehicle be cruising at a steady highway speed.

TYPES OF OBD-II CODES Not all OBD-II diagnostic trouble codes are of the same importance for exhaust emissions. Each type of DTC has different requirements for it to set, and the computer will only turn on the MIL for emissions-related DTCs.

TYPE A CODES. A type A diagnostic trouble code is emissions related and will cause the MIL to be turned on at the *first trip* if the computer has detected a problem. Engine misfire or a very rich or lean air–fuel ratio, for example, would cause a type A diagnostic trouble code. These codes alert the driver to an emissions problem that may cause damage to the catalytic converter.

TYPE B CODES. A type B code will be stored and the MIL will be turned on during the *second consecutive trip*, alerting the driver to the fact that a diagnostic test was performed and failed.

TYPE C AND TYPE D CODES. Type C and type D codes are for use with nonemissions-related diagnostic tests. They will cause the lighting of a "service" lamp (if the vehicle is so equipped).

OBD-II FREEZE-FRAME

To assist the service technician, OBD II requires the computer to take a "snapshot" or freeze-frame of all data at the instant an emissions-related DTC is set. A scan tool is required to retrieve this data. CARB and EPA regulations require that the controller store specific freeze-frame (engine-related) data when the first emissions related fault is detected. The data stored in freeze-frame can only be replaced by data from a trouble code with a higher priority such as a trouble related to a fuel system or misfire monitor fault.

The freeze-frame has to contain data values that occurred at the time the code was set (these values are provided in standard units of measurement). Freeze-frame data is recorded during the first trip on a two-trip fault. As a result, OBD-II systems record the data present at the time an emissions-related code is recorded and the MIL activated. This data can be accessed and displayed on a scan tool. Freeze-frame data is one frame or one instant in time. Freeze-frame data is not updated (refreshed) if the same monitor test fails a second time.

REQUIRED FREEZE-FRAME DATA ITEMS.

- Code that triggered the freeze-frame
- A/F ratio, airflow rate, and calculated engine load
- Base fuel injector pulse width
- ECT, IAT, MAF, MAP, TP, and VS sensor data
- Engine speed and amount of ignition spark advance
- Open- or closed-loop status
- Short-term and long-term fuel trim values
- For misfire codes—identify the cylinder that misfired

DIAGNOSING INTERMITTENT MALFUNCTIONS Of all the different types of conditions that you will see, the hardest to accurately diagnose and repair are intermittent malfunctions. These conditions may be temperature related (only occur when the vehicle is hot or cold), or humidity related (only occur when it is raining). Regardless of the conditions that will cause the malfunction to occur, you must diagnose and correct the condition.

When dealing with an intermittent concern, you should determine the conditions when the malfunction occurs, and then try to duplicate those conditions. If a cause is not readily apparent to you, ask the customer when the symptom occurs. Ask if there are any conditions that seem to be related to, or cause the concern.

Another consideration when working on an OBD-II-equipped vehicle is whether a concern is intermittent, or if it occurs only when a specific diagnostic test is performed by the PCM. Since OBD-II systems conduct diagnostic tests only under very precise conditions, some tests may be run only once during an ignition cycle. Additionally, if the requirements needed to perform the test are not met, the test will not run during an ignition cycle. This type of onboard diagnostics could be mistaken as "intermittent" when, in fact, the tests are only infrequent (depending on how the vehicle is driven). Examples of this type of diagnostic test are HO2S heaters, evaporative canister purge, catalyst efficiency, and EGR flow. When diagnosing intermittent concerns on an OBD-II-equipped vehicle, a logical diagnostic strategy is essential. The use of stored freeze-frame information and history codes can also be very useful when diagnosing an intermittent malfunction if a code has been stored.

SERVICE/FLASH PROGRAMMING

Designing a program that allows an engine to meet strict air quality and fuel economy standards while providing excellent performance is no small feat. However, this is only part of the challenge facing engineers assigned with the task of developing OBD-II software. The reason for this is the countless variables involved with running the diagnostic monitors. Although programmers do their best to factor in any and all operating conditions when writing this complex code, periodic revisions are often required.

Reprogramming consists of downloading new calibration files from a scan tool, personal computer, or modem into the PCM's electronically erasable programmable read-only

FIGURE 45–15 The first step in the reprogramming procedure is to determine the current software installed using a scan tool. Not all scan tools can be used. In most cases using the factory scan tool is needed for reprogramming unless the scan tool is equipped to handle reprogramming.

FIGURE 45–16 Follow the on-screen instructions.

memory (EEPROM). This can be done on or off the vehicle using the appropriate equipment. Since reprogramming is not an OBD-II requirement however, many vehicles will need a new PCM in the event software changes become necessary. Physically removing and replacing the PROM chip is no longer possible.

The following are three industry-standard methods used to reprogram the EEPROM:

- Remote programming
- Direct programming
- Off-board programming

REMOTE PROGRAMMING. Remote programming uses the scan tool to transfer data from the manufacturer's shop PC to the vehicle's PCM. This is accomplished by performing the following steps:

- Connect the scan tool to the vehicle's DLC. ● **SEE FIGURE 45–15.**
- Enter the vehicle information into the scan tool through the programming application software incorporated in the scan tool. ● **SEE FIGURE 45–16.**
- Download VIN and current EEPROM calibration using a scan tool.
- Disconnect the scan tool from the DLC and connect the tool to the shop PC.

- Download the new calibration from the PC to the scan tool. ● **SEE FIGURE 45–17.**
- Reconnect the scan tool to the vehicle's DLC and download the new calibration into the PCM.

CAUTION: Before programming, the vehicle's battery must be between 11 volts and 14 volts. Do not attempt to program while charging the battery unless using a special battery charger which does not produce excessive ripple voltage such as the Midtronics PSC-300 (30 amp) or PSC-550 (55 amp) or GR8 battery tester/charger (EL-50313), as specified by the vehicle manufacturer.

DIRECT PROGRAMMING. Direct programming does utilize a connection between the shop PC and the vehicle DLC.

OFF-BOARD PROGRAMMING. Off-board programming is used if the PCM must be programmed away from the vehicle. This is preformed using an off-board programming adapter.

IDENTIFYING AFTERMARKET (NON-GM) FLASH PROGRAMMING[1]

Engine transmission and catalytic converter part failures can be the result of non-GM (aftermarket) engine and transmission control module calibrations being installed.

When alteration to the GM-released engine or transmission control module calibrations occurs, it subjects powertrain and driveline components (engine, transmission, transfer case,

---

[1]General Motors TSB #09-06-04-026G

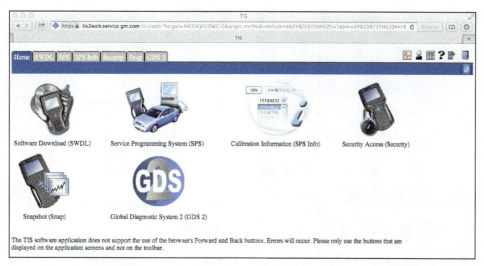

FIGURE 45–17 An Internet connection and access to TIS2WEB is required to perform updates and reprogramming. (*Courtesy of General Motors*)

driveshaft, and rear axle) to stresses that were not tested by General Motors.

It is because of these unknown stresses, and the potential to alter reliability, durability, and emissions performance, that GM has adopted a policy that prevents any unauthorized Service Agent Warranty Transaction submissions to any remaining warranty coverage, to the powertrain and driveline components whenever the presence of a non-GM calibration is confirmed—even if the non-GM control module calibration is subsequently removed.

Each calibration part number has a matching calibration verification number (CVN) that is unique to the calibration. The scan tool (Tech 2 or GDS 2) can be used to read the CVN, which is then compared with the calibration ID and CVN stored in the TIS2WEB database. If the vehicle CVN does not match the TIS2WEB CVN, current or past presence of an aftermarket (unauthorized) calibration is indicated. ● **SEE FIGURE 45–18**.

J2534 REPROGRAMMING
Legislation has mandated that vehicle manufacturers meet the SAE J2534 standards for all emissions-related systems on all new vehicles starting with model year 2004. This standard enables independent service repair operators to program or reprogram emissions-related ECMs from a wide variety of vehicle manufacturers with a single tool. ● **SEE FIGURE 45–19**. A J2534 compliant pass-through system is a standardized programming and diagnostic system. It uses a personal computer (PC) plus a standard interface to a software device driver, and a hardware vehicle communication interface. The interface connects to a PC, and

to a programmable ECM on a vehicle through the J1962 data link connector (DLC). This system allows programming of all vehicle manufacturer ECMs using a single set of programming hardware. Programming software made available by the vehicle manufacturer must be functional with a J2534 compliant pass-through system.

The software for a typical pass-through application consists of two major components:

- The part delivered by the company that furnishes the hardware for J2534 enables the pass-through vehicle communication interface to communicate with the PC and provides for all Vehicle Communication Protocols as required by SAE J2534. It also provides for the software interface to work with the software applications as provided for by the vehicle manufacturers. ● **SEE FIGURE 45–20**.

- The second part of the pass-through enabling software is provided for by the vehicle manufacturers. This is normally a subset of the software used with their original equipment manufacturer (OEM) tools and their Web site will indicate how to obtain this software and under what conditions it can be used. Refer to the National Automotive Service Task Force (NASTF) Web site for the addresses for all vehicle manufacturers' service information and cost, *www. NASTF.org*.

Since the majority of vehicle manufacturers make this software available in downloadable form, having an up-to-date computer and Internet access are required.

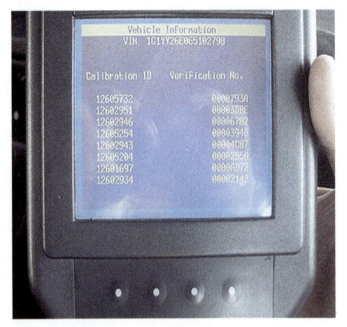

FIGURE 45–18 Use the scan tool to read and record the calibration ID and the calibration verification number (CVN). (*Courtesy of General Motors*)

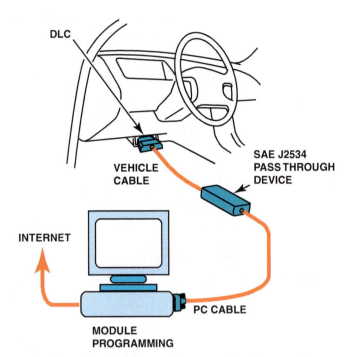

FIGURE 45–19 The J2534 pass-through reprogramming system does not need a scan tool to reflash the PCM on most 2004 and newer vehicles.

STRATEGY-BASED DIAGNOSIS[2]

The goal of **Strategy-Based Diagnosis** is to provide guidance when you create a plan of action for each specific diagnostic situation. Following a similar plan for each diagnostic situation, you will achieve maximum efficiency when you diagnose and repair vehicles. Although each of the Strategy-Based Diagnosis boxes is numbered, you are not required to complete every box in order to successfully diagnose a customer concern. The first step of your diagnostic process should always be "Understand and Verify the Customer's Concern." The final step of your diagnostic process should be "Repair and Verify the Fix." Refer to the following chart for the correct Strategy-Based Diagnosis.

1. **Understand and verify the customer's concern:** The first part of this step is to obtain as much information as possible from the customer. Are there aftermarket accessories on the vehicle? When does the condition occur? Where does the condition occur? How long does the condition last? How often does the condition occur? In order to verify the concern, the technician should be familiar with the normal operation of the system and refer to the owner or service manual for any information needed.

[2]General Motors Service Information document #1957622

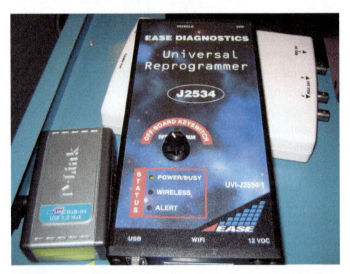

FIGURE 45–20 A typical J2534 universal reprogrammer that uses the J2534 standards.

2. **Vehicle operating as designed:** This condition exists when the vehicle is found to operate normally. The condition described by the customer may be normal. Compare with another like vehicle that is operating normally under the same conditions described by the customer. Explain your findings and the operation of the system to the customer. If the customer is dissatisfied, submit a Field Product Report.

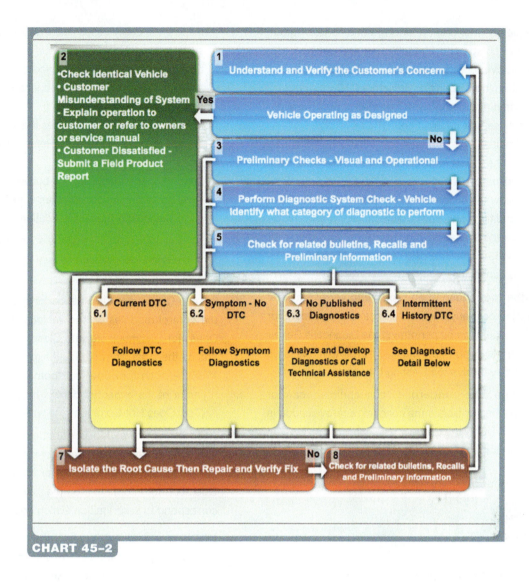

CHART 45-2

3. **Preliminary checks:** Conduct a thorough visual inspection. Review the service history. Detect unusual sounds or odors. Gather diagnostic trouble code (DTC) information in order to achieve an effective repair.

4. **Perform published "Diagnostic System Check – Vehicle":** The Diagnostic System Check – Vehicle (covered in the next section) verifies the proper operation of the system. This will lead the technician to an organized approach to diagnostics and identify what category of diagnostic to perform.

5. **Check for related bulletins, recalls and preliminary information (PI)**.

6. **Diagnostic categories:**

   6.1. **Current DTC:** Follow the designated DTC diagnostic in order to make an effective repair. Refer to "Diagnostic Trouble Code (DTC) List – Vehicle."

   6.2. **Symptom – No DTC:** Select the appropriate symptom diagnostic. Follow the diagnostic steps or

suggestions in order to complete the repair. Refer to "Symptoms – Vehicle."

   6.3. **No published diagnostics:** Analyze the concern. Develop a plan for the diagnostics. The service manual schematics will help you to see system power, ground, input, and output circuits. You can also identify splices and other areas where multiple circuits are tied together. Look at component locations to see if components, connectors, or harnesses may be exposed to extreme temperature, moisture, or corrosives (road salt, battery acid, oil, or other fluids). Utilize the wiring diagrams, system description and operation, and system circuit description.

   6.4. **Intermittent/history DTC:** An intermittent condition is one that does not occur continuously, may be difficult to duplicate, and will occur only when certain conditions are met. Generally, an intermittent DTC is caused by faulty electrical connections and wiring, malfunctioning components, electromagnetic/radio frequency interference, driving conditions, or after-market equipment. The following approaches/tools may prove to be beneficial in locating and repairing an intermittent condition or history DTC.

- Combining technicians' knowledge with the available service information.
- Evaluate the symptoms and conditions described by the customer on the Customer Concern Verification Sheets.
- Follow the suggestions on Testing for Intermittent Conditions and Poor Connections.
- Use the available scan tool, digital multimeter, or *J-42598-B* vehicle data recorder with data capturing capabilities.

7. **Isolate the root cause, then repair and verify fix:** After isolating the root cause, make the repairs and validate for the correct operation by performing the Diagnostic Repair Verification. Verifying that the DTC or symptom has been corrected may involve road testing the vehicle.

8. **Re-examine the concern:** If a technician cannot successfully find or isolate the concern, a re-evaluation is necessary. Reverify the concern. The concern could be an intermittent or normal condition.

DIAGNOSTIC SYSTEM CHECK – VEHICLE[3]

The **Diagnostic System Check** is the starting point for almost all vehicle concerns. Excerpted from General Motors Service Information (SI), following are the typical steps to perform this procedure:

1. This step is one of the key diagnostic steps that cannot be skipped. Often the cause of a customer concern will be discovered during these initial inspections. Before beginning vehicle diagnosis, the following preliminary inspections/tests must be performed:

- Ensure that the battery is fully charged. Refer to Battery Inspection/Test.
- Ensure that the battery cables are clean and tight.
- Inspect for any open fuses. Refer to Power Distribution Schematics and Electrical Center Identification Views.
- Ensure that the grounds are clean, tight, and in the correct location. Refer to Ground Distribution Schematics and Power and Grounding Component Views.

- Inspect the easily accessible systems or the visible system components for obvious damage or conditions that could cause the concern. This would include checking to ensure that all connections/connectors are fully seated and secured.
- Inspect for aftermarket devices that could affect the operation of the system. Refer to Checking Aftermarket Accessories.
- Search for applicable service bulletins.
- If the preceding inspections/tests resolve the concern, go to Diagnostic Repair Verification.

2. Install a scan tool. Verify that the scan tool powers up.
- If the scan tool does not power up, refer to Scan Tool Does Not Power Up.

3. Ignition ON, Engine OFF, verify communication with all of the control modules on the vehicle. Refer to Scan Tool Does Not Communicate with Class 2 Device for information on the modules you should expect to communicate.
- If the scan tool does not communicate with one or more of the expected control modules, refer to Scan Tool Does Not Communicate with Class 2 Device.

4. Access the Power Mode parameter on the scan tool. Verify the power mode parameter matches all the ignition switch positions. Refer to Power Mode Description and Operation for information on the power mode states that correspond to each ignition switch position.

NOTE: Open the driver's door to ensure retained accessory power mode (RAP) is inactive during this test. The engine may start during this test. Turn the engine OFF as soon as the crank power mode has been observed.

- If the power mode parameter does not match the ignition switch position for all ignition switch positions, refer to Power Mode Mismatch.

5. Attempt to start the engine. Verify that the engine cranks.
- If the engine does not crank, refer to Symptoms—Engine Electrical.

6. Attempt to start the engine. Verify the engine starts and idles.
- If the engine does not start and idle, refer to Engine Cranks But Does Not Run.

NOTE: Do not clear any DTCs unless instructed to do so by a diagnostic procedure. If any DTCs are powertrain-related DTCs, select Capture Info in order to store the DTC information with the scan tool.

[3]General Motors Service Information document #1830951

7. Use the appropriate scan tool selections to obtain DTCs from each of the vehicle modules. Verify there are no DTCs reported from any module. If any DTCs are present, refer to "Diagnostic Trouble Code (DTC) List – Vehicle" and diagnose any current DTCs in the following order:

1. DTCs that begin with a U.
2. Any of the following: B1000, B1001, B1004, B1007, B1009, C0550, P0601, P0602, P0603, P0604, P0606, P0607, P060D, P060E, P1621, or P2610.
3. Any of the following: B1372, B1373, B1390, C0899, P0562, or P0563.
4. Component level DTCs.
5. System level DTCs.
6. Any remaining DTCs.

If the customer concern is related to inspection/maintenance (I/M) testing, refer to Inspection/Maintenance System Check in service information.

COMPLETING SYSTEM REPAIRS

After the repair has been successfully completed, the vehicle should be driven under similar conditions that caused the original concern. Verify that the problem has been corrected. To perform this test-drive, it is helpful to have a copy of the freeze-frame parameters that were present when the DTC was set. By driving under similar conditions, the PCM may perform a test of the system and automatically extinguish the MIL. This is the method preferred by most vehicle manufacturers. The DTC can be cleared using a scan tool, but then that means that monitors will have to be run and the vehicle may fail an emissions inspection if driven directly to the testing station.

PROCEDURES FOR RESETTING THE PCM

The PCM can be reset or cleared of previously set DTCs and freeze-frame data in the following ways:

1. **Driving the Vehicle.** Drive the vehicle under similar conditions that were present when the fault occurred. If the conditions are similar and the PCM performed the non-continuous monitor test and it passed three times, then the PCM will extinguish the MIL. This is the method preferred by most vehicle manufacturers; however, this

method could be time consuming. If three passes cannot be achieved, the owner of the vehicle will have to be told that even though the check engine light (MIL) is on, the problem has been corrected and the MIL should go out in a few days of normal driving.

2. **Clear DTCs Using a Scan Tool.** A scan tool can be used to clear the diagnostic trouble code (DTC), which will also delete all of the freeze-frame data. The advantage of using a scan tool is that the check engine (MIL) will be out and the customer will be happy that the problem (MIL on) has been corrected. Do not use a scan tool to clear a DTC if the vehicle is going to be checked soon at a test station for state-mandated emissions tests.

3. **Battery Disconnect.** Disconnecting the negative battery cable will clear the DTCs and freeze-frame on many vehicles but not all. Besides clearing the DTCs, disconnecting the battery for about 20 minutes will also erase radio station presets and other memory items in many cases. Most vehicle manufacturers do not recommend that the battery be disconnected to clear DTCs and it may not work on some vehicles.

ROAD TEST (DRIVE CYCLE)

Use the freeze-frame data and test-drive the vehicle so that the vehicle is driven to match the conditions displayed on the freeze-frame. If the battery has been disconnected, then the vehicle may have to be driven under conditions that allow the PCM to conduct monitor tests. This drive pattern is called a **drive cycle**. The drive cycle is different for each vehicle manufacturer but a universal drive cycle may work in many cases. In many cases, performing a universal drive cycle will reset most monitors in most vehicles.

UNIVERSAL DRIVE CYCLE

PRECONDITIONING: PHASE 1.

MIL must be off.

No DTCs present.

Fuel fill between 15% and 85%.

Cold start—Preferred = eight hour soak at 68°F to 86°F.

Alternative = ECT below 86°F.

1. With the ignition off, connect scan tool.
2. Start engine and drive between 20 mph and 30 mph for 22 minutes, allowing speed to vary.

3. Stop and idle for 40 seconds, gradually accelerate to 55 mph.

4. Maintain 55 mph for 4 minutes using a steady throttle input.

5. Stop and idle for 30 seconds, then accelerate to 30 mph.

6. Maintain 30 mph for 12 minutes.

7. Repeat steps 4 and 5 four times.

   Using scan tool, check readiness. If insufficient readiness set, continue to universal drive trace phase II.

   Important: (Do not shut off engine between phases). Phase II:

1. Bring vehicle to a stop and idle for 45 seconds, then accelerate to 30 mph.

2. Maintain 30 mph for 22 minutes.

3. Repeat steps 1 and 2 three times.

4. Bring vehicle to a stop and idle for 45 seconds, then accelerate to 35 mph.

5. Maintain speed between 30 mph and 35 mph for 4 minutes.

6. Bring vehicle to a stop and idle for 45 seconds, then accelerate to 30 mph.

7. Maintain 30 mph for 22 minutes.

8. Repeat steps 6 and 7 five times.

9. Using scan tool, check readiness and I/M flags.

 **TECH TIP**

Drive the Light Out

If working on a vehicle that is subject to state emissions testing, it is best to not clear codes. When diagnostic trouble codes are cleared, all of the monitors have to be rerun and this can be a time-consuming job. Instead of clearing the code, simply drive the vehicle until the PCM clears the code. This will likely take less time compared to trying to drive the vehicle under varying conditions to run all of the monitors.

SUMMARY

1. Funnel diagnostics is a visual approach to a diagnostic procedure and involves the following steps:

   STEP 1 Verify the problem (concern)

   STEP 2 Perform a thorough visual inspection and basic tests

   STEP 3 Retrieve the diagnostic trouble codes (DTCs)

   STEP 4 Check for technical service bulletins (TSBs)

   STEP 5 Look carefully at scan tool data

   STEP 6 Narrow the problem to a system or cylinder

   STEP 7 Repair the problem and determine the root cause

   STEP 8 Verify the repair and check for any stored DTCs

2. Care should be taken to not induce high voltage or current around any computer or computer-controlled circuit or sensor.

3. A thorough visual inspection is important during the diagnosis and troubleshooting of any engine performance problem or electrical malfunction.

4. If the MIL is on, retrieve the DTC and follow the manufacturer's recommended procedure to find the root cause of the problem.

5. OBD-II vehicles use a 16-pin DLC and common DTCs.

6. General Motors recommends the use of Strategy Based Diagnostics when troubleshooting vehicle concerns.

REVIEW QUESTIONS

1. Explain the procedure to follow when diagnosing a vehicle with stored DTCs using a scan tool.

2. Discuss what the PCM does during a drive cycle to test emissions-related components.

3. Explain the difference between a type A and type B OBD-II diagnostic trouble code.

4. List three things that should be checked as part of a thorough visual inspection.

5. List the eight-step funnel diagnostic procedure.

6. Explain why a bulletin search should be performed after stored DTCs are retrieved.

7. List the three methods that can be used to reprogram a PCM.

8. List the steps of the strategy-based diagnosis (SBD) procedure.

1. Technician A says that the first step in the diagnostic process is to verify the problem (concern). Technician B says the second step is to perform a thorough visual inspection. Which technician is correct?
   a. Technician A only
   b. Technician B only
   c. Both Technicians A and B
   d. Neither Technician A nor B

2. Which item is *not* important to know before starting the diagnosis of an engine performance problem?
   a. List of previous repairs
   b. The brand of engine oil used
   c. The type of gasoline used
   d. The temperature of the engine when the problem occurs

3. A paper test can be used to check for a possible problem with _____.
   a. The ignition system (bad spark plug wire)
   b. A faulty injector on a multiport engine
   c. A burned valve
   d. All of the above

4. Which step should be performed *last* when diagnosing an engine performance problem?
   a. Checking for any stored diagnostic trouble codes
   b. Checking for any technical service bulletins (TSBs)
   c. Performing a thorough visual inspection
   d. Verifying the repair

5. Technician A says that if the opposite DTC can be set, the problem is the component itself. Technician B says if the opposite DTC cannot be set, the problem is with the wiring or grounds. Which technician is correct?
   a. Technician A only
   b. Technician B only
   c. Both Technicians A and B
   d. Neither Technician A nor B

6. The preferred method to clear diagnostic trouble codes (DTCs) is to _____.
   a. Disconnect the negative battery cable for 10 seconds
   b. Use a scan tool
   c. Remove the computer (PCM) power feed fuse
   d. Cycle the ignition key on and off 40 times

7. Which is the factory scan tool for the latest GM vehicles?
   a. Candi
   b. GDS 2
   c. Tech 2
   d. Modur 2

8. Technician A says that reprogramming a PCM using the J2534 system requires a factory scan tool, while Technician B says it requires Internet access. Which technician is correct?
   a. Technician A only
   b. Technician B only
   c. Both Technicians A and B
   d. Neither Technician A nor B

9. Technician A says that knowing if there are any stored diagnostic trouble codes (DTCs) may be helpful when checking for related technical service bulletins (TSBs). Technician B says that only a factory scan tool should be used to retrieve DTCs. Which technician is correct?
   a. Technician A only
   b. Technician B only
   c. Both Technicians A and B
   d. Neither Technician A nor B

10. Which method can be used to reprogram a PCM?
    a. Remote
    b. Direct
    c. Off-board
    d. All of the above

EDITOR'S NOTE: This information is included for reference purposes only. Much of it refers to older vehicles and depends on the type of scope and equipment being used. However, I find the secondary patterns very useful when explaining what is happening in the ignition system during a spark event.

appendix A

SCOPE-TESTING THE IGNITION SYSTEM

Any automotive scope with the correct probes or adapters will show an ignition system pattern. All ignition systems must charge and discharge an ignition coil. With the engine off, most scopes will display a horizontal line. With the engine running, this horizontal (zero) line is changed to a pattern that will have sections both above and below the zero line. Sections of this pattern that are above the zero line indicate that the ignition coil is discharging. Sections of the scope pattern below the zero line indicate charging of the ignition coil. The height of the scope pattern indicates voltage. The length (from left to right) of the scope pattern indicates time. ● **SEE FIGURES A–1 AND A–2** for typical scope hookups.

FIRING LINE The leftmost vertical (upward) line is called the **firing line**. The height of the firing line should be between 5,000 and 15,000 volts (5 and 15 kV) with not more than a 3 kV difference between the highest and the lowest cylinder's firing line. ● **SEE FIGURES A–3 AND A–4.**

The height of the firing line indicates the *voltage* required to fire the spark plug. It requires a high voltage to make the air inside the cylinder electrically conductive (to ionize the air). A higher than normal height (or height higher than that of other cylinders) can be caused by one or more of the following:

1. Spark plug gapped too wide
2. Lean fuel mixture
3. Defective spark plug wire

If the firing lines are higher than normal for *all* cylinders, then possible causes include one or more of the following:

1. Worn distributor cap and/or rotor (if the vehicle is so equipped)
2. Excessive wearing of all spark plugs
3. Defective coil wire (the high voltage could still jump across the open section of the wire to fire the spark plugs)

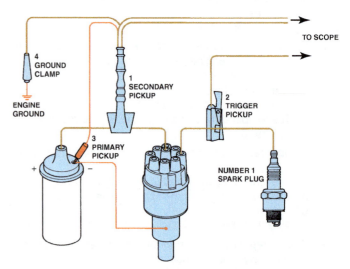

FIGURE A–1 Typical engine analyzer hookup that includes a scope display. (1) Coil wire on top of the distributor cap if integral type of coil; (2) number 1 spark plug connection; (3) negative side of the ignition coil; (4) ground (negative) connection of the battery.

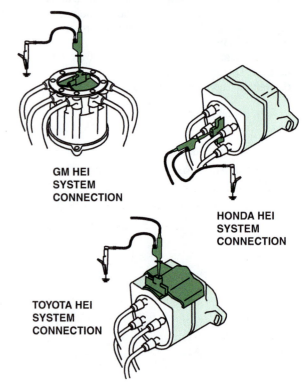

FIGURE A–2 Clip-on adapters are used with an ignition system that uses an integral ignition coil.

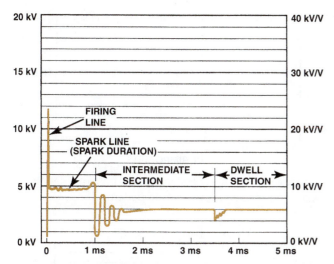

FIGURE A–3 Typical secondary ignition oscilloscope pattern.

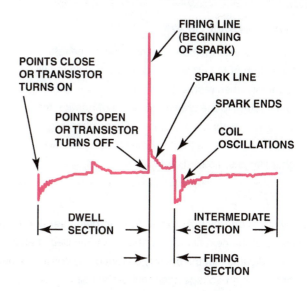

SECONDARY CONVENTIONAL (SINGLE)

FIRING LINE (BEGINNING OF SPARK)

POINTS CLOSE OR TRANSISTOR TURNS ON

SPARK LINE

SPARK ENDS

POINTS OPEN OR TRANSISTOR TURNS OFF

COIL OSCILLATIONS

DWELL SECTION

INTERMEDIATE SECTION

FIRING SECTION

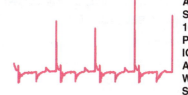

SECONDARY CONVENTIONAL (PARADE)

FIRING LINES SHOULD BE EQUAL. A SHORT LINE INDICATES LOW RESISTANCE IN THE WIRE. A HIGH LINE INDICATES HIGH RESISTANCE IN THE WIRE.

AVAILABLE VOLTAGE SHOULD BE ABOUT 10 K V ON A POINTS-TYPE IGNITION SYSTEM AND EVEN GREATER WITH AN ELECTRONIC SYSTEM

SPARK LINES CAN BE VIEWED SIDE-BY-SIDE FOR EASE OF COMPARISON

CYLINDERS ARE DISPLAYED IN FIRING ORDER

FIGURE A–4 A single cylinder is shown at the top and a four-cylinder engine at the bottom

SPARK LINE

The **spark line** is a short horizontal line immediately after the firing line. The height of the spark line represents the voltage required to maintain the spark across the spark plug after the spark has started. The height of the spark line should be one-fourth of the height of the firing line (between 1.5 kV and 2.5 kV). The length (from left to right) of the line represents the length of time for which the spark lasts (duration or burn time). The spark duration should be between 0.8 milliseconds and 2.2 milliseconds (usually between 1.0 ms and 2.0 ms). The spark stops at the end (right side) of the spark line, as shown in ● **SEE FIGURE A–5.**

INTERMEDIATE OSCILLATIONS

After the spark has stopped, some energy remains in the coil. This remaining energy dissipates in the coil windings and the entire secondary circuit. The **intermediate oscillations** are also called the "ringing" of the coil as it is pulsed.

The secondary pattern amplifies any voltage variation occurring in the primary circuit because of the turns ratio between the primary and secondary windings of the ignition coil. A correctly operating ignition system should display five or more "bumps" (oscillations) (three or more for a GM HEI system).

TRANSISTOR-ON POINT

After the intermediate oscillations, the coil is empty (not charged), as indicated by the scope pattern being on the zero line for a short period. When the transistor turns on an electronic system, the coil is being charged.

Note that the charging of the coil occurs slowly (coil-charging oscillations) because of the inductive reactance of the coil.

DWELL SECTION

Dwell is the amount of time that the current is charging the coil from the transistor-on point to

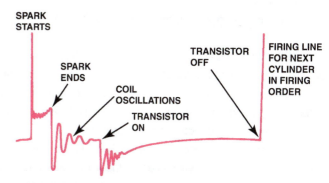

SPARK STARTS

SPARK ENDS

COIL OSCILLATIONS

TRANSISTOR ON

TRANSISTOR OFF

FIRING LINE FOR NEXT CYLINDER IN FIRING ORDER

FIGURE A–5 Drawing shows what is occurring electrically at each part of the scope pattern.

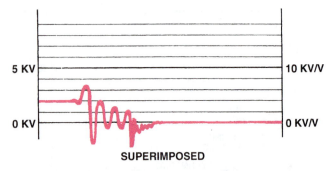
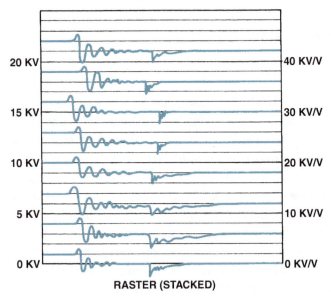

FIGURE A–6 Typical secondary ignition pattern. Note the lack of firing lines on superimposed pattern.

the transistor-off point. At the end of the **dwell section** is the beginning of the next firing line. This point is called "transistor off" and indicates that the primary current of the coil is stopped, resulting in a high-voltage spark out of the coil.

PATTERN SELECTION Ignition oscilloscopes use three positions to view certain sections of the basic pattern more closely. These three positions are as follows:

1. **Superimposed.** This **superimposed** position is used to look at differences in patterns between cylinders in all areas except the firing line. There are no firing lines illustrated in superimposed positions. ● **SEE FIGURE A–6.**

2. **Raster (stacked).** Cylinder 1 is at the bottom on most scopes. Use the **raster** (stacked) position to look at the spark line length and transistor-on point. The raster pattern shows all areas of the scope pattern except the firing lines. ● **SEE FIGURE A–7.**

3. **Display (parade).** Display (parade) is the only position in which firing lines are visible. The firing line section for cylinder 1 is on the far right side of the screen, with the remaining portions of the pattern on the left side. This selection is used to compare the height of firing lines among all cylinders. ● **SEE FIGURE A–8.**

READING THE SCOPE ON DISPLAY (PARADE) Start the engine and operate at approximately 1000 RPM to ensure a smooth and accurate scope pattern. Firing lines are visible only on the display (parade) position. The firing lines should all be 5 to 15 kV in height and be within 3 kV of each other. If one or more cylinders have high firing lines, this could indicate a defective (open) spark plug wire, a spark plug gapped too far, or a lean fuel mixture affecting only those cylinders.

A lean mixture (not enough fuel) requires a higher voltage to ignite because there are fewer droplets of fuel in the cylinder for the spark to use as "stepping stones" for the voltage to jump across. Therefore, a lean mixture is less conductive than a rich mixture.

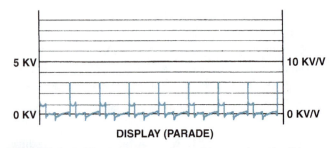

FIGURE A–7 Raster is the best scope position to view the spark lines of all the cylinders to check for differences. Most scopes display the cylinder 1 at the bottom. The other cylinders are positioned by firing order above cylinder 1.

FIGURE A–8 Display is the only position to view the firing lines of all cylinders. Cylinder 1 is displayed on the left (except for its firing line, which is shown on the right). The cylinders are displayed from left to right by firing order.

READING THE SPARK LINES Spark lines can easily be seen on either superimposed or raster (stacked) position. On the raster position, each individual spark line can be viewed.

NORMAL SPARK LINE LENGTH (AT 700 TO 1200 RPM)			
NUMBER OF CYLINDERS	MILLISECONDS	PERCENTAGE (%) OF DWELL SCALE	DEGREES (°)
4	1.0–2.0	3–6	3–5
6	1.0–2.0	4–9	2–5
8	1.0–2.0	6–13	3–6

CHART A–1

Spark line length depends on the number of cylinders and the engine speed.

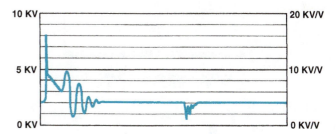

FIGURE A–9 A downward-sloping spark line usually indicates high secondary ignition system resistance or an excessively rich air-fuel mixture.

The spark lines should be level and one-fourth as high as the firing lines (1.5 to 2.5 kV, but usually less than 2 kV). The spark line voltage is called the **burn kV**. The *length* of the spark line is the critical factor for determining proper operation of the engine because it represents the spark duration or burn time. There is only a limited amount of energy in an ignition coil. If most of the energy is used to ionize the air gaps of the rotor and the spark plug, there may not be enough energy remaining to create a spark duration long enough to completely burn the air–fuel mixture. Many scopes are equipped with a **millisecond (ms) sweep**. This means that the scope will sweep only that portion of the pattern that can be shown during a 5- or 25-ms setting. Following are guidelines for spark line length:

- 0.8 ms—too short

- 1.5 ms—average

- 2.2 ms—too long

If the spark line is too short, possible causes include the following:

1. Spark plug(s) gap is too wide

2. Rotor tip to distributor cap insert distance gap is too wide (worn cap or rotor)

3. High-resistance spark plug wire

4. Air–fuel mixture too lean (vacuum leak, broken valve spring, etc.)

If the spark line is too long, possible causes include the following:

1. Fouled spark plug(s)

2. Spark plug(s) gap is too narrow

3. Shorted spark plug or spark plug wire

Many scopes do not have a millisecond scale. Some scopes are labeled in degrees and/or percentage (%) of dwell. The following chart can be used to determine acceptable sparkm line length. ● **SEE CHART A–1.**

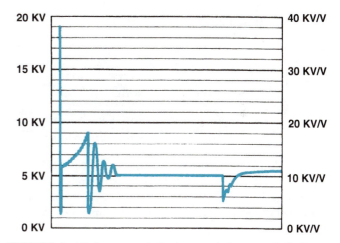

FIGURE A–10 An upward-sloping spark line usually indicates a mechanical engine problem or a lean air–fuel mixture.

SPARK LINE SLOPE Downward-sloping spark lines indicate that the voltage required to maintain the spark duration is decreasing during the firing of the spark plug. This downward slope usually indicates that the spark energy is finding ground through spark plug deposits (the plug is fouled) or other ignition problems. ● **SEE FIGURE A–9.**

An upward-sloping spark line usually indicates a mechanical engine problem. A defective piston ring or valve would tend to seal better in the increasing pressures of combustion. As the spark plug fires, the effective increase in pressures increases the voltage required to maintain the spark, and the height of the spark line rises during the duration of the spark. ● **SEE FIGURE A–10.**

An upward-sloping spark line can also indicate a lean air-fuel mixture. Typical causes include:

1. Clogged injector(s)

2. Vacuum leak

3. Sticking intake valve

● **SEE FIGURE A–11** for an example showing the relationship between the firing line and the spark line.

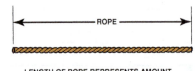

LENGTH OF ROPE REPRESENTS AMOUNT
OF ENERGY STORED IN IGNITION COIL

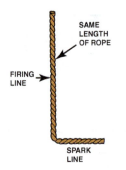

SAME
LENGTH
OF ROPE

FIRING
LINE

SPARK
LINE

SAME LENGTH OF ROPE (ENERGY).
IF HIGH VOLTAGE IS REQUIRED TO
IONIZE SPARK PLUG CAP, LESS
ENERGY IS AVAILABLE FOR SPARK
DURATION. (A LEAN CYLINDER IS
AN EXAMPLE OF WHERE HIGHER
VOLTAGE IS REQUIRED TO FIRE
WITH A SHORTER-THAN-NORMAL
DURATION.)

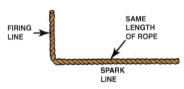

FIRING
LINE

SAME
LENGTH
OF ROPE

SPARK
LINE

IF LOW VOLTAGE IS REQUIRED TO FIRE
THE SPARK PLUG (LOW FIRING LINE),
MORE OF THE COIL'S ENERGY IS
AVAILABLE TO PROVIDE A LONG-
DURATION SPARK LINE. (A FOULED
SPARK PLUG IS AN EXAMPLE OF LOW
VOLTAGE TO FIRE, WITH A LONGER-
THEN-NORMAL DURATION.)

FIGURE A–11 The relationship between the height of the firing line and length of the spark line can be illustrated using a rope. Because energy cannot be destroyed, the stored energy in an ignition coil must dissipate totally, regardless of engine operating conditions.

READING THE INTERMEDIATE SECTION

The intermediate section should have three or more oscillations (bumps) for a correctly operating ignition system. Because approximately 250 volts are in the primary ignition circuit when the spark stops flowing across the spark plugs, this voltage is reduced by about 75 volts per oscillation. Additional resistances in the primary circuit would decrease the number of oscillations. If there are fewer than three oscillations, possible problems include the following:

1. Shorted ignition coil
2. Loose or high-resistance primary connections on the ignition coil or primary ignition wiring

ELECTRONIC IGNITION AND THE DWELL SECTION

Electronic ignitions also use a dwell period to charge the coil. Dwell is not adjustable with electronic ignition, but it does change with increasing RPM with many electronic ignition systems. This change in dwell with RPM should be considered normal.

Many EI systems also produce a "hump" in the dwell section, which reflects a current-limiting circuit in the control module. These current-limiting humps may have slightly different shapes depending on the exact module used. For example, the humps produced by various GM HEI modules differ slightly.

DWELL VARIATION (ELECTRONIC IGNITION)

A worn distributor gear, worn camshaft gear, or other distributor problem may cause engine performance problems, because the signal created in the distributor will be affected by the inaccurate distributor operation. However, many electronic ignitions vary the dwell electronically in the module to maintain acceptable current flow levels through the ignition coil and module without the use of a ballast resistor.

NOTE: Distributorless ignition systems also vary dwell time electronically within the engine computer or ignition module.

COIL POLARITY

With the scope connected and the engine running, observe the scope pattern in the superimposed mode. If the pattern is upside down, the primary wires on the coil may be reversed, causing the coil polarity to be reversed.

NOTE: Check the scope hookup and controls before deciding that the coil polarity is reversed.

ACCELERATION CHECK

With the scope selector set on the display (parade) position, rapidly accelerate the engine (gear selector in park or neutral with the parking brake on). The results should be interpreted as follows:

1. All firing lines should rise evenly (not to exceed 75% of maximum coil output) for properly operating spark plugs.
2. If the firing lines on one or more cylinders fail to rise, this indicates fouled spark plugs.

ROTOR GAP VOLTAGE

The **rotor gap** voltage test measures the voltage required to jump the gap (0.030 to 0.050 inch or 0.8 to 1.3 mm) between the rotor and the inserts (segments) of the distributor cap. Select the display (parade) scope pattern and remove a spark plug wire using a jumper wire to provide a good ground connection. Start the engine and observe the height of the firing line for the cylinder being tested. Because the spark plug wire is connected directly to ground, the firing line height on the scope will indicate the voltage required to jump the air gap between the rotor and the distributor cap insert. The normal rotor gap voltage is 3 to 7 kV, and the voltage should not exceed 8 kV. If the rotor gap voltage indicated is near or above 8 kV, inspect and replace the distributor cap and/or rotor as required.

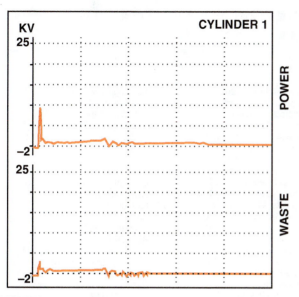

FIGURE A–12 A dual-trace scope pattern showing both the power and the waste spark from the same coil (cylinders 1 and 6). Note that the firing line is higher on the cylinder that is under compression (power); otherwise, both patterns are almost identical.

SCOPE-TESTING A WASTE-SPARK IGNITION SYSTEM

A handheld digital storage oscilloscope can be used to check the pattern of each individual cylinder. Some larger scopes can be connected to all spark plug wires and therefore are able to display both power and waste-spark waveforms. ● **SEE FIGURE A–12.** Because the waste spark does not require as high a voltage level as the cylinder on the power stroke, the waste form will be normally lower.

SCOPE-TESTING A COIL-ON-PLUG IGNITION SYSTEM

On a coil-on-plug type of ignition system, each individual coil can be shown on a scope and using the proper cables and adapters, the waveform for all of the cylinders can be viewed at the same time. Always follow the scope equipment manufacturer's instructions.

IGNITION SYSTEM SYMPTOM GUIDE

PROBLEM	POSSIBLE CAUSES AND/OR SOLUTIONS
No spark out of the coil	• Possible open in the ignition switch circuit
	• Possible defective ignition module (if electronic ignition coil)
	• Possible defective pickup coil or Hall-effect switch (if electronic ignition)
	• Possible shorted condenser (points-type ignition)
Weak spark out of the coil	• Possible high-resistance coil wire or spark plug wire
	• Possible poor ground between the distributor or module and the engine block
Engine misfire	• Possible defective (open) spark plug wire
	• Possible worn or fouled spark plugs
	• Possible defective pickup coil
	• Possible defective module
	• Possible poor electrical connections at the pickup coil and/or module